TOWARD
THE MILLENNIUM

STUDIES
IN THE HISTORY OF RELIGIONS
(*NUMEN* BOOK SERIES)

EDITED BY

H.G. KIPPENBERG · E.T. LAWSON

VOLUME LXXVII

TOWARD THE MILLENNIUM

MESSIANIC EXPECTATIONS FROM THE BIBLE TO WACO

EDITED BY

PETER SCHÄFER

AND

MARK COHEN

BRILL
LEIDEN · BOSTON · KÖLN
1998

This book is printed on acid-free paper.

Library of Congress Cataloging-in-Publication Data

Toward the millennium : messianic expectations from the Bible to Waco / edited by Peter Schäfer and Mark Cohen.
p. cm. —(Studies in the history of religions, ISSN 0169-8834 ; 77)
Papers presented in this book were read and discussed at a yearlong seminar at the Institute for Advanced Study and climaxed with a two-day international symposium in Mar. 1996.
Includes bibliographical references and index.
ISBN 9004110372
1. Messianism—Congresses. 2. Jewish messianic movements—Congresses. 3. Millennialism—Congresses. 4. Messianism, Political—Congresses. I. Schäfer, Peter. 1943- . II. Cohen. Mark R. , 1943- . III. Series.
BL475.T68 1998
291.2'3—DC21 98-17441
CIP

Die Deutsche Bibliothek - CIP-Einheitsaufnahme

Toward the millennium : messianic expectations from the Bible to Waco / ed. by Peter Schäfer and Mark Cohen. - Leiden ; Boston ; Köln : Brill, 1998
(Studies in the history of religions ; Vol. 77)
ISBN 90-04-11037-2

ISSN 0169-8834
ISBN 90 04 11037 2

PRINTED IN THE NETHERLANDS

CONTENTS

INTRODUCTION

To say that this book about messianism is being published toward the end of the second millennium because something apocalyptic is expected by many to take place around the year 2000 would be stretching things too far. The fact that many messianic phenomena have "made the news" in recent years, or that fundamentalism, often tinged with messianism, is "in the air" as we approach the end of the millennium, is probably also a coincidence. But, even if on the symbolic level, the conjuncture bears reflection.

Take the case of Waco. In April 1993, United States government authorities ended a fifty-one-day standoff at Mt. Carmel, a religious center near Waco, Texas, that housed a millennial Christian sect called the Branch Davidians. During the final, violent assault, most members of the sect remaining in Mt. Carmel died in a flaming inferno, along with their leader, David Koresh. Né Vernon Howell, Koresh had assumed a double messianic name—David, the future Messiah-King of Israel, and Koresh, Hebrew for Cyrus, king of ancient Persia and conqueror of Babylon, whom God (through his prophet Isaiah) had called his "annointed" (Hebrew: *mashiah*, whence the word "Messiah"). Koresh preached an apocalyptic message based on the "seven seals" of the Book of Revelation and on the Book of Daniel. His zealous messianic convictions and their biblical foundations were grasped by several religious scholars, though they were not well understood by the beleaguered and suspicious FBI. The Branch Davidians of Waco died in the flames sincerely believing they were taking part in the apocalyptical End of Days.

Or take the case of Habad. In 1994, Menachem Mendel Schneerson, Rebbe of the Lubavitch (Habad) Hasidim, died following a stroke. For years, the Rebbe had hinted to his followers that he was the Messiah. That he died childless and without designating an heir in the dynastic manner of Hasidic sects seemed consistent with a millennial understanding of his life. As his death approached, preparations for a joyous redemption of the world reached a fever pitch among the majority of his adherents, who persisted in the belief that he was the Messiah. Now, several years after his death, pictures of the Rebbe captioned "Moshiach (Messiah) Now" still spot roadsides, buildings, and automobiles.

Messianism has been "in the air" in other parts of the world, too, during these final years of the second millennium. In Islam, radical movements around the world stress pure practice of the religion of the Qur'ān, anti-government activism, and, especially in their Shiite variety, martyrdom in the battle against enemies as the prologue to a personal millennial reward. In Israel, extreme nationalists insist upon permanent control of Greater Israel, including the Temple site, as part of the messianic fulfillment of a biblical promise.

So it does not seem ill-timed that in 1995–1996, a group of scholars sitting in Princeton should have assembled to engage in the academic study of messianism. The inquiry centered in a yearlong seminar at the Institute for Advanced Study, supported by the Andrew W. Mellon Foundation. The seminar was led by Peter Schäfer, University Professor and Director of the Institut für Judaistik at the Freie Universität Berlin and Andrew W. Mellon Visiting Professor (1994–1996) in the School of Historical Studies at the Institute for Advanced Study. Scholars from the Institute, Princeton University, and other universities in the United States, Europe, and Israel participated. Biweekly meetings featured papers on a wide variety of related topics, including messianism in early, medieval and modern Jewish thought, messianism in the ancient pagan world, messianism in early, medieval, and early modern Christendom, messianism in Islam, and "secular" messianism. The seminar climaxed with a two-day international symposium in March 1996. Faculty in Jewish Studies at Princeton University joined forces with the Institute Seminar to celebrate the inauguration of its own Program in Jewish Studies, established through a gift from Ronald O. Perelman.

The intention of the symposium organizers was to have as broad a representation of topics as possible, particularly ones that had not been discussed in the biweekly seminar. This meant, also, inviting scholars who had not participated in the ongoing colloquy during the academic year. We were gratified by the response. The papers presented here, which include several that were read and discussed at the yearlong seminar, offer a varied and colorful mosaic of messianism in a variety of cultures, in history and in the contemporary world. Published on the eve of the close of the second millennium, we have entitled the book "Toward the Millennium." We offer it not only as the record of an academic seminar and conference, but also as timely food for thought at a moment in time when new messianic thinking, even new messianic episodes, may soon again fill the media.

The volume opens with several essays relating to Messiahs and messianic expectations in antiquity. Peter Schäfer's "Diversity and Interaction: Messiahs in Early Judaism," which also inaugurated the seminar, sets the stage. Jewish messianic expectations, evolving out of the framework of restorative and utopian ideas provided by the Hebrew Bible—and going well beyond it—lay the groundwork for most, if not all, messianic ideologies in Christianity and Islam as well as in modern secular movements, for instance, Zionism and Marxism. Postbiblical Judaism up to the beginning of Christianity reveals a plethora of different messianic ideas and expectations or of different messianic figures, partly divergent from each other, partly interdependent, which cannot and should not be harmonized; it is the stump out of which many shoots will grow, some anticipated and some rather surprising and wild. Only if the diversity and variety of Jewish messianic expectations in the formative era between the Hebrew Bible and the beginning of the second century C.E. are taken into consideration will further developments within Judaism itself and its daughter religions as well as in secular ideologies become comprehensible. Any attempt to unify or to standardize messianic expectations during antiquity and to condense them into some essence or basic idea runs counter to their complexity and the multitude of historical realizations they could and did take.

John Gagers's "Messiahs and their Followers" supports this point of view. It describes the era of concrete messianic movements in Palestine from the first century B.C.E. until 135 C.E., the end of the Bar Kokhba war, and re-emphasizes that the concept of a Messiah was anything but uniform. Nevertheless, they had some common features which can be summarized as follows: the leaders of these movements view themselves as fulfilling biblical prophecies; they are regarded as messianic leaders by their followers; they are described as reluctant to establish state authority; their religious and political restoration is centralized; they had many followers; the sources attempt to minimalize these movements or even to present them as criminal; most of their leaders suffered a violent death, though the movement they began did not die with their death; in the long term the only movement to succeed in establishing itself firmly was the Jesus movement. Several historical conditions paved the way for these movements. Gager emphasizes that Israel was occupied by the Romans, who introduced a system of heavy taxes and other duties, and that the Temple was governed by renegade priests. Different parties fought for supremacy, and a growing corpus of oral and literary traditions promised restoration. As for their members, he cautions against the tendency to limit them to the lower and underprivileged classes: as the Jesus movement makes clear, descriptions of this group are characterized by an "ideology of poverty" and a "rhetoric of disadvantage" which are not to be taken at face value.

Christian Habicht confirms the pride of place allotted to Judaism and Christianity in the history of messianism in his discussion of pre-Christian Graeco-Roman literature. He begins with savior figures like Brasidas, Alexander the Great and Demetrius Poliorcetes, who distinguish themselves by a particular and exceptional action but whom he regards as "far from what we might call a messianic figure." A more advanced stage is reached with Caesar and Augustus, who act as "mortal saviors, present on earth, their activity beneficial to all mankind, specifically by bringing about peace and prosperity, their birthday the beginning of a Golden Age." Nevertheless, Habicht hesitates to call this "messianic." Even Vergil's famous Fourth Eclogue was made to look like messianic prophecy only by its Christian interpretation. Habicht sees a "fundamental difference" between the pagan and the Christian concepts of the savior/Messiah: "In the Greco-Roman world the savior always operates in a real situation, delivering people from worldly evils such as war, enemies, oppression, or captivity. Christ . . . is a redeemer of the soul, delivering it from sins committed in the past." Interestingly enough, this description of the pagan savior goes very well with the early Jewish evidence of the Messiah/savior, which Gershom Scholem contrasts, using almost the same words, with the Christian messianic concept of inner salvation.[1]

After the failure of the Bar Kokhba revolt, Jewish messianic fervor waned. The Rabbis turned to a more theological interpretation of messianic traditions and were rather hesitant about transferring them to the realm of concrete historical events. Among the very peculiar strands of messianic thinking they developed is that of the suffering Messiah, a complement to the traditional concept of the

[1] See below, p. 16, n. 4.

Messiah-King from the house of David. Michael Fishbane discusses aspects of the Rabbinic concept of the suffering Messiah, especially as it expresses itself in the homilies of Pesiqta Rabbati. According to the Pesiqta, this "Messiah ben Ephraim" suffers but doesn't die. The midrash emphasizes the connection between suffering and salvation, and this connection is based on a correlation of Jeremiah 31 with Isaiah 53. With special reference to the "Mourners of Zion," to whom the preacher of Pesiqta Rabbati 34–37 may have belonged, the midrash points to the possible participation of humans in divine suffering. As God determined to be with Israel in their travails, these *'avelei tziyon* endure the sorrows of God.

Toward the end of the Rabbinic period apocalyptic literature started to flourish again, and with it new messianic expectations. Christianity had entered the plane of history and claimed for itself the very same traditions Judaism had hitherto used to express its hope for redemption, especially the early apocalyptic writings like Daniel, the Enoch literature and the Ezra apocalypse. In later apocalyptic literature both religions develop the concept of a "last enemy," the Antichrist, arising before the arrival of the true Messiah.

If for Christians the Antichrist is Jewish, the Jewish counterconcept is a Christ-like figure. Joseph Dan analyzes the first Jewish text in which such an individual appears, the enigmatic *Book of Zerubbavel.* The "Antichrist" is named Armilus, obviously reminiscent of Romulus, founder of Rome, and he is born out of a union of Satan with a beautiful female statue, a transparent parody on the birth of Jesus. Therefore Armilus figures as "a union between a false Messiah and a Roman emperor, expressing the Jewish counterpart of Christianity." Dan questions the origin and dating of the *Book of Zerubbavel.* The author seems to have had some acquaintance with the ancient apocalyptic literature as well as the Hekhalot corpus and some Christian traditions, but concrete literary influence cannot be proved. Because of the markedly individualistic nature of the work in general, the possibility "that he [the author] invented the whole myth" should not simply be ruled out. Dan finds none of the dates suggested for the book convincing. Only an approximate dating between the third and the sixth century C.E. can be ventured. The problem of the date is rooted in the literary nature of the work: "The messianic and apocalyptic language is so bare of any religious, ethical or theological elements that it can be accepted by all groups, in every country, in every historical set of circumstances."

Messianic expectations during the medieval period are characterized by a lively exchange between Jewish and Christian ideas. Israel J. Yuval's "Jewish Messianic Expectations towards 1240 and Christian Reactions" is devoted to a very peculiar chapter in this history of mutual influence and rejection. He analyzes the messianic hopes connected with the beginning of the sixth Jewish millennium in their appropriate historical context and refers to the dissemination of apocalyptic ideas in contemporary images at the beginning of the thirteenth century. The messianic excitement as described in thirteenth-century sources expresses the idea of a Jewish presence in the Holy Land as a precondition for the advent of the Messiah. Only after Jewish prayers are said at the Temple site the final scenario of redemption can take place. A Jewish army will defeat the Crusader and Muslim hosts, the Christians will be driven out of the Holy Land and Rome will be destroyed.

These messianic hopes, Yuval argues, led to new historical constellations: on the one hand, to the well-known immigration of 300 French Rabbis to the Land of Israel and to the obscure identification of a Mongol king with "the king of the Ten Tribes," and, on the other hand, to antisemitic reactions like the accusation of "ritual murder" and of Jewish collaboration with the Mongol invaders of Southwest Asia. As Yuval puts it, these reactions cannot be viewed independently of the accusation claiming that the shedding of Christian blood belongs to the Jewish concept of redemption. He concludes that Jewish messianism plays an important role "in our understanding of the mechanisms that produced the world of Christian antisemitism."

Next, Norman Housley deals with Christian messianic expectations between 1260 and 1556 and attempts to delineate the circumstances in which violence took place in late medieval and Renaissance Europe by focusing on the inspirational and organizational role of messianic individuals. He connects the emergence of texts which sanctify violence in pursuit of an eschatological objective to the history of the Crusades, as they share the goals of the recapture of Jerusalem and the final defeat of Islam.

The strands within Joachimite thought most important in this regard are the Angelic Pope and Last Emperor prophecies because these are messianic figures whose roles included waging war. The reform of the Catholic church, the Crusade to Jerusalem and the conversion of unbelievers became the essential ingredients of the Angelic

Pope's program. Last Emperor prophecies were from the start highly politically charged. They crystallized in the second Charlemagne prophecy in France, the third Frederick prophecy in Germany, the Arthurian prophecy in England, and the Hidden King (El Encubierto) in Spain. The basic difference between these messianic programs and the Crusades lay in the fact that the former were systems of ideas lacking any organizational structure to put the ideas into practice. This was a strength insofar as the messianic programs were flexible and immune to disillusionment; notable for their longevity and resilience, they could be tailored to fit contemporary political events.

Besides the messianic figures of emperor and pope who enjoyed their status *ex officio* there were revolutionaries who took up the task of bringing about the millennial phase in their own time, paving the way for Christ's return. This entailed the overthrow of established regimes and could only be accomplished by the use of armed forces, as the examples of Florence in the late Middle Ages and Anabaptist Münster at the time of the Reformation show. Hussite Tabor can be considered the best example of religious violence in the service of radical millenarianism. From the outset the chiliastic community at Tabor was militarized. Their doctrine of chiliastic total war could not be sustained for long, however. When Christ failed to reappear in 1420, the Taborites turned toward more moderate policies.

Finally national messianism, the application of the idea of divine election to ethnic groups, was a popular and recurrent theme in the Middle Ages. It became more common in the thirteenth century, and by the mid-sixteenth century there was scarcely a national, ethnic, or civic community in Europe which had not been saluted as a Chosen People, its territory deemed sacred soil, and its capital proclaimed to be the New Jerusalem.

Quite in contrast to the high millenarian expectations described by Housley, eschatological speculation was rarely used to justify political or social action in late medieval Spain. As Sara T. Nalle demonstrates, the only period which came close to producing some widespread messianic and millenarian movements was 1500–1530. Several events combined to make Spaniards more receptive to millenarian ideas: the union of the crowns of Aragon and Castile fed Joachimite spiritualism concerning the Last Days; the victory over the Muslims in Granada in 1492 raised hopes for the success of the Last Crusade; the approach of the chiliastic year of 1500 stimulated religious speculation among Christians and Jews; and the expulsion of the Jews in 1492 led to the belief in the imminent arrival of the Messiah to redeem his people. Throughout the sixteenth century rumors of a coming Messiah would sweep through *converso* communities.

The only example of a Spanish millenarian movement is the outbreak in 1520–1522 of twin revolutions in the kingdoms of Valencia and Castile. The radicalization of ideas expressed by the spiritual Franciscans led to uprisings against the monarchy, but only in Valencia did the rebellion turn into a millenarian movement. The large Muslim population of Valencia convinced the Christians of the necessity for a last crusade. In 1522, when the rebellion against the Muslim serfs was almost quashed, a messianic figure claiming to be the Hidden King (El Encubierto) stepped forth. He proclaimed the coming of a new age and led militias into the countryside against the Muslims and the local nobility. He was eventually killed on the order of the government and his soul condemned to hell by the Inquisition. It is possible that El Encubierto was not a Christian but a converted Jew who was well versed in Jewish messianic expectations.

In Castile the revolution did not produce a millenarian movement or messianic figure. After the revolution, however, Bartolome Sanchez personified the age's millennial and messianic hopes. In 1553 he proclaimed himself the Elijah-Messiah sent to punish the church, the Inquisition and the nobility, but no one listened to him since the revolutionary moment had passed. Perhaps without realizing it himself, Sanchez, who seems to have had some *converso* ancestry, attempted to reconcile Christian and Jewish traditions to create a syncretistic view of salvation with himself at its center. The inquisitors did not even consider him a heretic; for them he was a lunatic and consequently dismissed and forgotten.

The Jewish Messiah of the seventeenth century, Sabbatai Zvi, was considered both a heretic and a lunatic by his opponents and a true Messiah by his believers, even after his conversion to Islam (and by some even after his death). Distancing himself from Scholem's famous and influential book on Sabbatai Zvi, Moshe Idel argues in his article that the time has come for a new approach which liberates Sabbatai Zvi and his messianic mysticism or mystic messianism from the confines of particularistic historiography. Whereas Scholem had inscribed Sabbatianism "within the particularistic framework of historiography," interpreting it as "an event that belongs eminently to internal Jewish history and culture: the dissemination of Lurianic

Kabbalah and its messianism," Idel calls for a universalistic approach putting Sabbatai Zevi and the Sabbatian movement into "broader religious and cultural contexts."

These broader contexts are the connections between messianism, universalism and astrology which Idel describes in his essay. As far as the messianic strand within the history of Kabbalah and its influence on Sabbatai Zvi is concerned, he sees the late-thirteenth-century Kabbalah, especially the kabbalist Joseph ben Shalom Ashkenazi and those influenced by him, as having contributed much more to Sabbatai Zvi's self-awareness as Messiah than anything in Lurianic Kabbalah could possibly have done. Ashkenazi offered one of the most important and influential descriptions of the connection between the Messiah and the third sefirah [i.e., *binah* which is connected with Saturn]: "Unlike Abulafia, who did not connect Sabbatai with the human Messiah, R. Joseph ben Shalom Ashkenazi did so explicitly, his mention of the 'secret of Meshiyah YHWH' represents the most positive description of the planet in Hebrew literature." As far as astrology is concerned, it is precisely the fact that Sabbatai Zvi was born on a Sabbath under the sign of Saturn (Shabbtai) that speaks in favor of a new interpretation of Sabbatai Zvi's illness. Rather than diagnosing it as manic depression, as Scholem did, Idel prefers to call it melancholy because Saturn is connected with that emotional state. In addition, and more importantly, Saturn had been regarded as a god since late antiquity. Hence Idel considers the possibility that Sabbatai could have seen himself "not only as a Messiah, perhaps as someone ruled by the highest planet, or by the third *sefirah*, but also as someone who would achieve a divine status."

A very different perspective of Sabbatian messianism is put forward by Elliot R. Wolfson in "The Engenderment of Messianic Politics: Symbolic Significance of Sabbatai Sevi's Coronation." Wolfson sheds new light on the impact of Lurianic Kabbala on the Sabbatian ideal of redemption. Unlike Scholem, who stressed the correlation between a symbolic understanding of redemption and political reality, Wolfson locates a deeper stratum of the messianic theme in Lurianic Kabbala by focusing on the myth of restoring the divine *anthropos*. This process of reconfiguration is described both as the uplifting of the sparks of holiness to the fractured *anthropos* and in terms of the overcoming of gender dimorphism, which originated because of the division of the primordial androgyne into male and female.

According to Wolfson the most telling image for describing the unity of rectification (*tiqqun*) is the elevation of the female to the position of the crown, literally the corona of the phallus. Lurianic Messianism thus paved the way for the Sabbatian doctrine of redemption and its crucial interpretation of Sabbatai Zvi's conversion to Islam, which found its visible expression in his putting on the turban. As the author argues, this presumed coronation of Sabbatai Zvi was explained by his followers in the context of the mythology of the coronation of the Messiah. The turban was identified as the theosophic symbol of the crown, and as such the focus for many of the theological attempts, examined by Wolfson, to account for the conversion: "Putting on the turban assumed the soteriological significance of the ontic assimilation into the divine crown, which represents the restoration of the female to the male in the form of the corona of the phallus." Hence it is the ultimate task of the Messiah to overcome "gender dimorphism" in a unity wherein the female is contained in the male and the male in the female.

Much less known (and less influential) is the development of messianic ideas in the seventeenth century within the Christian context. Wilhelm Schmidt-Biggemann follows the strange life and destiny of the poet-Messiah Quirinus Kuhlmann, who was influenced by mystics like Jacob Böhme, Johann Rothe and Johann Amos Comenius and who saw himself as the divine executor of the course of history prophesied in Comenius' works. He not only travelled to the Turkish sultan to convince him to launch a "crusade" against Catholicism but also predicted the end of history for the year 1688. Like Sabbatai Zvi (who had predicted the year 1666) he failed, but unlike Sabbatai Zvi he didn't survive his failure and died at the stake in Russia in 1689.

His mystical-messianic message, which had appeared as early as 1670 in his *Kühlpsalter* and as of 1684 in his autobiographical poems, was nurtured by apocalyptic patterns current in the seventeenth century, especially the concepts of a Fifth Monarchy, the rule of the Holy Spirit and millenarian ideas. Kuhlmann is to be regarded "the most radical, surely the most poetical representative" of these ideas the messianic implications of which are explained with the help of the symbols engraved in the copperplate print of the *Kühlpsalter*'s title page and of the portrait of Kuhlmann.

The main idea of Kuhlmann's poems concerns the creative power of language: it is the German language which, according to Böhme and Kuhlmann, comes quite close to God's language of creation. Kuhlmann's aim as a Messiah was to imitate the process of creation through the word. Thus he used language and poetry as the guise of his apocalyptic-messianic thinking.

The modern period is opened by Yohanan Friedmann's essay on "The Messianic Claim of Ghulām Aḥmad." Friedmann deals with the beginnings of the Aḥmadiyya movement in India at the end of the nineteenth century. The founder of this movement, Ghulām Aḥmad Qādiyānī, claimed to be *Jesus redivivus*, whose second coming is also expected in the Muslim tradition. Ghulām Aḥmad's claim is to be seen in the context of the Muslim debate with Christianity, as represented by the colonial power on the Indian subcontinent. He propagated the idea that Jesus did not die on the cross but only swooned there and later went on to India where he died at a ripe old age. Since Jesus experienced a natural death his second coming must not be taken literally. Instead, Ghulām Qādiyānī proposed that the prophecy is about a person similar to Jesus (united with his "substance"), something the founder of the Aḥmadiyya movement claimed for himself.

Even more complex in the history of messianic ideas are modern, secular forms of messianism. Klaus Schreiner analyzes messianic strands in the political culture of the Weimar Republic in Germany. Beginning with revolutionary and restorative messianic expectations in the nineteenth century, he describes diffuse hopes for a strong, divinely sent leader who would bring about an epochal turn of events in state and society. Such hopes were voiced in the writings of historians, German-language scholars as well as sociologists, jurists and theologians. This phenomenon was evident in other areas of political life as well, for example in the youth movement. As a consequence of the economical, cultural and religious crisis after the First World War, these vague messianic expectations were accompanied by a skeptical attitude towards democratic institutions in the Weimar Republic.

Within the National Socialist movement itself, messianic-like elements were numerous and clearly rooted in the political climate of the period. Hitler as the *Führer* presented himself to his followers as having been appointed by superior forces and divinely gifted, but he never explicitly declared himself to be the savior or redeemer. He was a Germanic rather than a Christian "Messiah"; only in the doctrine of the "German Christians" did both become blurred. In academic circles, too, especially in literature, history and theology departments, Hitler was hailed as a savior figure. The National Socialist ideology drew pictures of the past and present which rejected democracy in favor of dictatorial ideologies of redemption. The success of the National Socialist religious imagery of salvation was due to its enormous appeal to the masses of insecure people in that period.

Among the most prominent Jewish thinkers in Germany during the Wilhelminian era and the Weimar republic were Hermann Cohen, Franz Rosenzweig and Walter Benjamin. Robert Gibbs in "Lines, Circles, Points: Messianic Epistemology in Cohen, Rosenzweig and Benjamin" starts from the assumption of some common denominators in the messianic thinking of these three philosophers: the epistemological truth lies in the messianic future; in order to understand it, a messianic view of history has to relate the past to the present. Gibbs analyzes the "idealistic linear progress" in Cohen's *Religion of Reason*, which culminates in the messianic vision of the world of peace: the idea of a personal Messiah is transformed into the concept of a messianic age beyond history—known through the idea of humanity with its origins in monotheism. Cohen's idealization of history is inseparably linked to the source of all "rigorous history"—Jewish history, which for the sake of introducing the messianic idea into the consciousness of the world can be interpreted as a line or chain of misery.

The author then turns to Cohen's student Franz Rosenzweig. In his *Star of Redemption* he finds a different concept of historical sequences and the future of redemption: the eternal circular movement in the Jewish cycle of festivals. Rosenzweig's concept of history does not progress in linear fashion from past to present to future but "allows for the discontinuity of messianism to break into time." Hence messianism produces history in circles.

Gibbs confesses "serious incompleteness" in dealing with the "Theses on the Philosophy of History" by the last of his German-Jewish thinkers, Walter Benjamin, focusing on "the constellation of points from past and present" as the place where "the future can interrupt and act." Comparing all three thinkers, he traces a straight line from the meaning of idealist historiography to the chain of misery in Hermann Cohen's work, establishes the circularity of Rosenzweig's commemorative celebrations of the eternal, and points out the flashes of the past in the present evident in Benjamin's ideas. Gibbs thus presents a penetrating study of the messianic dimension of historiography.

The most recent messianic phenomenon in Judaism is the Lubavitch movement. Rachel Elior traces the development of the Habad-Lubavitch movement's messianic ideology from the time of the Shoa until today. It was first formulated in reaction to the Shoa by Rabbi Yosef Yitzhaq Schneerson (1880–1950), who offered an apocalyptic explanation for the catastrophe, viewing it as the final stage of pre-messianic tribulations which would lead to divine redemption in the near future. When he arrived in New York in 1940 he called upon American Jews to accept responsibility for the fate of the Jews in Europe, to engage in *teshuvah* in order to end the pre-messianic tribulations and to usher in the Messiah. By 1945 it had become clear that the expected physical redemption would not take place; nevertheless he held on to "his vision regarding the salvation of the souls and the apocalyptic anticipation." The messianic motivation led to an outreach program encompassing the entire Jewish community; messianic hope was transformed into practical activity.

When his son-in-law Rabbi Menachem Mendel Schneerson (1902–1994) assumed the Habad leadership in 1951 he assured his followers that they were the last generation, urging them accordingly to broadcast the imminent appearance of the Messiah. The messianic resurgence rose to such new heights that the general expectation for imminent redemption in the near future was replaced by the expectation of a personal Messiah embodied in the Rebbe, who it was thought, would reveal himself in the present.

Shortly before Rabbi Menachem Mendel's death the movement split into the messianic majority, which believed that the Rebbe himself was the Messiah, and a self-proclaimed sane minority, which urged the moderation of messianic hopes. After the Rebbe's stroke, the messianic group saw him as the suffering servant of Isaiah 53, following Christianity's usage of the text. "Thus by applying the dialectical *divine* paradox to the hidden-revealed *human* Messiah, Habad could envisage a messianic movement which incarnated the mystical paradox within human dimensions." In summary the author points out that three principal elements are inherent in Habad's messianism: paradoxical spirituality, mystical leadership and social creativity.

Finally, some very recent implications and consequences of messianic expectations can be studied in the so-called Branch Davidian Community. James D. Tabor's "Patterns of the End: Textual Weaving from Qumran to Waco" analyzes the apocalyptic-messianic ideas of this community whose tragic end in the spring of 1993 created a great stir. Tabor explains the interpretation of biblical texts, especially of the Daniel apocalypse, by the leader of the sect, David Koresh, during the Gulf war and the operations of the FBI against the sect. He points to similarities of this contemporary biblical adaptation with texts from Qumran and illuminates the interrelation of text, interpretation and context. As Koresh in his preachings interpreted both prophetic texts *and* actual events, the *texts*—themselves fixed and unchanging—fatalistically mirrored in advance what had to happen.

The editors would like to express their thanks to the Andrew W. Mellon Foundation, Mr. Ronald O. Perelman, the Institute for Advanced Study, and Princeton University for their generous support. Johanna Hoornweg and Sabine Kößling kindly helped with the editing of the manuscripts, and Sabine Kößling prepared the indices.

DIVERSITY AND INTERACTION: MESSIAHS IN EARLY JUDAISM

Peter Schäfer

It seems only natural to open a seminar devoted to "Messianism" with a paper on Jewish Messianism, although the seminar is by no means limited to Jewish or its Christian offshoot's concepts of "Messianism" and the "Messiah." As the word "Messianism" reveals—it stems from the Hebrew root *mashah*, which means "anoint," hence the *mashiah* = the "anointed"—in our Western culture the understanding of the phenomenon it describes is deeply influenced by the Jewish-Christian paradigm. This certainly justifies making it the starting point of our consideration, even if it is to be hoped that we will be able to transcend it and to include concepts which are independent of the powerful Jewish-Christian model.

In its broadest sense "Messianism" denotes the belief in a salvation figure (savior, redeemer) who terminates the present order and ushers in a new order of justice and blessing.[1] Very often, but not always, the establishment of the new order is connected with the notion of the eschaton, the last days of the world (or at least of part of the world, depending on whether a universalistic or rather a more particularistic stance is adopted). This eschaton can come suddenly and unexpectedly, but may also be bound to certain times, especially to calculations of the millennium (millenarianism). In Early Judaism both parts of the broader definition are essential, the personal figure of the savior/redeemer as well as the new order inaugurated by his appearance and actions. However, the particular type of salvation figure he represents varies as greatly as do the circumstances and contents of the new order he brings about.

---

[1] H. Kohn, in: *Encyclopaedia of the Social Sciences*, ed. E.R. Anderson Seligman, New York [15]1963, vol. X, pp. 357ff. More concretely focussed on the situation of Early Judaism is the definition suggested by R.J. Zwi Werblowsky according to which the notion of Messiah "acquired the connotation of savior or redeemer who would appear at the end of days and usher in the kingdom of God, the restoration of Israel, or whatever dispensation was considered to be the ideal state of the world" ("Messianism: Jewish Messianism," in: *The Encyclopedia of Religion*, ed. M. Eliade, New York 1987, vol. IX, p. 472).

It goes without saying that the notion of the Messiah/the Messiahs in Early Judaism is a vast topic which cannot be dealt with adequately in a single paper. What we call Early Judaism extends over the time span from the Hebrew Bible until the beginning of the Rabbinical period in the first century C.E. I will therefore confine myself to a condensed survey in the form of a number of theses which in some cases, however, will be somewhat more elaborate and will deal also with the relevant textual evidence.

I would like to begin with three remarks which will serve as the methodological premisses of my presentation and which enjoy a growing consensus among scholars.[2] This consensus emerges, i.a., in response to Gershom Scholem's famous and influential[3] article "Toward an Understanding of the Messianic Idea in Judaism,"[4] based on a lecture that Scholem held at one of the Eranos conferences and originally published in 1959 in German under the title "Zum Verständnis der messianischen Idee im Judentum."[5] As the title already indicates, Scholem starts from the assumption that there is indeed something like "the" Messianic idea which can be traced throughout Jewish history: "The object of these remarks," he says in his essay, "is not the initial development of the Messianic idea but the varying perspectives by which it became an effective force after its crystallization in historical Judaism."[6] It is thus clear that according to Scholem the Messianic idea did crystallize at a certain point in time, most presumably at the end of the biblical period, and thereafter unfolded as an "effective force" in the course of history, though in "varying perspectives." Against this view, or rather against some misunderstandings which this view could evoke, it is argued:

1. Judaism of late antiquity is not a static, pre-determined entity whose essential elements remain unchanged throughout the course of history. On the contrary, there is not one single Judaism but rather

[2] See, e.g., J. Neusner, *Messiah in Context. Israel's History and Destiny in Formative Judaism*, Philadelphia 1984, especially the Preface, p. XI and pp. 227ff.; J. Neusner, W.S. Green, E.S. Frerichs, eds., *Judaisms and their Messiahs at the Turn of the Christian Era*, Cambridge 1987.

[3] See, e.g., the summary by J. Dan, "Gershom Scholem and Jewish Messianism," in: *Gershom Scholem. The Man and His Work*, ed. P. Mendes-Flohr, Albany, N.Y. and Jerusalem 1994, pp. 73–86.

[4] In his collection of essays entitled *The Messianic Idea in Judaism and Other Essays in Jewish Spirituality*, New York 1971, pp. 1–36, notes pp. 341–343.

[5] *Eranos Jahrbuch*, vol. 28, 1959, pp. 193–239, and republished in his collection of essays *Judaica*, vol. I, Frankfurt a. Main 1963 (reprint 1986), pp. 7–74.

[6] *Ibid.*, p. 2.

there are several "Judaisms" which, ideally, can be described as social groups to be located more precisely in time and history.

2. Accordingly, it cannot be the task to track down a pre-defined "idea" of the Messiah within the history of Judaism. On the contrary, the *dynamic* origin and development of diverse "ideas" and "notions" connected with Messianic expectations have to be traced throughout Jewish history. These "ideas" are, of course, not isolated monads, flowering in complete separation from each other, but are in many ways interrelated. However, in order to determine what is common among these various ideas one first needs to disclose the differences, the divergences, and those elements which cannot be easily harmonized and conceptualized.

3. Since the history of religious ideas in Judaism is mediated mainly through literature, the literary analysis of the respective sources is the indispensable prerequisite for any further investigation. However, since literature does not float in a vacuum, literary analysis must always be coupled with historical analysis. Statements about the Messianic expectations of the Jews are possible only in correlation with the progress of research on the history *and* literature of the respective period.

With these methodological premisses in mind I will proceed now to the survey of the variety of Messianic expectations in their most productive period, i.e., from the Hebrew Bible until the first century C.E. In doing so I will not attempt to establish a synchronic phenomenological structure, but instead will follow a chronological sequence in order to elucidate the historical dimension of the different Messianic ideas.[7]

1. *Hebrew Bible*

The Hebrew Bible is not *one* homogeneous work but a compilation of many different works edited after a long and complicated literary process which extended over several centuries. Accordingly, we cannot expect to find in the Bible the expression of one homogeneous Messianic expectation. As a matter of fact, we cannot take the Bible as evidence for a fully fledged Messianic idea in the later sense at

---

[7] Scholem's essay is particularly uninterested in the earlier history of the messianic "idea"; despite his frequent mentioning of apocalypticism, it starts more or less with Rabbinic Judaism.

all. What we do find are, for the most part, the following themes which are connected with the term Messiah and run through the various biblical books as a kind of leitmotif:[8]

(a) Emphasis is put first and foremost on the continuity of the Davidic kingdom, the Davidic dynasty, which is presented as perpetual (2 Sam. 7:12–29). The eternal kingdom of David refers mainly, but not only, to Israel: it can also include other nations and be understood as world domination (Ps. 2). In any case, what is expected is a real (legitimate) king from the house of David, not a utopian-mythic figure. In this sense even a foreign king can be designated "Messiah" instead of the "legitimate" representative of the Davidic dynasty, which in a particular historical situation is condemned to powerlessness—I refer to the famous passage which hails the Persian king Cyrus (539–529 B.C.E.) as the Messiah, who in 538 B.C.E. granted permission to the Jewish exiles to return to the Land of Israel and to rebuild the Jerusalem Temple (Is. 45:1–7):[9]

> (1) Thus said the Lord to Cyrus, His anointed one (*meshiho*)—whose right hand He has grasped, treading down nations before him. . . . (3) I will give you treasures concealed in the dark and secret hoards—so that you may know that it is I the Lord, the God of Israel, who call you by name. (4) For the sake of My servant Jacob, Israel My chosen one, I call you by name, I hail you by title, though you have not known Me. (5) I am the Lord and there is none else; beside Me, there is no god. I engird you, though you have not known Me, (6) so that they may know, from east to west, that there is none but Me. . . .

(b) An important factor is moreover the expectation of the restitution of the Davidic dynasty after the three crucial events in the history of biblical Judaism, i.e., the collapse of the Davidic-Salomonic empire and the division into the two separate states of Israel and Judah (931 B.C.E.), the downfall of the northern kingdom of Israel

---

[8] The classic contribution is still S. Mowinckel, *He That Cometh. The Messiah Concept in the Old Testament and Later Judaism*, New York 1955; and see now J.M. Roberts, "The Old Testament's Contribution to Messianic Expectations," in: *The Messiah. Developments in Earliest Judaism and Christianity*, ed. J.H. Charlesworth, Minneapolis 1992, pp. 39–51; P.D. Hanson, "Messiahs and Messianic Figures in Proto-Apocalypticism," *ibid.*, pp. 67–78.

[9] The translations are taken from the following editions: Hebrew Bible, except for Daniel: *Jewish Publication Society*; Daniel: L.F. Hartman and A.A. Di Lella, *The Book of Daniel*, New York 1978; Jesus Sirach: *Revised English Bible*; Apocrypha and Pseudepigrapha: J.H. Charlesworth, ed., *The Old Testament Pseudepigrapha*, vols. 1–2, London 1983–1985; Qumran literature: G. Vermes, *The Dead Sea Scrolls in English*, London [3]1987.

(722 B.C.E.), and the downfall of the southern kingdom of Judah (586 B.C.E.) which inaugurated the so-called Babylonian exile (586–538 B.C.E.). As one example out of many I quote Jer. 30:8–11 which was written in the second half of the seventh century B.C.E., i.e., after the demise of the northern and before the downfall of the southern kingdom:

> (8) In that day—declares the Lord of Hosts—I will break the yoke from off your neck and I will rip off your bonds. Strangers shall no longer make slaves of them; (9) instead, they shall serve the Lord their God and David, the king whom I will raise up for them.
>
> (10) But you, have no fear, My servant Jacob—declares the Lord—be not dismayed, O Israel! I will deliver you from far away, your folk from the land of captivity. And Jacob shall again have calm and quiet with none to trouble him; (11) For I am with you to deliver you—declares the Lord. I will make an end of all the nations among which I have dispersed you; but I will not make an end of you! I will not leave you unpunished, but will chastise you in measure.

(c) Essential for the unfolding of the Messianic expectation is what may be called the idealization of the future Messiah-king as a charismatic savior figure who is characterized in particular by the gift of the Spirit of God (*ruah adonai*), integrity and justice. Here we find increasingly utopian attributes, and probably the first attempts at eschatologizing the expectation. A famous example is Is. 11:1–9:

> (1) But a shoot shall grow out of the stump of Jesse,[10] a twig shall sprout from his stock. (2) The spirit of the Lord shall alight upon him: a spirit of wisdom and insight, a spirit of counsel and valor, a spirit of devotion and reverence for the Lord. (3) He shall sense the truth by his reverence for the Lord; he shall not judge by what his eyes behold, nor decide by what his ears perceive. (4) Thus he shall judge the poor with equity and decide with justice for the lowly of the land. He shall strike down the ruthless[11] with the rod of his mouth and slay the wicked with the breath of his lips. (5) Justice shall be the girdle of his loins, and faithfulness the girdle of his waist.
>
> (6) The wolf shall dwell with the lamb, the leopard lie down with the kid; the calf and the beast of prey shall feed[12] together, with a little

[10] Jesse (in Hebrew *Yishai*) is David's father.

[11] Emendation for "a land."

[12] Emendation with 1QIs.[a] and the Septuagint instead of "the calf, the beast of prey, and the fatling."

> boy to herd them. (7) The cow and the bear shall graze, their young shall lie down together; and the lion, like the ox, shall eat straw. (8) A babe shall play over a viper's hole, and an infant pass his hand over an adder's den. . . .

(d) Only in the post-exilic period do we encounter a priestly savior figure alongside, but clearly subordinated to, the king Messiah. This expectation, which plays an important role later, is attested only once in the Hebrew Bible, in the Book of Zechariah, who prophesied in Jerusalem around 520–518 B.C.E. (Zech. 6:9–15):

> (12) Behold, a man called the Branch[13] shall branch out from the place where he is, and he shall build the Temple of the Lord. (13) He shall build the Temple of the Lord and shall assume majesty, and he shall sit on his throne and rule. And there shall also be a priest seated on his throne,[14] and harmonious understanding shall prevail between them.

One may want to view these four thematic complexes as steps in the *historical* unfolding of the Messianic "idea" within biblical Judaism: from the continuity of the Davidic dynasty via the restitution of the kingdom of David and the idealization of David as the charismatic redeemer to the introduction of a priestly Messianic figure next to the kingly Messiah from the house of David. This is enticing but nevertheless wrong for it doesn't do justice to the complexity of the sources. We are not dealing here with evolutionary stages which can be derived "genetically" from each other, but with themes or motifs which are in many ways intertwined and emphasized differently in different periods. We do not yet find a Messianic figure in a clearly eschatological sense, however there can be no doubt that all four complexes greatly influenced the development of "the" Messianic "idea" in ancient Judaism and beyond.

2. *Jesus Sirach*

After the exile the Davidic dynasty vanishes, and so does the expectation of a redeemer from the house of David.[15] How well the Jews of Palestine could do without an offspring of David can be seen, as

[13] The "Branch" is the "Branch of David" (*semah David*).

[14] The Septuagint reads "seated on his right side."

[15] On Messianic traits in Jesus Sirach see A. Caquot, "Ben Sira et le Messianisme," *Semitica* 16, 1966, pp. 43–68.

in a snapshot, in the book called *Jesus Sirach*, or *The Wisdom of Ben Sira* or *Ecclesiasticus*. The book is dated to the period between 198 and 175 B.C.E., i.e., to the eve of the Hellenistic reform in Jerusalem which led to the Maccabaean uprising. Most of it belongs to the so-called Wisdom literature and praises Wisdom as well as provides exhortations for proper moral behavior. Only in the part which is called "Praise of the Ancestors of Old" (chs. 44–50) do we find a kind of historical retrospective which is almost completely obsessed with Aaron's and his descendants' priesthood; David and his kingship are mentioned only in passing, after the author has endlessly praised Aaron and the dignity of priesthood bestowed upon him "for ever": "As by a covenant with David son of Jesse of the tribe of Judah the royal succession should always pass from father to son." But then, as if he had said already too much about David, the author once more returns to Aaron and impresses upon the reader: "so the priestly succession was to pass from Aaron to his descendants" (Sir. 45:25).

The "Praise of the Ancestors of Old" does not at all culminate in the effusive praise of any random ancestor, but of the leading political figure of the author's own time, the High Priest Simeon, the son of Onias. He is the latest descendant of Aaron and hailed in Messiah-like tones (Sir. 50:1ff.). From this it becomes very clear that the author of Jesus Sirach is not interested in David and a restitution of the Davidic dynasty but in the perpetual rule of High Priests from the house of Onias who claim to be the only legitimate descendants of Aaron. No eschatological figure is to be expected in the future but a very "earthly" and powerful ruler: "May His (God's) mercy," he concludes, "be established with Simeon and may He raise up for him the covenant of Phinehas which shall not be revoked, either for him or for his descendants, forever" (Sir. 50:24). The Greek translator of the original Hebrew book, who published his translation some time after 117 B.C.E., saw fit to change this verse radically: "May he (= God) confirm his mercy towards us, and in his own good time grant us deliverance!" After the firm establishment of the rule of the Hasmonaeans, who did not belong to the family of the Oniades and therefore could not claim to be the true heirs of Aaron, it wasn't advisable to insist on God's "eternal" covenant with Simeon; and presumably the translator had had enough of high priestly rulers anyway.

3. *Daniel*

With the Book of Daniel's famous dream vision in chapter 7, which describes the vision of a lion, a bear, a leopard, and a fourth most dreadful beast, we enter a completely different realm. Chapters 7 to 12 of Daniel can be dated quite precisely between 167 B.C.E. (the peak of Hellenization with the dedication of the Jerusalem Temple to Zeus Olympios) and 164 B.C.E. (the recapture and reconsecration of the Temple by the Maccabees).[16] The dream vision was, therefore, written at the point when the efforts of the Seleucid king and his high priestly and noble Jewish accomplices met with fierce resistance on the part of the rural populace, led by the lowly priestly family of the Maccabees, however before the latter's decisive victory.

It is before this turning point of the struggle between the Seleucids and the Maccabees that the vision and its interpretation in Dan. 7 was composed (literally composed: the chapter is a highly complex and complicated literary construct which cannot be analyzed here in any detail). The climax of the vision is the judgment of the fourth beast, which represents the Hellenistic-Greek empire, and especially of its last horn which symbolizes King Antiochus IV Epiphanes who wages war against God's holy people. He is successful until the final judgment which takes place in heaven and is described as follows (Dan. 7:13–14):

> (13) In my night vision I then saw with the clouds of heavens there came one in human likeness (*ke-bar enash*: lit. like a human being). When he arrived where the Ancient One (*'atiq yomayya*: lit. the Ancient of Days) was, he was brought into his presence. (14) Then to him was given dominion—glory and kingship. Every nation, tribe, and tongue must serve him; his dominion is to be everlasting, never passing away; his kingship never to be destroyed.

The "one like a human being" is the enigmatic figure who has made his career as the "Son of Man" (which is a mistranslation of *bar enash*) and has preoccupied scores of scholars.[17] The interpretation of

---

[16] The dedication of the Temple to Zeus Olympios and the subsequent start of the Maccabaean revolt is presupposed; the military campaign of Antiochus IV in Asia, which started in 165, and the reconsecration of the Temple on the fourteenth of December 164 are not mentioned.

[17] See only J.J. Collins, "The 'Saints of the Most High' and 'One like a Son of Man'," in: id., *The Apocalyptic Vision of the Book of Daniel*, Missoula, Mont., 1977, pp.

the vision (Dan. 7:17–27) doesn't return to him: he appears with the clouds of heaven before the throne of the Ancient One (who is, of course, God) and is given everlasting kingship—that's that. The interpretation explains that the dominion "will be taken away, by final and utter destruction" (v. 26) from the fourth beast and its last horn and will be given to the "holy ones of the Most High" (vv. 18, 22) or the "people of the holy ones of the Most High" (v. 27) respectively. They "will receive the kingdom and possess it forever, yes, forever and ever" (v. 18); "their royal rule will last forever, and all dominions will serve and obey it" (v. 27). Hence vision and interpretation do not match completely in that the vision speaks only of the "one like a human being," and the interpretation of "(the people of) the holy ones of the Most High." But this obviously is the intention of the final redactor. One stands for the other, both are intermingled with each other, *both* are given dominion and kingship from the destroyed fourth beast and its last offspring. The one belongs to the heavenly realm, the other to the earthly realm, but heaven and earth are closely connected: the one given dominion in heaven looks "like a human being," and those who receive dominion on earth are "the holy ones," a designation which is clearly reminiscent of the angels. Therefore, the discussion among scholars, whether the "holy ones" are angels or the people of Israel, is a futile one—they are both.[18] Earth enters heaven, and heaven enters earth; what happens in heaven, happens also on earth.

This, I believe, is the message of our vision and interpretation. The one who is given dominion in heaven is the angel Michael who represents the people of Israel (in Jewish tradition he is the guardian angel of Israel) and who is at the same time the head of the angelic hosts; those who are given dominion on earth are the people of Israel who are identified with the angels. There is a clear similarity between what happens in heaven and what happens on earth, the only difference being a time-lag between the heavenly and the earthly event. The transference of dominion to the "one like a human being" in the vision has already taken place; the transference of dominion

123–147; W. Horbury, "The Messianic Associations of 'The Son of Man'," *Journal of Theological Studies*, N.S. 36, 1985, pp. 34–55.

[18] In the heavenly part of what happens we have only "the one like a human being," no angels, whereas in the earthly part we have only the angels and the people of Israel respectively (the expression "the people of the holy ones" in v. 27 makes it clear that both are meant), not "the one like a human being."

to "(the people of) the holy ones" in the interpretation will take place in the future,[19] however, in a future which is expected to be imminent. The interpretation argues that the rule of the hated oppressor of Israel is terminated precisely *because* the changeover of power has already taken place in heaven and will therefore immediately follow on earth. Israel, together with the angels, will rule forever.

Why am I dealing with this in the context of Messianic expectations? The "one like a human being" is certainly not a Messiah in the traditional sense of the word, yet I don't think we can exclude him from our considerations. He is definitely a heavenly figure and not a man, let alone a descendant of the Davidic dynasty, but his designation as "one like a human being" shows the close interrelation between the heavenly and the earthly realm. Moreover, he is an eschatological figure because he takes part in the final judgment, although his role in its proceedings (v. 10: "the court sat in judgment, and the books were opened") is a completely passive one: he arrives before the "Ancient One," and "then dominion was given to him" (v. 14)—he doesn't do anything in order to realize the changeover of power, it just happens. However, if we take into account chapter 12, which seems to belong to the same editorial layer as does chapter 7, we encounter a much more active Michael: "At that time, the great prince Michael, who stands beside the sons of your people, will appear. It will be a time of trouble, the like of which has never been since the nation came into being. At that time, your people will be rescued, all who are found inscribed in the book" (Dan. 12:1). Here the appearance of Michael signals and brings about the final rescue of the people of Israel, and the mention of those "inscribed in the book" clearly refers back to the books which were opened during the judgment in Dan. 7:10. The heavenly judgment which the "one like a human figure" witnesses now takes place on earth under the active participation of the "one like a human figure" who is Israel's guardian angel Michael.

Hence, I would like to argue that we do find here the notion of a savior figure who is expected in a time of suffering which is regarded as an eschatological crisis, and that it is precisely the Maccabaean period which marks the decisive turning point in the evolution of

---

[19] V. 21 which doesn't speak of the future but of the past seems to be an interpolation.

the Messianic expectation.[20] However, it is not *the* Messianic idea in Judaism which emerges but only *one* possibility within the multi-faceted and multi-colored set of potentials. It is no coincidence that at exactly this point in the history of Judaism there also arises the expectation of *individual* resurrection: "Many of those," the Book of Daniel continues, "who sleep in the dust of the earth will awake, some to eternal life, others to reproaches, to everlasting abhorrence" (Dan. 12:2). From now on it has become possible to connect the expectation of a Messiah with that of individual resurrection.

4. *The Animal Apocalypse* in the *Ethiopic Book of Enoch*

The so-called Animal Apocalypse, as part of the Ethiopic Book of Enoch, originated between 164 and 160 B.C.E., i.e., immediately after chapters 7–12 of the Book of Daniel were written and at the peak of the Maccabaean uprising. It contains a vision of the course of history from its beginnings to the erection of the Messianic kingdom. The course of history is described in symbolic images—different animals symbolize certain individuals—which can be easily deciphered. The climax of the whole account is the present time of the author, that of the Seleucid foreign rule which is being brought to an end by Judas the Maccabee. Michael, Israel's guardian angel, appears here again, mostly along the lines of what we know from the Book of Daniel: he is called "that man" (1 En. 90:14) and not only writes down what happens but also "helped him (= Judas) and revealed (to him) everything" (*ibid.*). This leads to the turning point: God himself intervenes, the Maccabees win the last battle, the final judgment begins, a new Jerusalem is created and all the nations acknowledge the rule of the people of Israel which now lives in everlasting peace: "The eyes of all of them were opened, and they saw the beautiful things; not a single one existed among them that could not see" (1 En. 90:35).

A later redactor of the apocalypse wasn't content with this description. He knew only too well that history hadn't come to an end

[20] I therefore do not agree with A. Caquot (and with J. Charlesworth who applauds him enthusiastically) "that the early Maccabaean crisis did not cause Jews to look for the coming of the Messiah": these are the words of Charlesworth, *The Messiah*, p. 27, n. 81, who refers to Chaquot's "Le messianisme qumrânien," in: *Qumrân: Sa piété, sa théologie et son milieu*, ed. M. Delcor, Leuven 1978, p. 237.

with Judas the Maccabee, and most probably he also wasn't very happy with Judas' and his successors' performance. He therefore added a new finale and also changed the role of the Messiah (1 En. 90:37–38). Redemption is now postponed to a remote future which starts with the birth of a "snow-white bull" who is regarded by most scholars to symbolize the Messiah. Since the first Adam is also allegorized by a "snow-white bull" (1 En. 85:3), this Messiah clearly is a new or second Adam. With his birth all humankind is also transformed into white bulls which certainly means the beginning of a new and eternal era of peace. Finally, the Messiah as the leader of this new generation, becomes a wild-ox with huge black horns, obviously in order to remain distinguished from his flock. This Adam-Messiah is no more active than the angel Michael, his birth simply signals the new era which is void of any historical events, an everlasting peace with no history. The dreadful course of history, of which the Seleucid oppression unfortunately wasn't the climax but only an episode, has finally come to an end—a new creation with a new humankind and a new Adam as its leader, who, however, doesn't lead anywhere.

5. The *Sibylline Oracles*

The complete counter-image to the eschatologically intense expectation during the Maccabaean period in Palestine can be observed almost simultaneously in the Sibylline Oracles. The third book of the Oracles is a Jewish compilation which originated in Egypt around 150 B.C.E. during the reign of Ptolemy VI Philometor (180–145 B.C.E.). It describes the rule of a "King from the sun" (3:652), most probably Ptolemy VI himself, "who will stop the entire earth from evil war" (3:653), "in obedience to the noble teaching of the great God" (3:656). He is the savior king; his reign brings about eternal peace, and even Greece will acknowledge the sovereignty of God who, of course, is the God of the Jews. The center of God's kingdom is Jerusalem with the Temple, in which Jews and Gentiles are united in the service of the one universal God. It is a truly eschatological kingdom, graphically characterized by precisely those features we know already from the biblical book of Isaiah (3:788–795):

> Wolves and lambs will eat grass together in the mountains. Leopards will feed together with kids. Roving bears will spend the night with

> calves. The flesh-eating lion will eat husks at the manger like an ox, and mere infant children will lead them with ropes. For he will make the beasts on earth harmless. Serpents and asps will sleep with babies and will not harm them, for the hand of God will be upon them.

Here we find ourselves in a completely different world from the one we have encountered so far, a world not of religious wars but of tolerance and candor toward the Gentiles. God intervenes in history in order to establish his universal kingdom of peace, yet his agent is not a Davidic king, not a High Priest, and not an angel but a foreign king—like Cyrus in the biblical period. The Messiah is once again a Gentile, another facet of the colorful Messianic expectation which adapts itself to different historical and social circumstances.

6. *Qumran*

Under the heading "Qumran" we refer to the Jewish community which is mainly known from the discoveries at the site close to the north-western shore of the Dead Sea called Khirbet Qumran with its archeological and literary remains, the famous Dead Sea Scrolls. Its "core group," Zadokite priests under a leader who called himself the "Teacher of Righteousness," withdrew into the wilderness in opposition to the ruling class in Jerusalem, most probably around 150 B.C.E. when the Maccabees assumed the High Priesthood (the first Maccabee to become formally High Priest was Jonathan in 153 B.C.E., and most scholars believe that he is the "Wicked Priest," the opponent of the Teacher of Righteousness). Hence the origin of the Qumran community and the literature attributed to it is connected to the radical change of power in Jerusalem when the victorious Maccabees laid claim to the High Priesthood to which they had no more right than the extreme Hellenists they had fought so successfully.

The literature of this community is as complex as its history, which came to an end only during the first Jewish war with Rome. This has a direct bearing on our subject. We find here a plethora of eschatological and Messianic expectations which reflects the diversity of Messianic beliefs not only in Early Judaism but also within the Dead Sea sect itself. It is an open question whether this pluralism testifies to different opinions or to a historical development within the community. Although there can be no doubt that all the diverse trends cannot, and should not, be lumped together, I would like to opt for an approach which at least tries to take into consideration what we know about the historical sequence of the sect's writings—despite the only too well-known pitfalls connected with such an undertaking.[21]

(a) Regardless of whatever historical sequence may be established, most if not all writings of the sect are characterized by an eschatological hope which expects the decisive change to be imminent and to include only those who belong to the right side (i.e., the Qumran community). The Qumranic expectation of salvation is absolute and exclusive, it pertains only to the "Sons of Light" as opposed to all the others, the "Sons of Darkness."

(b) The earliest Qumranic writings do not mention a Messiah at all. This applies to writings like the *Pesher Habakkuk*, the Thanksgiving Scroll (*Hodayot*) and, most notably, the recently published document called *Miqsat Maʿaseh Torah* (4QMMT) which contains a letter written around 150 B.C.E. by the Teacher of Righteousness himself or by someone from his entourage.

(c) The most significant contribution of the Qumran sect to Messianic expectation is the belief in a priestly, Aaronic, Messiah who supplements the Davidic Messiah. This follows the line inaugurated by the post-exilic prophet Zechariah and fits well, as is argued, with the predominantly priestly orientation of the sect. The two Messiahs are mostly mentioned together and called "the Messiahs" or "the Messiah of Aaron and Israel" (*meshiah/meshihe aharon we-yisraʾel*)[22] or "a Messiah from Aaron and from Israel" (*mashiah me-aharon u-mi-yisraʾel*).[23] The use of the singular or the plural doesn't seem to be relevant here (some scholars argue, that the singular phrase describes only *one* Messianic figure who represents the priest as well as the lay people); both phrases, I believe, refer to two distinct Messiahs, a

[21] J. Starcky's article "Les quatre étapes du messianisme à Qumran," *RB* 70, 1963, pp. 481–505, still has its merits, despite the fact that it is out-dated and that its conclusions are questionable; see the criticism by L.H. Schiffman, "Messianic Figures and Ideas in the Qumran Scrolls," in: *The Messiah*, ed. J.H. Charlesworth, p. 128. For the most recent literature see F. García Martínez, "Messianische Erwartungen in den Qumranschriften," in: *Jahrbuch für Biblische Theologie*, vol. VIII: *Der Messias*, ed. E. Dassmann, G. Stemberger *et al.*, Neukirchen and Vluyn 1993, pp. 171–209; L.T. Stuckenbruck, "'Messias' Texte in den Schriften von Qumran," in: *Mogilany* 1993, ed. Z.J. Kapera, Krakau 1996, pp. 129–139; J. Zimmermann, *Messianische Vorstellungen in den Schriftfunden von Qumran*, unpubl. Diss. theol., Tübingen 1996.

[22] 1QS 9:10 (plural); CD 12:23–13:1; CD 14:19; CD 19:10f. (singular).

[23] CD 20:1 (singular).

priestly and a lay Messiah. Whereas the former is explicitly connected with Aaron, the latter is never said to be Davidic. This has been emphasized by some scholars and taken as an argument against the notion of a Davidic Messiah in these texts.[24] I don't think, however, that this argument is valid here: who other than a Davidic Messiah can be meant by a Messiah of or from Israel as opposed to a Messiah of or from Aaron? Moreover, as can be seen from other texts, the Scrolls are certainly familiar with the notion of a Messiah from the house of David.[25]

If we inquire into the function of the two Messiahs we learn very little. The texts describe the law of the last days but nothing is said about the Messiahs' contribution in bringing the eschaton about, let alone about their actions. The coming of the two Messiahs merely marks a decisive turning point in history, nothing less but nothing more. What is made perfectly clear, however, is that the Messiah of Israel is subordinated to the Messiah of Aaron. One more detailed text outlines the eschatological assembly and the banquet presided over by the priest and the Messiah of Israel (1QSa 2:11–22):

> [The priest] shall come [at] the head of the whole congregation of Israel with all [his brethren, the sons] of Aaron the Priests, [those called] to the assembly, the men of renown; and they shall sit [before him, each man] in the order of his dignity. And then [the Mess]iah of Israel shall [come], and the chiefs of the [clans of Israel] shall sit before him, [each] in the order of his dignity. . . . And [when] they shall gather for the common [tab]le, to eat and [to drink] new wine . . . let no man extend his hand over the first-fruits of bread and wine before the Priest; for [it is he] who shall bless the first-fruits of bread and wine, and shall be the first [to extend] his hand over the bread. Thereafter, the Messiah of Israel shall extend his hand over the bread, [and] all the congregation of the Community [shall utter a] blessing, [each man in the order] of his dignity.

The two Messiahs are mentioned only in the so-called Damascus Document (CD), which did not originate in the Qumran community but was part of their library and probably was also redacted in

---

[24] Most notably Schiffman in his article, *op. cit.*, pp. 119ff.

[25] There is a certain tendency now among Qumran scholars to multiply the Messianic figures in Qumran almost infinitely; see H. Lichtenberger, "Qumran 3.5. Messianische und endzeitliche Erwartungen," in: *TRE*, vol. XXVIII, Berlin and New York 1997, p. 71.

Qumran, in the Rule of the Community (1QS) and in the Rule of the Congregation (1QSa), an appendix to the Rule of the Community. They all belong to the first century B.C.E., if 1QS is not to be dated to the end of the second century B.C.E., with the possible sequence 1QS, 1QSa, CD.[26] Hence we may assume that the belief in two Messiahs, with the predominance of the priestly Messiah, is not only the most prominent feature of the Messianic expectation in Qumran but also constitutes its earliest layer.

(d) A clearly Davidic Messiah alone with no priestly counterpart appears in the Rule of Benedictions (1QSb) which seems to belong to the same literary layer as does 1QSa. It mentions (1QSb 5:20) a "Prince of the Congregation" (*nesi' ha-ʿedah*) who will establish God's kingdom forever. The title "Prince" (*nasi'*) is taken from Ezekiel (34:24; 37:25) where it refers to David, and the visual imagery it uses is influenced by Isaiah (11:2–5; see above). There are several other references to this title: one appears in the Damascus Document (CD 7:18–21) which, however, couples it again with another, most probably priestly figure (the "Expounder of the Law" = *doresh ha-torah*) while the other is part of the War Rule (1QM 5:1) which is dated to the last period of the community[27] and also shows a clearly priestly bias.[28] One might argue, therefore, that the image of the Davidic Messiah tries to come out of the shadow of the all-powerful counter-image of the priestly Messiah—but never succeeded in liberating itself completely.

(e) Finally, reference to the "Branch of David" (*semah David*), another title undoubtedly referring to a Davidic Messiah, is made in a set of texts which also seems to belong to the latest literary layer.

---

[26] According to Starcky, *op. cit.*, 1QS dates from the period of the Maccabees (150–100 B.C.E.), 1QSa (as well as 1QSb) from the period of the Hasmonaeans (100–75 B.C.E.), and CD from the period of Pompey and Caesar (75–50 B.C.E.). Charlesworth, *op. cit.*, p. 27, dates all these texts—and accordingly "the first use of 'Messiah' to designate an eschatological figure in Jewish theology"—to the first century B.C.E.; see also Schiffman, *op. cit.*, p. 128. His approach is somewhat inconsistent in that he, on the one hand, opts for the plurality of Messianic expectations in Early Judaism but, on the other, follows a rather reductionist theory which is limited to the use of the term "Messiah." Both Charlesworth and Schiffman are certainly correct in arguing against Starcky (and Milik) that 1QS 8:15b–9:11 cannot be eliminated from 1QS and relegated to a second period in the history of the Qumranic literature.

[27] According to Starcky, the period of Herod and thereafter (50 B.C.E.–68 C.E.).

[28] On the shield of the "Prince of all the congregation" is written his name, "together with the names of Israel, Levi and Aaron."

The fragmentary commentary on Isaiah mentions[29] the "[Branch] of David" who will "arise in the end of days" (*be-'aha[rit ha-yamim]*) and rule over the nations as well as judge them according to the teachings of the priests (4QpJes.[a] = 4Q161, 18–25). The "priests" here do not represent a priestly Messiah, and yet they do have some influence on the "Branch of David." Again, in a commentary on 2 Sam. 7:11–14, it is proclaimed that the "Branch of David" will arise at the end of days, this time together with the "Expounder of the Law" (*doresh ha-torah*) who may or may not be a priestly Messianic figure (4Qflor. = 4Q174, 1:10–13). Another reference reflects the classical biblical expectation of the restoration of the Davidic dynasty without a priestly Messiah being mentioned expressly (4QPBless. 2–4),[30] and a recently published fragment which probably belongs to the lost end of the War Rule (1QM) explicitly equates the "Branch of David" with the "Prince of the Congregation" (4Q285 Frag. 5).[31] Hence it seems as if the Davidic Messiah has been revitalized and become dominant in the last stage of the Qumran community, probably as a result of the decline of the rule of the Hasmonaean kings.

7. *Psalms of Solomon*

At precisely this time, the middle of the first century B.C.E., another corpus of writings articulates what may be called the classical expression of the belief in a kingly, Davidic Messiah. The Psalms of Solomon have nothing to do with Solomon but are a pseudepigraphical work attributed by some scholars to Pharisaic circles. They reflect the capture of Jerusalem and the Temple by Pompey in the year 63 B.C.E. which terminated Hasmonaean rule and transformed Judaea into a

[29] Probably after referring in 1:2 to the "Prince of the Congregation," and therefore equating the "Prince" with the "Branch of David."

[30] This, however, is not clear evidence because the text (now also known as 4QpGen.[a] = 4Q252) is very fragmentary: "Whenever Israel rules there shall [not] fail to be a descendant of David upon the throne... until the Messiah of Righteousness (*meshiah ha-sedeq*) comes, the Branch of David. For to him and to his seed was granted the Covenant of kingship over his people for everlasting generations."

[31] Published by G. Vermes, "The Oxford Forum for Qumranic Research: Seminar on the Rule of War from Cave 4 (4Q285)," *JJS* 43, 1992, pp. 85–94. Another highly controversial fragment (4Q521) which most probably refers also to a Davidic Messiah (however, with no further designation) has been published by E. Puech, "Une apocalypse messianique (4Q521)," *RdQ* 15/60, 1992, pp. 475–522. On both fragments see F. García Martínez, *op. cit.*

client state dependent on Rome. Ps. 17, in particular, describes this radical political change and connects with it the hope that God may now once again send the promised king from the house of David who will put an end to the Roman oppression (which in turn had put an end to the unjust rule of the Hasmonaeans):

> (21) See, Lord, and raise up for them their king, the son of David, to rule over your servant Israel in the time known to you, O God. (22) Undergird him with the strength to destroy the unrighteous rulers, to purge Jerusalem from Gentiles who trample her to destruction. . . . (26) He will gather a holy people whom he will lead in righteousness; . . . (27) He will not tolerate unrighteousness (even) to pause among them, and any person who knows wickedness shall not live with them. . . . (29) He will judge peoples and nations in the wisdom of his righteousness. (30) And he will have gentile nations serving him under his yoke. . . . And he will purge Jerusalem (and make it) holy as it was even from the beginning, (31) (for) nations to come from the ends of the earth to see his glory . . . (32) . . . There will be no unrighteousness among them in his days, for all shall be holy, and their king shall be the Lord Messiah.

Here we have the classical arsenal of the Messianic expectation which later becomes mainstream Jewish Messianism: a Davidic Messiah sent by God who purges Israel of the Gentiles, judges Israel as well as the nations, gathers together the people of Israel in their holy land and holy city to which all the nations go on pilgrimage in order to render homage to him and his kingdom of justice and righteousness. It is important to note that there is no hint of a priestly counterpart, and that the Messiah doesn't operate on the basis of his own authority but solely as the agent of God. His kingdom is realized on earth and not in heaven, there is no indication of a transcendent-utopian expectation which takes place in a future world. If we take the historical background into consideration, it is striking that the figure of the Davidic Messiah-king pushes itself to the forefront at the very moment when the Hasmonaean rule has reached rock bottom. The irony of history is that the political change inaugurated by the Romans didn't lead to the longed-for Davidic king but paved the way for the king who was, in the eyes of the pious Jews, much worse than any Hasmonaean: the Idumaean Herod whom Josephus so contemptuously calls *hêmiioudaios*—"half-Jew."[32]

[32] Ant. XIV, 403.

8. *The Similitudes (Parables)* of the *Ethiopic Book of Enoch*

The Similitudes or Parables as part of the Ethiopic Book of Enoch are now recognized by most scholars as Jewish, Palestinian and dating from the end of the first century B.C.E. or, more likely, the beginning of the first century C.E. They are a kind of "hodgepodge" of previous Messianic notions and combine in a peculiar way the Messianic figures of the "Son of Man" (from Daniel) and a newly introduced "Elect One." Both can be called "Messiah" (48:10; 52:4), however only in passing; the title "Messiah" doesn't play an important role.[33] Both are described as much more active than the "Son of Man" in Daniel: their predominant function is the eschatological judgment, authorized by God, which inaugurates an eternal time of peace. Just as in the Psalms of Solomon, this peace takes place on earth, not in an extraterrestrial or celestial world.

9. The *Fourth Book of Ezra*

A last facet in the multi-colored Messianic expectation of Early Judaism takes shape in the so-called Fourth Book of Ezra[34] which can be dated quite reliably to around 100 C.E. It is a distinctly apocalyptical work, composed mainly as a question-and-answer-game between the "visionary" Ezra and the angel Uriel, and reflects the historical and theological situation after the destruction of Jerusalem and the Temple in 70 C.E.

A Messianic figure appears several times and blends elements of the Davidic Messiah with those of the "Son of Man" from Daniel. In one of his visions (11:37ff.) Ezra sees a "creature like a lion" announcing to an eagle, who is "the one that remains of the four beasts," that his rule has come to an end. The four beasts, of course, refer to Daniel, and the eagle symbolizes the rule of Rome, which according to the Fourth Book of Ezra is the last of the four kingdoms to rule over Israel. The lion is explicitly explained to be the "Messiah" (*unctus*), "who will arise from the posterity of David" (12:32). In another vision (ch. 13) Ezra sees "something like the figure of a

---

[33] Cf. J.C. VanderKam, "Righteous One, Messiah, Chosen One, and Son of Man in 1 Enoch 37–71," in: *The Messiah*, ed. J.H. Charlesworth, pp. 169–191.

[34] Cf. M. Stone, "The Question of the Messiah in 4 Ezra," in: J. Neusner *et al.*, *Judaisms and their Messiahs*, pp. 209–224.

man" (*homo*), flying "with the clouds of heaven," a clear reminiscence of the "Son of Man" of Daniel, waging war against an "innumerable multitude of men" and killing them not by "any weapon of war" but burning them by a stream of fire "sent forth from his mouth." The "man" is explained as "my son" (*filius meus*)[35] who, standing on the top of Mount Zion, destroys the nations "without effort by the law (which was symbolized by the fire)."

The Messiah-Son of Man of the Fourth Book of Ezra once again acts as God's agent, but his role in bringing about the last days is much more active than in most of the sources analyzed so far. However, this is only partly true, because at this stage a completely new element[36] is introduced into the eschatological scenario: the Messianic period is limited and even the days of the Messiah are numbered (7:26ff.):

> (26) For behold, the time will come, when the signs which I have foretold you will come to pass; the city which now is not seen shall appear [i.e., the heavenly Jerusalem], and the land which now is hidden shall be disclosed [i.e., the paradise]. (27) And everyone who has been delivered from the evil that I have foretold shall see my wonders. (28) For my son the Messiah (*filius meus Iesus*)[37] shall be revealed with those who are with him, and those who remain shall rejoice four hundred years. (29) And after these years my son the Messiah (*filius meus Christus*) shall die, and all who draw human breath. (30) And the world shall be turned back to primeval silence for seven days, as it was at the first beginning; so that no one shall be left. (31) And after seven days the world, which is not yet awake, shall be roused....

What is remarkable here is the radical distinction between two worlds, "this [earthly] world" and the "world to come," with the limited Messianic age as the intermediate period. The Messianic age is exclusively part of "this world," it takes place solely on this earth; the Messiah is part of history. The primeval silence following the death of the Messiah prepares the way for the new world which is a new creation. Only in this new world will the resurrection of the death and the final judgment take place, which will be carried out by God alone and will include Israel as well as the nations. The Messiah

[35] There is no reason to explain this expression as having been influenced by Christian terminology.

[36] The interpretation of 4Q285 as referring to the death of the Messiah is pure phantasy; see Charlesworth, *op. cit.*, pp. XVf., and García Martínez, *op. cit.*, p. 181.

[37] *Iesus* is certainly a Christian interpolation.

doesn't play a role in this new world, in contrast to the Animal Apocalypse in which, as we have seen, the Messiah belongs to the new creation. Here the new world is solely the world of God and his renewed creation. The relationship between the "world to come" and "this world," together with its concluding Messianic era, is not determined more closely. However, the "world to come" is undoubtedly the aeon which is sharply separated from "this world" in that it finally and fully completes salvation. Hence we recognize here for the first time in Jewish history the notion of a transcendent (not of this world) ahistorical expectation as opposed to an earthly (of this world) political expectation, something completely new which does not fit into the "old" categories of heaven and earth.

The broad spectrum of ideas we have reviewed represents a period in Jewish history which can be called, as far as the Messianic expectation is concerned, the formative period. The respective traditions range mainly within the triangle (Davidic) Messiah-king, priestly Messiah, and Son of Man. The most diffuse figure is the Son of Man who originally was an angel (Daniel, Animal Apocalypse) and later adopted attributes of the kingly Messiah (Similitudes, Fourth Book of Ezra). It is tempting to view the various facets of the Messianic expectation as stages of a certain historical development, and I confess that I couldn't resist this temptation completely. However, I should like to re-emphasize that the different Messianic figures cannot be reduced to a uniform underlying pattern; they are to be described adequately only as the *dynamic* interaction of various and changing configurations within different historical constellations. The concrete political expectation clearly dominates; only in the Fourth Book of Ezra do we encounter the transition to a transcendent expectation, one which would make its main impact not upon Judaism but upon Christianity.

I thank Aubrey Pomerance and Johanna Hoornweg for polishing my English.

MESSIAHS AND THEIR FOLLOWERS

John G. Gager

Although my topic today is messiahs and their followers, I intend to focus on the second part—messianic *followers*—rather than on the more familiar topic of messianic leaders or titles. I choose this emphasis for several reasons. First, there is little need to trace new furrows in the well-plowed field of semantic studies; the terms *maschiach* and *christos* have received more than their fare share of scholarly attention. Second, many of these semantic studies have limited themselves to literary manifestations of messianic titles and thus fall prey to the abstractness and rigidity that beset all forms of the history of ideas. Third, with the exception of the work of Richard Horsley, few studies have bothered to look at what constitutes 99% of all messianic movements—whether in first-century Palestine or anywhere else—namely, the followers of the movement.[1] Fourth and finally, I remain mindful of Yonina Talmon's caution that an overemphasis on messianic leaders may blind us to the possibility that messianic movements are often shaped by their following—that they grow from the bottom up—and that the leaders are in some sense produced by the movement as "a symbolic focus of identification rather than as sources of authority and initiative."[2]

But I cannot escape the fact that the terms *maschiach* and *christos* have generated much controversy in recent years and so I must indicate where I stand on their use and definition. In general, I favor a broader rather than a narrow use of the terms. As John Collins[3] and others have pointed out, not every use of the terms *maschiach* and *christos* indicates messianic thinking—by which I mean the enthusiastic expectation of decisive divine intervention in history—and conversely,

[1] Horsley, *Bandits, Prophets, and Messiahs. Popular Movements at the Time of Jesus* (Minneapolis, 1985). Somewhat older and still useful is Gerd Theissen, *Sociology of Early Palestinian Christianity* (Philadelphia, 1978), esp. pp. 31–95.

[2] Talmon, "Pursuit of the Millennium: The Relation between Religious and Social Change," in *Reader in Comparative Religion: An Anthropological Approach*, ed. W. Lessa and E. Vogt, 2nd ed. (New York, 1965), p. 528.

[3] Collins, *The Scepter and the Star* (New York, 1995).

we do not require the presence of these terms in an ancient source in order to qualify a figure or a movement as messianic. In line with Collins' recent work, I will assume that messianism in this broad sense was a common Jewish hope in first-century Palestine but that this hope was not uniform. It varied according to time, place and social setting. At the core of this hope stood the expectation of a human or human-like figure who, in the final days of history, would restore the fortunes of Israel to the imagined conditions of Israel's ideal past. At the heart of this dream was political independence and what we might call, somewhat anachronistically, perfect religious purity. Jews of the first century would have preferred a single comprehensive phrase like "restoration of the full covenantal relationship between god and his people" but for us it is hard to avoid the habit of differentiating between religion and politics.

As for the messianic figures themselves, they could be conceived as Kings (on the model of King David), as priests (often looking back to Aaron), as prophets (based on a variety of Biblical figures, including Moses) or even as heavenly figures (as with Daniel 7 and the enigmatic Son of Man). And finally, since I cannot deny my primary calling as a student of early Christianity, I will assume that the figures of Jesus and his early followers fall *completely* within the boundaries of first-century Jewish messianism. In line with this assumption, I will avoid the use of the term "Christian" and will speak instead of the early Jesus-movement. As we shall see shortly, the presence of the term *christos* in a first-century—text, even attached to one put to death by his enemies, does not place that figure outside or even at the periphery of messianic Judaism.

But let me turn to the real focus of my topic—messianic movements and followers. Here I must confess to a degree of unhappiness with some recent work on ancient Jewish messianism. For the most part, this work has tended to concentrate on abstract ideas (the history of terms) or intertextual traditions (how later texts interpret earlier ones). My sense of frustration here derives not just from the fact that the terms and titles themselves always point to collective action of one kind or another—messianic thinking is always a social fact—but also that these studies have generally ignored both the groups that put these ideals into action and the creative mechanisms by which texts were accommodated to social and political reality. My own starting-point is that there are no messiahs without followers. In line with this starting-point, I want to argue that we can identify something like a messianic reflex in Jewish Palestine, beginning early in the first century C.E. and extending at least to 135 C.E. In others words, a period of intense and recurrent messianic activity stretching over a period of more than 100 years.

Among the earliest of the attested movements (apart from Qumran which I will largely ignore), one of the most intriguing is the one that took shape around John the Baptist, dating from the 30's. Although the first-century Jewish historian Josephus (AJ 18.116), in typical fashion, has thoroughly de-eschatologized his portrait of John, the independent accounts of him in the gospels make it readily apparent that John led an important messianic movement, that he commanded a large following, that he expected the restoration of Israel in the imminent future and that his actions were inspired by Biblical models. John's death at the hands of Herod Antipas [tetrarch of Galilee, 4 B.C.E.–39 C.E.] failed to put an end to the movement. Indeed, his followers believed that he had been raised from the dead, and for a period of time thereafter the John-movement flourished as a dangerous rival to the Jesus-movement.

But there were other movements as well. In the year 45 C.E., a certain Theudas announced himself as a prophet and in Josephus' words (AJ 20.97–99: again de-eschatologized; see the account in Acts 5.36) "persuaded most of the common people (*ton pleiston ochlon*) to take up their possessions and follow him to the Jordan River". A decade or so later, another movement appears, led by a figure whom Josephus (BJ 2.2, 61; AJ 20.169; see the account in Acts 21.38—a Roman tribune asks Paul if he is the Egyptian who stirred up a revolt) calls simply "the Egyptian false prophet". This figure rallied a following of some 30,000 and sought to force his way into Jerusalem, in order to overpower the Roman garrison and establish himself as the new ruler of the city.

And the litany continues: under Pontius Pilate, a Samaritan led his followers to Mt. Gerizim under the hope of discovering the spot where Moses had buried the holy vessels of the Temple (Josephus, AJ 18.85). And in a summary statement (BJ 2.258) of the period around 60 C.E., Josephus says the following:

> Deceivers (*planoi anthropoi*) and impostors (*apateōntes*) under the pretense of divine inspiration, they fostered revolutionary changes; they persuaded the multitude (*to plēthos*) to act like madmen and led them out into the desert under the belief that god would there give them tokens of deliverance.

In addition to those mentioned—and others from the same period—the most explosive movements emerge in the disastrous Jewish revolts of 66–73, 115–117 and 132–135. There can be little doubt that messianic hopes and figures played a prominent role in each of these episodes. Writing about the first revolt, the one that culminated in the final destruction of the Second Temple, Josephus describes its origins as follows (BJ 6.312):

> But what more than all else incited them to war was an ambiguous oracle, likewise found in their sacred scriptures, to the effect that at that time one from their country would become ruler of the world.

Josephus records that the hapless messianists believed that this ruler would be, as he puts it, "one of their own" (the messiah), but he smugly concludes with the observation that the oracle in fact referred to the future emperor Vespasian.

As for the second revolt, centered in Egypt and Cyrene and poorly attested in the sources, we may take note of the fact that its leader was a self-proclaimed king, that it gathered a large following among Jews in the diaspora and that it features stories of outrageous violence on all sides. A recent interpreter of the revolt (S. Applebaum) has described it as follows: ". . . the spirit of the movement was messianic, its aim [was] the liquidation of the Roman régime and the setting up of a Jewish commonwealth, whose task was to inaugurate the messianic era."[4]

The third and final revolt (final in every sense) arose in Palestine in 132 under the figure known as Bar Kochba.[5] Once again an armed uprising against Rome failed miserably. So much so that the Roman historian Cassius Dio could write (66.12.1–14.4) that "nearly the whole of Judea was made desolate." This Bar Kosiba—Bar Kochba was his messianic name (the name itself means "Son of the Star" and refers to Numbers 24.17, a passage widely interpreted as a messianic prophecy)—gave an unmistakable messianic stamp to this mission. Eusebius (HE 4.6.1–4) reports that Bar Kochba claimed to be a luminary (*phōstēr*) (yet another reference to the star of Num. 24) who had come down to them from heaven and was

---

[4] Applebaum, *Jews and Greeks in Ancient Cyrene* (Leiden, 1979), p. 260.

[5] See Peter Schäfer, "Rabbi Aqiva and Bar Kokhba," in *Approaches to Ancient Judaism*, vol. 2, ed. W.S. Green (Chico, 1980), pp. 113–130, and *Der Bar Kokhba Aufstand. Studien zum zweiten jüdischen Krieg gegen Rom* (Tübingen, 1981).

miraculously enlightening those who were in misery. And in documents from the movement itself he is called "the prince of Israel" (*nesi Israel*).[6]

This rapid survey has revealed a striking portrait of what I have called the messianic reflex in Roman Palestine from the 30's of the first century to the 30's of the second century. For all of their diversity, they display a recurrent set of common traits:

- the leaders regularly presented themselves as fulfillments of Biblical prophecies or as imitators of Biblical heroes;
- each of the leaders can be called messianic—and was understood as such by his followers;
- they were all associated with resistance to established authorities—sometimes identified with Rome and sometimes with the ruling elites within Jewish society;
- the idea of restoration, both political and religious (our terms, not theirs), lies at the center of each movement; broadly speaking, they were eschatological-messianic movements;
- all of them generated considerable followings; in this sense they were popular movements and much more significant at the time than their contemporary reporters would like us to believe;
- through well-known rhetorical strategies these same reporters undertook not merely to minimize their popularity but to marginalize them in other ways: Eusebius speaks of Bar Kochba as a murderous bandit (*phonikos kai lesterikos aner*); Josephus repeatedly labels both leaders and followers as "dupes," "commoners," "impostors," "deceivers," and "bandits;" and a later Rabbi (Yochanan b. Torta—Ta'anit 4.8) mocked Rabbi Akiba's messianic proclamation of Bar Kochba with the words, "Akiba, grass will grow from your cheeks and he (the messiah) will not have come;"[7]
- predictably, most of these messianic figures and many of their followers came to a violent end at the hands of their enemies;
- less predictably, the demise of the leaders did not dash the hopes and dreams of their followers; or perhaps we should admit, based on the by now common phenomenon that the death, imprisonment or disappearance of a leader often increases rather than

[6] Collins, *Scepter*, p. 202.
[7] Collins, p. 202.

diminishes their stature,[8] that the survival of these movements demonstrates the manifold creative techniques used to adjust written texts and oral prophecies to the exigencies of historical reality;
- in the long run, only one of these messianic movements (the one around Jesus of Nazareth) survived its messianic origins; the rule here would seem to be that all messianic movements fail and that those that manage to survive do so only as post-messianic.

Among the many questions and issues that arise from these common traits, I would like to focus briefly on just three—(1) The social make-up of the group: What conditions of the times might have inclined some Jews in Roman Palestine to be attracted by messianic dreams in action? (2) Who joined? Are there any signs that the followers belonged to certain social groups, or classes or status, say, the lower orders of Palestinian Jewish society? (3) And finally, must we judge these messianic dreamers to be deluded and irrational, as they appeared to Josephus and most probably appear to us modern, rational-choice theoreticians?

The issue of what might be called pre-messianic conditions can be dealt with in summary fashion. Taken together, the following factors add up to a set of circumstances in which messianic movements become not just comprehensible but almost inevitable:

- the ancestral land of Israel lay in the hands of an oppressive foreign power;
- God's holy temple, though still functioning, was governed by renegade priests appointed not on the basis of sacerdotal descent but by appointment from the despised Romans;
- factionalism of various kinds generated hatreds, competition and murderous rivalries;[9]
- the heavy hand of Roman taxation intensified these rivalries, generated poverty and resentment, and gave rise to the recurrent phrase in the gospels—I assume that the words must have been common coin—"tax-collectors and sinners;"

---

[8] Talmon, "Pursuit," p. 134.

[9] Martin Goodman, in his *The Ruling Class of Judea. The Origins of the Jewish Revolt against Rome A.D. 66–70* (Cambridge, 1987) offers a useful survey of conventional explanations for the revolt of 66–70 (pp. 5–14) and argues for "the power struggle within the ruling class as one of the crucial factors which led to the outbreak" (p. 25). Virtually all the literary evidence from the period attests to intense rivalries and bitter hostilities.

– and finally, the presence of a large body of traditions—written and oral—which reiterated the promise of restoration through divine intervention.

Given these pre-conditions, we can no longer find it surprising that Josephus and others reflect a widespread messianic fervor in the 100 or so years between 30 and 135 C.E. But still we need to ask, "Who joined these movements?" Or perhaps we should turn the question around and ask, "What made it possible for certain individuals to emerge as the bearers of these broadly disseminated messianic ideals?"

In the first place, we can now assert with confidence that we are not dealing with numerically insignificant minority groups or with movements on the fringes of society. Josephus—who had every reason to play down their numbers—regularly speaks of large followings (*polloi*—AJ 20.97, 168, 169; BJ 2.264, 259; cf. BJ 7.438—*ouk oligous*). In the case of the anonymous Egyptian he gives a figure of 30,000; and the armed movement under Simon bar Giora, the messianic claimant in the revolt of 66–73, was strong enough for Josephus to call it an army (BJ 4.510).

The same Josephus proves much less helpful when it comes to identifying the social status of our followers. In the respectable style of many Greek and Roman historians, he is fond of dismissing them with an array of stock phrases: "the crowd" (*ochlos*—AJ 20.97, 160, 167); "ordinary folk" (*dēmos/laos*—AJ 2.102, 172, 286, 288); and "dupes" (*apateōntes*) are his favorites. But on at least one occasion—in his account of Simon bar Gioras—he is forced to admit that Simon's army "no longer consisted of mere slaves (*douloi*) and brigands but included numerous citizens who obeyed him as a king" (BJ 4.510).[10]

In the end, I am certain that Josephus' stock phrases tell us far more about the techniques of polemical historiography and about his own social location than they do about the catchment of the movements themselves.

[10] Goodman, *Ruling Class*, argues convincingly that "despite Josephus' rhetoric, there is evidence that many members of the Judean ruling class of the pre-war period remained actively involved in the revolt right up to the destruction of the city in A.D. 70" (p. 199). And speaking of the later revolt under Bar Kochba, he notes that "[R]ich Jews, like their poorer brothers, thus had no option in A.D. 132 but to fight to the end" (p. 251). Some of these elite members must have been motivated by messianic hopes, though concrete evidence is lacking.

If we turn for help on this matter to the one movement (again I exclude Qumran) that has left us a detailed self-portrait (the one around Jesus of Nazareth), we gain mixed results. Overall, there is little doubt that the early Jesus movement thought of itself as a body of disadvantaged outsiders. The poor are favored over the rich; the learning of the Pharisees is derided as hypocrisy; the rulers of the Temple are accused of turning the holy sanctuary into a den of brigands (*lestai*—that word again; the real meaning = "I don't like them"); and an atmosphere of anti-Romanism pervades the entire story. And yet we need to exercise caution before we translate this rhetoric of disadvantage into straightforward social description. Let me mention just a few of the obstacles:

- the rhetoric of disadvantage—we might also call it the ideology of poverty—does more than simply mirror social reality; it exaggerates, idealizes and thus distorts that reality;
- Jewish messianic thinking in particular stressed the positive redemptive value of outsiderness—God would redeem the weak and needy. This tendency is particularly visible in the role played by the Jordan River and the Judean desert in a number of movements (Qumran; John the Baptist; Josephus, AJ 20.97, 168, 188, 259). Such symbols not only attracted those who saw themselves as weak and needy but also tended to project an idealized—that is distorted—social portrait of the group as a whole;
- the theory of "relative deprivation," which has proven useful in the social analysis of millenarian and revolutionary groups, argues that deprivation is a relative concept and can be defined as the perception of an uneven relationship between expectation and access to the means of satisfaction. In other words, given the conditions of Roman occupation, a polluted temple, and oppressive taxation, the theory of relative deprivation alerts us to the likelihood that the pool of pre-messianic candidates in Jewish Palestine probably encompassed the majority of the population, excluding only those in command of the temple and those who, like Josephus, had made their peace with Rome;
- reinforcing this theoretical perspective is the distinctive nature of the social structure of the Roman world—and certainly of first century Palestine. With an exceptionally narrow power elite at the top and an equally broad band of dependent groups below, stretch-

> ing from just beneath the top all the way to the bottom, the possibilities for thinking of oneself as disadvantaged were virtually endless.

In the end, we will probably not find a better social description of messianic followers than the apostle Paul's terse description of the community of Jesus-followers in the Greek city of Corinth (1 Cor. 1.26): ". . . not many of you are wise in human terms, not many are powerful, not many are distinguished." Some perhaps, but not many.

But in the final analysis, one fact remains and one question. Most of the leaders and many of the followers of these messianic movements were put to death, by the sword or on the cross. And in light of their fate, how can we avoid Josephus' characterization of them all as charlatans or deluded lunatics? How can we treat them as anything but hopelessly irrational, given their repeated attempts to take up arms against the vastly superior forces of the Roman army? There may be no way out of this unhappy dilemma, but before we join hands with Josephus we would do well to consider whether he has told us the full story.

There are, I believe, two considerations worthy of attention. The first is the myth of the Maccabees, preserved (I suspect) not just in oral legend but in the widely circulated books that have come down to us as first and second Maccabees. At the heart of this myth lies the unlikely story of a small band of brothers who turn aside the might of the Seleucid army and restore sovereignty to the land of Israel. If *they* did—so the thinking must have run—so can we. The second consideration involves the notion, clearly visible at Qumran, in the Jesus-movement and hinted at by Josephus in his accounts of various prophetic figures on the eve of the first great revolt, that God and his heavenly hosts would intervene at the proper time to utterly defeat Israel's enemies. What the War Scroll from Qumran, several sayings of Jesus and the entire book of Revelation make unmistakably clear is that the final messianic drama would engage on the side of the righteous a military power from heaven which would annihilate the foreign oppressors once and for all. To be sure, this hope was never realized and may well seem foolish to us. But within the cultural setting of that time, it made sense and must be counted as rational. The hope was widely shared; there existed an ample library of writings to sustain and support it; and in the myth of the Maccabees it had received strong and recent confirmation. Even Josephus, who presents himself as the sole voice of reason in an ocean of irrationalism, reports as entirely believable, the following portent just prior to the great revolt (BJ 6.298f.):

> Before sunset, throughout all parts of the country, chariots were seen in the air and armed battalions hurtling through the clouds and encompassing the cities.

Of course, Josephus believed that the chariots were Roman. But the messianic dreamers knew that they belonged to God.

MESSIANIC ELEMENTS IN THE PRECHRISTIAN GRECO-ROMAN WORLD

Christian Habicht

A Messiah in the full sense of the word is not to be found in the Greco-Roman world. For one, ointment, an important (maybe even essential) feature of the Messiah, is never mentioned. We do find saviors and "messianic figures," that is to say: real persons reported as having inaugurated a new and better order, or ideal persons expected to come and to do so in the future. We will also find a "messianic message": a prophecy that such a figure will come (or is about to come), to inaugurate an idyllic age of peace and prosperity.

First, a few words about saviors in Greece. In classical antiquity, saviors were the gods, their beneficiaries individuals, or groups of persons, or states. The word *Soter* means "Savior" and is applied to many gods, its female form (*Soteira*) to goddesses. The first recorded case of a mortal hailed as savior occurred during the Peloponnesian War, in 422 B.C., when the Spartan general Brasidas was so honored by the city of Amphipolis (at the border of Macedon and Thrace). The city, founded only in 437 by the Athenians, had defected to the Spartans. The historian Thucydides, to whom we owe the story, was at the time the Athenian general in charge of the region and was held responsible for the loss. Another general, Kleon, attempted to recapture the city. In a battle under the walls both Kleon and Brasidas were killed, but the city was spared. Brasidas was given public burial within the city (a very rare honor) and was voted a hero's worship "as if he were the city's founder" (ὡς οἰκιστῆι), "since the citizens thought that he had become their savior" (νομίσαντες τὸν μὲν Βρασίδαν σωτῆρά τε ἑαυτῶν γεγενῆσθαι).[1]

Mortals as saviors became more common in the wars of the Successors after the death of Alexander the Great, and now, a century

[1] Thucydides 5. 11. 1–4: "After this all the allies gave Brasidas a public burial in the city . . ., following his body in full armour. And the Amphipolitans fenced in his monument and have ever since made offerings to him as a hero, giving honours and instituting games and yearly sacrifices. They also adopted him as founder of the colony . . ., thinking Brasidas to have been their savior."

after Brasidas, not only after their death, but while they lived. Consequently, they received not those honors bestowed on heroes and centered at the grave site, but those hitherto reserved for the gods, ἰσόθεοι τιμαί (godlike honors). In 307, when Demetrius Poliorcetes liberated the city of Athens from Kassander's despotic rule and restored democracy, he and his father Antigonus were hailed as Savior-Gods (θεοὶ σωτῆρες, dual σωτῆρε).[2] Three years later, the Rhodians granted Ptolemy I of Egypt godlike honors, since he had become their savior defending them against those same kings worshipped as saviors at Athens![3]

In all three cases (Amphipolis, Athens, Rhodes) the savior's activity was limited to a single community and restricted to a single beneficial act. Demetrius is the only one among them who introduced something like a *new order*, in restoring democracy. Even so he remains far from what we might call a messianic figure.

We come a step closer in 270 B.C. when the poet Theocritus of Syracuse, living in Alexandria in Egypt, praised king Ptolemy I and queen Berenice (both dead by then) as "saviors (he uses the poetic word ἀρωγός) of *all mankind*" (πάντεσσιν ἐπιχθονίοισιν ἀρωγούς).[4] Here, for the first time appears a savior for all humanity. If I am not mistaken, this is at variance with the activity of the Jewish Messiah which exclusively affects the Jews as God's chosen people—other nations come into the prophet's view but are irrelevant in this respect.

Another testimony also deals with the Ptolemies. It comes from a long decree of Egyptian priests of 238 B.C. written in Greek, hieroglyphs and demotic, the so-called Canopus decree. It reads: "The birth of king Ptolemy, son of the Brother-Sister Gods, took place on the 5th of Dios, which has been the beginning of many blessings to all mankind" (πᾶσιν ἀνθρώποις).[5] Similarly of a successor some forty years later, in the famous Rosetta stone. The universal aspect ("all mankind") is still there, but there is not much "savior" activity. The king is praised *qua* king, not for any specific deed. And the begin-

---

[2] Diodor 20, 46, 2. Plutarch, *Demetrius* 10, 4–5. Ch. Habicht, *Gottmenschentum und griechische Städte*, 2nd ed., Munich 1970, 44–48.

[3] Diodor 20, 100, 3–4. Pausanias 1, 8, 6. Habicht 109–110.

[4] Theocritus 17. 125.

[5] W. Dittenberger, *Orientis Graeci Inscriptiones Selectae* 56. 26. See also *Orientis Graeci Inscriptiones Selectae* 90. 47, the Rosetta stone of 196 B.C.

ning of his blessings for the human race is not the day he began to rule, but his birthday. He has not performed acts of a savior, but is born into this role.

Before long, Roman marshals and Roman emperors would replace the hellenistic kings. After his victory over Pompey in 48 B.C., Caesar was hailed by the Greek assembly of the province of Asia as "offspring of Ares and Aphrodite, god manifest (θεὸς ἐπιφανής) and common savior of mankind" (κοινὸς τοῦ ἀνθρωπίνου βίου σωτήρ)[6] or, on a Greek island, as "savior of the oecumene," the inhabited world (σωτὴρ τῆς οἰκουμένης).[7] He was not only a savior for all (as were the Ptolemies), but with an additional nuance, a god present and visible. This, too, was not new, for when king Demetrius (whom we have met before) returned to Athens in 290 B.C., he was praised in a hymn composed for the occasion.[8] It says among other things: "Other gods are either far away or have not ears, or are not, or heed us not at all; but thee I (King Demetrius) we can see in very presence, not in wood and not in stone, but in truth. And so we pray to thee. First bring peace, thou very dear! For thou hast the power." The message is "Bring us peace by delivering us from our enemies, the Aetolians!" This savior's function was limited, once more, to serve Athenian interests, not more. With Caesar, on the other hand, mankind's future is at stake. And so it is with Augustus, once he has finally, in 30 B.C., brought an end to civil war. A decree of the city of Halicarnassus (in western Turkey, once the residence of Maussollus, whose lavish tomb Augustus was later to imitate and outshine) calls him "Zeus the Fatherly (*Zeus Patroos*), savior of the common race of mankind" and continues: "Land and sea are at peace, the cities are flourishing through law and order, concord and prosperity; there is plenty of every good, of well-founded hopes for the future and of good feelings for the present."[9] And, as with the Ptolemies, Augustus' birthday is for the entire world (*Kosmos*) the beginning of "the good message

[6] *Inschr. Ephesos* 251 (province of Asia, 48 B.C.).

[7] IG XII 5. 557 (Carthaia on Ceus).

[8] Duris, *FGrHist* 76, F 13, vv. 15–22 (Athens, 290 B.C.).

[9] *Greek Inscriptions in the British Museum* 894, 4ff. (Halicarnassus, time of Augustus): Καίσαρα τὸν Σεβαστὸν . . . Δία δὲ Πατρῷον καὶ σωτῆρα τοῦ κοινοῦ τῶν ἀνθρώπων γένους . . . εἰρηνεύουσι μὲν γὰρ γῆ καὶ θάλαττα, πόλεις δὲ ἀνθοῦσιν εὐνομίαι, ὁμονοίᾳ τε καὶ εὐετηρίᾳ, ἀκμή τε καὶ φορὰ παντός ἐστιν ἀγαθοῦ, ἐλπίδων μὲν χρηστῶν πρὸς τὸ μέλλον, εὐθυμίας δὲ εἰς τὸ παρόν.

(εὐαγγέλια) to be brought about by him."[10] The wording is very close to the description of the birth of Christ in the Gospel of St. Luke, as has often been noticed. For young Augustus' Jewish biographer Nicolaus of Damascus, it was not Octavian's birthday, but his adoption by Caesar that marked "the beginning of good things for all mankind."[11]

So we find mortal saviors, present on earth, their activity beneficial to all mankind, specifically by bringing about peace and prosperity; their birthday the beginning of a Golden Age. They are, however, not expected in the future as the Messiah is; they are present, their work has already been done. They are recognized for what they are, not announced for what they might become one day. Also missing is another element: while these human saviors improve people's lives, they do not create a new order, and do not regenerate the world—at least, this aspect is not stressed.

It becomes, finally, dominant in the last testimony that I wish to present and to discuss a little more fully: Vergil's *Fourth Eclogue* or, to give it a title often used, "Vergil's messianic poem."[12] With it we remain at the lifetime of Augustus and, consequently, at the time Christianity was born.[13]

No other piece of lyrical poetry has been treated (and mistreated) as often as this poem of 63 lines. It is part of the ten *eclogues*, or pastoral poems, composed in imitation of Theocritus' *bucolics*. It does

---

[10] W. Dittenberger, OGI 458. 40 (province of Asia, 9 B.C.): ἦρξεν δὲ τῶι κόσμωι τῶν δι' αὐτὸν εὐαγγελί[ων ἡ γενέθλιος] τοῦ θεοῦ.

[11] *FGrHist* 90, F 130. 55: πᾶσιν ἀνθρώποις ἀρχὴ ἀγαθῶν. For the city of Ilion, as early as about 25 B.C., Augustus was "unsurpassed in benefactions for all mankind," ἀνυπερβλήτοις . . . κεχ[ρη]μένον . . . εὐεργεσίαις ταῖς εἰς ἅπ[αν]τας ἀνθρώπους (*Inschr. Ilion* 81).

[12] H. Hommel, "Vergils 'messianisches' Gedicht," *Theologia Viatorum* (Berlin, 1950) 182–212. W. Clausen, "Vergil's Messianic Eclogue," in J.L. Kugel (ed.), *Poetry and Prophecy* (Ithaca, 1990), 65–74.

[13] See the text on pp. 54–55. A select bibliography:

H. Lietzman, *Der Weltheiland*, Bonn 1909 (*Kleine Schriften* 1, 1958, 25–62).

E. Norden, *Die Geburt des Kindes. Geschichte einer religiösen* Idee, Leipzig 1924.

G. Jachmann, Die vierte Ekloge Vergils, *Annali della Scuola Normale Superiore di Pisa*, seconda ser. 21, 1952, 13–62.

P. Courcelle, Les exégèses chrétiennes de la quatrième églogue, *Revue des Études Anciennes* 59, 1957, 294–319.

R.G.M. Nisbet, Vergil's Fourth Eclogue: Easterners and Westerners, *Bulletin of the Institute of Classical Studies*, London, 25, 1978, 59–78.

W. Kraus, Vergils vierte Ekloge: Ein kritisches Hypomnema, *Aufstieg und Niedergang der römischen Welt* II 31, 1 (1980), 604–645.

W. Clausen, *A Commentary on Virgil, Eclogues*, Oxford 1994, 119–150.

not fit well into the genre and was probably composed separately and later included into the collection. The first three lines were then added to make it look closer to the world of shepherds in their utopian setting of an Italian Arcadia. It was written in 41 or 40 B.C., when the civil war that had begun in January 49 and seemed to have ended in the fall of 42 at Philippi, was again raging in Italy. It is addressed to Vergil's sponsor Asinius Pollio on the eve or in the course of Pollio's consulate which began on January 1, 40 B.C. The message is a prophecy (line 4) by the Sibyl of Cumae (near Naples) and goes, in much abbreviated form, like this: "The last age is about to come (l. 4); the birth of a boy is imminent (l. 8). He is Jupiter's offspring (l. 49) and will be born during Pollio's year as consul (l. 11). With this boy a new order is born (l. 5); as soon as the old sins are wiped out (l. 13), there will be an age of peace (ll. 17, 21ff.). The noble animals (like the lions) become innocuous (l. 22), the poisonous snakes and herbs disappear (l. 24)." At the end, the boy is born (l. 60), the prophecy fulfilled.

The problems most hotly debated are these: when was the poem composed? who is the boy? when exactly does the Golden Age begin? was there a model for the figure of the boy? I will comment briefly on these questions. First, date of composition: most scholars say: in the fall of 40 B.C., after an agreement was made at Brindisi between Antony and Octavian which avoided a new round of civil war that had seemed imminent. Asinius Pollio, we know, had a hand in bringing the pact about. A minority of scholars, however, say: composed a year earlier, in 41, on the eve of Pollio's consulship, to congratulate him at the occasion. I am inclined to agree with this second opinion.

Second, who is the boy? Is he divine (Jupiter's offspring, verse 49) or a mortal? If a mortal: perhaps Pollio's son?[14] His son Gallus later claimed to be this boy—but he was born the year before Pollio was consul and was for that reason found out in antiquity to be a false pretender. Most scholars say: a hoped-for son of Octavian;[15] but in 40 B.C. a daughter, Julia, was born, not a son. Others: a hoped-for son of Antony and Octavia,[16] since Antony and not Octavian was at the time regarded as the master of the world, and since Pollio

[14] So, among others, Lietzmann 26–29.
[15] So Jachmann 56–57, following scores of other, mainly German, scholars.
[16] Octavia, So Nisbet 63–64, Clausen 121–125 and other, mostly English, scholars.

was Antony's, not Octavian's, lieutenant—but the child born in 39 only was also a daughter, the elder Antonia. The marriage of Antony and Octavia was only arranged to seal the agreement at Brindisi, therefore a child from this marriage could not be born in 40—but Vergil explicitly speaks of ten months of pregnancy of the mother (line 61). It seems much better to acknowledge that no real person is meant, as already Gibbon concluded, saying: "The different claims . . . are found to be incompossible with chronology, history, and the good sense of Virgil."[17] Rather: the boy represents an ideal figure, be it the Golden Age or the Prince of Peace, or whoever.

Third, when exactly does the Golden Age begin? Vergil, in fact, gives two answers that contradict each other. First he makes it clear that the Golden Age is present with the birth of the boy; later he says that the new order will not be fully realized until the boy has grown into a man. Obviously, no real situation is depicted, despite the fact that the poet hopes to sing the praise of the boy's adult deeds when he himself will be an old man. The Golden Age, by the way, will be the last age (*ultima aetas*, line 4, which originally was the first line). That implies an eschatological element, familiar in the Jewish tradition, and at the same time reverses Hesiod, for whom the Golden Age is the first, to be followed by continuous decline.

Fourth, did Vergil have a model for the figure of the boy? This is possible, and passages of Isaiah have often been suggested as such, which he might have known through some intermediary (such as the Septuagint or a Sibylline oracle). Scholars pointed to Isaiah 9, 6–7: "For a boy has been born for us," who will become the "Prince of Peace." Or Isaiah 7, 14–15: "the Lord himself shall give a sign: A young woman is with child, and she will bear a son and will call him Immanuel." However, before Immanuel is able to bring about the new order, there will be a time of desolation—which is different from Vergil's prophecy. Therefore, no complete congruence—which we ought not to expect, anyway.

However much is disputed, *Vergil's boy comes as close to the figure of a Messiah as possible*. In fact, his message resembles the announcement of the birth of Christ (the virgin appearing in line 6: *iam redit et Virgo* was easily understood as being Mary). The poem was until the eighteenth and even the nineteenth century most often under-

---

[17] Ed. Gibbon, *The Decline and Fall of the Roman Empire* (ed. J.B. Bury, vol. 2, 1896), 308, note 61.

stood to be that announcement. The first Christian emperor, Constantine, read it so. In a speech delivered on Good Friday in the early 320s, he interpreted the Fourth Eclogue as the foretelling of the birth of Christ. His address *To the Assembly of the Saints* is a sermon spoken in Latin, but preserved only in a Greek translation appended to Eusebius' *Life of Constantine.* In chapters 19 and 20 the emperor quotes 56 of the 63 verses, a few at a time, and comments upon them (he omits the mention of Asinius Pollio). Gibbon has some marvelous remarks on the poem and on Constantine's speech: "Forty years before the birth of Christ, the Mantuan bard, as if inspired by the celestial muse of Isaiah, had celebrated, with all the pomp and oriental metaphor, the return of the Virgin, the fall of the serpent, the approaching birth of a god-like child, the offspring of the great Jupiter, who should expiate the guilt of human kind and govern the peaceful universe with the virtues of his father; the rise and appearance of an heavenly race, a primitive nation throughout the world, and the gradual restoration of the innocence and felicity of the Golden Age. The poet was perhaps unconscious of the secret sense and object of these sublime predictions which have been so unworthily applied to the infant son of a consul or a triumvir, but if a more splendid and indeed specious, interpretation of the fourth eclogue contributed to the conversion of the first Christian emperor, Vergil may deserve to be ranked among the most successful missionaries of the gospel."[18]

Vergil later wrote another prophecy: Anchises of Troy giving his son Aeneas a vision of things to come. They culminate in another savior: "whom thou so oft hearest promised to thee, son of a god, who shall again set up the Golden Age." This savior is none other than Augustus.[19] And this time, no doubt is possible: "Augustus Caesar" is called by name.

It was, however, the understanding of the Fourth Eclogue as announcement of the birth of Christ that contributed to make the poem look like messianic prophecy. There is, of course, a fundamental difference between a pagan and the Christian savior. In the Greco-Roman world the savior always operates in a real situation, delivering people from worldly evils such as war, enemies, oppres-

---

[18] Gibbon 307–308.

[19] *Aeneid* 6. 791–793: "Hic vir, hic est, tibi quem promitti saepius audis, Augustus Caesar, divi genus, aurea condet saecula."

sion, or captivity. Christ, on the other hand, is a redeemer of the soul, delivering it from sins committed in the past. He does not affect the conditions of life, but of afterlife. He looks for the spiritual, inner sphere of human beings. And he never does what he does collectively for groups of people, but only for individuals, even if the ultimate intention is universal: to redeem each one of them. His activity, furthermore, is not limited in time, but eternal. And unlike the pagan savior, he demands some measure of cooperation from those to be saved, at least faith in him.

Appendix: The Fourth Eclogue[20]

ECLOGA IV

Sicelides Musae, paulo maiora canamus!
non omnis arbusta iuuant humilesque myricae;
si canimus siluas, siluae sint consule dignae.
  Vltima Cumaei uenit iam carminis aetas;
magnus ab integro saeclorum nascitur ordo.
iam redit et Virgo, redeunt Saturnia regna,
iam noua progenies caelo demittitur alto.
tu modo nascenti puero, quo ferrea primum
desinet ac toto surget gens aurea mundo,
casta faue Lucina: tuus iam regnat Apollo.
teque adeo decus hoc aeui, te consule, inibit,
Pollio, et incipient magni procedere menses;
te duce, si qua manent sceleris uestigia nostri,
inrita perpetua soluent formidine terras.
ille deum uitam accipiet diuisque uidebit
permixtos heroas et ipse uidebitur illis,
pacatumque reget patriis uirtutibus orbem.
  At tibi prima, puer, nullo munuscula cultu
errantis hederas passim cum baccare tellus
mixtaque ridenti colocasia fundet acantho.
ipsae lacte domum referent distenta capellae
ubera, nec magnos metuent armenta leones;
ipsa tibi blandos fundent cunabula flores.
occidet et serpens, et fallax herba ueneni

[20] Text as printed in W. Clausen, *A Commentary on Virgil, Eclogues* (Oxford, 1994), pp. 11–13.

occidet; Assyrium uulgo nascetur amomum.
at simul heroum laudes et facta parentis
iam legere et quae sit poteris cognoscere uirtus,
molli paulatim flauescet campus arista
incultisque rubens pendebit sentibus uua
et durae quercus sudabunt roscida mella.
pauca tamen suberunt priscae uestigia fraudis,
quae temptare Thetim ratibus, quae cingere muris
oppida, quae iubeant telluri infindere sulcos.
alter erit tum Tiphys et altera quae uehat Argo
delectos heroas; erunt etiam altera bella
atque iterum ad Troiam magnus mittetur Achilles.
hinc, ubi iam firmata uirum te fecerit aetas,
cedet et ipse mari uector, nec nautica pinus
mutabit merces; omnis feret omnia tellus.
non rastros patietur humus, non uinea falcem;
robustus quoque iam tauris iuga soluet arator.
nec uarios discet mentiri lana colores,
ipse sed in pratis aries iam suaue rubenti
murice, iam croceo mutabit uellera luto;
sponte sua sandyx pascentis uestiet agnos.
"Talia saecla" suis dixerunt "currite" fusis
concordes stabili fatorum numine Parcae.
adgredere o magnos (aderit iam tempus) honores,
cara deum suboles, magnum Iouis incrementum!
aspice conuexo nutantem pondere mundum,
terrasque tractusque maris caelumque profundum;
aspice, uenturo laetentur ut omnia saeclo!
o mihi tum longae maneat pars ultima uitae,
spiritus et quantum sat erit tua dicere facta!
non me carminibus uincet nec Thracius Orpheus
nec Linus, huic mater quamuis atque huic pater adsit,
Orphei Calliopea, Lino formosus Apollo.
Pan etiam, Arcadia mecum si iudice certet,
Pan etiam Arcadia dicat se iudice uictum.
Incipe, parue puer, risu cognoscere matrem
(matri longa decem tulerunt fastidia menses)
incipe, parue puer: qui non risere parenti,
nec deus hunc mensa, dea nec dignata cubili est.

MIDRASH AND MESSIANISM: SOME THEOLOGIES OF SUFFERING AND SALVATION

Michael Fishbane

The theme of messianic hope is omnipresent in classical Jewish life and literature. It fills the Talmudim and Midrashim; is repeated in any number of prayers and rituals; dominates the choice of *hafṭarot* for Sabbaths and Festivals; structures homiletic perorations and the *shiv'ata'*-Piyyutim; and recurs in any number of other smaller and larger paytanic compositions. Reviewing all this material, one is struck by the deep structure of expectation and trust that constitutes Judaism in its many faces and forms—despite, or perhaps we should say, because of, the complete or incomplete realization of prophetic promises of final redemption. Paradoxes therefore abound, especially where the messianic manifestations are obscure or theologically problematic. In some cases the paradoxes even extend to the very formulation of standard prayers, as in the midrash that praises Israel for concluding its invocation that God redeem His people with the words: "Blessed art Thou, O Lord, *go'el yisrael*, who redeems Israel"—despite their present suffering.[1]

In the midrashim, the overall virtues of constancy and hopeful waiting often give way to a voice of insistent immediacy. Some dozens of cases express the urgency of a question. When will You redeem us, God?, when will King Messiah come?, and so on—*'Emati 'atah go'alenu; 'emati yavo' melekh ha-mashiaḥ; 'emat 'ati mashiah; 'am'ai la' 'ati melekh ha-mashiaḥ ha-yom; matai 'ati bar naphle?*[2] And then answers are given that encourage or curse calculations of the End, that set the conditions of human action or attitude, or that discuss the particular merit (or *zekhut*) of the Patriarchs or the Torah that may mitigate or facilitate rewards and protections in the judgment to come. The separate *logia* are usually brief, undoubtedly condensing longer fulminations and formulations on the subject.

In some cases, the midrashic sources preserve condensed apocalyptic

---

[1] See *Midrash Psalms*. S. Buber, ed. (Vilna, 1891), Psalm 31.8, p. 240.

[2] Cf. *Midrash Psalms*, 45.3, p. 269; *b. Sanhedrin* 96b, 98a, and 99a.

schemes and other statements of unexpected value. A teaching of Resh Lakish is exemplary in this regard, for he decodes the primal features of *"tohu"*, *"bohu"*, "darkness", and "deep" in Genesis 1:2 in terms of the four evil kingdoms (Babylon, Media, Greece, and Rome), and the "spirit of God" in terms of the Messiah who will come in the End.[3] Not only does the sage read eschatology into a formulation of protology—thus promising the end at the very beginning, but his interpretation preserves a striking teaching of the Messiah. Just how concretely one should take his identity of the *ruaḥ ʾelohim* ("spirit of God") and the *ruḥo shela-mashiaḥ* ("spirit of the Messiah") is not certain, but one cannot exclude the possibility that this midrash preserves an old notion that the historical Messiah will manifest a primordial divine form (either of God or created by Him).

There are other cases like this that indicate a rich (though largely lost or obscured) mythology of the Messiah. I shall choose two of these here, as they move us closer to my subject. The first is based on a homily interpreting Daniel's own revelation of the meaning of one of Nebuchadnezzer's dreams. Daniel praises God as He who "reveals deep and hidden things" (*galeʾ ʿamiqataʾ u-mesatrataʾ*) and concludes that *nehoraʾ ʿimeih shereiʾ* ("light dwells with Him"; Dan. 2:22). Concerning this light, Rabbi Abba Sarungaia said: "This is the King Messiah".[4] Nothing more is stated; but even this little says alot. For the Messiah is identified by the sage with the primordial light, whose origin was the subject of much rabbinic speculation. According to one view, the created light derives from an uncreated effulgence put on by God as a garment; according to another opinion, mundane light derives from "the place of the Temple", which I take to mean the heavenly Temple that various traditions mention as one of the things created or anticipated by God during the six days of creation. R. Sarungaia's position is different. For him the Messiah is the light (perhaps uncreated) that dwells with God on high. A later version of this sage's *logion* reduces the *nehoraʾ* to one of the primordial names of the Messiah. This too is an old notion, but seems to have somewhat neutralized the old myth, perhaps for polemical reasons.

---

[3] *Genesis Rabba*, J. Theodor & Ch. Albeck, eds. (Jerusalem: Wahrmann Books, 1965), 2.4, pp. 16f.

[4] Theodor – Albeck, pp. 3–4. The *editio princeps* and other mss. read *sheriy* for MT *shereʾ*.

The second point I wish to make at this stage bears on another of the old messianic names. In *b. Sanhedrin* 98b we read: "And the Rabbis say: His name is *Ḥivra'*, 'The Leper' of the House of Rabbi, as it is said (in Isaiah 53:4) 'surely he has borne our sickness (*ḥola-yenu*), our suffering he endured. . . .'" This is a puzzling sequence, since there is no connection between the name and the prooftext drawn from Isaiah 53. Something seems to have gone awry; and just this suspicion is confirmed by the reading of the midrash found in Raymundo Martini's polemical *Pugio Fidei*.[5] There, after the first name and some explanations, comes the following teaching: "The School of Rabbi says: His name is *Ḥulya'*", and goes on to give the aforementioned biblical citation. The verbal play between the name *Ḥulya'* ("The Afflicted One") and the word *ḥolayenu* is just right, and I am therefore inclined to suspect that Martini's citation preserves an authentic Jewish teaching of a suffering messiah, excised from the Talmudic tradition through internal or other censorship.[6] This may not have occurred until sixteenth-century Christian printings of the Talmud, since the name *Ḥulya'* with the prooftext from Isaiah 53:4 is cited by Don Isaac Abravanel, in his *Yeshu'ot Meshiḥo* (second *'Iyyun*).[7]

The existence of old rabbinic notions of a suffering Messiah can be further supported by R. Eleazar Kallir's *piyyuṭ* on the Messiah named *Yinnon* (which also connotes the sense of "Affliction"),[8] written for the *Musaf* service on *Yom Kippur*.[9] In it, the payyetan extensively utilizes passages from Isaiah 53 in his teaching that the Messiah will bear the sufferings of Israel, and will justify the people's sins before God. As a recitation for *Yom Kippur*, it anticipates a messianic atonement of sins, though with no mention of death or sacrifice.

Kallir's prayer indicates how deeply authentic the notion of a suffering Messiah was in classical Judaism. Indeed, in a homily found

---

[5] *Pugio Fidei*, ed. B. Carpzov, 1687 (reprinted, Farnborough, 1967), p. 862.

[6] I have found this view anticipated by A. Epstein, *Mi-Qadmoniyot Ha-Yehudim*, A.M. Haberman (Jerusalem: Mosad Ha-Rav Kook, 1957), 101. For other authentic midrashim in the *Pugio Fidei*, see S. Lieberman, *Shkiin* (second edition; Jerusalem Wahrmann Books, 1970), 52–67.

[7] However, he cites it in the name of "our Rabbis". Clearly, the manuscripts varied. The *Aruch* (s.v. *ḥvvr*) has "School of Rabbi Yishmael" for "School of Rabbi". This is undoubtedly a mistaken construal of *raby* as an abbreviation for *rab(bi) y(ishmael)*.

[8] Cf. *Songs Rabba* I. 6, "the nations of the world afflict (*monin*) Israel". See *Aruch Completum*, IV, p. 140b.

[9] See *Maḥzor*, D. Goldschmidt, ed. (Jerusalem, 1993), p. 410.

in *Pesikta Rabbati* 31, the sages even refer to the excessive suffering endured by the Messiah in every generation, according to the sins of that generation.[10] All this begs for a full inquiry, far beyond the bounds of this lecture. I shall therefore restrict myself to themes found in the cycle of *piska'ot* found in *Pesikta Rabbati* 34–37. These chapters have been ably discussed for over a century by G. Dalman[11] and A. Goldberg,[12] among others. But the importance of the material was not lost on earlier readers—being excerpted into *Pirkei Mashiaḥ*[13] and the *Apocalypse of Zerubavel*,[14] and commented upon by Azariah dei Rossi[15] and Nahman Krochmal.[16] Still, the last word has not been said. In what follows, I shall give particular attention to the theologies of messianic suffering found there, and some implied or obscure mythological features.

Pesikta Rabbati 34–37 are the final homilies in the cycle devoted to the 7 weeks of consolation following the fast of *Tisha Be-Av*. It thus runs parallel to the sequence in *Pesikta de-Rav Kahana*. Overall, these homilies draw on *hafṭarot* from Isaiah dealing with consolation, joy, and renewal. However, *Pesikta Rabbati* 34–37 is distinguished in several ways. First, by the unique occurence in *Piska* 34 and 35 of *hafṭarot* based on non-Isaianic passages;[17] second, by the very strong

---

[10] See M. Ish Shalom (Vienna, 1880), ed., 146b. Presumably, this suffering is endured in heaven.

[11] *Der leidende und der sterbende Messias der Synagoge* (Berlin, 1888).

[12] *Erlösung durch Leiden. Drei rabbinische Homilien über die Trauernden Zions und den leidenden Messias Efraim (PesR 34. 36. 37)* (Frankfurter Judaistische Studien. 4; Frankfurt am Main, 1978).

[13] A. Jellenik, *Bet HaMidrasch*, III, 70, 73.

[14] Wertheimer, *Batei Midrash*, I, 117–133.

[15] *Me'or 'Einayim le-Azzariah min ha-Adumim*, D. Cassel, ed. (Vilna, 1864–66; reprint: Jerusalem, 1969–70), 231–32.

[16] *Kitve Naḥman Krochmal*, S. Rawidowicz (London, 1961), 254–255.

[17] *Piska* 34, the fourth *hafṭarah* of consolation, begins with Zechariah 9:9; *piska* 35, the fifth one, begins with Zechariah 2:2. The treatment of messianic themes here is significant, along with allusions to Isaiah 53 (see below). But equally significant is the *explicit* omission of references to this text, which had taken a central place in Christian literature. The omission is quite glaring in the cycle of consolation in the *Pesikta de-Rav Kahana*. There, the fourth *hafṭarah* is Isaiah 51:12–52:12, and the fifth begins with Isaiah 54:1. Thus Isaiah 52:13–53:12 is missing from the sequence—and this is precisely the central passage dealing with the suffering servant of God! This significant gap was observed and commented upon by R. Loewe, in his "Prolegommenon" to the reprint of *The Fifty-Third Chapter of Isaiah According to the Jewish Interpreters*, with texts compiled, edited, and translated by S.R. Driver and Ad. Neubauer (1876; reprinted, The Library of Biblical Studies, New York: Ktav Publishing House, 1969), II, 21.

emphasis on the theme of suffering and a messianic figure called Ephraim; third, by the special structure of the four homilies, which are of the *ruaḥ ha-kodesh* type—thus giving a prophetic and even semi-apocalytic dimension to the sermons based on words of David, Solomon, Isaiah, and Jeremiah said to have been made in the "holy spirit";[18] and fourth, the literary coherence of the *piska'ot* separately and together, particularly in terms of themes and prooftexts. Most notable in the last regard is the recurrent (explicit and implicit) use of verses from Isaiah 53, Zechariah 9, and Psalm 22—all passages of importance in the New Testament and contemporary Christian literature. We shall consider these issues in due course.

Piska 34 sets the terms and themes to follow. As is typical of the *ruaḥ ha-kodesh* form, the opening biblical verse is applied to a historical entity through the question *keneged miy 'amaro P.N la-miqra' hazeh*, "With respect to whom did (David or Isaiah, etc.) say this passage? In the initial case, Isaiah 61:9 ("Their offspring shall be known among the nations") is applied to a group called the *'avelei tzion*, or "Mourners of Zion". This group is mentioned just earlier in that chapter as the one's to whom the Lord will bring "comfort" on the Day of Redemption, providing them with "a turban instead of ashes, a festive ointment instead of mourning, (and) a garment of splendor instead of a battered spirit" (vv. 2–3). Indeed, the polarities of these verses consititute the polarities of our whole cycle of *piska'ot*—beginning with the themes of mourning and sorrow in *piska* 34, and ending with the promised exaltation of the faithful in garments of splendor in *piska* 37. This deep structural integration of the homilies is another indication of their (final) compositional coherence.

The "Mourners of Zion" mentioned by Isaiah seem already to constitute an identifiable group after the destruction of the first Temple. No particular practices are identified by the prophet; but we have evidence from the nearly contemporary Elephantine papyri that after the destruction of the Jewish Temple in Yev the citizens performed such mourning practices as wearing sackcloth and fasting, abstaining from oils and wine, and sexual abstinence.[19] Mourning rites preserved from Tannaitic sources show related developments,

---

[18] Noted already by B. Bamberger, *Hebrew Union College Annual*; and also by Goldberg, *op. cit.*

[19] See *Aramaic Papyri of the Fifth Century C.E.*, edited, with translation and notes by A. Cowley (Oxford: The Clarendon Press, 1923), p. 112, ll. 20–22 (Papyrus 30; from 408 B.C.E.).

and the groups involved may have formed ascetic circles. Whether directly related or not, the group specifically designated in *Piska* 34 as *ʾavelei tziyon*, or "Mourners of Zion", are marked by two distinguishing characteristics. The first is their perpetual supplication of divine mercy; the second is their unabated hope in divine salvation. The two are related; and because of them the group was persecuted by other Jews,[20] but protected by God on high. In fact, the Isaianic passage cited earlier, referring to the "offspring" or *zarʿam* of the group, is reinterpreted to give the mourners assurance that God will stay "their hand", *zeroʿam*, in times of trouble.

According to the *piska*, one of the characteristics of the mourners is that they "arise early every morning to beseach (divine) mercy". The precise character of this vigil is not clear, though there can be little doubt that it must have involved rites of sorrow for the destroyed Temple and appeals for divine mercy in the sufferings of exile. But a deeper, more mythic dimension was involved. To appreciate this we need only look further on in the homily, where God declares that He will "Himself" testify on behalf of "the mourners who have sorrowed with Me (*she-nitztaʿaru ʿimmi*) for My destroyed Temple and ruined Shrine". The prooftext for this is taken from Isaiah 57:15, where God declares that He will be "with the downtrodden and humble of spirit (*ʾet dakkaʾ u-shephal ruaḥ*)". But this expression of divine comfort for humans says the opposite of what the preacher has declared—that is, until he indicates that the scriptural passage must be construed midrashically as *ʾitti dakkaʾ u-shephal ruaḥ*, which I take to mean that God will be "with" those who are "downtrodden with Me (*ʾitti*)". Such persons, the preacher adds, have humbly accepted derision, and all the while kept silent "and not attached merit to themselves" (*ve-loʾ heḥeziku ṭovah le-ʿatzmam*).

This notion of the participation by humans in divine suffering goes well beyond other midrashic expressions on the topic. For example, even the bold re-reading elsewhere in *Pesikta Rabbati* of Isaiah's word of comfort to Israel (*naḥamu, naḥamu ʿammi*, "Comfort ye, comfort ye, My people") in terms of God's appeal for consolation from Israel (*naḥamuni, naḥamuni ʿammi*, "Comfort Me, comfort Me, My people")

[20] I follow the reading of the Parma ms., *mi-yisrael*, against the reading *le-yisrael* by Friedmann. A. Marmorstein long ago observed, correctly, that only *mi-yisrael* makes contextual sense; see his "Eine messianische Bewegung im dritten Jahrhundert", *Jeschurun* 13, 1926), 18.

does not speak of humans sharing in divine sorrow. A certain distance remains between the people and the divine Mourner.[21] What is more, the sufferings the "Mourners of Zion" share with God in our homily invert the standard midrashic topos in which God Himself determines to be with Israel in her travail. In those cases, the prooftext "I (God) shall be with (Israel) in (her) trouble" (*ʿimmo ʾanoki be-tzarah*) is not immediately understood to mean that God will rescue Israel from travail, but rather, first and foremost, that He will participate in the people's bondage or exile. By contrast, the *ʾavelei tziyon* ritually endure the sorrows of God. Their behaviors led to derision and persecution, which only confirmed their self-understanding as suffering servants. We sense as much from the use of terminology from Isaiah 53 throughout the *piska*.

But I believe that more lies behind this persecution than a reaction of mockery at excessive rituals of mourning or expectation of salvation. To be sure, the "Mourners" are defined as those who "passionately desired (God's) salvation, evening, morning, and noontime" (*she-ḥamedu ha-yeshuʿah ʿerev va-voqer ve-tzohorayim*). But this alone is not noteworthy. More to the point is the preacher's contrast of the "righteous of the world" (*tzaddiqei ʿolam*) with the *ʾaveilim*. Speaking for God, he criticizes these righteous and says: "Even though words of Torah are necessary for Me (*she-divrei torah tzerikhim hem ʿalay*), you loved (*ḥibbiytem*) My Torah but did not love My Kingdom".[22] God then swears that those who truly desired the Kingdom are held in favor, and goes on to single out the "Mourners" and their suffering. The text is opaque. Just what is going on?

In my opinion, this passage can be explained through a version of a midrash on the verse "If I forget thee, O Jerusalem, let My right hand forget, etc." taught by R. Eleazar ha-Kappar. It occurs earlier in the homilies of consolation in *Pesikta Rabbati*. In it, the verse is presented as a word of God (and not the cry of human mourners). It goes as follows.

> My Torah is in your hands, and the End is in Mine, and the two of us need one another (*ve-sheneinu tzerikhim zeh la-zeh*). If you need Me to bring the End, I need you to observe My Torah in order to hasten

[21] The midrash appears in *Piska* 29, Friedmann, ed., 139a; it also occurs in the *Pesikta de-Rav Kahana*.

[22] Reading *ḥibbiytem*, with the Parma ms.

> (*kedei le-qarev*) the building of My Temple and Jerusalem. And just as it is impossible for Me to forget the End, which is (like having) "My right hand forget", so you have no permission (*reshut*) to forget the Torah written "From His right hand, a fiery law for them" (Deut. 33:2).[23]

It is not necessary to go into the full mythic background presupposed by R. Eleazar in order to observe that what is at issue in this midrash is a co-dependency between Israel and God with respect to the final End, and the centrality of Torah observance as a necessary catalyst. Indeed, the End is not presented as a divine reward for the merit of obedience, but somehow dependent upon the human performance of the commandments. This necessary nomism and the word *tzerikhim* explain the puzzling clause mentioned earlier from *Piska* 34. I would suggest that there too God testifies to the fact that "the words of Torah are necessary"; but the new issue is the spiritual focus on His messianic Kingdom. It is this which distinguishes the *ʾaveilim*; and one may suspect that what led to their persecution was a certain anomistic tendency, along with features of asceticism and social renunciation, that appeared in direct conflict with the world-affirmative character of Torah piety. Imposing laws of mourning upon themselves while the Temple was in ruins would have inevitably resulted in a suspension of many positive commandments. Several sources in rabbinic literature seem to me designed to neutralize just such activities.[24] By contrast, though without ever denying the Law, *Piska* 34 is all praise for those who yearn mournfully for salvation. Indeed, the righteous only merit their reward after they respond in tears to God's statement that only "the *ʾaveilim* merit (the Messiah), because (only) they acknowledged him and did not think of themselves (*ve-loʾ ḥeftzam ba-hem*)".

The turn to the figure of the Messiah brings the *piska* to its close. Two points deserve special note. The first is that this figure is named *ʿOni* (or "Sufferer"; based on a rereading of Zechariah 9:9 as "*ʿOni*, who rides on an ass"), because he is persecuted (*nitʿaneh*) in jail and reviled by fellow Jews (called *poshʿei Yisrael*). In this, the Messiah is like the "Mourners"—or as the text says, they are "like him" (*domim lo*)

---

[23] See *Pesikta Rabbati* 31, Friedmann, ed. 144b. A highly condensed and demythologized version is reported in *Pesikta de-Rav Kahana* 17, B. Mandelbaum, ed. (New York: The Jewish Theological Seminary of America, 1962), I, 286.

[24] See *Tosefta Soṭa* 15, Lieberman edition, 242–44; and the teaching of Rava in *b. Soṭa* 31a.

and will be exalted with him. This remark deepens our understanding of the structure of suffering and expectation of the *ʾaveilim*. They not only imitate divine sorrow, and participate in it, but they also live messianically in the strict sense. Their behavior and its consequences is a messianic posture that is vindicated by God. By contrast, the Messiah's own suffering vindicates the sinners and non-believers. This point is just adumbrated at the close of *Piska* 34—but it is a salient theme in subsequent homilies.

Before we get to that theme, let me mention the second notable issue at the close of the *piska*. It is the fact that the Messiah called *ʿOni* ("Sufferer") is also designated "Ephraim, My first born (*bekhori huʾ*)" (Jeremiah 31:9), and this passage leads to the prophetic assertion that "he" (*huʾ*) will be in the days of the Messiah *and* the world to come, "and (that) there will be none other with him (*ve-ʾein ʾaḥer ʿimmo*)". I take this to be a polemical assertion, stating in an unequivalent way that, for the preacher and his circle, there will be only one messianic figure—and that he will be the sufferer called Ephraim. Clearly, any other messianic figure, like David, is excluded; and by saying that Ephraim will be in *both* the days of the Messiah and the world to come, a sequence of figures (one, like Ephraim, who suffers at the messianic advent, and another, like David, who rules in the subsequent age) is also excluded. What is more—and this point is no less crucial—there is no notion here or in the subsequent *piskaʾot* that the sufferer is called "Ephraim, son of Joseph" (as in other sources), or dies in battle before the great End. Indeed, there is no mention whatever of a messianic death, or that death is part of the messianic scenario. The stress is solely on Ephraim's suffering and its salvific function. Indeed, as we shall now see from the sequel in *Piska* 36, that suffering links the Messiah to God's own suffering. And for this he is exalted on high.

Piska 36 expands the messianic scenario to mythic proportions, and both continues but also contradicts features found in *Piska* 34. The contradiction comes first. For through the verse from Psalm 36:10, "With You is the source of life, and in Your light we shall see light", the preacher first identifies the "source of life" with the Torah, through whose means one will enjoy light in the hereafter, and only then goes on to depict the pre-mundane nature of that light and its relationship to the Messiah. That is to say, obedience to the Law is exalted here as the means by which one may benefit in messianic glory; and nothing is said about the beatification of messianic mourners. Nevertheless, there is a strong thematic link to earlier motifs through God's naming of the Messiah as "Ephraim, My righteous Messiah (*meshiaḥ tzidqi*)", and the importance of suffering in the days of the End.

Although the preacher says that God "envisioned the Messiah and his deeds" before the creation of the world, we learn that his great commission scene of the Messiah takes place during "the six days of creation". Accordingly, the preacher has utilized or developed a myth that goes considerably beyond the well-known tradition that the "name of the Messiah" was one of the things thought of by God at this primordial time. Indeed, in our version, both the Messiah *and* his name are existent entities during the first six days.

The dialogue that enfolds between God and the future Messiah at this time is of crucial importance to the messianology (and apocalyptic theology) of the preacher. In it, God warns the Messiah of horrible sufferings that he will endure in the final Days because of the sins of the people, and asks him *ritzonekha bekhakh*, "Do you willingly accept this?", and adds that if the Messiah is unhappy at this prospect he is unacceptable. In response, the Messiah says: "With joy and gladness (*be-gilat naphshi uve-simḥat libbi*) I accept all this, so that no one in Israel will be doomed"; and he goes on to add that his salvific actions are not only for the living, but also for all those who have died since Adam. This notion was apparently more widespread in Judaism, being cited by Martini from a lost midrash by R. Mosheh Ha-Darshan,[25] and achieving notoriety in the Debates of Tortosa and San Mateo.[26] The Messiah's future suffering is thus joyfully embraced through an old legal phrase indicating willing and unreserved agreement;[27] and this suffering for sins anticipated before the creation will "save" every human that is or ever was.

Let me add parenthetically, that the notion of a willing acceptance of suffering is not unique to this source. Indeed, in old Near

---

[25] *Pugio Fidei*, 598. As in our midrash, the Messiah triumphs over Satan.

[26] See Ad. Posnanski, "Le Colloque de Tortose et de San Mateo (7 Fevrier 1413–13 Novembre 1414), *Revue des Etudes Juives* 74–75 (1922), 160–161.

[27] The language of "will" and "joy" are part of the technical vocabulary of legal volition clauses; see the important study by Y. Muffs, "Love and Joy as Metaphors of Willingness and Spontaneity in Cuneiform, Ancient Hebrew, and Related Literatures", Part I in his *Love and Joy: Law, Language and Religion in Ancient Israel* (New York: The Jewish Theological Seminary of America, 1997), Chapter 7, and especially Excursus III and V. Muffs doesn't bring the present example from *Piska* 36.

Eastern and Jewish legal sources, the range of terms used to indicate complete agreement includes the word love;[28] and so I would therefore propose that the meaning of the well-known expression that speaks of the acceptance of sufferings "in love (*me-'ahavah*)", as formulated in a detailed interpretation of Isaiah 53:10 preserved by Raba in the Talmud (*b. Berakhot* 5a), is in fact the willing and full-hearted acceptance of the travail. But this type of suffering only benefits the specific individual. By contrast, what is unique to the foregoing *Pesikta* passage is the joyful acceptance by a Messiah designate (at the beginning, in principle, and in the fullness of time, in actuality) of all the punishments due the unborn souls found with him before the creation[29]—and that this joyful endurance of universal sufferings for sin would save them all.[30]

But despite the Messiah's good intentions, we read in the *Pesikta* that the tribulations of the End are great and Ephraim cries out in suffering—claiming that he is but a creature of flesh and blood. God then answers him by recalling his agreement in primordial days, and by saying that "now your suffering will be like My own (*ʿakhshav yehei tzaʿar shelekha ke-tzaʿar sheli*)". God goes on to describe His suffering since the destruction of the Temple by Nebuchadnezzer, and even boldly applies the passage in Canticles that says "My head is filled with dew" (Cant. 5:2) to His own tears. Upon hearing this, the Messiah is consoled, and says *nityashevah daʿati; dayo la-ʿeved she-yehei ke-rabbo*, "I am reconciled; it is sufficient that a servant should be like his master". We thus have a recurrence of the earlier theme, in which the *'aveilim* suffered God's sorrow, although now an act of human suffering has word-redemptive effect. In recognition of this, the Patriarchs say to Ephraim (in *Piska* 37), that "you are greater than we; for though we are your ancestors, you have suffered the sins of our descendents (*she-savalta ʿavonot baneinu*)".

This last allusion to Isaiah 53, and the preceding reference to the salvation by Ephraim of all sinners who have died since Adam, allow

---

[28] See Muffs, *ibid.*, 144; and Part II, Chapter 8, especially pp. 180, 186 (with combinations of *'ahavah* and *ratzon*).

[29] Presumabaly, under the Divine Throne; alternatively, within the Cosmic Body (*guf*), out of which soul emerge to be incarnated on earth, and which must be depleted before the Messiah can come (cf. *b. Yevamot* 62a, 63b; *b. Niddah* 13b).

[30] R. Ḥiyya's statement in *yer. Shabbat* (Chapter 16, *kol kitvei*, hal. 1, at the beginning), to the effect that Rabbi Judah's sufferings were for the sins of the nation, and that this had a messianic dimension (see the prooftext from Lamentations 4:20), would be a middle position (i.e., suffering for the sins of others, but not *all* others).

us, I believe, to affirm the authenticity of a remarkable midrash on messianic suffering cited in Martini's *Pugio Fidei.*[31] It goes as follows:

> R. Yosi the Galilean said: You may learn the merit of the King Messiah and the reward of the righteous from Adam, who was given but one negative commandment, and having transgressed caused death for his generations and those to come until the end of time. Now which measure is greater, Goodness or Punishment? Conclude that Goodness is the greater and Punishment the lesser; for (if) the King Messiah was persecuted and sorrowed for the sinners (*mitʿaneh u-mitztaʿer beʿad ha-posheʿim*), as is said (Isaiah 53:5), "And he was wounded for our sins", how much the more will (this suffering) provide merit for all the generations (*kol ha-dorot kullan*), as it is written, (Isaiah 53:6) "And the Lord visited upon him the sin of all of us".

This teaching has a parallel in the *Sifra de-Vei Rav, Dibburaʾ de-Hovah* (12.10), as Lieberman noted many years ago.[32] In it, R. Yosi teaches the merit of the righteous using the same *a fortiori* argument as in the Martini version. The salient differences are that the *Sifra* says nothing about the Messiah, does not quote from Isaiah 53, and instead of referring to messianic suffering speaks of the merit of refraining from the sacrificial sins of *piggul* and *notar*, and of "self-affliction (*mitʿaneh*)" on Yom Kippur.[33] For these reasons (and assuming scribal changes), Lieberman concluded that the version in the *Pugio Fidei* is a Christian forgery.[34] I disagree. For one thing, the difference between the stress on the merits of the righteous and those of messianic suffering in our two texts is formally no different than the difference between *Seder Eliahu Zutta* 21 and *Pesikta Rabbati* 36—where the same two types occur. In both cases, I believe, we have either parallel versions, with different tendencies, or, more likely, the transformation of texts dealing *inter alia* with the sufferings of the righteous into teachings about messianic suffering.

In my view, a more important consideration in evaluating the Martini midrash is the fact that its key elements regarding suffering for sinners occur in *Pesikta Rabbati* 34, 36–37. In both cases the suffer-

[31] P. 866.

[32] See his *Shkiin* (second edition; Jerusalem: Wahrmann Books, 1970), 65. Martini cites it from the *Sifrei.* The text is also referred to in the Debates at Tortosa; see "Le Colloque", *op. cit.*, 163.

[33] I have used the *Sifra* edition of L. Finkelstein (New York: The Jewish Theological Seminary of America, 1983), II, 206–207.

[34] *Op. cit.*

ing goes back to the sin of Adam, on whose account death entered the world; in both cases, the suffering meritoriously saves all sinners; in both cases Isaiah 53 is a central text; and in both cases the suffering of the Messiah is limited to wounds. Nothing is mentioned about an atoning death for sin, and nothing is mentioned about a Davidic ancestry. I therefore see no more reason to assume Christian influence in the midrash gathered for Martini by his R. Rachmon than in our *Pesikta* cycle.[35]

Undoubtedly, these sources were part of an inner-Jewish development of messianic interpretations based on Isaiah 53. The antiquity of such need not be doubted. Already Justin Martyr has Trypho repeatedly say that the Jews expected a suffering Messiah, though he denied that it was Jesus.[36] But more to the point, hymns preserved in the Qumran scrolls describe the sufferings of a messianic figure (presumably the Teacher of Righteousness) with the language of Isaiah 53.[37] In addition, various rabbinic sources show the same exegetical tendency.[38] And finally, according to the testimony of the author of *'Avqat Rokhel* (preserved in Hulsius' *Theologia Judaica*) there is a striking alternate version to the reading found in *Pesikta Rabbati* 36, in which the messiah designate joyfully accepts suffering to atone for the sins of Israel. In this case, the prooftext used is the phrase (whose rabbinic usage we have already cited) *ḥolayenu hu' nasa'* ("he has borne our sickness") from Isaiah 53:4.[39] Indeed, this phrase and the subsequent v. 5 ("he was wounded because of our sins") seem to be the operative ones. They in fact served as the conclusion to

---

[35] Lieberman, *op. cit.*, 67–72, has reviewed the materials ascribed to R. Rachmon, and speculated that he was one of Martini's "helpers who gathered material from the Talmud" (p. 69). No doubt Martini had a helper; but I would suggest that the name Rachomon was chosen as a Hebrew play on his own name Raimundo, and perhaps even as a messianic allusion (*Raḥman* meaning "Merciful One").

[36] See *Dial. c. Tryphone* 36,1; 68,9; 99,1. A.J.B. Higgens, "Jewish Messianic Belief in Justin Martyr's *Dialogue With Trypho*", *Novum Testamentum* 9 (1967), 298, speculated that for apologetic purposes Justin Martyr put a mixture of Jewish and Christian views in the mouth of Trypho. But as seen from earlier examples his argument is not convincing; moreover, even calling the Messiah figure by the name "Lord" (68,9) is found in authentic Jewish sources (cf. *b. Baba Batra* 75b).

[37] Cf. 1Q Hod IX, 23–25 (Hodaya 17).

[38] In addition to the sources cited earlier, see the teaching of R. Simlai in *b. Soṭa* 14a and of R. Yoḥanan in *Ruth Rabba* V.16 (on 2:14). This latter tradition has been incorporated into the homily in *Leviticus Rabba* 34.8 in Ms. Munich 117 (see in the M. Margulies edition, p. 788).

[39] According to Hulsius, *Theologia Judaica*, p. 328; conveniently available in *The Fifty-Third Chapter of Isaiah* (*op. cit.*, n. 17), I, 9 (g).

a triennial *hafṭarah* recited for the *seder* Genesis 29:1–40:29, according to a precious manuscript first published by A. Büchler, and that reflects a practice from the end of the first millennium—if not much earlier.[40] Within this rich tradition, the uniqueness of the messianic *masekhet* in *Pesikta Rabbati* is its exalted theological correlation of human with divine suffering, and of course in the naming of the messiah Ephraim.

But why Ephraim? This is an old hedge of many thorns. Among the many explanations one may mention those that elide it with "a" or "the" messianic figure known as Ephraim ben Joseph and, also stressing that figure's death, suggest that Christian influence.[41] Other scholars have asserted that this figure was developed to separate David from sufferings in the end of Days.[42] I should like to try a different approach, based on the emphasis in the *Pesikta* on the name Ephraim alone, and the fact that he suffers but does not die. Starting from the notion of a suffering servant of God, whose tradition goes back to biblical antiquity, I would suggest that the choice of Ephraim achieves something that Isaiah 53 alone could not: namely, it links the theme of suffering to messianic expectation. This process, I would propose, was the result of a midrashic perception of a remarkable correlation in theme and language between Jeremiah 31—whose theme is the restoration of Ephraim, and Isaiah 53—whose theme is the redemptive suffering of a servant of the Lord.

Such an identification of Ephraim with the suffering servant of God in Isa. 53:4, 5 and 14—specifically, those verses where Ephraim says

---

[40] The text is Oxford MS. Heb. f. 21, leaves 24–31+Bodl.2727, published by A. Büchler in *JQR* o.s. 6 (1894), 39–42; see especially p. 40 (and pp. 13–14). The text was reprinted by J. Mann in *The Bible as Read and Preached in the Old Synagogue* (published 1940; reprinted, The Library of Biblical Studies, New York: Ktav Publishing House, 1971), I, 565–574; see especially pp. 565–566 and notes 70–71, and the discussion on pp. 298–299.

[41] For a review of some possibilities, see J. Klausner, *Ha-Raʿayon ha-Meshihi be-Yisraʾel*, 289–95; G.H. Dix, "The Messiah ben Joseph", *The Journal of Theological Studies* 27 (1926), 130–143; C. Torrey, "The Messiaḥ, Son of Efraim", *Journal of Biblical Literature* 66 (1947), 253–77. L. Ginzberg, *An Unknown Jewish Sect* (1922; New York: The Jewish Theological Seminary of America, 1970), 237, proposed that Ephraim was chosen so that the eschatological end would balance events during the exodus. In my view, this interpretation totally by-passes the theme of atoning suffering, perhaps because he wondered if texts like *Pesikta Rabbati* 36 were not "perhaps under Christian influence?;" see *ibid.*, 236, n. 113. I think that this approach impoverishes the Jewish theological tradition.

[42] See E.E. Urbach, *The Sages* (Cambridge, MA: Harvard University Press, 1987), 687.

that "I have been sorely afflicted (*yisartani va-ʾivaser*)" and "have borne the shame of my youth (*nasaʾti ḥerpat neʿurai*)" (Jer. 31:18–19)—would further result in Ephraim's association with the atoning function of the sufferings described there. All this, we may presume, would proceed at the level of midrashic intuition and yield the results of our passage.

As a final point, I would also suggest that the preacher of *Pesikta Rabbati* 34—clearly a sympathizer if not a member of the *ʾavelei tziyyon*—was drawn to this whole cluster of features in Jeremiah 31 by one more feature in it: namely, God's promise to the prophet that He will in the End turn Ephraim's "mourning to joy (*ʾevlam le-simḥah*; v. 13)". This phrase could only confirm to the "Mourners of Zion" that God's promise in Isaiah 61:2–3, to comfort "the Mourners of Zion (*ʾaveilei tziyon*)", and to give them "festive ointment instead of mourning (*shemen sason taḥat ʾeivel*; Isaiah 61:2–3)" would be fulfilled through one named Ephraim. Indeed, as we have seen, just this was the point made by the preacher in *Pesikta Rabbati* 34 in unequivocable terms.[43] For him and his audience—Ephraim was "he that cometh"—he and no other.

---

[43] This indeed is the concluding prophecy in *Piska* 34, where Ephraim is named for the first time.

ARMILUS: THE JEWISH ANTICHRIST AND THE ORIGINS AND DATING OF THE *SEFER ZERUBBAVEL*

Joseph Dan

I

The relationship between Judaism and Christianity in the early centuries of the Christian era is one of the most fascinating chapters in the history of religions. Many bonds united them in the beginning of their separate histories, and many remained in the following centuries. They differed in many points, but even then, very often, the common starting-point is discernible. This is especially true for the vast subject of messianism, because of the centrality of this element in their respective faiths; indeed, even the word Christianity, used to distinguish between Judaism and its daughter-rival, is linguistically identical with the term "messianism"; the same biblical term, Messiah, is the root of both terms, the difference being that the Hebrew word retained the Hebrew version of the term, whereas the Christian one preferred its Greek, Septuagint version. The concept of Antichrist is an integral part of the messianic concepts of both religions, and its study is indispensable for the understanding of the eschatological and apocalyptic components in both of them.

Antichrist, like the Messiah, is essentially a historical concept, concerned with the role of leadership. The language of messianism is the language of history, dealing with the impact of leadership—usually conceived as being of divine origin—on the history of the universe, and often bringing the historical process to its ultimate end. The language of messianism is distinctly different from that of mysticism. Mystical language usually denies itself and refrains from presenting a coherent historical message.[1] Messianism, on the other

[1] See the important recent discussion of the subject of mystical apophatic language in: Michael A. Sells, *Mystical Languages of Unsaying*, Chicago and London: University of Chicago Press, 1995; compare the articles collected in the volume: *Mysticism and Language*, edited by Steven T. Katz, Oxford: OUP 1992; J. Dan, "In Quest of a Historical Definition of Mysticism: The Contingental Approach," *Studies in Spirituality* 3 (1993), pp. 58–90. A detailed chapter on the relationship between

hand, even in the most obscure and seemingly incoherent apocalyptic texts, does present a concept of history which conveys a message concerning the future, and which demands that the attention of the public be directed to a linguistically communicated idea to be followed. The mystic craves to separate himself from history and unite his soul, in a meta-linguistic process, with the hidden divine realm. The eschatologist lives within history and craves to communicate his own concept of the approaching end of history to his religious society. Antichrist, like the Messiah, is a historical leader whose role demands communication with society; the language of anti-messianism, like the language of messianism, cannot therefore remain apophatic.

I started to study the subject of Antichrist many decades ago for two reasons: first, I was surprised and disheartened by the fact that so little could be found—at that time—in the library of scholarly books and articles dealing with early Christianity on this subject; it seemed to be deliberately neglected. The second reason was the clear statement by Irenaeus, never denied by subsequent Christian writers, that the Antichrist is a Jew from the tribe of Dan.[2] I felt that, if nothing else, I should write at least an article about this subject. My thanks are presented, therefore, to the Princeton Institute of Advanced Study and its seminar on messianism which gave me the opportunity to carry out this early promise to myself. I soon came to realize that in this case, like in many others, the understanding of a complex, religious and historical problem is dependent on a mundane detailed analysis of texts in their historical setting, no less than on ingenious theological generalizations. The following thesis

---

mystical and messianic languages included in my *On Sanctity* (Hebrew), Jerusalem: Magnes Press 1997.

[2] Irenaeus, *Adversus haereses* 5, 25–30. The subject has been presented in detail recently in a study by C.E. Hill, "Antichrist from the Tribe of Dan", *Journal of Theological Studies*, NS, vol. 46 (1995), pp. 99–117. Hill presents the various views of the first Church Fathers on the Jewishness and the geographical origins of the Antichrist figure. Various suggestions have been presented by Hill and others (see esp. Emmerson, note 8 below, pp. 80–82 *et passim*), concerning the reason for the selection of the tribe of Dan. One aspect neglected in these discussions is the image of this tribe as the origin of great military leaders in Jewish traditions, expressed, e.g., in the fact that Samson was from that tribe. The medieval mystical work, the *Zohar*, nominated Seraya from the tribe of Dan as the commander of the Messiah's armies (see, e.g., *Zohar* III, 194b). An early medieval wanderer, Eldad, from the tribe of Dan, who appeared in Babylonia and presented himself as an emissary from the Lost Ten Tribes, described the great military power of that tribe.

therefore rests mainly on an attempt to re-evaluate the dating and character of a short treatise, the *Book of Zerubbavel*, in the hope that this new approach, will also lead to the viewing of certain generalizations in a new light.

The figure of Christ separated Jews from Christians. It is interesting to note that the figure of the Antichrist, the evil tyrant who nearly conquers the whole world, was acceptable to both groups in a meaningfully similar fashion. For Christians, Antichrist is Jewish; for Jews, the Antichrist is a Christ-like figure. Is that a common element or a difference? Obviously, it is both at the same time, as are many other subjects in which the two religions differ, but use a common basis. It seems that Jews were ready to borrow from Christian apocalyptical descriptions of the final phase of the existence of the universe more than those of many other, more imminent and mundane spheres of ideas and myths. A comparison between Jewish and Christian descriptions of the "last enemy" may contribute to the understanding of a marginal, yet significant, aspect of the messianic drive which is so central to both religions and which serves to divide them so deeply.

II

Apocalyptic literature essentially brings Judaism and Christianity closer to each other, first and foremost because they have such obvious common roots. The book of Daniel is shared by them as the paradigmatic example of this genre, and many Jewish works, written between the second century B.C. and the first C.E. were either accepted completely by Christian culture or adapted into the new sets of ideas developed by the early Christian sects. Scholars debate whether a particular work is a Jewish or a Christian one, and often the answer is: both. There are also similar elements in the cultural attitude towards this genre: in both cultures the religious establishment often treated creativity in this realm with suspicion and tried to minimize the prevalence and impact of eschatological expectations. This is more evident in Judaism than in Christianity: Rabbinic tradition ignored ancient and contemporary apocalypses, and marginalized their position in the normative culture it sought to establish. In this way, many of the apocalypses which were written originally in "Jewish" languages—Hebrew and Aramaic—survived only in "Christian" languages: Greek, Latin, Armenian, Slavic, Ethiopian, etc.

It should be taken into account that when facing apocalyptic and eschatological phenomena, Jews and Christians are drawn into similar positions: the second coming of Christ, the *parousia*, is not so different from the "first" coming of the Messiah in a Jewish context. The upheavals of the last period before redemption, the overcoming of evil powers and the establishment of a divine kingdom on earth are phenomenologically similar in both religions.[3] This is most evident in the case of the figure of the "last enemy": Rabbinic Judaism was much more hesitant, compared to Christianity, in accepting the concept that there is an independent evil power in the universe, a Satan in the dualistic sense of the term;[4] in fact, this concept was adapted by some Jewish scholars only in the thirteenth century.[5] Yet full apocalyptic creativity is impossible without confronting the Messiah with ultimate evil; the core of the eschatological drama is the final struggle between the powers of good and those of evil. It is not surprising, therefore, that some of the earliest Jewish depictions of a satanic figure are to be found in this genre. The subject of this study is a prominent example of a meeting-point between Jewish and Christian apocalyptic creativity centered around a satanic figure.

Scholarship in the twentieth century seems to have ignored the presence of the Antichrist in Christian tradition, until almost its last decade. The classical study of the Antichrist by Bousset, published in 1894,[6] remained for nearly a century the only monograph on the subject. Scholars working on the history of Christianity devoted only

---

[3] As noted by Gershom Scholem in the beginning of his famous study, "The Messianic Idea in Judaism," in: *The Messianic Idea in Judaism and Other Essays on Jewish Spirituality*, New York: Schocken 1971, pp. 5–12 *et passim.*

[4] Elaine Pagels' recent study of the origins of the image of Satan in Christianity indicates that despite the common Jewish sources, this concept developed in opposition to Judaism, within a Christian social-cultural context; according to Pagels, social and religious conflict, within Judaism and later between Christians and Jews, can be perceived as the core of the development of the figure of Satan. See: E. Pagels, *The Origin of Satan*, New York: Random House 1995.

[5] See G. Scholem, *On the Mystical Shape of the Godhead*, New York: Schocken 1991, pp. 56–70; I. Tishby, *The Wisdom of the Zohar*, Oxford: OUP 1989, vol. II, pp. 447–458; J. Dan, "Samael, Lilith and the Concept of Evil in Early Kabbalah," *AJS Review* V (1980), pp. 17–40; *idem*, "Nahmanides and the Development of the Concept of Evil in the Kabbalah," in: *The Life and Times of Mosse ben Nahman*, Girona 1995, pp. 159–179; *idem*, "Samael and the Problem of Jewish Gnosticism," in: A. Ivry (ed.), *Proceedings of the Conference in Memory of Alexander Altmann*, London 1997 (in press).

[6] W. Bousset, *The Antichrist Legend: A Chapter in Jewish and Christian Folklore*, transl. by A.H. Keane, London 1896.

cursory attention to it when commenting on the relevant passages in the New Testament.[7] But in the last decade it seems that the Antichrist problem has been arousing renewed interest. Richard Kenneth Emmerson published a monograph on the Antichrist in medieval culture,[8] and, more recently, a detailed study of the early sources was published by Gregory Jenks.[9] The most important contribution is the comprehensive study by Bernard McGinn, covering the whole history of the subject, from ancient times to contemporary references.[10] These studies are a part of a discernible increase in the scholarly interest in the phenomenon of apocalypticism in general, which is expressed by numerous new studies.[11] The context of some of the most important contributions is that of the Last Emperor, which has been the subject of several studies in recent years.[12] There have been, however, very few attempts to study this subject in an inter-religious context, taking into account Jewish and Arabic sources.[13]

---

[7] A survey of the exegesis of mostly New Testament verses relating to this subject by the Church Fathers and modern scholars is presented by R.K. Emmerson (see following note), pp. 34–73.

[8] R.K. Emmerson, *Antichrist in the Middle Ages: A Study of Medieval Apocalypticism, Art and Literature*, Seattle: University of Washington Press 1981. See esp. the chapter dedicated to "The Life and Deeds of Antichrist", pp. 74–107, in which many of the ancient sources are discussed. A previous study of the image of Antichrist in the High Middle Ages was published by Hans Dieter Rauh, *Das Bild des Antichrist im Mittelalter, von Tyconius zum deutschen Symbolismus*, Münster: Aschendorf 1973; see esp. pp. 138–164.

[9] Gregory C. Jenks, *The Origins and Early Development of the Antichrist Myth*, Berlin and New York: Walter de Gruyter 1991. This is the most detailed analysis of the ancient sources available today.

[10] Bernard McGinn: *Antichrist: Two Thousand Years of the Human Fascination with Evil*, New York, San Francisco: Harper 1994.

[11] See, e.g., the important collection of studies centered around Joachim of Fiore and his impact on medieval religion and thought: *Prophecy and Millenniarism, Essays in Honor of Marjorie Reeves*, edited by Ann Williams, Harlow: Longman 1980; and recently: *The Apocalypse in the Middle Ages*, ed. by Richard K. Emmerson and Bernard McGinn, Ithaca and New York: Cornell University Press 1992 (several articles from these and other volumes are mentioned in the following notes). Concerning the early period, see esp.: Paula Frederiksen, "Apocalypse and Redemption in Early Christianity", *Vigilae Christianae* 45 (1991), pp. 151–181; Richard Landes, "Lest the Millennium Be Fulfilled: Apocalyptic Expectations and the Pattern of Western Chronography 100–800 C.E.", in: *Use and Abuse of Eschatology in the Middle Ages*, pp. 137–211.

[12] G.J. Reinink, "Pseudo-Methodius und die Legende vom Römischen Endkaiser," in: *Uses and Abuses of Eschatology*, pp. 82–111. Paul J. Alexander, "Byzantium and the Migration of Literary Works and Motifs: The Legend of the Last Roman Emperor," *Mediaevalia et Humanistica* NS 2 (1971): 47–82.

[13] David Flusser, "An Early Jewish-Christian Document in the Tiburtine Sibyl," in: *Paganisme, Judaisme, Christianisme: Mélanges offerts a Marcel Simon* (Paris: Boccard,

A similar situation prevailed in Judaica scholarship: no article with the Antichrist, or its Jewish counterpart, Armilus, in its title was published until the last few years,[14] and the most important text in which it is included, the *Sefer Zerubbavel*, was studied by only two scholars, one at the end of the last century[15] and the other in the middle of the twentieth.[16] The text was only recently translated by a scholar into English with an Introduction, analysis and notes.[17] The concept of the "Jewish Antichrist" in Hebrew apocalyptical literature did not receive significant attention.[18]

1978), pp. 153–183; Paul Alphendery, "Mahomet-Antichrist dans le Moyen Age," *Mélanges à Hartwig Derenbourg* (Paris: Leroux, 1909), 261–277.

[14] The exception is David Berger in his discussion of the name Armilus in *AJS Review* X (1985), and see below, note 45. Sections from this text and those which derived from it were included in Raphael Patai's anthology, *The Messiah Texts*, Detroit: Wayne State UP 1979. Patai presented the whole history of Hebrew messianic narratives as one whole, as if the scores of texts scattered over two millennia were parts of one coherent story; he did not contribute, therefore, to the understanding of the historical context of any of them.

[15] I. Levy dedicated to this subject a series of studies: "L'Apocalypse de Zerobabel," *Revue des Etudes Juives* LXVIII (1914), pp. 129–160; LXIX (1919), pp. 108–121; LXXI (1920), pp. 57–65, which served as a basis for the interpretation and dating of *Sefer Zerubavel* by subsequent scholars, including Y. Even Shmuel and S. Baron, as well as myself (see following note).

[16] Yehuda Even Shmuel (Kaufman), *Midreshey Geulah*, Jerusalem: The Bialik Institute 1954. Most of the volume is dedicated to *Sefer Zerubavel*, its predecessors and the numerous adaptations of the text, as well as a section dedicated to the various versions of the book. It is most unfortunate that this excellent volume has been out of print for many years. See also: Salo Baron, *Social and Religious History of the Jews*, vol. V, New York: Columbia UP 1957, pp. 138–168 and the notes there, pp. 353–367; J. Dan, *The Hebrew Story in the Middle Ages* (Hebrew), Jerusalem: Keter 1974, pp. 35–46, and the notes there, pp. 253–255.

[17] Martha Himmelfarb, "Sefer Zerubavel", in: D. Stern, M.J. Mirsky (eds.), *Rabbinic Fantasies: Imaginative Narratives from Classical Hebrew Literature*, Philadelphia: The Jewish Publications Society 1990, pp. 67–90. M. Himmelfarb made use in this edition of the work of her experience in the study of apocalyptic literature, which was presented in her recent monograph: *Ascent to Heaven in Jewish and Christian Apocalypses*, New York and Oxford: OUP 1993 (see esp. her discussion of the literary genre, pp. 95–114).

[18] In the important collection of studies of Jewish messianism in the Talmudic era, the subject is completely absent. See: Leo Landman (ed.), *Messianism in the Talmudic Era*, Hoboken New Jersey: Ktav 1979. The situation is not much better in a new anthology: *Essential Papers on Messianic Movements and Personalities in Jewish History*, ed. Marc Saperstein, New York and London: New York UP 1992. *Sefer Zerubbavel* is presented here only in the paragraphs dedicated to it in S. Baron's discussion in his *Social and Religious History of the Jews* (pp. 162–187).

III

The common source for both Jewish and Christian descriptions of the Antichrist is the book of Daniel, with its picture of the last beast and its evil ruler, which was identified with Antiochus IV Epiphanes,[19] whose persecutions (168–165 B.C.) caused the great rebellion of the Hasmoneans (165–161). Christian tradition retained the identification of this evil apocalyptic figure with a particular person, especially in the parallel sections of the Apocalypse of John; that figure was identified with the Emperor Nero, and became the paradigmatic evil enemy of Christians throughout the ages.[20] Jewish tradition was not so insistent on identifying the Antichrist figure with a particular person, and the individual, human characteristics which are found in the Christian sources are often absent from the Jewish parallel.

The sources in which the legend of the Antichrist took form differ considerably in the two religions, despite the common source. The Hebrew texts in which the myth is found are relatively marginal and do not directly represent normative Jewish literature. Most of them are fragments and brief treatises which are very difficult to date. The name of Armilus appears in the targumic literature, but in a way which does not allow us to determine the time and context of its evolvement. The Christian sources are much more central, and even though the earliest ones are anonymous and undated, their general time and context can be narrowed down with some confidence. This has been undertaken carefully and methodically by Bousset, Jenks and especially McGinn. As a result of this difference in the nature of the sources, it can be determined that the basic constituents of the myth of the Antichrist, including the term itself, were known among Christian communities by the end of the first century and the beginning of the second. Hebrew sources which name Armilus cannot have been dated with certainty; the texts which include this term hardly precede the fifth century,[21] even though there are

[19] It should be noted, however, than we do not have such an identification in an early Hebrew text, while Christian tradition included it in a relatively early age. See McGinn, *Antichrist*, pp. 26–27, 62 *et passim.*

[20] There is little doubt that this was done by Christians whose language was Hebrew. "The number of the Beast", 666, is a *gematria* of Neron Kesar in Hebrew (and the alternative number found in several texts, 616, is the equivalent of Nero Kesar). See McGinn, *Antichrist*, pp. 51–54.

[21] A suggestion concerning an earlier date is presented below.

good reasons to suppose that the legend originated at a considerably earlier date.

This gap of nearly half a millennium between the dated texts of the two religions demands that we assume that the Christian formulations preceded the Jewish ones. Indeed, this was the view I held and expressed for many years. There is, however, one major obstacle which does not permit us to discard the possibility that an independent Jewish tradition did take shape in Late Antiquity and was the basis for the Armilus legend. This concerns the name Armilus itself.

There can be little doubt that Armilus is a Hebraized form of the name Romulus, the co-founder and the first king of Rome.[22] His position at the end of history can be explained as reflecting the fact that one of the last Roman emperors happened also to be named Romulus, namely Romulus Augustus.[23] It is appropriate for a legend to utilize this name connecting the beginning and the end of the Roman millennium in human history. It should also be remembered that Judaism had not separated Christianity from Rome since the fourth century; the term "Edom" refers to both of them together, and the hatred directed towards the secular empire[24] was fused with the animosity shown to the rival religion. Yet if we accept this, the Hebrew Armilus legend cannot predate the fifth century, several centuries after the Christian legend acquired most of its important characteristics.

The main question is, why should a Jewish writer select the name Romulus from the many possibilities offered to him by the Roman-

---

[22] The problem of the origin of this name was discussed in detail in the studies by Levi, Even Shmuel, Baron, Patai, and Himmelfarb. The most important contribution to the subject was made by D. Berger, yet his ingenious suggestion does not fit the apocalyptic context; Balaam was never a participant in the mythical drama in any Jewish or Christian text.

[23] Romulus Augustus was crowned by his father, Orestes, *magister militium* in Gaul, in October 475, and his father ruled in his name until deposed in August 476, when Odoacer was crowned.

[24] It should be noted that Judaism never regarded the Roman empire as a secular entity. The clashes between the Jews and the Romans were viewed by ancient and medieval Jewish sources as religious in essence, as they really may have been in several instances. Even the earlier confrontation between Jews and the Hellenistic empire of Antiochus Epiphanes was regarded as a religious rather than a political one. For Jews, the Roman emperors represented the religious core of paganism. Viewing the empire as a secular structure into which any religious content can be inserted, is a typically Christian concept, though its development should be ascribed to the period after the adoption of Christianity by the Roman emperors.

Christian context? Romulus is not mentioned, to the best of our knowledge, in Jewish sources, and there seems to have been no interest whatsoever in this figure throughout the long period in which Rome exerted meaningful and terrible influence on Jewish affairs. It is a mystery why this name should suddenly become so central, when no other Hebrew or Christian source used it in the context of the apocalyptic messianic era, or, in fact, in any context at all. As long as we do not have any clue about the background and reasoning of the name, we cannot be sure of the time of the emergence of this myth, and the relationship between the Jewish and the Christian sources which were combined in it.

The complexity of this problem is the result of the constant tension between the proximity and distance of the Jewish and Christian concepts of the Messiah and his opponent. Christian sources describe Antichrist consistently as the opposite of Christ; his family, birth and fate resemble in an inverse way the biography of Christ. The Jewish apocalyptic author did not have such a prototype to mold the figure of Antichrist, because he did not have a clear tradition of the nature and biography of a Messiah; on the contrary, it is the *Sefer Zerubbavel* itself which is the most important source for the creation of a Jewish concept of an individual Messiah with a distinct biography. One may say that the author had to "invent" a Messiah and an anti-Messiah at the same time, as parts of the same apocalyptic vision. The author was not constrained, therefore, by the Christian insistence that the Antichrist should be human in the full sense of the term, a need which arose because of the incarnation of Christ; both of them were supposed to assume on earth the roles of human beings, at least for a certain time, as demanded by the concept of the incarnation. The Jewish writer did not have a "Christology"; there was nothing which demanded, as far as he was concerned, that the Messiah be human, and therefore nothing which demanded that the Antichrist be human. The story of the birth of Armilus is told, so it seems, without any reference to theological considerations, whereas the Christian writers concerned with the Antichrist had to insist on his birth to a woman and a man (the woman often described as a whore, and the man—as a wicked Jew from the tribe of Dan). Yet the basic concept of the Antichrist demanded that he be related in some way to the devil—he is often described as a "son of the devil", which is understood in a literal way. Therefore, the devil had to take part in the process of the Antichrist's birth. This was achieved by the concept that the spirit of the devil entered him when he was still in the womb; the "Rosemary's Baby" motif. The Jewish writer could tell his story freely—for him, Armilus was the son of the devil and a statue of a beautiful woman in Rome: a miraculous birth indicating the complete evil nature and non-humanity of the monstrous creature. There was no theological burden concerning the birth of the Messiah, and therefore the author had complete narrative freedom when telling the story of the birth of Armilus.

Yet the picture is even more complex. The Jewish writer did not have before him a biography of his Messiah, but he did have a detailed biography of a false Messiah, which is one of the main aspects of the figure of Armilus. That false Messiah, for him, was Jesus Christ. The narratives on Jesus were useful, to some extent, when the Jewish author described the appearance of the evil anti-Messiah in apocalyptic times. The story of Armilus' birth should be understood—and this has been pointed out by several scholars—as a reversal, and a parody, of the birth of Jesus. The image of an emperor and a seducer of souls was one which could be identified with the Christian Messiah after the Church became dominant in the Empire, uniting, as the Jewish writer believed, imperial power and spiritual-heretic forces. Armilus is perceived therefore as a union between a false Messiah and a Roman emperor, expressing the Jewish concept of Christianity.[25]

---

[25] The figure of Simon Magus plays a significant part in both the Jewish and the Christian concepts of the Antichrist. As several scholars have pointed out, some of the biographical details and the powers demonstrated by the Antichrist were based on the narratives about the first heretic, Simon the Samaritan. One of the main sources for this is the material included in the *Pseudo-Clementine Homilies*. It is important to note that the same sources also served Jewish traditions—but only those dealing with Jesus Christ. It is very probable that the anonymous author of the Hebrew or Aramaic original of the Jewish narrative on Jesus, the *Toledot Yeshu*, had access to sources similar to those used by the authors of the Pseudo-Clementine stories. In both cases, a biography of an arch-heresiarch is presented, which expresses no doubt about their actual powers to change nature and invoke supernatural phenomena, similar to those of the righteous, God-inspired heroes. This most intriguing subject has not yet been studied in any detail. See J. Dan, *The Hebrew Story in the Middle Ages*, Jerusalem: Keter 1974, pp. 188ff. On Simon Magus and the Antichrist see Emmerson, *Antichrist in the Middle Ages* (above, note 8), pp. 79–83; McGinn, *Antichrist*, pp. 71–74.

IV

The treatise in which Armilus makes its first appearance as a full-fledged Satanic figure, the *Book of Zerubbavel*, presents an enigma in Jewish literature concerning the relationship between Judaism and Christianity. This is the first and only Hebrew messianic treatise in which the leading role in the messianic drama is given to a woman, who is portrayed as the mother of the Messiah. Nowhere else in the vast literature dedicated to the subject do women take a meaningful part, and certainly not in a typically Christian role.[26] Hefzibah, the Messiah's mother, is described as the custodian of the miraculous instrument, the sacred staff of redemption, which had been passed from generation to generation since Adam, thus creating a connection between Adam and the Messiah, also found in the New Testament.[27] She is placed in the center of the messianic triad, which includes the Messiah son of Joseph and her son, Menahem ben Amiel, the Messiah son of David. They fight Armilus together, and when the Messiah son of Joseph is killed in battle, she resists with the remnants of the Jewish people and prevents Armilus from completely conquering Jerusalem, until the Messiah son of David takes command and defeats Armilus.

The apocalyptic role of Hefzibah is described as the culmination of a universal process. The text begins the narrative of the events of the redemption by presenting Hefzibah:[28]

> God[29] will give a staff of redemption to Hefzibah, the mother of Menahem ben Amiel. That staff is of *shoham*, and it is hidden in Rakat, the city of [the tribe of] Naphtali. This is the staff which God gave

---

[26] In actual fact, women did take meaningful parts in two Jewish messianic movements. They played a role in the court of Shabbatai Zevi in 1666–1676 and in the court of Jacob Frank in Offenbach, near Frankfurt, in the last quarter of the 18th century. Despite this, the writings of these movements do not include a theoretical systematization of a woman's role in the messianic drama.

[27] Messiah—Adam, see McGinn, and compare the talmudic sources, Adam, David Masman as the acronym of ADAM. It should be noted that the Daniel verse concerning the Son of Adam does not play in Judaism the same prominent role that it does in Christianity. The term can be read in Hebrew as "human being", and not only in the literal sense, son of Adam.

[28] This is Metatron's response to Zerubavel's question about the events of the time of the Messiah. See Even Shmuel, pp. 76–77; Dan, *The Hebrew Story*, 39–40, Patai, *The Messiah Texts*, pp. 125–126. The English translation is mine.

[29] Patai translated the name of God as "the Holy One blessed be He", which is the usual rabbinic reference to God, whereas the author, throughout the treatise,

> to Adam and to Noah and to Shem and to Abraham and Isaac and Jacob and Joseph and Moses and Aharon and Joshua and king David. Elijah will take it out of there and will give it to a person whose name is Nehemia son of Hushiel, son of Ephrayim son of Joseph. . . . And in the fifth year of Nehemia ben Hushiel's reign and for the ingathering of the holy people, the king of Persia will attack Nehemia and Israel, and it will be a very dangerous time for Israel. Then Hefzibah will appear, the mother of Menahem ben Amiel, with the staff given to her by Nehemia ben Hushiel, and will kill two kings, the name of the one is Nof the king of Yemen, and the other is Sargon the king of Antioch.

These sentences are unique in the number of completely original elements which they include. We do not know exactly when this paragraph was written, but the earliest possible date which can be ascribed to it is still one which is considerably later than dozens of Jewish traditions in Talmudic and midrashic literature concerning the Messiah, his origin and his time. The author decided to ignore the wealth of Talmudic-midrashic material, and to present a picture which is new in almost every detail. We do not know from any previous source about the existence of the "staff of redemption" and its being transmitted from generation to generation, being preserved in each historical period by the main representative of divine providence in that age. The central role of this "staff" in the events of messianic times is not known from any previous source. The full name of the Messiah son of Joseph is not disclosed in any text, and it was, most probably, invented by the author. The name of the father of the Messiah, Amiel, is not known from earlier literature. The kings mentioned here are completely different from those mentioned in previous apocalyptic literature, and seem to be artificial structures created from biblical materials. The town of Rakat in the Galilee, in the land of Naphtali, is not known from any other eschatological context.[30] This is an original presentation by an author who did not hesitate to innovate and present a dramatically new version of Hebrew messianic traditions.

---

insists on using the biblical names. Compare the version printed by Jellinek in *Beit ha-Midrash*, vol. 2, pp. 54–57.

[30] Jos. 19:35. It should be noted that Naphtali and Dan were regarded as neighbors and close to each other, yet this is not enough to connect this town with the Antichrist's ancestry or birthplace.

The most important new element is that of Hefzibah. The name is biblical,[31] but it does not represent any messianic or eschatological context in its biblical references. In Talmudic-midrashic literature it has no significance related to this subject. There is no connection in previous literature between this name and the names Amiel or Menahem. Other sources differ concerning the name of the Antichrist's father (though there is agreement about his own name, Menahem).[32] It should be noted that the author does not provide any information concerning the Messiah's father; his name is presented only as a part of Menahem's name. The only activity is reported to be that of Hefzibah, who, in this paragraph, is described as the one who gives the messianic role to the Messiah son of Joseph, and it is she who overcomes the first onslaught of the surrounding peoples against the people of Israel who have gathered in Jerusalem. In subsequent sections of this treatise, Hefzibah is presented as fighting alongside her son the Messiah; she is the one who carries on the struggle after Nehemia ben Hushiel's death. It is she who saves the last defenders of Jerusalem and prevents the fall of the city, and throughout the work she remains a dominant figure, a direct representative of God in the apocalyptic drama.

It is impossible to avoid the conclusion that some Christian influence came to bear when the figure of Hefzibah took shape in the mind of the author; this is especially important in investigating the relationship between the Jewish and Christian figures of the Antichrist. Yet at the same time, we should consider the differences between the *Sefer Zerubbavel* presentation and the mother of Christ. None of the central elements in the characterization of Hefzibah is typical of the image of Mary in early Christian traditions. Nothing is said or implied concerning anything unusual in the Messiah's birth. Hefzibah is not associated in any way with virginity, neither in this text nor in others. The messianic role, so it seems, has been assigned to Hefzibah before, and independently of her being the mother of Menahem.[33] She preserves the "staff of redemption", and gives it to

[31] For Hefzibah in the bible, see 2 Kings 21:1, but compare Isaiah 62:4 ("thou shalt be called Hefzi-vah . . . for the Lord delights in thee").

[32] See Num. 13:12, where Amiel son of Gamli represents the tribe of Dan. Menahem as the name of the Messiah is found in Talmudic literature (see, e.g., Bavli Sanhedrin 98b, Yerushalmi Berachot 17a). Usually his father's name is not mentioned; only in Bavli Sanhedrin it is stated to be Hezekiah.

[33] In the descriptions of Hefzibah in the sources collected by Wertheimer, she is

Nehemia ben Hushiel first, not to her own son. She is presented as a leader and a victorious warrior before the appearance of Menahem as a leader. It seems that besides the very concept of "mother of the Messiah", nothing connects Mary and Hefzibah.[34] If we could entertain the possibility that the work was written in a non-Christian culture, remote from detailed knowledge of the biography of Christ, this could be explained as a result of the author's having but a vague idea of the Christian concept of the mother of the Messiah. This, however, is impossible. The only non-Christian country in which such a work could have been written is Persia, and nothing in the work itself indicates this. The centrality of Rome in the narrative clearly reflects a historical reality dominated by Rome (western or eastern empire, or both).

V

The difficulty in determining the time and character of the *Sefer Zerubbavel* is a result of the diversity of sources which are employed in the creation of this apocalypse. Armilus' father is called in the various versions either Satan or Beliyal. The second version should be preferred, because "Satan" is a common, undifferentiated term for the power of evil, while Beliyal is almost unknown in this role in Hebrew texts. It is found in a central place in the pseudepigrapha,[35] but Talmudic-midrashic tradition did not use this name.

described as the wife of the prophet Nathan, the son of David. The problem of the Wertheimer versions of this text is a complex one and should be studied separately. Scholem tended to see it as a Sabbatian apocalypse, but it seems that it is actually a different version of the Zerubbavel original narrative.

[34] The subject of Hefzibah and the mother of the Messiah has been neglected in scholarship (and censored from Jewish apocalyptical literature). To the best of my knowledge there is only one book on the subject, published recently—*The Mother of the Messiah in Judaism*, by Jacob Neusner, Valley Forge, PA: Trinity Press, 1993. The book, however, is a translation into English of the midrash Ruth Rabba, and the figure in the title is that of Ruth. In the book, Hefzibah and *Sefer Zerubbavel* are not mentioned.

[35] Beliyal plays a most prominent part in the *Testaments of the Twelve Patriarchs*; he is mentioned in almost every segment of this work; he is also mentioned in *The Martyrdom of Isaiah* and other sources. In the original Hebrew form, Beliyal, he is found in several of the Dead Sea Scrolls. See: Michael E. Stone (ed.), *Jewish Writings of the Second Temple Period*, Philadelphia and Assen: Fortress Press and Van Gorcum 1984, index s.v.

It is conceivable that editors and copyists would replace the unknown "Beliyal" by the common "Satan", but not vice versa.[36] This seems to indicate that the author of this apocalypse had access to material which was not commonly used by his contemporary Hebrew writers; the material could be Christian, but could also be pre-Christian Jewish sources.[37]

Another possible context is that of Hekhalot and Merkavah mystical literature.[38] Two elements indicate such a connection: the names Metatron and Zerubbavel. One is the use of Metatron as the name of the celestial power revealed to Zerubbavel and transmitting heavenly secrets to him. Metatron appears in this particular role mainly in Hekhalot literature, especially in the Hebrew Book of Enoch.[39] The name itself is found several times in the Talmud and midrash,[40] but received a prominent place in the divine *pleroma* in the treatises of the early Jewish mystics. Some versions replace Metatron with Michael, and some use both as synonyms, but it seems that Metatron should be regarded as the original. Hekhalot mysticism is intensely individual in character, and the messianic element in it is at best marginal.[41] It cannot be said that the *Sefer Zerubbavel* was influenced by this literature or that it derived some of its major themes from

---

[36] Beliyal re-appeared in medieval Hebrew sources as a demonic name, sometimes indicating the king of the demons; its common form is "Beliar" or "Bilar", or "Bilad." G. Scholem studied the subject in detail, and concluded that its emergence in these contexts is the result of the influence of Arabic sources. See his studies: "Bilad King of the Demons" (Hebrew), *Madaey Hayahadut*, vol. 1 (1926), pp. 112–127; "New Chapters Concerning Ashmedai and Lilith" (Hebrew), *Tarbiz* 19 (1948), pp. 160–175.

[37] Some support for the Christian impact on this apocalypse can be found by the insistence in some versions of the work that the marble statue in Rome, Armilus' mother, is the image of a beautiful virgin. This is found in Wertheimer's versions, but it is impossible to determine whether this emphasis was part of the original text or inserted at some later date.

[38] Concerning the Hekhalot see the monographs: G. Scholem, *Jewish Gnosticism, Merkabah Mysticism and Talmudic Tradition*, New York: The Jewish Theological Seminary, 1960 (rev. ed., 1965); P. Schäfer, *The Hidden and Manifest God*, Albany, NY: SUNY Press 1992; J. Dan, *Ancient Jewish Mysticism*, Tel Aviv: MOD 1993.

[39] H. Odeberg, *Third Enoch or the Hebrew Book of Enoch*, Cambridge 1928 (reprint, with a Prolegommenon by J. Greenfield, Hoboken NJ: Ktav 1973); a new translation of the work with a commentary by P. Alexander is included in Charlesworth, *The Old Testament Pseudepigrapha*, vol. I.

[40] Detailed discussions of Metatron are found in the books listed above, note 38; the most comprehensive one is still that of H. Odeberg (note 39).

[41] Concerning the messianic element in Hekhalot, see J. Dan, *Ancient Jewish Mysticism*, pp. 95–115.

it; the presence of Metatron may only indicate some acquaintance with these treatises.

The problem is more complicated when it comes to the figure and the role of Zerubbavel in this treatise. On the one hand, the choice of Zerubbavel to be the one to whom the secrets of messianic redemption are revealed is easily understandable: as the last ruler of Judea from the house of David, and the builder of the Second Temple in Jerusalem, he could be entrusted with the secret of the renewed Davidic monarchy and the building of the third and last Temple. Yet Zerubbavel does not appear in this or any similar role in any other messianic text. His place in this treatise is unique. The only other context in which Zerubbavel holds a prominent place in a post-biblical Hebrew text is the Hekhalot treatise *Sar Torah*, which represents a separate Jewish mystical tradition, different in many respects from the main elements of Hekhalot traditions.[42] The *Sar Torah* treatise describes a collective mystical experience, shared by a large group of people—the builders of the Second Temple who returned from Babylonian exile and are obeying God's command to rebuild Jerusalem. Their leader is Zerubbavel, who represents them before God, and transmits the divine message to them. In this treatise God appears, in the Temple which is under construction, descending to meet the mystics and not the other way around they ascending to Him, as we find in other treatises. Scholars are in agreement that this treatise, in the version it has reached us, is one of the last works of Hekhalot and Merkavah literature, probably originating in the seventh or eighth centuries. In this form, therefore, it is probably later than *Sefer Zerubbavel* itself.

The question is whether these two sources taken together cannot serve as an indication for the existence of a Jewish tradition which placed Zerubbavel within the context of the messianic drama. While the *Sar Torah* cannot be described as a messianic text, the elements of utopia and memories of the distant past are most peculiarly interwoven in it. It is one of the texts presenting a mystical concept of meta-history.[43] The Temple which the mystics are constructing can be viewed as past and future at the same time. If there were a

---

[42] Concerning *Sar Torah* see my study, "The Theophany of the Sar Torah," *Jerusalem Studies in Jewish Folklore* 13–14 (1992), pp. 127–157.

[43] See J. Dan, "The Concept of History in Hekhalot Literature," *Binah* I, *Studies in Jewish History*, New York: Praeger 1989, pp. 47–58.

Hebrew tradition about Zerubbavel and the apocalyptic future, it could have served the author of the *Sar Torah*, as well as the author of the *Sefer Zerubbavel*.

Because of these diverse contexts and sources, it is very difficult to draw a conclusion about the origin of the figure of Armilus in the *Sefer Zerubbavel*.[44] The author was closer to some apocalyptic treatises than many Hebrew writers of the Talmudic period; he was aware, to some extent, of Hekhalot mystical traditions; he had some contact with Christian traditions. He could, therefore, have found Armilus in any of these, if indeed Armilus was present in any of them. The possibility that he invented the whole myth should not be ruled out. Apocalypses are not only reworkings of ancient formulas and the recombination of old traditions. They also express the individual imagination of the author and his creative urge, and this could be an example of such an unusual individual vision. Even so, there must be a reason for the selection of the name of Romulus, but so far, this seems to remain a mystery.[45] Yet another aspect of this figure has to be considered and studied: the image of Romulus as a divine figure in Imperial Rome and in the writings of the Church Fathers of Late Antiquity.

VI

Romulus, the founder of Rome, can be viewed as the prototype of the apocalyptical image of Armilus if we can successfully integrate a

[44] The ingenious suggestion by David Berger to understand the term Armilus as referring to a Greek translation of the name Balaam (*AJS Review* 1985, see above, note 14) is interesting and important, but it does not seem to fit the structure of the figure as presented here. Berger emphasizes correctly the Balaam-Moses connection, but Moses is completely absent from this apocalypse. Rome, on the other hand, is the center of the whole drama, and a Roman monarch is the natural candidate for this role. It is difficult to see why a Hebrew writer, who did not include non-Hebrew terms in the work, would choose a Greek form for the name of Balaam, nor why that prophet would be selected to be the evil emperor-messiah of the apocalypse.

[45] Another aspect of this problem is the possible connection between the figure of Armilus and the Islamic figure of a satanic, Antichrist-like entity, usually called Dajal. Several scholars have suggested that it may be connected with the figure of Armilus in the *Sefer Zerubbavel*; it has been suggested that this myth predates Islam, and may have been absorbed by pre-Islamic Arabic literature from Jewish sources. S. Baron tended to support this view. See his discussion and detailed bibliography in *Social and Religious History* (above, note 16), vol. V, pp. 358–359; I. Friedlander, "Ahmad, the Promised Messiah and Mahdi," *Review of Religions* XLVIII, part 10, pp. 24–34.

series of ancient Roman traditions concerning him with the Christian discussions of his figure, and see both as serving as a background for the image presented in the *Book of Zerubbavel.* This is possible, to a very large extent, thanks to the detailed presentation of the relevant material in Saint Augustine's *City of God.*[46] This masterpiece of Christian theology is relevant to this discussion because, like the *Sefer Zerubbavel*, it is concerned with two earthly cities: Jerusalem and Rome. This in itself contains the basic parallelism between Jesus and the Roman Emperor on the one hand[47] and that of the Messiah and Armilus on the other, each of them representing his respective city. Augustine, in his anti-pagan polemic, quotes many Roman sources[48] which designate the founder of Rome as a divine entity; coupled with Hercules, Romulus is presented as the perfect example of the deification of human beings by the ancient Romans, a process which serves the author as a decisive argument against the worship of such gods.[49] Yet Augustine emphasizes, at the same time, that Romulus (with his twin brother Remus), was the son of the god Mars.[50] An identification of Mars with Beliar or Belial, the satanic father of Armilus, would be a natural process. Another tradition used by Augustine to explain the "divinity" of Romulus is that his corpse was never found;[51] again, if one wishes, a close parallel to Christ can be found here too. The mother of all the Roman gods, Cybele, was the subject of a magnificent statue in Rome, a fact mentioned

---

[46] I am using the translation by Gerald G. Walsh and Grace Monahan, in the series: *The Fathers of the Church: A New Translation*, founded by Ludwig Schopp, ed. Roy Joseph Deferrari, New York: The Fathers of the Church Inc., 1952. On this subject see also: Walter Burkert, "Caesar und Romulus-Quirinius," *Historia* XI (1962), pp. 356–376.

[47] Thus, for instance, in Book XXII, Ch. 6, Augustine compares Romulus, the founder of Rome, to Christ, the founder of Jerusalem, and points to parallels between the love of the Romans for the founder of their city to the love of the Christians for Christ (p. 427). A parallel between Romulus and Christ is also presented in the beginning of the work, Book I, Ch. 34, p. 71.

[48] The source which Augustine relies on most is Cicero (see, e.g., Book XXII, Ch. 4, p. 421, quoting from *De re publica*). Compare also Ch. 6 (p. 426).

[49] See, e.g., Book VIII, Ch. 5 (pp. 29–30); this argument is repeated several times in the work.

[50] In Book XVIII, end of Ch. 21 (p. 112), Augustine quotes the sources which state that Rhea, who is identified with Ilia, a vestal virgin, and the god Mars were the parents of the twins. This is one more link between Romulus and Christ—a virgin mother, though with very different meanings of the term.

[51] *Ibid.* Ch. 24 (p. 118). In the same way, the divinity of Aeneas is explained.

by both Augustine and the Roman historians on whom he relies.[52] He most often quotes Cicero on this subject, probably because Cicero expressed emphatic objections to the deification of human beings, be they as prominent as Romulus himself.

Augustine puts forward the parallel between Romulus, the founder of Rome, and Jesus Christ, whom he describes as the founder of Jerusalem; he equates the love of the Christians for Jesus to that of the Romans for Romulus, thus associating him with a messianic role. Book XVIII and other parts of the *City of God* are dedicated to the presentation of a historical parallel between the history of the kings of Israel (and later, of Judah and Israel) with the history of the Roman kings, rulers and emperors,[53] a process known to us also from Talmudic sources. Augustine makes the comparison in the context of contrasting the history of prophecy and the history of idolatry, but from the point of view of a Jewish writer, this brings Romulus deeper into a Jewish framework.

Augustine's numerous references to the Roman god Romulus, and the other details which he connects with this story, represent a possible connection between the founder of Rome and the Jewish Antichrist. Romulus is actually some kind of an Antichrist in Augustine's presentation, which represents prevalent Roman and Christian views and not the isolated speculations of a systematic theologian. Many of the facts and structures which he presents could have been known to people who had not read the complete *City of God.* To this we should add some obvious negative characteristics of Romulus, also emphasized by Augustine as well as by others: his responsibility for the murder of his twin brother,[54] which brings him into a biblical context as a Cain-like figure (a parallel especially potent if Abel is identified as a typological prototype of Christ); and his association with rape,[55] which made it easy to present him as a satanic figure, especially for someone who, unlike all the others who wrote about him, hated Rome passionately, as the Jewish apocalyptic writer undoubtedly did.

There is no doubt, therefore, that a good case could be presented,

---

[52] See his description of the statue of Cybele as mother of all the gods in Book III, Ch. 12 (pp. 144–145).

[53] See, e.g., Book XVIII, Ch. 22 (p. 113).

[54] On Romulus as a murderer, see Book III, Ch. 6 (p. 135).

[55] On Romulus as a rapist, see Book II, Ch. 17 (p. 98).

suggesting that the figure of Armilus in the *Sefer Zerubbavel* is derived from the Roman traditions concerning Romulus as a deity, which were re-invoked by the Christian theologians in their discussions of pagan gods, and were associated in this way with a messianic figure, namely Christ. This would also give a meaningful basis for determining the date of the Hebrew apocalypse, probably in the first half of the fourth century. A historical background could be supplied by the struggles between Rome and Persia at that time. Such a hypothesis would also indicate that the author was familiar with Christian culture, thus explaining other elements of Christian influence found in the work.

Unfortunately, I find this hypothesis unacceptable. It is reasonable, and, as is often claimed today, undoubtedly "it could have happened". History, however, is concerned with what happened, and not with what could have happened. This concept assumes that a Jewish writer in the Roman empire was familiar, to a degree not found in any of our sources, with Roman traditions and legends, as well as with the Christian literature and thought of the time. There is no example in Hebrew works indicating such an awareness of these sources. There is no proof that Romulus was appreciated by, or even known to, Jewish sages, or that there was any interest in this figure or any similar Roman historical or mythological character. Furthermore, despite all these parallels between Christ and Romulus, Augustine does not ascribe to the founder of Rome any apocalyptic role; Romulus is never removed, in these discussions, from his historical context and planted in another, later or future one. It seems to me to be extremely far-fetched to assume not only that a Jewish writer knew all these traditions and speculations, but that he alone made the significant leap from history into eschatology, which, to the best of my knowledge, no Christian writer made. Such structures are very tempting, but a historical approach must insist on differentiating between the probable and the actual. In this case, no links are to be found between the Roman Romulus myth and its Christian versions and Hebrew apocalypticism.

VII

This lacuna in our knowledge prevents us from reaching a definite conclusion about the date of the legend which served as a basis for the messianic apocalypse of the *Sefer Zerubbavel*. The vague hint referring to the king of Persia, utilized by Levy and the scholars who followed him, is insufficient to decide this matter. In the absence of an indication of the date, it is impossible to determine with any certainty the nature of the relationship between the Christian Antichrist myth and the Jewish parallel.[56] This is further complicated by the ambiguous nature of the portrayal of Armilus in the Jewish sources when compared to the Christian concepts of Antichrist on the one hand and the Last Emperor on the other.[57]

The image of Armilus in the *Sefer Zerubbavel* and the following sources includes many elements which, in the Christian apocalyptical descriptions, are emphasized mainly as those of the Last Emperor. From a Jewish point of view, the Satanic figure is that of a world-conqueror and a Roman emperor, besides his being a seducer of the soul of the people. Armilus is, in these sources, an intricate combination of Christ, Antichrist, and a successful and victorious Roman emperor. The fact that scholars found no difficulty in identifying him with the emperor Heraclios of Byzantium is a clear indication of this aspect in his image. Because of this, and because we do not have an alternative to the explanation of his name as derived from

[56] It is important to note that the realization of the proximity of the figures of Armilus and Antichrist destroys any basis for the insistent designation of the *Sefer Zerubbavel* as a seventh century work. Israel Levi, Yehudah Even Shmuel (Kaufman) and Raphael Patai followed the identification of Armilus with the last Byzantinian conqueror of the Near East before the emergence of the Arab hosts, namely Heraclios. Because of this, the date given to the *Sefer Zerubbavel* is circa 630, just before the Islamic conquest of the region. This conclusion follows the persistent notion that an apocalypse should be dated by the last historical event which it describes, before going on to utopian myth. In this case, these scholars believed that the *Sefer Zerubbavel* describes Armilus as having appeared (born from the statue at Rome), and conquered the earth, and the transition to utopia is only the story of his demise at the hands of the Messiah. This seems to be a completely erroneous structure. There is no evidence that the author regarded his own time as that of the reign of Armilus. Besides, if the prototype of Armilus is Antichrist, then the whole work remains in the realm of legend, and neither Heraclios nor any other political figure played a part in it in any way. Without this artificial identification, we do not have an indication of the historical period in which the *Sefer Zerubbavel* was written, and it could be dated anywhere between the second and the seventh centuries (the exclusion of a later date is justified, because it is evident that the map of the world which was known to the author did not include Islam; after 634 such a treatise could not have been written). The formulation of Armilus in the image of the Antichrist prevents his identification with any historical figure. Thus, I think that there can be no doubt that the *Sefer Zerubbavel* is the earliest detailed source describing this apocalyptical narrative, and Y. Even Shmuel was correct in his designation of the other texts as "following *Sefer Zerubbavel*".

[57] Concerning this figure, see McGinn's presentation in *Antichrist*, pp. 85–91 *et passim*.

Romulus, the first and last monarch of Rome, we should take into consideration the wealth of apocalyptic material which was created in a Christian context in Late Antiquity and the early Middle Ages about the Last Emperor.

Jews differed considerably from Christians in their attitude towards the image of a Roman emperor. History imposed upon Christianity an ambiguous attitude towards such a figure: On the one hand, the Emperor of Rome is the arch-enemy, the source and focus of all the persecutions of Christians during the early centuries after Christ. On the other hand, after the fourth century, he is in many cases the defender of the faith and the empire he governs is the earthly, secular representation of the realms of Christianity. The establishment of the Holy Roman Empire and the crowning of Charles the Great as emperor in 800 gave a tangible political expression to this second attitude towards the empire and its ruler. It is a long way indeed from the Rome of Nero and the Rome of the Pope, and the latter is expressed in the envisioned empire of the Middle Ages, a dream which survived in one way or another until the crowning of Napoleon Bonapart as emperor a thousand years after Charles the Great. In the Christian apocalypse, the two figures are constantly present. Many scholars view the portrayal of the Last Emperor in the Antichrist apocalypse as an attempt to resolve this ambiguity: Antichrist himself remains a representation of the evil emperor, but before his coming the empire will be redeemed, restructured and its dominions expanded by this figure, and the renewed, purified empire will be submitted by the emperor to Christ.

From the point of view of Jewish apocalypticism, the transformation of the Roman empire into a Christian entity meant the unification of two enemies. From both secular and religious points of view Rome was hated as the embodiment of all evil and because of the evils it brought to the Jewish people its destruction was the subject of many visions of the future. One of the most important expressions of this feeling is to be found in the main treatise of Hekhalot mysticism, the *Hekhalot Rabbati*. According to the basic narrative of this text, the emperor of Rome decided to torture and execute ten sages; his wish was endorsed by God because of the unresolved guilt of the ten sons of Jacob arising from the selling of Joseph, their brother, into slavery, a crime for which the Torah demands the death penalty. God gave Samael, the celestial prince of Rome, the power to execute the sages, but as part of a deal which required that Samael agree to the ultimate destruction of Rome and its emperor in a horrible way. When the sages who are destined to be martyred by the emperor hear the details of this destruction, they make it a day of celebration. This narrative, which originated in a circle of mystics, probably in the third century, was retold as a popular martyrological legend and converted into a poetic work, which became part of the Jewish prayer ritual.[58] This narrative, in all its forms, does not make any distinction between an Antichrist figure, the last emperor and the actual emperor of Rome: they are all, without differentiation, the intense representation of all earthly evil.[59] The religion to which this emperor adheres is not mentioned and is completely immaterial. Furthermore, the ancient Jewish terms which used to denote the evil empire, Esau and especially Edom, were extended to include Christianity. There was no need, therefore, within the Jewish apocalypse to differentiate between the evil emperor, the Antichrist, and the good emperor, presented in the Last Emperor legends; there is no "good emperor" anywhere in Jewish concepts of Rome and everything associated with it.

It is important to consider the role of a celestial power, that of Samael, in this narrative. As will be shown below, there was probably a competition between Samael and Armilus for the role of the ultimate satanic figure in Jewish tradition, one which was won by Samael. Samael in this narrative is the supreme, meta-human embodiment of Rome, the current and the last emperors, and of all the evil inherent in all of them. Yet, at the same time, he is an obedient servant of God, representing Rome in His celestial court.

---

[58] See concerning this: J. Dan, "The Story of the Ten Martyrs and Hekhalot Rabbati," *Simon Halkin Festschrift*, Jerusalem 1973, pp. 15–22. The relevant texts have been edited in a synoptic form with a detailed Introduction and Commentary by G. Reeg, Tübingen 1988, with comprehensive bibliography.

[59] They do not, however, represent any celestial or theological evil. The figure of Samael in this narrative is almost identical to that of Satan in the book of Job or that of the *kategor* in Talmudic and midrashic literature. He is part of the celestial court of God, and cannot do any evil without explicit divine permission. He does represent the inclination to harm and destroy, but this is conceived of as an inevitable aspect of existence, which is governed and regulated by God. If this idea were to be followed with theological consistency, Rome could not be seen as evil: it is only the instrument chosen by God to fulfil a certain aspect of His designs for the universe, and it is the power by which God punishes those who sin, including prominent Jews. But the texts did not follow this theological reasoning; they attributed to Rome intrinsic evil, and directed all their hatred towards the empire and its ruler.

VIII

One of the ambiguities about the Antichrist of the Christian apocalypses is the problem of his origin. The early tradition seems to insist that he comes from the Gallilee, from the towns near the Sea of Gallilee which were cursed by Christ.[60] Another tradition insists that he was born in Babylon, the origin of all that is sinful and evil.[61] This contradiction was often resolved by including in the narrative a parallel to Christ's early move from Nazareth to Bethlehem.[62] Also the Hebrew apocalypse includes a geographic ambiguity, but its background is completely different. The vision of Zerubbavel begins with the transportation of the narrator to the place where the Messiah was staying:

> A wind carried me between heaven and earth and brought me to Niniveh the great city, which is the city of bloodshed. And he[63] said to me: Go to the House of Idolatry. I went as I was commanded. He then told me: Continue on your way. I turned, and a hand touched me. I then saw a wounded and despicable man. The wounded and despicable man told me: Zerubbavel, what are you doing here? I answered and said: The wind of God carried me to a place I do not know, and brought me to this place. He said to me: Do not be afraid, for you have been brought here in order that you will see [this]. When I heard his words I was encouraged and asked him: What is the name of this place? He said to me: This is the great [city] of Rome. I asked him: Who are you and what is your name, and what are you doing in this place? He said to me: I am God's Messiah, and I am bound here in prison until the time of the end.[64]

---

[60] The first among these is Chorazin, which is, therefore, often cited as his birthplace. See Luke 10:13, 15, and R.K. Emmerson, *Antichrist in the Middle Ages*, pp. 80–81. This element seems to be unconnected to his origin as a son of the tribe of Dan; the area described was not in Dan's lot (neither the early one in the central plain nor the second area of its settlement in the far north). It should be understood as one of the motifs which create parallelism between Christ and the Antichrist, and the fulfillment of a prophecy preserved in Luke.

[61] Emmerson, *ibid.*, 80–81.

[62] See, e.g., Adson's narrative, analyzed in: B. McGinn, *Visions of the End: Apocalyptic Traditions in the Middle Ages*, New York: Columbia University Press 1979, pp. 82–87; D. Verhelst, "La Préhistoire des conceptions d'Adson concernant l'Antichrist", *Recherches de Théologie ancienne et médiévale* 40 (1973), pp. 52–103.

[63] The angel leading Zerubbavel, who is called Metatron or Michael.

[64] Y. Even Shmuel, p. 71.

This first meeting between Zerubbavel and the Messiah happens in a place which is called Niniveh by Zerubbavel, but the Messiah informs him that its name is Rome. This should be understood as a literary element, expressing loyalty to the pseudepigraphic format. Zerubbavel could not have known the name of the city of Rome, which did not exist in his own time and is not mentioned in the bible; the narrative, pretending to be biblical and using many biblical phrases and syntax, has to use a biblical term for the city. Niniveh, the city of bloodshed,[65] could have been the term used by Zerubbavel. Babylon is another possibility, but this is difficult because Zerubbavel has just come to Jerusalem from Babylon, appointed by the Persian king who lived in that city, and therefore, if the author wished to be loyal to the biblical background, it could not be designated as the place of supreme evil. Niniveh was thus chosen, but immediately replaced by Rome. In the Hebrew tradition, there is no ambiguity whatsoever about Rome being the birthplace and center of power of the Antichrist-Armilus.[66]

Another meaningful difference between the Jewish apocalypse and the Christian one is that of the humanity of the evil figure. As scholars have repeatedly shown, Antichrist must be a human being, the incarnation of evil, in the same way that the Messiah, Christ, is the incarnation of goodness in an actual human being. The definition of Antichrist in a Christian context includes an insistence on this aspect, which differentiates him from other images of evil, like Satan, Devil, Lucifer, Belial(r) and others, which are conceived as celestial, super-human figures. This distinction is irrelevant when an apocalypse is presented in a Jewish context, where there is no insistence that the Messiah himself be a human being in the full sense of the term (unless, of course, a particular human being, like Shabbatai Zevi or Menahem Mendel Shneersohn, is elevated to the role of a Messiah; in these cases there is a tendency to minimize his humanity rather than insist on it, as is often found in Christology). Armilus is presented in a way which does not allow for a clarity about the kind of combination of humanity and super-humanity he represents. Neither does his miraculous birth to a non-human mother and

[65] Compare Jonah 1:2, 3:2.

[66] But the term "Rome" itself is ambiguous: it could be either the Italian Rome or Byzantium.

father[67] nor anything else in his biography indicate unambiguously whether he is either a human being or a celestial power; he is undoubtedly a combination of both, but no effort is made to reflect definitively about the nature of this combination.

IX

It seems that it is necessary to relegate the *Sefer Zerubbavel* together with the *Sefer Yezira*, several Hekhalot treatises and many midrashic works to the category of Late Antiquity Hebrew works whose exact date cannot be determined within the range of the third to the sixth centuries. It is evidently later than the mishnaic context, and prior to the Arabic onslaught, but within this span of nearly half a millennium, it is impossible to pinpoint it with any confidence. The artificial nature of the pseudo-biblical language prevents us from using language as an indicator, and the deliberate absence of any distinguishing historical, geographical or even religious element precludes the use of standard philological criteria in attempting to date it. We are left with the enigma of the name Armilus as the only possible indicator of the date and circumstances of the writing of the whole treatise.

If we postulate that the name Romulus in this apocalypse reflects some knowledge of the last emperor of Rome, we are faced with the following possibilities:

1) The book was written when Romulus Augustus was crowned emperor, in the few months between this event and the onslaught of the German conquerors against Rome and the end of the direct imperial succession. Someone in Palestine could have seized on the fact that a Roman emperor—a boy—was crowned, bearing the name of the founder of the city, and believed that this boy was destined to renew the power and glory of Rome and again make it into the military, cultural and spiritual center of the world. The name was regarded as a sign for the impending renewal. The fact that besides the name of the founder of Rome this boy-emperor also bore the name of the greatest of all Roman emperors, Augustus, may have

[67] Because of this, it is impossible to accept the suggestion presented in several studies that there is an element of parody of Christian beliefs in the story of Armilus' birth.

added to the author's concept (he may not have been aware how common the title "Augustus" was among Roman emperors). This process thus heralded, for that writer, the apocalyptic saga which would bring about the fall of Rome and the victory of the Jewish Messiah. The political and military turmoil described in imprecise terms in the *Sefer Zerubbavel* is a reflection of the enormous turmoil throughout the Roman Empire and the surrounding lands in this period of the deterioration of Roman power. If we pursue this concept, we can pinpoint the time of the writing of the treatise within a range of a few months in the year 476.

The advantage of such an approach is that it follows the traditional lines of interpretation of apocalyptical material, that is, the quest for the point of departure between actual history and imaginary, prophetic descriptions. In this case, the point of departure is the crowning of Romulus Augustus, before his weakness and the helplessness of the empire became apparent. The treatise, according to this approach, could never have been written in 475 or 477. From a historical-philological point of view, this seems to be a great advantage.

The weaknesses of this hypothesis are many. It is improbable that such a concept about the last Roman emperor could have occurred in an isolated manner to a writer in a remote province, which did not even belong to the Western Empire but had been ruled for nearly two centuries by Byzantium; indeed, the term "Rome" itself could be a reference to Byzantium and not to the Italian Rome. If indeed the crowning of Romulus made such an impression, we would expect additional material, from other sources, reflecting similar attitudes and expectations concerning this young monarch. We should also expect some kind of pre-prophecy, an expectation that the last emperor would bear the name of the founder; to the best of my knowledge, no such material has been found. Another objection is that we have no report of any unusual circumstances regarding the birth and the nature of Romulus Augustus. If we postulate that the whole story concerning the birth and image of Armilus is pure fiction, it is very difficult to associate it with the actual person who assumed the monarchy in Rome. Another objection may be that the events that seem to us, in hindsight, momentous, seemed less extraordinary viewed from Palestine in the fifth century. A quick succession of Roman emperors in the West was the norm, and the attacks by Germanic hosts were rather usual. The view that this was the end of a millennium-long era is one formulated after the fact. For most people in the East, the Roman empire continued to prosper in Byzantium, and the turmoil in the West was not remarkably different from that of previous decades.

2) A variation of this suggestion might be the utilization of the fact that Romulus Augustus vanished from the historical arena after the fall of Rome. He was exiled to a small town near Naples, and nothing is known about his fate. History does not tolerate such lacunae, and some visionary may have surmised that Romulus, like many rulers before and after him, from King David to Frederick II, was in hiding, waiting for his time to re-appear, re-assert his rights and re-establish his empire. If so, the treatise was written in the years following 476.

The same objections also apply to this variation, especially as it is very difficult to imagine that such an expectation of the return of Romulus would be confined to a single Jewish messianic writer, and completely absent in European literature. Jewish writers usually picked up such legends from the surrounding culture and did not invent them themselves. Another objection is that the detailed descriptions of Armilus, which have no counterpart in the image of Romulus Augustus, become more difficult to apply if we assume that years have passed, and that the historical figure of Romulus did not change to accommodate such supernatural characteristics.

3) Another variation of the same approach would be to assume that the *Sefer Zerubbavel* was not written in Palestine or indeed anywhere in the Byzantine empire, but in Rome or in another place close to the events of the year 476. Such a proximity would explain the importance given to the crowning of Romulus. Nothing in the work, however, supports such a possibility. It cannot be rejected, because a negative can never be proven, but without positive proof such a hypothesis can not be adopted.

X

In conclusion, it seems that rejecting the seventh-century dating of *Sefer Zerubbavel* and the figure of Armilus-Romulus does not produce an alternative which can be stated with confidence. It is reasonable to assume that the legend preceded the seventh century by many generations, but it is impossible to decide whether it originated with Romulus Augustus, which would have given it a fifth-century date, or with the Roman god Romulus as described by St. Augustine, which would give it a fourth-century date. These possibilities are open, and any conclusion depends on further material which may be discovered either in a Jewish context or a Christian one, or both. Until then, no final decision on the exact relationship between Christianity and Judaism concerning the evolution of the Antichrist apocalypse can be made.[68]

The impossibility of identifying Armilus and defining the moment in history which inspired his advent into Hebrew apocalyptic myth has not prevented the *Sefer Zerubbavel* from becoming the standard description of the events of the messianic era for more than a millennium; apocalypses thrive on such vagueness, whereas a more precise relationship to a particular period makes them shrivel when the historical arena changes and they become irrelevant. Armilus acquired eternal dimensions because this figure could be applied to any time and place, like the even less precise images of the beasts and monsters of *Daniel* and the *Apocalypse of John*. The power of apocalyptic and messianic literature resides no less in what it does not say than in what it explicitly states. The historical picture drawn in it needs to be, at one and the same time, vague enough to be applied to any set of historical circumstances, and precise enough to make this application seem to be the one and only possible explanation of the narratives. Such is the basic paradox of this literary genre: to be effective, it must be shown to have one and only one true meaning, describing accurately the age of the interpreter, but it must also allow many interpreters in different ages to make this application with complete confidence. Messianic language involves a literal, unambiguous usage of language: it denotes events and personalities which are unique, well-defined and recognizable in mundane terms. It derives its message from texts which are opaque and highly imaginative, but it translates them into historical actualities described literally and precisely. The figures of the Messiah son of David, the Messiah son of Joseph and Armilus as presented in *Sefer Zerubbavel* proved to be open to such repeated literal translations in dozens of different historical circumstances.[69]

---

[68] It is hoped that the recent interest in the subject will yield new sources which can elucidate this problem. See, e.g.: Paul Speck, "The Apocalypse of Zerubbavel," *Jewish Studies Quarterly*, 1997.

[69] How effective this process can be was proved to me a few years ago, when I

However, an even more important characteristic of apocalyptic messianism is expressed by the *Sefer Zerubbavel*: the absence of any particular religious demands, or even particular religious characteristics. The treatise is a recounting of future events, presenting them as happening without any dependence on the deeds of human beings. The future has been decided by God, and nothing can change it. This determinism, paradoxically, produces a text which is free from the limitations of any particular religious ideology. The prophecies are completely neutral as far as the concept of God and His demands of humanity are concerned. In fact, God is almost absent from this work (this is often the case with other apocalyptic-messianic works, too). If we understand religion as a system which directs human beings how to fulfil God's expectations of them, *Sefer Zerubbavel* is not a religious work. It contains no didactic elements: it does not "point the way", and—most important—it does not include the concept of spiritual crossroads: if you do that, this will happen, or if you do this, that will happen. The prophecy will materialize independently of any individual choice made by human beings.

This absence of a religious message does not mean distance from religion, on the contrary. The fact that no specific religious demand is presented makes this treatise—like others before and after it—acceptable to every religious system. It is completely neutral in all theological, ethical and religious debates, and therefore it can reside comfortably with all of them. If it were more specific and demanding, it would evoke controversy and discussion. The fact that it does not demand any particular concept of God, of ethics, of religious precepts and their meaning, or any specific kind of human activity, makes its appeal universal and eternal. Only in this way can a satanic figure like Armilus be accepted both by a rationalist-scientist like

---

participated in a discussion on the subject on Israeli television. One of the participants was a well-known professor of physics in an Israeli university, who put on the table a bundle of recently published books from the United States which presented a radical criticism of current American society, education, politics etc., and asked us in full confidence: "How can one doubt that this is the beginning of the messianic era? All the traditional signs of messianic times are so obviously expressed in these books. The situation in the world today is exactly as portrayed by our ancient apocalyptical texts." The argument that such books are published in every decade, and that the prophecies can be easily interpreted as reflecting any historical situation, did not impress him at all. Of course, in this and other cases the belief in the approaching redemption came first, and then the "signs" were collected, interpreting the texts accordingly.

Saadia Gaon in the tenth century and a Lurianic kabbalist, believer in Shabbatai Zevi, who converted to Islam in the second half of the seventeenth century. The worldviews of these two writers are so far apart in all the essential and non-essential elements of religion that they could never create a common agenda. The framework of *Sefer Zerubbavel*, however, was equally comfortable for both of them, because of the absence of any particular religious norm or demand. The messianic and apocalyptic language is so bare of any religious, ethical or theological elements that it can be accepted by all groups, in every country, in every historical set of circumstances.

When we are looking at the broad picture of Jewish messianic history covering nearly two millennia, it is evident that Armilus has remained a relatively secondary figure, whereas the apocalypse of *Sefer Zerubbavel* as a whole is a central element. It has to be admitted that the more influential parts of *Sefer Zerubbavel* were those which elaborated and systematized earlier motifs, while the completely new ones did not have the same impact. Hefzibah was ignored or deliberately censored, while Armilus became a secondary name of Satan. This occurred despite the fact that there was nothing in the image of Armilus to prevent it from becoming a more central one; on the contrary, the figure which eventually came to dominate the role of the satanic power in Jewish apocalypse was associated with Rome as deeply as was Armilus, namely Samael, who emerged in Late Antiquity as the main power in the realm of evil in Judaism.

Three main processes gave Samael his central position in Jewish apocalyptic literature: one was a gradual application of his name instead of the general reference to "Satan" in Talmudic literature, culminating in the early Middle Ages when Samael is called "the head of all these satans". The second was the depiction of Samael as the leader of the fallen, rebellious angels and the introducer of sin to Adam and Eve in the Garden of Eden. This happened in the midrash *Pirkey de-Rabbi Eliezer*, in the beginning of the Islamic era, when the legend of the rebellion of angels appeared, or re-appeared, in Hebrew literature.[70] The third process—which was probably the earliest one chronologically—is the description of Samael as the

[70] PRE chapter 13. In the same work, Samael appears also in the traditional role of the "kategor", the prosecutor, of Israel on Yom Kippur. This chapter was copied, almost verbatim, in the *Book Bahir* (last section, § 200 in Margoulioth's edition), and thus became a part of the earliest work of the Kabbalah.

celestial prince of Rome in *Hekhalot Rabbati*.[71] From these sources, the figure of Samael became central to the Kabbalah in the late twelfth century and during the thirteenth; in the *Zohar* this became the main name of an evil power so meaningful that its pronunciation was forbidden in later custom.

It seems that Judaism in the Middle Ages accepted as its main satanic figure a power deeply connected with Rome; Christianity was identified with Rome and Edom, and came to represent earthly as well as celestial evil. Both Armilus and Samael had all the qualifications for this position. Both emerged from relatively marginal treatises, *Hekhalot Rabbati* and *Sefer Zerubbavel*. In addition to the above mentioned reasons, the question of why Samael won this "race" against Armilus should also be considered in the context of the meanings of their names in the context of Jewish culture.[72] Samael could, and was, connected to several Hebrew terms, while Armilus was a foreign, meaningless name; his roles as the founder of Rome, the ruler of Rome, the last ruler of Rome and a god of Rome did not become components of Jewish literature and myth. Samael, on the other hand, besides being the prince of Rome, was regarded as the power of the left side (his name could be read also as "left"), together with the north, which is the source of all evil.[73] The possibility of describing him as blind could also be utilized. On the other hand, the colorful story of Armilus' birth found no parallel in the descriptions of Samael; it seems that myths on the origins of the devil did not find an echo in later Jewish narratives. Armilus was thus marginalized, and the monster born of a statue of a virgin in Rome was replaced by Messiah the blind snake in which all evil resides.

---

[71] On the history of Samael see Scholem, *Kabbalah*, Jerusalem: Keter 1974, pp. 385–389; J. Dan, "Samael and the Problem of Jewish Gnosticism," in: A. Ivry (ed.), *Studies in Jewish Philosophy and Mysticism in Honor of A. Altmann* (in Press); *idem*, "Nachmanides and the kabbalistic Concept of Evil," in: *The Life and Times of Mosse ben Nahman*, Girona 1995, pp. 159–179; *idem*, "Samael, Lilith and the Concept of Evil in Early Kabbalah," *AJS Review* 5 (1980), pp. 17–40 (repr. in: L. Fine (ed.), *Studies in the Kabbalah*, New York: NYU Press 1995, pp. 154–178).

[72] A secondary reason could be the connection between Samael and figures like Rabbi Akibah and Rabbi Ishmael in the Hekhalot tradition, which gave Samael an advantage, especially for the Jewish mystics who actually decided the matter; the *Sefer Bahir*, Nachmanides, Rabbi Isaac ha-Cohen and the *Zohar* were much more impressed with the ancient mystical treatise and the authority of the speakers in it.

[73] See Jer. 1:14; "left" and "north" are synonymous in Hebrew, because when one is facing east, as one should, north is to his left. In the same way, the term for "right" in the Bible is "south".

JEWISH MESSIANIC EXPECTATIONS TOWARDS 1240 AND CHRISTIAN REACTIONS

Israel Jacob Yuval

Calculations of the "End of Days" have always been a favorite Jewish hobby. True, the Talmud says, "Death to those who calculate the End of Days,"[1] but it would seem that there is life after death. Perhaps that is why so many of the "calculators" themselves did not take their own calculations too seriously. Lipman Mühlhausen, in his polemical anti-Christian tract *Sefer Nizahon* written in 1400, warned his readers against calculating the End of Days, but proceeded immediately to predict that the Messiah would come in 1410.[2] To make sure, he went on to warn his readers not to be disappointed if his prediction failed to materialize. A few years after 1410 the work was recopied. What happened to the author's unfulfilled calculation? The copyist left the calculation itself untouched but altered the result to 1426.[3] To be on the safe side, he "proved" the new date with his own calculation, going on to say that if the Messiah should nevertheless fail to come in 1426—that would be due to "our sins".

Such calculations are not really different from today's horoscopes, and they should be regarded as an arithmetical pastime. It would be wrong, therefore, to treat all calculations of the End of Days as active messianic movements. Nevertheless, one should surely not go to the other extreme, that is, to deny them any significance whatsoever. I would like to describe here a major calculation of this sort, which aroused extensive reactions and great excitement; its historical weight was considerable, both in internal Jewish life and in shaping Christian-Jewish relations. I am referring to the Jewish messianic expectations that emerged as the year 1240 drew near.

The Municipal Library at Darmstadt owns a Hebrew manuscript containing an anonymous work entitled "Homilies of the King

---

[1] BT Sanhedrin 97b.

[2] Yom-Tov Lipman Mülhausen (sic!), *Sefer Hanizzahon*, ed. F. Talmage, Jerusalem 1984 (reprint of Hackspan's edition, Altdorf-Nürnberg 1640), p. 187, § 335.

[3] Ms. Oxford, Bodleian Library, Opp. 592, § 335 (A. Neubauer, *Catalogue of the Hebrew Manuscripts in the Bodleian Library*, Oxford 1886, No. 2162).

Messiah and Gog and Magog".[4] The author identifies himself as a disciple of R. Isaac b. Abraham (known by the acronym Rizba), one of the most important French Tosafists of the early thirteenth century.[5] The direct motive for writing the work was the conviction that the Messiah would be revealed before the year 5000 Anno Mundi, i.e., before the year 1240. The calculation is based on a Talmudic saying that the world would survive for 6000 years, including two thousand years of "chaos" (תהו), two thousand years of "Torah", and two thousand years of "Messiah."[6] The messianic era was supposed to begin in the year 4000; at any rate, it could be no later than 4999 (i.e., before 1240 A.D.); for otherwise the Talmud would not have told us that the last two thousand years were the era of the "Messiah". The author attributes the calculation to his mentor, Rizba; and since the latter died in 1210, messianic expectations of the end of the fifth millennium surfaced at least one generation before 1240. As that year approached, these hopes intensified.

The messianic excitement of which we are speaking is well documented and we shall return to some of the sources later.[7] Before that, however, I would like to describe what the author of the "Homilies" has to say about the necessary preparations for the Messiah's coming. He writes as follows:

> Let no man take it upon himself to say that the King Messiah will reveal himself on an impure Earth . . . and let no men err and say that he will reveal himself in the Land of Israel among gentiles. . . . But it is clear that the Land of Israel will be the home of Torah scholars and pious men and men of virtue from the four corners of the

[4] Ms. Darmstadt, Cod. Or. 25. A small part of this treatise was quoted by authors in the second half of the thirteenth century, but only this late citation was published both by S. Assaf, *Texts and Studies in Jewish History*, Jerusalem 1946, p. 90 and in: Abraham ben Nathan of Lunel, *Sefer Hamanhig. Rulings and Customs*, ed. Y. Raphael, 1, Jerusalem 1978, pp. 81–82, n. 6. Therefore, the original text of the Darmstadt manuscript was not mentioned in recent publications, although it was already known to scholars such as Moritz Stern (below n. 24) and Harry Breslau, "Juden und Mongolen", *Zeitschrift für die Geschichte der Juden in Deutschland* 1 (1887), p. 102; *idem*, "Ein Nachtrag", *ibid.*, 2 (1888), pp. 382–383.

[5] E.E. Urbach, *The Tosafists: Their History, Writings and Methods*, Jerusalem 1980, pp. 261–271, esp. p. 270 and n. *46.

[6] BT Sanhedrin 97a.

[7] Most of the relevant sources were collected and analyzed by A.Z. Aescoly, *Jewish Messianic Movements*, Jerusalem 1956, pp. 180–192. A detailed survey of all the sources will appear in my forthcoming book, *"Two Nations in Your Womb": Perceptions of Jews and Christians in the Middle Ages* (provisional title), chapter 5.

> Earth, one from a city and two from a family, each person moved by his heart, and a spirit of purity and love of holiness shining within him. Only then will the King Messiah reveal himself among them.

This passage is known to scholars from secondary sources written around the end of the thirteenth century;[8] but we can now state categorically that it expresses views current in France as early as one generation before 1240. Its basic idea is completely new: In the past, Jews had immigrated to the Holy Land for ascetic purposes, to mourn the destruction of Jerusalem, or to fulfill the religious commandments of מצוות התלויות בארץ. They had no intention of initiating any messianic activity.[9] On the contrary, the traditional view was that the Messiah would gather the Jews from their lands of exile and bring them back to Zion, just as God had redeemed Israel from Egypt while they were still on unholy land.[10] After all, the Exodus from Egypt had always been a typological model for the Messianic Era, implying that the return to Zion would occur after the redemption. Our anonymous author, however, contests this view. Following his great teacher, he believes that a Jewish presence in the Holy Land is a precondition for the advent of the Messiah. As he continues:

> And when the congregation in the Land of Israel increases and they will pray at the holy mountain and their cry for help shall rise up to heaven, the King Messiah will reveal himself among them and gather in the remaining exiles, for Israel shall hear that the King Messiah has revealed himself. . . . And the warriors of Israel will be gathered unto him from the four corners of the Earth, and he will assemble a great army and smite the princes of Ishmael and Edom that are in Jerusalem and evict the gentiles therefrom.

The expression "their cry for help shall rise up to heaven" is taken from Ex. 2, 23. Just as in Egypt God first heard the cry of the groaning Jews and then redeemed them, so in the last Redemption He will first hear the Jews' prayers at the site of the Temple, and only then will He redeem them. Thus the immigration of an elitist

---

[8] E. Reiner, *Pilgrims and Pilgrimage to Eretz Yisrael 1099–1517* (Ph.D. dissertation submitted to the Hebrew University), Jerusalem 1988, pp. 114–118, 151–155.

[9] The Karaite's attitude towards Jewish immigration to Eretz Israel during the tenth century is the only exception. See the letter of Daniel al-Kumisi in: J. Mann, "A Tract by an Early Karaite Settler in Jerusalem", *Jewish Quarterly Review* 12 (1922), pp. 257–298, esp. pp. 283–285.

[10] See Maimonides, *Iggeret Teiman*, in: ed. J. Kafih, *Iggerot (Letters) by Moshe ben Maimon (Maimonides)*, Jerusalem 1972, p. 52.

group to Eretz Israel is a necessary stage in the messianic scenario. Once it has been realized, Redemption will continue in the natural way. When it becomes known that a Jewish king has risen in the Holy Land, the Jews still in the Diaspora will willingly immigrate. A Jewish army will be mobilized from those Jews, and it will defeat the Crusader and Muslim hosts; the Christians will be expelled from Jerusalem. The text goes on to describe the opposing measures—a crusade will be initiated ("And the king of Edom will gather his entire force to wage war"); but the Jewish king will also organize a "crusade" and send the "warriors of Ephraim" to do battle. Ultimately, the Christians will be driven out of the Holy Land, and Rome itself will be destroyed.

As one might expect, this scenario is modeled on the political realia of the Crusades. The King Messiah is portrayed rather like a Crusader king. The idea that the Messiah will be revealed only when Jews have resettled the Holy Land is reminiscent of the Crusader ideal of the custodianship of the Holy Land. Jewish messianic hopes in the Crusader period had to cope with the real situation: Palestine was an arena of struggle for only two religions—Christianity and Islam. This treatise, however, betrays a Jewish attempt to alter this situation and restore matters to their former glory, to the days when Jews were present in the Holy Land.

The appeal to prepare for the coming of the Messiah by immigrating to the Land of Israel, even before 1240, fits what we know of the elitist groups of French Jews who came to Palestine in 1212—an event known in the sources as "The immigration of the three hundred rabbis."[11] Scholars have offered a variety of hypotheses as to the motives for this wave of immigration. L. Zunz, E.N. Adler and E.E. Urbach suggested a messianic motive, a view rejected by later historians, such as G. Cohen, A. Kanarfogel and, more recently, E. Reiner.[12] In light of this new source, the messianic explanation deserves reconsideration. The most prominent scholar among the

[11] Ephraim Kanarfogel, "The Aliyah of 'Three Hundred Rabbis' in 1211: Tosafist Attitude Toward Settling in the Land of Israel", *Jewish Quarterly Review* 76 (1986), pp. 191–215; Reiner (above n. 8), pp. 39–40, 55–69.

[12] L. Zunz, *Gesammelte Schriften*, III, p. 227; E.N. Adler, "Notes sur l'émigration en Palestine de 1211", *Revue des Etudes Juives* 85 (1928), p. 71; Urbach (above n. 5), I, p. 334 (cf. his explanation in pp. 125–126!) versus: G. Cohen, "Messianic Postures of Ashkenazim and Sefardim", *Studies of the Leo Baeck Institute*, New York 1967, p. 124; Kanarfogel, *ibid.*, p. 196; Reiner (above n. 8), pp. 116–117, 153–154.

French immigrants was R. Samson of Sens, the brother of Rizba—whom we have already encountered in this context. Rizba himself had died one year before his brother came to Palestine and was therefore unable to realize his messianic teachings, but he did write a halakhic work on the religious precepts specific to the Holy Land. Accordingly, I suggest that his disciple's "Homilies" was the French immigrants' ideological manifesto.

The author notes, with some satisfaction, that "a spirit from on high inspires the worthy to go up to Zion", thus indicating that a certain immigration movement in his time entertained objectives that fit his expectations of redemption sometime before 1240. Linguistically speaking, this sentence is highly reminiscent of our major source for the story of the three hundred rabbis: the chronicle *The Kings of Edom*, an appendix to Solomon Ibn Verga's *Shevet Yehuda*. There we read that in 1211 "The Lord inspired rabbis of France and rabbis of England to go into Jerusalem."[13] These two sentences are parallel. The expressions I have translated as "a spirit from on high inspired" and "the Lord inspired . . ." in fact use the same Hebrew root ער"ה; "the worthy" (Hebrew: כשרים) is parallel to "rabbis of France and . . . England"; and "to go up to Zion" is of course matched by "to go into Jerusalem". Most probably, Ibn Verga's account is based on this Darmstadt manuscript, that assigns messianic significance to the French immigration to Zion. Moreover, the immigrants are described as "scholars, pious and worthy men", a phrase corresponding to the pietistic-messianic goals of the French immigration to the Holy Land in the first quarter of the thirteenth century.

The messianic expectations towards 1240 also had other manifestations. In 1236, R. Moses ben Jacob of Coucy traveled through the Jewish communities of Spain, exhorting them to repent their sins. His sermons on that journey were incorporated in his great *Sefer Mitzvot Gadol*—one of the most important legal Jewish codices of the Middle Ages. In this respect R. Moses may be compared with the mendicants, Franciscans and Dominicans, who wandered the roads of Europe preaching repentance. There was "a cause from the heavens", he wrote, "that I should wander the lands to rebuke the exiles of Israel".[14] The expression "a cause from the heavens" is

---

[13] *Shevet Yehuda*, eds. Y. Baer & A. Shochat, Jerusalem 1946/47, p. 147.

[14] *Sefer Mitzvot Gadol*, part 2: Asse (positive precepts), No 3. In his introduction

somewhat reminiscent of the aforementioned "a spirit from on high inspired...", and it may be a hint of messianic designs.[15] Moreover, Moses of Coucy's teacher and mentor, R. Judah b. Isaac Sir Leon of Paris, was associated with circles in France and Germany which expected the advent of the Messiah in 1236.[16] Israel Ta-Shma recently published a sermon of R. Moses of Coucy, throbbing with messianic fervor, but expressing the fear that his generation would suffer the same fate as the generation of the wilderness—those who were fortunate enough to be redeemed and leave Egypt, but died in the wilderness because of their sins and were not permitted to reach the Promised Land.[17] The implication is clear: the messianic scenario dictated a massive campaign of repentance.

The two reactions discussed above to the messianic expectations on the eve of 1240 clearly reflect the two major religious phenomena of thirteenth-century France: the Crusades and the emergence of the Mendicant orders. But these are only two expectations out of many. The considerable extent of the messianic expectations before 1240 is indicated by further reports in both Jewish and Christian sources.[18] The wave swept from Egypt to Spain, from Sicily to Germany. We may justifiably ask, then, what was the Christian attitude to the Jews' messianic agitation? My thesis is that Christians did not remain indifferent. The messianic scenario was supposed to restore the political and religious status of the Jews, to convert a humiliated nation into a victorious one. The messianic scheme implied the approach of a universal Day of Judgment, when God would pass sentence on the nations that had enslaved Israel and punish them. Divine messianic justice would culminate in the fall of Edom, the Christian Church, the mythical successor to Rome, the destroyer of Jerusalem. Such a scenario could not possibly pass without a Christian reaction.

---

to part 1: Lo-ta'asse (negative precepts), he uses again the same expression "there was a cause from the heavens" to explain the reason for his preachings.

[15] According to this concept, repentance must precede the messianic age, since following the Messiah's coming there will remain no more room for repentance. See Jakob Molin, *The Book of Maharil*, ed. S.J. Spitzer, Jerusalem 1989, p. 305.

[16] A. Marx, "A Tract on Years of Salvation", *Hazofe le-Chochmat Yisrael* 5 (1921), p. 198.

[17] I.M. Ta-Shma, "*Iggeret udrashat hit'orerut*" (Hebrew), *Moriah* 19/5–6 (1993/4), pp. 7–12; I. Gilat, "Two *Baqqashot* of Moses of Coucy", *Tarbiz* 28 (1958), pp. 54–58; J. Katz, *Exclusiveness and Tolerance. Studies in Jewish-Gentile Relations in Medieval and Modern Times*, New York 1962, p. 80.

[18] Aescoly (above n. 7).

There are indeed a good many textual indications of Christian interest in the Jews' messianic activities. Christians made no secret of their fears that the ancient Jewish kingdom of the Ten Tribes was hidden beyond the Dark Mountains, as evidenced, for example, by the Legend of Alexander.[19] Andrew Gow discusses the legend of the "Red Jew" that spread through Germany from the thirteenth century on, portraying the Jews as harboring evil designs and planning the downfall of Europe.[20] Various explanations have been suggested for the color "red". One possibility is a reversal of the role that the Jews assigned the Christians in their messianic scenario. The Christians are categorized as "Edom", a word already associated in the Bible with the color red (derived from the same root in Hebrew). Biblical prophecies predict absolute doom for Edom at the End of Days. The Christian legend of the "red Jew" perhaps assigns the Jew the same messianic fate that the Jews claimed was in store for the Christians.

The fact that such Jewish eschatology foretold such a terrible fate for the Christians may explain the relatively moderate tone of messianism in Germany—German Jews were presumably fearful of Christian reactions.[21] German Jewry lived under the protection of the Holy Roman Empire, the main target for destruction in the messianic era; it was only natural, therefore, that Jews should exercise great care. Here, perhaps, lies an explanation for the surprising fact—already pointed out by E. Kanarfogel—that not one single German Jew came to the Holy Land with the "Three Hundred Rabbis". In fact, a text written among Hasidei Ashkenaz in the first half of the thirteenth century, published by I. Ta-Shma, issues a stern warning, "not to take steps to hasten the end of days, and not to immigrate to the Land of Israel before the proper time, [...] Any person who hastens to immigrate to the Land of Israel shall surely die"![22] Such a statement reads like a direct rejoinder to the French messianic program described above. The sharp tone of the passage gives one the

[19] A. Neubauer, "Where are the Ten Tribes?", *Jewish Quarterly Review* 1 (1889), pp. 14–28, 95–114, 184–201; B. McGinn, *Visions of the End*, 1979; C.F. Beckingham & B. Hamilton (eds.), *Prester John, the Mongols and the Ten Lost Tribes*, 1996.

[20] Andrew C. Gow, *The Red Jews: Antisemitism in an Apocalyptic Age 1200–1600*, Leiden/New York/Köln 1995.

[21] Cohen (above n. 12).

[22] I.M. Ta-Shma, "The Attitude to *Aliya* to Eretz Israel (Palestine) in Medieval German Jewry", *Shalem. Studies in the History of the Jews in Eretz Israel*, 6, ed. J. Hacker, Jerusalem 1992, pp. 315–318.

impression that the Ashkenazi author considered any practical messianic program a real danger, because of the influence it might exert on the Christian host society.

Indeed, in the German chronicle *Gesta Treverorum*, we read explicitly of the danger facing the Jews in Germany as a result of their messianic agitation:[23]

> Many of the Jews began to rejoice, believing that their Messiah would come at that time and liberate them. The year was then 1241. Some of the Christians suspected that the Jews wished to perpetrate some evil against the Christians, and therefore the Jews were no longer held in favor. However, they were granted imperial protection.

Moritz Stern suggested that the *Gesta Treverorum* might be alluding to the anti-Jewish riots of 1241 in Frankfurt.[24] This event—to which I will presently return may also be connected with the messianic expectations around 1240; but the chronicle is also referring to imperial protection of the Jews, and this can mean the privilege granted to all the Jews of the *Reich* by Frederick II in 1236, in which he first defined their status as *servi camerae nostrae* ("servants of our chamber").[25] This radical change in the legal status of the Jews was the emperor's response to the Fulda ritual murder accusation, which took place on Christmas Eve of 1235.[26] During that year there were three other blood libels in Germany: in Lauda, Tauberbischofsheim and Wolfesheim—it was a year marked by an outbreak of blood libels against the Jews.

Upon hearing of the accusation made against the Jews, the emperor immediately ordered an investigation. He summoned the heads of the church and the nobles of his realm to attend court at Haguenau, but owing to disagreement among those present no unanimous decision could be reached. Frederick II therefore convened a further council, this time at Augsburg, to which he summoned converts from

---

[23] *Gestorum Treverorum Continuatio IV*, in: *MGH SS*, XXIV, p. 404; J. Aronius, *Regesten zur Geschichte der Juden im fränkischen und deutschen Reiche bis zum Jahre 1273*, Hildesheim/New York 1970 (reprint), p. 228.

[24] M. Stern, "Analekten zur Geschichte der Juden", *Magazin für die Wissenschaft des Judenthums* 15 (1888), pp. 113–114.

[25] *MGH Constitutiones*, II, pp. 274ff., No. 204; R. Hoeniger, "Zur Geschichte der Juden Deutschlands im Mittelalter", *Zeitschrift für die Geschichte der Juden in Deutschland* 1 (1887), pp. 136–151.

[26] G.I. Langmuir, "Ritual Cannibalism", in: *idem, Toward a Definition of Antisemitism*, Berkeley/Los Angeles 1990, pp. 263–281.

outside Germany—England, Spain and France. In July 1236 these "experts" reached the conclusion that the blood libel was false.

At the same time that he refuted the blood libel, Frederick proclaimed that the Jews would henceforth be considered "servants of his chamber", in order to protect them from future accusations of this sort.[27] The *Gesta Treverorum* is referring, I submit, to this privilege. The sentence "Some of the Christians suspected that the Jews wished to perpetrate some evil against the Christians" can allude to events that took place before the Jews were granted "imperial protection", i.e., to the Fulda blood libel. These blood libels reflected Christian suspicions that the Jews "wished to perpetrate some evil against the Christians", perhaps on the background of the Jews' belief that "their Messiah" was about to come. The link between Christian accusations of ritual murder and Jewish expectations of redemption had already been made a century earlier, by the convert Theobald of Canterbury, who proclaimed in 1149, shortly after the ritual murder accusation of Norwich, that the Jews believed the Messiah would not come unless Christian blood was spilled.[28] Here was the connection between the avenging messianic beliefs of the Jews and the accusation of ritual murder. A Jewish reflection of this accusation may be found in the thirteenth-century apocalyptic text, "Prayer of R. Simeon bar Yohai".[29] The author, perceiving the Crusader wars in the Holy Land as harbingers of the Redemption, accused the Christians of "extracting the brains of babes and slaughtering babes daily for Jesus". Thus the messianic and ritual-murder motifs are linked in a Jewish source as well, undoubtedly in reaction to similar Christian accusations.

Clearly, then, Jewish messianic hopes as 1240 approached were a backdrop for major political events. They fueled the outbreak of four blood libels in 1235; but they also indirectly caused the proclamation of the Jews as "servants of the imperial chamber". This proclamation contradicted the political dimension of the Jewish messianic

[27] S.W. Baron, "'Plenitude of Apostolic Powers' and Medieval 'Jewish Serfdom'", *Yitzhak F. Baer Jubilee Volume*, ed. S.W. Baron *et al.*, Jerusalem 1960, pp. 102–124; A. Patschovsky, "Das Rechtsverhältnis der Juden zum deutschen König (9.–14. Jahrhundert). Ein europäischer Vergleich", *Zeitschrift der Savigny-Stiftung für Rechtsgeschichte: Germanische Abteilung* 110 (1993), pp. 331–371.

[28] *The Life and Miracles of St. William of Norwich*, ed. A. Jessop and M.R. James, Cambridge 1896, pp. 93–94.

[29] Y. Even Shmuel, *Midreshei Ge'ula. Chapters of the Jewish Apocalyptic*, Jerusalem 1954, pp. 281–282.

aspiration of liberation from the servitude and subjection to a Christian king. It was also a clever political move on Frederick's part. Bernhard Diestelkamp has pointed out the close involvement of the Dominicans, then the pope's supporters and allies, in the instigation and investigation of the Fulda blood libel.[30] Diestelkamp has shown that the investigation in Fulda had all the characteristics of an Inquisitional trial, and he notes, moreover, that it coincided in time with a wave of persecution of heretical movements in Germany. Frederick's councils at Haguenau and Augsburg were a direct reaction to Dominican interference in the affairs of his kingdom. He understood that this interference concerned the Jews not only of Fulda but of the entire *Reich*. Frederick II therefore used the Dominicans' own weapon against them: he initiated court proceedings, in the style of the Inquisition, in order to prove the Jews' innocence. It was for this purpose that witnesses were summoned to Haguenau and Augsburg to testify as to future accusations against the Jews, and herein lies the intimate connection between the exoneration of the Jews, on the one hand, and their definition as "servants of the imperial chamber", on the other. Both acts served the emperor's purpose: to defend his own interests against the pope and his allies. Frederick was protecting the Jews not only out of integrity and broad-mindedness, but also because he was a shrewd politician, well aware that what was good for the pope was bad for the emperor.

We do not know the identities of the converts who took part in the second council, at Augsburg, except for one. He was Nicolaus Donin, who later became notorious for his accusations against the Talmud which led to the Paris trial of 1240. We learn this from a letter of R. Jacob b. Elijah of Venice:[31]

> This convert [= Donin] went before the king superior to all kings in name and honor, and spoke lies and made false accusations that on Passover nights we slaughter young boys still accustomed to their mothers' breasts, and that the Jews had adopted this custom, and that

[30] B. Diestelkamp, "Der Vorwurf des Ritualmordes gegen Juden vor dem Hofgericht Kaiser Friedrichs II. im Jahr 1236", *Religiöse Devianz. Untersuchungen zu sozialen, rechtlichen und theologischen Reaktionen auf religiöse Abweichungen im westlichen und östlichen Mittelalter*, ed. D. Simon, Frankfurt 1990, pp. 19–39.

[31] Ed. J. Kobak, *Jeschurun* 6 (1868), Hebrew Section, p. 29, transl. by S. Grayzel, *The Church and the Jews in the Thirteenth Century*, New York 1966, pp. 339–340 and again by R. Chazan, "The Condemnation of the Talmud Reconsidered (1239–1248)", *Proceedings of the American Academy for Jewish Research* 55 (1988), p. 15.

> the hands of merciful women cook the children and we eat their flesh and drink their blood.... This wicked man sought to destroy us, and gave sword in the hands of the king to kill us. He lied to him. But God returned to him double his iniquity.... The honored king, in his piety and cleanness of hands, did not believe his words, and paid no heed to him, knowing that they are folly and nonsense and vanity.

The association with the Fulda blood libel was suggested correctly, first by Solomon Grayzel and later by Joseph Schatzmiller.[32] The description "the king superior to all kings in name and honor" could refer only to the Holy Roman Emperor, Frederick II. And indeed, we have already seen that French converts were among those summoned to Augsburg; one of them, then, was Nicolaus Donin. He failed, however, to convince his audience. Frederick rejected his accusations and accepted the position of other converts, who categorically denied the libel that the Jewish ritual required human blood. Donin's defeat at Augsburg drove him to try his fortune elsewhere. He went to Rome to meet the pope, just as expected from someone who had failed to convince a German emperor.

The pope Gregory IX was not a sworn enemy of the Jews. In the autumn of that year, 1236, he had taken action to defend the Jews of Anjou, Poitou and Brittany against rioting Crusaders—after some 2,500 Jews had already been massacred.[33] It took Donin three

---

[32] Grayzel, *ibid.*; J. Schatzmiller, "Did Nicholas Donin Promulgate the Blood Libel?", *Studies in the History of the Jewish People and the Land of Israel* 4, Haifa 1978, pp. 175–182. For another opinion see Ch. Merchavia, "Did Nicholas Donin Instigate the Blood Libel?", *Tarbiz* 49 (1980), pp. 111–121.

[33] S. Grayzel (above n. 31), pp. 226–229. A similar piece of information is reported by *Chronicon Brittanie* (Grayzel, *ibid.*, p. 345 n. 1): "Statim post Pascha crucesignati Jerusolymitani qui tunc temporis multi erant, interfecerunt Judeos per totam Brittaniam, Andegeviam, et Pietaviam". Around the same time (twentieth of Adar 1236) the Jews of Narbonne were close to face a severe pogrom. For a Jewish report of this event see A. Neubauer, *Medieval Jewish Chronicles and Chronological Notes*, Oxford 1887, p. 251; D. Kaufmann, "Le Pourim de Narbonne", *Revue des Etudes Juives* 32 (1896), pp. 129–130. For a Christian report see J. Régné, *Etudes sur la condition des Juifs de Narbonne*, Narbonne 1912, pp. 68–71. Later on, in 1239, the Jews of Brittany were expelled (Grayzel, *ibid.*, pp. 344–345). The Hebrew protocol of the Paris trial against the Talmud in 1240 mentions a series of persecutions in Brittany, Anjou and Poitiers, in which "tens of thousands of Jews were killed" (Yehiel ben Joseph of Paris, *Wikkuach*, ed. R. Margaliyot, 1975, p. 22). R. Hillel of Verona knows of 3000 Jews killed in France after the burning of the books of Maimonides (ed. Z.H. Edelmann, *Chemda Genuza*, Königsberg 1856, p. 19). Across the channel, the Jews of Oxford were accused in 1236 of having circumcised a Christian child before crucifying him on Easter. See Z.A. Rokéah, "The Jewish Church-Robbers and Host Desecrators of Norwich (ca. 1285)", *REJ* 141 (1982), p. 340, n. 26. A

years to win Gregory over to his side. In June 1239, shortly before Frederick was excommunicated for the second time—permanently—by the pope, Gregory dispatched letters to the most important monarchs of Europe (except, of course, Frederick), instructing them to search Jewish homes and confiscate their books on the Sabbath, 3 March 1240, during synagogue services.[34] That specific date was chosen carefully: it was Shabbat "Zakhor", the special Sabbath before Purim—the festival that marks the downfall of the Jews' enemies. Purim possessed a profound symbolic significance for Jews in medieval times; it was the festival of revenge prior to the festival of Freedom, Passover.[35]

Accusations of this kind were indeed leveled against the Jews at Paris.[36] After failing in his attempt to persuade those present at Augsburg that the Talmud required ritual murder, Donin seems to have moderated his charges. Now he cited the talmudic saying, "The best of the gentiles should be slain" (*optimum Christianorum occide*).[37] So much has been written about this saying and its meaning; nevertheless, it is perhaps worth trying once again to determine its original literary context. It was said of the Egyptians in pursuit of the Children of Israel. The midrash is essentially saying: Events during the Exodus from Egypt demonstrate that one cannot rely even on the best of the non-Jews, for they joined Pharaoh's host in pursuit of the fleeing Israelites. In keeping with the typological pattern of

---

similar accusation was raised against the Jews of Norwich (*ibid.*, pp. 340–346). On a ritual murder accusation in Hampshire 1236 see Z.E. Rokéah, "Crime and Jews in Late Thirteenth-Century England", *Hebrew Union College Annual* 55 (1984), p. 101 n. 13.

[34] Grayzel (above n. 31), pp. 240–241.

[35] E. Horowitz, "'And It Was Reversed': Jews and Their Enemies in the Festivities of Purim", *Zion* 59 (1994), pp. 129–168; G. Mentgen, "Über den Ursprung der Ritualmordfabel", *Aschkenas* 4 (1994), pp. 405–416.

[36] Ch. Merchavia, *The Church versus Talmudic and Midrashic Literature (500–1248)*, Jerusalem 1970, pp. 227–360; J. Cohen, *The Friars and the Jews. The Evolution of Medieval Anti-Judaism*, Ithaca/London 1982, pp. 60–76; Chazan (above n. 31).

[37] A close reading of Donin's accusations during the Paris trial against the Talmud reveals their accuracy. It is unlikely that he would have risked to tell lies about his former religion to Frederick II by claiming that Jews were in need for human blood for their rituals. It seems more reasonable to assume that his allegations in Augsburg were of a more general character, stating for instance that in certain cases Jewish law might have indeed justified killing of Christians (*optimum Christianorum occide*). That would be the case in the messianic era. An assertion of this kind in an environment that blamed Jews with ritual murder could have been understood by Jews as a dangerous confirmation of the Christian accusations. This assumption explains why Frederick II rejected after all the charges against the Jews.

the Exodus, this sentence therefore has a messianic significance: when the redemption is in progress it will be forbidden to spare even the best of the gentiles. Donin was not implying that the Jews would kill Christians for no particular reason, but that their messianic doctrine decreed the slaughter of even the best of the Christians. Judaism was being tried at Paris, accordingly, as the implacable enemy of Christianity. Although the messianic motif did not explicitly come up at the Paris trial—and it surely cannot be seen as the only motive for the assault on Judaism—one cannot discount the possibility that it was the motif that most readily made Donin's accusations timely and relevant. The question of Jewish loyalty now took the center of the political stage, on the background of the Jews' messianic expectations and Christian society's awareness of the implications.

But now Christian apprehensions with the approach of the year 1240 were heightened by the appearance of a new player on the European stage: the Mongols.[38] As the trial in Paris was in progress, the Mongols stormed the gates of Eastern Europe. It is difficult to determine just when the first news of their rapid conquests reached Europe; it seems that by the late 1230s the fears that they would take the heart of Europe by storm began to be real.[39] Many thought the Mongols to be the descendants of the Ten Tribes.[40] According to the Marbach Chronicle, the Jews believed that the Mongolian king Genghis Khan was the Messiah, son of David.[41] A contemporary, the English chronicler Matthew Paris, wrote that German Jews

[38] For a detailed survey of the relevant sources see S. Menache, "Tartars, Jews, Saracens and the Jewish-Mongol 'Plot' of 1241", *History. The Journal of the Historical Association* 81 (1996), pp. 319–342. The author was unaware of my article, "Towards 1240: Jewish Hopes, Christians Fears", *Proceedings of the Eleventh World Congress of Jewish Studies*, Division B, Bd. II, Jerusalem 1994, pp. 113–120, in which I already proposed a link between the messianic aspirations of the Jews towards 1240 and the Christian anti-Jewish reaction.

[39] Breslau (above n. 4); Aronius, *Regesten* (above n. 23), No. 531, pp. 227–230; G.A. Bezzola, *Die Mongolen in abendländischer Sicht (1220–1270). Ein Beitrag zur Frage der Völkerbegegnung*, Bern/München 1974, pp. 34–36, 44; J. Fried, "Auf der Suche nach der Wirklichkeit. Die Mongolen und die abendländische Erfahrungswissenschaft im 13. Jahrhundert", *Historische Zeitschrift* 243 (1986), pp. 287–332; F. Schmieder, *Europa und die Fremden: Die Mongolen im Urteil des Abendlandes vom 13. bis in das 15. Jahrhundert*, Sigmaringen 1994, pp. 24–30, 258–261, esp. p. 259 n. 327.

[40] R. Lerner, *The Powers of Prophecy. The Cedar of Lebanon Vision from the Mongol Onslaught to the Dawn of the Enlightenment*, Berkeley/Los Angeles/London 1983, pp. 21–22.

[41] *Annales Marbacenses*, ed. G.H. Perts., *MGH SS*, XVII, p. 174; Breslau, *ibid.*, pp. 100–101; Schmieder, *ibid.*, p. 24.

believed the Mongols to be the Ten Tribes, come to release their brethren from Christian servitude and subjugate the whole world.[42] A Hungarian bishop, in a letter to a colleague in Paris in 1241, calls the Mongols "Gog and Magog", and reports that they used Hebrew script.[43] The Jews, for their part, were accused of supplying the invaders with arms.[44]

The role of the Mongols in Jewish eyes is demonstrated by an obscure document from Sicily, telling of "the king who was concealed"—the king of the Ten Tribes—who sent twelve messengers to all the kings of Europe, commanding them to permit the Jews to leave their countries and immigrate to Palestine.[45] Otherwise, he warned, he would declare war upon them. A great fear, we are told, fell upon the kings of Spain, France, Germany and Hungary, who tried to appease "the concealed ones" (הגנוזים) with money. It seems very reasonable to assume, that "the concealed ones" are the Mongols;[46] but it is less clear when this document was written. The date of the document has long been discussed.[47] The earliest date proposed is the eleventh century, but some place its time as late as the sixteenth century. All the views proposed till now are based on the assumption that the text is a historical document, describing events that actually took place. I would like to suggest here a different reading, which I shall illustrate with one passage. The text relates that the rumors of the advent of the Jewish Messiah king created a dangerous situation:

> The people of Alleman [= Germany] prepared to slay all the Jews. The monks (Heb. גלחים) stood up and said to them: Beware ye, do not harm them, for he who harms them and anyone who touches them is as if touching the apple of his eye, causing harm not only to

---

[42] Matthaeus Parisiensis, *Chronica maiora*, ed. H.R. Luard (7 vols., *Rolls Series*, 1872–1883), IV, pp. 131–133, transl. by J.A. Giles, *Matthew Paris's English History*, 3 vols., 1852–1854.

[43] Richer, *Gesta Senonensis Ecclesiae*, ed. G. Waitz, *MGH SS*, XXV, p. 310; Breslau (above n. 4), p. 101.

[44] Menache (above n. 38), p. 339.

[45] Published for the first time by J. Mann, *Texts and Studies*, I, Cincinnati 1931, pp. 38f. and again recently by N. Zeldes, "A Magical Event in Sicily: Notes and Clarifications on the Messianic Movement in Sicily", *Zion* 58 (1993), pp. 347–363.

[46] Matthaeus Parisiensis (above n. 42) calls the Mongols *inclusi*: "quos dominus in montibus Caspiis precibus Magni Alexandri quondam inclusit".

[47] A full account of the different opinions concerning the dating of this document is presented by Zeldes (above n. 45).

> himself but to the whole world, for if they [= the concealed ones] come and they hear that Jews have been slain, they will slay you in retribution.

Did such an event ever occur? The monks' warning includes two parts. First: "he who touches them is as if touching the apple of his eye"; and second: the "concealed ones" are liable to punish whoever harms the German Jews. The first argument is a direct quote from the Babylonian Talmud (Gittin 57a), which quotes Jesus as propounding Augustine's doctrine of tolerance, as if Jesus commanded his followers to keep the Jews alive. As formulated here, therefore, this argument does not reflect the language of the Church and its priests, but that of Jewish propaganda.[48] The same applies to the warning that those who harm the Jews will be punished—for it is inconceivable that German monks could ever have voiced such sentiments. What we have here, therefore, is Jewish propaganda, valid and relevant in any period and adaptable to changing circumstances. To my mind, those who date the document as a whole as late as the fifteenth century are correct, although this specific passage, with its reference to the "concealed ones", reflects the atmosphere in the Jewish camp in the thirteenth century, during the Mongolian invasion. It clearly betrays the messianic hopes beating in Jewish hearts, the hostility aroused against them among the German masses and their need to seek the protection of the ruling circles.

Yet another episode that may be tied in with this train of events is the anti-Jewish pogrom of 1241 in Frankfurt.[49] On 9 April 1241, just after the Passover festival, the armies fighting the Mongols were defeated at Liegnitz, Poland. From now on the Mongols posed a real threat to the German *Reich*.[50] Relations between Jews and Christians in Frankfurt deteriorated rapidly. The Jews tried to prevent the baptism of a Jewish youth who wanted to convert to Christianity; on May 24 street fights broke out, and a few Christians were injured. The incident infuriated the Christian townspeople, who massacred

---

[48] In his letter to Rabbenu Tam immediately following the Blois incident of 1171, Nathan ben Meshullam informs him that Louis VII, the king of France, granted protection to the Jews. The author places in the king's mouth the same talmudic expression (A.M. Haberman, *Sefer geseroth Ashkenaz ve-Zarfat,* Jerusalem 1971, p. 145).

[49] Ed. F. Backhaus, *"Und groß war bei der Tochter Jehudas Jammer und Klage. . . ." Die Ermordung der Frankfurter Juden im Jahre 1241,* Sigmaringen 1995.

[50] Schmieder (above n. 39), p. 28. The panic spread from Hungary to Germany, and reached France and Spain as well.

some 180 Jews. The fact that the defeat at Liegnitz and the May anti-Jewish riots took place at approximately the same time, as well as the bold behavior of the Jews, reinforces the impression that the news of the debacle at Liegnitz caused heightened tension. It is not hard to imagine the excitement generated by the Mongolian victory, if not in the Jewish Quarter then, at least, in Jewish hearts.

I have briefly reviewed a series of seemingly unrelated events: the French immigration of rabbis to the Holy Land, R. Moses of Coucy's campaign in Spain, the blood libels in Germany in 1235, Frederick II's privilege of 1236, the trial of the Talmud in Paris, the Mongol invasion and the Frankfurt pogrom in 1241. All these occurred against a backdrop of messianic expectations that intensified as the year 1240 drew near. It is not my contention that the messianic context provides a direct, causal explanation in all cases; I merely wish to suggest that it served as a triggering factor, which stood in the background of these events. As Andrew Gow has aptly pointed out: "Antisemitism and apocalypticism are so inextricably intertwined in medieval Europe that they must be studied together if a coherent and accurate picture of both phenomena is to emerge".[51] Any discussion of Jewish messianism must, therefore, take into consideration not only internal developments within Jewry, but also reactions on the part of the Christian environment.

A comparative analysis of the Jews' messianic hopes, on the one hand, and the Christian reactions, on the other, indicates the rather complex nature of a basic assumption underlying scholars' attitudes to antisemitism, namely, the assumption that antisemitism is produced by irrational fantasies. Blood libels, accusations of desecration of the host, the belief that Jewish men menstruate or have a tail—all these are, of course, irrational. However, one must ask where these fantasies came from, and for what purpose.

Jewish messianism had an important part to play in our understanding of the mechanisms that produced the world of Christian antisemitism. There was a tragic asymmetry between the mutual messianic expectations of Christians and Jews. The Christians expected the Jews to convert, whereas the Jews prayed for the extinction of Christianity. On the eschatological level, Judaism was more aggressive than Christianity; this was, of course, a natural response to the reality in which Jews were a subject minority. The asym-

[51] Gow (above n. 20), p. 3.

metry in eschatological matters influenced the relationship on the real level, because the eschatological narrative of the two religions was founded on mutual negation and reversion. The Jewish Messiah is the Christian anti-Christ, and vice versa. Each side's messianic scenario allotted the other side a very active, even dangerous role. Jewish messianic visions were not mere esoteric fantasizing; they influenced the Christians' understanding of reality. Jewish messianic expectations thus played a certain role in the creation of Christian anti-Jewish perceptions and behaviour. The story of 1240 brings to a head these contrasting perceptions and their potential impact on Jewish-Christian relations.

THE ESCHATOLOGICAL IMPERATIVE: MESSIANISM AND HOLY WAR IN EUROPE, 1260–1556

Norman Housley

My interest in this topic was first aroused by three texts written in very different circumstances but possessing a common theme: sanctified violence in pursuit of an eschatological objective. The first is a letter written by Sigismund, king of Hungary and Emperor-elect, in September 1427 to Henry Beaufort, papal legate in Germany, to the effect that when Sigismund had stabilized his frontier with the Turks, received the imperial crown at Rome, and suppressed the Hussite rebellion, he would journey to the Holy Land to recover Christ's Tomb.[1] Two years later, in her *Ditié de Jehanne d'Arc*, Christine de Pisan prophesied that once Joan's victory over the English was complete, she would proceed to fight the heretics and the unbelievers, and that she and Charles VII would "put paid to the Saracens by conquering the Holy Land".[2] And in 1501 Christopher Columbus, in an extraordinary letter to Ferdinand and Isabella, drew on his credentials as the discoverer of the western sea passage to the Indies to urge the Catholic Monarchs to recover Jerusalem, quoting Arnau de Vilanova's prophecy that "he who will rebuild the [Holy] House upon Mount Zion will come from Spain".[3]

These three texts, and others like them, all pertain to the history of crusading.[4] The popularity of eschatological programmes, featuring such cherished crusading goals as the recapture of the holy city of Jerusalem and the final defeat of Islam, had a part to play in keeping the crusade idea alive in late-medieval and Renaissance

---

[1] Bayerische Akademie der Wissenschaften (eds.), *Deutsche Reichstagsakten* (Munich, Gotha and Göttingen, 1867), ix. 72–4.

[2] A.J. Kennedy and K. Varty (eds.), *Christine de Pisan: Ditié de Jehanne d'Arc* (Oxford, 1977), pp. 35–6.

[3] C. Varela (ed.), *Cristóbal Colón, Textos y documentos completos* (Madrid, 1982), doc. 63, pp. 252–6. Appropriately enough in view of what follows, Columbus attributed this prophecy wrongly to Joachim of Fiore.

[4] Translations can be found in my *Documents on the Later Crusades, 1274–1580* (Basingstoke, 1996), docs. 40, 43, 54, pp. 120–3, 132–3, 169–73.

Europe. But they are not simply about the crusade. They are a long way distant from the world of actual crusading, with its indulgences and taxes, its hard-nosed political negotiations and its armies of papal preachers and collectors. They also reach out beyond traditional crusading, for in this period the crusade was part of a bigger canvas in which the deployment of armed force on a large scale in the hope of achieving religious goals was predicted, called for, or actually occurred, in an eschatological or apocalyptic context. This was particularly the case during the early Reformation, when the militancy of certain groups generated passions which bring to mind the fervour and xenophobia of the early crusading period. This paper represents a first attempt to delineate the circumstances in which violence took place, focussing on the inspirational and organizational role of messianic individuals. Recent research on the eschatological writings of these centuries has been rich in both quantity and quality,[5] but it seems to me that to date nobody has asked two questions which are surely worth posing. First, how far and by what means did the messianic figures who achieved prominence in this period manage to translate their programmes into military action, crusading or otherwise? And secondly, did this action make more than a transient impact on the political and religious landscape of Europe?[6] It is useful to investigate these issues in terms of two approaches which may be termed the mainstream and radical traditions. I shall conclude with some remarks about a third approach which was less electrifying but arguably more productive.

1. *Messiahs in Power: Joachimist Programmes of the Last Days*

It is hard to avoid starting with Joachim of Fiore. The renown which he achieved in the late Middle Ages is well reflected in the tradition, which arose in Franciscan circles during the second half of the

[5] Useful bibliographical essays are B. McGinn, "Apocalypticism in the Middle Ages: An Historiographical Sketch", *Medieval Studies* 37 (1975), 252–86, reprinted in his *Apocalypticism in the Western Tradition* (Variorum Collected Studies Series 430, Aldershot and Brookfield, VT, 1994), study II; M. Bloomfield, "Recent Scholarship on Joachim of Fiore and his Influence", in A. Williams (ed.), *Prophecy and Millenarianism: Essays in Honour of Marjorie Reeves* (London, 1980), 21–52; B. McGinn, "Awaiting an End: Research in Medieval Apocalypticism, 1974–1981", *Medievalia et Humanistica* ns 11 (1982), 263–89.

[6] I am not considering the New World, which calls for separate treatment.

fourteenth century, that he drew up the entire plan for the mosaics in San Marco, Venice, as a prophetic programme.[7] Joachim's influence on late-medieval and Renaissance eschatology seems to have been as dominant as that of the rediscovered Aristotle on political ideas. Nor does the comparison between the two end there. In the same way that the study of Aristotle generated optimism about the fruitfulness of political activity, so Joachim's placing of his millennial third *status* within human history, and his concept of the "bridging" or transitional sixth *etas* of tribulations and triumph, made it possible to construct imaginative prophetic agendas based on the here and now. These agendas lessened (though they could not resolve) the tension inherent in all monotheistic eschatologies between providence and human agency. There existed the initial constraint that Joachim himself tried to pinpoint the sixth *etas* with undue exactitude, but once the fateful year 1260 was past, the way was clear for Joachites and those influenced by Joachimism to cast their prophecies in terms of political and religious configurations which appeared to meet the criteria set by the abbot, and by such early Joachimist texts as the *Super Hieremiam* and the *Super Esaiam*.

The massive corpus of eschatological prophecy which resulted has been much examined, although many of the most important texts still await definitive editions.[8] The strands most important for us are those of the Joachite Angelic Pope and Last Emperor prophecies, because we are here dealing with messianic figures whose roles included the waging of wars. The *pastor angelicus* makes his appearance right at the start of our period, when Roger Bacon wrote that "because of the goodness, truth, and justice of this pope the Greeks will return to the obedience of the Roman Church, the greater part of the Tartars will be converted to the faith, and the Saracens will be destroyed. There will then be one flock and one shepherd (*unum*

---

[7] O. Niccoli, *Prophecy and People in Renaissance Italy* (tr. L.G. Cochrane, Princeton, 1990), p. 24. John Phelan commented (*The Millennial Kingdom of the Franciscans in the New World* [2nd, revsd edn., Berkeley and Los Angeles, 1970], p. 125) that "the Joachimite tradition captivated apocalyptic mystics for half a millennium".

[8] Amidst the dauntingly large literature, reference must be made to two books. M. Reeves, *The Influence of Prophecy in the Later Middle Ages: A Study in Joachimism* (Oxford, 1969), remains the most authoritative and comprehensive treatment, while B. McGinn's *Visions of the End: Apocalyptic Traditions in the Middle Ages* (New York, 1979), is an excellent collection of translated texts, some by Joachites and most of those written after 1200 influenced by Joachimism.

ovile et unus pastor, John 10:16)".[9] The different fate allocated to each group of non-Catholics accurately reflected the hopes and fears of Bacon's contemporaries. A few years later a prophetic agenda set out for Pope Gregory X (1271–76), and reported by Salimbene, included the recovery of Jerusalem.[10] Reform of the Catholic church, crusade to Jerusalem, the conversion of the unbelievers: these became the essential ingredients of the Angelic Pope's programme, although after the *débâcle* of Celestine V's brief reign in 1294, many Joachites, especially the Spiritual Franciscans, juxtaposed their ideal figure with the current occupant of the Holy See, to whom they gave the role of *antichristus misticus*.[11]

Last Emperor prophecies originated in the midst of the conflict between the papacy and the last Staufen, so they were from the start highly charged politically.[12] Even after the Guelf and Ghibelline context was long gone, the polarities survived by being subsumed into rival French and German prophetic traditions which persisted for some three centuries, until the abdication of Charles V in 1555–56.[13] The French tradition began with prophecies concerning Charles of Anjou, the brother of St Louis and papal champion against the descendants of Frederick II. In *Rex novus adveniet*, probably written after the death of Conradin in 1268 although purporting to date from 1256, the "new king" would conquer Sicily and defeat the last Staufen, then "by battle (*Marte*) [he and the pope] will drag the followers of Mohammed to Christ so that there will be one flock and one shepherd".[14] The *Liber de flore* of c. 1305 prophesied an alliance between the Angelic Pope and a French Last Emperor which

---

[9] Translation from McGinn, *Visions of the End*, p. 190. See also Reeves, *The Influence of Prophecy*, pp. 46–8.

[10] Translation in McGinn, *Visions of the End*, p. 191.

[11] B. McGinn, "Angel Pope and Papal Antichrist", *Church History* 47 (1978), 155–73, reprinted in *Apocalypticism in the Western Tradition*, study V; *idem*, "*Pastor Angelicus*: Apocalyptic Myth and Political Hope in the Fourteenth Century", in *Santi e santità nel secolo XIV: Atti del XV Convegno Internazionale, Assisi, 15–17 ottobre 1987* (Perugia, 1989), 221–51, reprinted in *Apocalypticism in the Western Tradition*, study VI; Reeves, *The Influence of Prophecy*, Part Four *passim*.

[12] See R.E. Lerner, "Frederick II, Alive, Aloft, and Allayed, in Franciscan-Joachite Eschatology", in W. Verbecke, D. Verhelst and A. Welkenhuysen (eds.), *The Use and Abuse of Eschatology in the Middle Ages*, Mediaevalia Lovanensia series 1, studia XV (Leuven, 1988), 359–84.

[13] D. Kurze, "Nationale Regungen in der spätmittelalterlichen Prophetie", *Historische Zeitschrift* 202 (1966), 1–23; Reeves, *The Influence of Prophecy*, Part Three *passim*.

[14] Translation from McGinn, *Visions of the End*, p. 179.

would culminate in the recovery of Jerusalem.[15] Between 1345 and 1356 the Franciscan Jean de Roquetaillade, probably the greatest fourteenth-century Joachite, energized Francophile prophecies with a series of predictions linked very firmly to the current political situation. Thus according to his first major book, his lengthy commentary on the Joachimist text *Oraculum Cyrilli* (1345–49), Antichrist would be elected as Emperor in Rome together with an Antipope, but they would be overthrown by the king of France, the true pope and the Franciscans. Unbelievers would be converted and the third *status* inaugurated. Its end would come with the appearance of Gog and Magog, that traditional sign of the imminence of the Second Coming, derived from Revelation 20:7–8. The most striking feature of this prophecy is Roquetaillade's daring historicization of the forces of good and evil, the latter comprising the Sicilians and the Emperor Louis IV. A few years later, not surprisingly, the English joined them.[16] Shortly after Roquetaillade's death, in about 1380, the French prophetic tradition crystallized in the famous Second Charlemagne prophecy, which was first applied to Charles VI and was to retain a magnetic appeal for many generations. A French king would pacify his realm, subjugate his neighbours, and destroy Rome and Florence. He would be crowned as Emperor by the Angelic Pope, enforce conversion on the nations of the East, and finally die after surrendering his crown on the Mount of Olives.[17]

From its beginnings in the 1260s, the German-imperial tradition vested its main hope in the arrival of a Third Frederick, a messianic figure who for some would be a chastiser and for others a renovator. The urge to respond in kind to the Second Charlemagne prophecy

---

[15] H. Grundmann, "Liber de Flore: Eine Schrift der Franziskaner-Spiritualen aus dem Anfang des 14. Jahrhunderts", *Historisches Jahrbuch* 49 (1929), 33–91; McGinn, "*Pastor Angelicus*", pp. 239–45.

[16] J. Bignami-Odier, *Etudes sur Jean de Roquetaillade (Johannes de Rupescissa)* (Paris, 1952), pp. 53–112, 123 (reprinted in "une nouvelle édition, corrigée et completée", as "Jean de Roquetaillade, théologien, polémiste, alchimiste", in *Histoire littéraire de la France XLI: Suite du quatorzième siècle* [Paris, 1981], 75–240); C. Morerod-Fattebert (ed.), *Johannes de Rupescissa: Liber secretorum eventuum*, Spicilegium Friburgense: Textes pour servir à l'histoire de la vie chrétienne, vol. 36 (Freiburg, 1994). On Roquetaillade, see also S. Barnay, "L'Univers visionnaire de Jean de Roquetaillade", in *Fin du monde et signes des temps: Visionnaires et prophètes en France méridionale (fin XIIIe–début XVe siècle)* (Toulouse and Fanjeaux, 1992), 171–90.

[17] Translation in McGinn, *Visions of the End*, p. 250. See also M. Chaume, "Une Prophétie relative à Charles VI", *Revue du moyen âge latin* 3 (1947), 27–42; Reeves, *The Influence of Prophecy*, pp. 320–31.

was clearly strong. Thus in the prophecies of "Gamaleon", which circulated in the early fifteenth century, a French tyrant who seized the imperial title would be cast down by a German prince who would also crown a new pope at Mainz, reform the church, exterminate the Jews and lead "the last, great expedition to the Holy Land".[18] The fact that the name Frederick was held by only one late-medieval Emperor, and he one of the least inspiring, was not an insuperable obstacle to German hopes, for both Sigismund and Maximilian attracted attention as candidates for the role of Last Emperor.[19] As we saw at the beginning, Sigismund was prepared to refer to this role even in the midst of his struggles against the Hussites and Turks, when he wanted to accentuate his imperial ambitions. In 1488 the most learned of the German prophetic texts, Johann Lichtenberger's *Prognosticatio*, was published, to massive acclaim, and in 1519 the imperial tradition embarked on its Indian Summer with the "constellation of prophecies" which were generated by the election of Charles V.[20] At key events in Charles's reign, such as the election itself, the sack of Rome in 1527, the Tunis expedition in 1535, and the battle of Mühldorf in 1547, the prophecies came thick and fast. For example, following Charles's great victory over Francis I at Pavia in 1525, his secretary Alfonso de Valdés commented that "It seems that God, by a miracle, has granted the emperor this victory so that he may not only defend Christendom and resist the power of the Turk . . . but that . . . he may also seek out the Turks and Moors on their own lands and . . . recover the empire of Constantinople and the holy mansion of Jerusalem. . . . Thus it may come about, as is prophesied by many, that under the rule of this most Christian prince, the whole world may receive our holy Catholic faith and the words of our Redeemer may be fulfilled: *Fiet unum ovile et unus pastor*".[21] For Giles of Viterbo, the Emperor was "the Messiah, or at any rate the Messiah's agent and reflection".[22]

---

[18] Translation in McGinn, *Visions of the End*, pp. 251–2. See also Reeves, *The Influence of Prophecy*, p. 332.

[19] *Ibid.*, pp. 340–1, 350–3.

[20] McGinn, *Visions of the End*, pp. 270–6; Reeves, *The Influence of Prophecy*, pp. 347–74; Niccoli, *Prophecy and People*, pp. 172–88.

[21] Quoted by A. Terry, "War and Literature in Sixteenth-Century Spain", in J.R. Mulryne and M. Shewring (eds.), *War, Literature and the Arts in Sixteenth-Century Europe* (Basingstoke, 1989), pp. 101–18, at p. 101.

[22] F. Secret (ed.), *Egidio da Viterbo, Scechina e libellus de litteris Hebraicis*, Edizione nazionale dei classici del pensiero italiano, serie 2, 10–11 (2 vols., Rome, 1959), ii. 281.

These principal traditions of political prophecy were flanked by others. In England Joachimism was overshadowed by the Arthurian prophecy of the king who would wear three crowns, defeat the French and conquer as far as Jerusalem. It was applied not just to Edward I and Edward III, in whose cases the cap fitted well, but even to a *rex inutilis* like Edward II. In 1313 Adam Davy wrote of five prophetic dreams in which Edward featured as Emperor, pilgrim and crusader.[23] Far more richly textured was the Iberian, and particularly the Aragonese prophetic tradition. The latter was fertilized after 1282 by that of Sicily, and soon afterwards produced in Arnau de Vilanova a major Joachite whose prophecies were repeatedly deployed to place kings of Aragon and later Castile in a messianic capacity, so much so that Gutierre Diez de Games made fun of people who greeted each new monarch with prophecies.[24] Spain also created, in *El Encubierto*, the only socially radical Last Emperor figure, whose culminating crusade to Jerusalem would fit the pattern of the peasants' crusades rather than the imperial or royal *passagia* usually considered appropriate for the Second Charlemagnes.[25] We shall return to *El Encubierto* later.

Even from this brief summary the imaginative riches and variety of the eschatological programmes envisaged by Joachites, and their significance in terms of "l'histoire des mentalités", will be apparent. Let us now turn to what Marjorie Reeves described as "the delicate problem of the interplay between word and action". There are two interlocking aspects to this: the degree of fruitful exchange which took place between these Joachimist programmes and crusading activity, and the broader issue of the relationship between prophecy and the political goals of rulers to whom it was addressed. Clearly the two motifs which connected many Joachites with the crusades were the recovery of Jerusalem and the defeat of Islam. Both were somewhat problematic. Regaining Jerusalem did not enjoy an automatic priority on the practical crusading agenda once the Ottomans began

---

[23] C. Beaune, "Perceforêt et Merlin: Prophétie, littérature et rumeurs au début de la guerre de Cent Ans", in *Fin du monde et signes des temps*, pp. 237–55.

[24] See A. Milhou, "La Chauve-souris, le Nouveau David et le Roi caché (trois images de l'empereur des derniers temps dans le monde ibérique: XIIIe–XVIIe s.)", *Mélanges de la Casa de Velazquez* 18 (1982), 61–78; M. Aurell, "Eschatologie, spiritualité et politique dans la confédération catalano-aragonaise (1282–1412)", in *Fin du monde et signes des temps*, pp. 191–235.

[25] See the study by Sara Nalle in this volume, which first alerted me to this.

making their Balkan conquests, and there was a tendency, which the papal *curia* was bound to find disconcerting, for Joachites to precede their last great *passagium* with the *renovatio ecclesie*. In some cases the latter meant the wholesale reform of the papal office through the Angelic Pope, and the more apocalyptic prophets, particularly the Spiritual Franciscans, predicted the humiliation of the secular clergy, even the sack or destruction of Rome and the translation of the papacy elsewhere.[26] Few would be content with the relatively modest proposals set out by those popes who pursued the traditional Innocentian programme of reform and crusade. As for the final defeat of Islam, this was often construed as a victory of persuasion rather than arms. All non-believers (except for Gog and Magog, and a few peripheral *gentes*) would be converted by the Joachite *viri spirituales* to achieve the longed-for "unum ovile et unus pastor".[27] The relationship between crusade and conversion was always a delicate one, and the prominence of John 10:16 in Joachimist programmes was not helpful in passing from ideas to action.[28]

Nonetheless, the interaction between prophecy and crusade was on the whole a fruitful one, from a number of viewpoints. Fantastic as some of their ideas were, Joachites were realistic enough in the way they approached the problem of mobilizing sufficient resources to achieve their aims; they appreciated the need for figures of established authority to act in order to get crusades off the ground. The brief awaiting the Angelic Pope was breathtakingly wide, but it mirrored, albeit in an exaggerated way, the crusading claims and missionary aspirations of thirteenth-century popes like Innocent III and IV, and Gregory X.[29] Some Joachites showed a considerable degree of knowledge both about the circumstances of past crusades and about the preconditions and mechanics of whose which they pre-

[26] For example, Bignami-Odier, *Etudes*, p. 80; Reeves, *The Influence of Prophecy*, pp. 328, 334–5, 339, 342, 356–7, 367, 439; Niccoli, *Prophecy and People*, pp. 175–7.

[27] Bignami-Odier, *Etudes*, pp. 103, 163; Reeves, *The Influence of Prophecy, ad indicem*. E.R. Daniel, "Apocalyptic Conversion: The Joachite Alternative to the Crusades", *Traditio* 25 (1969), 127–54, at pp. 137–9, explains the pivotal place of conversion in the eschatological schema of Joachites.

[28] Cf. *ibid.*, pp. 141, 153, for opposition to crusading on the part of some early Joachites.

[29] J. Riley-Smith, *The Crusades. A Short History* (London, 1987), pp. 119–77; M.W. Baldwin, "Missions to the East in the Thirteenth and Fourteenth Centuries", in K.M. Setton (gen. ed.), *A History of the Crusades*, 2nd edn. (6 vols., Madison, Wisconsin, 1969–90), v. 452–518, at pp. 452–89.

dicted. Arnau de Vilanova was dispatched to the papal court by James II during the siege of Almería in August 1309 to request extra privileges for the Aragonese crusade against Granada; his speech at Avignon did not please the king, but it was an astute attempt to wring further concessions out of Clement V by setting James's campaign within a broader context of crusading goals.[30] Jean de Roquetaillade's *Liber secretorum eventuum*, completed in November 1349, contains references to two *passagia* to the East during the period before Antichrist's appearance which bring to mind the several small expeditions and phased crusades which had characterized the movement throughout Roquetaillade's lifetime.[31] In other writings Roquetaillade showed himself to be well-informed about the crusade.[32]

This familiarity with crusading may have sprung from a desire to harness the movement for the benefit of the Joachite programme, but the crusading cause stood to gain. In the broadest sense, Joachimism furnished a varied menu of prophetic insights within which such events as Columbus's Atlantic crossings, and the overseas discoveries of the Spanish and Portuguese, could be interpreted providentially, to balance out such forbidding developments as the Ottoman advance and to instill a feeling of hope.[33] In Last Emperor programmes, a useful shift of emphasis occurred from the culminating surrender of the crown, which was necessarily passive, to the leadership of the final, great *passagium* to the East.[34] Joachite prophecy was one source among many which reminded secular rulers, particularly the Emperor and the king of France, of the expectations attached to title, dynasty and race. Serving popes were not consistently viewed as mystical antichrists, to be swept away in favour of Angelic Popes. Leo X, for one, was actually acclaimed as the Angelic

---

[30] P. Miquel Batllori (ed.), *Arnau de Vilanova: Obres catalanes*, Els nostres clàssics, Colleccio A, vols. 53–4, (2 vols., Barcelona, 1947), i. 72, 74, 217, 220; Aurell, "Eschatologie", pp. 195–7.

[31] Morerod (cf. n. 110) Fattebert (ed.), *Johannes de Rupescissa: Liber secretorum eventuum*, pp. 167–8.

[32] Bignami-Odier, *Etudes*, pp. 67, 74, 77–8, 84, 137–8, 172.

[33] See text quoted above, at n. 3; J.W. O'Malley, "Fulfillment of the Christian Golden Age under Pope Julius II: Text of a Discourse of Giles of Viterbo, 1507", *Traditio* 25 (1969), 265–338, esp. p. 273 (reprinted in *his Rome and the Renaissance: Studies in Culture and Religion*, Variorum Collected Studies Series 127 [London, 1981], study V; R.E. Lerner, *The Powers of Prophecy: The Cedar of Lebanon Vision from the Mongol Onslaught to the Dawn of the Enlightenment* (Berkeley, Los Angeles and London, 1983), pp. 189–97, provides an excellent analysis of expectations from prophecy.

[34] *Ibid.*, p. 56.

Pope.[35] Giles of Viterbo, general of the Augustinians and a leading Joachite and church reformer under Julius II and Leo X, issued his most important call for a crusade to meet the challenge of the upcoming End of Days in that most orthodox of settings, the Fifth Lateran Council.[36] Giles was capable of attributing a messianic role to Julius II, who in his eyes was presiding over a Golden Age of the Church and should cap his achievements by reconquering the Holy Land.[37] But even if the pope in office proved disappointing, placing the Angelic Pope in the imminent future enabled men to set out their prophetic stall without causing either offense or loss of hope about the possibility of change occurring.[38]

In fact the Joachimist programme not only helped keep people interested in crusading, it also shaped crusading ideology and policies, perhaps more so than crusade historians have hitherto perceived. Eschatology was always important in crusading, and in the thirteenth century it entered papal crusading bulls. For example, Innocent III alluded to apocalyptic prophecy on the end of Islam when he proclaimed the Fifth Crusade in 1213, and in 1265 Clement IV referred to prophecies in Revelation in a crusade bull against Baybars.[39] It is clear that some people in the papal *curia* found the imaginative and intellectual appeal of Joachimism irresistible, for the crusade bulls against the last of the Staufen contained references to Joachimist prophecies circulating at the time, in which Frederick II featured as the serpent, Conradin as the adder or basilisk, and Charles of Anjou as the lion.[40] It seems too that crusade preachers grasped

[35] See D. Weinstein, *Savonarola and Florence: Prophecy and Patriotism in the Renaissance* (Princeton, 1970), p. 352: "The new crusade I see arise through him with great celebration to make all one sheepfold. . . ."

[36] See C. O'Reilly, "'Without Councils we cannot be saved . . .' Giles of Viterbo addresses the Fifth Lateran Council", *Augustiniana* 27 (1977), 166–204. A report of a phantom battle witnessed at Verdello, near Bergamo, at the end of 1517, and construed as a sign of the imminence of the Last Days, was seized on by Leo X to promote his planned crusade. See Niccoli, *Prophecy and People*, pp. 65–6, 79, and cf. pp. 79–85 for later elaboration of the report into pro-imperial myth.

[37] J.W. O'Malley, "Fulfillment of the Christian Golden Age", pp. 325–6.

[38] Reeves, *The Influence of Prophecy*, p. 503.

[39] G. Tangl, *Studien zum Register Innocenz' III* (Weimar, 1929), pp. 88–97, at p. 91; C.T. Maier, "Crusade and Rhetoric against the Muslim Colony of Lucera: Eudes of Châteauroux's 'Sermones de Rebellione Sarracenorum Lucherie in Apulia'", *Journal of Medieval History* 21 (1995), 343–85, at p. 358.

[40] *Ibid.*, p. 358; N. Housley, *The Italian Crusades: The Papal-Angevin Alliance and the Crusades against Christian Lay Powers, 1254–1343* (Oxford, 1982), p. 42. I did not take note of the clear Joachimist content of such phases in my analysis of the crusade bulls.

Joachimism's wider popularity and so geared their message to it. As Christoph Maier has shown, Joachimist prophecies about the Staufen were cleverly meshed with biblical exegesis in a series of sermons delivered against the Muslim colony at Lucera by one of the century's finest crusade preachers, Eudes of Châteauroux, in 1268–9.[41]

Furthermore, as the popes tried to deal with their Italian problems by bringing the French in, they drew up crusading agendas which look remarkably similar to Joachimist programmes. Bulls in favour of Charles of Anjou copied, or were copied by, Joachimist prophecies when they depicted the French conquest of southern Italy as an essential first step towards assisting the beleagured Latins in the East.[42] And in the *Liber de Flore* of c. 1305 we have the alliance of an Angelic Pope and a French Last Emperor followed by the reunification of the Catholic and Orthodox churches, the "pacification" (i.e., conquest) of Sicily, and the stabilization of the turbulent Italian peninsula. At the end the Last Emperor will regain Jerusalem.[43] The entire package is very similar to that allocated by Boniface VIII to Charles of Valois in 1300, with a few additions all based on other policies which were much discussed at the Capetian and Valois courts.[44] There would appear to be a traffic of ideas here between the *Liber* and papal policy, and it is probably based on a traffic of individuals, perhaps Arnau de Vilanova, who was a crusade enthusiast, is praised in the *Liber*, and travelled widely in the early years of the fourteenth century. But the period between the fall of Acre and the end of Clement V's reign was marked by hectic crusade planning and activity, and by much eschatological excitement, and it is questionable whether the precise nature of the exchange can be uncovered now.[45]

What is most striking, however, is that the Second Charlemagne tradition established a prophetic template of enduring worth, and closely bound up with France's crusading past, to which future French interventions in Italy could be fitted. The Franco-guelf axis created

---

41 Maier, "Crusade and Rhetoric", pp. 355–69.

42 Housley, *The Italian Crusades*, p. 68.

43 Grundmann, "Liber de Flore", *passim*.

44 G. Digard *et al.* (eds.), *Les Registres du pape Boniface VIII* (4 vols., Paris, 1884–1935), no. 3917.

45 See S. Schein, *Fideles crucis: The Papacy, the West and the Recovery of the Holy Land, 1274–1314* (Oxford, 1991); Lerner, *The Powers of Prophecy*, pp. 37–61. This is not to suggest that Boniface VIII was a closet Joachite: see his sceptical remark, quoted in R.K. Emmerson, *Antichrist in the Middle Ages: A Study in Medieval Apocalypticism, Art, and Literature* (Seattle, 1981), p. 53.

in the second half of the thirteenth century was subsumed for decades at a time by the disasters of the Hundred Years War, when the king of France was militarily incapable of playing his messianic role. But the prophetic hopes were sustained by individuals like Jean de Roquetaillade, the anonymous author of a prophecy addressed to Charles VI in 1380, Christine de Pisan in 1429, and Jean du Bois, who exhorted Charles VII in 1455 to carry out the task allotted to him.[46] Since the basic political geography did not alter, old ideas could be dusted down and used afresh.[47] The overall prophetic template, after all, was not chronological but broadly referential: a growing threat from Islam, the need for reform in the church, Christendom sunk in sin and disunity. None of this was to change between the thirteenth and sixteenth centuries. So in 1494 the Second Charlemagne prophecy again made its appearance, this time in vernacular verse addressed by Guilloche de Bordeaux to the young Charles VIII. And with it came the idea of a French crusade to the East launched from bases in the kingdom of Naples, just as in the days of Charles of Anjou and Charles of Valois.[48]

The basic difference between these messianic programmes and crusading lay in the fact that the former, as a system of ideas, had at its disposal no structures of organization. This was at once its weakness and its main strength. Joachites could provide no men, money, ships or allies. However, this gave them immunity from the disillusionment which was the price paid by advocates of crusading, when the repeated use of its ample machinery of preaching and tax collection brought little or no actual military activity. By contrast, messianic programmes were notable for their longevity and resilience; few people appear to have renounced their Joachimist beliefs in disenchantment.[49] After the sack of Rome in 1527, Girolamo Casio de'

---

[46] Bignami-Odier, *Etudes, passim*, esp. p. 123; Chaume, "Une Prophétie"; N. Valois, "Conseils et prédictions adressés à Charles VII en 1445 par un certain Jean du Bois", *Annuaire Bulletin de la Société de l'histoire de France* 46 (1909), 201–38. For Christine de Pisan, see above, at n. 2.

[47] For Roquetaillade, writing in 1356, the kingdom of Sicily was still the *regnum Karoli*: Lerner, *The Powers of Prophecy*, pp. 139–40 n.

[48] See Reeves, *The Influence of Prophecy*, pp. 354–8; Y. Labande-Mailfert, *Charles VIII et son milieu (1470–1498): La jeunesse en pouvoir* (Paris, 1975), pp. 188–9.

[49] The most famous example is Salimbene, but he was a special case since his disillusionment sprang from the passing of specific years which had been designated as the End, 1250 and 1260: see McGinn, *Visions of the End*, p. 167. For a more interesting later example see Reeves, *The Influence of Prophecy*, pp. 425–7.

Medici prophesied that this terrible event must be the prelude to the recovery of the Holy Land, which had erroneously been considered to be the job of Charles VIII.[50] Flexibility was another strength. When John I of Aragon objected to the prophecies of Francesc Eiximenis because of his prediction that the only royal house to survive the upcoming *tribulatio* would be the French one, the chastened prophet wrote a new scenario stating that John was the messianic "Bat" (*vespertilio*) which would conquer Mecca and subdue the sultan of Babylon (i.e., Egypt).[51] The prophetic interpretation of Charles VIII's role was sufficiently flexible for contemporaries to see him both as a new David, a liberator, and as a Cyrus, a rough but ultimately beneficial *flagellum Dei*. Even some of the Jews in Italy became excited at the messianic prospects.[52] The main traditions we have looked at were far from being cast in stone, for names could be changed and agendas brought up to date. When considering the tribulations of the church, outdated reference to the Great Schism could be dropped in favour of the chaos caused by the Lutherans.[53] In 1516, in a rare period of Anglo-French amity, Silvestro Meuccio brought the king of England into his Francophile programme in order that England's burgeoning naval forces could combine with those of Venice.[54] Nor were the two principal traditions irreconcilable: Charles V's prophetic career embraced, among other things, both the Eagle and (through his Burgundian ancestors) the Lily.[55]

The fact that writers like Roquetaillade, Eiximenis and Meuccio were astute enough to tailor their prophecies to fit contemporary political events and expectations implies that prophecy and political decisions were elements of a dialectical process. Granted that some individuals, such as the bizarre Revolutionary of the Upper Rhine (c. 1490–1508), were so isolated and extreme as to be totally divorced from reality,[56] most belonged to a political culture in which prophecy was expected to shape planning and action, and vice versa. The

[50] Niccoli, *Prophecy and People*, p. 179.
[51] Aurell, "Eschatologie", pp. 208, 228–9.
[52] A. Denis, *Charles VIII et les Italiens: Histoire et mythe* (Geneva, 1979), 31–66.
[53] Niccoli, *Prophecy and People*, pp. 133–4.
[54] Reeves, *The Influence of Prophecy*, pp. 375–8.
[55] *Ibid.*, pp. 359–74. Cf. Lerner, *The Powers of Prophecy*, pp. 157–74, on the way the Tripoli prophecy was adapted first by Lutherans and then by Catholics to cast Charles in a messianic role which would be acceptable to the opposing camps at different stages of his political career.
[56] For a recent study see K. Arnold, "'Oberrheinischer Revolutionär', oder

vigour and self-confidence of the Joachimist tradition constitute a strong argument that description and prescription were interwoven: Joachites were not passively awaiting events but making them clearer for the benefit of those in power.[57] As so often, Giles of Viterbo is a revealing example. He regarded his predictions as a means of spurring into action those in authority. When Charles V was crowned as Holy Roman Emperor and appeared to offer hope of bringing about the *renovatio* of Giles's tenth age, he shifted from papal to imperial messianism. His greatest work, the *Scechina*, was commissioned by Clement VII but dedicated to Charles V.[58]

It is not being cynical to say that prophecy exerted its strongest impact on policy when it ran in harmony with other considerations, dynastic, economic and religious. This was in part because prophecy functioned as a veiled expression of political goals, even, if we accept the word's applicability to this period, as propaganda.[59] Some prophets and commentators held office with the rulers they addressed: Vilanova was Clement V's physician, Lichtenberg Frederick III's astrologer, Wolfgang Lazius court historian for Ferdinand I.[60] Given a favourable eschatological atmosphere the dissemination of messianic programmes could make expensive policies more palatable. Perhaps the most illuminating example of this is the circulation during the gruelling Granada war of 1482–92 of the entire package of Iberian prophecies (*El Encubierto*, the Bat, and the New David).[61] Undoubtedly this helped "sell" the war, which as an anti-Islamic crusade carried escha-

'Elsässischer Anonymus'? Zur Frage nach dem Verfasser einer Reformschrift vom Vorabend des deutschen Bauernkrieges", *Archiv für Kulturgeschichte* 58 (1976), 410–31.

[57] I cannot therefore agree with the passivity implicit in Lerner's remark (*The Powers of Prophecy*, p. 196) that "Medieval eschatological prophets hardly wrote as reformers or revolutionaries; their aim was to comprehend and make known God's plan without thinking that they or others could do anything to change it". This seems to miss the point about the malleability inherent in the most successful prophecies, including the one which Lerner was analyzing.

[58] J.W. O'Malley, *Giles of Viterbo on Church and Reform: A Study in Renaissance Thought*, Studies in Medieval and Reformation Thought, vol. 5 (Leiden, 1968), pp. 116, 130–1, 181ff.

[59] Aurell, "Eschatologie", p. 231, argues this with some vigour in the case of Aragon.

[60] The most interesting case is that of Roquetaillade, who is compared by Lerner (*The Powers of Prophesy*, p. 136) to John the Baptist in Herod's cistern. Rulers were of course capable of treating the prophetic offerings of their office-holders as the irrelevant sidelines of people whose services were valued for quite different reasons.

[61] Milhou, "La Chauve-souris", pp. 70–1, and cf. Aurell, "Eschatologie", pp. 204–6 on Aragon in the late-fourteenth century.

tological overtones anyway. However, the message would not have got far had there not existed a readiness to hear about the apocalyptic, which is dramatically present in Columbus's letter of 1501.[62]

The issue of impact has been greatly clarified by Ottavia Niccoli's study of popular prophecy in Italy, in which she demonstrated the broad social base which characterized prophecy in the late fifteenth and early-sixteenth centuries, as well as the myriad lines of connection between piazza, study and court. As she expressed it, prophecies were "a unifying sign connecting nature to religion and religion to politics and coordinating all the scattered shreds of a culture".[63] The sources for Niccoli's period are unusually rich (particularly the diaries of Marin Sanudo), but recent research on Roquetaillade points in the same direction.[64] This cultural approach is far more fruitful than attempting to find specific examples of rulers who were driven by their messianic role. As the example of Charles VIII and the French invasion of Italy has amply shown, the latter all too easily becomes a sterile business of lining up one authority against another.[65] It follows that the wars conducted by such messianic figures as Charles VIII and Charles V cannot be pigeon-holed as religious or secular activities. Rather, they should be portrayed as conflicts shaded by religious expectations, the intensity of which depended on the degree of eschatological awareness in existence at the time. The latter appears to have had its own pattern, created by such factors as military disasters in the East, climactic trends, and of course the incidence of plague.[66]

---

[62] See above, at n. 3. Columbus's eschatological views have received a lot of attention recently. See, for example, P.M. Watts, "Prophecy and Discovery: On the Spiritual Origins of Christopher Columbus's 'Enterprise of the Indies'", *American Historical Review* 90 (1985), 73–102; L.I. Sweet, "Christopher Columbus and the Millennial Vision of the New World", *Catholic Historical Review* 72 (1986), 369–82, 715–16.

[63] Niccoli, *Prophecy and People*, p. xvi.

[64] Barnay, "L'Univers visionnaire".

[65] See the excellent discussion in Labande-Mailfert, *Charles VIII et son milieu*, pp. 169–218. For two contemporary sceptics see Denis, *Charles VIII et les Italiens*, pp. 131, 142. But as she remarks (*ibid.*), "Charles VIII représente le cas-type du Messie, rejeté avec la violence avec laquelle il a été attendu".

[66] See Lerner, *The Powers of Prophesy*, pp. 115–24, 197 (military disasters); Niccoli, *Prophecy and People*, pp. 140–67 (floods); R.E. Lerner, "The Black Death and Western European Eschatological Mentalities", *American Historical Review* 86 (1981), 533–52.

2. *Radical Messiahs, Millenarian Movements and Armed Force*

The messianic figures we have examined so far enjoyed their status *ex officio*: popes, emperors and kings, they were looked to because they possessed the power, either individually or in partnership, to destroy and renovate within Christendom, ultimately to annihilate Islam and, in so many cases, to regain Jerusalem. There were also, however, a number of messianic individuals without the benefit of ancestry or rank, revolutionaries who took up the task of bringing about the millennial phase of Christian history in their own time, so paving the way for Christ's return.[67] Building the New Jerusalem, which entailed both the overthrow of established regimes and the defence of the millennial order against attack, could hardly be done without resort to armed force, even if much of the preparatory dirty work could be left to the Turks.[68] Indeed, some of the favourite scriptural texts of the millenarians, including Ezekiel, Daniel and Revelation, if followed literally, enjoined on them violence in the name of the Lord as a necessary, purgative process. Ezekiel 9 depicted a divinely-mandated purging of Jerusalem by six executioners, in which even women and children were killed and only the Elect were spared death; while in Revelation 7 the task of destruction was assigned to four angels, and the number of the Elect specified as 144,000. But those who took it upon themselves to enact such scenes had limited access to established secular channels for raising armed forces, nor did they have any desire to tie their aims in with crusading. This they associated with the old, corrupt order, even if they occasionally paid homage to its remarkable success in mobilizing armies.[69] What therefore did they do?

---

[67] Useful introductions are S.L. Thrupp (ed.), *Millennial Dreams in Action: Essays in Comparative Study* (The Hague, 1962), especially the essays by Kaminsky and Weinstein; and N. Cohn, *The Pursuit of the Millennium: Revolutionary Millenarians and Mystical Anarchists in the Middle Ages* (revised and expanded edn., New York, 1970). Cohn's book has been heavily criticized but has the virtue of being ceaselessly thought-provoking.

[68] See W. Klaassen (ed.), *Anabaptism in Outline: Selected Primary Sources* (Kitchener, Ontario, and Scottdale, PA, 1981), pp. 321–2; J.M. Stayer, *Anabaptists and the Sword* (Lawrence, Kansas, 1972), pp. 115–24, 154–5.

[69] P. Matheson (ed. and tr.), *The Collected Works of Thomas Müntzer* (Edinburgh, 1988), p. 155: "I will lift up my voice against you for all the world to hear, and all the brethren will be ready to risk their life blood, as they have been hitherto against the Turk".

The problem is seen at its most acute in the career of Thomas Müntzer, whose writings reveal in highly colourful language the stress and frustration which arose from powerless passion. Müntzer rejected the Lutheran view that Old Testament Law had been superceded by New Testament Gospel, and he believed that the Elect were not just permitted to fight, but mandated by God to kill Christ's enemies. He was also convinced that such events as the Ottoman capture of Belgrade in 1521 were signs of the imminence of the Last Days. Theological radicalism and eschatological urgency were vitalized by his bellicose temperament. For himself he adopted a series of biblical role models, ranging from the prophet Elijah to Jeremiah, Daniel and John the Baptist. His final letters to his opponents in May 1525, brimming over with personal abuse and violent threats, were signed "Thomas Müntzer with the sword of Gideon". As Johann Agricola complained to him, "You breathe nothing but slaughter and blood".[70]

Such threats were, however, to a large extent bluster, for Müntzer was unable to find suitable sword-bearers. His favourite device for mobilizing force against his enemies was the league. He seems to have assembled the first before 1513 against the archbishop of Magdeburg,[71] but the search for followers became more urgent once the reform crisis began. Müntzer's journey to Prague in 1521 was probably motivated by the hope that the Czechs would act as the defenders of the Gospel, as they had done a century previously.[72] When the Czechs failed to respond to his preaching, Müntzer fell back on his leagues. He organized a Christian League in July 1524 and an "Eternal League of God" in the spring of 1525.[73] These bodies of men were loyal, dedicated and well-armed; but they comprised at most a few hundred soldiers, and during the last year of his life Müntzer made two attempts to expand his military base. In July 1524 he delivered a famous sermon before Duke John of Saxony and his son John Frederick, in which he demanded that they use

---

[70] Stayer, *Anabaptists and the Sword*, pp. 76–89; Matheson (ed.), *Collected Works*, pp. 151, 156, 157, 248, 300, 371; T. Scott, *Thomas Müntzer. Theology and Revolution in the German Reformation* (Basingstoke, 1989), p. 23 and *passim*. A useful introduction to recent scholarship is *idem*, "From Polemic to Sobriety: Thomas Müntzer in Recent Research", *Journal of Ecclesiastical History* 39 (1988), 557–72.

[71] Scott, *Thomas Müntzer*, p. 6.

[72] *Ibid.*, pp. 28–39.

[73] On the leagues, see *idem*, "The 'Volksreformation' of Thomas Müntzer", *Journal of Ecclesiastical History* 34 (1983), 194–213.

their influence and military strength much more actively in promoting evangelical reform. The text used was Daniel 2, a classic of eschatological exegesis, and Müntzer did not mince his words: if the princes failed to act then the sword would be taken from them, in accordance with Daniel 7:27.[74] Within a few months he and his Eternal League had thrown in their lot with the rebel peasants. But the marriage between Müntzer's apocalyptic theology and the peasants' economic demands was, as a recent biographer put it, "fitful, fragile and fortuitous".[75] After the climactic battle of Frankenhausen Müntzer himself criticized the peasants for putting their self-interest first.[76]

Müntzer was clearly unable to locate a group which was both willing to accept the proferred mantle of the Elect, and powerful enough to ride out the storms of the 1520s. What was needed was a compact base for action, and in a period of rapid urbanization the city, with its established political and military structures, its economic potential and its susceptibility to the spread of religious radicalism, offered such a base *par excellence.* So it is not surprising that two important examples of violent millenarianism were urban ones. Florence in the late middle ages developed a distinctive civic millenarianism compounded of *campanilismo*, populism, the radical preaching of the Spiritual Franciscans and a Francophilia derived from the city's guelf associations. On these foundations, as Donald Weinstein showed in his classic study, Girolamo Savonarola created his millenarian vision of Florence as the New Jerusalem in 1494, the catalyst being the political crisis brought on by Charles VIII's invasion. In December, with the Medici regime overthrown and the French packed off to Rome, Savonarola outlined a programme for the transformed city which combined spiritual and temporal glory. Pisa, which had rebelled against Florentine rule in 1494, would be reconquered, and other lands would be won, so that Florence's fame would be such that "the Turks will convert to the faith of Christ".[77] This "benevolent imperialism" was trumpeted by the *piagnoni*, Savonarola's supporters, but the search for a translation of ideas into military practice is not rewarding. While one of the leading *piagnoni*, Domenico

[74] Matheson (ed.), *Collected Works*, pp. 226–52.

[75] Scott, *Thomas Müntzer*, pp. 174–5.

[76] Matheson (ed.), *Collected Works*, pp. 160–1.

[77] Weinstein, *Savonarola and Florence, passim.* He has recently written a useful bibliographical update: "Hagiography, Demonology, Biography: Savonarola Studies Today", *Journal of Modern History* 63 (1991), 483–503.

Cecchi, wrote a lengthy treatise on the need for a regenerated popular militia in February 1496, its language is secular and there is no hint that these armed *cives* would be fighting for the sacred cause preached by Savonarola.[78] Discussion of military reform was unaffected by the millenarians' exuberant rhetoric: to this extent Savonarola deserved Machiavelli's title of "the unarmed prophet".[79] Details were not the prophet's strong point, and he was enough of a Joachite to invest all his hopes in Charles VIII, even after the French retreat in 1495. The millennial Elect and the Second Charlemagne were after all linked in "a divinely ordained partnership".[80]

A more promising example of urban millenarianism is Anabaptist Münster in 1534–35, at the height of Germany's Radical Reformation. The need to establish and work from an urban base was clear to the radical sectarians, and at various times a number of European cities were mooted as potential New Jerusalems.[81] A plot was forged to seize Erfurt in 1528 but failed, and it was only in February 1534, when the Anabaptists won political control of Münster, that a suitable platform existed for translating into practice millenarian ideas which were no less extreme than those of Müntzer had been.[82] Münster was a major city and the Anabaptist cause was well-entrenched in Westphalia and the neighbouring Low Countries. Under Jan Matthijs and Jan van Leiden Münster was transformed into the New Jerusalem and those within its walls became the Chosen. On 8 September 1534 van Leiden was proclaimed king of the New Israel. His elaborate regalia asserted universalist claims, even though his rule extended only to the city's ramparts. Communism was practised and polygamy introduced, the latter, it has been suggested, constituting an attempt to increase group coherence among the city's inhabitants.[83]

---

[78] C.C. Bayley, *War and Society in Renaissance Florence: The "De Militia" of Leonardo Bruni* (Toronto, 1961), pp. 237–9.

[79] T.J. Lukes, "To Bamboozle with Goodness: The Political Advantages of Christianity in the Thought of Machiavelli", *Renaissance and Reformation* 8 (1984), 266–77, esp. p. 268.

[80] Weinstein, *Savonarola and Florence*, p. 177. Cf. Weinstein's comment on p. 312: "Nowhere in his sermons or in his writings does [Savonarola] concern himself with the details of the new order".

[81] W. Klaassen, *Living at the End of the Ages: Apocalyptic Expectation in the Radical Reformation* (Lanham, New York and London, 1992), pp. 84ff.

[82] Stayer, *Anabaptists and the Sword*, pp. 191–3.

[83] Good recent introductions, with up-to-date bibliographies, are R.P. Hsia, "Münster and the Anabaptists", in R.P. Hsia (ed.), *The German People and the Reformation*

The regime's chief theologian and propagandist was Bernhard Rothmann, the reforming preacher who had introduced the Anabaptist cause to Münster. As late as November 1533 Rothmann wrote a "Confession of the Two Sacraments" which has been described as "a classic peaceful Anabaptist statement".[84] Rothmann's views on war were radicalized by the Anabaptist seizure of power, which the Anabaptists saw as a miraculous event comparable to the parting of the Red Sea.[85] He believed that it marked the close of the Second Age of world history and the approach of the millennium, which must be ushered in by a literal enactment of Ezekiel 9, the purging of Babylon's evil through fire and sword. References to the Sermon on the Mount or other texts in favour of passivity were irrelevant since the Age of the Gospel was past. Instead, vengeance would be exacted under the direction of van Leiden, a Davidic Messiah, to prepare the way for the return of Christ, which would be peaceful in the manner of Solomon.[86] "This is the kingdom and the throne of David, in which, through the sword of righteousness, the kingdom among us is to be cleansed and extended."[87] The time had therefore come to listen to Joel rather than Isaiah, and turn ploughshares into swords.[88] The fantastic idea was entertained of the 144,000 saints of Revelation 7 first converging on Münster, and then, once the predicted forty-two months of tribulation were past, marching out from the city to occupy the purged world.[89] Jan Matthijs even

(Ithaca and London, 1988), pp. 51–69; and J.M. Stayer, "Christianity in One City: Anabaptist Münster, 1534–35", in H.J. Hillerbrand (ed.), *Radical Tendencies in the Reformation: Divergent Perspectives* (Kirksville, Missouri, 1988), 117–34. Stayer, *Anabaptists and the Sword*, pp. 227–80, provides a detailed analysis of the theory and use of violence in Anabaptist Münster.

[84] "Bekenntnisse van beyden Sacramenten": R. Stupperich (ed.), *Die Schriften Bernhard Rothmanns* (Münster-i-W., 1970), 139–95. The description is Stayer's, in "Christianity in One City", p. 121.

[85] Stayer comments (*Anabaptists and the Sword*, p. 251), that "fundamentally, Rothmann was a propagandist, preparing an *ex post facto* justification of what had already occurred and a summons to a crusade".

[86] See especially Rothmann's "Bericht von der Wrake", Stupperich (ed.), *Die Schriften*, pp. 285–97. There are some translated extracts of Rothmann's eschatological views in Klaassen (ed.), *Anabaptism in Outline*, pp. 330–5.

[87] *Ibid.*, p. 253 (= Stupperich, p. 278).

[88] Stupperich (ed.), *Die Schriften*, pp. 296, 353, referring to Isaiah 2:4 and Joel 3:10.

[89] C.A. Cornelius (ed.), *Berichte der Augenzeugen über das münsterische Wiedertäuferreich* (Münster, 1983: repr. of photographic reproduction of 1st edn., 1853), p. 97.

advocated killing all the inhabitants of Münster except the Anabaptists, although thankfully he was overruled on this.[90]

Anabaptist Münster got closer to chiliastic holy war than Savonarolan Florence had done, but for all its drama it remained a short-lived episode. The New Jerusalem was defended by only 1500–2000 fighting men against a powerful coalition of Catholic and Lutheran forces. Attempts to arouse Anabaptists in the neighbouring Low Countries to come to the assistance of Münster failed, although there were a few local uprisings and the extent of the support which the Münsterites enjoyed remains problematic. More might have been achieved to bring relief to the beleagured "kingdom" had the rescue efforts been better co-ordinated.[91] Jan van Leiden, like Müntzer some years earlier, blamed defeat on the inadequacy of his instrument, claiming that the Elect had proved sinful.[92] The hopeless situation in which the besieged Anabaptists found themselves led even the bellicose Rothmann, in a treatise written in February 1535, to emphasize the need to endure suffering for God's cause.[93] Once the city had fallen, moreover, most other Anabaptists made haste to distance themselves from the violent millenarianism which it had espoused. Menno Simons, for example, wrote in 1539 that while the Last Days were imminent, the promised kingdom of Christ was spiritual, not tangible, it had no king but Christ himself, and "neither this King nor His servants bear any sword but the sword of the Spirit".[94] A few groups of Anabaptists adhered to the Münsterite tradition, especially Jan van Batenburg, who saw himself as a second Gideon, but all they could achieve was scattered acts of terrorism, not the holy war waged, albeit briefly, at Münster.[95]

In fact it is to Hussite Tabor that we have to look for the best example of sacred violence in the service of radical millenarianism. And it was one of the achievements of Howard Kaminsky to establish both the circumstances in which Tabor's chiliasm developed,

---

[90] R. Van Dülmen (ed.), *Das Täuferreich zu Münster 1534–1535: Berichte und Dokumente* (Munich, 1974), pp. 71–2.

[91] Stayer, *Anabaptists and the Sword*, pp. 262–78; *idem*, "Christianity in One City", pp. 122–4.

[92] *Idem, Anabaptists and the Sword*, p. 278.

[93] See Stupperich (ed.), *Die Schriften*, pp. 299–372.

[94] J.C. Wenger (ed.) and L. Verduin (tr.), *The Complete Writings of Menno Simons c. 1496–1561* (Scottdale, PA, 1956), p. 217.

[95] Stayer, *Anabaptists and the Sword*, pp. 282–97.

and the effects which this had for the Hussite cause generally. The Prague chronicler Lawrence of Březová, who is generally our best source for the early phase of Hussitism, remarked that in January 1420 some priests on the movement's Taborite wing, so called because of their practice of holding open-air, hill-top services, began preaching "a new coming of Christ, in which all evil men and enemies of the Truth would perish and be exterminated, while the good would be preserved in five cities [cf. Isaiah 19:18]". They were reacting in despair to Prague's dilatory response to Sigismund's threat of a crusade, and "urged that all those desiring to be saved from the wrath of almighty God . . . should leave their cities, castles, villages and towns . . . and should go to the five cities of refuge".[96] Initially the two towns of Plzen and Písek functioned as the designated "arks of salvation", but in late February a Taborite force occupied Hradiště, renaming it Tabor.[97]

The chiliasts had already made their move from passivity to resistance, and from its origins the new community at Tabor was militarized to a remarkable degree. Organized into four military and political divisions, the Taborites set about capturing fortresses and establishing a lordship of their own over the surrounding countryside. In John Žižka of course they possessed a military tactician of genius.[98] With the aid of such scriptural texts as Deuteronomy 11:24, Isaiah 30:32 and Revelation 17:14, a doctrine was developed of expropriative holy war by the Elect against their persecutors in the Last Days. It found its fullest expression in the tracts of John Čapek, whose writings were described as "more full of blood than a fishpond is of water". For Čapek, as for Rothmann ninety years later, the unique circumstances of his age swept away all customary juridical constraints on warfare: the Taborites were "an army sent by God through the whole world to inflict all the plagues of vengeance". Tabor's initial communism, its practice of common chests, was reflected in Čapek's insistence that not only the clergy but also the nobility must be killed, "chopped down like pieces of wood".[99] As

[96] H. Kaminsky, "Chiliasm and the Hussite Revolution", *Church History* 26 (1957), 43–71, at p. 47; *idem, A History of the Hussite Revolution* (Berkeley and Los Angeles, 1967), pp. 311–12.

[97] *Ibid.*, pp. 329–36.

[98] See F.G. Heymann, *John Žižka and the Hussite Revolution* (Princeton, 1955).

[99] Kaminsky, *History*, pp. 347–60. See also the translation of Articles against the Taborites in McGinn, *Visions of the End*, pp. 266–8.

Kaminsky put it, "The new violence was indeed religious violence, orgiastic and ritualistic as well as practical in character".[100]

Of course this doctrine of chiliastic total war had no long-term future, even at Tabor itself. Any belief that the Second Coming is imminent cannot by definition last long, so ideologies constructed around it were bound to be exciting but of short duration. Christ's failure to reappear in 1420 was rationalized in terms of a two-stage Second Coming, the first of which was secret (1 Thess. 5:2) and had supposedly occurred; but this was unconvincing.[101] Furthermore, two developments occurred in the course of 1420 which rapidly propelled the Taborite confederation towards more moderate policies. One was the fact that the millenarians, in particular their leading prophet Martin Húska, embraced the heresy of Pikartism, the denial of Christ's real presence in the sacrament. This robbed *utraquism* of most of its point, and was just as obnoxious to most Taborites as it was to more conservative Hussites. Meanwhile, Sigismund's intransigence and the immediate need to defeat his crusading army compelled the Hussite centre party to be more resolute in organizing its own defence. A doctrine of legitimate war was expounded by the Prague University masters, based on scholastic Two Swords theory. In contrast to the views of the chiliasts, this war was to be waged by the noble elite and would accord with the normal laws of war. The Four Articles of Prague, formulated in March 1420, paved the way for the Hussite coalition which successfully defended Prague against Sigismund in the summer of 1420, but when the conservatives denounced millenarianism alongside Pikartism in December, the leading Taborites declined to defend it.[102]

In 1421 the Pikarts and the even more extreme Adamites were expelled, hunted down and massacred by forces mobilized by Tabor and Prague in harmony. Húska was burnt in August 1421.[103] Tabor ceased to be an avowedly millennial community and gradually shed the social radicalism which had been associated with it; it has been plausibly suggested that Münster's development would have been similar had it survived for long enough.[104] The chiliast total war

100 Kaminsky, *History*, p. 347.
101 *Ibid.*, pp. 345–6.
102 *Ibid.*, pp. 361–83, 412–18.
103 *Ibid.*, pp. 418–33.
104 Stayer, "Christianity in One City", p. 134.

doctrine had lasted for less than a year. Kaminsky stressed its importance in supplying the urgency with which Tabor had been founded and fortified, and its control established over what had previously been solidly Catholic territory in southern Bohemia.[105] It is tempting to agree with him, but it is impossible to weigh the significance of this compelling dynamic compared with Žižka's purely military contribution. Certainly the Hussite coalition's defence of Bohemia against the series of crusades forms one of the clearest examples in this period of a religious war fought outside, indeed in plain opposition to, the crusading movement. But this quickly became a notably conservative venture, and the depiction of the new faith as millennial was displaced by a drive to create a national, Bohemian cause. If Hussitism was to be associated with the linguistic, historical and religious traditions of the *gens bohemica*, it would obviously be disastrous to impose a clean break with the past.

Tabor in 1420 was not the only example in this period of a movement which combined energetic holy war, a socially radical programme and a millenarian view of contemporary events. The anonymous *El Encubierto* who seized control of Játiva (another urban base) during the *Germanías* revolt in 1522 in Valencia appears to be another one. In fact his case is even more intriguing than early Tabor in so far as this enterprising individual made use of Iberia's indigenous Last Emperor tradition to provide a forceful and able leadership.[106] This was an ongoing problem for the radical Messiahs. Self-portrayal as a reincarnated Enoch or Elijah, prophets of the End, meant accepting the constraints of a purely civilian role,[107] while posing as the bearer of Gideon's sword or the like was little more than metaphorical.[108] Bernhard Rothmann's depiction of Jan van Leiden as the Davidic Messiah was ingenious but, like the two-stage Second Coming of the Taborite chiliasts, improvisatory and unsatisfactory. It robbed the appearance of Christ himself of its full

[105] Kaminsky, "Chiliasm", pp. 63–4.

[106] For this I am indebted to Sara Nalle's paper.

[107] See the exhaustive treatment by R.L. Petersen, *Preaching in the Last Days: The Theme of "Two Witnesses" in the Sixteenth and Seventeenth Centuries* (New York and Oxford, 1993). For Joachites, Enoch and Elijah were useful but secondary *dramatis personae*: see, for example, Bignami-Odier, *Etudes*, p. 170.

[108] For Thomas Müntzer, Jan van Batenburg and the sword of Gideon see above at nn. 70, 95. There is a good discussion of Anabaptist role models in Klaassen, *Living at the End of the Ages*, pp. 79–84.

drama.[109] *El Encubierto*, on the other hand, tapped into Joachimism's accumulated wealth of expectation. The image of *El Encubierto* decreeing that the possessions of the clerics and nobles of Játiva be confiscated and used for the pursuit of a rebellion which was simultaneously a millennial holy war bears comparison with the creation of Tabor's *seigneurie* in southern Bohemia. Perhaps it was only possible thanks to Aragon's uniquely subversive Joachimist legacy. For Joachites elsewhere, such as Jean de Roquetaillade, social disturbances were one of the tribulations of the sixth *etas*: purgative and necessary they may be, but they did not form a feature of the millennium itself, when social divisions would continue to exist no matter what other momentous changes took place.[110]

3. *National Messianism? The Chosen People*

So far the fruits of our search for holy wars in messianic settings are somewhat limited. Arguably the root reason is that the violence we have considered was in design or reality apocalyptic. Whether it was one feature of a prophetic agenda, or the expression of the Elect pursuing a millennial vision, apocalyptic violence suited the printed page or the pulpit better than it did the military camp or battlefield. To find a more powerful and lasting impact on warfare in this period, it is necessary to look not at messianic figures or millennial programmes and their apologists, but at the concept of the Chosen People, what one might term "national messianism".[111]

Applying the idea of divine election to ethnic groups was of course a popular and recurrent theme in the Middle Ages: one finds it at least as early as the Carolingians. But it became more common from the thirteenth century onwards, and the process was illuminated by

---

[109] Although one Anabaptist still clung to this view in 1538, three years after the fall of Münster: Stayer, *Anabaptists and the Sword*, p. 293.

[110] Morerod-Fattebert (ed.), *Johannes de Rupescissa: Liber secretorum eventuum*, pp. 77ff.; Bignami-Odier, *Etudes*, pp. 164 and especially 95: a fascinating suggestion that the destruction of the wicked might be the work of another uprising of the *pastoureaux*, acting "sub titulo passagii". For a Florentine prophecy incorporating the *Ciompi* revolt of 1378, see Weinstein, *Savonarola and Florence*, pp. 50–1.

[111] The arguments outlined in the final three paragraphs are explored at greater length in my paper entitled (English version) "*Pro deo et patria mori*: Sanctified Patriotism in Europe, 1400–1600", in P. Contamine *et al.* (eds.), *Guerre et compétition dans la croissance des états européens (XIIIe–XVIIIe siècle)* (Paris: PUF, forthcoming).

two of Princeton's finest medievalists. Ernst Kantorowicz showed how in the thirteenth century the Thomists transferred the concept of the church as a *corpus mysticum* to the state, laying the foundations for the sanctification of a *respublica* rather than a *gens*.[112] And Joseph Strayer illustrated how in the case of the French a similar transfer of the idea of the "Holy Land" occurred, from a unique territory in Palestine to the *patria* of the Christian believer.[113] This development was made possible by a mixture of the French crusading legacy, the political astuteness of the last Capetian kings and their advisors, and the encouragement or at least acquiescence of the popes. Strayer quoted Joan of Arc's remark that "all those who wage war against the holy kingdom of France, wage war against King Jesus".[114] It is true that the French evinced a peculiarly strident form of "sacred patriotism", but it was far from being unique or even unusual. Not to be outdone by their neighbours, the English were scarcely less ebullient in their assertions. And although some came to the idea late, by the mid-sixteenth century there was scarcely a national, ethnic or civic community in Europe which had not been saluted as a Chosen People, its territory deemed to be sacred soil, and its capital city hailed as the New Jerusalem. Victories were seen as proof of God's election, defeats as a sign that the *populus Dei* must repent of its sins to regain His favour.[115] One is tempted to say that this scriptural way of construing national identity and giving it purpose was inevitable, in a period in which ways of formulating national bonds other than in terms of religion and dynastic allegiance remained fairly inchoate.

Interactions with the eschatological prophecies and movements which we have examined were naturally manifold. The French and, to a lesser extent, the Germans attempted to tie in the theme of the

---

[112] E.H. Kantorowicz, *The King's Two Bodies: A Study in Mediaeval Political Theology* (Princeton, 1957), pp. 193–272.

[113] J.R. Strayer, "France: The Holy Land, the Chosen People, and the Most Christian King", in T.K. Rabb and J.E. Seigel (eds.), *Action and Conviction in Early Modern Europe: Essays in Memory of E.H. Harbison* (Princeton, 1969), 3–16. See also C. Beaune, *The Birth of an Ideology: Myths and Symbols of Nation in Late-Medieval France* (tr. S.R. Huston and ed. F.L. Cheyette, Berkeley, Los Angeles and Oxford, 1991), pp. 172–93.

[114] Strayer, "France", p. 16n.

[115] As, for example, in Gerónimo de Mendieta's assertion that Spain's problems during the final decades of the sixteenth century were a providential judgement on the government's abusive treatment of the Indies. See Phelan, *The Millennial Kingdom*, pp. 106–7.

Chosen People with Last Emperor prophecies.[116] So during the Italian wars, the imaginative Jean Lemaire de Belges wrote of a king of France defeating and converting the Turks, dominating Europe and the East, and becoming Emperor. He would also enjoy a vision of the walls of Troy, the mythical ancestral homeland of the *gens Francorum*, from which it had been led by God to the Promised Land of France.[117] German national pride is apparent in the "Gamaleon" prophecies, with their prediction that a German Emperor would bring about the *translatio* of the reformed papacy to the patriarchate of Mainz.[118] The claim that the Castilians were a Chosen People was powerfully assisted by the eschatological reading given to their conquests and missionary work in Granada and the New World, and it ran like a constant theme through the sixteenth century to the Armada and beyond.[119] There was a vigorous tradition of divine election at Florence which Savonarola picked up and incorporated into his millenarian preaching.[120] And the Hussites argued that the *gens bohemica* were chosen by God to defend and propagate the reformed faith of Hus because of its historic piety.[121]

This interlacing of patriotic sentiment with the concept of a divinely mandated mission was bound up with the period's bellicosity. Without doubt it lacked the emotional charge of the apocalyptic or millennial. But it allowed for a steadier infusion of purpose and morale, one which was more subject to control and direction. The belief in providential destiny, usually teleological though sometimes eschatological, joined dynastic ambition, damaged pride and economic advantage *inter multa alia* among the myriad reasons for going to war, while scriptural texts like the books of Maccabees furnished inspiring material for galvanising the defence of the God-given *patria* in the face

---

[116] Roquetaillade, noted for his precocious patriotism, remarked in his *Liber ostensor* (1356) that "ce royaume est plus honorable que n'importe quel royaume temporel, depuis l'origine du monde": Bignami-Odier, *Etudes*, p. 204. Compare Symphorien Champier, in his *De monarchia Gallorum* (1537): Reeves, *The Influence of Prophecy*, pp. 380–1.

[117] Beaune, *The Birth of an Ideology*, p. 240.

[118] McGinn, *Visions of the End*, pp. 251–2; Reeves, *The Influence of Prophecy*, p. 332.

[119] Phelan, *The Millennial Kingdom*, pp. 5–38. See in particular A. Milhou, *Colón y su mentalidad mesiánica en el ambiente franciscanista español* (Valladolid, 1983).

[120] Weinstein, *Savonarola and Florence*, pp. 27–66. See too his conclusion (p. 375) that "civic republicanism had emerged, in ideology as well as fact, as an alternative to the medieval *respublica christiana*".

[121] F. Smahel, "The Idea of the 'Nation' in Hussite Bohemia", *Historica* 16 (1969), 143–247, 17 (1969), 93–197.

of "gentile" aggression. Perhaps the best indication of what it gained rulers is the fact that by the early sixteenth century men like Erasmus, who placed a premium on peace and Christian unity, and wanted to dissociate religion from warfare, were appalled by the trend.[122] By this point it was apparent that the universalist, inclusive outlook of traditional Catholic eschatology, which had found expression in the crusading movement and had remained important in some features of the Joachimist programme,[123] especially its passion for conversion, was out of touch with the increasingly xenophobic, exclusive reality of European political life. Even as Erasmus wrote religious division was joining political disunity. When the last "Last Emperor" to assume office in a confessionally intact *respublica christiana* abdicated in 1556, it was clear that in future messianic individuals would have to be even more politicized than past ones had been, if they were to make any impact on their world.[124]

[122] J.-C. Margolin, *Guerre et paix dans la pensée d'Erasme* (Paris, 1973), pp. 194, 224–5.

[123] Reeves, *The Influence of Prophecy*, pp. 503–4, 507–8.

[124] Although as Reeves pointed out (*The Influence of Prophecy*, pp. 381–4, 479–81), it remained possible for individuals like Guillaume Postel to combine strongly patriotic feelings with universalist aspirations. See also W.J. Bouwsma, *Concordia mundi: The Career and Thought of Guillaume Postel (1510–1581)* (Cambridge, Mass., 1957), pp. 216–30.

THE MILLENNIAL MOMENT: REVOLUTION AND RADICAL RELIGION IN SIXTEENTH-CENTURY SPAIN

Sara T. Nalle

The connection between religious radicalism and social-political dissent in late medieval and early modern Europe remains to this day one of the most fascinating areas of historical inquiry. In this respect there is a striking contrast between the experience of northern Europe and that of Spain. Although during the later Middle Ages Spaniards of all religious backgrounds were familiar with messianic and millenarian beliefs, they rarely, if ever, used such notions to justify collective social or political action. Even in fifteenth-century Catalunya, where eschatological speculation ran deep, contemporary peasant revolts failed to make the connection between the desire for social justice and millennial prophecies.[1] Later, while in northern Europe the radicalism of millennial movements gave way to the Anabaptist fringes of the Reformation, in Spain there were few cases of religious radicalism, and these remained largely within the Catholic tradition.[2]

Scholars have been tempted to explain this lack of radicalism by pointing to the action of the Inquisition as a braking influence. The Inquisition's presence on the Iberian peninsula provides only a partial answer, however. The modern tribunals were established in the late fifteenth century (replacing the medieval Papal Inquisition which

---

[1] See Paul Freedman, "The German and Catalan Peasant Revolts," *American Historical Review*, Feb. 1993, pp. 39–54. "Rebellion did not require a dramatic external stimulus such as millenarian expectation or imported urban concepts of equality . . ." (p. 52).

[2] The only native-born heresy of this period is illuminism, which to this day remains hard to classify. The inquisitors at first thought that they were dealing with a Jewish heresy because virtually all those arrested were of converso background.

Several scholars have examined the general phenomenon of Messianism in the Iberian world: Américo Castro, *Aspectos del vivir hispánico: espiritualismo, mesianismo, actitud personal en los siglos XIV al XVI* (Santiago de Chile, 1949); Jacques Lafaye, *Mesías, cruzadas, utopías. El judeo-cristianismo en las sociedades ibéricas* (Mexico, 1984); and Mariano Delgado, *Die Metamorphosen des Messianismus in den iberischen Kulturen* (Freiburg, 1994).

had operated in the Kingdom of Aragon), but for the first sixty years of their existence they focused almost exclusively on punishing Judaizing. In terms of their ability to censor religious speculation by the Catholic majority, the courts did not come into their own until the second half of the sixteenth century.[3] Moreover, the one period in Spanish history which came closest to producing some wide-spread messianic and millenarian movements (1500–1530), the period studied in this article, occurred while the Inquisition was in operation; paradoxically, the religious enthusiasm of those years was in no small measure owing to the sponsorship of the Inquisitor General himself, Cardinal Francisco Jiménez de Cisneros (1436–1517).

Several events combined at the end of the fifteenth century to make Spaniards as a whole more receptive to messianic and millenarian ideas. First, oddly enough, was the marriage in 1469 of the two princely heirs, Ferdinand of Aragon and Isabella of Castile. Since the days of Fr. Arnold of Villanova (1220–1309), royal confidant, physician and Joachimite visionary, the kings of Aragon had been closely associated with prophecies concerning the Last Days, reform of the church, and the final crusade which would recover Jerusalem, annihilate Islam and schismatics, and usher in an age of universal peace. The empire over which the kings ruled—Aragon, Catalunya (including Rousillon and Cerdanya), Valencia, the Balearic Islands, and Sicily—was the melting pot of notions of Joachimite spiritualism and evangelical poverty among the numerous Beguins, Tertiaries, and Spiritual Franciscans of the western Mediterranean.[4] The union of the crowns of Aragon and Castile simultaneously fed Aragonese imperial ambitions and served to introduce to the interior of the peninsula a tradition which had remained for two hundred years confined to the shores of the Mediterranean.[5]

The events of 1492 also fed into expectations. The year began with the surrender of the last Muslims on the Iberian Peninsula after a long and expensive campaign jointly managed by Isabella and Ferdinand. The victory in Granada raised hopes for the success of

[3] See J.-P. Dedieu, *L'administration de la foi: L'Inquisition de Tolède (XVe–XVIIIe siècle)* (Madrid, 1989); and Sara T. Nalle, "Inquisitors, Priests, and the People during the Catholic Reformation in Spain," *The Sixteenth Century Journal* 18 (1987): 557–87.

[4] H. Lee, M. Reeves, and G. Silano, *Western Mediterranean Prophecy. The School of Joachim of Fiore and the Fourteenth-Century Breviloquium* (Toronto, 1989), pp. 27–66.

[5] Alain Milhou, *Colón y su mentalidad mesiánica en el ambiente franciscanista español* (Valladolid, 1983), p. 101.

the mythic Last Crusade which would come at the end of millennium, itself only just around the corner (counting half millennia). If the Catholic Monarchs could drive Islam from Spanish soil after an occupation of seven hundred years, then perhaps these same monarchs, particularly the Aragonese king Ferdinand, could expel Islam from other formerly Christian lands, even Jerusalem itself. In 1509, Cardinal Cisneros completed the first leg of the Last Crusade by personally leading the campaign against Oran in North Africa. Cisneros, an observant Franciscan, saw no contradiction between this and his many other religious activities, such as his reform of the Dominican and Franciscan orders, founding of the University of Alcalá, leadership of the Inquisition, and support for spiritual Christianity. This last included encouraging female visionaries and sponsoring the publication in Castilian of many classics of mysticism—all of which later would come under the suspicion of the very same Inquisition which Cisneros once led.

But 1492 is remembered in Spain for two other momentous events: the expulsion of the Jews and the discovery of the New World. Naturally, when Spaniards grasped the magnitude of the discovery and its possible ramifications, many, particularly the Franciscans and Columbus himself, easily made the connection between the predictions of the earlier spiritual Franciscans and an Iberian mission in the New World.[6] Many left in pursuit of their own American millennium, perhaps—although this is pure speculation—even siphoning off the most committed and radical of the evangelical visionaries.[7]

The expulsion of the Jews, however, was another matter altogether. Normally, one would not think to mix instances of Jewish messianism with Christian millenarianism, but the unique history of the peninsula's three religious groups led to an extraordinary melding of influences.[8] This blurring of boundaries increased with the

---

[6] Particularly useful is Milhou, *Colón y su mentalidad mesiánica*.... See also *El Libro de las profecías of Christopher Columbus*. An en face edition, trans. and commented by Delno C. West and August Kling (Gainesville, 1991).

[7] On utopian efforts by Spanish missionaries in the New World, see John L. Phelan, *The Millennial Kingdom of the Franciscans in the New World: A Study of the Writings of Gerónimo de Medieta (1525–1604)* (Berkeley, 1956); and Marcel Bataillon, "Evangélisme et millénarisme au Nouveau Monde," in *Courants religiuex et humanisme à la fin du XVe et au début du XVIe siècle* (Paris, 1959).

[8] Nonetheless Milhou is quite emphatic that for Christians in Spain, Messianism, "far from being related in a privileged manner with the Jewish inheritance, was no more than a variation, although powerful and relatively late, of European messianism." Milhou, *Colón y su mentalidad mesiánica*..., p. 10.

conversion to Christianity of many Sephardim during the fifteenth century. The approach of the chiliastic year of 1500 sparked a great deal of religious speculation among both Christians and Jews. Particularly among the Jews, messianic speculation had a long tradition in Spain. Virtually all of Spain's medieval Talmudic scholars had confirmed that belief in the Messiah was a tenet of Judaism.[9] The anguish created by the expulsion order of 1492 brought these beliefs into sharp focus: instead of a distant, theoretical coming, the Messiah was on his way now to redeem his suffering people. The last of the Sephardic scholars to write on messianism was Isaac Abravanel, the minister of finance in Isabella and Ferdinand's government. After the Edict of Expulsion, Abravanel emigrated to Italy, where between 1496 and 1498 he published three messianic treatises. On the basis of careful study and calculation, Abravanel was convinced that the messianic age was at hand and that redemption would occur between 1503 and 1573.[10]

Abravanel's prognostications, coupled with the diaspora of Sephardim around the Mediterranean world and the advances of the Ottoman empire, led to decades of intense messianic ferment among Castilian Jews and converted Jews known as *conversos*. Around 1500, there were several outbreaks of messianic fervor in the villages and towns of Andalusia and New Castile. In the most disturbing case, conversos in the city of Córdoba fell under the spell of a young slave girl, who foretold that the Messiah was at hand and would soon redeem them. The Inquisition found this outbreak of Jewish messianism so threatening that it put to death over one hundred people—a high number even for the time.[11] Throughout the sixteenth century, rumors of a coming Messiah would sweep through converso communities. For example, David Reubeni, claiming to be an emissary from a king in distant lands, arrived in southern Portugal in 1526 and promised that the Portuguese marranos would soon return to Jerusalem.

---

[9] Joseph Sarachek, *The Doctrine of the Messiah in Medieval Jewish Literature* (New York, 1932).

[10] B. Netanyahu, *Don Isaac Abravanel, Statesman and Philosopher* (Philadelphia, 1968), pp. 216–226.

[11] For an overview, see Stephen Sharot, *Messianism, Mysticism and Magic. A Sociological Analysis of Jewish Religious Movements* (Chapel Hill, 1982), pp. 62–85. The best article on the subject is John Edwards, "Elijah and the Inquisition: Messianic Prophecy among *Conversos* in Spain, c. 1500," *Nottingham Medieval Studies* 28 (1984): 79–94, which is a longer and more accurate discussion of the cases noted by Yitzhak Baer in *A History of the Jews in Christian Spain* 2 vols. (Philadelphia), 1961, 1978, 2:356–358.

Reubeni caused such a stir across the border in Spain that an inquisitor in Badajoz was obliged to write to the King of Portugal in protest.[12] The Messiah's coming was foretold for 1520, 1524, 1531, and 1540, the latter prophecy arousing enough interest in southern Spain that one inquisitor kept personal notes on the case until his death in 1547.[13]

Conversos and Jews lived in close proximity to Old Christians in Spain, and as a result the three groups were quite familiar with each others' messianic and religious traditions, often mixing, parodying, or confusing the two. In Herrera del Duque and Córdoba, the messianic movements among the conversos there bore a strong similarity to Christian millenarianism, and incorporated Christian-inspired rituals and doctrines. Members of the Córdoba group, for example, participated in a parody of the Mass in which Hebrew books and objects were employed, and went, bare-backed and with whips in hand, on penitential processions. In Herrera del Duque, a young prophetess claimed she had been taken to Heaven on the wings of angels, passing through Purgatory (!) on the way.[14]

An inquisitorial case from a different region of Spain which illustrates well the conversos' religious versatility as well as their hopes for redemption is the trial of Nicolás de Zaragoza, a bookbinder who was originally trained as a copyist of Hebrew books.[15] When the Edict of Expulsion was proclaimed in 1492, Nicolás, who had been born in Zaragoza about thirty years before, chose exile over conversion. After a few years in North Africa, like so many others, Nicolás returned to Spain, converted to Christianity, and began a new career as a semi-itinerant bookbinder. In 1526, Nicolás was arrested by the Inquisition of Cuenca, where he had lived for a few years, for allegedly predicting that "a new composer of the law, and a composer of a new law would come," which was taken as proof that Nicolás had remained Jewish at heart. When contradicted by

[12] Maria Jose Ferro Tavares, "O Messianismo Judaico em Portugal (ca. metade do século XVI)" *Luso-Brazilian-Review* 28 (1991): 141–152; Carlos Carrete Parrondo and Yolanda Moreno Kock, "Movimiento mesiánico hispano-portugués: Badajoz 1525" *Sefarad* 52 (1992): 65–68. On the most important case of Messianism in Portugal, see Elias Lipiner, *O Sapaterio de Trancoso e o Alfaiate de Setúbal* (Rio de Janeiro, 1993).

[13] Archivo Diocesano de Cuenca (henceforth "ADC"), Secc. Inq., exp. 2311.

[14] Edwards, "Elijah and the Inquisition."

[15] All information on Nicolás de Zaragoza is derived from his trial preserved in the ADC, Secc. Inq., leg. 117, exp. 1596, unfoliated.

those who heard him prophesy, he allegedly replied, "I guarantee that within a year you will no longer be going to mass." The Inquisition's prosecutor also found suspicious the fact that Nicolás had used scripture to buttress his predictions of a new composer of the law.

Drawing on his knowledge of the Bible and his reading of various messianic and apocalyptic tracts, Nicolás tried several ruses to turn aside the accusations. At first he explained that what he really had said was that in 1524 an astrologer named Luca Agnorrico had predicted that in that year a false prophet would come to Spain.[16] As it was normal to prove that Jesus was the Messiah by using proofs from the Old Testament, Nicolás could not see anything wrong with his use of such citations.

Since Nicolás denied the charges, the inquisitors had the witnesses' incriminating testimony read back to the defendant to break down his resistance. The witnesses related how they had been sitting around talking about predictions of the Antichrist and some great floods and Nicolás had told them about various prophecies that had been made for 1520 and 1524.[17] In response to these more specific charges, Nicolás explained that what had really taken place was that he had read two printed pamphlets on the Last Judgment which foretold that a false prophet would come to Spain in 1524 and mass would be suspended. Nicolás had taken this to mean that the Messiah would come and make a new law, and had believed this for a few days, but later he had realized his error.

Nicolás' changing story failed to convince the inquisitors of his innocence. After some months in prison, Nicolás seized on a new

---

[16] Possibly the Italian astrologer, Luca Guarico. For an introduction, see Ottavia Niccoli, *Prophecy and People in Renaissance Italy*, trans. Lydia G. Cochrane (Princeton, 1990).

[17] In 1524 the unusual planetary conjunction of Saturn and Jupiter in the sign of Pisces inspired many astrological predictions. One prophecy discussed by Nicolás' group, of a deluge, reflects the widespread fear across Europe that 1524 would bring a huge flood. General calamities for 1524 had been predicted as early as 1499 by the German astrologer Stöffler and were discussed in print by several Spanish writers in the early 1520s. [F. Díaz Jimeno, *Hado y fortuna en la España del siglo XVI* (Madrid, 1987), pp. 55–68.] A heavy rain in Burgos in 1524 led to panic, and there was general fear in Spain that the world would come to an end. [J. Caro Baroja, *Vidas mágicas e Inquisición* (Madrid, 1967), v. II, pp. 166–67 based on the *Floreto de anécdotas y noticias diversas*, n. 124 in MHE vol. 48, pp. 103–104.] Stöffler's predications also sowed panic in Italy, with which Valencia maintained close trade ties (O. Niccoli, *Prophecy and People*, ch. 6).

line of defense—that what the witnesses had heard him say had really been in reference to the Antichrist. If Nicolás could convince the inquisitors that he had been speaking about the Antichrist, he would be off the hook on the charges of Judaizing. So now he had to prove that he knew perfectly well the difference between the Messiah and the Antichrist, and could not possibly have been speaking about the Messiah when he predicted that a new composer of the law would come. (Never mind that the Messiah *he* had been thinking of was the Jewish one.)

To prove his familiarity with the subject, Nicolás recited several prophecies in connection with the end of the world that he had seen in a book published in Valencia. This book predicted that the reign of the Antichrist would last three and a half years and afterwards a saintly pope would come to reform the church and restore it to the way it had been in the days of St. Paul. Also predicted was that the Antichrist would be conceived in sin and would perform false miracles, and that Elijah and Enoch would come again but this Antichrist would have them beheaded. In yet another long letter written several months later, Nicolás continued his strategy of proving that everything he had said was in reference to the Antichrist. One of his arguments was quite original. Focusing on the word "composer" [*componedor* in Spanish], Nicolás launched into a discussion of the true meaning of the word "compose", which, he explained, was always used in connection with made-up things, like chivalric novels and such lies, but never in connection with the truth. Thus, "componedor de una ley nueva" can only refer to the Antichrist, because, as everyone knows, the Antichrist's deeds are all false while those of Christ are true.[18] Now Nicolás was able to remember more about the book that he had read: "I have seen many times in Valencia

[18] ADC, 117:1596 ". . . se toma conponer cosa yncierta y falsa y mintrosa y fingida como dizimos, 'fulano, ¡cómo supo componer la mentira o mentiras!' y en cosa verdadero no cabe este vocablo de conponer. Assi mismo cuando se conpone hun libro de cosas fingidas y inciertas y de muchas mentiras como libros de ystorias como de Amadies de Esplantian, de Clarian de Floriseo y do otros semejantes dizese, 'conpone aquel tal libro' [por] lo qual no cabe este vocablo ni estras en cosa de verdad, saluo en cosas ynciertas y fingidas como an de ser las cosas del antixpo segun que lo estan en los doctores catholicos. . . ." Covarrubias, in the *Tesoro de la lengua castellano* (Madrid, 1611) writes "componer vale también mentir, porque el mentiroso compone y finge la mentira, haziéndola verisímil." In legal settings, the noun *componedor* also has the meaning of arbitrator, but "lawgiver" in the Bible is translated as "legislador" or "dador de leyes".

a book which has been reprinted several times which is called 'Treatise on the Antichrist, reply of the Alcocha, and prophecies of Fray Juan Aleman'", which he then proceeded to summarize quite accurately. According to this book, the Antichrist will seduce the weak in faith with promises of riches and false miracles and threats of storms; thereafter his followers will be known by the seal ("*carachte*") on their foreheads; the Antichrist will reward those who wear his seal and punish those who do not; by means of diabolical art he will ascend to the heavens and fire will fall from the sky; ultimately, the Antichrist will fall to earth and be killed, at which point the people will recognize their error and clamor for the true Christ, who will unite all three faiths into one flock.[19] To clinch his argument, Nicolás then respectfully offered his own original point-by-point comparison of the attributes of the Antichrist and the true Christ.

Ultimately, Nicolás was unable to prove his innocence, and he was punished for Judaizing. One of the several interesting facets of this case is Nicolás' familiarity with various books of Christian prophecies, including Fray John Alamany's *Venguda del Antichristo.* As noted above, Catalan-speaking lands had been introduced to a rich mixture of millennial ideas in the thirteenth and fourteenth centuries, where they had become a part of the religious landscape.[20] Because of the crown of Aragon's imperial designs on the eastern Mediterranean and its self-appointed role as protector of pilgrims on their way to Jerusalem, Aragonese kings became associated with the legends of the Last Emperor. In this Iberian reworking of the legend, however, the Aragonese king ultimately would destroy Islam, restore Jerusalem, and through his opposition to the papacy and the crown of France, usher in the days of the Antichrist.[21] Alamany's tract, a sum-

---

Zaragoza seemed unaware of the fact that according to the doctrine of the Messiah as defined in the Tortosa Disputation (1413), the Messiah will not declare a New Law because he has come to fulfill the Old (Baer, *op. cit.*, v. 2, p. 188).

[19] This idea of the three religions united into one flock can be found in the Joachimite *Breviloquium* of the late fifteenth century (West, p. 35). Although Zaragoza states his source as the *Venguda del Antichristo*, his summary more closely follows M. Martínez Ampiés, *El libro del Antichristo*, published in Zaragoza, 1495 (and reprinted in facsimile in 1982 [R. Alba, ed., Madrid: Editora Nacional]).

[20] An exhaustive study is J.M. Pou y Martí, *Visionarios, beguinos y fraticelos catalanes (s. xiii–xv)* (Vich, 1930), now available in a reprint edition with introduction by J.M. Arcelus Ulibarrena (Madrid, 1991).

[21] Alain Milhou, "La chauve-souris, le nouveau David et the Roi Caché (trois images de l'empereur des derniers temps dans le monde ibérique)" *Mélanges de la Casa de Velázquez* 18 (1982), p. 66; *idem, Colón y su mentalidad mesiánica* . . ., pp. 165–168.

mary of the ideas of the Calabrian Joachim of Fiore and the Valencian Arnold of Villanova, was first written in Latin in the early fifteenth century. After circulating in manuscript form throughout the century, a Catalan version was printed for the first time in the 1490s and then reprinted, with tremendous effect, in Valencia in late 1520.[22] At that moment in time, the city of Valencia was in the midst of the rebellion of the Germanías.

The outbreak in 1520–1522 of twin revolutions in the kingdoms of Valencia and Castile provides historians with the only example of a millennial movement in Spanish society, when the ideas expressed in the prophecies of the spiritual Franciscans took radical, collective form in an actual revolution. In both instances, the Comunidades of Castile and the Germanías of Valencia were uprisings against the monarchy which acquired radical tendencies, but significantly, only in Valencia did the rebellion turn into a millenarian movement. In Castile, at first the nobility and textile-producing cities joined together to protest the rule of the foreign king, Charles V, and within weeks many villages joined the Comunidades in order to throw off the yoke of their seigneurial obligations. Although at times the *comuneros* availed themselves of religious language and several leaders were likened to messiahs, the revolution, whether in the cities or rural areas, remained resolutely secular in its outlook. Despite the presence of a pamphlet and manuscript literature predicting the arrival of a new David and a new era of justice, no individual or group claimed to be sent specially by God to effect wide-ranging social justice or to usher in a new kingdom and utopian age.[23] The religious language employed by the *comuneros* was traditional and mild (for example, *Santa* Comunidad, recalling the popular and legitimate Santa Hermandad of the Catholic Monarchs' reign) and comparisons of certain leaders to the messiah came not from the *comuneros*

[22] A comparison of the title and content of Nicolás de Zaragoza's summary of this book with a ms. version printed in Ramón Alba, *Acerca de algunas particularidades de las Comunidades de Castilla tal vez relacionadas con el supuesto acaecer Terreno del Milenio Igualitario* (Madrid, 1975) pp. 180–200; and with Milhou's summary of the only known surviving printed version (A. Milhou, "La chauve-souris . . ."), leads one to think that more than one version of the book was in circulation, although only one printed edition is known today.

[23] Alba, *Acerca de algunas particularidades. . . .* Although his compilation of millennial and apocalyptic tracts proves that such ideas were rife at the time of the Comunidades, he was unable to show that the revolt or its leaders were explicitly viewed in those terms by those who participated in the events.

themselves, but from hostile chroniclers desiring to discredit and ridicule the leaders' popular acclaim.[24]

In contrast with Castile, Catalan-speaking lands had a long tradition of millenarian speculation, and in Valencia there lived a large Muslim population (nominally converted to Christianity) whose presence served to convince Christians of the necessity for a last crusade. From the onset the rebellion of the Germanías was markedly more popular in tone. In 1519, the Christian artisans of the city were given permission to form militias to defend Valencia from Berber pirates, but instead they turned the militias against the kingdom's nobility and their Muslim serfs. At the eleventh hour, just when it appeared that the rebellion had been quashed, early in 1522 a messianic figure claiming to be the Hidden King of medieval prophecy stepped forward and infused a new spark into the failing revolt. From his stronghold in Játiva, surrounded by his followers, El Encubierto (as he was known in Spanish) dressed like a king, proclaimed the coming of a new age, and led sorties into the countryside against the hated Muslim serfs and royal troops sent to support the local nobility.[25]

About fifteen years ago, Alain Milhou linked the appearance and popular success of the Hidden King with the messianic expectations of late-medieval Iberia.[26] This mysterious figure so completely owed his identity to the millennial prophecies that, were it not for the fragmentary eyewitness accounts of his activities and statements, one would be tempted to put down the entire episode of El Encubierto to the over-active imagination of later chroniclers. In 1520, Fray Alamany's book had predicted that during a time when nation fought

---

[24] Joseph Pérez, "Moines frondeurs et sermons subversifs en Castille pendant le premier séjour de Charles-Quint en Espagne" *Bulletin Hispanique*, LXVII (1965), pp. 217–224.

[25] From the moment of his appearance, the story of El Encubierto has fascinated chroniclers, historians, even playwrights and novelists, but despite this interest, the documentation remains slight. Most of the documentary sources can be found in M. Dánvila y Collado, *Las Germanías de Valencia* (Madrid, 1886); and *idem*, "El Encubierto de Valencia," *El Archivo* (1889), IV:123–138. A good general discussion may be found in Ricardo García Cárcel, *Las Germanías de Valencia*, 2nd. ed. (Valencia, 1981), pp. 132–138. Joan Fuster, *Rebeldes y heterodoxos* (Barcelona, 1972), devotes two chapters to El Encubierto, one of which deals with the "doctrine" of El Encubierto. As Fuster neither read the complete documentary record nor was aware of Christian eschatalogical thought in Valencia, the work has limited usefulness.

[26] A. Milhou, "La chauve-souris. . . ."

nation, and civil war reigned, a hidden king would come to Spain to punish the bad Christians, evil nobility, corrupt church, the Jews, and above all else, the Moors.[27] In alliance with the New David, the Hidden King would redistribute the wealth to Spain's poor. Once triumphant he would return to the east to reign in Jerusalem. Alamany even described the appearance of this Hidden King: "know that the Hidden One has a handsome figure, [is] fair-skinned with red hair, is well and true spoken, and a lover of justice and an enemy of evil-doers. He has beautiful eyes, a handsome face and well-made limbs. . . ."[28] Strangely, in a region which spoke Catalan, El Encubierto would speak Castilian.

Contemporary accounts of El Encubierto are extremely sketchy as well as biased.[29] After all, this was a man whose movement could only be checked by the viceregal government's paying five killers to assassinate him on the outskirts of Valencia. His statements and revolt were so heinous to the establishment that after his murder, El Encubierto's body was dismembered and displayed in an iron cage and later burnt, while his heretical soul was condemned to hell by the Inquisition.[30] Hostile or not, the eye-witnesses did agree on several points: that the man claimed to be of the lineage of the Aragonese king Ferdinand the Catholic (accounts vary as to whether he was Ferdinand's son or grandson, Jewish or Christian) and that he had been sent by God to redeem Spain; he was popularly acclaimed as the Encubierto or Hermano (another messianic term); he spoke Castilian extremely well; and he delivered a heretical sermon in Játiva in March 1522 to a large crowd of people. After his murder, two more men claiming to be the Hidden King stepped forward in succession to continue the rebellion in Valencia, and a book of

---

[27] Don't forget that the language here is very similar to Matt. 24:5–28. All of the ideas contained in the Joachimite prophecies are there as well, including, "como el relámpago que sale del oriente y se muestra hasta el occidente, así será también la venida del Hijo del Hombre."

[28] Milhou, "Le chauve-souris", p. 70.

[29] For a list and summary, see R. García Cárcel, *Orígenes de la Inquisición Española. El tribunal de Valencia, 1478–1530* (Barcelona, 1976), pp. 101–108. Such was the horror El Encubierto inspired among those who chronicled his intervention in the Germanías that after sifting through the surviving documentation, García concluded that it is probably impossible to uncover the man's true identity and purpose. Among the lists of rebels, however, there is one "Anthoni Navarro, alias Lo Encubert o ermano Miguel" (*idem, Las Germanías de Valencia*, p. 136).

[30] G. Escolano, *Décadas de la Historia de la Insigne y coronada ciudad Reino de Valencia*, 2a parte, tom. II (Valencia, 1879), col. 708a.

his sayings circulated on the island of Mallorca, which was also in revolt against Charles V.

A few accounts survive concerning the eschatological ideas contained in El Encubierto's sermons. Prior to delivering a sermon just before Easter, 1522 in Játiva's main square, El Encubierto forced the city's secular and religious leaders to attend in the presence of 300–400 armed followers. Within days of the sermon's delivery, several Franciscans managed to denounce El Encubierto's heresies to the local tribunal of the Inquisition in Valencia, which preserved their testimony for posterity. In addition, a layman by name of Miquel García included in his memoirs of the Germanías a brief second-hand account of El Encubierto's ideas. He recalled that among many other heresies, El Encubierto declared that Christ would be incarnated four times, that instead of the Trinity there was a Quaternity, and that there would be four Judgments in all: two had occurred in the past, the third was taking place at that moment, and a last would soon take place.[31]

The longer testimony preserved by the Inquisition corroborates and greatly expands on García's brief comments, although it does not record the structure or sequence of El Encubierto's thoughts. Instead, the sermon is recorded as a series of propositions, each unrelated to the next, and some quite fanciful.[32] It is left to the historian to reconstruct the argument that originally connected the various points recorded in the document. El Encubierto's sermon clearly took as its theme the contemporary belief that the Antichrist and a social revolution in Valencia were at hand. For example, two witnesses remembered that El Encubierto foretold that many clergy would follow the Antichrist and lose their souls, and that the viceroy

---

[31] Eulàlia Duran, *Crònique de les germanies de Guillem Ramon Català i de Miquel Garcia (segle XVI)* (Valencia, 1984), pp. 394–95. Garcia was a hostile witness.

[32] The most striking proposition, which was used as a way of discrediting El Encubierto's other statements, was his explanation for why the mule is a sterile animal. According to the witnesses, "Dijo que en el diversorio do parió Nuestra Señora a Jesú Christo dicen algunos locos letrados que no habían sino el asno y el buey y dice él que también era la mula y que se comía feno y por eso la maldijo Christo y por esta causa la mula no concibe, ni puede concebir y si concibe es de poderío del Diablo" (Archivo Histórico Nacional. Sección Inquisición, Valencia, Leg. 799–3, f. 363v). Absurd though it is to those who know how mules are bred, apparently this explanation for the mule's sterility is still in circulation in Latin America (oral communication from Asunción Lavrín). Thus, El Encubierto's explanation would not appear quite so silly to his lower-class audience.

of Valencia, then waging war against the Germanías, was the second Antichrist (the first being his superior, Charles V). El Encubierto warned the clergy that if they did not turn away from this second Antichrist and stop speaking badly of the revolution, they would be burned in the town's main square. To prepare for the coming Day of Judgment, El Encubierto ordered the wealth of the church and the nobility in Játiva to be confiscated, heaped up in the main square, and sold by his legal agents. The proceeds would be used to support the Holy War (i.e., the Germanías) and the starving poor. The Hidden King concluded by addressing his enemies directly: "*your* King Don Carlos," he admonished them, would become king only when God wished and with El Encubierto's approval ("yo que demostraré como es rey y no es rey").[33]

Messianic figures typically see themselves as possessing special knowledge and powers; hence El Encubierto's boast that he together with God would determine when Don Carlos actually would become king. He claimed that he was invulnerable to harm, and through his naked sword of virtue (which he brandished at the crowd) he would effect justice. The agents of El Encubierto's enlightenment and empowerment were the prophets Elijah and Enoch, who figured prominently in El Encubierto's sermon. First, he claimed that the pair had appeared to him when he had been a shepherd, and had carried him to Valencia on a mission of faith and justice. Because he was illiterate, the two had revealed to him his special knowledge, but everything he said could be found also validated in the Book of the Apocalypse. Later, the prophets would go to Rome and kill the Antichrist in a plaza there. But contrary to what the "crazy" preachers predicted, after the Antichrist's death the world would not come to an imminent end—it would last as long again as it had from the birth of Adam down to the present. We might conclude that this was offered as a comforting thought to those who may have been attracted by El Encubierto's millennial message but were frightened by the idea that their newly created just world would vanish just as quickly as it had appeared.

El Encubierto's reliance on the authority of Elijah and Enoch to validate his mission fits perfectly with medieval popular eschatology, which held that the Second Coming would be heralded by the two

[33] AHN, Inq. Valencia, Leg. 799–3 (libro de testificación), ff. 363r–365v. Milhou also summarizes this testimony in "Le chauve-souris", pp. 76–77.

prophets, who would preach against the Antichrist, be killed by him, and then would be resurrected.[34] We saw virtually the same idea in Nicolás de Zaragoza's account of Elijah and Enoch being beheaded by the Antichrist. In a back-handed way, El Encubierto showed some vague familiarity with Joachimite thought in his references to multiple ages of man, each leading to a higher spiritual plane, multiple Antichrists, and the uniting of peoples into one flock under one shepherd. El Encubierto also tied cleverly into the legends of the crusading kings of Aragon by claiming descent from Ferdinand the Catholic and announcing his own crusade against the Muslims of Valencia. However, by using the idea of a Hidden King, which was relatively new in Spain, El Encubierto gained access to a more subversive millenarian tradition than the legends of the last Emperor.[35]

It is just possible, however, that the man who postured as the Hidden King was not Christian, but a converted Jew from Andalusia, an allegation offered in passing by one of the Franciscans who denounced El Encubierto to the Inquisition.[36] If true, we might speculate that El Encubierto, well versed in the lively messianic hopes of his native province, and sporting the red hair of a Davidic Messiah, effectively manipulated not only the millenarian anxieties of Old Christians but also the messianic hopes of *conversos* in Valencia, who had joined in the revolt as well. But, here we need a word of caution: in sixteenth-century Spain, the standard method of discrediting an individual was to call him a *converso*.

---

[34] For central Europe, see Norman Cohn, *The Pursuit of the Millennium*, 2nd ed. (New York, 1974), pp. 145, 261; on Italy, see O. Niccoli, *Prophecy and People*, p. 94. Enoch and Elias were identified with the two witnesses who appear in the book of the Apocalypse: "Cuando hayan acabado su testimonio, la bestia que sube del abismo hará guerra contra ellos, y los vencerá y los matará. Y sus cadáveres estarán en la plaza de la grande ciudad que en sentido espiritual se llama Sodoma y Egipto, donde también nuestro Señor fue crucificado." (Apocalypse 11, 7–8, trans. Casiodoro de la Reina, 1569.) Note that for El Encubierto, the great city had become Rome.

[35] The first documented reference in Spain to "the hidden king" comes in the fifteenth century, although the concept had been circulating in other parts of Europe during the Middle Ages. See Milhou, "Le chauve-souris . . .", pp. 61–79; and Yves-Marie Bercé, *Le roi caché. Sauvreurs et imposteurs. Mythes politiques populaires dans l'Europe moderne* (Paris, 1990) (which includes a few pages on the Valencian case).

[36] The Castilian chroniclers Santa Cruz and Sandoval reproduce an elaborate, well-developed fable about the origins of El Encubierto, whom they identify as Juan de Bilbao, a converted Jew from Oran who seduced his master's daughter and generally was thoroughly despicable. The tale seems to originate with Miquel García, whose animadversion to El Encubierto is evident throughout his chronicle.

While El Encubierto was preaching in Játiva, about one hundred miles to the northwest, the villages and towns across the border in Castile were recovering from the aftermath of the Comunero Revolt. Although the Comunidades deeply disrupted the political and social fabric of Castile, the revolution did not produce a millenarian movement or messianic figure, despite the fact that in the early sixteenth century Castile was fairly pullulating with visionaries and their predictions. To take but one example, in that fated year of 1524, when Nicolás de Zaragoza thought a false prophet (or the Messiah) would come to Spain, a small group of Franciscans in Escalona were convinced that the overthrow of the pope and revision of the scriptures was at hand. Nothing whatever came of their convictions, and we only know of the group's existence via a reference in the trial of the *alumbrado* Pedro Ruiz de Alcaraz.[37] One reason for this curious lack of political activism may lie in the fact that, as Milhou notes, Castilian eschatalogical speculation tended to be more religious in nature and was not explicitly political. Moreover, unlike Valencia and Catalunya, the Castilian fascination with millennial and apocalyptic prophecies was of very recent origin. The extremism of Catalan prophecy did not reach Castile until the late fifteenth century via the Franciscan reform movement. At this time, many in Castile began to find a compelling convergence between the last days of the Reconquista and the Joachimite prophecies of the coming of a third age, defeat of the infidel, and the recovery of Jerusalem.[38] Perhaps the most famous of these predictions was the prophecy that Ferdinand the Catholic, having just recovered Granada from Islam, would not die until he completed the Reconquista by taking Jerusalem itself. Fueling the era's apocalyptic fears was the publication in Zaragoza and Burgos (1495; 1497) of Martín Martínez de Ampiés' *Libro del Antichristo*, which was both a translation into Castilian of Adson's *Libellus de Antichristo* and a paraphrase of the Valencian St. Vincent Ferrer's sermons on the Apocalypse.

Before the memory of the Comunidades and the age of wonders died with the last survivors of the revolt, Castile did produce a man who took upon himself the mantle of the age's millennial

[37] Geraldine McKendrick and Angus MacKay, "Visionaries and Affective Spirituality during the First Half of the Sixteenth Century" in *Cultural Encounters: the Impact of the Inquisition in Spain and the New World*, ed. M. Perry and A. Cruz (Berkeley, 1991), pp. 93–104.

[38] Milhou, *Colón y su mentalidad mesiánica*..., p. 101.

and messianic hopes. However, when Bartolomé Sánchez concluded in 1553 that he was the Elijah-Messiah sent by God to punish the church, the Inquisition and the nobility, he found no one to listen to him—the revolutionary moment had passed. Nonetheless, we should see at least part of Sánchez's homespun eschatological vision as the natural endproduct of this age of religious radicalism. To understand this, we need to return to the winter of 1521, when the Germanías and Comunidades were still raging.

Sánchez, who was born around 1501, was from an area of Castile known as the marquisate of Moya, which bordered on the frontier with Valencia. During the Comunero revolt, with the help of the nearby town of Requena and troops from revolutionary Valencia, the villages of the marquisate of Moya expelled their lord and declared themselves free of his seigneurial authority. After several months, the region was pacified by the royal governor in the spring of 1521.[39] As punishment for their part in the rebellion in Moya, men from Requena were drafted into the royal army to fight against their former allies in Valencia.[40] At the battle of Gandía (25 July 1521) the conscripts from Requena broke ranks and brought about the defeat of the royal army.[41] Afterwards, we can imagine that some of these men joined the Germanía forces that moved on to Játiva, and that some eventually returned home bearing news of El Encubierto, just as Nicolás de Zaragoza arrived in Cuenca around 1523 with his memories of Valencia and the *Venguda del Antichristo*.

The revolt in the marquisate of Moya had been led by men from the town of Moya and the village of Cardenete, the unofficial second capital of the marquisate. The marquis was particularly harsh in his punishment of the villagers of Cardenete, where he began to enforce his seigneurial rights with a vengeance.[42] At the time Bartolomé Sánchez was in his early twenties, and thus witnessed the revolt and the marquis's brutal attempts at reprisal. Sánchez's family of farmers was not prominent or wealthy, but one uncle turns up in the

---

[39] For the only modern account of this revolt, see J.I. Gutiérrez Nieto, *Las comunidades como movimiento antiseñorial* (Barcelona, 1973), pp. 200–204.

[40] Archivo General de Simancas, Cámara de Castilla, 24 julio 1521.

[41] AGS, Patronato Real, leg. 2, exp. 85, ff. 78r–v.

[42] Sara T. Nalle, "Moya busca nuevo señor: aspectos de la rebelión comunera en el Marquesado de Moya" in *Moya: estudios y textos*, ed. Diputación Provincial del Cuenca (1996), pp. 35–44.

lists of comunero leaders from the village. After the revolt, the family seems to have faltered economically: the menfolk emigrated to the next province, and Bartolomé, who waited until his early thirties to marry (an indication of a late inheritance or poor economic position), eventually lost his land and was forced to become a migrant laborer and woolcarder.[43]

By his own account, Sánchez had been a devout Catholic until 1550, when a series of increasingly upsetting events turned him away from the church and convinced him that God had chosen him for a special mission. First, on Midsummer's Eve 1550, after a day of working in the fields, Sánchez experienced a vision of a woman flanked by two men, and over her head was a bird with outstretched wings. This he interpreted as the true Trinity: God the Father, Son, and Mother. On account of the bird representing the Holy Spirit, sometimes he allowed that what he saw was actually a quaternity. The vision upset him, but not as much as did the next episode: during Lent of 1551, Sánchez bought a used printed book of hours in Spanish, and opening it up, discovered an illustration exactly representing what he had seen in his vision.[44] In 1552, Sánchez experienced several frightening fits, including visions of the devil coming to kill him. At the same time he was excommunicated by his parish priest for failure to pay his tithes. Early in 1553, Sánchez discovered his prophetic voice, and began disputing theology with his fellow villagers.

Just before his arrest by the Inquisition in October 1553, Sánchez experienced his last vision, in which Mary revealed to him the nature of God's plan for him. Sánchez believed that God had selected him to be his messenger—Elijah—who would exact justice for all the crimes that the Inquisition and priests had committed, especially against those who believed that the Messiah had yet to come. This second Messiah was not Christ, who had been murdered against his will in Jerusalem, but his avenger Elijah. Sánchez quoted Scripture to prove this point: "to avenge that death and injustice that was done to Him while He was on the cross, He said, 'heli heli lama

[43] ADC, Inq., leg. 196, exp. 2216.

[44] Only a handful of copies of printed Spanish books of hours survive today, rendering identification of Sánchez' book nearly impossible. The closest candidate thus far is a 1565 edition of the *Horas de Nuestra Señora* printed by Juan de Ayala in Toledo. Although the publication date is later, the edition easily could be a reprint of a book dating from the first half of the century.

zabatani': come Elijah, come Elijah to avenge my death for they've killed me."[45] Most often, Sánchez referred to Elijah as Elijah-Messiah, in the sense that salvation could not take place until Elijah avenged Christ's murder. Like Elijah, Sánchez believed he would not suffer an earthly death; as long as he was a witness to God's message, the Lord would protect him from the Inquisition's bonfires. "Pile on the wood!" Sánchez would dare the court.

Sánchez' troubles with the Inquisition went on for several years after he declared that he was Elijah; what interests us at this moment is how he fits into sixteenth-century currents of messianism and millennialism. As we have seen, the figure of Elijah held enormous significance for Sánchez's contemporaries Nicolás de Zaragoza and El Encubierto, who were well aware of the prophet's role in ushering in the second coming and the Last Judgment. This was the popular Christian view of Elijah in the apocalyptic literature. It was not by accident that both Sánchez and Melchior Hoffmann, one of the leaders of the Anabaptist revolution in Münster, believed that they were led by Elijah on a mission of justice (although in Sánchez's mind he had *become* Elijah).[46] For Sánchez justice meant that God would punish the church, the Inquisition, the rich, and the mighty, all of whom were standing in the way of the poor laypeople.

However, there were two other meanings of Elijah available to Sánchez: Joachim of Fiore believed that the third, final, spiritual age would be the age of Elijah, and then again, the Jews still believed the original story, that Elijah would herald the coming of the true Messiah. Only fifty years before, *conversos* in Córdoba were executed for believing that Elijah would lead them to the promised land. Which tradition held sway over Sánchez? He admitted to seeking out religious men and friars, listening to sermons, and talking to anyone who would listen to him. In the 1550s, it was still possible in Castile to acquire fairly radical religious texts, such as the 1545 apocalyptic tract *Leche de la fe* by the Franciscan Luis de Maluenda,

---

[45] ADC, Inq., leg. 196, exp. 2216, f. 37v: "para vengar aquella muerte e synjustiçia que se le hizo estando en la cruz, dixo 'heli heli lama zabatani'—ven helias ven helias a vengar mi muerte que me han matado." Compare Matt. 27:46–47 ". . . Jesús exclamó con gran voz diciendo: Elí, Elí, lamá sabachthnai? Esto es: Dios mío, Dios mío, ¿por qué me has desamparado? Y algunos de los que estaban allí, oyéndolo, decían: A Elías llama éste."

[46] On Hoffmann, see Klaus Deppermann, *Melchior Hoffmann. Soziale Unruhen und apokalyptische Visionen im Zeitalter der Reformation* (Göttingen, 1979).

who violently attacked wealthy laymen and prelates for their abuse and neglect of the poor.[47] On the other hand, Sánchez's own village harbored a small *converso* community, which was wiped out by the Inquisition sometime in the first half of the sixteenth century, and Sánchez himself seems to have had some *converso* ancestry. When he spoke of redemption in his prayers, he used the words "the people of Israel," which he would then qualify by adding, "who are the lay people." Sánchez's complicated theology of the two messiahs, the first a failure and the second the true redeemer, could be a faint recollection of the Jewish doctrine which taught that two messiahs, one from the house of Joseph, and the other from that of David, would come to the world. Could it be that Sánchez, like Nicolás de Zaragoza, was holding out for a Jewish redeemer, and his anticlerical and anti-inquisitorial invective sprang from an outraged sense of Jewish persecution?

Before we leap to the conclusion that Sánchez was a crypto-Jew, let us go back to the question of the Book of Hours. Just as Fray Alamany's *Venguda del Antichristo* paved the way for El Encubierto, a key element to Sánchez's enlightenment was a printed book. Sánchez bought the book in order to prepare for confession as a Christian, and was awestruck by the resemblance between an illustration in the book and the vision he had experienced a year or so before. The iconography of both derive from a common late-medieval theme in Marian devotions, the crowning of the Virgin as Queen of Heaven by Jesus and God, attended by the Holy Spirit. Such representations were known as "quaternities" and seemed to have helped foster the misunderstanding held by more than one person in the sixteenth century that the Godhead included the Virgin Mary.[48] But Sánchez did more with his book than to look at the illustrations. When we compare his quotations of scripture with surviving examples of similar books, it is quite clear that Sánchez absorbed the language

---

[47] Luis de Maluenda, O.F.M., *Tratado llamado leche dela fe del principe christiano. Con lxij milagros de Jesu christo nro dios y redẽptor. Y con los misterios del antechristo: Y con las ropas de las virtudes Morales y Teologales* . . . (Burgos: Juan de Junta, 1545). Thanks to Inquisitorial censorship, only one copy of this book survives; it has been commented on by Eugenio Asensio, "Fray Luis de Maluenda, Apologista de la Inquisición, condenado en la Indice Inquisitorial" *Arquivos do Centro Cultural Português* IX (1975): 87–100. Eleven copies of *Leche de la fe* were for sale at Ayala's bookstore in Toledo in 1556 at four reales each (A. Blanco Sánchez, "Inventario de Juan de Ayala, gran impresor toledano [1556]," *Boletín de la Real Academia de Historia* 62 [1987]: 207–50).

[48] Milhou, *Colón y su mentalida mesiánica* . . ., pp. 25, 80–87, 127.

and contents of his book of hours as well, and like the prophet he thought he was, he could draw on a fund of biblical knowledge, and speak with the cadence and the rhetoric of scripture. In Sánchez' mind, Mary *was* the mother of God, and Jesus really had been the Messiah, but he had been murdered by the pharisees and priests of the synagogue because they were angered by his message. As a result, God's intended redemption of mankind was frustrated. The priests of the synagogue were succeeded by the pope and his clergy, who continued to keep salvation from the people. Salvation would come only with the second messiah, the Elijah-Messiah who would avenge the first Christ's murder. Perhaps without realizing it, Sánchez was attempting to reconcile both Christian and Jewish traditions to fashion a syncretistic and idiosyncratic view of salvation which incorporated key elements of both religions, and placed himself at its center![49]

Like El Encubierto, Sánchez stood in front of his community and demanded social justice. Borrowing the words of the Magnificat, Sánchez called on God to create a fortress in his might, humble the proud and rich, and raise up the poor and hungry. Given what had happened in Cardenete in the 1520s, the words of the prayer needed little elaboration, yet no one in the village was moved to action. Despite the many similarities between El Encubierto's and Sánchez' ideas, an all-important difference separates the two men. The Hidden King was made possible by the revolutionary situation in Valencia. When he was killed, others stepped forward to take his place. In Valencia, there was a convergence between the causes of the Germanías and the conditions that, according to Norman Cohn, were ideal for the creation of millennial movements. These included the presence of landless peasants and artisans whose economic position had eroded in the last generation.[50] By contrast, the participants in the Comunero

[49] Such a delusion was not without precedent. There are many examples of both Christians and Jews in Spain who believed themselves to be Elijah or Jesus Christ. Juan de Horozco y Covarrubias, in his *Tratado de la verdadera y falsa prophecia* (Segovia, 1588), devotes a chapter to the many who have pretended to be Jesus Christ. He takes his first example from Sulpicius Severus's *Life of St. Martin* (fifth century C.E.), who told about a Spaniard who believed he was Elijah. When people believed him, he was emboldened to claim that he was Jesus Christ himself (f. 30v). For Christian examples, see Menéndez Pelayo, *Historia de los heterodoxos españoles*; for Jewish ones, see Yitzhak Baer, *A History of the Jews in Christian Spain.*

[50] See García Cárcel, *Las germanías de Valencia* and Norman Cohn, *The Pursuit of the Millennium: Revolutionary Millenarians and Mystical Anarchists of the Middle Ages* (New York, 1970), pp. 281–84.

revolt generally seem to have been the artisans and merchants of still-prosperous Castilian cities. Although the popularity of apocalyptic and millenarian ideas seems to have reached its apogee during the Comunidades, that revolt never produced its own charismatic leader, as did happen in Valencia. Perhaps such ideas, only recently popularized in Castile, were not sufficiently rooted to provoke a true millenarian movement. For all its justice, Sánchez' personal revolution was about thirty years too late and perhaps one hundred miles too far west. The many who heard him speak were provoked not to righteous indignation but to disgust and outrage. For them, Sánchez was the furthest thing from a charismatic leader; instead he threatened the status quo and had to be silenced. Ultimately, Sánchez suffered the most humiliating of defeats. The inquisitors assigned to his case found that he was not a prophet, nor even a heretic. He was merely insane, and with that, he was dismissed and forgotten.[51]

The millennial moment in Spain had passed, but the ideas which inspired Nicolás de Zaragoza, El Encubierto, and Bartolomé Sánchez continued to circulate in the Iberian peninsula and occasionally find converts.[52] In the 1570s and 1580s, Madrid was home to two street people (or prophets) who prophesied the end of Spain, and in faraway Peru, Fr. Francisco de la Cruz believed that he was a New David and rightful king of the Indies. In 1590, a small group of highly placed courtiers in Madrid were transfixed by Lucrecia de León's disturbing dreams of the destruction of the Spanish empire and prepared for the end. Although these individuals enjoyed notoriety, the Inquisition easily dealt with them as false prophets or madmen.[53] Support for prophecy of the sort patronized by Cisneros had been replaced with official suspicion and repression. Never would Spain experience such a conjuncture of conditions that would allow an Encubierto to take the stage again.

---

[51] A fate which awaited El Encubierto as well in the seventeenth century at the hands of the historian, Gaspar de Escolano, who recasts El Encubierto as an amusing madman.

[52] Portugal and her American colony, Brazil, in fact exhibited far more interest in messianism and eschatology. See note 35, Bercé, *Le roi caché*, and R. Cantel, *Prophétisme et messianisme dans l'oeuvre d'Antonio Vieira* (Paris, 1960).

[53] Richard L. Kagan, *Lucrecia's Dreams: Politics and Prophecy in Sixteenth-Century Spain* (Berkeley, 1990).

SATURN AND SABBATAI TZEVI: A NEW APPROACH TO SABBATEANISM*

Moshe Idel

1. *Introduction: Reflections on Jewish Culture*

One of the most interesting characteristics of the various forms of Jewish culture is their continuous undulation and oscillation between two poles: the "particularistic" and the "universalistic". Preserving and cultivating some major forms of ritualistic attitudes, different Jewish communities have sometimes flourished, often suffered and eventually perished, in cultural ambiances different from the main centres where the particularistic attitudes were initially articulated. This oscillation affected both the more popular and the elitist forms of Judaism: the former have adopted popular practices cultivated in their local areas, while the Jewish elites often opened themselves to some of the major forms of the majority elite cultures.

The two poles represent, on the one hand, the common denominators—understood here as the particularistic attitude—while the "universalistic" aspects represent the adoption of the forms of culture embraced by the non-Jewish communities where the Jews lived. Or, expressed in nonjudgmental terms, the particularistic approach is much more centripetal, while the universalistic one is more centrifugal. It should be mentioned that by using the term universalism, we should be well aware of the specific and often limited nature of the forms of those cultures that hosted the Jewish ones. Even today, "universalism" does not mean more than a reification of values accepted by some cultures that reflect only minorities in the global population, but are nevertheless powerful enough to impose their values as worthwhile.

* Substantial parts of this article were written in 1994, during the period I served as a Stewart Distinguished Professor in the Department of Religious Studies at Princeton University. I am very grateful for this kind of invitation, which facilitated the completion of a study on Messianism, now in print. A first version of this study was delivered at the Israel Academy for Science and Humanities, Jerusalem, in March 1995. I hope that a much more detailed exposition of topics dealt with here will be completed in the near future.

The two poles attracted two main types of attitudes among the historians of Judaism: while the integrative aspects were more emphasized by nineteenth-century Jewish historiosophy, in our century the opposite approach has become more dominant. The nineteenth-century historians operated in various European diasporas, especially Germany, at a time when acculturation to the Christian Enlightenment culture was still conceived of as an ideal—a phenomenon related to Jewish Emancipation. The latter historians, on the other hand, attempted to create a dichotomy between the "centrifugal" elements, described as negative, and the "centripetal" ones, described as positive. So, for example, an historian like Heinrich Graetz, conceived of Kabbalah as the bête noire of the Jewish Middle Ages, while Maimonides was portrayed as the paragon of Jewish culture; in the historiography of Yitzhaq Baer, the most important Israeli historian, the situation is exactly inverse: Jewish medieval philosophy was considered a major reason for the conversion of Jews.

The positive attitude to Kabbalah as a centripetal type of lore is, to a very great extent, due to the pivotal change in the nature and role of Jewish mysticism produced by the magisterial studies of Gershom Scholem. His positive and sympathetic approach to this lore opened the way, and the hearts of some of the historians, to integrating mysticism as an active factor in shaping Jewish history. Most outstanding in this context was Scholem's chef d'oeuvre, his monograph on *Sabbatai Ṣevi.*[1] A broad description of the historical aspects of Sabbateanism and an incisive analysis of the conceptual and mystical underpinnings of this movement, this book is also the most important discussion of messianism in Judaism, as it deals in detail not only with an important "Messiah" but also with the history of messianism in Judaism—and sometimes also in Christianity—and with the emergence of a popular messianic movement of great dimensions.

Scholem's hypothesis concerning the emergence of Sabbateanism has become one of the best known theses of modern scholarship in Judaica.[2] His assumption is that the diffusion of Kabbalistic mes-

---

[1] G. Scholem, *Sabbatai Ṣevi, the Mystical Messiah 1626–1676*, tr. R.J.Z. Werblowsky (Princeton UP, Princeton, 1973).

[2] This thesis, which may be described as a hyperthesis, has been repeated so many times that a list of those scholars who reiterated it, without adducing any additional material to strengthen it, would amount to a short booklet. More recently it has been summarized by R.J. Zwi Werblowsky, "Shabbetai Zevi," in H. Beinart,

sianism via the dissemination of Lurianism, served as the indispensable background for the emergence of Sabbateanism as a collective messianic phenomenon. This major rationale, in fact the single major one according to Scholem, inserts Sabbateanism into the history of Jewish mysticism in a dramatic manner. Though Sabbateanism affected the lives, the beliefs and the thoughts of so many Jews, common folk as well as learned rabbis, living in different geographical and cultural centres, Scholem considered Lurianism a common denominator sufficient to create a relatively uniform cultural substratum nourishing Sabbatean messianism and embedded in it. Relying on a monocausal explanation, Scholem's view of Sabbateanism is deeply rooted within the particularistic framework of historiography; its main cause allegedly is an event that belongs eminently to internal Jewish history and culture: the dissemination of Lurianic Kabbalah and its messianism.[3] This more particularistic approach differs from the way Scholem described the emergence of Kabbalah as a synthesis between Neoplatonism and Gnosticism, or Jewish Gnosticism, namely as a lore that was generated by the confluence of two spiritual trends that were different, or even antagonistic to rabbinic Judaism.[4] With the development of Kabbalah, as envisioned by Scholem's historiography, it become more and more an inner Jewish affair. This is also evident in his description of the emergence of Hasidism as a reaction to, and neutralization of Sabbatean trends.

Does indeed Kabbalah represent such a definitive turn from an initially greater openness toward external factors, to a much more

---

ed. *The Sephardi Legacy* (The Magnes Press, Jerusalem, 1992), vol. II, pp. 207–216, where he offers, in wonderful English, a very faithful version of Scholem's views, consistently ignoring all the scholarship published after the master's death. On the other hand, see the innovative approach to the subject by Y. Liebes, *Studies in Jewish Myth and Jewish Messianism*, tr. Batya Stein (SUNY Press, Albany, 1993), pp. 93–114, and his *On Sabbateanism and Its Kabbalah, Collected Essays* (Mossad Bialik, Jerusalem, 1995) [Heb.]. For an innovative treatment of Nathan of Gaza's thought see A. Elqayam, *The Mystery of Faith in the Writings of Nathan of Gaza* (Ph.D. Thesis, Hebrew University, Jerusalem, 1993) [Heb.]. See also notes 3, 10 below.

[3] For a critical review of Scholem's overemphasis on the role of messianic Lurianism in the emergence of Sabbateanism see M. Idel, "'One from a Town, Two from a Clan'—The Diffusion of Lurianic Kabbala and Sabbateanism: A Re-examination," *Pe'amim*, vol. 44 (1990), pp. 5–30 [Heb.], and an English version, printed in *Jewish History*, vol. 7 no. 2 (1993), pp. 79–104.

[4] G. Scholem, *Kabbalah* (New York, 1974), p. 45; *ibid., Origins of the Kabbalah*, tr. A. Arkush, ed. R.J. Zwi Werblowsky (Princeton UP, Princeton, JPS, Philadelphia, 1987), pp. 404–414.

internal, "purely" Jewish story? The answer seems to be rather complex: In my opinion, the sources of the nascent Kabbalah are to be sought much more, though not exclusively, within the various Jewish traditions.[5] This lore, in all its different forms, became gradually more and more open to the cultural ambiences that hosted the various centres of Kabbalah, either by responding to the challenges of these centres or by being influenced by certain conceptual views found there. This holds true for the *Zoharic* Kabbalah, that has absorbed more Christian elements than the earlier theosophical Kabbalah;[6] the ecstatic Kabbalah, that absorbed more Neoplatonic and Sufic elements in the second phase of its development, but initially had been strongly influenced by Neoaristotelianism,[7] and the Kabbalah in Italy, that was developed in a much more philosophical approach from the end of the fifteenth century until the first third of the seventeenth century.[8] Even the Lurianic Kabbalah, which emerged out of an originally particularistic mode of thought, was interpreted only one generation after its inception, in strong Renaissance terms.[9] Does Sabbateanism, a basically messianic movement, represent an exception to this greater turn of major forms of Kabbalah toward external forms of thought? The messianic nature of this movement may, indeed, point in this direction. However, it seems that a much more complex explanation for the emergence of this movement, than that offered by Scholem is in order; recently, the importance of the Marranos for the reception of this messianic theory has

[5] See M. Idel, *Kabbalah: New Perspectives* (Yale UP, New Haven, London, 1988).

[6] See Y. Liebes, *Studies in the Zohar*, tr. A. Schwartz, S. Nakache, P. Peli (SUNY Press, Albany, 1993), pp. 139–161.

[7] A. Altmann, "Maimonides' Attitude toward Jewish Mysticism," *Studies in Jewish Thought*, ed. A. Jospe (Detroit, 1981), pp. 200–219; M. Idel, "Maimonides and Kabbalah," in ed. I. Twersky, *Studies in Maimonides* (Cambridge, MA, 1990), pp. 54–70.

[8] M. Idel, "Major Currents in Italian Kabbalah between 1560–1660," *Italia Judaica* (Roma, 1986), vol. II, pp. 243–262; reprinted in D.B. Ruderman, ed. *Essential Papers on Jewish Culture in Renaissance and Baroque Italy* (New York UP, New York, 1992), pp. 345–368.

[9] This strategy started before the emergence of Lurianism; see M. Idel, "The Magical and Neoplatonic Interpretations of Kabbalah in the Renaissance," in ed. B.D. Cooperman, *Jewish Thought in the Sixteenth Century* (Cambridge, MA, 1983), pp. 186–242; and for later phenomena see A. Altmann, "Lurianic Kabbalah in a Platonic Key: Abraham Cohen Herrera's Puerta del Cielo," *Hebrew Union College Annual*, vol. 53 (1982), pp. 321–324; N. Yosha, *Myth and Metaphor, Abraham Cohen Herrera's Philosophic Interpretation of Lurianic Kabbalah* (Ben Zvi Institute, The Magnes Press, The Hebrew University, Jerusalem, 1994) [Heb.].

been reiterated, as well as the contribution of the pogroms of 1648/9.[10] These two explanations are of a more sociological nature, as they deal with the conditions which fostered the dissemination of this type of messianism and less with its inception. Here I would like to deal with the possible contribution of an additional factor to both the emergence of Sabbateanism and to its reception. This factor is the interpretation of Saturn as the planet that is related to the change of religion, as found in Arabic, Christian and Jewish astrology, its reinterpretation in Kabbalistic sources as dealing with the Messiah, and, finally, the Sabbatean interpretation of Saturn, in Hebrew *Shabbatai*, to Shabbatai Tzevi.[11] By suggesting the importance of the astrological factor, I do not intend to reduce the emergence, the evolution or the reception of Sabbateanism to this factor alone, and create thereby a new unilinear explanation of this mass phenomenon. Rather, I would like to propose the presence of a multiplicity of causes, of different natures, some of them already mentioned above, and allot to the astrological factor, a more modest role than the main, or a main, cause. Nevertheless, it is my claim that while the explanations accepted nowadays in scholarship deal much more with the reception of Sabbateanism, in the following I shall be concerned with the emergence, and only marginally with its reception.

2. *Astrology, Messianism, and "Universalism"*

Like some other corpora of knowledge that reached medieval Europe, by the mediation of and development by Arab authors, astrology evolued into a form of knowledge accepted by different intellectual and popular circles, and become a kind of common meeting ground, a science accepted by many in both East and West. Arguments based on the book of heaven, were adopted in some circles as much as those in that other widely accepted book, the Sacred Scriptures. We may see in astrological language and concepts a rather universal

---

[10] Y. Barnai, "Christian Messianism and the Portuguese Marranos: The Emergence of Sabbateanism in Smyrna," *Jewish History*, vol. 7 (1993), pp. 119–126; Y. Barnai, "The Outbreak of Sabbateanism—The Eastern European Factor," *Journal for Jewish Thought and Philosophy*, vol. 4 (1994), pp. 171–183. See also now S. Berti, "A World Apart? Gershom Scholem and Contemporary Readings of 17th-century Christian Relations," *Jewish Studies Quarterly*, vol. 3 (1996), pp. 212–214.

[11] On Kabbalah and astrology in general see J. Halbronn, *Le Monde Juif et l'Astrologie* (Arche, Milano, 1985), pp. 289–334, as well as note 117 below.

nomenclature, widespread and influential in many of the areas where Jewish mysticism flowered in the Middle Ages. Unlike all the forms of Jewish mysticism, astrological terminology was much easier to understand in broader Jewish circles, and ostensibly also facilitated communication between intellectuals who did not otherwise share the same religious assumptions. If Jewish mysticism was, for some of the first centuries of its existence a particularistic language, the astrological one may be described as universalistic.

As pointed out by several scholars, the astrological character of Saturn in the Middle Ages is a composite one, reflecting different traditions: on the one hand, the ambivalent nature of Kronos in the Greek mythology, on the other, the more positive nature of Saturn in the Roman one; in any case the complex figure emerging from this synthesis was associated with the negative characteristic of the melancholic.[12] Appointed in the Golden Age on the Islands of the Happy, Saturn is also the paramount planet of the solitary and under its aegis numerous spiritual qualities are enumerated, as well as quite unpleasant occupations. We cannot deal here with the rich literature concerning this quite complex planet and the "influences" attributed to it. Let me point out solely some basic facts for the point I would like to make. Already in ancient texts, but much more so in the Middle Ages, the nexus between Jews and Saturn was suggested on the grounds that this planet dominates, according to some texts, the seventh day, which was held holy by the Jews.[13] This is the reason why this planet has been designated in Hebrew as *Sabbatai*, a derivative of the name Sabbath, the Hebrew term for Saturday. In the Middle Ages, this nexus reverberates in many texts, most of them

---

[12] See the up-to-date French translation of R. Klibansky, E. Panofsky, F. Saxl, *Saturne et Mélancholie*, tr. L. Evrard (Eng.: *Saturn and Melancholy*), London and New York, 1964) (Galimard, Paris, 1989), pp. 210–212; For the ancient psychology of melancholy, afterwards connected to Saturn see J. Pigeaud, *Aristote, L'Homme de génie et la Mélancholie* (Rivages, Paris, 1988); J. Starobinski, *La mélancolie au miroir* (Julliard, 1989).

[13] See the important text of the tenth-century Al-Gabisi, known as Alcabitius, discussed in *Saturne et Mélancholie*, p. 208. More on Saturn and the Jews see E. Zafran, "Saturn and the Jews," *Journal of the Warburg and Courtauld Institutes*, vol. 42 (1979), pp. 16–27. Saturn surfaces often in fourteenth- and fifteenth-century Hebrew texts, which mingled philosophy, astrology, and magic, studies in recent years by D. Schwartz, see notes 15 and 119 below. On Saturn and the Golden Age see G. Guastella, "Saturn, Lord of the Golden Age," in *Saturn from Antiquity to the Renaissance* (U. of Toronto Italian Studies, 8) (Dovehouse Editions Inc., Ottawa, 1992), pp. 1–23.

of an astrological nature. So, for example, R. Abraham ibn Ezra, one of the most influential Jewish thinkers, is quoted as maintaining that "from the nations Sabbatai has, [under his aegis are], the Jews."[14] I would like to emphasize that in those few cases of astrological discussions where Sabbatai is mentioned by Jewish authors before the impact of Arabic astrology is discernible, all the descriptions of Saturn are negative. Positive qualities were added to the negative ones only after the twelfth century, and it seems to me that precisely this positive addition may explain the subsequent developments in Judaism.

Toward the end of the thirteenth century, R. Abraham Abulafia writes as follows:

> Among the stars, the power of *Sabbatai* corresponds to it[15] because it[16] is the highest among its companions, and behold, the supernal is appropriate to the supernal, and the nation of Israel is superior to all the nations, "for there is a high one who watches over him that is high, and that there are yet higher ones."[17] And the high one is the dust[18] of the land of Israel, and higher than it, that is appointed on it, is *Sabbatai*, and Israel are higher than them.[19]

---

[14] *Reshit Hokhmah* as quoted by the fourteenth-century commentator on Ibn Ezra's writings, R. Joseph Bonfils Tuv 'Elem, *Sefer Tzafnat Pa'aneah* (Cracaw, 1912), p. 49. On this quote see M. Idel, "Hitbodedut as Concentration in Jewish Philosophy," in (eds.) M. Idel, Zeev W. Harvey, E. Schweid, *Shlomo Pines Jubilee Volume on the Occasion of His Eightieth Birthday* (Jerusalem, 1988), vol. I, pp. 41–42 [Heb.]. For more on Ibn Ezra's view on the Jews and Saturn see Y.T. Langermann, "Some Astrological Themes in the Thought of Abraham Ibn Ezra," in (eds.) I. Twersky and J.M. Harris, *Rabbi Abraham Ibn Ezra: Studies in the Writings of a Twelfth-Century Jewish Polymath* (Harvard UP, Cambridge, MA, 1993), pp. 59–60.

[15] To the land of Israel. On the nexus between the land of Israel and Saturn later on see D. Schwartz, "The Land of Israel in the Fourteenth-Century Jewish Neoplatonic School," in (eds.) M. Hallamish and A. Ravitzky, *The Land of Israel in Medieval Jewish Thought* (Yad Izhak ben-Zvi, Jerusalem, 1991), p. 148 and note 40 [Heb.].

[16] Sabbatai.

[17] Ecclesiastes 5:7.

[18] On the relation between "the power of dust" and Sabbatai see also Abulafia's *Commentary on Sefer Yetzirah* (ed.), I. Weinstock (Mossad ha-Rav Kook, Jerusalem, 1984), p. 34.

[19] *Sefer Gan Na'ul*, MS. München 58, fol. 327a. This text is quoted in *Sefer ha-Peliy'ah* (Premislany, 1883), part I, fol. 76c, a book known to Sabbatai Tzevi, as we shall see below. On this book see M. Kushnir-Oron, *The Sefer Ha-Peli'ah* and the *Sefer Ha-Kanah, Their Kabbalistic Principles, Social and Religious Criticism and Literary Composition* (Ph.D. thesis presented to the Hebrew U. of Jerusalem, 1980), esp. pp. 75–76, where Abulafia's influence on the book is discussed [Heb.]. For more on Sabbatai, the image of the Jew, and the land of Israel, see Abulafia's *Sefer 'Otzar 'Eden Ganuz*, MS. Oxford 1580, fol. 95c. See also *ibid.*, fol. 102a. On Sabbatai and

Unfortunately, Abulafia did not elaborate upon the relation between Israel and Saturn, the former being conceived of as superior to the latter. This is an unusual hierarchy, as the much more common assumption is that Saturn is presiding over the nation of Israel. I have no good explanation for Abulafia's passage, but in any case, the nexus between the two entities is explicit. However, what seems to be important for our further discussion is the fact that the term *'Eretz*, mentioned in the above quote, has been interpreted in our context as pointing to 1290, the date of redemption: the *'Aleph* stands for thousand; the *Reish* for two hundred, and the *Tzade* for ninety. Thus, at least implicitly, and as we shall see below in another passage from this book, in a rather more explicit manner, Saturn-*Sabbatai* is related to redemption.

However, much more important is the existence of the concept that the conjunction between Saturn and Jupiter, the so-called *conjunctio maxima*, in Hebrew *ha-dibbuq ha-gadol*, is the moment of the emergence of new religions.[20] This view was well known to Jewish writers since the twelfth century and sometimes even connected explicitly with messianic expectations.[21] So, for example, we read in a mid-thirteenth-century treatise, widespread in manuscripts, by R. Moses ben Yehudah, entitled *Commentary on the Hebrew Alphabet*[22]

> all [the data] amount to five thousand and twenty years,[23] and [then] the rule of Saturn[24] will commence and during it our redemption will be, with the help of Shadday, blessed be His Name.[25]

---

the black bile see *ibid.*, fol. 109a. On another issue, the pronunciation of the divine name by a messianic figure, as shared by both Abulafia and Sabbatai Tzevi, see M. Idel, *Messianic Mystics*, appendix 1 (Yale UP, New Haven, London, 1998) (forthcoming).

[20] See O. Loth, "Al-Kindi als Astrolog," *Morgenländische Studien* (Leipzig, 1875), pp. 263–309; Halbronn, *Le Monde juif et l'astrologie*, pp. 139–142, 156–159; F.A. de Armas, "Saturn in Conjunction: From Albumasar to Lope de Vega," *Saturn from Antiquity to the Renaissance* (U. of Toronto Italian Studies, 8) (Dovehouse Editions Inc., Ottawa, 1992), pp. 151–171.

[21] See R. Abraham bar Hiyya, *Sefer Megillat ha-Megalleh* (eds.), A. Poznanski and J. Guttmann (Berlin, 1924), pp. 119, 128, 153–154.

[22] MS. Paris, Bibliothèque Nationale 711, fol. 66b.

[23] 1260.

[24] Sabbatai.

[25] See also there fol. 66a, and in the rather contemporary astrological view printed in Alexander Marx, "Ma'amar 'al Shenat ha-Ge'ullah," *ha-Tzofeh le-Hokhmat Yisrael*, vol. 5 (1921), p. 198, mentioning the coniunctio maxima between Saturn and Jupiter. On the origin of religions as linked to the great conjunctions of Saturn and Jupiter,

This is by no means an exceptional stand. The conjunction between the two planets was also thought to indicate the arrival of a messianic figure by a contemporary of R. Moshe, R. Yehudah ben Nissim ibn Malkah.[26] Moreover, we learn about the importance of the *coniunctia maxima* for the emergence of an important Jewish figure, a prophet or Messiah, from several sources at the end of the fifteenth and the beginning of the sixteenth century.[27] A contemporary of Abraham Zakut, R. Yohanan Alemanno, describes Saturn as appointed over the Torah of Israel, the Temple in Jerusalem and the Hebrew language.[28] As we shall see in the next paragraph, Saturn played a more visible role in the descriptions of Judaism at the end of the sixteenth century in Italy.

3. *Saturn, Binah and Messiah*

In some Kabbalistic writings, the planet Saturn was connected to the third *sefirah, Binah*, whose affinity to concepts of redemption is known from several types of kabbalistic sources. The origins of this view may date to the very beginnings of Kabbalah, and led to the great importance of this *sefirah* in the theosophy of R. Isaac Sagi-Nahor and his school, where it is often designated as *Teshuvah*, repentance or return.[29] However, it seems that both the book of the *Zohar* and Joseph Gikatilla used redemptive terms in their depiction of this *sefirah* much more than the earlier Kabbalists had done. In the *Zohar*, for example, the fifty gates of *Binah*, mentioned in the Talmud, are described as having been opened by God at the time of the exodus from Egypt, "in order to take out the people of Israel . . . as will He

---

see also G. Vajda, *Recherches sur la philosophie et la kabbale dans la pensée juive du Moyen Age* (Paris, 1962), p. 264, n. 3.

26 M. Idel, "The Beginning of Kabbalah in Northern Africa? A Forgotten Document by R. Yehuda ben Nissim ibn Malka," *Pe'amim*, vol. 43 (1990), pp. 4–15 [Heb.], esp. p. 10 note 42. On the author and his views on astrology see G. Vajda, *Juda ben Nissim ibn Malka, Philosophe Juif Marocain* (Collection Hesperis, Paris 1954), pp. 45–46, 136–141, 143.

27 See M. Beit-Arieh and M. Idel, "An Essay on the End and Astrology by R. Abraham Zacut," *Qiriat Sefer*, vol. 54 (1979), pp. 174–194; *ibid.*, pp. 825–826 [Heb.].

28 See the texts collected and translated in Idel, "The Magical and Neoplatonic Interpretations," pp. 209–210.

29 See *idem*, "On R. Isaac Sagi Nahor's Mystical Intention of the Eighteen Benedictions" (eds.) M. Oron and A. Goldreich, *Massu'ot, Studies in Kabbalistic Literature and Jewish Philosophy in Memory of Prof. Ephraim Gottlieb* (Mossad Bialik, Jerusalem, 1994), pp. 28–29 [Heb.].

do also in the days of the Messiah."[30] In a manner quite similar to Gikatilla, the *Zohar* would say that this *sefirah* is the source from where the redemption of Israel would come.[31]

For the time being, the first instance of a plausible identification of the third *sefirah* with Saturn is found in a book by Abraham Abulafia, *Gan Na'ul*, already mentioned above. While interpreting a verse related to David, the quintessential messianic figure, "His seed shall endure for ever, and his throne shall be like the sun before me,"[32] he wrote:

> *Leil Shmarim*[33] whose secret is *'Et Qetz*,[34] and by combination of letters is *haker ha-nefesh*,[35] "and His throne shall be like the sun[36] before me".... The secret of *Negdi*[37] is *Binah*,[38] which comprises *Gedi*[39] and *Deli*[40] which are the servants[41] of the star[42] Sabbatai,[43] whose secret is *mahashavti* and everything is *Binah Mahashavti*, and whoever comprehends it he comprehended *Mahashavti*. And see that *Levanah* is *Ke-Binah*[44] and also *Hokhmah* is *Ke-Hamah*[45] and know them and when you will understand them and recognize the linkage of *Moladot* during the periods of equinox and solipses,[46] you will understand from them the influx that emanates

---

[30] Zohar, I, fol. 261b.

[31] II, fol. 46b. Similar views recur in Kabbalistic literature; see, e.g., the late fifteenth-century Italian Kabbalist R. Elijah ben Benjamin of Genazzano, *'Iggeret Hamudot*, ed. A. Greenup (London, 1912), p. 60, analyzed by C. Mopsik, *Les grands textes de la Kabbale* (Verdier, Lagrasse, 1993), pp. 303–304.

[32] Psalm 89:37. See esp. *ibid.*, verse 41 where the term *meshihekha*, your annointed, which was later understood as your Messiah, is mentioned. The eschatological interpretation of these verses is standard, though Abulafia's extraction of precise dates seems to be unparalleled.

[33] The night of watchfulness. This is apparently a deficient spelling of *Leil shimmurim*, an expression found in Exodus 12:42, a verse understood as pregnant with messianic implications.

[34] Both expressions amount to 660, as it is the phrase. See below, note 36.

[35] The recognition of the soul, a phrase that amounts also to 660.

[36] *Ka-shemesh*, amounts also to 660.

[37] Namely "before me".

[38] *Negdi* and *Binah* amount numerically to the same figure: 67, as do the combination of the words *Gedi* and *Deli.*

[39] Capricorn.

[40] Aquarius.

[41] On Saturn and the two zodiacal signs see the paintings adduced in Klibansky, Panofsky, Saxl, *Saturne et Mélancholie*, pp. 304–306, 312–313, and see also below, note 75.

[42] Namely the planet.

[43] *Kokhav Shabbatai* amounts to *gematria* 760 like *Mahashavti.*

[44] Like *Binah.* In *gematria* both are equivalent to 87.

[45] Like the sun. *Hokhmah* and *ke-Hamah* amount to 73.

[46] *Ba-tequfah.*

> from the emanator to its recipient. And know that the paths of the *sefirot*[47] that I wrote to you, are—according to their secret—*Binah*,[48] whose meaning is twelve [times fifty-five amounts to "the time of][49] *Qetz*",[50] and all is *Seter*[51].[52]

There can be doubt that for Abulafia, the terms *Binah* and *Sabbatai* on the one hand, and redemptive secrets on the other, are related to each other. For his own person, who pretended to be the Messiah, redemption would start soon after writing the book, no more than two years. In other instances, he claimed that the time of redemption would be 1290, while *Sefer Gan Na'ul* was composed in circa 1289.[53] The nexus between *Mahashavti*, namely thoughtful, and Saturn, is well documented in astrological texts, where this planet is conceived of as being appointed to govern "the power of thought"—*koah ha-mahashevet*—according to Abraham ibn Ezra, for example, who also claims that the power of foretelling the future is also connected to this planet.[54] The nexus between thought or understanding and Saturn however, is much older. It is implied in the alleged etymology of Kronos, the partial correspondent of Saturn, which has

---

[47] Abulafia differentiates between the higher form of Kabbalah dealing with the divine names and the lower one dealing with the *sefirot*. See M. Idel, "The Contribution of Abraham Abulafia's Kabbalah to the Understanding of Jewish Mysticism," in (eds.) P. Schäfer and J. Dan, *Gershom Scholem's Major Trends in Jewish Mysticism, 50 Years After* (J.C.B. Mohr, Tübingen, 1993), pp. 124–127.

[48] *Binah* as a term for Kabalah see M. Idel, "Secrecy, Binah and Derishah," in eds. H. Kippenberg and G. Stroumsa, *Secrecy and Concealment* (Brill, Leiden, 1995), pp. 331–333.

[49] The phrase in brackets is found in *Sefer ha-Peliy'ah*, but not in MS. München.

[50] The time of the End, in Hebrew *'Et Qetz*, amounts *Seter*, namely 660. Elsewhere in this book Abulafia proposes the *gematria Qetz* = 190 = *ne'elam*, namely hidden, like *seter*. See MS. München 58, fol. 338b. See also the next footnote.

[51] In many places in this book *Seter, arcanum*, stands for the figure 660, which has a messianic meaning in Abulafia. See e.g. MS. München 58, fol. 328b. In other words, the quintessential arcanum is the eschatological one. This figure is also the result of the multiplication of 12 by 55, which is *Yod Bet*, and *Nun Hei*, the consonants of *Binah*, and it is also the numerical value of the sun, *ka-shemesh*. For more on Abulafia's calculations of the end see M. Idel, "'The Time of the End': Apocalypticism and Its Spiritualization in Abraham Abulafia's Eschatology," (forthcoming).

[52] See his *Gan Na'ul*, MS. München 58, fol. 323b, copied in *Sefer ha-Peliy'ah* part I, fol. 75a, where the version is deficient. See also above, the previous paragraph for another discussion of Saturn in Abulafia.

[53] See M. Idel, *Abraham Abulafia's Works and Doctrines* (Ph.D. thesis, Hebrew University, 1976), p. 19 [Heb.].

[54] See the quote in his name adduced and discussed in M. Idel, "Hitbodedut as Concentration in Jewish Philosophy," vol. I, pp. 41–42. Compare also below, note 101.

been understood to point to *koros*, plenitude, and *nous*, intellect.[55] The nexus to *virtus intellectiva* is conspicuous in the Middle Ages,[56] and, according to Abulafia, connected with the reception, apparently by the human intellect, of the influx from above. Whether or not this reception of intellectual influx is related to knowledge of the future, contemplation, or prophecy, as in the other instances when Abulafia mentioned Saturn, is a matter of speculation, but this is quite a plausible assumption. In any case, the above passage not only deals with secrets of the immediate future, but also interprets a biblical verse that has obvious "messianic" implications. The meaning of the phrase *Binah Mahashavti*, apparently "Understand My Thought", may refer to the fathoming of the secret of redemption found in divine thought. As the other phrase, "*Binah* Twelve End", indicates that within the term *Binah* one finds the figure 660, which stands for "the end", according to Abulafia. Moreover, the discussions on *Hokhmah* and *Binah*, may well point to the verse of Isaiah 11:2, where the spirit of *Hokhmah* and *Binah* is described as resting upon the messianic figure, a verse that was exploited in quite specific messianic terms by a contemporary of Abulafia's, as we shall see shortly. A cautious assessment of the content of the passage would therefore emphasize its eschatological dimension, whereas a more audacious one would insist upon its messianic cargo.

Let me speculate on the significance of the term *Binah*: it means understanding, and it may be understood in a non-sefirotic framework. However, any attempt to discount a sefirotic reading is mistaken, because Abulafia mentions explicitly "the paths of the *sefirot*". If this is a plausible explanation, then *Binah* points also to the third *sefirah*, and is connected with Sabbatai. If this guess is correct, the above text represents the first nexus between the planet Sabbatai, *Binah*, and redemption.

Whether or not Abulafia's text itself had an impact on a much more influential passage, to be discussed immediately below, is a difficult question and cannot be determined here.[57] In any case, of

---

[55] See Klibansky, Panofsky, Saxl, *Saturne et Mélancholie*, p. 247. On Sabbatai and men of understanding—*Binah*—see also R. Abraham ibn Ezra's *Hai ben Meqitz*, (ed.), Jacob Egers, *Diwan des Abraham ibn Ezra mit seiner Allegorie Hai ben Mekiz* (Berlin, 1886), p. 143 [Heb.].

[56] *Saturne et Mélancholie*, p. 255.

[57] There are some points of resemblance between R. Joseph Ashkenazi's Kabbalah and some topics in Abraham Abulafia, despite the huge differences between them.

utmost importance for the further history of this interpretation of the function of the third *sefirah* was the echo of this view in the writings of a Kabbalist of Ashkenazi extraction. R. Joseph ben Shalom Ashkenazi, a prolific Kabbalist of the late thirteenth century, offered one of the most important and influential descriptions of the connection between the Messiah and the third *sefirah*:[58]

> He has appointed the letter *Bet* over life and bound a crown to it and formed [the planet] by it *Sabbatai* in the world, and Sunday in the year [namely in the dimension of time], and the right eye in the person, namely that He elevated the letter *Bet* so that it is the head on "the power of the *Keter 'Elyon*." And he put in it the power of *Hokhmah* and formed in it the planet of *Sabbatai*, which is beneath the [divine name] 'ABG YTTz,[59] and the latter gave wisdom to *Sabbatai*. Why is *Sabbatai* the planet of destruction, and nevertheless informed by the wisdom of [the name] 'ABG YTTz? The explanation is that despite the fact that *Sabbatai* is the power of destruction, by the [dint of the] *Shemittot*, it possesses the power of *Hokhmah*,[60] and the reason it is appointed over destruction is that it is not concerned with any of the corporeal issues and this is the reason why it destroys them and also does not begrudge them their adornments, but is concerned with the separated intelligences that are the *sefirot*, [and the comprehensions of the heptades] and the comprehension of God, blessed be He, . . . and it is appointed over the Jews and this is the reason they are in trouble in this world. . . . And because it is appointed over the gravity, it designates darkness and [is appointed] over everything that is black and [is] over the black bile[61] . . . and the planet of *Sabbatai* is appointed

A more detailed discussion of the possible contacts between the two is still a desideratum of the research of the thirteenth-century Kabbalah.

[58] On this Kabbalist see the important study of G. Vajda, "Un Chapitre de l'histoire du conflit entre la Kabbale et la philosophie: la Polémique anti-intellectualiste de Joseph b. Shalom Ashkenazi," *Archives d'histoire doctrinale et littéraire du Moyen Ages*, vol. XXXIII (1956), pp. 45–127.

[59] This is the first unit of letters that constitutes the name of forty-two letters, each of the six letters corresponding, according to Joseph Ashkenazi's *Commentary on Sefer Yetzirah*, to each of the seven planets. The phrase "the power of the supernal Keter" which is characteristic to the style of R. Joseph Ashkenazi, has been applied by Nathan of Gaza to Sabbatai Tzevi. See e.g., A. Amarillo, "Sabbatean Documents from the Archive of R. Shaul Amarillo," *Sefunot*, vol. V (1961), p. 270 [Heb.]. The expression "Koah Keter 'Elyon" recurs again in *Sefer ha-Peliy'ah*, part I, fol. 57c, again under the influence of R. Joseph ben Shalom Ashkenazi's *Commentary on Sefer Yetzirah.*

[60] See notes 55–56 above.

[61] *Marah Shehorah*, namely melancholy. The nexus between Saturn and melancholy is quintessential in many ancient, medieval and Renaissance texts, as the

> over them and because it is appointed for eternity, when it reaches the ascendant, it will never decline, as it is said that[62] "the spirit of God rests upon him, the spirit of *Hokhmah* and of *Binah*." See and understand that this is the secret of "*Mashiyah YHWH*" . . . See and understand that the planet *Sabbatai* has the crown of *Binah*.[63]

This is one of the richest, and, as we shall see below, most influential discussions about the nature of Saturn, but also the one most ignored in the vast scholarly literature on the metamorphoses of this planet-god. As I cannot engage here in a detailed analysis of its content, I shall only remark that astrological opinions were combined with eschatological ones, some of which dealt with cosmic eschatology, or *makrokronos*, while others, more important from my point of view, dealt with the *mesokronos*, the historical time of the national redeemer.[64] Unlike Abulafia, who did not connect Sabbatai with the human Messiah, R. Joseph ben Shalom Ashkenazi did so explicitly in fact, his mention of the "secret of *Mashiyah YHWH*" represents the most positive description of the planet in Hebrew literature.

Let me address now the repercussions of this view in lesser-known writings; the first of them is authored by a Spanish Kabbalist,

---

monograph of Klibansky, Panofsky, Saxl, amply demonstrates. In several Hebrew sources, which escaped the attention of those authors, this nexus is also evident. See, in addition to the astrological literature starting in the twelfth century, the Zoharic literature: *Zohar Hadash*, (ed.) R. Margoliot (Mossad ha-Rav Kook, Jerusalem, 1978), fols. 32a, 33d; *Zohar*, vol. III, fol. 237b (Ra'aya' Meheimna'); *Tiqqunei Zohar*, no. 21, fol. 56b; no. 70, fol. 124ab. I hope to deal with the Zoharic stands in the more detailed version of the present study.

[62] Isaiah 11:2.

[63] *Commentary on Sefer Yetzirah* (Jerusalem, 1961), fols. 51b–52a. On this passage see also H. Pedayah, "Sabbath, Sabbatai, and the Diminution of the Moon—The Holy Conjunction, Sign and Image," in (ed.) H. Pedayah, *Myth in Judaism = Eshel Beer-Sheva*, vol. 4 (1996), pp. 150–153 [Heb.].

This quote was echoed by many authors. See, e.g., R. Moses of Kiev's *Commentary on Sefer Yetzirah*, called *'Otzar ha-Shem*, *ibid.* A version of this passage, with some slight differences, is found in R. Joseph ben Shlomo Al-Ashqar, *Sefer Tzafnat Pa'aneah*, MS. Jerusalem 40 154, facsimile edition (ed.), M. Idel (Jerusalem, 1989), fol. 71a. See also *ibid.*, fol. 37ab, where another eschatological understanding of Saturn is mentioned.

On the identification between Saturn and the third *sefirah*, without, however, messianic implications, see another book by Ashkenazi, his *Kabbalistic Commentary on Genesis Rabbah* (ed.), M. Hallamish (The Magnes Press, The Hebrew University, Jerusalem, 1984), p. 236. On the affinity between Saturn, a third power within the pleroma and an eschatological figure seen already in *Ismaiyliah*, cf. the discussion of Henry Corbin, *Cyclical Time and Ismaili Gnosis* (London, 1983), pp. 91–92, 94.

[64] On the two terms see M. Idel, "Some Concepts of Time and History in Kabbalah" (forthcoming).

R. David ben Yehudah he-Hasid, whose Kabbalah is haunted by Joseph Ashkenazi's ideas; one of the most explicit descriptions of the Messiah as a symbol of the third *sefirah* argues as follows:

> The king Messiah is the secret of *Binah*; and when the time of the redemption of Israel arrives, the Holy One, Blessed be He, who is *K[eter] 'E[lyon]* will cause him to smell all those fine smells and perfumes . . . that attribute called Messiah as it is written[65] "and the spirit of 'Elohim hovers over the face of the water"; this is the spirit of the Messiah. . . . Then, the *Binah* which is the Messiah judges the poor in a right manner, namely *Knesset Yisrael*, because she arouses the stern judgement and the justice of the nations of the world.[66]

The mythology of redemption is construed here in terms of the emanative drama in the higher realm of the three *sefirot*; the first *sefirah* provokes the arousal of the third one by means of smells and perfumes, symbols of the divine influx. Then, by means of this arousal, and apparently of the power received from the higher instances, the third *sefirah* distributes its influx onto the last *sefirah*, symbolized by the Assembly of Israel, while withholding that influx from the demonic powers, symbolized by the nations. This description is characteristic of a whole series of symbolic readings of the meaning of redemption: this is not an extraordinary moment, a rupture with the past, or an upheaval. In fact, it is depicted as being just the distribution of the divine forces from the first to the last *sefirah*. The Messiah is an agent that is active in differentiating the distribution of the influx. The apocalyptic judgement which takes place in history is presupposed: not negated but also not explicated. What is important for this Kabbalist is rather the understanding of the supernal, divine processes rather than lower history. The fourteenth-century Kabbalah classic,[67] the anonymous *Sefer ha-Temunah* also envisions a link between the third *sefirah* and the Messiah, apparently under the impact of the views already surveyed above:

---

[65] Genesis 1:2.

[66] *Sefer Mar'ot ha-Tzove'ot* (ed.), D.Ch. Matt (Scholars Press, Atlanta, 1982), pp. 100–101.

[67] On the tentative datation of this book at the end of the thirteenth-century see G. Scholem, *Origins of the Kabbalah*, pp. 460–461, note 233; I hope to devote a special study to this issue; see, for the time being, M. Idel, "The Meaning of *Ta'amei ha-'Ofot ha-Teme'im*' of R. David ben Yehudah he-Hasid," in (ed.) M. Hallamish, *'Alei Shefer, Studies in the Literature of Jewish Thought Presented to Rabbi Dr. Alexander Safran* (Bar-Ilan UP, Ramat Gan, 1990), pp. 18–21 [Heb.].

> "The Son of David will not come until the souls are exhausted from the Body"[68] and then the supernal and lower redemptions will be united to the supernal light... because everything will return to the first redeemer, who has safely redeemed everything, and "that who has been sold, will be redeemed and he will be free at the Jubilee"[69] which are the days of the "Supernal Messiah".[70]

From the context, as well from some parallels found in the writings of R. Joseph Gikatilla dealing with terms relating to redemption,[71] it stands to reason that the first redeemer, identical to the "Supernal Messiah" refers to the third *sefirah*, which is considered to be linked to both the redemption of the higher entities, namely the last seven *sefirot*, and the lower, mundane world. Redemption here stands not for national or individual salvation but for a cosmic process involving both the corporeal and the spiritual components of reality. This is a deterministic process, deeply influenced by astrological concepts, which resorts to eschatological concepts in order to make his points in more traditional terms. Thus, we find in the emphasis on the redemptive nature of the third *sefirah*, designated as redeemer and upper Messiah, a clear tendency to depict the return of the emanative process to the source, a restoration of the primordial, a circular concept of what I propose to call a "cosmic makrokronos", and not a rectilinear vision of history which ends, or culminates, in the messianic era.[72]

However, the most important repercussion of the views from the circle of R. Joseph Ashkenazi and R. David ben Yehudah he-Hasid, is found in the late fourteenth- or early fifteenth-century *Sefer ha-Peliy'ah*; composed in the Byzantine empire, this vast compilation of various Kabbalistic sources includes the passage from R. Joseph Ashkenazi's *Commentary on Sefer Yetzirah* quoted above.[73] This passage should be understood as the continuation of the school of the Kabbalists

---

[68] *Yevamot*, fol. 62a.

[69] Leviticus 25:24.

[70] *Sefer ha-Temunah* (Lemberg, 1892), fol. 44b. In this book, the planet Saturn, and some of its qualities, are connected, as in R. Isaac of Acre's *Sefer Me'irat 'Einayyim*, to the ninth *sefirah*, Yesod. See fols. 3b, 16a.

[71] See those sources in M. Idel, "Types of Redemptive Activities in the Middle Ages," in (ed.) Z. Baras, *Messianism and Eschatology* (Merkaz Shazar, Jerusalem, 1983), pp. 264–265, 270–271 [Heb.] and *Sefer ha-Temunah* itself, fol. 55ab.

[72] See above, note 64.

[73] *Sefer ha-Peli'yah*, I fol. 57ac. On the influence of R. Joseph Ashkenazi on this book see Kushnir-Oron, The *Sefer Ha-Peli'ah*, p. 94, note 48, 187–193.

mentioned above; this means that the Messiah was understood to be connected to the third *sefirah*, as we learn from the use of the term *Binah*, the mention of the *Shemittot* and of the heptade, which are related, as seen above, to the third *sefirah*. However, what is especially significant in this text is the recurrence of the name of the planet *Sabbatai*, which corresponds to the well-known Latin deity and planet Saturn.

The ambiguity of the qualities associated with this planet is well-known in scholarly circles, and reflects much older traditions, psychological, mythical and astrological, which I would like not to elaborate on here; numerous astrological texts attribute to the planet not only the celestial power to govern wisdom, thought by some post-Renaissance authors and artists to be the source of genius, but, at the same time, also the responsibility for passive, destructive and melancholic dispositions. An awareness of the nexus between Sabbatai and Saturn was seen already by the sixteenth-century Christian Kabbalist, Francesco Giorgio of Venice, in his very influential book *De Harmonia Mundi*, I, 4,5.[74]

The formative impact of R. Joseph ben Shalom Ashkenazi's passage on the late sixteenth-century Italian thinker, R. Abraham Yagel, is evident:

> You should know that Capricorn and Aquarius are the constellations of Israel;[75] their planet is Saturn, since these constellations are its [Saturn's] houses, as [Abraham] ibn Ezra explains in *Sefer ha-ʿAtzamim*,[76] and R. Abraham ben David in his commentary on the *Sefer Yetzirah*. Because of these constellations, they [the Jews] are liable to plunder and destruction, to toil and to burdens, like those of our ancestors in Egypt. None of the heavenly hosts are as devastating as these two in summoning evil and suffering to this world. Accordingly, the astrologers assigned as its [Saturn] lot the black plague, illness, slaves, graves, prison, and a place of corpses.[77]

---

[74] See note 86 below. For Saturn in a sixteenth-century Jewish thinker, R. Abraham ibn Migash, see S. Rosenberg, "Exile and Redemption in Jewish Thought in the Sixteenth Century: Contending Conceptions," in (ed.) B.D. Cooperman, *Jewish Thought in the Sixteenth Century* (Harvard UP, Cambridge, MA, 1983), pp. 406–407 and the pertinent footnotes.

[75] See also above, note 41.

[76] On this book of Renaissance magic, spuriously attributed to Ibn Ezra, see M. Idel, "The Magical and Neoplatonic Interpretations," p. 195; *idem*, "The Study Program of Yohanan Alemanno," *Tarbiz*, vol. 48 (1979), p. 312 n. 76 [Heb.].

[77] *Gei Hizzayon*, cf. *A Valley of Vision, The Heavenly Journey of Abraham ben Hananiah*

The present plight of the Jews, however, is to be compensated for by their success in the future; speaking of the six lower planets, he wrote that "all of them will give strength to Saturn, although the latter will not give strength to any of them."[78] And, according to an Indian sage,

> Since Saturn signifies to the Jews, all the gentiles will acknowledge their Torah and bow down to them while they [the Jews] will not acknowledge them [the gentiles], as the prophet stated:[79] "For then I will make a pure speech to the nations so that they will all invoke the Lord by name."[80]

The two quotes treat the two extremes of the situation of the Jews: their subordination in the present, reminiscent of the negative qualities of the Greek god Kronos, while the positive future, very reminiscent, as we shall see in a moment, of the messianic age, seems to reflect more the character of Saturnus, the Latin god, before he was conflated with the Greek one. Indeed, this last quote adumbrates the subsequent, much more articulate discussion where the ascendancy of the planet Saturn is described in strikingly utopian terms. No less than the great philosopher Aristotle,—in fact a pseudo-Aristotelian source circulated in the Middle Ages,[81]—has been adduced from a work by the famous Jewish thinker Joseph Albo, to the effect that in the golden future "everyone will accept Israel's Torah."[82] After invoking the authority of the Indian astrologer and that of the great Greek philosopher, Yagel approaches the opinion of the Kabbalists. He formulates his view, on the basis of ideas already presented above, that

> *Binah*, the supernal mother, nourishes these constellations and their planets. She is called in the language of the rabbis "the constellation of Israel" and also "repentance," by which all repent. [She also is

Yagel, tr. D.B. Ruderman (U. of Pennsylvania Press, Philadelphia, 1990), p. 171. On this author in general see D. Ruderman, *Kabbalah, Magic, and Science, The Cultural Universe of a Sixteenth-Century Jewish Physician* (Harvard UP, Cambridge, MA, 1988).

[78] *Ibid.*, p. 173.

[79] Zephaniah 3:9.

[80] *Ibid.*, p. 173.

[81] See S.M. Stern, *Aristotle on the World-State* (U. of South Carolina Press, Columbia, SC, 1968), pp. 78–85, esp. p. 85, note 1.

[82] *Gei Hizzayon, ibid.*, p. 173.

> called] "jubilee," and through [her power] the slaves were liberated and Israel went out from Egypt.[83]

Afterwards he introduces a lengthy citation from R. Joseph ben Shalom Ashkenazi's *Commentary on Sefer Yetzirah*, in part quoted above.[84] Thus, the astrological view about the messianic character of Saturn and the higher power that rules it, the third *sefirah*, was combined with various eschatological views, certain messianic verses and Talmudic discussions.[85] However, interesting as Yagel's views may be in themselves, they remained on the margin of Jewish culture. Nevertheless the fact that a similar view was expressed by a older contemporary, the above-mentioned Christian Kabbalist Francesco Giorgio, writing about the nexus between Sabbatai, Saturn and *Binah* in his *De Harmonia Mundi*[86] seems to be quite significant. It points to the impact of Kabbalah on the cultural mood in Italy, and to a certain extent in Europe—as the French translation and printing of the book in 1556 show. However, I assume that the inverse would also be correct, namely that the vigorous culture of the Renaissance would have an impact on certain Jewish audiences, including Kabbalists, at the end of the sixteenth century and later.

4. *Sabbatai Tzevi and Saturn*

Sabbatai Tzevi, the most famous and notorious of the Jewish Messiahs, was named Sabbatai, like some other Jewish infants, because he was born on Sabbath; thus a certain affinity between his name and an event that may be astrologically interpreted is found from the very moment of his birth. However, what seems to be much more pertinent is the fact that already in his youth he studied *Sefer ha-Peliy'ah*, and, as Scholem pointed out, he was also influenced by it. Three quotations, analyzed above—two by Abulafia and the third by R. Joseph of Shalom Ashkenazi—had been anonymously included in this large compendium of early Kabbalah. The very fact that the three main passages on the planet Saturn-*Sabbatai* found here have eschatological and messianic implications, could not, in my opinion,

[83] *Ibid.*, p. 173.
[84] See Ruderman, *ibid.*, pp. 173–174 and the pertinent notes.
[85] *Ibid.*, pp. 174–175.
[86] I,4,5. See C. Swietlicki, *Spanish Christian Cabala* (U. of Missouri Press, Columbia, 1986), pp. 140–145 esp. p. 143.

have escaped the attention of a careful reader. One of the Sabbatean ideologues has quoted R. Joseph Ashkenazi's passage from *Sefer ha-Peliy'ah* as follows:

> These are the words of Metatron to the holy Qanah (re)called in *Sefer ha-Peliy'ah* and he is a wondrous man and this is found in our hands in a manuscript, and his words had been copied by Rabad in his *Commentary on Sefer Yetzirah* . . . and these are the words of Metatron to the holy Qanah, and these are his [Qanah's] words.[87]

Sefer ha-Peliy'ah, the source used by the student of Nathan of Gaza, is attributed to a second-century Tannaitic figure, a revered mystic named R. Nehuniah ben ha-Qanah, who is described as engaging in various mystical dialogues with Metatron, the highest of the angels. Both the mention of this mystic's name and the belief that this book had been revealed from above, were bound to add to the authority of the affinity between Sabbatai-Saturn and the Messiah. Actually the name of the planet connected in the above quote to the "secret of the Mashyiah YHWH" is, in Hebrew, identical with the proper name of Sabbatai Tzevi. This coincidence may, however, be more than a mere accident, for Sabbatai Tzevi studied the book too, and might have been influenced by this passage. In any case, his prophet used it explicitly in order to prove his messianism. I am inclined to attribute to this quote, which has also left other traces in the Sabbatian literature,[88] a much greater role than that of a belated and retro-

---

[87] The epistle of R. Abraham Peretz, entitled "Magen Abraham" printed in G. Scholem, *Studies and Texts, Concerning the History of Sabbetianism and its Metamorphoses* (Mossad Bialik, Jerusalem, 1974) [Heb.], pp. 175–176, differs from the original in *Sefer ha-Peli'yah* as printed later in the eighteenth-century, only in insignificant details. On the recurrence of manuscripts of *Sefer ha-Peliy'ah* in circles of Sabbateans see the important remarks of M. Benayahu, *The Sabbatean Movement in Greece* (Jerusalem, 1971–1977), pp. 350–354 [Heb.]. The Sabbateans were aware of the literary nexus between Joseph ben Shalom's *Commentary on Sefer Yetzirah* and *Sefer ha-Peliy'ah*; see M. Benayahu, *The Shabbatean Movement in Greece*, Jubilee Volume Presented to Gershom Scholem (Ben-Zvi Institute, Jerusalem, 1971–77), pp. 369–370 [Heb.], and see also *ibid.*, p. 151. Cf. also the note printed by Amarillo, "Sabbatean Documents," p. 269. See also the important additional material concerning the affinity between Sabbateanism and astral magic, and between Sabbatai Tzevi and melancholy, discovered and analyzed by Avraham Elqayam—after reading a first version of this presentation—in his study "The Rebirth of the Messiah," *Kabbalah, Journal for the Study of Jewish Mystical Texts*, (eds.) D. Abrams and A. Elqayam, vol. I (1996), pp. 104–111, 129, 136, 139–140, and notes 57, 162 [Heb.].

[88] See G. Scholem, *Studies and Texts*, p. 267 and note 288 and the text hinted at in Scholem, *Researches in Sabbateanism*, (ed.) Y. Liebes ('Am 'Oved, Tel Aviv, 1991), p. 44 and Y. Liebes' remark, *ibid.*, p. 175 note 143 as well as the quote from *Sefer*

spective proof text. I assume that Tzevi conceived of himself as the Messiah, at least in part, because of the content of the afore cited passage, where the planet Saturn, alias *Sabbatai*, was described as the "secret of the Messiah." The manner of reference is rather ambiguous because it is not altogether clear whether the reference is to a planet or to a human individual. Thus, someone could, plausibly enough, either understand the passage as dealing with the expected Messiah, who is considered to be related to Sabbatai, or understand that he is called Sabbatai. If this hypothesis is correct, and I hope to elaborate elsewhere much more on this topic, then the late thirteenth-century Kabbalah from the circle of Joseph Ashkenazi must have contributed to Tzevi's self-awareness as Messiah more than anything in Lurianic Kabbalah could possibly have done.[89]

Let me adduce some significant instances of the possible contribution of what may be called the Saturn-clue to the understanding of an important passage authored by Nathan of Gaza. In one of his famous epistles he mentions that the faith in Sabbatai Tzevi, if accepted by the believers, will ensure the reception of

> "the inheritance of the Lord"[90] which is the mystery of the Jubilee Year that will become manifest at this time and the "rest", which is the mystery of the manifestation of ʿAttiqa' Qaddisha', within the configuration of Zeʿir 'Anppin, in the year 1670.[91]

Two different topics are explicated in this passage. Let me start with the more obvious one: in 1670 a high revelation is to take place, when the highest divine hypostasis, *ʿAttiqa' Qaddisha'*, will illuminate the lower configuration within the intradivine world.[92] Then those

ha-Peli'yah adduced in R. Elijahu of Smyrna *Midrash Talpiyyot* (ed. Smyrna, reprinted in Jerusalem, 1963), fol. 163a.

[89] As Scholem has correctly indicated, both *Sefer ha-Temunah* and *Sefer ha-Qanah*—in fact he might have included *Sefer ha-Peliy'ah* as being even more—"influenced the Sabbatians tremenduously"; cf. his *The Messianic Idea in Judaism* (Schocken Books, New York, 1972), p. 111. In general I would say that the trend of Kabbalah represented by the writings of R. Joseph Ashkenazi, and adopted by some other important Kabbalists, has been one of the most influential schools in Kabbalah in general. See M. Idel, "An Anonymous Commentary on *Shir ha-Yihud*," eds. K.-E. Grözinger and J. Dan, *Mysticism, Magic and Kabbalah in Ashkenazi Judaism* (Walter de Gruyter, Berlin, New York, 1995), pp. 151–154.

[90] See I. Tishby's remark in *Tzitzat Novel Tzvi*, by Yaʿaqov Sasportas, eds. Z. Schwartz and I. Tishby (Mossad Bialik, Jerusalem, 1954), p. 7, note 8 [Heb.].

[91] *Tzitzat Novel Tzvi*, pp. 7–8; G. Scholem, *Sabbatai Sevi*, p. 270 and his notes there.

[92] This is a view found both in Zoharic theosophy and in Lurianic Kabbalah,

who merit it will gain the "rest", *menuhah*. This redemptive significance is alluded to by the term "secret". However, a precursor of the salvific drama is already evidenced "at this time", by the reference to the "secret of the Jubilee". I assume that this secret designates a lower form of deliverance—but one already present in 1665. However, what is the theosophical significance of this mystery of the Jubilee? To judge from its almost unanimous agreement with Kabbalistic symbolism and on the basis of the above discussions, the Jubilee is a symbol of the third *sefirah*. This symbolism points to the then governing power, namely the *sefirah* of *Binah*.

This distinction between the two phases was overlooked in Scholem's analysis; nevertheless, he did quite correctly point out the salvific meaning of *Binah* in this context. However, he did not pay attention to its possible implications, leaving the reader with the impression that the reference here is to one global redemptive event.[93] Moreover, in one of the later sentences of the same epistle, describing future events during the next seven years, Nathan writes explicitly that the miracles mentioned in the book of the *Zohar* will take place until

> the year of the next Shemittah.[94] And in the seventh [year] ben David will come[95] and in the seventh year is Shabbat, which is the king Sabbatai, and at that time the above-mentioned rabbi, [namely Sabbatai Tzevi] will come from the river of Sambatiyon together with his spouse, the daughter of Moses, our master.[96]

The emphasis on the seventh is obvious; it is quite reminiscent of the mystery of the Jubilee and, at the same time, of the description cited above from *Sefer ha-Peliy'ah*, where Saturn-Sabbatai is described as being connected to "the secret of Shemittot". However, even more explicit is the mention in the last quote of King Sabbatai. The reign of this king should not, in my opinion, be confused with that of

---

and connected sometimes with the glory of redemption. See *Zohar*, III, fol. 136b and Y. Liebes, *Studies in the Zohar*, pp. 44–46, 60–62.

93 *Sabbatai Ṣevi*, pp. 275–276.

94 Namely within the span of maximum six years.

95 I. Tishby, *Tzitzat Novel Tzvi*, p. 11, note 9, mentions the parallel to *BT, Megillah*, fol. 17b.

96 *Tzitzat Novel Tzvi*, p. 11, G. Scholem, *Sabbatai Ṣevi*, pp. 273–274. On the distinction between the plene spelling of Sabbatai, with an 'Aleph, which points to a maleficent spirit, very similar to Saturn, and the deficient spelling, without an 'Aleph, as pointing to a private name, see Ba'alei ha-Tosafot, *Gittin*, fol. 11a.

Tzevi himself, because immediately after mentioning King Sabbatai Nathan introduces the "Rabbi", namely Tzevi himself, thus precluding a possible mix-up between the two. In other words, from this quote we can see that the importance of the reign of *Sabbatai*-Saturn, which is in fact the seventh planet, as part of the redemptive drama was utilized beyond the direct quotes from the thirteenth- and fourteenth-century passages that served as possible sources of inspiration. We may assume that Tzevi, while studying *Sefer ha-Peliy'ah* in his youth, has been attracted by the afore-cited text and he might have been influenced by the nexus between *Sabbatai*, namely Saturn as a planet, and the Messiah. His vision passed over to Nathan, who within one discussion integrated both the man and the planet with the same name. Provided that the above presuppositions are correct, we have an interesting example of how certain items in Kabbalistic books could have infused their ideas in certain kinds of personalities, and thus have constituted starting points for wide-reaching personal developments, even more than historical events.

Indeed, on the basis of the above texts, it would be plausible to propose another clue to the inner spiritual life of Tzevi: Scholem proposed to diagnose a mental illness that may explain Tzevi's emotional up and downs: mania depressiva[97] or what is called nowadays a bipolar personality. It is not my aim here, or in general, to dispute the accuracy of this modern diagnosis of the mental malady of a patient who died so many decades ago. What will suffice now (and I hope to be able to elaborate on this issue at length elsewhere) is that, influenced by his perception of a personal affinity to *Binah* and Saturn, Tzevi also internalized the peculiar emotional characteristic associated with this planet: *marah shehorah* or melancholy. As is better known today, since the Renaissance more and more historical personalities born under the aegis of Saturn, have been haunted by fears of having a troubled fate.[98] I hope that with the help of this clue, some aspects of Tzevi's behavior will be better understood, but the psychological aspects of absorbing the melancholic aspects of Saturn is an issue that still awaits a fuller discussion.

Let me adduce an explicit statement about the affinity between the Messiah and the planet, in a poem dedicated to Tzevi by a contemporary of his:

---

[97] *Sabbatai Ṣevi*, pp. 125–138.
[98] See R. Witkover, *Born Under Saturn* (London, 1963).

> Come together like brethren—
> All the planets, in order to praise
> . . . . To Thee,
> the supernal Sabbatai, the head of the seven—
> greatness and dominion is appropriate.
> This is why God put on you broad knowledge—
> Your name was called by his name on the day of circumcision.[99]

To interpret these verses I propose that they deal with Sabbatai the Messiah in terms of his status as the first among the seven planets, namely Saturn, which also offers the reason for the name given to the infant Sabbatai at the moment of circumcision. Again, I would like not to deduce the development of the self-awareness of Tzevi from the reception of Sabbatai as a planet, but at least we may argue that the nexus between the very high status of the planet Sabbatai and the Messiah Sabbatai could not have escaped many of his followers, as it could not have escaped, in my opinion, Tzevi himself. In other words, the relatively young Tzevi, who studied a classic of Kabbalistic literature in the geographical area he was born, was shaped by a statement that connected his name to the homonym planet and with the Messiah.

Another very important nexus between Sabbatai the Messiah and the planet, in a conspicuous astrological context, is found in the epistle of R. Raphael Sopino.[100] Moreover, according to another text preserved by Sasportas, Tzevi was described as transmitting the gift of prophecy to his close friend, R. Abraham ha-Yakhini, as follows:

> The Master [Tzevi] put upon him his spirit of prophecy. Thereupon something resembling a brilliant star grew on his forehead—and it seems to me that it was the planet Saturn—and it is said that he [ha-Yakhini], too, then prophesied.[101]

---

[99] S. Bernstein, "The Letters of Rabbi Mahalujah of Ancona," *Hebrew Union College Annual*, vol. 7 (1930), p. 515, and G. Scholem, in the Hebrew version of *Sabbatai Ṣevi* (Tel Aviv, 1957), p. 405, (not translated in the English version p. 493).

[100] Printed in R. Yaʿaqov Sasportas, *Tzitzat Novel Tzvi*, p. 93; See also G. Scholem, *ibid.*, p. 647, note 155. Sopino, like Mahaleluyah, was an Italian Rabbi, and the importance of the Italian context is obvious in the astrological one. See also below note 111.

[101] Cf. G. Scholem, *Sabbatai Ṣevi*, p. 430, *Tzitzat Novel Tzvi*, pp. 165–166. See also *ibid.*, p. 186. On Saturn and prophecy see the passage from R. Joseph ben Shalom Ashkenazi, part of which was dealt with above, as copied in *Sefer ha-Peliy'ah*, part I, fol. 57b. See also above, note 54. It should be emphasized that from the formulation of the last sentence, it appears that Tzevi, too, was conceived of as a prophet.

Both the spirit of prophecy, and the mentioning of the star—even without the explicit reference to Saturn—point to Saturn, which was linked to the faculty of prophecy. For an astral understanding of Tzevi we have a very reliable testimony, emanating from the most intimate circle of the Messiah, but independent of the testimonies of Nathan of Gaza and his followers, who merely reiterated the views of *Sefer ha-Peliy'ah*. If this assumption is correct, we are witness to a classical situation of personality interacting with ways of thought, in this case an astrological model capable of influencing not only an abstract messianic claim, but also other aspects of his inner life. At any rate, it is quite possible that Tzevi's "melancholy" is not only part of his personal spiritual constitution and due to his having read the passage from *Sefer ha-Peliy'ah* but also indicative of the more general attitude toward melancholy in his time.[102] In addition to the possible contamination of the young Tzevi by ideas connecting Sabbatai-Saturn to the future Messiah, from the point of view of our discussion here it would be pertinent to examine a major issue related to the role of the myth: Saturn the deity became a planet, but despite this astral role some qualities of the ancient god remained alive. As pointed out by Seznec, in the Middle Ages astral concepts were carriers of mythical concepts concerning the ancient gods.[103] Might we, however, find an even greater revival of the ancient myth in Tzevi's thought and self-perception? Or, to ask the question more bluntly: could Sabbatai conceived of himself not only as a Messiah,

---

See also Giacomo Saban, "Sabbatai Sevi as Seen by a Contemporary Traveller," *Jewish History*, vol. 7 (1993), p. 106.

[102] For a very recent outstanding treatment of melancholy in Tzevi's time see M. Heyd, "Be Sober and Reasonable," *The Critique of Enthusiasm in the Seventeenth and Early Eighteenth Centuries* (E.J. Brill, Leiden, 1995), pp. 44–70; S.L. Macey, *Patriarchs of Time, Dualism in Saturn-Cronus* (U. of Georgia Press, Athens and London, 1987), pp. 23–39; H.S. Versnel, *Transition and Reversal in Myth and Ritual* (E.J. Brill, Leiden, New York, Koeln, 1993), pp. 136–227; F.E. Manuel and F.P. Manuel, *Utopian Thought in the Western World* (Belknap, Harvard, Cambridge, MA, 1980), pp. 64–92; V. Teti, *La melanconia del vampiro, Mito, Storia, Immaginario* (Manifestolibri, Roma, 1994), pp. 161–200. For more on the recurrence of the idea of melancholy in Tzevi's lifetime see L. Babb, *The Elizabethan Malady, A Study of Melancholia in English Literature from 1580 to 1642* (Michigan State College Press, East Lansing, 1951), and J.O. King III, *The Iron of Melancholy, Structures of Spiritual Conversion in America from the Puritan Conscience to Victorian Neurosis* (Wesleyan UP, Middletown CT, 1983), as well as the huge scholarly literature about Robert Burton's *Anatomy of Melancholy*, the most important discussion on melancholy, printed in Oxford in 1621, shortly before the birth of Sabbatai Tzevi.

[103] J. Seznec, *The Survival of the Pagan Gods: The Mythological Tradition and Its Place in Renaissance Humanism and Art* (Princeton UP, Princeton, 1972).

perhaps as someone ruled by the highest planet, or by the third *sefirah*, but also as someone who would achieve a divine status? In a rather explicit passage, the ascent of Tzevi to the *sefirah* of *Binah* this is quite evident; in a Yemenite apocalypse, stemming from a rather early period of the Sabbatean movement, the Messiah is described as ascending from "one degree to another, [all] the digression of the seven sefirot from Gedulah to Malkhut . . . after two years he ascends to the degree that his mother is there."[104]

Scholem correctly interpreted this text as pointing to the third *sefirah*, which is commonly represented by the symbol for "mother", and he even proposed, on the basis of this passage, to presuppose a mystical event in the spiritual life of Tzevi in 1650, and again, he correctly intuited that the meaning of this happening would be the understanding of the "secret of divinity."[105] What Scholem did not specify was the nature of the "secret of divinity." On the strength of the above quotes and some other dealt with above, I suggest that this secret was not only understood by reaching the third *sefirah*: This *sefirah* may in fact be the very secret of divinity, namely the most intimate secret of Sabbatean theology as proposed by Tzevi himself. This suggestion invites a more detailed investigation, which may find that the Sabbatean secret of divinity changed over time as part of a development both alongside the vector of time and of the ontic hierarchy of the *sefirot*, meaning that the closer the messianic drama approaches the final stage, the higher is the status of the divine power appointed over or related to Sabbatai, and this is what constitutes the "secret of divinity." In any case, elsewhere in the same epistle, the nest of the bird, the mystical place of the Messiah, is none other than the third *sefirah*.[106]

However, whatever the details of Sabbatai's own secret of divinity may have been—and this secret is far from being clear—the apoth-

---

[104] G. Scholem, *Researches in Sabbateanism*, pp. 214–215. For more, on the possible non-Yemenite background of this treatise, see recently Y. Nini, "Sabbatean Messianism in Yemen," *Pe'amim*, vol. 65 (1995), pp. 5–17 [Heb.]. For a Freudian interpretation of this passage which emphasises the importance of the mention of "his mother" see A. Falk, "The Messiah and the Qelippoth: On the Mental Illness of Sabbatai Sevi," *Journal of Psychology and Judaism*, vol. 7 no. 1 (1982), pp. 25–26. For a Jungian interpretation see S. Hurwitz, "Sabbatai Zwi, Zur Psychologie der häretischen Kabbala," *Studien zur analytischen Psychologie C.G. Jungs, Festschrift zum 80. Geburtstag von C.G. Jung* (Rascher Verlag, Zürich, 1956), vol. II, pp. 239–263.

[105] *Idem*, *Sabbatai Ṣevi*, pp. 119–123, 146–147, 149; Y. Liebes, *Studies in Jewish Myth*, pp. 107–113.

[106] G. Scholem, *Researches in Sabbateanism*, p. 222.

eosis described in the above text presupposes that the Messiah, ascending to the third *sefirah*, has been divinised in one way or another. In the many discussions dealing with the nexus between the Messiah and *Binah*, it is only the Messiah named Sabbatai to whom this specific form of apotheosis is attributed; none of the others mention the ascent of an historical Messiah to that *sefirah*.[107] Unlike Marsilio Ficino, Girolamo Cardano and Robert Burton, among many others, whose mood was profoundly affected by their belief that they were born under Saturn,[108] Sabbatai Tzevi attempted, or at least has been portrayed so, to ascend to the celestial source governing his character. As in the case of the divinisation of Solomon in a fourteenth-century Kabbalistic text,[109] the divinisation of the Messiah in Sabbateanism restores some mythical traits of Greek themes lost over the centuries. It is quite plausible to assume that the seventeenth-century Messiah did not even know about the classical Greek mythological material about Saturn, and I have little doubt that he did not intend to restore Saturn's status as the father of the gods. However, what seems pertinent to our discussion is that the use of the hermeneutical apparatus of the median line of the divine powers,[110] gave a certain dramatic coloring to certain vestiges of ancient myths that makes them look closer to the ancient sources than to the medieval versions of these myths.

5. *Some Conclusions*

Let me distinguish between two main suggestions in the above pages related to Sabbateanism: one deals with what seems to me to be a demonstrated claim, namely that the astrological background of both

---

[107] On the apotheotic impulse in Jewish mysticism see M. Idel, "Metatron: Comments on the Development of Jewish Myth," (ed.) H. Pedayah, *Myth in Jewish Thought = Eshel Beer Sheva*, vol. 4 (Beer Sheva, 1996), pp. 29–44 [Heb.]. See also M. Idel, "The Contribution," p. 127.

[108] See Klibansky, Panofsky, Saxl, *Saturne et Mélancholie*, pp. 389–432; D.P. Walker, *Spiritual and Demonic Magic, From Ficino to Campanella* (U. of Notre Dame Press, Notre Dame, London, 1975), pp. 45–50.

[109] See M. Idel, "Prometheus in a Jewish Garb," *Eshkolot*, (NS) vol. 5/6 (1981), pp. 119–122 [Heb.].

[110] As I shall show elsewhere, the symbolism of the median line, that comprises mainly the *sefirot* of *Malkhut* and *Tiferet*, was used also in other cases in order to introduce Greek mythical concepts. Here is not the place to discuss the possible affinities between Tzevi's sexual problems and the Saturnine character, as well as between the Sabbatean sexual orgies and Saturnalia.

the messianic and melancholic nature of Sabbatai Tzevi were instrumental in his reception as a melancholic Messiah. Indeed, even in the criticism of the movement, the astrological element was adduced.[111] Given the fact that both the supporters and the opponents introduced astrological concepts of Saturn, I see no reason not to attach a great importance to this type of speculation in the diffusion and reception of Sabbateanism, at least in some cultural areas in Europe. Indeed, as I have suggested elsewhere, it would be more reasonable not to look for only one basic and universally valid explanation for the emergence of Sabbateanism, which allegedly unified all the Jewish communities, but to allow different explanations that may fit different communities.[112] In our case, the Renaissance concern with Saturn may have influenced some Jews in Italy or in West Europe more than those living in the East.

The second suggestion deals with the plausibility of the impact of the Kabbalistic discussions of Saturn in *Sefer ha-Peliy'ah* on the emergence of Tzevi's self-perception as Messiah. For the time being, no attempt has been made to explain why the young Kabbalist Sabbatai did adopt a messianic claim. My proposal, based upon what seems to me to be a plausible inference, combines the undisputed testimony regarding the early study of this book by Tzevi, and its role in helping to spread positive treatments of the planet, one of which mentions the Messiah of God. Though such an explanation includes an imponderable factor, the psychological impact of the content of these discussions on the young Sabbatai seems to be, for the time being, the sole significant proposal that explains the emergence of the messianic consciousness. I would like to emphasize that, in theory, one could accept the validity of the "reception" theory, without accepting the second suggestion. Though such an attitude is possible, I regard it as not very plausible.

The above proposals are not intended to substantially mitigate the

---

[111] See Sasportas' resort to the argument of astronomers, *ha-Tokhenim*, who described Saturn as a bloody star, in order to criticize Sabbatai Tzevi. Cf. *Tzitzat Novel Tzvi*, pp. 99–100, and Tishby's remark p. 100 note 2. See also *ibid.*, p. 298 and the similar claim of Isaac Cardoso in Yosef Hayim Yerushalmi, *From Spanish Court to Italian Ghetto, A Study in Seventeenth-Century Marranism and Jewish Apologetics* (U. of Washington Press, 1981), p. 345: "What save sadness did Sabbatai, who was born on a funeral day, predict? He was unfortunate in his very name, since, in the Hebrew language, Saturn is called Sabbatai, a sad and malignant star regarded as a rather great misfortune by the astrologers."

[112] See Idel, "One in a Town," p. 94.

place of the Sabbatean ideology within the history of Jewish mysticism by overemphasizing the astrological component, nor to inscribe it forcefully in the history of the legacy of Greek or Roman mythology. Nevertheless, the astral mythology should be taken in account, in the forms it inspired after having been adopted within Kabbalistic writers. My proposals strive, nevertheless, to broaden the pertinent contexts of the emergence and expansion of Sabbateanism. In lieu of scholarly overemphasis of the role of Lurianic Kabbalah—which was rejected, or at least ignored by Tzevi—in order to create a unilinear explanation of the history of Jewish mysticism, I propose a much less developmental picture which emphasizes the importance of cross-currents,[113] and the importance of pre-Lurianic forms of Kabbalah, and in our specific instance, the continuous relevance of quite heterogenous Kabbalistic elements preserved in *Sefer ha-Peliy'ah*. The heterogeneity of the Kabbalistic trends represented in this book is emblematic for how I propose to describe the history of Kabbalah, and of Kabbalistic messianism. Various distinct schools, in our case, ecstatic Kabbalah and astrologically oriented treatments, survived in manuscripts, from which important excerpts were incorporated in Kabbalistic classics. Thus their views could inspire later forms of Jewish mysticism, even after the emergence and canonization of later forms of Kabbalah, like Lurianism.

My further argument is that astrological concepts in serving as a conduit for messianic perceptions relating to Saturn-Sabbatai, were much more important than Lurianic concepts, allegedly full of acute messianic overtones, in preparing the ground for Sabbatean ideas and ferment. A proper understanding of the phenomenon of Sabbateanism as proposed above assumes the need to transcend the often artificial distinctions between literary genres and literature belonging to a certain type of religion. The reliance on analyzing Kabbalistic literature alone in order to understand religious developments with a broad impact, as in Scholem's monograph, seems to overlook other types of sources which could shed a different light on the emergence of certain moments in Sabbateanism.

The above suggestion to incorporate the emergence and diffusion of Sabbatean messianism within broader religious and cultural contexts is, however, a necessary approach in a variety of topics relating to

---

[113] See *idem*, "Metatron," pp. 32, 44.

Judaism, and especially to Jewish mysticism. It is not my purpose here to deal in detail with examples of the necessary readings of Jewish topics against backgrounds which are much larger than scholars have heretofore imagined. However, some suggestions, connected to the line we have adopted above, may be in place. Greek mythological themes, for example, are turning up in Hekhalot literature,[114] in the views of the Golem,[115] some eschatological and other Kabbalistic themes in Kabbalah, and some topics in Jewish Renaissance mysticism.[116] Too stark and artificial a separation between Jewish mysticism and other forms of occult knowledge *en vogue* in late antiquity and the Middle Ages[117] or between Kabbalah and philosophy,[118] as cultivated in the dominant scholarly forms of treating the history of this mystical lore, hardly helped to advance the study of the field. Only the work of gradually freeing analyses of Jewish material from the intellectual ghettoes created by scholars who portrayed Jewish thinkers as reflecting narrow concerns dealing predominantly with ritual or history, together with the examination of Jewish texts beyond the often artificial walls of literary genres or historical circumstances, may open gates that would otherwise remain closed because of the limited expertise of modern forms of scholarship.[119]

---

[114] See G.G. Stroumsa, "Mystical Descents," *Death, Ecstasy, and Other Worldly Journeys*, (eds.) John J. Collins and Michael Fishbane (SUNY Press, Albany, 1955), pp. 137–151. On a Greek mythologoumenon in the Hekhalot literature I hope to devote a separate study.

[115] See M. Idel, *Golem: Jewish Magical and Mystical Traditions on the Artificial Anthropoid* (SUNY Press, Albany, 1990), pp. 4–5.

[116] See *idem*, "Prometheus"; Liebes, *Studies in Jewish Myth*, pp. 65–93.

[117] For the importance of astrological-magical terminology for a better understanding of Kabbalah and Hasidism see *idem, Hasidism: Between Ecstasy and Magic* (SUNY Press, Albany, 1995), index sub voce Astrology. On Kabbalah and astrology in general see Halbronn, *Le Monde Juif et l'Astrologie*, pp. 289–334; R. Kiener, "Astrology in Jewish Mysticism from the *Sefer Yesira* to the *Zohar*," *Jerusalem Studies in Jewish Thought*, vol. VI (1987), pp. 1–42; On astrology and magic in the Renaissance in general see E. Garin, *Astrology in the Renaissance* (Arkana, London, 1983); F. Secret, "L'Astrologie et les kabbalistes chrétiens a la Renaissance," *Le Tour Saint-Jacques*, vol. 5 (1956), pp. 45–49.

[118] See M. Idel, "Abulafia's Secrets of the Guide: A Linguistic Turn," in eds. Alfred Ivry and Elliot Wolfson, *Perspectives in Jewish Thought and Mysticism* (London, 1997), pp. 269–272.

[119] See also Idel, "Saturn, Sabbath, Sorcery and the Jews," (forthcoming).

THE ENGENDERMENT OF MESSIANIC POLITICS: SYMBOLIC SIGNIFICANCE OF SABBATAI ṢEVI'S CORONATION

Elliot R. Wolfson

Sabbatianism as a Religious Factor

Much scholarship has been written on the historical and theological contours of the seventeenth-century Sabbatian heresy, which Gershom Scholem referred to as the "largest and most momentous messianic movement in Jewish history subsequent to the destruction of the Temple and the Bar Kokhba Revolt."[1] Without denying the many refinements and modifications in recently published work, the magisterial edifice of intellectual history constructed by Scholem to a great degree remains intact. Particularly influential was Scholem's contextualization of the messianic movement in terms of the history of Jewish mysticism, and especially the primary role that he assigned to Lurianic kabbalah as the ideational basis for Sabbatian theology, articulated most elaborately by Nathan of Gaza (1644–1680) and Abraham Miguel Cardoso (1627–1706). Other scholars have contributed in significant ways to the study of the ideological and philosophical aspects of Sabbatianism, but the religious dimension of this astonishing chapter in the spiritual history of the Jews is a story that is for the most part still told along the lines established by Scholem.

Indeed, Scholem insisted that despite the political and social explanations that one could posit to explain the spread of this movement in Palestine and throughout the Jewish Diaspora, in places as distinct as Syria, Yemen, Persia, Turkey, North Africa, the Balkans, Italy, Germany, the Netherlands, England, and Poland, the central and unifying factor was of a religious nature, which he traced to the convergence of mystical and messianic tendencies in kabbalistic teachings disemminating from the mouth of Isaac Luria. For Scholem, there is no conflict between the "traditional national and political

---

[1] G. Scholem, *Kabbalah* (Jerusalem, 1974), p. 244.

content of the messianic idea" and the "new spiritual and mystical note which it acquired in Lurianic kabbalah."[2] The intensification of the spiritual quest in the mystical theosophy promulgated in the later period of Luria's career (refracted primarily through the prism of his disciples) only deepened the messianic impulse, for the particular redemption of the Jewish people and the return from exile to the land were viewed as external symbols of an internal cosmic redemption and the restoration of the unity of all being within the divine.

Thus, in *Major Trends in Jewish Mysticism*, Scholem readily acknowledged that the eschatological goal in Lurianic kabbalah entails the "restoration of the ideal order, which forms the original aim of creation. It is also the secret purpose of all existence. Salvation means actually nothing but restitution, re-integration of the original whole, or *Tikkun*, to use the Hebrew term."[3] In a second passage from this work, Scholem observed that the "true nature of the redemption is mystical," and he insists that the "historical and national aspects are merely ancillary symptoms which constitute a visible symbol of its consummation."[4] Rather than deny the literal belief in the coming of the messiah, however, Scholem was of the opinion that the Lurianic kabbalists viewed this actual historical event as the external sign that the redemption of being in general (on the cosmic, human, and divine planes) is complete. In a third passage, Scholem adopts an even bolder stance, emphasizing that for the disciples of Luria messianic redemption was transformed from the conception of a "national restoration" into a "drama of cosmic importance," which entailed the "restoration of that great harmony which was shattered by the Breaking of the Vessels and later by Adam's sin." The sign of redemption, therefore, is "not so much the end of exile, which began with the destruction of the Temple," but "the end of that inner exile of all creatures which began when the father of mankind was driven out of paradise." Scholem draws the inevitable conclusion: "The kabbalist laid far greater emphasis on the spiritual nature of redemption than on its historical and political aspects." After reaching that conclusion, however, Scholem immediately qualified his position by asserting that the historical and political aspects "are by no means

---

[2] *Ibid.*, p. 245.
[3] G. Scholem, *Major Trends in Jewish Mysticism* (New York, 1954), p. 268.
[4] *Ibid.*, p. 274.

denied or discounted, but they tend more and more to become mere symbols of that mystical and spiritual process. The historical redemption is as it were a natural by-product of its cosmic counterpart, and the kabbalists never conceived the idea that a conflict might arise between the symbol and the reality which it was supposed to express."[5]

Similarly, in his magisterial intellectual biography, *Sabbatai Ṣevi: The Mystical Messiah*, Scholem again emphasizes that the "decisive innovation" of Lurianic kabbalah "was the transposition of the central concepts of exile and redemption from the historical to a cosmic and even divine plane." These concepts are "numinous symbols of a spiritual reality of which historical exile and redemption are merely the concrete expression."[6] And in like fashion, in his seminal essay, "Toward an Understanding of the Messianic Idea in Judaism," Scholem refers to the "double glance" of the doctrine of redemption in Lurianic kabbalah, which is "cast upon the inner and outer aspect of the world," a particular phenomenon that is illustrative of the more general "dialectics of Jewish mysticism."[7] According to Scholem, as any number of scholars have noted, the dialectical merging of the national and the universal, the political and the cosmic, the material and the spiritual, holds the key to understanding the latent potency of Lurianic messianism and its volcanic eruption in the Sabbatian movement.[8] But Scholem himself was careful to

---

[5] *Ibid.*, p. 305.

[6] G. Scholem, *Sabbatai Ṣevi: The Mystical Messiah 1626–1676*, translated by R.J. Zwi Werblowsky (Princeton, 1973), p. 26.

[7] G. Scholem, *The Messianic Idea in Judaism and Other Essays on Jewish Spirituality* (New York, 1971), p. 17. See *ibid.*, p. 48. Similarly, I. Tishby, *The Doctrine of Evil and the "Kelippah" in Lurianic Kabbalism* (Jerusalem, 1942), 134–143 (in Hebrew), interprets the references to messianic redemption in the relevant Lurianic texts as betraying a convergence of the cosmic redemption, related specifically to the elevation of the sparks, and the national redemption of the Jewish people (see esp. pp. 137–138). See below, n. 14.

[8] *Major Trends*, p. 287; *Sabbatai Ṣevi*, pp. 7–8; *Kabbalah*, pp. 75–76; *Messianic Idea*, p. 59. Scholem's position has been challenged by several scholars. See S. Sharot, *Messianism, Mysticism, and Magic: A Sociological Analysis of Jewish Religious Movements* (Chapel Hill, 1982), pp. 98–101; M. Idel, *Kabbalah: New Perspectives* (New Haven, 1988), pp. 257–260. Idel's own acknowledgment that the "theological language" of Sabbatai Ṣevi's followers was "predominantly Lurianic" (p. 259) is, in my opinion, still the essential point. That is to say, even if we acknowledge that the Lurianic dimension of Sabbatai Ṣevi's own messianic and spiritual comportment was minimal (a point acknowledged by Scholem, *Sabbatai Ṣevi*, pp. 116–117, 904), and indeed it appears that his own sources of literary influence were primarily the *Zohar* and *Sefer ha-Qanah* (which includes *Sefer ha-Peli'ah*), the theological presentation of the Sabbatian movement at the hands of the rabbinic elite was still very much indebted to the technical symbols and modes of discourse of the theosophic kabbalah

distinguish between Lurianic kabbalah and Sabbatianism on this very important issue. That is, in the case of the former the spiritualization of the messianic ideal did not lead to a split between the inner-symbolic and the external-historical since the messianic expectations were not put to the test of history. In the case of the latter, by contrast, the internalization of the messianic ideal without any apparent application in history did indeed lead to a suppression of the this-worldly emphasis of Jewish messianism, which in turn occasioned the break between symbol and reality.[9]

Even from this very brief sketch, it should be evident that Scholem's interpretation of Sabbatianism rises or falls with the correctness of his reading of the Lurianic material. It lies beyond the scope of this study to enter into great detail regarding the latter, but it is incumbent upon me to say something about this subject for my own interpretation of the theological content of the Sabbatian material will likewise depend on how I understand the Lurianic texts. I am in agreement with Scholem's basic claim that Sabbatianism is, first and foremost, a religious phenomenon. To be sure, I do not think one can ever isolate religion from social, economic, political, cultural, or psychological factors, but I subscribe to the view that "religious" as an autonomous category in the realm of human experience should be upheld. In terms of the specific phenomenon of Sabbatianism, the rabbinic elite who accorded religious credibility to this movement by providing theological justifications for Sabbatai Ṣevi's messianic pretenses were primarily concerned with constructing a messianic reality that derived its doctrines, symbols, and rituals from the complex world of Jewish mysticism, principally as filtered through the *Zohar* and the Lurianic material.[10] Furthermore, in the sociological climate of the seventeenth century, belief in a messiah would have

---

promulgated by Luria and his disciples. For a criticism of Idel's view, see I. Tishby, "Upheaval in the Research of Kabbalah (On: M. Idel, *Kabbalah: New Perspectives*)," *Zion* 54 (1989): 220–222 (in Hebrew), and the response of Idel, "'What is New is Forbidden,'" *op. cit.*, 238–239. For a fuller statement of Idel's position, see his "'One from a Town, Two from a Clan'—The Diffusion of Lurianic Kabbala and Sabbateanism: A Re-Examination," *Jewish History* 7 (1993): 79–104; *idem, Messianism and Mysticism* (Tel-Aviv, 1992), pp. 78–83 (in Hebrew).

[9] *Major Trends*, p. 306; *Messianic Idea*, pp. 87–88, 109, 121–123.

[10] I accept the criticism of Scholem's attempt to underplay the influence of Christian millenarian speculation on the immanent development of eschatological traditions within Jewish circles. It cannot be a mere coincidence that the year 1666 was designated as the time of redemption and the second coming of Christ to defeat the antichrist Rome, precisely the year when the messianic fervor surrounding

been impossible without rabbinic approbation, which entailed as a principal component the sanction of prophetic and paranormal experiences.[11] The legitimization of the messianic pretense, therefore, derived from kabbalists whose claim to authority was buttressed by appeal to revelation.

Sabbatai Ṣevi reached its peak. It goes without saying that the particular expression of messianic beliefs has to be evaluated in terms of the symbols and modes of language characteristic of the kabbalistic tradition, but this is no way minimizes the likelihood of external influence. See Sharot, *Messianism, Mysticism, and Magic*, pp. 105–106.

[11] Even if we accept the criticism of Scholem that he neglected to focus on popular religious culture in his construction of the Sabbatian movement, there is little question that the rabbinic elite were the ones who provided the theological justification for the messianic beliefs and actions of the lay communities. Moreover, it is clear from the earliest documents that the authority of the rabbis in this matter derived from claims to prophetic inspiration. Regarding Nathan's acclaim as a master of mantic powers who was worthy of prophetic visions on a par with Ezekiel, see Baruch ben Gershon of Arezzo, *Zikkaron li-Venei Yisra'el*, in *'Inyenei Shabbatai Ṣevi*, edited by A. Freimann (Berlin, 1912), pp. 43, 46–47, and the testimony of Nathan himself concerning his vision of the chariot cited in one of his epistles included in this chronicle, p. 61. See also the epistle of Nathan regarding Sabbatai Ṣevi and his apostasy edited by G. Scholem, *Studies and Texts Concerning the History of Sabbatianism and Its Metamorphoses* (Jerusalem, 1982), p. 236 (in Hebrew); *The Story of Shabbetay Zevi by R. Leib ben R. Ozer Amsterdam, 1711–1718*, translation, introduction and notes by Z. Shazar, edited by S. Zucker and R. Plesser (Jerusalem, 1978), pp. 10–11, 16 (in Hebrew and Yiddish); the version of Nathan's chariot vision reported by Abraham Cuenque in Jacob Emden, *Torat ha-Qena'ot* (Altona, 1752), 18a; the letter of Nathan cited by G. Scholem, *Researches in Sabbateanism*, edited by Y. Liebes (Jerusalem, 1991), p. 19 (in Hebrew), and the prophecy of Nathan in the visionary account attributed to Abraham the Pious, in G. Scholem, *Be-'Iqvot Mashiaḥ* (Jerusalem, 1934), pp. 59–61 (another version of this text is published by Scholem, *Researches*, pp. 68–69). Nathan describes his visions to Moses Pinhero in a text published in *'Inyenei Shabbatai Ṣevi*, p. 95 (cited in Scholem, *Sabbatai Ṣevi*, p. 206). Nathan's prophetic status and the role that it played in the Sabbatian phenomenon is also noted in the text of Cardoso published in Scholem, *Studies and Texts*, p. 280. For an extended analysis of the role of prophecy and Nathan's messianic mission, see Scholem, *Sabbatai Ṣevi*, pp. 205–213, 224–233, 267–268; and the briefer comment in *Messianic Idea*, p. 60. This point is corroborated by external documentary evidence as well. Consider, for example, Michel Fèvre's account of Sabbatai Ṣevi transcribed in G. Saban, "Sabbatai Ṣevi as Seen by a Contemporary Traveller," *Jewish History* 7 (1993): 107 (corresponding English translation on p. 112). This non-Jewish author relates that what convinced the Jews of the veracity of Sabbatai Ṣevi's messianic claim was the rabbinic authority of Nathan of Gaza and his widespread reputation as a prophet. Needless to say, prophetic and paranormal tendencies are attributed to Sabbatai Ṣevi himself as part of his messianic portfolio. See *Zikkaron li-Venei Yisra'el*, p. 45. On the renewal of prophetic revelations associated with Sabbatai Ṣevi's professed messiahship, with special reference to the phenomenon of mass prophecy involving men, women, and children (particularly in Smyrna), see *Zikkaron li-Venei Yisra'el*, pp. 49–50; Jacob Sasportas, *Sefer Ṣiṣat Novel Ṣevi*, edited by I. Tishby (Jerusalem, 1954), pp. 60, 96, 147–148, 156, 182; Scholem, *Sabbatai Ṣevi*, pp. 254, 256–258, 417–426, 464–465, 532, 606–607, 707. Regarding the self-proclaimed prophetic status of Cardoso, see the remark of Sasportas, *Ṣiṣat Novel Ṣevi*,

I am also in general agreement with Scholem's contention regarding the messianic posture of the kabbalah promulgated by Luria and his colleagues in the wake of the Spanish expulsion.[12] With respect to the nature of the messianism implicit in Lurianic doctrine, however, I would take issue with Scholem's insistence that there is a necessary harmony between the symbolic understanding of redemption on the inner, spiritual plane and the reality of redemption in the national, political arena. In my judgment, Scholem did not go far enough, for the impact of the Spanish expulsion on Luria's thinking did not take the form of a messianic utopianism with a national

---

p. 368. On the prophetic nature of Cardoso's messianic calling, see, *op. cit.*, pp. 270–271, 289–291, 297; N. Yosha, "The Philosophical Elements in the Theology of Abraham Miguel Cardoso," MA. thesis, Hebrew University, 1985, p. 10 (in Hebrew). It must be pointed out, however, that in his disputations Cardoso emphasized the role of the intellect in discerning the mysteries of Godhead and downplayed the role of paranormal or revelatory experience. See, for example, I.R. Molho and A. Amarilio, "Autobiographical Letters of Abraham Cardozo," *Sefunot* 3–4 (1960): 233–234 (in Hebrew): "I have not made any student swear that he would conceal the secret, but rather they should discourse about what I have notified them by way of kabbalah, and not in accordance with what spiritual, angelic voices (*maggidim ruḥaniyyim*) told me, for with respect to the matter of the divine they have already heard from me that I do not believe in any spirit or angel, and not in Elijah or Meṭaṭron.... The ancients have said with respect to he who does not strive to know the secret of the faith of the Holy One, blessed be He, it is better for him not to have been created... From here it is known that every Jew has the ability to discern his Creator, for God has placed in his intellect the ability to discern him through the way of wisdom just as Abraham our patriarch accomplished, for he had no Torah, Prophets, or Writings." The mandate, therefore, is for every person to come to knowledge of God through the exercise of one's reason. Cardoso also affirms in his voluminous writings the position that the distinctive feature of the messiah is that he knows the divine nature from his own intellectual power of discernment and thus Abraham serves as the messianic prototype. See, for example, *Derush Ẓeh 'Eli Wa'anvehu*, in Scholem, *Studies and Texts*, pp. 340, 342, 356, 362–363. The rationalist orientation of Cardoso reflected in this document is noted by Scholem, *op. cit.*, p. 333. This approach is most fully developed in *Derush Ḥokhmat 'Avraham 'Avinu*, extant in MS New York, Jewish Theological Seminary of America 1677. By contrast, in the document of Cardoso published in Scholem, *Studies and Texts*, p. 280, the author remarks that Meṭaṭron, Elijah, angels, and prophets were revealed to him and to his students as a sign of the messianic redemption. On the presence of *maggidim* and prophets in the circle of Cardoso, see *op. cit.*, p. 285. To date, the most comprehensive treatment of the philosophic dimension of Cardoso's thinking is found in Yosha, "Philosophical Elements," and *idem*, "The Neoscholastic Terminology of Miguel Cardoso's Doctrine of Divinity," *Proceedings of the Eleventh International Congress on Jewish Studies*, sec. 3, vol. 2 (Jerusalem, 1994), pp. 77–84 (in Hebrew).

[12] Scholem, *Major Trends*, pp. 245–250, 284–286. For a critique of the Scholemian position regarding the link between the expulsion and Lurianic kabbalah, see Idel, *Kabbalah: New Perspectives*, pp. 265–266; *idem, Messianism and Mysticism*, pp. 72–77.

or political focus.[13] There is little evidence that in the later stages of his thinking Luria (or his disciples) understood the messianic quest in these terms. To be sure, these kabbalists employ the traditional language of a personal messiah and the anticipated return to the land and rebuilding of the Temple, but the attuned ear will understand that these expressions have been radically transformed in the crucible of theosophic symbolism.[14] The expulsion from the Iberian Peninsula at the end of the fifteenth century did not encourage Luria and his circle in sixteenth-century Safed to believe that the temporal redemption was near.[15] On the contrary, the sufferings of the exile, which is understood in kabbalistic terms as a spiritual and not merely spatial condition,[16] led to a pietistic and ascetic quietism[17]

[13] I am deliberately avoiding the issue of the identification of Luria and Vital as messianic figures, although I would just note in passing that these identifications support the hypothesis that messianic redemption propagated by this circle of kabbalists had little national or political application. Regarding these messianic identifications, see Ḥayyim Vital, *Shaʿar ha-Kawwanot* (Jerusalem, 1963), 37a; *Peri ʿEṣ Ḥayyim* (Jerusalem, 1980), pp. 245–246; *Sefer ha-Ḥezyonot*, edited by A. Aescoli (Jerusalem, 1954), pp. 5, 92–93, 106, 241–242; M. Benayahu, *The Toldedoth Ha-Ari and Luria's "Manner of Life" (Hanhagoth)* (Jerusalem, 1967), pp. 41, 64, 199, 258, 275 (in Hebrew); D. Tamar, "R. Isaac Luria and R. Ḥayyim Vital as the Messiah son of Joseph," *Sefunot* 7 (1963): 167–177 (in Hebrew); *idem*, "Messianic Dreams and Visions of R. Ḥayyim Vital," *Shalem* 4 (1984): 211–229 (in Hebrew). See also the studies of Meroz and Liebes cited below in n. 29.

[14] Tishby, *Doctrine of Evil*, pp. 142–143, remarked that redemption in Lurianic kabbalah is "first and foremost the redemption of good from the dominion of evil, and the transformation of all realms of being, including the human being, into a world that is entirely good." (Scholem, too, recognized that in the Lurianic texts the redemption is tantamount to the destruction of the forces of evil in the world. See *Major Trends*, p. 246; *Messianic Idea*, p. 47.) The national redemption, therefore, is principally the "liberation of the souls of Israel from the bonds of the shells, and the freedom from the yoke of enslavement to the foreign kingdoms is but an external symbol for the completion of internal processes." In accord with the orientation of Scholem, Tishby notes that the messianism in Lurianic kabbalah is transferred from the external sphere to the internal plane, but he goes beyond Scholem in emphasizing the marked indifference in these sources towards concrete issues related to a personal messianic figure. He thus concludes: "The messiah that is mentioned is almost always only an abstract concept."

[15] Scholem, *Major Trends*, pp. 244–251; *Sabbatai Ṣevi*, pp. 18–22; *Messianic Idea*, pp. 43–48.

[16] More specifically, the esoteric significance of exile refers to the imprisonment of the sparks in the demonic shells and the sustenance of those shells by the overflow of the divine efflux. See *Shaʿar ha-Gilgulim* (Jerusalem, 1903), § 21, 21a.

[17] The ascetic tendencies in sixteenth-century Safed have been discussed by a number of scholars. See Scholem, *Major Trends*, pp. 284–285; *Kabbalah*, p. 245; R.J. Zwi Werblowsky, *Joseph Karo: Lawyer and Mystic* (Philadelphia, 1977), pp. 38–83, 113–118, 133–139, 149–152, 161–165; M. Pachter, "The Concept of Devekut in the Homiletical Ethical Writings of Sixteenth Century Safed," in *Studies in Medieval*

and a rather negative, perhaps even gnostic, assessment of the physical world and human history.[18]

The real goal of the mystical path set forth by Luria in the advanced stages of his teaching was to overcome the fragmentation of finite existence. The coming of messiah is consequent to the obliteration of evil and impurity from the world, a process of purification that is mythically depicted as the extrication of the sparks of holiness (derived from the seven primordial kings of Edom who died)[19] from the limbs of the human form submerged in the depths of impurity, beginning with the head and culminating with the feet.[20] This

---

Jewish History and Literature, vol. 2, edited by I. Twersky (Cambridge, Mass., 1984), pp. 200–210; L. Fine, "Purifying the Body in the Name of the Soul: The Problem of the Body in Sixteenth-Century Kabbalah," in *People of the Body: Jews and Judaism From an Embodied Perspective*, edited by H. Eilberg-Shwartz (Albany, 1992), pp. 117–142; and D. Biale, *Eros and the Jews: From Biblical Israel to Contemporary America* (New York, 1992), pp. 113–118. In *Major Trends*, p. 286, Scholem described the "new moral idea of humanity" propagated by Lurianic kabbalah as the "ideal of the ascetic whose aim is the Messianic reformation, the extinction of the world's blemish, the restitution of all things in God." See also *Sabbatai Ṣevi*, p. 19. Despite his very accurate depiction of the connection between the messianic ideal and asceticism in Lurianic kabbalah, Scholem falls short of drawing the logical conclusion regarding the decidedly apolitical nature of this mystical notion of redemption.

[18] On the gnostic dimension of Lurianic kabbalah, associated primarily with a mythical tendency that is contrasted with a philosophical orientation, see Scholem, *Major Trends*, pp. 260, 267–268, 269, 279–280, 286; *Sabbatai Ṣevi*, p. 253; *Kabbalah*, pp. 74, 143; I. Tishby, "Gnostic Doctrines in Sixteenth Mysticism," *Journal of Jewish Studies* 6 (1955): 146–152. By using the term "gnostic" to characterize Lurianic kabbalah, neither Scholem nor Tishby meant to suggest an actual historical connection. The issue is rather the ideational and symbolic parallelism between ancient gnostic sources and Lurianic texts. Curiously, while both Scholem and Tishby duly note the gnostic dimension of the Lurianic notion of the cataclysm within the Godhead resulting in an exile of an aspect of the divine, neither one relates the gnostic character of Lurianic kabbalah to the desire to escape from corporeal existence, a fate that is linked to the doctrine of metempsychosis. On the comparison of Sabbatianism to ancient gnosticism, see Scholem, *Sabbatai Ṣevi*, pp. 312, 797; *Messianic Idea*, pp. 104–107.

[19] Following the lead of the *Zohar*, Luria and his disciples use the biblical image of the Edomite kings to refer to the unbalanced forces of judgment that must be discharged from the divine prior to the emanation of the holy forces. See Scholem, *Major Trends*, p. 266; Tishby, *Doctrine of Evil*, pp. 28–34. R. Meroz, "Redemption in the Lurianic Teaching," Ph.D. dissertation, Hebrew University, 1988, pp. 128–142 (in Hebrew), argues that the myth of the death of the Edomite kings is associated with the doctrine of the divine configurations in the second of the five stages of Luria's development.

[20] *Sha'ar Ma'amerei Rashbi* (Jerusalem, 1898), 34a–d; *'Eṣ Ḥayyim* (Jerusalem, 1910), 3:2, 17a; 19:3, 91c; 39:1, 65d; *Sha'ar ha-Gilgulim*, § 15, 16b. In several of these instances, the Lurianic idea is related exegetically to a messianic passage from *Zohar* 2:258a. Regarding this text, see E.R. Wolfson, "Images of God's Feet: Some Observations on the Divine Body in Judaism," in *People of the Body*, pp. 170–171. On the

is the esoteric significance attributed by Ḥayyim Vital to the rabbinic dictum, "The son of David will not come until all the souls in the body are consumed,"[21] i.e., the messiah will come only when all the sparks are uplifted and restored to the configuration of the primordial anthropos (*'adam qadmon*).

Prima facie, it might seem that the traditional idea of a personal messiah is preserved, for in this system the messianic figure heralds a new stage of history in which only the holy forces have dominion. Some texts may allow for such an interpretation, but others clearly suggest that the messianic coming is transformed into a figurative trope that signifies the cessation of the historical process rather than the inauguration of a new epoch, for the liberation of the sparks results in the elevation of the various planes of being (referred to in the technical terminology of the kabbalah as the four worlds of emanation [*'aṣilut*], creation [*beri'ah*], formation [*yeṣirah*], and doing [*'asiyyah*])[22] to their infinite source in the Godhead.[23] The messianic era is thus depicted as the time of ascent (*'aliyyah*) and integration (*hitkallelut*) of all of the worlds, when *Malkhut*, divine kingship, shall be restored as the crown on the head.[24]

---

description of coming of the messiah consequent to the purification of all evil from the divine image, see *'Eṣ Ḥayyim*, 49:3 (parallel in *Qehillat Ya'aqov* [Jerusalem, 1992], p. 83).

[21] B. Yevamot 62a.

[22] On the kabbalistic doctrine of the four worlds, see G. Scholem, "On the Development of the Concept of Worlds in the Early Kabbalah," *Tarbiz* 2 (1930): 415–442; 3 (1931): 33–66 (in Hebrew). For brief discussions of this notion in Lurianic kabbalah, see Scholem, *Major Trends*, pp. 272–273; *Kabbalah*, pp. 119, 137, 142.

[23] *Sha'ar ha-Kawwanot*, 59a–b. See Meroz, "Redemption in the Lurianic Kabbalah," pp. 14, 17, 370. Tacitly elaborating the position of Scholem, Meroz concludes that with the development of Luria's teaching the cosmic perspective regarding redemption overcomes the political to the point that the former emerges as the real goal, which entails the elevation and restoration of all things in their ontic source.

[24] A foretaste of the messianic reality is experienced on the Sabbath, which is described by Vital and other disciples of Luria as a time when all the worlds ascend and are bound together as one ontic unity. See *Sha'ar ha-Kawwanot*, 62b; *Sha'ar Ma'amerei Rashbi*, 37d; *Peri 'Eṣ Ḥayyim*, p. 378; *Sefer ha-Derushim* (Jerusalem, 1996), p. 141; *Derushei ha-Kawwanot le-Rabbi Yosef 'ibn Tabul*, edited by Y. Avivi, *Studies in Memory of the Rishon Le-Zion R. Yitzhak Nissim*, edited by M. Benayahu (Jerusalem, 1985), vol. 4, pp. 93–94; *Sefer Kawwanot Gedolot*, MS Oxford, Bodleian Library 1701, fol. 101a; Moses Yonah, *Kanfei Yonah*, MS Sassoon 993, pp. 537–538, 548–551, 561–563; Scholem, *Major Trends*, p. 275. Needless to say, many more examples could have been provided, but in the present context the ones I have cited will suffice to illustrate the point. It should be noted, however, that the characterization of Sabbath in terms of the ascent of the divine gradations is a motif found in earlier sources, especially in zoharic texts, and it played an important role in the

Scholem is certainly correct, therefore, when he characterizes redemption in the Lurianic kabbalah as "synonymous with emendation or restoration," but I think he errs when he further describes redemption as signifying "the perfect state, a flawless and harmonious world in which everything occupies its proper place."[25] On the contrary, restoration entails the elevation of the worlds to the Infinite rather than the constitution of a perfect world in space and time.[26] Moreover, as I have suggested in several studies, the unity of rectification (*tiqqun*) is expressed in terms of the overcoming of gender dimorphism, the condition of being that came about through the division of the primordial (male) androgyne (i.e., the process whereby the female is contained in the male in the aspect of the male) into male and female.[27] The most telling image to describe the state of reconstituted androgyny is the elevation of the female to the position of the crown, which is depicted alternatively as the corona of the phallus, the crown of the husband, or the crown worn by the righteous in the world to come.[28]

Needless to say, I am not denying that the messianic rectification is described in terms of the standard kabbalistic emphasis on the unification of male and female, a point generally acknowledged by scholars.[29] But beyond the union of male and female, there is a

---

different stages of Luria's thinking about the nature of redemption. See Meroz, "Redemption in the Lurianic Kabbalah," pp. 118–121, 171–176.

[25] *Messianic Idea*, p. 47.

[26] On the essential connection of the secret of redemption (*sod ha-ge'ullah*) and the elevation of the feminine forces from the demonic realm by means of the phallic gradation of *Yesod*, see *Peri 'Eṣ Ḥayyim*, p. 209.

[27] Wolfson, *Circle in the Square*, pp. 116–119; "Coronation of the Sabbath Bride: Kabbalistic Myth and the Ritual of Androgynisation," *Journal of Jewish Thought and Philosophy* 6 (1997) pp. 301–344; "*Tiqqun ha-Shekhinah*: Redemption and the Overcoming of Gender Dimorphism in the Messianic Kabbalah of Moses Hayyim Luzzatto," *History of Religions* 36 (1997): 289–332; "Re/membering the Covenant: Memory, Forgetfulness, and the Construction of History in the *Zohar*," to appear in the Festschrift in honor of Yosef Hayyim Yerushalmi. See also Meroz, "Redemption in the Lurianic Kabbalah," p. 125.

[28] *Sha'ar ha-Haqdamot* (Jerusalem, 1909), 28c; *Mavo' She'arim* (Jerusalem, 1903), 2.3:2, 12a; *'Eṣ Ḥayyim*, 1:1, 14c; 10:3, 48d; 14:2, 70d; *Sha'ar ha-Kawwanot*, 18d; *Peri 'Eṣ Ḥayyim*, pp. 158 and 458 (parallel in *Sefer Kawwanot Gedolot*, MS Oxford, Bodleian Library 1701, fol. 45b); *'Arba' Me'ot Sheqel Kesef* (Cracow, 1886), 27c–d; *Sefer ha-Derushim*, pp. 28, 30. In *Sefer ha-Ḥezyonot*, p. 186, Vital identifies the aspect of *Malkhut* within *'Atiq Yomin*, the uppermost configuration, as the encompassing light (*'or ha-maqif*), which is the element of the feminine that rises above the masculine. On the ascent of *Malkhut* to the Infinite, see Meroz, "Redemption in the Lurianic Kabbalah," pp. 208–211.

[29] See Tishby, *Doctrine of Evil*, pp. 139–140; Scholem, *Sabbatai Ṣevi*, p. 17. The

unity wherein the female is contained in the male and the male in the female, a unity, that is, wherein the gender dimorphism is transcended through the constitution of the one, male androgyny. To illustrate the point I will refer here to the description of the two kinds of unification offered by Ephraim Penzieri, a disciple of Vital, in his account of the three aspects of *Keter*,[30] the first of the ten luminous emanations, which is the crown: One kind of union entails the integration of two lights in one instrument (*shenikhlalim shenayim bi-kheli ʾeḥad*). In this state, the "lights are contained one within the other in the mystery of male and female, and they illuminate one another, the male in the female and also the female in the male. Thus there are four letters of *ʾahavah*."[31] Eros, *ʾahavah*, is configured by the male and female and the two ways of relating that pertain between them, the male in the female or the female in the male.[32]

There is another kind of union, however, wherein the "two lights are integrated without an instrument" (*shenikhlalim shenei ʾorot bilti keli*). In this state, "the male and the female of *Keter*, when they do not touch *Keter*, ascend to their source above, for within the mouth there is a root for these ten lights, from *Keter* to *Malkhut*." In its elevation, the light of *Keter* "does not return anymore to *Keter*, but it remains beneath the root of *Malkhut*, and from there it shines upon the ten lights, and according to the actions of the lower beings so shall be their illumination." When the lower beings desire to receive the efflux, "the male and the female, which are within *Keter*, ascend to the place of the light of *Keter* that is beneath the root of *Malkhut*. And if the light of *Keter* is greater than them in stature such that they cannot stand together in one place, then the light of *Keter* ascends

heterosexual nature of the messianic rectification has been emphasized as well in two of the more recent treatments of the idea of redemption in the Lurianic kabbalah: Meroz, "Redemption in the Lurianic Kabbalah," and Y. Liebes, "'Two Young Roes of a Doe': The Secret Sermon of Isaac Luria Before His Death," *Jerusalem Studies in Jewish Thought* 10 (1992): 113–169 (in Hebrew). See *idem*, "The Messiah of the *Zohar*," in *The Messianic Idea in Jewish Thought: A Study Conference in Honour of the Eightieth Birthday of Gershom Scholem* (Jerusalem, 1982), pp. 109–110 (in Hebrew).

[30] Penzieri's comments correspond to the discourse included in *ʿEṣ Ḥayyim* 7:4, 33b–c, and parallel in *Sefer ha-Derushim*, pp. 71–72.

[31] Introduction to *Sefer ha-Derushim*, p. 7.

[32] A source for the Lurianic interpretation of the word *ʾahavah* may have been the discussion of this term, connected more specifically with the union of spirits (*devequt de-ruḥaʾ be-ruḥaʾ*) occasioned by the kiss of the mouth (exegetically linked to Song of Songs 1:2) in *Zohar* 1:146a–b. In that context, moreover, the four letters of the word *ʾahavah* are related to the Tetragrammaton.

to the place of the root of *Malkhut*, and since *Malkhut* is greater than *Keter*, for the one is the root and the other the branch, *Malkhut* ascends to the place of *Yesod*, and then the two roots are in one place and the root of *Keter* is aroused to disseminate upon them."[33] The ascent of the male and the female within *Keter* in order to receive the overflow triggers the emanation of light from *Keter* to the light of *Keter*, and then to the male and the female. As a result of the overflow, male and female are united, and the three are equal in the one gradation. Afterwards the light of *Ḥokhmah* descends to the place of *Binah* in order to overflow upon the branch of *Ḥokhmah*, and, consequently, the root of *Malkhut* descends from the aspect of *Yesod* to her place, and *Keter* assumes its position beneath *Malkhut*. But this state, too, is described as a unity of three, for *Keter*, the male, and the female stand together in one place. "Then the male is contained in the female for she receives from the root of *Ḥokhmah*, and he is beneath her, in the secret of 'a capable wife who is a crown for her husband' (Prov. 12:4)."[34]

The elevation of *Keter* to *Malkhut* results in the ascent of *Malkhut* to the aspect of *Yesod* (the containment of the female in the male), whereas the descent of *Keter* beneath *Malkhut* results in the metamorphosis of the feminine into the aspect of the crown (the containment of the male in the female). The attribution of the crown to the feminine indicates a state wherein the female rules over the male, which is to be contrasted both with the exilic state wherein the female is beneath the male and the beginning of the rectified state wherein there is a face to face union of male and female such that the two are equal in stature.[35] I would emphasize here (as I have in previous work) that the ultimate consequence of the union of male and female for the latter is that she is restored to her ontic source in the male, and more specifically in the form of the penial corona.[36] In this state, heterosexual union gives way to an ideal of

---

[33] *Sefer ha-Derushim*, pp. 7–8.

[34] *Ibid.*, p. 8.

[35] See *Sha'ar Ma'amerei Rashbi*, 5a; *Sefer ha-Derushim*, pp. 39–40, 153.

[36] On coitus as the masculinization of the female, see Wolfson, *Circle in the Square*, pp. 92–98. From this perspective circumcision serves as the ultimate symbol for redemption insofar as it is by means of this rite that the feminine as the sign of the covenant (the letter *yod*) is disclosed in the exposure of the corona. Analogously, in the redemptive state the female is restored to this position. See the "secret of circumcision" (*sod ha-milah*) according to the teaching of Luria in the version of *Sha'ar ha-Nevu'ah we-Ruaḥ ha-Qodesh*, MS New York, Jewish Theological Seminary of America

unity that transcends the erotic yearning of one sex for the other, or in the words of Penzieri, a union of the two without an instrument. Through this union the aspect of *Malkhut* is elevated to the position wherein it rectifies the primordial death of the kings (*mitat ha-melakhim*) and the shattering of the vessels (*shevirat ha-kelim*).[37] The psychosexual dynamic of bondage/release at this stage is expressed in the ascetic abrogation of carnal sexuality.[38]

9005, fol. 35a: "When one pulls back the membrane, one should concentrate on the disclosure of the corona (*'aṭarah*), which is the image of a *yod*, the seal in the small body (*guf qaṭan*), from the name Shaddai, for beforehand the *yod* was concealed. . . . Through the pulling back of the membrane the *yod* is revealed, and thus [is formed the name] Shaddai."

[37] See Y. Jacobson, "The Aspect of the Feminine in the Lurianic Kabbalah," in *Gershom Scholem's Major Trends in Jewish Mysticism 50 Years After: Proceedings of the Sixth International Conference on the History of Jewish Mysticism*, edited by P. Schäfer and J. Dan (Berlin, 1993), pp. 250–255; Wolfson, *Circle in the Square*, pp. 116–117.

[38] On the role of sexual renunication in kabbalistic doctrine and practice, see E.R. Wolfson, "Eunuchs Who Keep the Sabbath: Becoming Male and the Ascetic Ideal in Thirteenth-Century Jewish Mysticism," in *Becoming Male in the Middle Ages*, edited by J. Cohen and B. Wheeler (New York, 1997), pp. 151–185. It lies beyond the scope of this study to provide a detailed account of the nexus between asceticism and redemption. Such an account will appear as part of my chapter on eroticism and asceticism in a forthcoming monograph on eros and the construction of gender in kabbalistic ritual and myth. Suffice it to note here that descriptions of the world-to-come in kabbalistic literature are often predicated on the fact that the great Sabbath is beyond the union of male and female, which is characteristic of Sabbath itself. The ascetic dimension is highlighted in kabbalistic literature by the identification of the world-to-come and *Binah*, which is also identified as Yom Kippur, a day in which physical pleasures are prohibited. A particularly important passage in this regard is *Zohar* 2:116a (*Ra'aya' Meheimna'*): "Therefore, on Yom Kippur . . . sexual intercourse is forbidden. There the sign of the covenant, which is the *yod*, is the crown on the Torah scroll (*taga' 'al sefer torah*) . . . as it has been established [B. Berakhot 17a], 'In the world-to-come there is no eating, drinking, or sexual intercourse. Rather the righteous sit with their crowns upon their heads.' Since there is no intercourse (*shimmush*) in this world with the crown (*taga'*), the masters of the Mishnah established [M. 'Avot 1:13], 'the one who makes use of the crown perishes' (*kol ha-mishtammesh be-taga' ḥalaf*)." In this context, the sexual abstinence required on Yom Kippur is linked explicitly with the feminine assuming the posture of the crown. The eschatological image of the righteous sitting with crowns on their heads is thus interpreted as a symbolic depiction of their celibacy. This dynamic is reflected in the course of the normal Sabbath, for the emphasis on heterosexual intercourse, which relates specifically to the elevation of the feminine *Malkhut* on Sabbath eve (see *Peri 'Eṣ Ḥayyim*, p. 393), gives way to ascetic renunciation, which is reflective of the ontic status of the divine potencies on the afternoon of Sabbath, i.e., the "time of favor" (*'et raṣon*) when (following the symbolic language of the Idrot sections of the *Zohar*) the supernal will of *'Atiqa' Qadisha'* shines upon the forehead of *Ze'eir 'Anpin*. According to the Lurianic application of the zoharic imagery, at this time *Ze'eir 'Anpin* ascends to the beard of *'Arikh 'Anpin*, while *Nuqba'* remains in the bosom of *'Abba'*. See *Sha'ar ha-Kawwanot*, 75a–b; *Peri 'Eṣ Ḥayyim*, pp. 403, 441; *Kanfei Yonah*, MS Sassoon 993, p. 563. In effect, therefore, the union

By way of summary, we may say that, for Luria, the messianic theme of the ingathering of the exiles did not signify primarily the return of the Jewish people to the concrete land of Israel, but the reintegration of the scattered soul sparks of the fractured divine anthropos.[39] The reconfiguration of the anthropomorphic divine form signals the end of history, marked by the ontic restoration of all particularity in the one that is beyond limit. Expressed from the vantage point of human consciousness, the soteriological teaching of Luria is predicated on the presumption that right action affords the soul the opportunity to complete the cycle of birth and death and thereby escape the wheel of transmigration.[40] The eschatological task is to be redeemed from rather than in historical time.

As I noted above, Scholem contrasted Lurianic kabbalah and Sabbatianism on the grounds that in the latter, unlike the former, the symbolic sense of redemption was severed from its concrete manifestation in history. Scholem astutely perceived that the Sabbatian ideal of redemption is principally spiritual/individualistic rather than political/nationalistic.[41] Clearly, in the mind of Sabbatian thinkers,

---

at this moment is that of the lower male and the upper male. On the homoerotic nature of this intrasefirotic dynamic, see Wolfson, *Circle in the Square*, pp. 196–197 n. 6. The link between asceticism and redemption is highlighted as well in the following contrast between the first and seventh nights of Passover: On the first night carnal intercourse is prohibited because the union between the masculine and the feminine aspects of God was complete and the aspect of *Yesod* was in an enlarged state (*gadlut*), whereas on the seventh night intercourse is permissible since the union is incomplete. See *Peri ʿEṣ Ḥayyim*, p. 517. Regarding the messianic implications of the seventh night of Passover, see Liebes, "Messiah of the *Zohar*," pp. 109–110 n. 97; "'Two Young Roes of a Doe'," p. 142; Meroz, "Redemption in the Lurianic Kabbalah," pp. 306–315.

39 See Scholem, *Major Trends*, pp. 278–280.

40 That the ultimate purpose of *gilgul ha-neshamot*, the reincarnation of souls, is the elevation of the souls from their imprisonment in the demonic realm and their restoration to the divine is underscored by the reenactment of this drama on every eve of Sabbath. See *Peri ʿEṣ Ḥayyim*, p. 403. Scholem, *Major Trends*, pp. 281–283, discusses the Lurianic doctrine of transmigration as part of the process of *tiqqun*, but he does not go far enough in understanding how the ultimate goal of the restoration is the cessation of the wheel of reincarnation, which leads to the end of the cycle of birth and death, i.e., the end of temporal existence governed by generation and corruption. A difficult problem, which I will mention here with no attempt at a resolution, is the meaning that would be accorded the traditional notion of resurrection of the dead, a doctrine that is indeed affirmed in the relevant sources. For example, see *Mavoʾ Sheʿarim*, 2.3:7, 15b. How this doctrine is to be squared with the emphasis of overcoming the wheel of metempsychosis is a problem that would require an extensive analysis, which lies beyond the scope of this paper.

41 See also Y. Liebes, "Sabbatean Mysticism," *Peʿamim* 40 (1989): 4–20 (in Hebrew); English version in *idem*, *Studies in Jewish Myth and Jewish Messianism*, translated by

the inner aspect of redemption is based on a substantial change in the external nature of reality as a whole such that the primordial fissure of the divine is mended and all the forces of being are realigned in a configuration of true unity. But the rupture between fact and fiction, truth and image, so prevalent in Sabbatian theology, titled the balance of interpretation. Concern for the inward condition far outweighs concern for how the spiritual ideal would be practically implemented. As I will argue, moreover, the critical metaphysical change is linked to the symbol of the crown, which figures prominently in the Sabbatian doctrine of redemption, specifically as it relates to the presumed coronation of Sabbatai Ṣevi and those who gave witness to his messianic calling.

Myth of Coronation in Sabbatian Theology

The focus of the remainder of this study is on the rite of Sabbatai Ṣevi's coronation and Sabbatian myth. By the coronation of Sabbatai Ṣevi I have in mind his putting on the turban, which is related in some accounts to the moment of conversion that arose in his meeting with the Turkish authorities (including Meḥmed Van Effendi, the chief preacher of the sultan) in Adrianople on September 16, 1666. In its simplest meaning, as scholars have generally noted,[42] the image of Sabbatai Ṣevi's setting the turban on his head, which is expressed in the language of Zechariah 3:5, signifies his conversion to Islam, for the turban was the Muslim headgear forbidden to Jews in the Ottoman empire.[43] In a recent study, David Halperin has noted that the coronation of Sabbatai Ṣevi in the turban (*miṣnefet*) of the sultan, together with his putting on a special robe (*levush*), indicate that the heroic figure has undergone a promotion that involves an ontic transformation. Halperin suggests that the literary model for the description of Sabbatai Ṣevi's promotion was the legend of

---

B. Stein (Albany, 1993), pp. 93–106; Idel, *Messianism and Mysticism*, pp. 80–83. To date, the fullest discussion of the Sabbatian phenomenon in terms of spiritual redemption and religious renewal is A. Elqayam, "The Mystery of Faith in the Writings of Nathan of Gaza," Ph.D. dissertation, Hebrew University, 1993 (in Hebrew).

[42] See Scholem, *Sabbatai Ṣevi*, p. 707 n. 52.

[43] I owe this insight to D.J. Halperin, "Sabbatai Zevi, Meṭaṭron, and Mehmed: Myth and History in Seventeenth-Century Judaism," in *The Seductiveness of Jewish Myth: Challenge or Response?*, edited by S. Daniel Breslauer (forthcoming). I thank the author for providing me with a copy of his study prior to its publication.

Enoch's transformation into Meṭaṭron in early Hekhalot literature, especially *3 Enoch*.[44] There is indeed much evidence to support Halperin's thesis, for Sabbatian documents (theological treatises, liturgical commentaries, and amulets) are replete with references to the fact that Sabbatai Ṣevi is the earthly representation of Meṭaṭron. This is underscored, for instance, by the fact that the numerical value of the full spelling of the name Shaddai is 814, which is the numerical value of the name Sabbatai Ṣevi.[45] The three letters of the name Shaddai also equal 314, which is the numerical value of the name Meṭaṭron. The former numerology only makes sense in light of the latter, that is, the attempt of Sabbatians to link Sabbatai Ṣevi and Shaddai reflects their assumption that the messiah is the mundane manifestation of that angel.[46] For instance, according to the testimony of Azariah ha-Levi, cited by Cardoso in a lengthy autobiographical epistle recounting his activities until 1702, Sabbatai Ṣevi himself repeatedly (the exact figure mentioned is 100 times) instructed some of his followers that "in the future he would govern the supernal and lower realms, elevated above Meṭaṭron, and thus they understood that he would ascend to the level of God."[47] In this context, Cardoso is critical of those Sabbatians who blurred the ontological boundary separating the human Sabbatai Ṣevi and the divine level that is above the angelic Meṭaṭron; according to these Sabbatians, this ontic identification implied the apotheosis of the messiah into

---

[44] See reference in previous note.

[45] See Scholem, *Sabbatai Ṣevi*, pp. 234, 240 n. 115, and 512 (citing the letter of Samuel Primo, Sabbatai Ṣevi's secretary in Gallipoli, published in Sasportas, *Ṣiṣat Novel Ṣevi*, p. 129, and in *Zikkaron li-Venei Yisra'el*, p. 56); the *hanhagot* of Nathan of Gaza published by M. Benayahu, *The Shabbatean Movement in Greece* [*Sefunot* 14] (1971–1977): 277–278, and further references cited in n. 4. Concerning the identification of Sabbatai Ṣevi and Meṭaṭron, see the comment of Abraham Yakhini discussed by Scholem, *Sabbatai Ṣevi*, p. 879 n. 125. Consider also the remark of Hosea Nantawa cited by Sasportas, *Ṣiṣat Novel Ṣevi*, p. 156: "R. Nathan Ashkenazi the prophet . . . wrote concerning our lord, may his glory be elevated, that 'his name is like the name of his Master' [the description of Meṭaṭron in B. Sanhedrin 38b], Shabbatai Ṣevi has the numerical value of Shaddai written out in full, *shy''n dl''t yw''d*." See the response of Sasportas, *op. cit.*, p. 178.

[46] On the description of Sabbatai Ṣevi as an angelic being, see the account of Leib ben Ozer in Emden, *Torat ha-Qena'ot*, 2a: "The appearance of his face was like that of an angel of God verily, and none could look upon his face, for 'the skin of his face was radiant' (Exod. 34:29)." The parallel in *The Story of Shabbetay Zevi by R. Leib ben R. Ozer Amsterdam*, p. 6, emphasizes the luminous quality of Sabbatai Ṣevi's visage without specifying his angelic status.

[47] Molho and Amarilio, "Autobiographical Letters," p. 203.

the higher aspect of Meṭaṭron.[48] In another epistle, written to his disciples in Smyrna sometime after 1700, Cardoso reports his own visionary experiences according to which the special relation between Sabbatai Ṣevi and Meṭaṭron is affirmed: "When Meṭaṭron departed and descended to talk to me, he left his place to Sabbatai Ṣevi, may his splendor be elevated, [and he adorned him] in a turban (*be-miṣnefet*), and to Ro'shi, who was my angelic mentor (*maggid*), in a hat that is called *somrero*, and they extended the discussion with me for about half an hour."[49] This passage is particularly relevant insofar as the ontic identification of Sabbatai Ṣevi and Meṭaṭron is expressed in terms of the headgear that is bestowed upon the human messianic figure by the priestly angel. Sabbatai Ṣevi's receiving of the hat, referred to by the Hebrew *miṣnefet*, from Meṭaṭron parallels

---

[48] Cf. Cardoso's characterization of the belief of some of the supporters of Sabbatai Ṣevi in Salonica that he presents in another epistle, published by Molho and Amarilio, "Autobiographical Letters," p. 211: "The messiah is fully divine, and [he is] Meṭaṭron as well, and all the more so is he the absolute Samael, for the divine *sefirot* of *Malkhut* of [the world of] emanation are clothed within him and through them he is aggrandized and exalted." The text is cited (in a slightly different translation) and analyzed by Halperin, "Sabbatai Ẓevi, Meṭaṭron, and Meḥmed." Cardoso repeatedly attacked those Sabbatians who attributed a divine status to Meṭaṭron. See, e.g., Molho and Amarilio, "Autobiographical Letters," pp. 191 and 195. It is reasonable to assume that underlying Cardoso's comments is an implicit identification of Meṭaṭron and Jesus, on the one hand, and the Jewish messiah and the Christian savior, on the other hand. At the very least, it is clear that in Cardoso's mind the belief in Sabbatai Ṣevi's divinity is on a par with the Christological doctrine of incarnation. Consider, for example, Cardoso's remark in an untitled work extant in MS New York, Jewish Theological Seminary of America Mic. 1723, fols. 135b–136a; and the passage from *Derush ha-Kinnuyim* published in Scholem, *Researches*, pp. 415–416. See Scholem, *Messianic Idea*, p. 107. With respect to several doctrinal issues, including the suffering of the messiah, salvation through faith, the incarnation of the messiah, the second coming of the messianic figure, the Trinity, antinomianism, and the mystical rationalization of historical crisis, it has been suggested that Sabbatianism may have been influenced by Christianity. See Scholem, *Major Trends*, p. 307; *Sabbatai Ṣevi*, pp. 282–286, 332–354, 545–548, 795–799; *Messianic Idea*, pp. 123–125; C. Wirszubski, *Between the Lines: Kabbalah, Christian Kabbalah, and Sabbatianism*, edited by M. Idel (Jerusalem, 1990), p. 131; Y.H. Yerushalmi, *From Spanish Court to Italian Ghetto Isaac Cardoso: A Study in Seventeenth-Century Marranism and Jewish Apologetics* (New York and London, 1971), p. 307 n. 11; Sharot, *Messianism, Mysticism, and Magic*, p. 120. For a detailed discussion of the applicability of the doctrine of incarnation to Sabbatian theology, see Scholem, *Researches*, pp. 359–374. On the suffering messiah, see the letter of Abraham Cardoso to his brother, Isaac, printed in Jacob Sasportas, *Ṣiṣat Novel Ṣevi*, pp. 291–292, and the analysis of this document in Yerushalmi, *From Spanish Court to Italian Ghetto*, pp. 314–320.

[49] "Autobiographical Letters," p. 192. On the role of Sabbatai Ṣevi as the *maggid* of Cardoso, see the comment of Scholem, *Researches*, p. 427 n. 7. On the use of the abbreviation *ro'shi* for the name of Cardoso's *maggid*, see the comments of Scholem, *Researches*, pp. 430–431. I am grateful to David Halperin for this reference.

the donning of the maggid in a *sombrero*, and thus it signifies his angelic transformation.

It is likely, therefore, that the prototype for the Sabbatian writers was indeed the figure of Enoch-Meṭaṭron. However, it is necessary to contextualize better the identification of Sabbatai Ṣevi and Meṭaṭron in terms of the complex kabbalistic symbolism absorbed by Sabbatian thinkers. Simply put, Meṭaṭron is the two-faced being, fallen angel and risen god.[50] The duplicity is represented by a number of images, including the bipolarity of the symbol of the bow, shrouded in darkness in a state of exile but cloaked in luminosity when redeemed,[51]

---

[50] The doublefaced nature of Meṭaṭron as angel and god, related by some authors to the double spelling of the name with six or seven letters, is one of the root ideas in Jewish esotericism. See E.R. Wolfson, *Through a Speculum That Shines: Vision and Imagination in Medieval Jewish Mysticism* (Princeton, 1994), pp. 228, 255–263 (the two ways of spelling the name are discussed on p. 261, and see references given in n. 312). According to most kabbalists, the spelling with seven letters (the extra letter is the *yod*) corresponds to the upper aspect of Meṭaṭron, which relates to the *Shekhinah*. An interesting exception is Moses Cordovero who assigns this spelling to the angelic form of Meṭaṭron, which corresponds to the phallic dimension of the *ṣaddiq* in whom the *Shekhinah* is garbed during the week so that there is unity between male and female. Cordovero thus describes the angel Meṭaṭron as the "corporeal righteous male" (*ṣaddiq gashmi*) who assumes the role of the female waters below for he induces the overflow of the male waters from the *ṣaddiq* above (*Yesod*). Meṭaṭron is called *sar ha-panim* (literally, "archon of the faces") because (like *Yesod*) he unites the face of the male and the face of the female. See *Pardes Rimmonim* (Jerusalem, 1962), 16:4, 79a, and 23:13, 27b, s.v. Meṭaṭron; *Tiqqunei Zohar ʿim Perush ʾOr Yaqar*, vol. 2 (Jerusalem, 1973), pp. 139–141; *Zohar ʿim Perush ʾOr Yaqar*, vol. 9 (Jerusalem, 1976), p. 128, and vol. 11 (Jerusalem, 1981), p. 62. On the phallic nature of Meṭaṭron in Cordovero's writings, see also *Zohar ʿim Perush ʾOr Yaqar*, vol. 5 (Jerusalem, 1970), p. 162; *Tiqqunei Zohar ʿim Perush ʾOr Yaqar*, vol. 2, p. 222. Cordovero's position reflects the particular influence of the later strata of zoharic literature. See *Zohar* 3:228b (*Raʿayaʾ Meheimnaʾ*); *Tiqqunei Zohar*, edited by R. Margaliot (Jerusalem, 1978), Introduction, 4a and 7a; 70, 119b. Regarding the symbolic association of Meṭaṭron and the phallus, see below, n. 60. On the homologous relationship of Meṭaṭron and the *Shekhinah*, see *Zohar* 2:94a–b. In that context, Meṭaṭron is identified as the "body of the princess" as well as the "maidservant of the *Shekhinah*." See also *Tiqqunei Zohar*, Introduction, 114b; *Zohar Ḥadash*, edited by R. Margaliot (Jerusalem, 1978), 117a (*Tiqqunim*). During the weekdays the *Shekhinah* is garbed in the image of the servant and maidservant, the masculine and feminine aspects of Meṭaṭron, but on Sabbath the *Shekhinah* ascends and is divested of these angelic garments. The double nature of Meṭaṭron is also implied in *Zohar* 2:131a.

[51] *Zohar* 1:72b, 117a; 3:215a–b (*Raʿayaʾ Meheimnaʾ*); *Tiqqunei Zohar* 18, 36b. For discussion of the eschatological significance of the symbol of the rainbow, related especially to the gender transformation of the *Shekhinah* on her way out of exile, see Wolfson, "Re/membering the Covenant." On the androgynous nature of the symbol of the rainbow, see Wolfson, *Through a Speculum That Shines*, pp. 334 n. 30, 337–338 n. 40, 340–341 n. 48, 368–369 n. 149. On the relation of Meṭaṭron and the rainbow, see Wolfson, *Along the Path*, p. 137 n. 165; *Through a Speculum that Shines*, pp. 334, 337–338 n. 40.

the female throne elevated to the masculine crown,[52] the heel of Jacob contrasted with the head of Israel.[53] The twofold nature of Meṭaṭron is linked in the later strata of zoharic literature with the duality of good and evil,[54] symbolized by the Tree of Knowledge,[55] the Torah of Creation in contrast to the Torah of Emanation, also related to the Oral Torah or the Mishnah, which is predicated on the distinction between what is forbidden and what is permissible,[56] and the rod of Moses that turns into the serpent.[57] Particularly significant is the last image, for the metamorphosis of the serpent into the rod is related in some of the relevant passages to the messianic function attributed to Moses, the figure of the redeemer who mediates between the messiah son of Joseph and the messiah son of David.[58] Additionally, it is evident from at least one text that the

---

[52] On the identification of the throne and crown in German Pietistic esoteric lore and the kabbalistic symbolism, see Wolfson, *Along the Path*, p. 43, and further references given on p. 166 n. 279.

[53] The representation of the female by the heel of Jacob in contrast to the representation of the male by the head of Israel is a kabbalistic notion that has its roots in older Jewish esoteric lore, attested, for example, by the secret teaching of the German Pietists and the explicit pronouncement by Abraham Abulafia. See Wolfson, *Along the Path*, pp. 21–22, 135–136 n. 156. On the elevation of Meṭaṭron to the place of Jacob, and the consequent transformation of the name Shaddai to YHWH, see *Zohar* 1:149a (*Sitrei Torah*). In that context, Meṭaṭron ascends from the gradation of *Yesod*, represented by Shaddai, to that of *Tif'eret*, the place of Jacob to which is assigned the Tetragrammaton. On the specific application of the names "Jacob" and "Israel" to Sabbatai Ṣevi, see the letter of Sabbatai Ṣevi published by A. Amarillo, "Sabbatean Documents from the Saul Amarillo Collection," *Sefunot* 5 (1961): 252 (in Hebrew), and analysis in Y. Liebes, *On Sabbateanism and its Kabbalah: Collected Essays* (Jerusalem, 1995), pp. 187–188 (in Hebrew).

[54] See P. Giller, *The Enlightened Will Shine: Symbolization and Theurgy in the Later Strata of the Zohar* (Albany, 1993), pp. 41, 54, 72–73.

[55] *Zohar* 1:27a (*Tiqqunim*); 3:124b (*Ra'aya' Meheimna'*), 277a (*Ra'aya' Meheimna'*); *Tiqqunei Zohar* 40, 80b; 66, 97a–b; 67, 98a; 69, 99b, 109a; 70, 133b; *Zohar Ḥadash*, 106c (*Tiqqunim*); Y. Liebes, *Sections of the Zohar Lexicon* (Jerusalem, 1976), pp. 109–110, 124 (in Hebrew); Giller, *Enlightened Will Shine*, pp. 41–42, 85, 116. In some contexts, the duality of the good and evil in the Tree of Knowledge refers respectively to Meṭaṭron and Samael rather than to two aspects of Meṭaṭron. See *Zohar* 2:115a (*Ra'aya' Meheimna'*); *Tiqqunei Zohar* 53, 87b.

[56] *Zohar* 1:27a (*Tiqqunim*); 3:29b (*Ra'aya' Meheimna'*); *Tiqqunei Zohar*, Introduction, 14b; 40, 80b; *Zohar Ḥadash*, 106c (*Tiqqunim*); G. Scholem, *On the Kabbalah and Its Symbolism*, translated by R. Manheim (New York, 1969), pp. 68–70; I. Tishby, *The Wisdom of the Zohar*, translated by D. Goldstein (Oxford, 1989), pp. 1101–1108; Giller, *Enlightened Will Shine*, pp. 41, 59–63, 72–77.

[57] *Zohar* 1:27a (*Tiqqunim*), 263a; 3:255a (*Ra'aya' Meheimna'*), 277a (*Ra'aya' Meheimna'*); *Tiqqunei Zohar* 60, 93b; 67, 98a; 69, 108b; 70, 133a.

[58] *Zohar* 1:25b, 27a, 263a. Also relevant is the fact that Sabbatai Ṣevi identified himself as the serpent, in part related to the numerical equivalence of the Hebrew words for serpent and messiah, *naḥash* and *mashiaḥ*. See Scholem, *Sabbatai Ṣevi*, pp.

transfiguration of the serpent into the rod is understood in terms of the gender transformation from female to male.[59] The elevated nature of Meṭaṭron corresponds, therefore, to the rod of Moses that is connected more specifically with the phallic potency of *Yesod*.[60] It is my contention that the coronation of Sabbatai Ṣevi conveys the apoth-

---

227, 235–236, 391, 813; Liebes, *On Sabbateanism*, 172–182. Regarding the role of Moses as mediating between the two messianic figures, see *Zohar* 3:153b (*Ra'aya' Meheimna'*). On the messianic status of Moses in *Tiqqunei Zohar* and *Ra'aya' Meheimna'*, see Scholem, *Sabbatai Ṣevi*, p. 53; Giller, *Enlightened Will Shine*, pp. 52–53; and the comprehensive analysis of A. Goldreich, "Clarifications in the Self-Perception of the Author of *Tiqqunei Zohar*," in *Massu'ot: Studies in Kabbalistic Literature and Jewish Philosophy in Memory of Prof. Ephraim Gottlieb*, edited by M. Oron and A. Goldreich (Jerusalem, 1994), pp. 459–496, esp. 469–473 (in Hebrew). See also reference to Liebes in n. 60. For a recent study on the role of the messiah son of Joseph in Sabbatian theology, see A. Elqayam, "The Absent Messiah: Messiah Son of Joseph in the Thought of Nathan of Gaza, Sabbatai Ṣevi, and Abraham Miguel Cardozo," *Da'at* 38 (1997): 33–82 (in Hebrew).

[59] *Tiqqunei Zohar* 70, 133a. See *ibid.*, 68, 99a, where the staff of God, related exegetically to the "fiery ever-turning sword" (Gen. 3:24), is associated with the transformation of judgment into mercy, attributes that are generally assigned the respective gender valences of female and masculine.

[60] On the relationship of Moses and Meṭaṭron, see references to various scholarly publications cited in E.R. Wolfson, "Meṭaṭron and Shi'ur Qomah in the Writings of Ḥaside Ashkenaz," in *Mysticism, Magic and Kabbalah in Ashkenazi Judaism*, edited by K.E. Grözinger and J. Dan (Berlin, 1995), p. 91 n. 151. This identification is enhanced by the fact that the letters of the name of Moses in Hebrew can function as an acrostic for *meṭaṭron sar ha-panim*, i.e., Meṭaṭron the archon of the face (or presence). See, for instance, Moses of Kiev, *Shoshan Sodot* (Korets, 1784), 70b. On the phallic nature of Meṭaṭron, see Wolfson, *Through a Speculum That Shines*, pp. 259 n. 304 and 337–338 n. 40; *Along the Path*, pp. 128–129 n. 121 and 150–151 n. 204; "The Doctrine of the Sefirot in the Prophetic Kabbalah of Abraham Abulafia," *Jewish Studies Quarterly* 2 (1995): 368–369 n. 100; and the further evidence adduced by N. Deutsch, *The Gnostic Imagination: Gnosticism, Mandaeism, and Merkabah Mysticism* (Leiden, 1995), pp. 112–119. See also the passages of Cordovero mentioned in n. 49, and Vital, *'Eṣ Ḥayyim*, 46:7, 104b–c. Although Moses is generally associated with *Tif'eret*, which corresponds to the torso of the divine body, rather than with *Yesod*, which is in the position of the phallus, it is evident from some zoharic passages (not to mention other kabbalistic literature) that there is a close proximity between the two gradations such that the phallic characteristics are easily applied to Moses. For example, see *Zohar* 1:21b; 2:68a. On the phallic characteristic associated with Moses in zoharic literature, connected especially to his messianic status, see Liebes, "Messiah of the *Zohar*," pp. 105–107, 200 (English version in *Studies in the Zohar*, translated by A. Schwartz, S. Nakache, and P. Peli [Albany, 1993], pp. 15–17, 73). More importantly, according to some Lurianic texts, Moses symbolically corresponds to *yesod de-'abba'*, the phallic aspect of *Ḥokhmah, da'at 'elyon*, which is the aspect of supernal consciousness that is homologous to the phallus below. See *'Eṣ Ḥayyim*, 32:1, 35c; *Sha'ar ha-Kelalim*, chs. 10 and 11, mentioned by Scholem, *Sabbatai Ṣevi*, p. 306 n. 286. See also Meroz, "Redemption in the Lurianic Kabbalah," pp. 256 n. 9, 264–265. That the identification of Moses with the messiah has phallic implications is evident from the words of Nathan in his letter concerning the heresy of Sabbatai Ṣevi, in Scholem, *Studies and Texts*, pp. 239, 243,

eosis of the messiah to this supernal aspect of Meṭaṭron. Putting on the turban assumed the soteriological significance of the ontic assimilation into the divine crown, which represents the restoration of the female to the male in the form of the corona of the phallus (*ʿaṭeret berit*), the metamorphosis that signals the culmination of the eschatological process, the reversal of positioning such that the female sits atop the head of the male. As I will set out to demonstrate, moreover, this act, whether performed literally or symbolically, emerged as the engendering rite of passage that marked someone a true follower of the apostate redeemer. Not only the messiah but his supporters as well were to be absorbed into this aspect of the divine. Wearing the turban thus translates in Sabbatian theology to the means by which one enters into or is clothed by the *ʿaṭeret berit*,[61] the ritual that confirmed the divine status of Sabbatai Ṣevi and thereby localized the myth of messianic redemption in historical context. Previous scholars have noted that in Sabbatian theology, particularly as it is formulated by Nathan and his followers, Sabbatai Ṣevi symbolically corresponds to, or indeed is the incarnation of, *Tifʾeret* or *Keter*, although some have also recognized that in a number of texts the messianic figure represents the earthly manifestation of *Yesod*.[62] By focusing on the motif of coronation and the related symbol of the crown, however, a new dimension is added to this

---

and 252. On the analogy between the first deliverance through Moses and the final deliverance through Sabbatai Ṣevi, see Scholem, *Sabbatai Ṣevi*, pp. 584–586; *Researches*, p. 363; *Messianic Idea*, p. 98; Wirszubski, *Between the Lines*, p. 186. Scholem's assessment that interpreting the figure of Moses as a type of the messiah betrays the typological exegesis of a Christian hermeneutics seems to me gratuitous given the midrashic and kabbalistic precedent for identifying the link between Moses as the first redeemer and the final redeemer, although I do not deny the striking assonance between the Sabbatian and Christian positions. Regarding the symbolism of the three messianic figures of Moses, Joseph, and David in Sabbatian thought, see Scholem, *Sabbatai Ṣevi*, p. 53; and Liebes, *On Sabbateanism*, pp. 169–170. On the development of this idea in Lurianic kabbalah, see Meroz, "Redemption in Lurianic Kabbalah," pp. 256–257.

[61] The expression *likkanes ba-miṣnefet*, "to enter the turban," is used in a Dönmeh text published by Scholem, *Researches*, p. 302. (According to a variant reading, noted by Scholem, the text should read *likkanes be-ʾemunat ha-miṣnefet*, "to enter the faith of the turban," i.e., to adopt the Islamic religion.) According to Scholem, *op. cit.*, p. 292, the eighteen rituals specified in this text, which was composed around 1760, may go back to the time of Sabbatai Ṣevi himself. See also Liebes, *On Sabbateanism*, pp. 290–291 nn. 207–208.

[62] See Wirszubski, *Between the Lines*, p. 186; Scholem, *Researches*, p. 363; Y. Nadav, "A Kabbalistic Treatise of R. Solomon Ayllion," *Sefunot* 3–4 (1960): 319–320 (in Hebrew); Liebes, "Messiah of the *Zohar*," p. 111; *idem*, *On Sabbateanism*, pp. 54, 62, 72–73, 279 n. 65, 304–306 n. 29.

discussion. The crowning of Sabbatai Ṣevi as messiah represents his assuming the position of the divine crown, which is related more specifically to the female that crowns the male. In this act of crowning, the lowest of the sefirotic potencies, the female aspect of *Malkhut* is elevated to the highest gradation, the male aspect of *Keter*. Messianic redemption reflects the transposition of the ontological hierarchy such that the branch of the crown is placed beneath the root of kingship.

Apostasy and the Esoteric Significance of Donning the Turban

The particular association of the messianic crown and the turban that Sabbatai Ṣevi reportedly wore on the momentous day of his public apostasy is made by both his opponents and supporters. Predictably, however, this image was used either to demean or to exalt the apostate messiah. According to his adversaries, as may be deduced, for example, from the recounting of the apostasy in a letter written in November 1666 by Joseph Halevi of Livorno to Jacob Sasportas, Sabbatai Ṣevi's casting off his skullcap and putting on the turban represented his rejection of Judaism and the public profanation of the divine name.[63] The promise of the glorious crown of the messiah degenerated into the turban, symbolic of the degradation and the shamefulness of the apostasy. Thus, in a second passage, Joseph Halevi derides Hosea Nantawa of Alexandria, who reported in a letter to the sages of Livorno the ecstatic vision that Mordecai Ashkenazi had in Constantinople during the summer of 1666, which led to his affirmation of Sabbatai Ṣevi's messiahship and his own transformation into a venerated prophet. The precise object of that vision was said to be a royal crown of fire that extended from

[63] *Ṣiṣat Novel Ṣevi*, p. 172. On the expression "putting on the garment" as signifying Sabbatai Ṣevi's conversion to Islam, see the text of Abraham Cardoso printed in I.H. Weiss, *Bet ha-Midrash* (Vienna, 1865), p. 64 (text edited by N. Brüll). The editor remarks (n. 8 *ad locum*) that a similar expression is found in Christian works describing the conversion of Sabbatai Ṣevi. The connection of putting on the turban and forsaking the Torah in the case of the apostasy in Salonika in 1683 is made by Cardoso in the passage published in Scholem, *Studies and Texts*, p. 279. In the same document, p. 280, Cardoso recounts the donning of the turban on the part of Sabbatai Ṣevi himself, although in that case he emphasizes that the turban was placed on the messiah by others (*hilbishuhu ha-miṣnefet*), language that deliberately removes the responsibility of the action from Sabbatai Ṣevi himself. See also Cardoso's recounting of this episode in the letter to his brother in *Ṣiṣat Novel Ṣevi*, p. 293. On the wearing of the turban and antinomian behavior, see Molho and Amarilio, "Autobiographical Letters," p. 224.

Sabbatai Ṣevi's head to the middle of heaven. In an utterly cynical and sarcastic tone, Joseph Halevi writes: "I pray you ask that elderly sage, whose name is Mordecai, concerning whom you said that he saw the crown of fire on the head of your messiah rise to the middle of heaven, what was its color? Was it the color of silver, which he collected from those who came from the ends of the earth to see his face and from whom he profited . . . or was it the color of the white turban that is now on his head?"[64] In the eyes of Joseph Halevi, the crown envisioned by Mordecai Ashkenazi could be explained either as a symbol of Sabbatai Ṣevi's greed or in terms of the turban that emblematized his apostasy.

In the mind of his supporters, by contrast, the donning of the turban was interpreted as a symbol of the messianic coronation they had long predicted and anticipated. According to reports written by both believers (e.g., Aaron Ṣarfati of Amsterdam)[65] and critics (e.g., Sasportas,[66] Joseph Halevi,[67] and Jacob Frances[68]), in the aftermath of the conversion (November–December 1666), the turban was identified as a crown (in some cases based on the language of Ezekiel 21:31, *hasir ha-miṣnefet we-harim ha-ʿaṭarah*, "remove the turban and lift off the crown," or that of Psalm 21:4, *tashit le-roʾsho ʿaṭeret paz*, "You have set upon his head a crown of fine gold") and Sabbatai Ṣevi's placing the turban on his head was viewed as the messianic coronation. According to one of Nathan's prophetic revelations, which is reported by Leib ben Ozer, Sabbatai Ṣevi "will take the royal crown (*keter malkhut*) from the king of Ishmael and will place it on his head, and the king of Ishmael will follow him like a Canaanite slave for the dominion will belong to him."[69] The textual evidence indicates, moreover, that many of the theological attempts to account for the conversion were linked especially to the image of the turban or crown. In one of his letters, Nathan considered the donning of the

---

[64] *Ṣiṣat Novel Ṣevi*, pp. 156–157; see Scholem, *Sabbatai Ṣevi*, pp. 606–607.
[65] *Ṣiṣat Novel Ṣevi*, pp. 27–28.
[66] *Ibid.*, p. 13.
[67] *Ibid.*, p. 189.
[68] *The Poems of Jacob Frances*, edited by P. Naveh (Jerusalem, 1969), p. 443 (in Hebrew). Concerning the Frances brothers and their attacks on the Sabbatian movement, see Scholem, *Sabbatai Ṣevi*, pp. 516–518.
[69] The text is translated into Hebrew in Emden, *Torat ha-Qenaʾot*, 2b–3a. For a slightly different version of this passage, see *The Story of Shabbetay Ẓevi by R. Leib ben R. Ozer Amsterdam*, p. 12. Cf. the language of Abraham Cuenque's memoir in Emden, *Torat ha-Qenaʾot*, 20a.

turban as a sign of the elevation of the *Shekhinah* out of exile: "Even though he wore the holy turban (*ha-ṣanif ha-ṭahor*)[70] his holiness was not profaned on account of this, for he is holy and every act of Sabbath is holy.[71] One must also believe that the *Shekhinah* ascended to her primary source and she no longer dwells in the exile."[72] A precise parallel to this formulation is found in a letter that Nathan wrote to Joseph Ṣevi on February 7, 1668, but in that context Nathan further identifies the evil garment worn by Sabbatai Ṣevi (according to the locution of *Tiqqunei Zohar*, "he is good on the inside but his garment is evil," *tav mi-legaw u-levusha' dileih bish*),[73] as "the turban that he wore. Therefore the verse says 'yet humble, riding on an ass' (Zech. 9:9) . . . for the situation that will come to him on account of the evil garment is that he must wear it and he will be impoverished from the Torah and impoverished from the commandments."[74] Wearing the garment (*levush*), which is the turban, signifies the transvaluation necessary for redemption: the messiah must sink to the depths of impurity in order to redeem the fallen sparks of his soul-root.[75]

---

[70] This expression is derived from Zechariah 3:5. In that context, the *ṣanif ha-ṭahor* refers to the "pure diadem" placed on the head of Joshua the high priest.

[71] The identification of Sabbatai Ṣevi with Sabbath is a commonplace in Sabbatian texts. See below, n. 105.

[72] Letter of Nathan published in Amarillo, "Sabbatean Documents," p. 253.

[73] *Tiqqunei Zohar*, 60, 93b.

[74] *'Inyenei Shabbatai Ṣevi*, p. 60; *Ṣiṣat Novel Ṣevi*, pp. 260–261; see Scholem, *Sabbatai Ṣevi*, pp. 742–743. The same language is used in a letter written by Nathan to Samuel Primo published in Amarillo, "Sabbatean Documents," pp. 270–271. See also the formulation of Nathan in his letter on Sabbatai Ṣevi's apostasy, in Scholem, *Studies and Texts*, p. 244, and the letter of Nathan cited by Mahallallel Halleluyah of Ancona, published in Scholem, *Researches*, p. 67. The view of Nathan is paraphrased in Abraham Cuenque's memoir cited in Emden, *Torat ha-Qena'ot*, 21a. In another letter of Nathan published by Amarillo, "Sabbatean Documents," p. 263, reference is made to Zechariah 9:9 as it is interpreted in *Zohar* 3:69a. According to Nathan's understanding of the zoharic passage, the "riding on an ass" refers to the strange acts committed by the messiah, which are related more specifically to his conversion of Jews to Islam. These heretical acts are in emulation of God who "copulates in a place that is not his own."

[75] As is well known, a key component of the religious history of Sabbatianism is related to the blatant acts of breaking traditional halakhic practice, culminating in the ultimate act of betrayal, the conversion of Sabbatai Ṣevi to Islam. These intermittent acts of antinomianism and the fateful apostasy were transformed by faithful followers of Sabbatai Ṣevi, especially Nathan of Gaza, into a theology of paradox largely based on certain presuppositions of Lurianic kabbalah. That is, the abrogation of Jewish law and the adoption of the Muslim faith, which Nathan and other Sabbatians referred to as the *ma'asim zarim*, the "strange acts," afforded the pseudo-messiah the opportunity to descend to the realm of the demonic shells (*qelippot*) in order to perform the ultimate rectification (*tiqqun*). In a document written in 1666

In another Sabbatian text, *Mar'ot ʿal Raza' de-Malka' Meshiḥa'*, written in 1667–1668 by Jacob ben Isaac Sirojon,[76] the turban of Sabbatai Ṣevi is associated with the headdress (*miṣnefet*) of the high priest.[77] The implication of this association, drawn explicitly by the author, is that the messiah had the priestly task of atoning for the sins of Israel. Indeed, the means of atonement was putting on the turban:

> This is the secret of this soul, which is the anointed high priest, and he is called Sabbatai Ṣevi, may his majesty be exalted, and in this holy turban there is a secret, for it is the turban of Aaron the priest, as it is written, "Let a pure diadem be placed on his head" (Zech. 3:5), "to make atonement for the Israelites" (Lev. 16:34), and it is said, "For on this day atonement shall be made for you" (*ibid.*, 30). The holy king wore this turban on that day that is called Yom Kippur.... Aaron the priest would offer sacrifices there and he would intend the explicit name, so too this messiah atones for Israel through his prayer and intends his own name. Come and see the secret of this holy turban when it has been revealed in this lower world.... This turban was given to Moses and Aaron the priest.... It was necessary [for Sabbatai Ṣevi] to wear this turban to complete the commandment given to Aaron the priest, as it is written, "he shall wear a linen turban" (Lev. 16:4).[78]

The symbol of wearing the turban was extended by various Sabbatian writers to designate the circle of true believers who followed the path of Sabbatai Ṣevi and converted to Islam. For example, according to the chronicle of Jacob Najara, on the 19th of Shevat in 1671, Sabbatai Ṣevi revealed to Jacob several matters including the subject of the turban. Reportedly, Sabbatai Ṣevi identified the "masters of faith" (*baʿalei 'emunah*)—a term that is based on the technical expression *ma'arei meheimanuta'* used in zoharic literature to designate the mystical

---

prior to Sabbatai Ṣevi's conversion, *Derush ha-Tanninim*, Nathan already explained the entrapment of the messiah in the demonic shells in terms of the task of uplifting the fallen sparks. See Scholem, *Be-ʿIqvot Mashiaḥ*, pp. 39–40; *Major Trends*, pp. 291, 296–299; *Sabbatai Ṣevi*, pp. 302–306; *Messianic Idea*, p. 95.

[76] See Scholem, *Sabbatai Ṣevi*, pp. 736–737.

[77] B. Giṭṭin 7a: "What is the matter of the headdress (*miṣnefet*) doing alongside the diadem (*ʿaṭarah*)? It is to indicate to you that when the headdress is on the head of the high priest, the diadem is on the head of every person, but when the headdress is removed from the head of the high priest, the diadem is removed from the head of every person."

[78] R. Schatz, "Mystic Visions of King Messiah—An Early Document by an Apostate Sabbatean," *Sefunot* 12 (1971–78): 230 (in Hebrew), and see Schatz's analysis on pp. 222–223.

fraternity[79]—as the ones "who wear the turban (*lovshei ha-ṣenif*) for they comprehend the sublime wisdom and the great level."[80] The wearers of the turban put aside the Torah of truth (*torat ʾemet*), which is the law of Moses (*torat mosheh*), and adopt the Torah of mercy (*torat ḥesed*), which is the Islamic faith.[81] In the continuation of this text, Jacob relates the story of some believers putting on the turban as a sign of support for the apostate messiah. The disciples are thus referred to as *baʿalei ʾemunat lovshei ha-ṣenif le-maʿalah*, "masters of faith [who] wear the turban above."[82] From another passage in this chronicle, which describes the conversion of Abraham Gamaliel of Constantinople and Joseph Karillo, it is apparent that the wearing of the turban was not forced on everyone but was limited to only a small number of Sabbatai Ṣevi's entourage.[83] Analogously, in the commentary on Psalms, written in Kastoria between 1678–79 by Israel Ḥazzan, the disciple and personal secretary of Nathan of Gaza, one reads that Sabbatai Ṣevi proclaimed that "there are some who wear the turban for good and others for evil, and there are some who wear our bonnet for good and others for evil. . . . The masters of faith, whom I have entered into this trial, will remain in the turban for good and for the rest of our brothers in Israel their hat is for good."[84] The truly worthy of Sabbatai Ṣevi's adherents are those who "entered this crucible and broke the law of Moses to bring about the rectification of the world through the wearing of the tur-

---

[79] On the designation of the entourage of apostates as *baʿalei ʾemunah*, see Scholem, *Researches*, p. 112.

[80] Amarillo, "Sabbatean Documents," p. 255. See *ibid.*, p. 257, where the believers are referred to as those "who wear the turban," *lovshe ha-ṣenif.*

[81] Cf. the commentary on Psalms by Israel Ḥazzan, MS Budapest-Kaufmann 255, fol. 101b: "'His faithful ones' (*ḥasidav*), this refers to those who enter the Torah of mercy (*torat ḥesed*). . . . The Torah for its own sake (*torah lishmah*) is the Torah of mercy (*torah shel ḥesed*). This is connected to what the [rabbis] blessed be their memory, said [B. Nazir 23b; Horayyot 10b], 'Greater is a transgression for its own sake' (*ʿaveirah lishmah*), that is, for the sake of the [letter] *he*ʾ [i.e., the consonants of the word *lishmah* can be broken into *le-shem he*ʾ], for the sake of the rectification of the Presence (*le-ṣorekh tiqqun ha-shekhinah*), as it is written, 'It is time to act for the Lord, for they have violated Your Torah (Ps. 119:126), this is the Torah of Moses (*torat mosheh*), in order to rectify the rectification of the Presence (*letaqqen tiqqun ha-shekhinah*).'"

[82] Amarillo, "Sabbatean Documents," p. 261.

[83] *Ibid.*, p. 259; see Scholem, *Sabbatai Ṣevi*, p. 850.

[84] MS Budapest-Kaufmann 255, fol. 124b, cited in Scholem, *Researches*, p. 111 (the reference to fol. 133a needs to be corrected to 133b; I have cited the manuscript according to the pagination in Arabic numerals, which is more consistent than the scribe's original Hebrew characters). See Scholem, *Sabbatai Ṣevi*, pp. 727 and 858.

ban (*tiqqun ha-ʿolam bi-levishat ha-ṣanif*)."[85] Wearing the turban is thus endowed with eschatological significance: What appears on the outside as the ultimate act of betrayal is in truth the ultimate act of self-sacrifice and devotion, indeed an act of cosmic redemption.

It is precisely this practice to which Cardoso refers in an autobiographical letter in which he bitterly criticizes the followers of Sabbatai Ṣevi led by Samuel Primo. The heresy of these individuals took the form of preaching that Sabbatai Ṣevi was the incarnation of God who instructed his disciples in the abrogation of normative halakhah:

> All those who had angelic guides, when they wished to write or to speak about the secret of divinity, they went out to false beliefs and they became dependent on wells that have no water but only snakes and scorpions. They wrote heretical beliefs, as, for example, R. Nathan and R. Joseph ibn Ṣur, and others like them. But I and my students, who had angelic guides, never were caught. . . . Our angelic guides always commanded us to perform the *tiqqun* and they did not allow a prayer to be offered to God, blessed be He, that was not in the Torah or [in the works of] prophecy, according to the [accepted] law and practice, and they were always bound to the knowledge of and faith in God, to worship Him in truth through the commandments and by means of charity. But all the other people, apart from my students, who had revelations of the spirits, abandoned the commandments. It was not enough that they wore the turban (*lavshu miṣnefet*), but they transgressed the Written Torah and the Oral Torah. There was amongst them the principle that in order to bring the redemption, it is necessary to desecrate the Sabbath, to eat leavened bread on Passover, and not to accept the words of the rabbis, blessed be their memories, who speak about the divine matter.[86]

On one level, then, the turban represents for both Sabbatai Ṣevi and a select number of his supporters the outward sign of assuming the messianic role of perfecting the world. This task is linked to the turban because the latter is the sign of the Islamic faith and only by accepting this religion could the messiah and his followers descend to the depths of the demonic to elevate the entrapped sparks. I would suggest, however, that the turban assumed another critical connotation, and one that is related more generally to the theosophic symbol

---

[85] MS Budapest-Kaufmann 255, fol. 87a, cited in Scholem, *Researches*, p. 111. Cf. MS Budapest-Kaufmann 255, fol. 107a: *baʿalei ha-ʾemunah shelavshu ha-ṣenif.*

[86] Molho and Amarilio, "Autobiographical Letters," p. 212.

of the crown. An allusion to this symbolism is found in a decree sent by Sabbatai Ṣevi on the second day of Rosh Ḥodesh of the month Tammuz in the year 1667. In that document, it is reported that when Sabbatai Ṣevi reached the line "do not substitute God and do not rebel against His religion" of the traditional *yigdal* hymn, he said: "The wearing of the turban should no longer [be understood] from the perspective of a punishment for the sake of rectification (*ha-ʿonesh le-ṣorekh tiqqun*), but as referring to a great secret."[87] The reader is not informed about the content of the secret, but it is reasonable to assume that it has something to do with entering an eschatological stage in which the paradox of having to redeem the world by converting to Islam has been transcended.[88] I propose that the turban has been transformed from a token of apostasy (the Turkish headgear) to an emblem of eschatological transfiguration (the theosophic crown).

Apotheosis of Sabbatai Ṣevi and the Assimilation into the Crown

The utilization of the symbol of the crown on the part of Sabbatians to refer to the hypostatic dimension of the messiah's being is a well attested phenomenon. The point is underscored, for example, in Israel Ḥazzan's commentary on Psalm 21:4:

> Before his kingship was revealed "you proferred him blessings of good things"... afterward you "set upon his head a crown of fine gold." Thus you know that Amirah,[89] prior to his kingship being publicized, would mention God in his blessings when he was in a lucid state. And this is the simple meaning, "You have proferred him," You proferred him good things in his blessings when he mentioned [the name of] the Lord. But when his kingship will be revealed and quickly disclosed to us, then the holy name will be a crown of fine gold on his head before the eyes of all nations.[90]

---

87 Amarillo, "Sabbatean Documents," p. 252.

88 For a different explanation of this enigmatic line, see Liebes, *On Sabbateanism*, p. 29.

89 The initials of the expression, *ʾadonenu malkenu yarum hodo*, "our lord and king, his majesty be exalted," the customary designation of Sabbatai Ṣevi by his followers. See Scholem, *Sabbatai Ṣevi*, p. 110 n. 25, and his suggestion on p. 263 that this title may have been related phonetically to the Arabic word *ʾamir*.

90 MS Budapest-Kaufmann 255, fol. 25a, cited in Scholem, *Researches*, p. 94.

Ḥazzan thus characterizes the metamorphosis of Sabbatai Ṣevi from a private mystic to the publicly acclaimed messiah in terms of the divine name. Prior to his proclamation, Sabbatai Ṣevi would mention the name in moments of mental lucidity.[91] By contrast, after he announces his messianic status, the name will become a crown of fine gold on his head. In addition to the kingly dimension of the symbol of the crown, there is a theosophic connotation, for the crown symbolizes a particular aspect of God. It is precisely that aspect into which Sabbatai Ṣevi is ontically assimilated when he assumed his role as messiah. The crown, therefore, represents both Sabbatai Ṣevi's assumption of the messianic reign and his apotheosis into the attribute of the Godhead that corresponds to the crown, which is the divine name.

The association of the crown and the name, a very old idea in Jewish esotericism,[92] is underscored as well in the second testimony of the *Sahaduta' di-Meheimanuta'*, which recounts an event that occurred on the seventh day of Passover in 1668.[93] God is said to have invited Sabbatai Ṣevi to the festival meal and in preparation for that meal "dressed him in a crown" (*hilbisho ba-keter*). In the course of that meal, Sabbatai Ṣevi learns that God will avenge the Jews who have refused to acknowledge the veracity and legitimacy of his messianic claim. Upon hearing this Sabbatai Ṣevi threatens to remove the crown that God has placed on his head in an act of protest, but before he is able to do so the divine decree is changed from judgment to mercy. At this point the author describes a second coronation of Sabbatai Ṣevi by God, based on the description of the adornment of Aaron in the headdress and holy diadem in several Priestly sources (Exod. 29:6, 39:30; Lev. 8:9):

> At that moment the Holy One, blessed be He, had a diadem (*ṣiṣ*) in His hand, the holy crown (*nezer ha-qodesh*), and there were twelve stones fixed in it, which shine with an incomparable splendor, and He placed

---

[91] On the messianic rationale for Sabbatai Ṣevi's pronouncing the name of God in public, see Scholem, *Sabbatai Ṣevi*, pp. 142–143.

[92] See Scholem, *Major Trends*, p. 358 n. 17; *idem, Jewish Gnosticism, Merkabah Mysticism, and Talmudic Tradition* (New York, 1965), pp. 54–55.

[93] Concerning the authorship of this tract, see I. Tishby, *Studies in Kabbalah and Its Branches: Researches and Sources* (Jerusalem, 1993), p. 338; Scholem, *Sabbatai Ṣevi*, p. 829 n. 22. In the latter source, Scholem cites manuscript evidence that suggests that this work was composed by Solomon Laniado. My thanks to Avraham Elqayam who reminded me of these references.

> it on the head of our master. . . . He said before the Holy One, blessed be He, "Master of the world, why aren't these stones inscribed?" He said to him, "This will be a sign in your hands. The diadem will be on your forehead always, and any time that you make use of it you will see the stones upon which are written and inscribed twelve permutations of My great name. You will know that the time of redemption has come, and it will be a great and awesome day." Then our master said this verse, "He has exalted the horn of His people for the glory of all His faithful ones, Israel, the people close to Him. Hallelujah" (Ps. 148:14).[94]

There is ample evidence in Sabbatian literature to illustrate, moreover, that the crown functions even more specifically as a symbol of the attribute of the corona of the divine phallus, which was linked to Sabbatai Ṣevi. Here I will cite but a few examples. This first illustration is taken from Nathan's commentary on his own apocalyptic vision, falsely attributed to Abraham the Pious, which was composed in the spring of 1665. Commenting on the description of Sabbatai Ṣevi in the vision, "he is my beloved, my darling, like the apple of my eye" (*ʾahuvi ḥavivi kevavat ʿeini*),[95] Nathan writes:

> "He is my beloved" (*ʾahuvi*): he called him "beloved" (*ʾahuv*), for the love of a woman for her husband is known through her adornment in the secret of the twenty-four adornments of the bride, which is the numerical value of the word *ʾahuvi*. The Holy One, blessed be He, adorned him in all of these adornments in the secret of "a woman spreads rouge over her face,"[96] for the twenty-four permutations of [the name of] sovereignty (*ʾadnut*) are the aspect of judgment, the secret of blood. Thus the woman who adorns herself paints her face red in order to pass before the gate and afterward she is mollified [and becomes white] like milk. Furthermore, he said, "my darling" (*ḥavivi*), as the love of a woman (*ḥibbat ʾishshah*) for her husband when she is bound to the thirty-two paths[97] in the secret of "the Lord established the earth in wisdom" (Prov. 3:19). He said, moreover, "like the apple of my eye" (*kevavat ʿeini*), this is the secret of the crown of David (*ʿaṭeret dawid*), which was the pupil of the eye (*bat ʿayin*), the secret of the "crown of their king" (*ʿaṭeret malkam*) (2 Sam. 12:30), the secret of the

[94] *Be-ʿIqvot Mashiaḥ*, p. 76.
[95] *Ibid.*, p. 59.
[96] B. Moʿed Qaṭan 9b.
[97] That is, the thirty-two paths of wisdom mentioned at the beginning of *Sefer Yeṣirah*.

corona of the phallus (*ʿaṭeret ha-yesod*), which encompasses as well the aspect of their king.[98]

In this passage, Nathan characterizes Sabbatai Ṣevi as the female beloved who stands in relation to the male lover.[99] *Prima facie*, it would seem that the gender dynamic should be translated simply into the hierarchical relationship that pertains to the human being vis-à-vis God. However, each of these female attributes relates to a dimension of the feminine *Shekhinah*. Thus, the word *ʾahuvi*, "my beloved," alludes to the twenty-four adornments of the bride, which symbolize the attribute of judgment; the word *ḥavivi*, "my darling," refers to the thirty-two paths of wisdom by means of which the masculine potency established the feminine earth; and, finally, the expression *bavat ʿeini*, the "apple of my eye," is linked to the aspect of the *Shekhinah* identified as the pupil of the eye (*bat ʿayin*),[100] the midpoint of the circle,[101] which is also depicted as the royal crown of David as well as the corona of the phallus. In this third characteristic, therefore, Sabbatai Ṣevi represents the female element that is localized in the male organ, the crown that encircles the head of the king.

Nathan returns to this symbolic identification of Sabbatai Ṣevi in his *Derush ha-Taninim*, composed in 1666 prior to the apostasy. Toward the beginning of that work, Nathan describes his own historical moment as the time when the "additional element of the holiness of Sabbath" (*tosefet qedushat shabbat*) began to take effect in the world.

---

[98] *Be-ʿIqvot Mashiaḥ*, p. 63.

[99] The point is duly noted by Elqayam, "Mystery of Faith," p. 254 n. 11. The author does not, however, focus on the fact that in the last of the three images employed by Nathan in this context the female is contextualized as part of the male in the form of the royal crown of David (*ʿaṭeret dawid*) or, more graphically, as the corona of the penis (*ʿaṭeret yesod*). The feminization of Sabbatai Ṣevi is also implied in the analogy that Sabbatian writers make between the messiah and the biblical figure of Esther who epitomizes the virtue of dissimulation. See below, n. 147. Also relevant is the testimony of Cardoso (in Scholem, *Studies and Texts*, p. 287) that some followers of Sabbatai Ṣevi remarked that "the *Shekhinah* was garbed within him and on account of this he ascended to her level since he possessed the unity of emanation (*ha-yeḥidah de-ʾaṣilut*)."

[100] On the symbolism of *bat ʿayin*, see E.R. Wolfson, "Weeping, Death, and Spiritual Ascent in Sixteenth-Century Jewish Mysticism," in *Death, Ecstasy, and Other Worldly Journeys*, edited by J.J. Collins and M. Fishbane (Albany, 1995), pp. 241–242 n. 69, 244 n. 92. See also the passage from *Tiqqunei Zohar* discussed below at n. 117.

[101] I have discussed the phallic connotation of the symbol of the midpoint of the circle, which is generally applied to the *Shekhinah*, in "Coronation of the Sabbath Bride."

Just as on Friday, from the fifth hour of the day, the worlds and the *Shekhinah* begin to ascend, so from the year 1657 the holiness of Sabbath began to manifest itself in history and the *Shekhinah* ascended from the exile. Citing a passage from the *Zohar*,[102] Nathan further describes the Sabbath as the name of God, "for it is already known that the restfulness (*shevitah*) is in the Cause of Causes, and it is the name of the Holy One, blessed be He, to indicate that the potency of this one is given to that one, and he ascends through the secret of Sabbath, which is constantly in the supernal beard after the sixth millennium. Concerning this the rabbis, blessed be their memory, said,[103] 'the world exists for six millennia and for one it is desolate.'"[104] The six millennia are governed by *Zeʿeir ʾAnpin*, the configuration of the divine that corresponds to the son, but in the seventh, which is the cosmic sabbatical, this gradation ascends in the secret of Sabbath[105] to one of the highest aspects of the Godhead, graphically portrayed in the distinctive language of the Idrot sections of the *Zohar* as the beard of *ʿAtiqa Qadishaʾ*, the "holy ancient one,"[106] and the

---

[102] *Zohar* 2:88b.

[103] B. Sanhedrin 97a.

[104] *Be-ʿIqvot Mashiaḥ*, p. 15.

[105] See Scholem, *Sabbatai Ṣevi*, pp. 313–314. On the identification of Sabbatai Ṣevi as the "great Sabbath" (*shabbat ha-gadol*) or the "holy Sabbath" (*shabbat qodesh*), see the letter of Nathan published in *Zikkaron li-Venei Yisraʾel*, p. 59, and in *Ṣiṣat Novel Ṣevi*, p. 260. A slightly different version appears in Scholem, *Researches*, p. 67. It is obvious from that context as well that the attribution of the name *shabbat* to Sabbatai Ṣevi implies the fact that the messianic figure is elevated to the highest aspect of the Godhead. Thus, Nathan remarks that Sabbatai Ṣevi is the "holy Sabbath, the source of the supernal and holy *Ḥokhmah*, the power of the supernal *Keter*." See below, n. 135; and Liebes, *On Sabbateanism*, p. 285 n. 112. On the identification of Sabbatai Ṣevi as the aspect of Sabbath, see also Nathan's letter to Raphael Joseph in *Ṣiṣat Novel Ṣevi*, p. 11 (translated in Scholem, *Sabbatai Ṣevi*, p. 273); and the letter of Primo, *op. cit.*, p. 129. In light of this identification, it is of interest to note the remark of Nathan in his *hanhagot*, published by Benayahu, *Shabbatean Movement in Greece*, p. 278: "Our master, his majesty be exalted, merited the honor of his greatness on account of the fact that he greatly honored the Sabbath with his body and his money and with all his ability."

[106] *Zohar* 3:130b–134b; 288a–289b, 292b–293b. It should be noted that the messianic element is already associated with the beard in *Zohar* 3:132b; see Liebes, *Studies in the Zohar*, p. 102. The connection of Sabbatai Ṣevi to the highest configuration (*parṣuf*) of the divine, referred to by the technical zoharic terminology, *ʿAtiqaʾ Qadishaʾ*, is also underscored by Nathan's remark that the messianic figure symbolized the state of rest (*menuḥah*), which is characterized (following *Zohar* 3:136b) by the disclosure of *ʿAtiqaʾ Qadishaʾ* in the lower configuration of *Zeʿeir ʾAnpin*. *Ṣiṣat Novel Ṣevi*, p. 8. See the citation from Nathan's penitential devotions cited below at n. 140. Regarding this dimension of Nathan's teaching, see Scholem, *Sabbatai Ṣevi*, pp. 275–276. A similar formulation regarding the identification of the holy king, which

world is governed by the configurations of *ʾAbbaʾ* and *ʾImmaʾ*, the divine father and mother.[107] Having established the contours of the messianic dynamic in the divine sphere, Nathan turns to a portrayal of the messianic figure below, Sabbatai Ṣevi, who reflects this dynamic in his mundane existence:

> Just as the Holy One, blessed be He, ascends to this level, so, too, the messianic king will ascend to a high level in body and soul, for his body will be purified like the pavement of sapphire, and this is the secret of "under His feet there was the likeness of a pavement of sapphire" (*we-taḥat raglav kemaʿaseh livnat ha-sappir*) (Exod. 24:10).[108] The word *we-taḥat* is numerically equivalent to his name and to his cognomen.[109] And he is [referred to in the expression] *raglav* ("His feet") because he is in the secret of the heels. *Raglav* ("His feet") is *regel yah*, which is the secret of the corona of the phallus of the Father (*ʿaṭeret yesod ʾabbaʾ*), for *Yesod*, too, is called foot (*regel*). "The likeness of a pavement of sapphire," this refers to the crown (*ʿaṭarah*) in the secret of the "crown of her husband" (*ʿaṭeret baʿlah*) (Prov. 12:4), for it ascends to the supernal world above which there is nothing.[110]

By means of an extraordinary reading of Exodus 24:10, Nathan is able to establish that Sabbatai Ṣevi is to be identified as the feet of God, an identification that entails as well the idea that the root of the messiah is in the heels of the primordial anthropos, the locality of the most difficult sparks that are redeemed only in the time right before the messianic coming, the "footheels of the messiah," *ʿiqvot mashiaḥ*.[111] Insofar as the foot functions as an euphemism for the

---

is *Tifʾeret*, and *ʿAtiqaʾ Qadishaʾ* is found in the *Razaʾ di-Meheimanutaʾ* in Neḥemiah Ḥayyon, *ʿOz Leʾlohim* (Berlin, 1713), 79a. See Scholem, *Sabbatai Ṣevi*, pp. 905–909; Liebes, *On Sabbateanism*, p. 63. On the attribution of this text to Cardoso, see Liebes, *op. cit.*, pp. 35–48.

107 Nathan's description of the messianic epoch reflects the idea expressed in Lurianic texts regarding the ascent of *Zeʿeir ʾAnpin* (together with his feminine counterpart, *Nuqbaʾ*) to the configurations of *ʾAbbaʾ* and *ʾImmaʾ* on Sabbath as a result of the overflowing of mercy from *ʿAtiqaʾ Qadishaʾ*. See *Shaʿarei Maʾamerei Rashbi*, 18b–c, 19b, and analysis in Meroz, "Redemption in the Lurianic Kabbalah," pp. 117–118, as well as my own discussion in "Coronation of the Sabbath Bride."

108 Cf. the text of Nathan in Scholem, *Researches*, p. 67.

109 I surmise that the meaning of this remark is that the word *we-taḥat*, which means "and under," is equal to 814, which is the numerical value of the letters of the name Sabbatai Ṣevi as well as the numerical value of the letters of the name Shaddai written out in full. See above, n. 45.

110 *Be-ʿIqvot Mashiaḥ*, pp. 15–16.

111 On the Lurianic background of this motif, see Scholem, *Sabbatai Ṣevi*, pp. 49, 303; Tishby, *Doctrine of Evil*, pp. 134–135.

phallus,[112] Nathan identifies the foot of God mentioned in the biblical verse as the corona of the phallus of the Father. When the aspect of the foot ascends, it assumes the position of the diadem on the head of the masculine potency, a secret related to the biblical expression, "crown of her husband." In his discussion of this passage, Scholem marvels at what he considers to be the incompatible positions expressed by Nathan with respect to the alternative localization of the messiah's soul in the lowest and the highest configurations of the divine.[113] According to my interpretation, however, there is no contradiction at all in Nathan's remarks, for the messiah is portrayed as the phallic crown that rises until it becomes ontically integrated into the highest realm of the Godhead. The elevation of the feminine is related exegetically to the words "the likeness of a pavement of sapphire," which also serves as the textual basis for the idea that Sabbatai Ṣevi purified his body. In the final analysis, Sabbatai Ṣevi's purification of his body, and one may assume that control over sexual passion figures prominently in this purification, is the mundane act that parallels the ascent of the feminine in the divine sphere. In line with this symbolic parallelism, Nathan asserts that the revelation of Sabbatai Ṣevi as messiah represents the restoration of the feminine to the masculine:

> The root of the messianic king is in the corona of the phallus of the Father (*ʿaṭeret yesod ʾabbaʾ*) . . . and the messiah son of David . . . his place is in *ʿAṭarah*, for he is in the corona of the phallus of *Zeʿeir* (*ʿaṭeret yesod di-zeʿeir*). Therefore, it says concerning him, "The crown was taken from the head of their king [and it was placed on David's head]" (2 Sam. 12:30) . . . and it says, "Mordecai left the king's presence in royal robes [of blue and white] with a magnificent crown of gold" (Esther 8:15). "Mordecai left," this is the secret of the phallus of the Father (*yesod ʾabbaʾ*) that protrudes. It says a "crown of gold" (*ʿaṭeret zahav*) . . . for when the phallus of the Father goes out he takes the crown of gold. . . . and when that phallus projects he contains that crown in him, according to the secret of [the verse] "I have set my bow in the cloud" (Gen. 9:13).[114]

---

[112] Regarding the phallic symbolism of the foot, see Wolfson, "Images of God's Feet," pp. 164–170.

[113] *Sabbatai Ṣevi*, p. 307.

[114] *Be-ʿIqvot Mashiaḥ*, p. 20. Scholem, *Sabbatai Ṣevi*, pp. 306–307, relates this text to Lurianic sources wherein Mordecai is symbolically associated with the aspect of God known as *yesod de-ʾabbaʾ*, the foundation of the Father, the element of consciousness that corresponds to the phallus. According to Sabbatai Ṣevi's disciples,

The messianic moment is marked by the reintegration of the feminine in the masculine, symbolically portrayed as the corona of the extended phallus, the crown of gold atop the head of Mordecai.[115] Following earlier kabbalistic sources, especially passages from the zoharic corpus, Nathan portrays the reconstituted androgyne as well in terms of the biblical image of the rainbow in the cloud, the sign of the covenant established by God with Noah. Symbolically, the covenant signals that the phallic bow is manifest through the (holy) covering, the cloud that stands in relation to the bow as the feminine crown on the head of the messianic king.[116] Hence, the cloud, without which the bow is not visible as a sign, is transformed into the crown of the bow that extends. From another perspective, however, the covering can be imaged in negative terms as that which obstructs the vision of the bow in its luminous colors like the foreskin that covers the sign of the covenant, the letter *yod* inscribed on the head of the penis. Thus, in his lengthy epistle on Sabbatai Ṣevi's

---

Mordecai is a spark from the soul of the messiah. Regarding the symbolic association of Sabbatai Ṣevi and Esther, see below, n. 147. Finally, let me note that despite the many differences in approach between Nathan of Gaza and Abraham Cardoso, with respect to the issue of the phallic source of the messianic figure, they are in basic agreement. Thus, for example, see the text of Cardoso in Scholem, *Researches*, p. 436: "Now it is known that the messiah son of David is from *Malkhut*, which is the end and the terminus of the *sefirot* of emanation. Similarly, the messiah son of David is the terminus, and he is from the side of the root of his soul from the foundation of the Father (*yesod de-ʾabbaʾ*), from the corona of the foundation (*ʿaṭarah shel ha-yesod*), which is the aspect of *Malkhut*... and the messiah son of Ephraim is from *Yesod*... and from the side of his root, which is from the corona of the foundation of the mother (*ʿaṭeret yesod de-ʾimmaʾ*)." See *op. cit.*, p. 444.

115 See E.R. Wolfson, "Woman—The Feminine As Other in Theosophic Kabbalah: Some Philosophical Observations on the Divine Androgyne," in *The Other in Jewish Thought and History: Constructions of Jewish Culture and Identity*, edited by L. Silberstein and R. Cohn (New York, 1994), pp. 166–204; *idem*, "On Becoming Female: Crossing Gender Boundaries in Kabbalistic Ritual and Myth," in *Gender and Judaism: The Transformation of Tradition*, edited by T.M. Rudavsky (New York, 1995), pp. 209–228, and the expanded version of this study, in *Circle in the Square*, pp. 79–121.

116 A particularly succinct formulation of this idea is given by Cordovero, *Tiqqunei Zohar ʿim Perush ʾOr Yaqar*, vol. 2, p. 222. Commenting on the remark in the introduction to *Tiqqunei Zohar*, 7a, "The eighth vision, 'such was the appearance of the surrounding radiance' (Ezek. 1:28), is the lower *Shekhinah*, concerning whom it says, 'the female surrounds the male' (Jer. 31:21)," Cordovero writes: "Since he saw the appearance of the bow, that is, the secret of *Yesod* that is seen within *Malkhut*, and *Malkhut* crowns (*koteret*) him." In the continuation of this passage, Cordovero explains that this state is referred to as the female surrounding the male since the union of male and female arises from the side of the feminine judgment, the lower form of union that must be contrasted with the male surrounding the female, the higher union that arises from the attribute of masculine mercy.

heresy, Nathan builds on a messianic discourse in *Tiqqunei Zohar*[117] and depicts redemption as the cutting away of the three shells that surround the corona. When these shells are cut away, the three colors of the rainbow shine through the letter *yod*, the three colors that constitute the pupil of the eye (*bat ʿayin*), which is the point of the sign of the covenant (*nequddah ʾot berit*).[118] Concerning this moment, the voice of Scripture portends, "When the bow is in the clouds, I will see it and remember the everlasting covenant between God and all living creatures, all flesh that is on earth" (Gen. 9:16). When the sign is covered by the shells, the Sabbath is desecrated, for she has fallen into the hole of impurity, but when the shells are removed, the Sabbath is sanctified and the *Shekhinah* is elevated to the position of the crown. In line with the view of Menaḥem de Lonzano, Nathan posits two stages to the redemption, the symbolic ascent of Moses and the *Shekhinah* from a state of entrapment in the demonic shells, and the historical redemption of the Jewish people. What prevents the second stage and the final *tiqqun* are human transgressions, and especially the crisis of faith that is epitomized in the failure to recognize that Sabbatai Ṣevi is the messiah.[119] Naturally, the elevation of the divine presence (*ʿilluy ha-shekhinah*) to the aspect of the corona of the phallus is predicated on the heterosexual union that results from the stiffening and the extending forward of the sign of the covenant (i.e., the erection and the ejaculation of the penis in the act of coitus). Hence, Nathan refers explicitly to the union of Sabbatai Ṣevi and the feminine presence of God: "We have already said that our master is in the gradation of the *ṣaddiq* who is united with the *Shekhinah*, and he is the youth, and this is the secret of the verse 'For the youth at a hundred years [shall die]' (Isa. 65:20), for this is the secret of the time of his occultation."[120] Sabbatai Ṣevi is thus linked explicitly to the phallic potency of the divine, the *ṣaddiq*, which is also associated with the figure of Meṭaṭron referred to as

[117] *Tiqqunei Zohar* 37, 78a.

[118] On the symbol of *bat ʿayin*, see above, n. 100.

[119] Nathan's epistle on Sabbatai Ṣevi's heresy in Scholem, *Studies and Texts*, p. 264; see *ibid.*, p. 271. Compare the words of Abraham Rovigo cited and analyzed by Scholem, *Messianic Idea*, pp. 107–108.

[120] *Be-ʿIqvot Mashiaḥ*, pp. 16–17. See parallel passage in Nathan's *Derush ha-Menorah*, in *op. cit.*, p. 124: "This is the secret [of the verse] 'For the youth at a hundred years shall die' (Isa. 65:20), this is the mystery of the messiah son of David whose root is in *Yesod*, the youth (*naʿar*) whose root is dependent on [the attribute of] the *ṣevi*." The two passages are already cited by Scholem, *Researches*, pp. 362–363.

na'ar, the "youthful one" or the "servant,"[121] and in virtue of that correlation he is united with the *Shekhinah*. The consequence of that union, however, is the restoration of the feminine to the masculine, a process, in which the female is transformed into the crowning aspect of the male. If male and female were not united, it would not be possible for the female to be assimilated into the male. By identifying Sabbatai Ṣevi as *'aṭeret yesod*, therefore, Nathan intended to communicate the idea that he embodies the androgynous unity of the divine as it is contextualized specifically in the male organ.

This gender transformation also underlies Nathan's insistence that the critical role assigned to Sabbatai Ṣevi was his rectifying the sin of spilling semen in vain, the primordial sin of Adam that set history in motion.[122] According to a passage in *Derush ha-Taninim*, the protoype of this messianic action is Bar Kokhba, a spark from the soul of the Davidic messiah, concerning whom the rabbis said that he cast stones with his feet.[123] Nathan remarks that this alludes to the "wondrous rectification that he performed above in the secret of the soul of the footheels of the messiah. The stones are the rectification of the seed that they cast aside with their hands, for *Malkhut* is in the heel, and [this rectification occurs] by means of *Yesod*, which is *ben koziba'*."[124] The function of rectifying the sin of spilling semen in vain is attributed to Sabbatai Ṣevi on account of his being the incarnation of the corona of the divine phallus. However, not only the messiah but also the souls of the generation of the messiah, who are distinguished by their comprehension of a "wondrous wisdom," derive from the same gradation of the divine.

> You must know that these souls have their source in the world of circles (*'olam ha-'iggulim*) for the shattering was in them, and they were contained in a straight line in the secret of the crown (*'aṭarah*) that is in each and every limb, and they are in the secret of the mouth of the penis (*pi ha-'amah*), for these souls are the eighty-five[125] sparks from

---

[121] See Scholem, *Jewish Gnosticism*, pp. 49–50.

[122] Nathan appropriated the idea that the chief task of the messiah was to rectify the sin of spilling semen in vain from the Lurianic material. This messianic task is applied, for instance, to Moses in *Sha'ar ha-Pesuqim* (Jerusalem, 1912), 21b–d. See Meroz, "Redemption in Lurianic Kabbalah," pp. 329–335, 343–344; Liebes, "'Two Young Roes of a Doe'," p. 141.

[123] Nathan paraphrases the rabbinic dictum in *Midrash Eikhah Rabbah*, edited by S. Buber (Vilna, 1899), 2:47, 51a.

[124] *Be-'Iqvot Mashiaḥ*, p. 45.

[125] The number eighty-five is written in Hebrew with the letters *pe* (= 80) and *he'* (= 5), which can also spell the word *peh*, i.e., mouth.

> the two hundred and eighty-eight sparks that remained in the shattered vessels. Moses, our master, elevated two hundred and two sparks ... and these sparks that Moses elevated returned to the shells and they were elevated by all the generations that have passed. There remained eighty-five sparks that were not elevated except by means of the messianic king who is also in the mouth of the penis (*peh ha-ʾamah*). ...[126] The mouth of the messianic king is forever open and it is built magnificently ... and it says, "like the tower of David" (Song of Songs 4:4), this is the foundation of the corona (*yesod ha-ʿaṭarah*), which is "built magnificently" (*banuy le-talpiyyot*), sometimes the lower mouth and sometimes the upper mouth, and this is the elevation of *Malkhut*. This requires a lengthy explanation and this is not its place. ... Therefore there is one additional spark that binds them all, and the eighty-six sparks of the shattered vessels, which are in the [aspect of] *Malkhut* of the masculine, ascend and the rectification of the aspect of unity (*beḥinat ha-ʾaqqudim*) that was mentioned. At the end of this sabbatical year the aspect of the mouth of the feminine will be rectified when the messianic king will come from the Sambaton river in order to rectify the aspect of these eighty-six sparks.[127]

The sparks redeemed in the messianic era derive from the same root as the soul of the messiah. From that perspective Sabbatai Ṣevi is not only the redeemer but also the one who is redeemed.[128] What is most important for the purposes of this study is that the ontic source of these souls is in the mouth (or head) of the penis, which corresponds to the *ʿaṭeret berit*, the aspect of the feminine contextualized in the masculine. The liberation of these sparks, which are the fragments of the messiah's own soul, results in the constitution of this aspect of the divine.

The characterization of the messianic age in terms of the elevation of the female to the position of the crown that rests on the head of

---

[126] The point made by Nathan is not intelligible unless one keeps in mind the fact that the numerical equivalence of the consonants that make up the word *peh* equal eighty-five (see previous note). On the basis of this numerology Nathan links the uplifting of the eighty-five remaining sparks to the messiah who is the mouth of the male organ (*peh ha-ʾamah*).

[127] *Be-ʿIqvot Mashiaḥ*, pp. 45–46.

[128] This idea of the "redeemed redeemer" is affirmed in older kabbalistic sources, including, most importantly, in the zoharic corpus, where it is linked exegetically to the description of the king in Zechariah 9:9, "righteous and saved is he." See Liebes, "Messiah of the *Zohar*," pp. 88, 205–206 (English translation, pp. 3, 73). Particularly germane to Sabbatian theology is the interpretation of this verse in *Zohar* 3:69a.

the male is found as well in the letter that Nathan wrote to Raphael Joseph of Egypt:

> In our time, with the help of God, the matters will be clarified and the lights will disseminate, and *Malkhut* will be in the mystery of the "crown of her husband," and the Tetragrammaton will be articulated as *yah, yah* repeated twice, and this is what the verse said, "[YHWH will be the king over all the earth;] in that day, YHWH will be one and his name will be one" (Zech. 4:9), for the *waw/he'* of YHWH will be coupled like the *yod/he'*, and they never are separated. In this time, you know with certainty that no spark of the *Shekhinah* is amidst the external ones, and the worlds are now in the secret of the *lamed* of [the word] *ṣelem* [image] as they are on the eve of Sabbath. We should no longer seek to perform rectifications (*tiqqunim*), but only to adorn the bride, to restore her face to face [with the bridegroom]. . . . Therefore, she is in [the world of] emanation in the secret of face to face, beneath the foundation (*hi' ba-'aṣilut be-sod panim be-fanim taḥat yesod*), and the other worlds are in the secret of the hinder parts (*we-ha-ʿolamot ha-'aḥerim hem be-sod 'aḥorim*).[129]

In the messianic period, the feminine rises from the submissive position characteristic of the state of exile to her restoration in the realm of emanation. Nathan perceived that his own time was akin to the eve of Sabbath, the time before the messianic coming, encoded in the enlarged *lamed* of the word *ṣelem*, the image, which stands metonymically for *ṣelem 'elohim*, the divine image that refers more specifically in the complex theosophy of Lurianic kabbalah to the three aspects of the internal and the encompassing consciousness (*moḥin penimiyyim u-maqifin*) of *Zeʿeir 'Anpin*.[130] At such time it is appropriate to stop reciting the *tiqqunim* instituted by Luria, and in their place it is necessary to adorn the bride and to prepare her for union with the male.[131] In this state, the *Shekhinah* has already been uplifted from

---

[129] *Ṣiṣat Novel Ṣevi*, pp. 8–9.

[130] *ʿEṣ Ḥayyim* 23:1, 105d. On the expansion of the *lamed* in the word *ṣelem* on the eve of Sabbath, see *Shaʿar ha-Kawwanot*, 64a–b; *Peri ʿEṣ Ḥayyim*, pp. 374–375, 376–377, 394; *Kanfei Yonah*, MS Sassoon 993, p. 548.

[131] This theme is repeated in a number of Nathan's writings. For example, in *Derush ha-Taninim*, in *Be-ʿIqvot Mashiaḥ*, p. 15, Nathan writes that, insofar as the messianic redemption has already begun in the form of the eve of Sabbath, it is no longer necessary "to perform the *tiqqun* and to weep over the exile of the *Shekhinah* as we used to do, but rather [it is necessary to perform] the *tiqqun* that was established by the Amirah, as it is known to you." See Scholem, *Sabbatai Ṣevi*, p. 250 n. 149; *Messianic Idea*, pp. 102–103. In his letter on the heresy of Sabbatai Ṣevi, Nathan expressed the matter as follows: The *Shekhinah* and Moses had already been

the dust of exile and she is thus characterized as being "in the secret of face to face, beneath the foundation," that is, she is situated beneath the phallic *Yesod* in her restoration to the divine realm. In this state, moreover, the *Shekhinah* is also referred to as *ʿaṭeret baʿlah*, the "crown of her husband," for the heterosexual union facilitates the process by which the female becomes integrated as the crowning part of the male. The reconstitution of the androgynous phallus is marked as well in the transformation of the four-letter name, *yhwh*, to the repetition of *yh yh*, a transposition occasioned by the union of the upper male and female (*yod/he*ʾ) and the lower male and female (*waw/he*ʾ) to form the complete name.[132]

A similar characterization of the eschaton is reiterated by Nathan in the first part of his theosophical *magnum opus*, *Sefer ha-Beriʾah*, composed sometime around 1670. In that work, Nathan emphasizes several times that the root of the attribute of *Malkhut* at the time of the *ṣimṣum* (the withdrawal of the infinite divine light) was on the right, i.e., the attribute of mercy that is generally valorized in theosophic kabbalah as male. However, as this attribute emerged from the primordial space (*ḥalal* or *ṭehiru*), it assumed the character of the left, the attribute of judgment, or the backside. The goal of the historical process is for *Malkhut* to be restored to the right. This restoration is portrayed by Nathan, following earlier kabbalistic sources, as the transmutation of *Malkhut* into the crown that is elevated to the uppermost gradation, the attribute of *Keter*. In Nathan's own words:

> Understand what the sages, blessed be their memory, said, regarding the fact that in the future her name will be the "crown of her husband" (*ʿaṭeret baʿlah*) . . . for her nature is to resemble *Keter*. . . . In the time of the *ṣimṣum* she was the right, but immediately after the *ṣimṣum* she turned into the left, and afterward she will be restored to the right. *Keter* acquired its essence immediately in the act of the chariot (*maʿaseh merkavah*), but *Malkhut* does not acquire her essence until the end of the act of creation (*maʿaseh bereʾshit*). . . . On account of this reason they

uplifted from the state of oppression, and thus the one who continues to weep or lament over the downtrodden condition of the *Shekhinah* in exile is like one who weeps and laments on the Sabbath. What there is to weep about, concludes Nathan, is the fact that our sins have caused the messiah to be defiled. See Scholem, *Studies and Texts*, p. 264.

[132] For Scholem's insightful discussion of this text, see *Sabbatai Ṣevi*, pp. 275–282. Scholem duly notes the use of the motif of the ascent of the *Shekhinah* to mark the coming of the redemption (pp. 277–278, 281), but he does not engage in any gender analysis of the symbolism.

> said that she will be a "crown of her husband," for after her root, which is entirely the right, is purified, she has a greater ascension than her husband, and she indeed resembles *Keter*.[133]

A parallel to this formulation is found in *Liqquṭei Raza' de-Malka' Qadisha'*:

> The intention of those sages who said that this sabbatical cycle (*shemiṭ-ṭah*) corresponds to the attribute of *Malkhut* is related to the fact that they comprehended all the act of creation (*ma'aseh bere'shit*) that took place, and they determined that in this sabbatical cycle the attribute of *Malkhut* would be rectified, for she came last in the act of creation, whence she was produced through the secret of the left in relation to the attributes above her. In accordance with *Yesod*, which placed within her the source of everything, her nature was in the secret of the right, but they turned her into the left, and now, in the act of the chariot (*ma'aseh merkavah*), we return her to the right. Therefore, we see that most of the actions of the souls of Israel are to rectify this attribute until they restore her to be the crown of her husband (*'aṭeret ba'lah*) in the manner of *Keter*, which is the right in accordance with the foundation of the Infinite (*yesod 'ein sof*). She was produced on the left and afterwards she returns to the right.[134]

I surmise that the symbolic depiction of Sabbatai Ṣevi's coronation signifies his ontic transformation into *'aṭeret ba'lah*, which marks the eschatological state in which *Malkhut* is restored to the masculine *Keter*,[135] the state in which she acquires an ascension greater than her

---

[133] MS New York, Jewish Theological Seminary of America Mic. 1851, fol. 12a.

[134] MS New York, Jewish Theological Seminary of America Mic. 1549, fols. 3b–4a.

[135] The relationship of the messiah and the supernal *sefirah* is underscored by the numerological equivalence of the name of Sabbatai Ṣevi and the expression *koaḥ keter 'elyon*, the "power of the supernal crown," i.e., both equal 814. See the letter of Nathan to Joseph Ṣevi in *Zikkaron li-Venei Yisra'el*, p. 59, and *Ṣiṣat Novel Ṣevi*, p. 260; *Songs and Hymns of the Sabbatians*, edited and translated by M. Attias, with notes by G. Scholem, and introduction by I. Ben-Zvi (Tel Aviv, 1948), p. 206 n. 2 (in Hebrew). The source of this expression, *koaḥ keter 'elyon*, from Joseph ben Shalom Ashkenazi's commentary on *Sefer Yeṣirah*, falsely attributed to Abraham ben David of Posquierés, is duly noted by Scholem (standard edition of *Sefer Yeṣirah* 4:5 [Jerusalem, 1962], 51c): "He enthroned *bet* in life and tied a crown to it, creating through it Saturn in the world, the first day [of the weekly cycle] in time, and the right eye in the person, that is, he elevated the *bet* to be the head through the power of the supernal crown (*lihyot ro'sh be-khoaḥ keter 'elyon*). And he placed therein the power of wisdom (*koaḥ ha-ḥokhmah*), and he formed in it the planet of Saturn, which is beneath the name AB"G YT"S [i.e., the first of seven pairs of six letters that make up the forty-two-letter name, and this is the one that transmits wisdom

husband. *Malkhut* is transferred from her lowly station at the bottom of the divine pleroma to the exalted position of being the crown that sits atop the head of the king. Here we confront the profound dialectic of gender symbolism in Sabbatian soteriology: Messianic time is marked by a reversal of the positioning of male and female, which betokens concurrently the masculinization of the divine feminine and the feminization of the earthly messiah. In my opinion, this same symbolic structure underlies the statement repeated in several contexts by Nathan that Sabbatai Ṣevi "caused the king to sit on his throne."[136] The formulation of Nathan in a small treatise dedicated to clarifying the faith of Sabbatai Ṣevi, *Kawwanat ʾEmunat ʾAdonenu*, is particularly noteworthy: "Concerning this faith our master the king, may his majesty be elevated, labored until he placed the king, which is *Tifʾeret*, on his throne. Therefore, regarding him Habakuk the prophet prophecied, *ṣaddiq be-ʾemunato yiḥyeh* ['the righteous man shall live in his faith'] (Hab. 2:4) the first letters of which spell *ṣevi*.[137] After he placed the king on the throne, he was greatly elevated until the point that he alone was given permission to inquire of *ʿAtiqaʾ Qadishaʾ*."[138] The placing of the king on the throne signifies the union of the masculine and the feminine aspects of God, *Tifʿeret* and *Shekhinah*, which results in the elevation of Sabbatai Ṣevi, who represents in his own being the union enacted in the world of ema-

to Saturn." Nathan refers explicitly to the continuation of this passage (*Sefer Yeṣirah* 4:5, 52b), as well as to its citation in *Sefer ha-Peliʾah* ([Cracow, 1894], pt. 1, 57c), wherein Saturn is identified as the messiah, in his writings, for example, in his epistle on the heresy of Sabbatai Ṣevi in *Studies and Texts*, p. 267. On the nexus of the Christian-pagan idea of the renewal of Saturn and the kabbalistic notion of the revival of divine kingship in the form of Sabbatai Ṣevi, see Yosha, "Philosophical Elements," p. 63 n. 13.

136 See the beginning of *Derush ha-Taninim* in *Be-ʿIqvot Mashiaḥ*, p. 14. Also relevant are the words of the angelic *maggid* to Nathan regarding the placing of Sabbatai Ṣevi on the divine throne, which is related more specifically to the identification of the messiah and Moses. See Scholem, *Be-ʿIqvot Mashiaḥ*, p. 59; *Researches*, p. 68. On the possibility that this already implies the idea of the apotheosis of Sabbatai Ṣevi according to Nathan, see Elqayam, "Mystery of Faith," p. 33.

137 For an extensive discussion of the use of this verse, which informed Sabbatian theology, see Elqayam, "Mystery of Faith," pp. 34–48.

138 I have translated from the version of the text published by G. Scholem, *Shabbetai Ẓevi and the Shabbetaian Movement During his Lifetime* (Tel Aviv, 1987), p. 255 (in Hebrew). For a slightly different version, see *ʿInyenei Shabbetai Ṣevi*, p. 93. This motif in Nathan's thought has been noted by Scholem, *Sabbatai Ṣevi*, p. 317, and Liebes, *On Sabbateanism*, pp. 285 n. 112 and 289 n. 176. My interpretation, however, differs from the explanation of Scholem and Liebes. On the identification of Sabbatai Ṣevi as *ʾemunah*, see n. 143.

nation, to the uppermost gradation of the divine, *ʿAtiqaʾ Qadishaʾ*. As I mentioned above, Nathan appropriates the zoharic motif of the disclosure of *ʿAtiqaʾ Qadishaʾ* in the configuration of *Zeʿeir ʾAnpin*, or, alternatively, the Lurianic description of the elevation of *Zeʿeir ʾAnpin* to *ʿAtiqaʾ Qadishaʾ*, in order to characterize the quality of restfulness that is indicative of the messianic reality operative in the time of Sabbatai Ṣevi.[139] What is necessary to emphasize here is that the ascent of the messiah to the top of the sefirotic realm is connected by Nathan to the elevation of the *Shekhinah* and her transformation into the crown that rests on the head of the male. The phallic implication of this process is underscored in Nathan's remark in his penitential devotions: "The manifestation of the light of the name Shaddai will be disclosed through the messianic king, and through him the light of *ʿAtiqaʾ Qadishaʾ* will be manifest in *Zeʿeir ʾAnpin*, and by means of this the souls of this generation will be rectified."[140] The souls rectified in the generation of the messiah, as I noted previously, are those sparks lodged in the heels of the anthropomorphic form submersed in the demonic shells. But these sparks can be redeemed only when the full light of the name Shaddai is revealed through the messianic king, a disclosure that facilitates the illumination of *Zeʿeir ʾAnpin* by the light of *ʿAtiqaʾ Qadishaʾ*. The name Shaddai clearly refers to *Yesod*, the phallic potency of the divine, which is rendered complete when the feminine crown is restored to it, a process set into motion by Sabbatai Ṣevi's placing the king upon the throne. From a symbolic point of view, therefore, enthronement signifies the same gender transformation as coronation.

Sabbatai Ṣevi incorporates male and female, and thus he represents the reconfigured Adam, the male to which the female is restored. This symbolic matter is related in a number of images utilized by the Sabbatian theologians, especially Nathan and his colleagues and disciples. For example, Nathan writes that the name *shabbetai* can be decomposed into *shabbat yod*, which is an alternative way of noting that Sabbatai Ṣevi embodied the two Sabbaths, clearly a reference to *Malkhut* and *Yesod*, the feminine night and the masculine day.[141] According to another text, Sabbatai Ṣevi shone with the illumination

---

139 See above, n. 107.

140 I. Tishby, "Nathan of Gaza's Penitential Devotions," *Tarbiz* 15 (1944): 164–165 (in Hebrew). See Scholem, *Sabbatai Ṣevi*, pp. 275–276, 296.

141 Nathan's epistle in Scholem, *Studies and Texts*, p. 268. On the symbolic correlation of Sabbatai Ṣevi and the Sabbath, see above, n. 105.

of the sun and moon, again an obvious reference to the masculine and feminine potencies of the divine.[142] The presumption that Sabbatai Ṣevi embodies the divine androgyne in his being also underlies Nathan's repeated identification of Sabbatai Ṣevi as the personification, embodiment, or incarnation of faith (*ʾemunah*), a theme repeatedly linked exegetically, as we have already seen, to the verse *ṣaddiq be-ʾemunato yiḥyeh* (Hab. 2:4).[143] The true believer has faith in the proclamation of divinity (*pirsum ʾelohut*) through the person of Sabbatai Ṣevi.[144] That is, according to an older kabbalistic symbol, especially prominent in zoharic literature,[145] the mystery of faith refers to the unification of the masculine and feminine potencies of the divine, a unity that is realized in the personhood of Sabbatai Ṣevi;[146] there

142 See the version of Nathan's letter published by Scholem, *Researches*, p. 67; and another letter of Nathan in *op. cit.*, p. 69.

143 The apocalypse of Nathan attributed to Abraham the Pious in Scholem, *Researches*, p. 69 (alternative versions in Scholem, *Be-ʿIqvot Mashiaḥ*, p. 60, and *Ṣiṣat Novel Ṣevi*, p. 159); the letter of Nathan on Sabbatai Ṣevi's heresy in Scholem, *Studies and Texts*, pp. 238–239, 261, 272. In the latter context, Sabbatai Ṣevi is identified as the "holy faith" (*ha-ʾemunah ha-qedoshah*) such that being rooted in it is equivalent to fulfilling the Torah in its entirety. See also *Zikkaron li-Venei Yisraʾel*, p. 43; and references in the following note. The nexus between the secret of faith and the Torah is an important aspect of Nathan's teaching, which is intrinsically related to his eschatological justification of antinomianism. See the passage from Nathan's *Liqquṭei Razaʾ de-Malkaʾ Meshiḥaʾ*, MS New York, Columbia University x893 z8, fol. 10a, cited from another manuscript by Elqayam, "Mystery of Faith," p. 47, and further discussion on p. 255 n. 18. On Nathan's doctrine of faith, see Scholem, *Sabbatai Ṣevi*, pp. 211–212; 282–284; *Messianic Idea*, pp. 91–92. Scholem duly noted the similarity of Nathan's view and the Christological doctrine. For a more recent analysis of Nathan's position in light of the secret of faith promulgated by Sabbatai Ṣevi, see the aforementioned study of Elqayam.

144 Scholem, *Studies and Texts*, p. 266. Nathan thus connects the theosophic doctrine regarding the identification of Sabbatai Ṣevi as the embodiment of faith and the halakhic ruling of Maimonides (*Mishneh Torah*, Melakhim, 11:3) that the messiah, in contrast to the prophet (see Yesode Torah, 7:7), requires no external sign or miracle to legitimate his claim. See the language of Nathan in the letter published by Scholem, *Researches*, p. 20. In that context, moreover, Nathan emphasizes that the rabbis rejected Jesus because of all the wonders and signs he performed, and not because he identified himself as divine, since the messiah indeed does assume the position of the incarnational form of the divine: "Is it not the level of the messiah to rectify the lower world and to be a chariot for the light of life? Therefore his name is YHWH, for he comprises the chariot of the three worlds."

145 See Liebes, *Sections of a Zohar Lexicon*, pp. 398–401.

146 The erotic union of gender in the personhood of the messiah is conveyed as well by the application of the expression *ʾish ʾemunot*, "a man of faith" (Prov. 28:20), to Sabbatai Ṣevi. See the text published by Scholem, *Shabbetai Zevi*, p. 255, and analysis of Elqayam, "Mystery of Faith," pp. 32 and 253–254 n. 8. Elqayam correctly notes that this biblical expression is applied to Moses in earlier midrashic sources; hence the attribution of the same phrase to Sabbatai Ṣevi is predicated on

is no mention of a feminine counterpart to Sabbatai Ṣevi, for in his own being he encompasses and thereby transcends the male/female polarity.[147]

Iconic and Figural Representations of the Crown

In support of my hypothesis, let me mention several iconographic representations of Sabbatai Ṣevi's crown in sources both prior to and after the apostasy. For example, in some synagogues, Psalm 21, which was interpreted in a Sabbatian vein, was inscribed on a wooden board decorated with floral designs and surmounted by a crown with the words "the crown of Sabbatai Ṣevi."[148] The iconographic portrayal of the crown was, no doubt, suggested by the end of the fourth verse of this psalm, *tashit le-ro'sho ʿaṭeret paz*. The symbolic significance of the messianic coronation, which I have explored from a number of texts, is iconically depcited in a copperplate engraving facing the title page of Nathan's *Tiqqun Qeri'ah le-khol Laylah wa-Yom*, published in Amsterdam in 1666 (see figure 1).[149] Two distinct scenes

the implicit identification of the latter with Moses. See above, n. 60. On the erotic implications of Sabbatai Ṣevi's relationship to faith, which refers both to his existential religious state and to the corresponding divine gradation of *Malkhut*, see Liebes, *On Sabbateanism*, p. 279 n. 67.

[147] This is not to deny the occasional references to the wives of Sabbatai Ṣevi who play an important role in the messianic drama as it is portrayed in the imagination of the Sabbatian theologians. Especially interesting are the remarks of Nathan in his letter to Raphael Joseph in *Ṣiṣat Novel Ṣevi*, pp. 11–12 (translated in *Sabbatai Ṣevi*, pp. 273–274). The enigmatic nature of the traditions about the status of Sabbatai Ṣevi's wives is underscored by Nathan's insistence that to understand the matter one must receive an oral tradition. The mystical significance of Sabbatai Ṣevi's marriage and divorce is emphasized in Nathan's letter published in Amarillo, "Sabbatean Documents," pp. 263–264. In that context, the Jewish woman that Sabbatai Ṣevi married after he wore the garment of Islam is compared to Esther who hid her identity from Ahasuerus. Regarding the marriage of Sabbatai Ṣevi to the daughter of Joseph Filosoff, whose name may indeed have been Esther, see Benayahu, *Shabbatean Movement in Greece*, pp. 27–32, and the poem of the father-in-law celebrating the marriage of his daughter to the messiah, *op. cit.*, pp. 365–366. See Scholem, *Sabbatai Ṣevi*, pp. 851 and 887 n. 153. On the comparison of the fate of Sabbatai Ṣevi to Esther, see the letter of Nathan in *Zikkaron li-Venei Yisra'el*, p. 60; *Ṣiṣat Novel Ṣevi*, p. 262; Scholem, *Sabbatai Ṣevi*, p. 743. See also letter of Joseph Halevi to Sasportas, *Ṣiṣat Novel Ṣevi*, p. 256, and the letter of Cardoso to his brother, *op. cit.*, p. 295.

[148] *Sabbatai Ṣevi*, p. 424. The source for Scholem's comments is Thomas Coenen, *Ydele verwachtinge der Joden* (Amsterdam, 1669).

[149] For a bibliographic description of this edition, see Scholem, *Sabbatai Ṣevi*, p. 938 n. 32. The picture is reproduced in *ibid.*, plate III, opposite p. 546.

Fig. 1. Crown of Ṣevi. From: *Tiqqun Qeri'ah le-Khol Laylah wa-Yom.* (Amsterdam, 1666), titlepage. (Photo: S. Kaufman, courtesy The Library of the Jewish Theological Seminary of America, New York).

are depicted in the frontispiece. In the upper half, Sabbatai Ṣevi is portrayed as sitting on the royal throne, holding a scepter in his right hand, and his left hand is on an open book that is resting on his lap. Four men stand on either side of the throne, all gazing at the enthroned messianic king. Above the head of Sabbatai Ṣevi is a celestial crown held by four angels and bearing the inscription *ʿaṭeret ṣevi*. The three steps leading up to the throne are inscribed with the verse "In those days and at that time, I will raise up a true branch of David's line, and he shall do what is just and right in the land" (Jer. 33:15). In the lower part of the picture, Sabbatai Ṣevi is portrayed as sitting and studying at a round table with twelve disciples.[150] At the very bottom of the lower picture are the words "Meditate on it day and night" (Josh. 1:8) and on the top the word *tiqqun* appears in bold letters.

It is evident that the picture represents the transformation of Sabbatai Ṣevi from charismatic teacher to messianic king. The redemptive potency of the mystical fellowship engaged in study depicted in the lower picture is fully realized only when Sabbatai Ṣevi occupies his place on the throne and is crowned as messiah as is portrayed in the upper picture. The expression on the crown is derived from the biblical verse, *ba-yom ha-huʾ yihyeh yhwh ṣevaʾot la-ʿaṭeret ṣevi we-li-ṣefirat tifʾarah li-sheʾar ʿammo*, "In that day, the Lord of Hosts shall become a crown of beauty and a diadem of glory for the remnant of His people" (Isa. 28:5). The inscription *ʿaṭeret ṣevi* thus has a double connotation: On the one hand, it is the crown that belongs to Sabbatai Ṣevi, but, on the other hand, it is the crown to which Sabbatai Ṣevi himself refers. I would suggest, therefore, that the implication of this inscription is that Sabbatai Ṣevi has been transformed into the crown. Support for my interpretation may be gathered

---

[150] Scholem (see reference in previous note) describes the lower scene as "the Ten Tribes studying with the messiah." Scholem's comment is perplexing insofar as there are clearly twelve figures sitting at the table with Sabbatai Ṣevi at the head. In his fuller description of this engraving (*Sabbatai Ṣevi*, p. 526), Scholem correctly notes that "the lower picture shows twelve bearded men, together with an oversized thirteenth—evidently the Twelve Tribes and the messiah—seated at a round table and studying from a book." On the significance of the selection of twelve rabbinic scholars on the part of Sabbatai Ṣevi to represent the twelves tribes and its possible analogy to the Gospel account of the apostles, see Scholem, *op. cit.*, pp. 222–223, and references supplied in n. 69; see also the document published by Scholem, *Researches*, p. 63, where mention is made of the twelve sages surrounding Sabbatai Ṣevi who correspond to the twelves sons of Jacob whence emerged the twelve tribes.

from an edition of the *Hafṭarot* published in Amsterdam in 1666. The title page shows a large crown and a diadem, on which are written the words *ʿaṭeret ṣevi*, and underneath it the inscription, "Sabbatai Ṣevi, king of Israel and the anointed of the God of Jacob."[151] These iconic images graphically represent a cornerstone of Sabbatian theology, which involves the identification of Sabbatai Ṣevi as the incarnation of the attribute of God that corresponds to the *ʿaṭeret ṣevi*, i.e., the corona of the phallus.[152] The image of the crown relates both to the exoteric fact that Sabbatai Ṣevi will be crowned as the Davidic messiah and to the more esoteric claim that he is ontically on a par with the divine crown, which is localized anatomically in the male organ.

The significance of this particularly ornate depiction of Sabbatai Ṣevi's coronation is underscored when compared to another frontispiece of a second *tiqqun* also published in Amsterdam in 1666 (see figure 2). In this case there are three different scenes. The upper scene depicts the receiving of the Tablets of the Covenant by Moses from God (represented by the letters *bet he*ʾ, i.e., *barukh hu*ʾ, "blessed be He") on the top of Mount Sinai, which is surrounded by the people of Israel. Flowing out from the two sides of the mountain is the verse, "By day may the Lord vouchsafe His faithful care, so that at night a song to Him may be with me" (Ps. 42:9). In the center of the picture is the title of the special prayer book, *tiqqun liqro*ʾ *laylah wa-yom*, the liturgy that is to be read night and day. The second scene is a depiction of Sabbatai Ṣevi sitting and studying a text with nine disciples seated at or standing around the table. The third scene beneath this one is the coronation and anointment of Sabbatai Ṣevi who sits at the left side of the table. The messianic crown is represented as the wreath held by two (presumably angelic) hands above the head of Sabbatai Ṣevi. Directly below the wreath is the jar of oil that is being poured over Sabbatai Ṣevi's head. The disciples turn

[151] The title page is reproduced in A.M. Haberman, *A History of the Hebrew Book* (Jerusalem, 1945), p. 104, and discussed by Scholem, *Sabbatai Ṣevi*, p. 528.

[152] My symbolic decoding of the expression *ʿaṭeret sevi* is based on the fact that the word *ṣevi* refers to *Yesod*, the phallic gradation of the divine. See *Zohar* 1:49a; 3:175a (*Piqqudin*). Especially relevant is the interpretation of the expression *ṣevi laṣaddiq*, "glory to the righteous" (Isa. 24:16), in *Zohar* 3:284a–b: "to be joined in one union with the Holy One, blessed be He, and to be sanctified in one holiness." The "glory to the righteous" thus denotes the union of male and female through the phallus. It is reasonable to suggest, therefore, that the *ʿaṭeret ṣevi* is the corona of the phallus.

Fig. 2. Siddur Sabbatian (Tiqqun), Amsterdam, RBR 97:16. (Photo: S. Kaufman, courtesy The Library of the Jewish Theological Seminary of America, New York).

their attention from the books opened before them to the miraculous scene of their teacher's coronation and anointment as the messiah. In contrast to the first frontispiece that I discussed, in this case the crown is a simple wreath in the style of ancient Greece and it is not overlaid with the added symbolic significance of the *ʿaṭeret ṣevi*. I surmise, nevertheless, that one is justified in interpreting this wreath as a symbolic allusion to the divine crown to which the messiah ben David corresponds.

One of the most interesting iconic representations that alludes to the symbolism of the messiah's identification as the divine crown is found in the frontispiece of *Ḥemdat Ṣevi*, Ṣevi Chotsh's commentary on *Tiqqunei Zohar*, published in Amsterdam in 1706 (see figure 3). On the top of this picture are two deer holding a crown upon which is inscribed Isaiah 28:5. On the bottom of the page it is written in Aramaic that the "one who wants to understand the secret of this supernal gate should look at the introduction to the *Tiqqunim* at the beginning of the first passage." The Aramaic word for gate, *tarʿaʾ*, like its Hebrew equivalent, *shaʿar*, can also refer to the title page. Hence, the hint implies that if one wants to understand the esoteric significance of the images, one must consult the passage that is specified.[153] From an examination of that text it may be deduced that the secret relates to the fact that the word *ṣevi* designates the attribute of *Yesod*, the phallic potency that enters the *Shekhinah* from above. Moreover, it is clear from that passage that *ṣevi* refers to Moses, an association that highlights the redemptive dimension of this gradation. Thus Chotsh comments on the citation of the verse "This the gateway to the Lord, the righteous shall enter through it" (Ps. 118:20) at the very beginning of *Tiqqunei Zohar*:

> The opening of his words illumines the seventy *tiqqunim*, for the *Shekhinah* is called the "gateway"... and the abbreviation [of the expression] *ṣaddiqim yavoʾu vo* ["the righteous shall enter through it"] is *ṣevi* . . . for *Yesod* is called *ṣevi*. . . . "From the end of the earth we hear singing: Glory to the righteous. And I said: *razi li, razi li*[154] (Isa. 24:16), for all the mysteries of Scripture (*razei torah*), which are the secret of the *Zohar*, are related to Moses . . . and Moses in [the letter permutation of] a"t

[153] *Ḥemdat Ṣevi* (Amsterdam, 1706), 50a.

[154] My rendering of the original Hebrew reflects the meaning imputed to it by the kabbalistic author rather than its contextual sense. See the letter of Cardoso to his brother in *Ṣiṣat Novel Ṣevi*, pp. 294–295.

Fig. 3. *Ḥemdat Ṣevi* by Ṣevi Hirsch Chotsch, Amsterdam, 1706. (Courtesy The Library of the Jewish Theological Seminary of America, New York).

> ba"sh is *ṣevi*[155] . . . the secret of the crown (*ʿaṭarah*) of *Zeʿeir*, the glorious diadem, for all of the *Tiqqunim* are dependent on Moses.[156]

With this hint in hand, we can surmise that the idea conveyed by the ornate picture on the frontispiece is that *ʿaṭeret ṣevi* corresponds to the crown of *ṣevi*, i.e., the corona of the phallus, which is the glorious diadem (*kelil tifʾeret*) placed on the head of Moses,[157] the aspect of consciousness (*daʿat*) that is the inner reality of *Yesod*.[158] The secrets of Torah, which are expounded in the different parts of the zoharic corpus, derive from this gradation of the divine.[159] One must further assume that there is a cryptic allusion here to the fact that the crown stands symbolically for Sabbatai Ṣevi, the messianic figure identified as the generational embodiment/reincarnation of Moses. This secret is alluded to in the two biblical verses cited on the very top of the title page. On the right hand side Proverbs 18:10 appears, *migdal ʿoz shem yhwh bo yaruṣ ṣaddiq we-nisqav*, "The name of the Lord is a tower of strength to which the righteous man runs and is safe," and on the left side Psalm 118:20, *zeh ha-shaʿar la-yhwh ṣaddiqim yavoʾu vo*, "This the gateway to the Lord, the righteous shall enter through it." In the former verse, the letters *waw*, *yod*, and *ṣaddi* in the words *bo yaruṣ ṣaddiq* are starred,[160] and in the latter verse the same letters

---

[155] That is, the name of Moses can be read as *ṣevi* through the exegetical technique of letter substitution following the pattern of a"t ba"sh, the first letter (*ʾalef*) represented by the last letter (*taw*), and so on. The use of this technique by Nathan is noted by Scholem, *Sabbatai Ṣevi*, p. 306.

[156] *Ḥemdat Ṣevi*, 50a.

[157] Based on the liturgical refrain in the Sabbath morning prayer describing Moses, "a glorious crown You placed on his head," *kelil tifʾeret be-roʾsho natata lo*.

[158] On Moses as the supernal consciousness, *daʿat ʿelyon*, which is depicted as the inner reality of *Yesod*, and connected, moreover, with the three colors of the rainbow, which is the sign of the messianic redemption, see *Ḥemdat Ṣevi*, 67b. Interestingly, these three colors are also identified in that context as the crown (*ʿaṭarah*) that Solomon's mother bestowed upon him (Song of Songs 3:11). See *ibid.*, 8a, where the emergence of the messianic figures from the womb of *Malkhut* is attributed to *daʿat* entering into *Yesod*. Needless to say, many more textual examples could have been cited, but that clearly lies beyond the scope of this study. I plan on presenting a more systematic analysis of the kabbalistic doctrines of Chotsh in a separate essay.

[159] On the relationship of Moses and the divine emanation whence the zoharic corpus derived, see Wolfson, *Through a Speculum That Shines*, pp. 386–391.

[160] A similar exegesis of Proverbs 18:10 occurs in a document published by Scholem, *Researches*, p. 65. In that setting, the "tower of strength" (*migddal ʿoz*) is identified with the fortress of Abydos in Gallipoli where Sabbatai Ṣevi was incarcerated. Regarding this locution, see Scholem, *Sabbatai Ṣevi*, pp. 460, 469, 512, 598, 606, 626–627, 670, 678.

in the words *ṣaddiqim yavo'u vo* are starred.[161] Encoded in the two verses, therefore, is an allusion to *ṣevi*, which refers metonymically to Sabbatai Ṣevi. The *ṣaddiq* who runs in the tower of strength, identified as the divine name, and the *ṣaddiq* who enters through the gate of the Lord is none other than Sabbatai Ṣevi, who is crowned by the figural crown inscribed with the words *yhwh ṣeva'ot la-ʿaṭeret ṣevi we-li-ṣefirat tif'arah* (Isa. 28:5), a verse read as a sign of the incarnation of the divine in the messiah.

Coronation and the Engenderment of Messianic Politics

By way of recapitulation, it can be said that on the simple level, as most scholars have noted, wearing the turban, *levishat ha-ṣenif*, signifies the conversion to Islam. Halperin is to be given credit for pointing out another dimension of this phenomenon. The literary model that Sabbatian theologians probably drew upon was the translation of Enoch to heaven and his transformation into the angelic Meṭaṭron. There is, indeed, an obvious and special connection between Meṭaṭron and Sabbatai Ṣevi. My own analysis builds on and supports the view of Halperin, but I have tried to broaden the discussion by examining the act of putting on the turban in terms of the theosophic symbology of the crown in Sabbatian sources. When the phenomenon is viewed in that light, it becomes clear that on a more profound level donning the turban denotes the ontological assimilation of the messiah and his followers into the corona of the phallus, which is their psychic root in the divine anthropos. This assimilation symbolizes the feminization of those who wear the turban, for by means of this action they are integrated into the *ʿaṭeret berit*, but at the same time this process signifies the masculinization of the divine feminine, for in the eschaton the *ʿaṭeret berit* rises to the metaphysical status of *ʿaṭeret baʿlah*, and *Malkhut* ascends to the position of *Keter*.

I suggest that this is the "great secret" to which Sabbatai Ṣevi referred when he spoke of wearing the turban. Beyond serving as an obvious sign of the conversion to Islam, the donning of the turban designates the crowning of the messiah with the *ʿaṭeret ṣevi*, an

---

[161] The same allusion to Sabbatai Ṣevi in Psalm 118:20 is found in Nathan of Gaza, *Sefer ha-Beri'ah*, MS New York, Jewish Theological Seminary of America Mic. 1851, fol. 28a. See also the account of Nathan reported by Mahallallel Halleluyah of Ancona, published in Scholem, *Researches*, p. 65.

act that symbolically represents his apotheosis into the *ʿaṭeret berit.* The restoration of the feminine to the male organ underlying this rite is the fulfillment of the messianic myth as it has evolved in the kabbalistic tradition. By putting on the turban, therefore, Sabbatai Ṣevi and his followers were reintegrating the feminine in the masculine and thereby the blemish in the Godhead, which resulted in the primordial splitting of the male androgyne, was rectified. This, it seems to me, is the connotation of Nathan's remark that Sabbatai Ṣevi "restored the crown to its former splendor in the secret of the Tree of Life," *heḥezir ʿaṭarah le-yoshnah be-sod ʿeṣ ḥayyim.*[162] Insofar as Sabbatai Ṣevi is the manifestation of the *ʿaṭeret berit*, he is able to accomplish the ultimate *tiqqun* by restoring the feminine crown to the masculine Tree of Life.

The symbolism of the crown was well captured by Baruch of Arezzo in his summary account of Nathan's theological orientation: "When the sage, R. Nathan of Gaza, heard that he placed the holy turban on his head, he knew wholeheartedly that our master gave himself to the [demonic] shell in order to purify from there the sparks of holiness, just as Abraham took Hagar the Egyptian, Jacob the daughters of Laban, and Moses the daughter of Jethro. . . . He had to do this in order to rectify the world in the kingdom of Shaddai."[163] Putting on the turban signifies the act of apostasy, which is framed in Lurianic terms as the descent to the demonic that is necessary for the liberation of the holy sparks. But in this passage the issue is expressed as well in gender terms. It is surely not insignificant that Sabbatai Ṣevi's donning of the turban is compared to the taking of a non-Israelite wife on the part of Abraham, Jacob, and Moses. In each of these instances, the demonic is associated with the feminine. By contrast, Sabbatai Ṣevi's descent to the depths of the demonic is not portrayed as his taking a non-Jewish woman as a wife. It is related instead to the Muslim headgear that he dons as the external sign of his apostasy. Symbolically, however, the author of this passage is certainly conveying the idea that the wearing of

[162] *Be-ʿIqvot Mashiaḥ*, p. 50. For an altogether different interpretation of this passage, see Scholem, *Sabbatai Ṣevi*, p. 321; and the recent suggestion by Elqayam, "Mystery of Faith," p. 255 n. 18. Also relevant are the words of the *maggid* in the apocalypse of Nathan to the effect that "Sabbatai Ṣevi would restore the crown to its former splendor." See *Be-ʿIqvot Mashiaḥ*, p. 60; *Researches*, p. 69.

[163] *ʿInyenei Shabbatai Ṣevi*, p. 58.

the turban, rendered as the holy crown, is equivalent to the taking of a wife.

The sexual implications of this act are underscored in the comment that Sabbatai Ṣevi had to put on the turban in order "to rectify the world in the kingdom of Shaddai," *letaqqen ʿolam be-malkhut shaddai*, an expression derived from the second part of the *ʿAleynu* prayer.[164] This rectification relates to the union of male and female, *malkhut* and *shaddai*, *Shekhinah* and *Yesod*. The name Shaddai is written out in full, *shin dalet yod*, which equals 814, the numerical value of Sabbatai Ṣevi. The integration of the male and female, which in the final analysis entails the restoration of the female to the male, is accomplished by the donning of the turban. In short, the coronation of Sabbatai Ṣevi is an act of phallic empowerment that results in the masculinization of the divine feminine. But, as I have noted above, this process concomitantly entails the feminization of the earthly messiah.

The gender implications of the act of coronation are implied in a legendary remark that Baruch makes on two separate occasions in his hagiographical chronicle: Sabbatai Ṣevi did not engage in intercourse with his wife until after he had put on the turban.[165] From one perspective this is simply meant to convey the idea that until he assumed his messianic role he was not complete and therefore he was not permitted to know his wife carnally. But, from another perspective, this comment may relate to the fact that the coronation symbolically enacts the androgynisation of Sabbatai Ṣevi. Only after he attained the state of androgyny in his own being was he worthy to unite sexually with his wife. Ascetic renunciation, therefore, served as the necessary condition for his assumption of the messianic task.[166] With respect to this issue there is an interesting reversal of what is

---

[164] On Sabbatai Ṣevi's application of this phrase, *letaqqen ʿolam be-malkhut shaddai*, to himself, see Scholem, *Sabbatai Ṣevi*, pp. 239–240.

[165] *Zikkaron li-Venei Yisraʾel*, pp. 46 and 63. Regarding the mystical significance attributed to Sabbatai Ṣevi's marital relationships, see above n. 147.

[166] The ascetic dimension may also be implied in the motif of Sabbatai Ṣevi's ascension to the highest grade of the divine, which is occasioned by or reflects the theosophic process whereby *Tifʾeret* is elevated to *Keter*. See above nn. 38, 105, and 106. Especially relevant is the comment in *Zohar* 3:261b on the verse, "You [Moses] shall stand here with Me": "From that point you shall separate entirely from your wife, and cleave and ascend to the other place that is masculine without any feminine." It is likely that this is an enigmatic reference to *Binah*, the world of the masculine to which Moses cleaves after having adopted a celibate lifestyle. Cf. *Zohar* 1:22a, 152b; 2:222a. It is nevertheless instructive that the nature of Moses'

attributed in the zoharic corpus to Moses, the messianic prototype of Sabbatai Ṣevi. That is, following earlier rabbinic sources, the author of the *Zohar* emphasizes that after Moses united with the *Shekhinah* he had to separate from his physical wife.[167] In the case of Sabbatai Ṣevi, by contrast, the celibate denial precedes the consummation of sexual union with his wife.[168] The wearing of the turban is the external sign that he has realized the unity of the divine in his own being. To achieve that end, it was necessary for him to avoid carnal intercourse with his wife. After realizing this unity, however, Sabbatai Ṣevi was free to engage in matrimonial sex, another sign that the Sabbath of the messianic era had been initiated by his donning the holy crown.[169]

---

conjunction to the divine is phrased as a cleaving of the male to the potency that is masculine without any admixture of the feminine.

[167] *Zohar* 1:21b, 236b, 239a; 2:5b, 245a; 3:4b, 148a, 180a. Interestingly enough, the tradition regarding sexual renunciation on the part of Moses is criticized in the zoharic text itself. See *Zohar* 1:234b and *Zohar Ḥadash*, 58b. On the mystical marriage of Moses to the *Shekhinah*, see Scholem, *Major Trends*, pp. 200, 226–227; Tishby, *Wisdom of the Zohar*, p. 1333; M. Idel, "Sexual Metaphors and Praxis in the Kabbalah," in *The Jewish Family: Metaphor and Memory*, edited by D. Kraemer (New York, 1989), p. 206; Liebes, *Sections of the Zohar Lexicon*, pp. 182–184; "Messiah of the *Zohar*," pp. 107, 122 (English translation, p. 15); "Zohar and Eros," *Alpayyim* 9 (1994): 102 (in Hebrew).

[168] A similar argument has been made with respect to Moses Ḥayyim Luzzatto. That is, prior to his marriage to Zipporah, a marriage that clearly symbolized the recreation of the biblical scene, Luzzatto adopted a celibate life on account of his union with the *Shekhinah*. See Tishby, *Studies in Kabbalah and Its Branches*, pp. 730 and 748 n. 18; Liebes, "Messiah of the *Zohar*," p. 112.

[169] An extreme application of this logic is found in the comment of Nathan Neṭa, the son of Jonathan Eybeschütz, cited by Jacob Emden, *Sefer Hit'abbequt* (Altona, 1762), 11a, to the effect that the patriarchs came to the world to rectify four senses and Sabbatai Ṣevi the fifth sense of touch, an act that is manifest in the overturning of the law prohibiting illicit sexual relationships in public. Scholem, *Messianic Idea*, p. 117, cites this source from a later edition. See also Idel, "Sexual Metaphors and Praxis," pp. 212–213.

SALVATION THROUGH PHILOLOGY: THE POETICAL MESSIANISM OF QUIRINUS KUHLMANN (1651–1689)

WILHELM SCHMIDT-BIGGEMANN

I. *Outlines of Kuhlmann's Messianic Career*

1. *Erudite Poetry and Juvenile Melancholy*

Sometimes, the most radical figures in history are the most characteristic ones as well. This seems to be the case with Quirinus Kuhlmann, a seventeenth century philologist, mystic, and philosopher who, in his lifetime, had a very particular reputation as a millenarian mystic and poet between London and Moscow.[1] Quirinus Kuhlmann was born in Breslau on February 26th 1651. His parents were merchands; his father died only two or three years after Quirinus' birth, his mother survived her son more than 30 years. In the first years of his life, young Quirinus suffered from a speech impediment, he was—as he described it later—often mocked for this desease. This may be one of the reasons why he begun to study very early in the libraries of his native town. Seventeenth century Breslau in Silesia was one of the most cultivated towns in the former Reich; Silesia was famous for the erudite poetry of Martin Opitz, Andreas Gryphius, Hofmann von Hofmannswaldau and Daniel Casper von Lohenstein; they formed the "Schlesische Dichterschule". The Breslau educational institutions were excellent, there were two Lutheran gymnasia, the Elisabeth and the Magdalena school. The Lutheran

[1] For Kuhlmann cf. esp.: Walter Dietze: *Quirinus Kuhlmann. Ketzer und Poet. Versuch einer monographischen Darstellung von Leben und Werk.* Berlin 1963. Neue Beiträge zur Literaturwissenschaft, vol. 17. L. Parker and A.A. Forster: "Quirinus Kuhlmann and the Poetry of St. John of the Cross". *Bulletin for Hispanic Studies* XXV, 1958, pp. 1–23. Claus Victor Bock: *Quirinus Kuhlmann. Ein Beitrag zur Charakteristik des Ekstatikers.* Bern 1957 (Basler Studien zur deutschen Sprache und Literatur, Heft 18). Heinrich Erk: *Offenbarung und heilige Sprache im Kühlpsalter Quirinus Kuhlmanns.* Diss. (Masch.) Göttingen 1953. The outstanding recent interpretation, including critical remarks on the secondary sources of Kuhlmann is the essay of Sibylle Rusterholz: "Klarlichte Dunkelheiten. Quirinus Kuhlmanns 62. Kühlpsalm". In: Martin Bircher und Alois M. Haas (eds.): *Deutsche Barocklyrik. Gedichtinterpretationen von Spee bis Haller.* Bern and Munique 1973, pp. 225–264.

erudite public schools competed with a Jesuit gymnasium. Erudite and pious theater and poetry, both Latin and German, were performed regularly, declamations and rhetoric displays were common on every school term. The fame of these performances and their poetical results was so wide-spread, that Gianbattista Vico reported in his Scienzia Nuova, some 80 years later, that Silesia's peasants were born poets.[2]

Quirinus did not grow up in a wealthy situation; since his mother was a widow, he needed a scholarship for his education at school. In 1661 he indeed received a stipend for the "Ratsgymnasium bei Maria Magdalena". When he left this Gymnasium nine years later he had become a famous man, widely known for his erudition and his vers. In these years he wrote a song of praise to the German language[3]—this item of the peculiar commission of the German language will be of some importance in his later poetical representation of his own revelations.

In 1671, he began his studies at the university of Jena, then 20 years of age, again supported by a stipend donated by the Breslau burgher Georg Schöbel. After Kuhlmann's messianic conversions, Schöbel became one of Kuhlmann's closest disciples. In his first year at Jena Kuhlman began to study jurisprudence. It was in Jena, too, that Quirinus systematically began his career as a poet and polymath. This intensive life as an erudite poet did not leave much time for a serious study of jurisprudence. Instead of a juridic dissertation he finished two collections of poems: "Himmlische Liebesküsse", a collection of poems in the spirit of the biblical Song of Songs, and an anthology entitled "Sonnenblumen", which embodied poems on the particular commitment of the German language[4] and a reedition of

---

[2] Vico: *La Scuienza nuova secondo l'edizione del MDCCXLIV.* (Introduzione e note di Paolo Rossi) Milano 1982, p. 332: Abbiam veduto i primi scrittori nelle novelle lingue d'Europa essere stati verseggiatori; e nella Silesia, provincia quasi tutta di contadino, nascon poeti. Libro secondo. Della sapienza poetica II Della Logica Poetica, 5. Corollari d'intorno all' origini della locuzion poetica, degli episodi, del torno, del numero, del canto e del verso. Corresponds 3d ed. No. 471.

[3] Dietze, p. 30.

[4] Dietze, pp. 71f.

Der Teutsche hat noch mehr / als dort das Grichen Land.
Auf Teutsche! Teutsche auf! ihr könnt den Welt-kreis lehren!
Der Teutschen Erdreich trägt / was fremden unbekand.
Auf Helden! pflanzet fort di Weißheit-dattel-Früchte!
Ein steter Nach-ruf ist der schönste Ehren-lohn

his juvenile poems which had already appeared in 1668, entitled "Grabesschriften".[5]

During his time in Jena, Quirinus became aquainted with the Jesuit Athanasius Kircher's philosophy of universal language following the ideas of the medieval philosopher Raimundus Lullus.[6] What Kuhlmann was fascinated by was the *ars combinatoria* of the thirteenth century Catalan philosopher which had again achieved a peculiar reputation in seventeenth century Germany, because it was considered as the logical science of all possible cognition, *scientia omnium possibilium*. It was especially in Kuhlmann's university of Jena, that Lullism was influential through Leibniz's and Kuhlmann's professor Erhard Weigel. Leibniz wrote his "Dissertatio de arte combinatoria" in 1664, a few years later Kuhlmann began his correspondence with Athanasius Kircher on the subject of Lull's *ars combinatoria*. With the Lullistic techniques of universal logical and linguistical invention he tried to improve the German language, which the baroque scholar Justus Georg Schottelius had demonstrated to be one of the world's original "Haupt-Sprachen",[7] close to the divine Hebrew. During Kuhlmann's studies in Jena one of his fellow-students mocked him: "He sends letters to the most eminent people, like the Father Kircher in Rome, whom he raises to heaven at one moment, and pulls into the depths the next. This time he situates him in his wisdom before gods and goddesses, the other time he throws him as stultitious below blockheaded guys. . . . As Schottelius study was so imperfect in quarto size, he wants to edit a book in folio to provide the German language with an improved function, in a Lullistic way."[8]

Macht ihr die Teutsche Sprach nicht selber gantz zunichte:
So geht si allen vor: Ich wett um Kron und Thron.

[5] Dietze, p. 36.

[6] For Kircher cf. Thomas Leinkauf: *Mundus combinatus. Studien zur Struktur der barocken Universalwissenschaft am Beispiel Athanasisus Kirchers.* SJ. Berlin 1993. Wilhelm Schmidt-Biggemann: *Topica universalis. Eine Modellgeschichte humanistischer und barocker Wissenschaft.* Hamburg 1983, pp. 156ff.

[7] Justus Georg Schottelius: *Ausführliche Arbeit von der teutschen Haubt-Sprache.* Braunschweig 1666. Cf.: Wolf Peter Klein: *Im Anfang war das Wort. Theorie- und wissenschaftsgeschichtliche Elemente frühneuzeitlichen Sprachbewußtseins.* Berlin 1992.

[8] Dietze, p. 77: Letter of Joachim Heinrich Hagen to Siegmund von Birken. "Schickt Brieffe an die Vornehmsten leute, als nach Rom, an den P. Kircher, quem coelo tenus jam tollit, mox in profundem trahit; mox Dijs Deabusque Sapientà praeponit, rursus ceu stultissimum infra pureros abjict. Ingleichen in Engelland, und anderweit. Neulich erwehnte Er, wie ein Unversuchter Vorschlag in ängste. Nemlich, Er sey gesonnen, Seine Briefe, und teutsche Send-schreiben, an grosse Personen, in

In this juvenile caricature one finds already two of Kuhlmann's philological obsessions: *Ars combinatoria* and high esteem of the German language;[9] though still without the spiritual context that will rule his later ideas.

As early as in his Jena period, Quirinus seems to have suffered from melancholy. He was reported to have covered his walls with reflecting "turkish papers" to brighten the room; the sources say that he wanted to be transferred by this into a mystic mood. He may have suffered from depression of darkness, those situations reoccurred frequently during his lifetime.[10] He often rested in his room for several days without leaving it. This habit corresponded his very intensive poetical attempts and his idiosyncratic philosophy mainly concentrated on his importance as a poet of a universal language.

In fact, Kuhlmann's melancholic temper and his efforts in poetry and letters made it impossible for him to finish his studies. A promise to postpone his German poetry in favour to work for a juridical doctorate[11] was never fulfilled. In the fall of 1673 Kuhlmann, together with his friend Abraham Plagge, left the university of Jena to go to Leiden.

Such a change was not unusual at those times, many Silesians studied in Leiden. But Kuhlmann's case became peculiar. It was in Leiden that Kuhlmann had his conversion to Jacob Böhme. In his later reminiscences he wrote that his friend Plagge caused that decisive event of Kuhlmann's life by giving him a copy of Böhme's

---

etlichen Centurien (so hoch sollen sie noch wachsen) der Welt durch den druck zu communiciren. Er wundere, worum es Gelehrte leute nicht lange schon angefangen? da wir doch im latein so viel vorgänger hetten. Ob Sie ihrem Stylo, oder Verstand mißgetraut, wäre ihm zweiflich. Beydes wisse er zu zeigen. Weil Schottelij opus in 4t. unvollkommen, wolle er in foliô eines edieren, und den Grund der teutschen Sprache, auf eine Lullianische Weise, heben."

9 The Poem "Der Wechsel menschlicher Sachen" in the "Himmlische Liebesküsse" is a result of his vernacular poetic Lullism. Cf. Hans Aarsleff: Language, Man and Knowledge in the Sixteenth and Seventeenth Centuries (Unpubl. Manucript cited with the author's permission), pp. 52–61.

10 Cf. Gottlieb Wernsdorf (+1729) (Praes), G. Liefmann, (Def), *Dissertatio historica de fanaticis Silesiorum speciatim Quirini Kuhlmanno.* Wittenberg 1733. Dietze, p. 143.

11 "Er will nun das teutsche etwas ruhen lassen, und Jura so ämsig studiren, daß Er inner Jahres-Frist doctoriren könne." Letter from Hagen to Birken, cf. fn. 7.

"Mysterium magnum".[12] The "Mysterium Magnum" is a detailed allegorical and theosophical commentary on the book of Genesis. In 1688, more than 14 years later, Kuhlmann considered this event as a divine revelation, "received in Christ's year of 1674, written down in the Christ-month 1675, first published in 1676".[13]

Kuhlmann described the content of his vision in two very different ways; the first was in a latin text of 1674 which was rather close to the event of his conversion: "Inflamed with Böhmian fire, I read Böhme with fiery eagerness and capacity. I did not know the Böhmian texts and I knew them the same day. What an admiration (o Jesus!) overcame me when I heard Böhme tell his revelations which I had learned from the universe of nature, with God as my teacher, it were the revelations the first outlines of which I just had begun to delineate in my own works".[14] Looking back to a Messianic career from a distance of about 14 years, Kuhlmann's judgement of his Böhmian conversion had considerably changed: in 1688 he understands his conversion as an instruction of God the Father to fell the great whore Babylon (which was of course identified with the pope).

Whatever the correct interpretation of this conversion may be: from this time the Messianic career of Quirinus Kuhlmann began. His conversion cannot have happened very abruptly, since he continued his correspondence with the Jesuit Athanasius Kircher; slight differences to his former habits, however, could be recognized. He now emphazised his own individual knowledge as deriving from divine indulgence and grace: "All people will love my sweetness, if they love truth and their salvation. They do not follow the philosophers and their philosophy, but simply obey the wisdom that is written into all creature, and they do not attribute this wisdom to me, a humble man that I am, but completely to God, whom I praise to be my solely teacher."[15] The allusion to Saint Paul's second letter

---

[12] Cf. the Latin description of the conversion Dietze, p. 100.

[13] Amsterdam printed for the author 1688. Bibliography *Kühlpsalter* vol. 2, p. 408.

[14] "Boehmiano ardore accensus, Böhmium flammea rapacitate & capacitate perlustro, unoque die textum Böhmium nesciveram et sciveram. Quanta, (Prô Jesum!) admiratio me involvit audientem, Böhmium ex revelatione referre, quae ex universâ Naturâ Deo Doctore didiceram, quaeque in monumentis meis editis primis lineis delineaveram?" (Dietze, p. 100.)

[15] "Omnes candorem meum amabunt, si veritatem suamque salutem amabunt, nec Philosophos, simulatamque Philosophiam, sed sapientiam simplicem, Universalem,

to the Corinthians (2. Cor. 12:10: "I please myself in my infirmities") is evident. This self-interpretation directed Kuhlmann's further way of life: He perceived himself to be God's chosen instrument.

In this idiosyncrasy Kuhlmann stood not alone in the seventeenth century neither in England nor in the Netherlands.

The most prominent case in seventeenth century England was the one of James Naylor. Being one of Cromwell's famous officers, i.e. quarter master in General Lambert's army, he was converted to Quakerism by John Fox himself. In October 1656 he "made a triumphant entry into Bristol, which was a parody of Christ's entry into Jerusalem. A man went before him bare-headed; two women led his horse, some threw their garments before him; others sang hosannas and cried, 'Holy, Holy, Lord, God of Israel'."[16] In a long process the "bare bones" Parliament in London sentenced him to death, but after Cromwell's intervention he was "pardonned" to be pillored, whipped, his tongue bored with glowing iron, and to be finally imprisoned. A year later he died in his gaol in the Tower of London. The process had a huge parliamentarian and constitutional echo, since Cromwell had argued, that the Parliament being a legislative power had no right to sentence anyone.

The city and the region of Amsterdam had plenty of Messiahs, prophets and prophecies. Three of them became important for Kuhlmann: the Amsterdam prophet Johann Rothe, his friend Friedrich Breckling, the editor of the famous 1682 Amsterdam edition of Böhme's collected works, and Johann Amos Comenius (1670) who died four years before Kuhlmann entered the Netherlands.

Johann Rothe, born 1628, had his conversion—"Erlebnis" in 1652. From that date he preached the kingdom of Christ. He was very successful in preaching, came to England and was considered to be a "Fifth Monarchist"—a member of the radical anabaptist and spiritual opposition against Cromwell. He was arrested, exiled and, after Cromwell's death, he came back to England in 1660. Here he witnessed the preparation and attempt of the Fifth Monarchists' riot against the restoration of an earthly kingdom,[17] their suppression and the execution of the leaders in January 1661. He returned to Hol-

---

omnibus creatis inscriptam sequentur, mihi nihil adscribentes, indignissimo homini, sed omnia Deo, quo praeceptore unio glorior." (Dietze, p. 106.)

[16] Charles Harding Firth: *The Last Years of the Protectorate*. I. London 1909, p. 85.

[17] Cf. fn. 31.

land, continuing to preach repentance. From 1674 on, Kuhlmann saw Rothe as his first prophet, his John the Baptist. The Titel of Kuhlmann's "Neubegeisterter Böhme" displays how he interpreted Rothe's message: "New Inspired Böhme Including 150 Prophecies in Agreement with the Fifth Monarchy or the Reign of Jesus of the Dutch Prophet Johann Rothe."

In 1657, the famous pedagogue, theosopher and polymath Comenius, had anonymously edited a book named "Lux in tenebris". The volume was reedited under his name in 1665/67 and became very influential for Kuhlmann's career. It was a collection of prophetical and millenarian treatises and contained the prophecies of the most prominent Thirty Years' War seers Christoph Kotter, Christina Poniatova and Nicholas Drabic. Later, Kuhlmann interpreted this book as his Old Testament, because it contained the prophecies which were completed by his own millenarian kingdom. The prophecies were newly and perfectly formulated by the poems of his "Kühlpsalter"; and so Kuhlmann's poems became his New Testament. The role of Comenius' collection "Lux in tenebris" in its time and in Kuhlmann's life is complicated. The collection's three prophecies concern the "Winter-King" Frederic of Bohemia (1596/1610–1632), the Palatine prince who, in 1620, became King of Bohemia for one Winter and then lost the Battle at the White Mountain in 1621. In the course of the expulsion of the Lutheran and the Calvinistic Bohemians as well as the Bohemian Brethren, who were all allies of the Winter-King, anti-Habsburg prophecies arose, the three most famous of which Comenius published in his "Lux in tenebris". These prophecies reflected the protestant crisis of the Thirty Years' War, in which Comenius had suffered severely and in which he had participated as an adviser and propagandist of the Calvinist and Lutheran side. He was, e.g., one of the responsible intellectuals who persuaded Gustav Adolf to intervene in the war.[18]

The first prophecy of the "Lux in tenebris"—it is the one of Christoph Kotter—dated from 1616, and it prophesied the divine kingdom of the protestants. It was hoped to be fulfilled by the Winter-King but it failed with the battle at the White Mountain in Prague, 1621. The second prophecy, the one of Christina Poniatowa, was supposedly dated in 1627 and prophesied the coming of a second

[18] Milada Blekastad: *Comenius. Versuch eines Umrisses von Leben, Werk und Schicksal des Jan Amos Komensky*. Oslo/Prag 1969, pp. 166–172.

Frederic. This prophecy seemed to be fulfilled with Gustav Adolph's invasion into the Reich in 1630; but it failed in 1632, when Gustav Adolf died in the battle of Lützen. The third coming of the "Lion of midnight" in order to establish the "Kingdom of Christ", was predicted by Nicolas Drabic (who was burnt in Bratislawa in 1671 and therefore considered to be a martyr). He foretold the arrival of the third reign, the reign of the apocalyptic millennium.

Comenius himself believed that the prophecies he published would be fulfilled during his lifetime.[19] The prophecies he published had the form of all the antipapistic as well as anti-Habsburg prophetical pamphlets from the times of the Reformation on: The abolition of the House of Habsburg, both the Austrian and the Spanish branch, was connected with the prediction of the end of popery. No question that this tendency fitted the antipapistic propaganda of all parties of the English Revolution, The Fifth Monarchy men, the levellers, Cromwell's independents, the presbyterians, and most of the episcopalian parties joined these aims.[20]

2. *The Instrument of God's Reign*

Backed by this political theology, Kuhlmann saw himself as God's fulfilling instrument of the third reign and of the Fifth Monarchy which was propagated in Comenius' prophetical collection "Lux in tenebris", Kuhlmann's "Old Testament". According to his own opinion he was proceeded by his baptizing arch-prophet Johann Rothe. Even if Rothe did not acknowledge or accept Kuhlmann to be the Messiah of the millennium, Kuhlmann began to slip into his position as the unfolder and fulfiller of the instant kingdom of Christ. This millenarian reign was more and more identified with the "Kühlreich", Kuhlmann's coming kingdom that he visioned arriving after the pouring of the apocalyptical "sixth vial": "Now the end of the sixth vial is the total exclusion of the curved Pope, the period of the Four Monarchies, and the full conversion of the Turks; upon which shall immediately follow that interval of the seventh vial, in

[19] Wilhelm Schmidt-Biggemannn: "Enzyklopädie, Eschatologie und Ökumene. Die theologische Bedeutung von enzyklopädischem Wissen bei Comenius". In: *Frühneuzeit-Info.* 1992, Heft 2, pp. 19–28.

[20] For the development of antipapistic propaganda s. Christopher Hill: *Antichrist in Seventeenth Century England.* London 1971. C.A. Patrides, Joseph Willreich (eds.): *The Apocalypse in English Renaissance Thought and Literature.* Manchester 1984.

which the universal conversion of all nations shall be carried on, and way made for the Thousand Years' Apocalyptical reign."[21]

Even the outlines of Kuhlmann's biography witness his Messianic task: In march 1674 he officially finished his universal studies and began to travel. From 1675 on he lived in Lübeck, together with Magdalena von Lindau, his servant, and her three children. Magdalena von Lindau had been recommended to Kuhlmann by the Dutch prophetess Tanneke Denijs. One year later, Kuhlmann travelled to England, where he stayed for two years without his "family" (he was not legally married to Magdalena). His family remained in Hamburg. In England, Kuhlmann lived in the house of John Bathurst and had intensive contacts with Franciscus Mercurius van Helmont, then physician of Lady Conway and friend of Knorr von Rosenroth as well as of Henry More.[22] In London he adopted the old Calvinistic plan of a coalition between the protestants and the Sultan in Byzanz to destroy catholicism.[23] He decided to bring a copy of Comenius' "Lux in tenebris" to the Bosporus and to donate it personally to the Sultan in order to convert him.[24] It was Sultan Mechmed IV (1648–1687), the one who had convinced Sabbathai Zwi to become a Muslim. The journey to Constantinople was a complete catastrophe: Of course he was not admitted to the Sultan's court, while his family

---

[21] Quirinus Kuhlmann: *The General London Epistle. The prophecy of John Kegel, the 12th Jan. 1626, Kuhlman, his Fulfilling and Explication of the Fifth Section of the Fare-Going Prophecy, written by him in Smirna in Natolia, in October 1678.* London 1679. Nr. 26, p. 77.

[22] Cf. Serge Hutin: *Henry More. Essai sur les doctrines théosophiques chez les Platoniens de Cambridge.* Hildesheim 1966. Kurt Salecker: Christian Knorr von Rosenroth (1638–1689). Leipzig 1931, (Palaestra 178) pp. 39f., 88f.

[23] This was part of the "calvinoturkish" alliance which first emerged in sixteenth century netherlandes. Cf. M.E.H.N. Moud: "Calvinoturkisme in de zeventiende eeuw. Comenius, Leidse orientalisten en de urkse bijbel". In: *Tijdschrift vor Geschiedenis,* 91, 1978, pp. 576–607. Id.: "Calvinoturcismus und Chiliasmus im 17. Jahrhundert". In: *Pietismus und Neuzeit* Bd. 14. Chiliasmus in Deutschland und England im 18. Jahrhundert. Ed. Klaus Deppermann. Göttingen 1988, pp. 72–85. K. Westerink: "Liever Turks dan paaps: en devies tijdens de Opstand in de Nederlanden." In: *Topkapi en Turkomanie. Turks-Nederlandse ontmoetingen sinds 1600.* H. Theunissen, A. Abelmann and W. Meulenkamp (eds.). Amsterdam 1989, pp. 75–89.

[24] This was not the first attempt of radical independents to convert the Sultan. In 1653 two Quaker Women Elizabeth Williams and Mary Fisher from Yorkshire were whipped in Cambridge for their missionary activities. In 1660, Mary Fisher tried to convert the Sultan Mohammed IV in Adrianopel. She was accepted friendly, but her attempts were in vain. She died in South Carolina in 1697. Cf. S.W. Scott-Giles: *Sidney Sussex College. A Short History.* Cambridge 1975, pp. 70f.

travelling together with him rejected him when he came back to the ship. In March 1679 he returned to Holland, in May of the same year he definitely left his adopted family. The rest of his life Kuhlmann travelled through protestant, especially Calvinistic Europe including England. He preached in radical conventicles, supported more or less by rich burghers and nobles who were themselves members of those tiny independent congregations.

In 1683 Kuhlmann met Maria Gould (Maria Anglicana), a learned woman and doctor of medicine practising in London. Maria became disciple of Kuhlmann, went with him to Amsterdam in 1684, the two married in the following year. It was in that period that the "Kühlpsalter", Kuhlmann's most important series of spiritual autobiographic poems was systematically collected and printed (first vol. 1684).

The period between 1683 and 1686 when Maria Anglicana died (16th Nov.) is the most intensive time of Kuhlmanns mystical poetry. On the first of January 1684, John Beresford, a disciple in London, saw him in a midnight's vision appearing as the king of the Fifth Monarchy, the beautiful king with the shining countenance.[25] After 1686 Kuhlmann's Messianic consciousness apparently came into in a more and more nervous tension. It seems that he now was totally possessed by his commitment to fulfill the Fifth Monarchy which he had predicted to arrive in 1688: "What so ever therefore the Holy Scripture hath fore-told concerning the Papal and Turkish State under the Time, Times, and Half a Time [i.e., Rev. 11:11] of 1176

[25] Cf. Ernst Sackur: *Sibyllinische Texte und Forschungen. Pseudomethodius, Adso und die Tiburtinische Sibylle.* Halle 1898, p. 185. "Et tunc surget ex Grecorum, cuius nomen Constans, et ipse erit rex Romanorum et Grecorum. Hic erit statura grandis, aspectu decorus, vultu splendidus atque per singula membrorum lineamenta decenter compositus." The visioner is John Beresford, and a German translation of his vision has survived. "Den wolte ich schlaffen, doch konte nicht, und umb Mitternacht, als ich ganz wachend, drang auf mich ein Gesichte, und sogleich befand ich mich bey fleetbrüg /: in der Stadt London unter einer großen Menge von Menschen, unter welchen Quirin Kühlmann erschien, sizend auf einem Pferdte syende umbringet von der Menge, die mit Verwunderung zulieffen ihn zu sehen, da ich unter andern Ihn auch ansahe, sein Kleid war herrlich und glänzende, sein Angesicht leüchtete als wie die Strahlen von göttliche Krafft, auf seinem Haupte hatte er eine gekrönte Müze od. hut mit einem Lober Kranz umbgeben, die Krone war von erhobenen Massiven Gold mit weiß und blau amulirt, und rund umbglänzende mit Perlen und Edelgesteinen, so daß es an Köstlichkeit und Pracht die Königliche Krone weit übertraff, und fest auf seinem Haupte saß." Dietze, p. 243.

years[26] will be accomplished in the year 1688."[27] He married again in 1687 in order to fulfil his Messianic task together with his third wife Marie Ackerlot, the mother of his daughter who died after her birth. Even encouraged by those blows of fate which typologically made him a representative of the biblical "man of grief and sorrows" he made a new attempt to get political support from the east: The light in the darkness, "Lux in tenebris" which was prophesied by the third of Comenius' prophets, Drabic, could also come from the third Rome, from Moscow. So he wrote a new "Kühljubel", the 23rd of a second series, in which he tried to move the Russian Szar into an alliance with the Sultan and to fight against the House of Habsburg and the Pope. When Vienna and Rome were destroyed—that was his hope—the world would be united and the four winds would join for the unique Kingdom of Jesus.[28] In summer 1689 Kühlmann made his second and last attempt to get political support for his millenarian projects. Under the name "Ludvig Ludovicin" he travelled to Moscow. In the German colony in Moscow, where he lived in the house of an adherent, Conrad Nordermann, he immediately began to preach his millenaristic prophecies. However, Kuhlmann and Nordermann were soon denounced to the local orthodox authorities as both theologically and politically dangerous; they were arrested, interrogated and seriously tortured. Nonetheless Nordermann confessed his belief in Kuhlmann, and Kuhlmann insisted on having a divine commitment. Both men were held in prison for three months and finally burnt on October 4th 1689.

II. *Apocalyptical Patterns in the Seventeenth Century*

Kuhlmann was deeply involved in the struggles of political spiritualism of his epoch, his horrible end was then an unescapable event.

---

[26] These are the years Kuhlmann reckoned in his apocalyptic calculus: "Twelve months are one time, Four and twenty are two times, and six are half a time [the amount can either be counted as two and a half or three and a half]; which according to the course of the Moon make three years, and near an half more; and so are the three days and a half. But according to longer time (28 years reckoned for one month) this is one time, two Times and a half time, and thus to be numbered: One time is 336 years, two times 672, and a half time is 168, which being added together make 1176. In this time the Treader down [i.e., the Katechont] will have power, and afterwards he shall be converted." *The Great London Epistle*, pp. 5f.

[27] *The Great London Epistle*, p. 74, nr. 23.

[28] *Kühlpsalter* II, 363v.

His biography shows clearly how important a role millenarian patterns played in the seventeenth century. This spiritual force was, of course, due to religious and theological power in politics, but it also depended on the longlasting symbols of political theology in western traditions. In times of crisis the most ancient topics always had a surprising revival because they were considered to be the stabile patterns by which the present times could be interpreted. This is especially apparent in the apocalyptic thought and imagery of the seventeenth century.

a. *Fourth and Fifth Monarchy*

The theory of the four monarchies is an interpretation of Daniel's biblical vision of the four reigns which stems from St. Jerome and remained vivid through the medieval Glossa ordinaria[29] of the bible. Here the four animals of his vision are identified with the Assyrian, the Persian, the Greek and the Roman empires. The idea of the fourth reign is crucial in political theology. The medieval German "Heiliges Römisches Reich" drew its legitimation from the continuity of the Roman and the medieval Empire. This concept remained basic for Lutherans in the Reformation: the Lutheran church needed the legitimacy of a religious institution. If the Reformation was God's commitment for the reformators, they needed a divine institution in the real historical world for their reform. Only this institution guaranteed the continuity of the history of salvation and the transmission of revelation. After the delegitimation of the papacy in Lutheran theology both Luther and Melanchthon used the theological interpretation of the Reich to legitimate the earthly existence of their church. Of course, they wanted the Reich completely to be converted to Protestantism, however, that did not happen. Melanchthon and Luther expected the apocalypse to come within a short period, after the conversion of the Emperor, the conversion of the Jews and the failure of the Turks.

This pattern changed in the course of the late sixteenth century, when it became apparent that the catholic world remained stabile.

[29] The Babylonian, Persian, Greek, and Roman empires are parallelizised with the four reigns in Daniel's visions. Cf. Franz Kampers: "Die Idee der Ablösung der Weltreiche in eschatologischer Bedeutung". In: *Hist. Jb.* hg von der Görresgesellschaft 1898, p. 425. For the Glossa ordinaria see the Article in TRE "Glossa ordinaria".

Now anti-Habsburg and anti-Spanish propaganda emerged, which condemned catholicism as even worse than the Turks.

From the beginning of their reformation, the Calvinistic churches did not favour the German interpretation of the "translatio imperii". The Calvinist congregations interpreted the theologico-political concept of the Four Monarchies as secular. With their judgement, that the Reich remained in catholic hands, it became the last empire of the world that was to be succeeded by a fifth, millenarian monarchy. This theory flourished in the Thirty Years War and had a second blossoming time in Cromwells England.[30] In 1661 there was a riot of Fifth Monarchy men in England, which Kuhlmann's[31] prophet Rothe witnessed.

---

[30] For the term of "Quintomonarchism" that appears in the writings of Ludwig Friedrich Giftheil (+1661) s. Gottfried Arnold: *Unpartheyische Kirchen- und Ketzerhistorie.* Leipzig 1699/1700. Pt. III, pp. 98–102, nos. 8–13, esp. no. 9. Cf. Ludwig Eylenstein, Friedrich Giftheil: "Zum mystischen Separatismus des 17. Jahrhunderts in Deutschland". In: *Zs. für Kirchengeschichte* hg. von Otto Schee und Leopold Zscharnak. Jg. 1922, vol. XLI, pp. 1–62.

[31] The Name of Fifth Monarchist emerged in England during the Puritan Revolution. It signified a group of republican radicals among the army that expected the final reign of Christ to come. "Ever since Cromwell had become Protector he had been bitterly assailed by the 'Fifth Monarchy men'. The theocratic republic which was their political ideal was incompatible with any species of monarchy; and the Protector's maintenance of a national church increased their hostility to his rule" (Firth, p. 207). They reached the top of their influence in 1653. As late as April 1657, when a group of radical millenarian opponents of Cromwell tried to plot against the government. They met at two head quartes, at All-Hallors and in Swan Alley, Coleman Street (id. p. 208). Their leader was Thomas Venner, a cooper, who was imprisoned till 1659. Jan. 6, 1661 again he set up with a considerable following to overthrow the government. They marched the streets with the cry "Long live King Jesus" until they were dispersed by the guards. Three days later the remnant of them was captured. Venner was hanged and quartered on Jan. 19. Lit: Charles Harding Firth: *The Last Years of the Protectorate* (1656–1658), vol. 1, London 1909, pp. 207–219. Vavasour Powel: *A Word for God*, 1655. William Medley: A Standart Set-up: Whereunto the true Seed and Saints of the most High may be gathered together into one, out of their several Forms: For the Lambe against the Beast, and False Prophet in this good and honorable Cause. Or the Principles and Declaration of the Remnant, who have waited for the blessed Appearance and Hope. Sewing, how Saints as Saints, men as men, and the Creation shall have their blessings herein, as in the Deliverance of the true Church out of Babylon, and all Confusion; as in the most Righteous and Free Common wealth State; as in the Restitution of all things. Subscribed W. Medley Scribe. Gen. xlix. 2. Who shall rouse him up? Deut. xxxiii. 27. Isai. Ix. 22. Isai. Ixii. 10. Rev. xix. 2. Printed in the Year 1657. Tai Liu: *Discord in Zion. The Puritan Divines and the Puritan Revolution 1640–1660.* The Hague 1973. Richard H. Popkin: *Millenarianism and Messianism in English Literature and Thought 1650–1800.* Clark Library Lectures 1981–1982. Leiden etc. 1988. B.S. Capp: *The Fifth Monarchy Men. A Study in Seventeenth Century English Millenarianism.* London 1972.

b. *The Reign of the Spirit*

The Idea of the third reign, the reign of the Spirit after the reign of the Father (Old Testament) and the Son (New Testament) depends on the Christian dogma of the Holy Trinity. The theology of the third reign became popular at the end of the twelfth century with Joachim of Fioris. The most influential formulation of this theology of history is to be found in Joachim's "Concordia Veteris cum Novo Testamento", (Venice 1516), in his "Explanatio in Apocalypsin" and in the "Psalterium decem chordarum" (Venice 1527).[32] The first public riot these radical Joachimite thoughts provoked was the scandal of the "Evangelium aeternum" preached by radical adherents of Joachim's in Paris in 1260.[33] In the pseudo-Joachimite commentary in Jeremiah, which was written about 1250, before the death of the Emperor Frederic II of Hohenstaufen, both, the Pope and the Emperor are identified as antichrists, and the coming of an Emperor of peace and the Angelic Pope are prophesied.[34]

The idea of a third reign remained extremely provocative throughout the Middle Ages, the Reformation, from the seventeenth to the twentieth century: It first formulated the apocalyptic ending of Christianity by the abolition of the external institutions of the church, the decline of "outward" papacy in favour of a spiritual one, and the decline of the external reign of the Emperor in favor of a spiritual hidden king. The first person who was typologically identified with the angelic pope was St. Francis. The debates about the Franciscan life of poverty, which emerged from this identification, were part of the public riots in the course of the theological and political discussion of Joachim of Fioris' ideas. In the late medieval political theology of the empire, which saw itself confronted to a French papacy in Avignon, the ideas of the spiritual Third Reign and the New Kingdom grew to more and more strength. The political and theological propaganda of the Reformation agitated with the topics of the "new reign of spirit", the Spirit of the Holy Trinity and the spirit of the holy Scriptures.

In the famous Rabbinical "Vaticinium Eliae" the time of the world was prophesied to last 6000 years; and in the most influential world-

---

[32] Dempf: *Sacum Imperium.* 2nd ed. Darmstadt 1954, pp. 280ff.

[33] Marjorie Reeves: *Prophecies in the Late Middle Ages.* Oxford 1969. Franz Kampers: *Kaiserprophetien und Kaisersagen im Mittelalter.* München 1895.

[34] Dempf, p. 333.

chronicle of the Venerable Bede six eras of the world were counted. The seventh era to come was the one of the millennium, before in the eighth era the world would return into its divine beginning. Therefore the end of the sixth era was coincident with the beginning of the spiritual third reign of the Holy Spirit, with the Fifth Monarchy and the beginning of the millennium.

The anabaptist kingdom of God in Münster of 1530 was the first attempt to realize the millenarian reign of the Spirit in a political way. This theologico-political experiment was ended brusquely by the siege and the conquest of Münster by its catholic bishop and by the punishment and the execution of the leaders. But the ideas still remained vivid.

In the later middle-ages the "Prognosticon" (1488) of Johannes Lichtenberger was famous for its prophecy of a juvenile spiritual king with the bright shining countenance,[35] directed to the young Emperor Maximilian I.[36] The topic, of course, has a lot in common with Isaiah's prophecy of the Child born,[37] with the fourth Ekloge of Vergil, and with the prophecy of the Tiburtian Sibylle.[38] Lichtenbergers "Prognosticon" was widely diffused, translated, reprinted and

---

[35] The source ist the Sybilla Tiburtina (Ed. Sackur, s. fn. 37); and Kampers, p. 15; referring to Flavius Josephus, *Bellum Iudaicum* VI, chapt. 4,5.

[36] S. Dietrich Kurze: Johannes Lichtenberger (+1503). *Eine Studie zur Geschichte der Prophetie und Astrologie.* Lübeck und Hamburg 1960. Here the idea of the spiritual emperor in national commitments is reported: "Der widerspenstige Franzose wird zuletzt dem König mit dem keuschen Angesicht unterliegen, der dann die Herrschaft vom Orient bis zum Okzident innehaben wird.... Manche glauben, so berichtet Lichtenberger, daß dieser Kaiser Friedrich sei. 'Ich aber will, daß es Maximilian sei'." pp. 21 ff. Kurze refers to Ps. 45,3 to Henoch 46,1–5 (E. Kautzsch: *Die Apokryphen und Pseudepigraphen des Alten Testaments.* Tübingen 1900, vol. 2, pp. 262f.).

[37] Isaiah 9.6:
For to us a child is born,
to us a son is given;
and the government will be upon
his shoulder,
and his name will be called
"Wonderful Councellor, Mighty God,
Everlasting Father, Prince of
Peace"
Of the increase of his government
and of peace
there will be no end.

[38] Sackur, p. 185.

commented many times until the eighteenth century.[39] Of course Lichtenberger's prophecies were used in the English Revolution, when a battle between the French king and the Pope was previewed.[40] This was the very topic Nicolas Drabic, Kuhlmann's prophet, used when he predicted: "And the house of Babylon will be cleaned by a young man, whom God will prepare the way, so that he flies through the midst of God's house, illuminates and cleans the filthy Babylon, amazing all inhabitants of the world. In this day the sun will shine and the moon will no longer be darkened."[41]

It goes without saying, that the editor of the prophecies "Lux in tenebris", Johann Amos Comenius, expected the third reign of the Spirit: All his pedagogical efforts were directed towards the advent of the third reign,[42] in this context he saw himself as a follower of the Rosicrucians, a tradition he shared with Quirinus Kuhlmann.[43]

c. *Millenarianism*

Millenarianism contained very specific difficulties in the Lutheran theology of the sixteenth and seventeenth centuries. Though the doctrine rested on St. John's Revelation (Chapter 20) it was nevertheless judged to be heretical by the Confessio Augustana[44] ("opiniones Iudaicae") of 1530 and by the Consensus Helvetica posterior

---

[39] The last I found in the British Museum Catalogue stems from 1790 and is directed against Marie Antoinette, Marie Caroline and Marie Christine. BM Catalogue s.v. Johann, Lichtenberger: *De dry Gezusters of arglistige Staekunde van Marie Antoinette, Marie Caroline en Marie Christine.* 1790.

[40] Spectators, make a ring, that you may see . . . (Paraphrase of a prophecy attributed to Johann Lichtenberger respecting the Quarrel between the French king and the pope) London 1663.

[41] "Et Domus Babylon expurgabitur ab Adolescente quodam, cui Dominus viam parabit, ut domus ejusdem medium pervolet, Babylonumque immundam mundet et illuminet, ad stuporem omnium in terra habitantium; in illo die lucebit Sol & Luna non obtenebrabitur amplius." Dietze, p. 149. Cf. the title engraving No. 3 of the "Kühlpsalter".

[42] Cf. Schmidt-Biggemann: Enzyklopädie, pp. 19–28.

[43] Cf. *Neubegeisterter Böhme* 1674, p. 379: Auf / auf ihr Rosenkreutzer! Wo seid ihr? was verberget ihr euch ferner? die zeit ist gebohren / daß alles Veborgene wird ans Tageslicht gebohren / und mus euer Unschuld klar erscheinen! Auf / auf! gedenket / was in der Bekäntnis durch Himmlische Erkänntnis geweissaget / weil der HErr eure Weissagung / di vormals verspottet / nun vollendet." On the same page Kuhlmann announces a latin tract "von den Wundern der 6sten zeit oder den Rosenkreutzern". Cf. Dietze, p. 415.

[44] Art. XVII "Damnat Anabaptistas, qui sentiunt hominibus damatis ac diabolis finem poenarum futurum esse (those are the Origenists). Damnant et alios, qui nunc

(Art XI): The millenarians were condemned to be "enthusiastici", "Schwärmer". But Millenarianism remained a theological provocation for the sixteenth and the following centuries, especially since many Calvinistic congregations outside Switzerland saw themselves not bound by the ban of millenarianism.

Johann Heinrich Alsted, the teacher of Comenius, a German Calvinist professor at the then very famous university of Herborn (which was the model for many Calvinistic universities in the seventeenth century) wrote the most influential millenarian treatise: "Diatribe de mille annis apocalypticis", printed in Herborn 1627. The book was reedited in 1630 and translated into German in the same year. The essence of Alsteds "Diatribe" consisted in the reckoning of Daniel's prophecies, and the prophetic polyhistor set the date of 1694 for the beginning of the millennium. In 1642 an English summary of Alsted's Diatribe was edited in London: "The Worlds Proceeding Woes and Succeeding Joyes", and a complete translation by W. Burton was printed in London in 1643: "The Beloved City: Or the Saint's Reign on Earth A Thousand Years."[45] This translation was part of the project for the reformation of the world, which Harlib, Dury, and Comenius tried to execute in Cromwell's England.[46] The undertaking stemmed from Rosicrucian traditions that had emerged in Germany in the second decade of the seventeenth century. In Cromwell's England the famous three reformers tried to change the English society into a Christian community after Rosicrucian ideals,[47] an undertaking which was shared by circles interested in Jacob Böhme. In 1649 a collection of prophecies appeared in London: "Mercurius Teutonicus, or a Christian Information Concerning the Last Times

spargunt Iudaicas opiniones, quod ante resurrectionem mortuorum pii regnum mundi occupaturi sint, ubique oppressis impiis."

[45] Wilhelm Schmidt-Biggemann: "Apokalyptische Universalwissenschaft. Johann Heinrich Alsteds 'Diatribe de mille annis apocalypticis'". *Pietismus und Neuzeit*, vol. 14, pp. 50–71.

[46] Cf. John Dury's letter of thirteenth Jan. 1642 to Sir C. (i.e., Sir Cheny Culpeper) of Leeds Castle and Hollingbourne: Pious education is "that good which is to be sought for, in the kingdom of God"..., and in the institutions of free Christian education "lastly Christ's rule is observable". In: *Comenius in England. The Visit of Jan Amos Komensky (Comenius) the Czech Philosopher and Educationist to London in 1641–1642; its Bearing on the Origins of the Royal Society, on the Development of the Encyclopaedia, and on Plans for the Higher Education of the Indians of New England and Virginia as Described in Contemporary Documents*, Selected, Translated, and Edited with an Introduction, and Tables of Dates, by Robert Fitzgibbon Young. Oxford and London 1932, pp. 77, 79.

[47] G.H. Turnbull: *Hartlib, Dury, and Comenius*. London 1947, H.-E. Trevor-Roper: Religion, Reformation und sozialer Umbruch. Berlin 1970. Peter Toon ed.:

Being Divers Prophetical Passages of the Fall of Babel and the New Building in Zion. Gathered out of the Mystical Writings of that Famous German Author, Jacob Behmen, aliàs Teutonicus Phylosophus." Among other millenarian quotations of Böhme's works the collection published a passage which originally probably hinted to the Swedish king, but it fitted perfectly to the new English political theology: "Know; that a Lilly blossometh unto you, Yee Northern Countries; if you destroy it not with the Sectarian Contention of the Learned, then it will become a great Tree among you. . . ."[48]

III. *The Emblems of Millenarianism*

Concerning this context it is obvious, that Kuhlmann then was no isolated figure. But he was perhaps the most radical and surely the most poetic representative of millenarianism in the seventeenth century. He felt himself to be God's seed, through which the new millenarian age was to come into existence.

Kuhlmann's career as a Messiah was not untypical. So he is an interesting figure both biographically and because of the remarkable symbolic force of his thoughts. Kuhlmann sees himself as a divine instrument, as the germ and living ground pregnant with the third period of the world to come. He considers himself personally responsible for the coming of the millenarian age. The new time will arrive only through him; he is blessed and therefore beaten as the preacher, servant, and king of the fifth, the millenarian monarchy.[49] His unique rank consists in the fact that he is the only Messiah who describes his own commitment through his poems. As an erudite he connects the historical topics of the Fifth Monarchy with millenarian

---

Puritan, the Millennium, and the Future of Israel: Puritan Eschatology 1600 to 1660. Cambridge 1970. R.G. Clouse: The Rebirth of Millenarianism. *Ibid.*, pp. 42–65.

[48] *Mercurius Teutonicus of a Christian Information Concerning the Last Times Being Divers Propheticall Passages of the Fall of Babel, and the New Building in Zion. Gathered out of the Mystical Writings of that famous German Author, JACOB BEHMEN, aliàs Teutonicus Phylosophus. Despise no Propheceyings. Prove all things, hold fast that is good. I Thess. 5:20.21.* London. Printed by M. Simmons, for H. Blunden at the Castle in Cornhill 1649, p. 14.

[49] That Kuhlmann considered himself as a Quintomonarchist and as the king of this new time is visible in his pamphlet of 1682: *Salomon a Kaiserstein cosmopolita De monarchia Jesuelitica, ultimo aevo reservata, Ad politicos aulicosque orbis terrarum.* London 1682. For the history of the Fifth monarchist see the highly informative study of B.S. Capp: (fn. 31). The book includes a short, very useful history of the term of

traditions and the prophecies of the third, spiritual reign according to the Joachimite prophecies; and these patterns of a universal theology of history are joined with the traditional doctrine of the six ages of the world. In his poetry, the clusters of theological speculations grow together to a unique power of metaphysical imagery: it evokes the new world to come by the force of the poetic word. The linguistical force is the realizing power of the verbum "fiat": "Vollzieh!" "Perform!" This speculation is the heart of his poetry.

Kuhlmann's poetical efforts reach their summit in his "Kühlpsalter". This "Kühlpsalter" was Kuhlmann's gospel: In a series of poems beginning in Breslau 1670 it shows Kuhlmann's own way of fulfilling his divine commission up to his present in 1686. The poems describe located and dated personal mystical experiences. So the "Kühlpsalter" is the evangelium aeternum[50] of the times fulfilling through Kuhlmann's life in order of the world's instant new era of glory. In his own view, Kuhlmann's biography unfolds the secret of the coming; the reign of the 1000 apocalyptic years is committed to him, Kuhlmann—and it is about to begin. His wife Maria Gould (Maria Anglicana) plays the correspondent female role as the incarnation of biblical wisdom, drawn from the apocryphic book of wisdom as the reincarnation of Eve in paradise and of the cosmic wife (Maria) in St. John's Revelation (Rev. 12:1,2).[51] The wife: "clothed with the sun"—that is the alchemical "gold" of Maria Gould's name—"with the moon under her feet, and on her head a crown of twelve stars. She was pregnant and was crying out in birthtangs, in the agony of giving birth."

In the engravings of the Kühlpsalter's title-pages (1684–1686) this apocalyptic claim is immediately apparent. The emblems stem from Böhme's "Mysterium Magnum", a vast allegorical commentary to the book of Genesis that caused Kuhlmann's Böhmistic conversion, and this emblematic ensemble is completed by symbols of Kuhlmann's own Messianic commitment.

In his allegorical interpretation of the book of Genesis, one of the striking examples of Christian Kabbala, Böhme interpreted the name

---

"Fifth Monarchy", pp. 23–45. Unfortunately he does not deal with the continental part of this group and therefore doesn't know Kuhlmann.

[50] Cf. Dietze, p. 129.

[51] This interpretation goes back to Irenaeus of Lyon, *Adv. Haer.* 3, 12, 4. Migne PG 7, col. 959f.

of Henoch as "divine breath". The triple cross, Henoch's symbol derives from the letter H consisting of three lines which just have to be enhanced by another three lines. This meaning of the name Henoch was evident for him because of the two aspirated "h" in it. Representing the divine breath it was possible to see Henoch as the allegory of spiritual space, created by the power of the divine sound, as the allegory of the space of primordial creation and of the epochs in the history of salvation. "This shows the inner, holy, omniscient Spirit through the outward one; as through the miracles of the matrix of the outward beings, as through the spirit of the outward world, what would happen to the human reigns on earth: For the inner spirit speculated itself through God's formated Wisdom and contemplated itself in the formated spirit of its miracles: This signifies the name 'Henoch'".[52]

In the course of universal history, the reign of Henoch signifies the last, the sixth period of the world that is equivalent with the unclosing of the millennium, when Christ himself will reappear for the first time (Christ's second apocalyptic advent is the last revelation of the Celestial Jerusalem): "This sixth reign begins after the Apostles' death and longs with its outward regiment until the mountain of Zion, when the enthusiasted Henoch will reappear in spirit and power: For Henoch is the prophetic root, and holds in his regiment Noah, Moses and the sword of Elija: At the end of the sixth time the outward Jared will fall and together with him the outward building which is the city of Babel.

The sign of the end is visible in the figure which can be seen in the engraving and it signifies the time in which the triple cross reveals itself in Henoch's voice, as a revelation of the Holy Trinity, and can be recognized in its similitude to all visible beings. The picture also signifies the conquest of the Cherub's sword in Babel, since for the power of the city of Babel the top of the Cherub's sword points downwards. Thirdly it signifies the great rod and punishment over Babel, a rod mightily handling its power. Fourthly it signifies God's

[52] *Mysterium magnum XVII*, chap. 30, 29. Jacob Böhme: *Sämtliche Schriften* (1730), Ed. Peuckert, Stuttgart 1958, vol. 7, p. 269: "Das deutete der innere, heilige, allwissende Geist durch den äussern, als durch die Wunder der Gebärerin der äußern Wesen, als durch den Geist der äussern Welt an, wie es mit dem menschlichen Reiche auf Erden ergehen würde: denn der innere Geist spiegulierete sich durch die geformte Weisheit Gottes, und beschauete sich in den geformten Geistern der Wundern; Dieses deutet uns der Name Henoch an."

wrathful furious fire which will divour the sword and the rod. This will be the end of the sixth era: the triple cross also shows the time when this will occur; when Christ's reign will have such a [triadic] number, the sixth era will be finished."[53] (See Fig. 1).[54]

III. *Title Engravings of the "Külhpsalter"*

Böhme's allegory of Henoch is the emblematical background of the title engravings found in the Kühlpsalter. Three triple crosses—the signs of the ending sixth era—are set together and framed by bushes of lilies and roses. The lilies and roses are Böhme's emblems for eternal blessed life.[55] Three crowns are found above the upper triple cross, and the letters Q(uirinus) K(uhlmann) are set between the

---

[53] *Ibid.*, pp. 272f. 43. Dieses sechste Reich fänget an nach der Apostel Tode, und währet mit seinem äusserlichen Regiment bis an den Berg Zion, bis der verzückte Enoch im Geist und Kraft wieder erscheinet: Denn Enoch ist die prophetische Wurtzel, und hält in seinem Regiment Noam, Mosen und das Schwert Eliä: Am Ende der sechsten zeit fällt der äussere Jared, und mit ihme dasselbe äusserliche gebäu, als die Stadt babel. 44. Des Endes Zeichen stehet also mit einer solchen Figur, wie sie hier im Kupferstich zu sehen ist, und deutet an die Zeit, als da sich das dreyfache Creutz in der Stimme Henochs eröffnet, als eine Offenbarung der H. Dreyfaltigkeit, dieselbe in der Figur und Gleichniß an allen sichtbaren Dingen zu erkennen: Mehr deutets an die Überwindung des Schwerts Cherubs in Babel, da der Gewalt der Stadt Babel sein Schwert mit der Spitze unter sich kehret. Zum dritten deutets an die grosse Ruthe und Straffen über Babel, welche Ruthe ihren Gewalt mächtig über sich führet. Zum vierten deutets an das grimmige Zorn-Feuer Gottes, welches das Schwert und Ruthe verschlingen soll. Dieses wird das Ende der sechsten Zeit seyn: Das dreyfache Creutz zeiget auch an die Zeit, wenn das geschehen soll; wenn das Reich Christi wird eine solche Zahl haben, so ist die sechste Zeit ganz vorüber."

[54] This emblem appears also on the title page of the 1649 London collection of apocalyptical and millenarian extracts from Böhme's writings: *Mercurius Teutonicus*. For Böhme's English disciples see Wilhelm Struck: *Der Einfluß Jakob Böhmes auf die englische Literatur des 17. Jahrhunderts*. Berlin 1935.

[55] Cf. Jakob Böhme: Von den drei Principien II, 19; Sämtliche Schriften II, (1730), ed. Peuckert 1988, p. 316: "Die rechte Porten des Eingangs in Himmel oder Hölle. 64. Die Vernunft suchet immer das Paradeis, daraus sie ist ausgegangen, und spricht: Wo ist dann die Stätte der Ruhe der armen Seelen? Wo kommt sie hin, wann sie vom Leibe scheidet? fähret sie weit weg, oder bleibet sie hier? 65. Wiewohl es ist, daß wir in unser hohen Erkentniß mögen schwer verstanden werden: denn so eine Seele dis schauen will, so muß sie eine neue Geburt eingehen, sonst stehet sie hinter der Decke, und fraget immer, wo ist der Ort? 66. Jedoch wollen wir's setzen um der Lilien-Rosen willen: Da der H Geist im Wunder wird manche Pforten eröffnen, das man ietzt für unöglich hält, und in der Welt niemand daheime ist, sondern sie sind zu Babel."

Fig. 1. Böhme, *Mysterium Magnum*. Sämtliche Werke (1730). Ed. Peuckert. (Stuttgart, 1958), Bd. 7, facing p. 273[54].

Fig. 2. Fig. 3.

Title engravings of the *Kühlpsalter*, vol. 1 and 2.

Fig. 4. Fig. 5.

Title engravings of the *Kühlpsalter*, vol. 3 and 4.

crowns. The first field shows Adam, Eve, the serpent and the edenic tree. In the following title engravings Adam and Eve are surrounded by a halo, in order to show that they signify the primoridial spiritual first men. The second field of the triple cross shows Christ and the two thieves crucified with him. The third, lower triple-cross undergoes a considerable change in the course of the four engravings. In all four pictures this field is surrounded by a wall with twelve towers and doors symbolizing the Celestial Jerusalem of St. John's Revelation. In the first engraving this field has in its center the apocalyptic lamb; in the second engraving the portraits of Q(uirinus) K(uhlmann) and M(aria) A(ngelica) are set on both sides of the lamb; in the third engraving Q(uirinus) K(uhlmann), is presented as the apocalyptic kosmokrator of St. John's Revelation (Rev. 1:12–18), he is crowned with seven stars, surrounded by the sun and the moon—as it was prophecied by his Prophet Drabic[56]—and holds a sword and a sceptre in his hands; M(aria) K(uhlmann), his wife, appears as the apocalyptic Madonna (Rev. 12) with the crowned divine child on her arms. The fourth title engraving does no longer display these attributes of the rising apocalypse. The apocalyptic emblems are now replaced by symbols of the final state of glory: in the upper, edenic field the serpent has disappeared, Adam points to the restored tree and Eve to the lily above her. Quirinus and Maria are surrounded by halos, they have become the new Adam and Eve, three hands hold Quirinus' crown,[57] a couple of hands connects Quirinus to the new Eve, and she points to the lamb, as well as to her mystic bridegroom: The Thousand Years' Reign has arrived.

This program of the engravings shows, that Kuhlmann saw himself in 1686, in the time of the printing of the third engraving, as the prophet of the apocalypse and as the *ektypus* of the archetypical *kosmokrator* who was revealed in the opening verses of St. John's Revelation.

At first glance, Kuhlmann's portrait looks just alike other portraits

---

[56] Cf. above p. 267.

[57] This symbol appeared first in a prophecy of Christian Kotter, reported in Comenius' *Lux in Tenebris* s.l. 1657, p. 35.

Fig. 6. Quirinus Kuhlmann's portrait.

of learned or noble men in the seventeenth century. But this impression is deceiving. You do not find any attributes of erudition or political power, it is just the portrait of a man with a wide garment which is hold by a buckle. This buckle, however, displays Böhme's symbol of the divine world and Henoch's breath, the triple cross. The typological names of the subscription of Kuhlmann's portrait finally open the complex meaning of the portrait. Names of famous philologists figure together with biblical and historical kings, and the text ends with a prayer. At its whole, the subscription is composed in steps of remarkable spiritual ranking:

The first two lines mark Kuhlmann's claim as an architype of a philologist. *Philo-logy* means love of God's word, being in the beginning with God and being God, through whom the world was made, and the word was the light in the darkness. So he is, as an erudite Philologist also a learned poet featuring in his first typological series: "Alter Scaligerorum,[58] Taubmanus, Grotius, Opitz, Barthius, Iscanus,[59] Gryphius, Muretus, Erasmus!"

The second series, like every series marked by an exclamation mark, shows Kuhlmann as the arch-prophet, representing Henoch, who, according to Böhme, was the type of edenic wisdom, and ending with the last of the Old Testament's prophets, John the Baptist. "Henoch, Josephus, Davides, Iosua, Moses, Elias, Daniel, Salomon, Elisa, Johannes!"

The third series is the one of kings, representing symbols of heavenly power and political theology in the course of world-history. Kuhlmann's garment shows his kingship, he wears the purple "vestis regia".[60] In the subscription of the portrait there are five kings featuring; a hint to the Fifth Monarchy: "Cyrus, Alexander, Constantine, Karl, Fridericus!" The line begins with Cyrus, the founder of the Persian empire, who let Israel return from Babylonia to Jerusalem,[61]

[58] Both, the father and the son, are pointed to.

[59] Iscanus, Joseph of Exeter, f. 1190, medieval Latin poet. His *De bello Troiano* was first printed at Basel in 1558 as *Dareti Phrygii de bello Troiano, Libri 6 a Cornelio Nepote in Latinum conversi* and again in 1583 with the Iliad in folio, also Antwerp 1608 and Milan 1669. It was published under Joseph's name with notes by Samuel Dresenius, Frankfurt 1620 and 1623, by J. More, London 1675, with Dictys Cretensis and Dares Phrygius in usum Delphini, Amsterdam 1702 and London 1825.

[60] Sackur, p. 168.

[61] Isai 41:2: The just one from the east.

to be continued by the Greek Alexander the Great and the Roman Constantine, the first christian emperor. Karl—the German version of the name—probably means Charlemagne and can be interpreted as the specific commitment of the German empire in the course of universal history. This is a change in the traditional interpretation of Daniel's four reigns. According to St. Jerome, Daniel's four apocalyptical animals are interpreted as the Assyric, Persian, Greek and Roman Empires, and the continuity of the Roman and German empires, the *translatio imperii*, was part of the self-interpretation of the Italo/German Holy Roman Empire of the Middle Ages. Be that as it may, Fridericus certainly hints to the Winter-King, the one who was prophesied to realize the final victory of Protestantism in Bohemia. Fridericus is considered the true heir of Charlemagne's reign—and the real, final Friedrich will be the king of the Fifth Monarchy, namely Kuhlmann.

Exactly this is the climax of the remarkable enhancement of the subscription's forth series, featuring Kuhlmann's millenarian commitment: "Liliger, Juvenis, Frigerans, Artista, Sophata!" "Liliger" is the one who supports Böhme's reign of lilies and roses. As a symbol of his royal and prophetic commission Kuhlmann, in his portrait, wears a buckle holding his coat with the three crowns of the eternal Trinitarian reign and the triple cross of Henoch's edenic wisdom. "Iuvenis" hints to the juvenile King who was expected since the Jewish riot against the Romans and who was prophesied again by the Sibylla Tiburtina.[62] The portrait itself displays that shining countenance. "Frigerans" is the biblical hint to Kuhlmann's apocalyptical role from Acts of the Apostles 3:20, where a "cooling time" is prophesied. "Artista" is Elias Artista who was, besides Henoch, considered to be one of the two witnesses in St. John's Revelation, to announce the Apocalypse.[63] "Sophata" is the wisest, this title hints to the book of Wisdom; here Kuhlmann sees himself as the Father's purely shining mirror (Sap. 7:26).

From the typological incarnation of Wisdom in Kuhlmann the step to the final, the fifth rank can only be the closest approximation to God. The genre of this last step is prayer and the present

[62] Cf. fn. 36: Flavius Josephus, *Bellum Judaicum* VI, 4,5. Cf. Sackur, p. 185.

[63] Sackur, p. 112, Bousset, Der Antichrist, pp. 134ff. The best book on this topic, still indispensable, is Thomas Malvenda: De Antichristo libri undecim. Rome 1604. for Henoch and Elia see *Liber nonus: De Henoch & Elia*, pp. 452–479.

one displays the divine commission Kuhlmann claims to have received: "O Pater haec tua sunt. Haec ad te cuncta reflexit."

IV. *Speculative Philology*

1. *The Creating Word*

The title of Kuhlmann's collection of mystical poems is "Kühlpsalter". This strange word alludes of course the biblical psalter: Kuhlmann claimes to rewrite the psalms for the beginning of his Fifth Monarchy and the third period of the world, the Kühl-reich. The meaning of the term "Kühl" derives from Kuhlmann's interpretation of the vulgate translation of the Acts of the Apostles (3:20): "Poenitemini igitur, et convertimini ut deleantur peccata vestra: Ut cum venerint tempora *refrigeri* a conspectu Domini, et miserit eum qui praedictus est vobis: Jesum Christum". Kuhlmann related this promise of "refrigeri", "cooling", after the time of the punishment to his own name[64] and hence to his revealed poetry.

The word that Kuhlmann writes as the reincarnated Sophia/Christ is claimed to be the poetic appearance of the "cooling" time to come and at the same time the reality of that new arrival. God's word has the power to command the emergence of the third period: and the aim of the "Kühlpsalter" is to provoke this command for the new time. This book claims poetically that the new third period, the millennium of the world, is just arriving. The performance of magical and poetic words will unclose the new time of roses and lilies. That is why the book has two genres of poems: The first are the "jubilees" of the time that already had arrived and the second genre contains anxious and urgent prayers for the new period to come; both species are, of course, complementary.

Kuhlmann, as a Böhmist, shared Böhme's doctrine of creation that had its center in the theology of the word. This doctrine was rooted in the Philonian and Augustinian commentaries on the book of Genesis. For the Judeo-Christian context the argument was evident, that the divine word had a creating power: "In the beginning God created the heavens and the earth. The earth was without form and void, and darkness was upon the face of the deep; and the Spirit of God was moving over the face of the waters. And God said: 'Let

[64] Cf. Dietze, p. 239.

there be light'—'Fiat lux'—and there was light." These first three verses of the book of Genesis mark the creation of the world by the force of the word: the decisive, crucial word is "Fiat".

Of course creation is considered to be creation out of nothing: And so the word "Fiat" is the command for things to emerge into existence. This "Fiat" signifies the central meaning of language: Language does not denote something which already exists. It is just the contrary: God's word, his primordial idea of the things to be created, is considered to exist before the things were evoked into their external existence; and the command to execute God's will is "Fiat". In this theory the essence of language is command, not denotation. The commanding of the "Fiat" brings the things God had in mind into outward existence. This interpretation of the "Fiat" in Genesis 1:3 was not extraordinary, it was shared by Böhme and by Kuhlmann.

The doctrine of the creating "Fiat" can easily be connected to the first verses of the prologue of St. John's Gospel: "In the beginning was the Word, and the Word was with God and the Word was God. He was in the beginning with God; all things were made through him , and without him was nothing made what was made. In him was life, and the life was the light of men. The light shines in the darkness, and the darkness has not overcome it. . . . And the Word became flesh and dwelt among us." This text was the most important source of speculative Christology in the Christian tradition. Christ appears here in three functions: 1. He is the inner trinitarian logos, the Son of the Father. 2. He is the Word by which the world was created. 3. He was made flesh.

For our purpose, the doctrine of creation through the word that is through Jesus Christ is the most important topic. How could creation be explained? Böhme, as standing in the Philonian and Origenistic traditions, imagined the creation in two steps. The first step was the conception of the world through the word: The result consisted in an ideal, spiritual world, the "causae primordiales" of the Stoic and Platonic traditions, sometimes conceived as the hypostasis of Sapientia, Schechina, Wisdom. In this Wisdom God's complete conception of the world attained a spiritual unity. God's ideas were conceived as the spiritual existence of the world, and the ideas emerged into their extramental existence by the divine word "Fiat". This Judeo-Christian adaptation of the Stoic concept of the "logos spermatikos" confronted a crucial difficulty: Its original existence was merely spiritual, before time and space, located only in God's wisdom. This divine wisdom contained the *logoi spermatikoi*, the primordial living spirits of all things to emerge. For the step into outside special and timely existence the command of the "Fiat" was absolutely necessary. This transition from an eternal mental existence into an extramental existence was the moment of the "beginning", it was the rise of the living word into its outward essence. The "Fiat" commanded the mental seminal causes, the concepts of things into their external perfection; "es bringt zu Stand und Wesen". The emergence of the things, their arrival in extramental existence displayed the eternal presence of God's creating word in the course of time.

This is also the apocalyptic function of the "verbum fiat": the rise of the millenarian Messiah could only be imagined as a process of becoming reality, as the emergence of still concealed events "from darkness to light". The millenarian Messiah disclosed the rising new world, just as the word "Fiat" disclosed the spiritual ideas into the outward existence of things. His power was the same as the mighty "Fiat" of the first creation. Men who enjoyed God's grace could already perceive the times to come in their innermost hearts[65] and thus enjoy the dawn of the coming "Rose and Lily Time".

The seeds of the things were the divine ideas which had survived unruined the times of sin; they had to be evoked by the eternal power of God's words. So future perfection was hidden in the creation. The one who could conceive the hidden beauty of the things felt the yearning foreshadowing of the "Rose and Lily times".[66] It was the heavenly power of the new heaven and the new earth predicted in the last chapter of St. John's Apocalypse: 21:2,10–12 that could be perceived in the hearts of the devote people: "And I saw the holy city, New Jerusalem, coming down out of heaven from God, prepared as a bride for her husband. . . . 'Come, I will show you the Bride, the wife of the Lamb'. And in the Spirit he carried me away to a great, high mountain, and showed me the Holy City of

[65] Cf. Caspar Schwenckfeldt: "Catechismus. Vom Worte des Creutzes / und vom Unterscheide des Worts des Geistes und Buchstabens, was auch propriè und eigentlich Gottes Wort sey". In: *Der Erste Theil der schrifftlichen und orthodoxen Bücher und Schrifften des Edlen / theuren / von Gott hochbegnadeten und Gottseligen Mans Caspar Schwenckfelds.* Frankfurt 1564.

[66] For quotations see Dietze, p. 414, fn. 27 and p. 415, fn. 30; especially the titles of the prophetess' Tannecke Denijs pamphlets: *Die Christliche Lilie-Blum.* Amsterdam 1662 etc.

Jerusalem coming down out of Heaven from God, having the glory of God, its radiance like a most rare Jewel, like a Jaspe, clear as crystal. It had a great, high wall, with twelve gates. . . ."

The concept of the creating word also forms the core of Böhme's appreciation of his German mother-tongue. Böhme saw the German language as quite close to God's creating language, for he saw in its roots the traces of God's originating words. So the German language was able to evoke the eternal ideal power in the spiritual seeds of the things. This concept of the creative "Ursprache" which had a close linkage to the essence of the things was adopted by Kuhlmann, and he tried to work it out in an analogical way: he verbalized the nouns—which is easily possible in German. Thus his language reveals by its temporalizing, its mimetic forming of time the temporal character of rising and becoming. This temporalizing of language means, theologically, that Kuhlmann tried to imitate the process of creation through the word in order to reestablish the primordial state which is God's third, apocalyptic revelation.

Exactly this is the function of the Messiah, the role which Kuhlmann saw himself in. By his poetry he re-presented the eternal divine word, he made the word present which had been incarnated first in the creation—and which was typologically displayed by the primordial Adam and in Eve. In a second realization the word had been made flesh in the crucified Jesus Christ. The word will be finally fulfilled by Quirinus Kuhlmann, the new "Jesuel", and by his wife, the new Eve, Maria Angelica.

Kuhlmann names himself Jesuel, and his congregation will be the "Jesuelits". He uses a specific interpretation of the hebraic "El", featuring as the first divine name in Isidor's of Seville Etymologiae: "Primum apud Hebraeos Dei nomen 'El' dicitur, quod alii Deum, alii etymologiam eius exprimentes, ἰσχυρός, id est 'fortem', interpretati sunt. Ideo quod nulla infirmitate opprimitur, sed fortis est et sufficiens ad omnia perpetranda."[67] Kuhlmann interprets God's power in the sense of Dionysius the Areopagite's celestial hierarchy as an hypostatic person, an angel: "The holy 'El', the name of the great angel, who triumphs with the soul over the heavens, is given back to us through all 10 L [probably the ten 10 Sephiroth as the ten divine powers] in the name of *Jesueliter*; and we soon will be able

[67] Isidore of Seville *Etymologiae lib. VII*, chap. I,3. Ed. W.M. Lindsay, Oxford 1911.

to welcome the *Israel* of the *Christs* [the 144,000 elected of the Millennium], the three unique kingdom of Jesus Christ.

Rejoice, you heavens, rejoice you earth! The Cooling Time [Cf. Act. III:20][68] of which all prophets spoke from the beginning of the world, begins already with the gemmae of the lilies and the roses. . . ."[69]

2. *Poetical Apocalypse*

This is the moment when the apocalypse begins, a moment that is enchanted in the perhaps most intensive poem of the Kühlpsalter, trying to use the magic power of the word and to entreat God's final revelation from darkness into light, from weakness to strength; it enchants the very first moment of God's upshining presence.[70] The poem is dated: "When he [Kuhlmann] secretly left Amsterdam the 19th of August, remembering through Rome and Alcair to Jerusalem; even more secretly was driven back to Amsterdam by miracles in the 144th hour, and resounded Jerusalem's most secret concealments on August 29th, 1680."[71]

1.11. Recht dunkelt mich das dunkel,
Weil Wesenheit so heimlichst anbeginnt!
O seltner Glükkskarfunkel! Es stroemt, was euserlich verrinnt,
Und wird ein Meer, was kaum ein baechlein gründt.

---

[68] Cf. fn. 28.

[69] *Kühlpsalter* I, p. 203. "29 Das heilige El, der nahme des grossen Engels, der mit der Seelen über di Himmel triumfiret, ist Uns durch alle Zehen L nun in dem nahmen *Jesueliter* widererstattet, und wird bald das *Israel der Christen* der *Jesueliter*, das dreieinige Königreich Christi begrüßet werden. 30. Freuet euch, Ihr Himmel! Frohlokke, du Erde! Die Kühlungszeit, davon alle Propheten vom anbeginne der Welt gesprochen, knospet albereit seine lilien- und Rosenknospen, und mus nunmehro das Unkraut von dem Weitzen in der grossen Erndte der letzen Weltstunde geschiden werden."

[70] Sibylle Rusterholz describes the relationship between Kuhlmann and St. John of the Cross in detail. Cf. Rusterholz. For the mystical tradition of this theme cf. Alois M. Haas: "Die dunkle Nacht der Sinne und des Geistes. Mystische Leiderfahrung nach Johannes vom Kreuz". In: *Mystik als Aussage. Erfahrungs-, Denk- und Redeformen christlicher Mystik.* Frankfurt 1996, pp. 446–464.

[71] "Zweiter Theil. Als er aus Amsterdam den 19. August geheim ausreiste, durch Rom und Alcair nach Jerusalem gedenkend; noch geheimer in der 144 stunde mit wundern nach Amsterdam zurückgetriben ward; und am allergeheimsten zukünfftige Jerusalemsche Verhohlenheiten austhönte den 29. Aug. 1680." Quirinus Kuhlmann: *Der Kühlpsalter.* Buch V–VIII, Paralipomena. Hg. v. Robert L. Baere. Tübingen 1971, pp. 12f. = the 2. (62.) Kühlpsalm 2. Theil. The english translation stems from Anthony Grafton, whom I thank very much for his kindness. The double counting of the verses indicates that it is the second poem within a series; here the series contains three poems of 10 verses. The verses have 5 lines, the scheme of rhyme is a b a b b.

This first verse connects darkness and beginning. The beginning is the first shining of essence (Wesenheit), of the essence of the things according to God's primordial ideas which will reappear in the last times. It is a rare fortune to participate in such a decisive moment of the history of salvation, the first light is shining as a garfunkel of fortune, a gem reflecting the brightness and flash of the first beginning which is the brighter the darker the darkness was. This is, however, a mere inner event, the inner stream nourishing an ocean is hardly perceivable outwards as a rill.

[The dark, how deep it darkens me
For essence begins secretly.
O fortune rare, o fortune's gem.
Inside me rises high the stream
which outside hardly ever seems
a brook to normal men
An ocean groes and swells and fills
Though only trifling slender rills
provide its fundament.]

2.12. I dunkler i mehr lichter:
I schwaerzer A.L.L.S. i weisser weisst sein sam.
Ein himmlisch Aug ist richter:
Kein Irdscher lebt, der was vernahm;
Es glaenzt i mehr, i finster es ankam.

The verse starts with the paradox of darkness a light. The strange writing of "A.L.L.S." signifies the cabbalistic usage of the letters: the L, pronounced as "El", is the representative of the "El", the Power of God's name.[72] If "A." means "A(nfang)" and "S." means "S(chluß) A.L.L.S. is the symbol of God's almighty and endless power. "El" is the name of God's power and light, it is his essence that becomes his seed. The confrontation of black and white has an alchemistical meaning: black is the coldest grade in the process of glowing and white is the hottest. That the white colour carries the seed of the coming, is due to a concept of beginning deriving from neoplatonic traditions. The second aphorism of the "Book of XXIV Philosophers" consists in one verse describing God's spontaneous generating power:

---

[72] The A.L.L.S. may correspond to Sibylle Rusterholz's Interpretation as Amsterdam, London, Lutetia [Paris], Edinburgh, Smyrna. Cf. Rusterholz, p. 237. It may also mean A[nfang] EL, EL, S[chluß].

"Monas, monadem gignens, in se reflectens ardorem".[73] The process describes the spontaneous beginning of reflection from the unpredictable One into the reflection of itself: in the moment of that reflection the heating of love between the monade and its image instantly produces a flashing light. Since this movement of speculation is the absolute first movement, the absolute beginning, this originating of light is as well the origin of life, for life is the faculty of moving. That is the reason why the seed of life is white. This eternal process of becoming is the theogony which has its eternal source in the everlasting inner trinitarian life. It is only God's heavenly eye that can perceive this inner divine process and which can determine the transmission of this divine life to earth in order to begin the final times. No being on earth was hitherto (except Kuhlmann?) able to perceive this process of God's eternal self creation which will now become visible in its brightness.

3.13. Ach nacht! Und nacht, di taget!
O tag, der nacht vernünfftiger Vernunfft!
Ach Licht, das Kaine plaget,
Und helle strahlt der Abelszunfft!
Ich freue mich ob deiner finstern Kunfft.

"Ach"—is the most expressive syllab displaying innermost feelings, it returns in the verb "ächzen". With such intensity the night is addressed as the time when the source of every process becomes visible. "Ach Nacht!" It is the moment when the night disappears and becomes day; this is the moment of the true revelation of good and evil; and this is a revolutionary moment. The brightness of God's final day will be darkness for earthly reason (vernünfftige Vernunfft). God's light is the one that tortures the adherants of Cain and is bright for the followers of Abel. Still in his darkness, Kuhlmann is delighted of the dark advent of God's light.

The topic of the dark advent of light stems from Plotinus and occurs in Ps. Dionysius the Areopagite. In his "Mystical Theology" Dionysius advises his student Timothy to ascend the steps of mystical knowledge, to get rid of everything, even of being and not being, "and to be raised aloft unknowingly to the union, as far as attainable, with Him Who is above every essence and knowledge. For by

[73] *Le livre de XXIV philosophes.* Ed. Francoise Hudry. Grenoble 1979.

the resistless and absolute ecstasy in all purity, from thyself and all, thou will be carried on high, to the *superessential ray of the Divine darkness*, when thou hast cast away all, and become free from all".[74]

4.14. O laengsterwartes Wunder!
Das durch den kern des gantzen Baums auswaechst!
Du faengst neu Edens zunder!
Ei liber, sih mein hertze laechst!
Es ist genug: Hoehr, was es innigst aechst.

Böhme, in his "Mysterium magnum", described the process of creation as the real mysterium, since by this process God created the difference of himself.[75] It was this original mystery by which the primordial world was created. This primordial world is the type of the coming one as well. The return to that primoridal world is the mystery long since expected. Therefore the garden of Eden is the type of the world to return in final times: from the kernel unfolding to the perfect tree of paradise this eternal mystery will be displayed. In an immediate address the poet entreats God to begin his work as he created the world with his fiery life—"Du fängst neu Edens zunder", you begin again Eden's tinder—and he offers his heart to the beloved: "mein herze laechst", my heart is yearning for you. This yearning is a common topic of mystical literature to describe the thirst of the mystic for the reception of his beloved. "Es ist genug" quotes Elija in the deserts (1. Kings 19:4). "Hör" alludes the "sih" of the verse above, and the verb "ächst" is a verbalisation of the "ach" of the beginning of verse 3.13.

5.15. O unaussprechlist Blauen!
O lichtste Roeth! O übergelbes Weis!
Es bringt, was ewigst, schauen
Beerdt di Erd als Paradeis;
Entflucht den fluch, durchsegnet iden reis.

After Kuhlmann delineated the type of the world to arrive, the process of becoming is described as the lightening in the process of glowing. The enhancement reminds the alchemic order of colours:

---

[74] Dionysius Areopagita. *Mystic Theology* I,1. Tr. John Parker. London 1899, repr. New York 1976.

[75] Cf. Wilhelm Schmidt-Biggemann: "Das Geheimnis des Anfangs. Einige spekulative Betrachtungen im Hinblick auf Böhme". In: Jan Garewicz und Alois Maria Haas (eds.): *Gott, Natur, Mensch in der Sicht Jacob Böhmes und seiner Rezeption.* Wiesbaden 1994, pp. 113–127.

The first stage of glowing is blue, the medium is red, the hottest colour is white, even more than yellow/gold—and white is also the colour of the divine seed. This process of becoming light brings into apparition what God conceived in his eternal wisdom. For Böhme theses colours are the main ones of the rainbow which, for him, is a "figure" of the last judgement.[76] Here the primordial edenic world is reminded and its final realisation is described by a bold word "ewigst", meaning either "ewig ist" or the superlative of "ewig" (eternal). This eternal existence will become reality on earth. This realisation of the heavenly paradise on earth is conceived as "beerden"; and it will finish the curse of the first parents "entflucht den fluch" uncurses the curse and it will newly and completely bless the whole nature: "durchsegnet iden reis" blesses every twig growing.

6.16. O Erdvir! Welches Strahlen?
Der finsterst ist als vor die lichtste Sonn.
Krystallisirtes Prahlen!
Die Welt bewonnt di Himmelswonn:
Sie quillt zurükk, als wäre si der Bronn.

The unfolding of divine grace and glory on earth, described as beginning in the last verse is here continued and enhanced: Now the earth becomes the mirror reflecting God's glory. "Erdvier" hints to the four elements of the world: fire, water, air, and earth. These elements begin to shine after having received again their primordial form; and their darkest ray shines even brighter than the brightest sun (der finsterste ist noch vor der hellsten Sonne). "Kristallisiertes Prahlen", christallized boasting—for my opinion the most intensive image and formulation in this poem. The earth appears as a christal reshining from God's overabundant power. The world raises and renders heavenly joy to heaven, it is the reflowing of grace from earth onto heaven as if the world were the fountain of divine grace and glory.

7.17. Welch wesentliches Bildnis?
Erscheinst du so Geheimste Krafftfigur?
Wi richtigst, was doch wildnis?

[76] Cf. Böhme, *Mysterium magnum* ch. 33, 27–33. The colours are as well symbols of the holy trinity, according to St. John of the Cross, whom Kulmann quotes. Blue is the colour of the Holy Spirit, red the One of the Father, and white and yellow the ones of the Son. Cf. Rusterholz, p. 244.

O was vor zahl? Ach welche spur?
Du bists, nicht Ich! Dein ist Natur und Cur!

"Essential image" alludes the dogmatics of Christology: The first image is Christ being the image of God, and from this image derives the primordial Adam, the man before the sin. This essential, primordial image is also the divine *logos*, who has the power to realize things. For this process of pushing primordial conceptions into reality divine power is required, and the symbol of this power is the El or L.[77] As a rectangle it forms also a constructive element of the cross, as it was enhanced by Böhme's Triple Cross. The figure of power appearing is the form of forms, it is the symbol of divine power and order, by which the original chaos was tamed in the first creation and which reappears rectifying the wilderness by God's final coming. Order and essence have the character of numbers, so the traces of God's order are perceivable throughout. The L or El is especially the Symbol of God's presence in his Messiah Kuhlmann; thus, in the return of God's grace from earth to heaven, the mystical Messiah is present, too. In this process God is always present; and even if God and man seem to become undiscriminable in the process of the returning grace to heaven—it remains God's will, choice, and order that will be established: Du bist's nicht ich! Dein ist Natur und Cur.

8.18. Di Kron ist ausgefüllet,
Di Tausend sind auch uberall ersaezt:
Geschehen, was umhüllet;
Sehr hoher roeth, hoechst ausgeaetzt,
Das alle kunst an ihr sich ausgewetzt.

The crown of the rulers of the Millennium is complete—it becomes clear that the divine order to be installed is not only a natural but rather a political one; this is the rule of the 24 Oldest of St. John's Revelation. Their Thousand Years' Reign is instant; the "Tausend" hints to Daniel 7:10: "Thousands of Thousands ministered to him, an ten thousand times a hundred thousand stood before him: The judgement sat and the books were opened."(Cf. Rev. 20:4f) So the history of the world is finished, everything has happened that was

[77] By the way it is the reverse form of the Hebrew letter Waw, which was considered to be the symbol of the edenic tree.

hidden before and had to be fulfilled in earthly times. These times were times of suffering. The past period is described in alchemistical terms as the time of purifying glow: it is the red glow, that purified everything; all the art of purifying metals has been exercised in the last period before the Millennium.

9.19. Di Lilien und Rosen
sind durch sechs tag gebrochen spat und früh:
Si kraenzen mit libkosen
Nun dich und mich aus deiner müh.
Dein VVil ist mein, mein will ist dein: Vollzih.

Lilies and roses, Böhme's symbols of the Millennium, have been broken during six days, symbolizing the 6000 years of the world-history. The caressing symbolic flowers garland you and me—the saints of the instant Thousand Years, and the true people of Zion?—or God/Christ and Kuhlmann? The Millennium being instant, it has not yet come. So the almost desperate entreating prayer to the Father, quotes Jesus' words and transforms them into a mystical exchange formula, connected with a reminder of the originating power of the divine command "Fiat": "Dein VVil ist mein, mein will ist dein: Vollzieh!" Thy will is mine, my will is thine: Complete!

[Six days—our earthly histories—
Have made the roses and lilies
A little broken heap;
But now His flowers, red and white,
Caress and garland us. Their might
Will obstacles oer'leap.
Thy will is min my will is thine: Complete.]

10.20. Im Jesuelschen schimmer
Pfeiln wir zugleich zur Jesuelschen Kron:
Der Stoltz ist durch dich nimmer!
Er ligt zu fus im hoechsten hohn.
Ein ander ist mit dir der Erb und Sohn.

It seems that in the last verse God's final coming and with it the deification of man blissfully has happened. God's power is present in Jesuel, which is Kuhlmann's spiritual name. In Jesuel's shimmering light appears the power of the new mediator between the world and God; and in his shimmering light—the power of the "El"—we fly like arrows (the German has the bold verbalisation "pfeilen", to arrow) to the heavenly reign of the "Kühlreich": "Jesuel's crown". Because of the new mediator God's love of mankind is mirrored in man's love of God, so that the pride—the satanic origin of sin, is overcome and lies humbled under God's feet.[78] The devil is bound. The sin has disappeared. God reigns and a new man, obviously the third Adam, has become, together with Christ, the Father's Heir and Son.

> [In Jesuel's schimmering light
> To Jesus' crown we take our flight.
> The pride that once defiled now lies,
> All humbled, never more to rise.
> And with you another one:
> The Lord's true heir, and the Lord's son.]

---

[78] Cf. I. Cor. 15:21–28: For by a man came death, and by a man the resurrection of the dead. And as in Adam all die, so also in Christ all shall be made alive. But every one in his own order, the first-fruits Christ: then they that are of Christ, who have believed in his coming. Afterwards the end: when we shall have delivered up the kingdom to God the Father, when he shall have brought to naught all principality, and power, and virtue. For he must reign, until he hath put all his enemies under his feet. And the enemy death shall be destroyed last: For he hath put all things under his feet. And whereas he saith: All things are put under him, undoubtedly he his excepted, who put all things under him. And when all things shall be subdued unto him, then the Son also himself shall be subject unto him that put all things under him, that God may be all in all.

THE MESSIANIC CLAIM OF GHULĀM AḤMAD

Yohanan Friedmann

I

Messianism would probably not be the first thing which comes to the mind of a student of Islam when reminded of the Aḥmadī movement, which has been active in India and elsewhere since the late nineteenth century. The controversy surrounding the Aḥmadiyya and its notoriety was caused primarily by the fact that the founder of the movement made a claim which in the Islamic context is even bolder than a messianic one. He claimed for himself a certain type of prophethood, and this claim was widely seen as contradicting the Muslim perception of Muḥammad as the last prophet. Because of this prophetic claim of its founder, the Aḥmadiyya has become—since its inception in India in 1889—one of the most controversial movements in modern Islam. The Muslim mainstream received the movement with scathing criticism, and countered its activities and ideas with numerous demands calling for the exclusion of Aḥmadīs from the Muslim fold. As long as India was under British rule, the controversy was confined to the religious sphere, and could be described as a doctrinal dispute between private individuals or voluntary organizations. However, when the headquarters of the movement and most of its members moved, after the partition of India in 1947, into the newly established and professedly Islamic state of Pakistan, the Aḥmadī issue was transformed into a constitutional problem of major significance. Almost immediately upon the establishment of the new state, a radical Muslim organization launched a campaign designed to remove Aḥmadīs from senior positions in the public administration. Muḥammad Zafrullah Khān, a prominent Aḥmadī who was then serving as the foreign minister of Pakistan, was singled out for attack. These attempts were not successful in the early 1950s, but the issue came to the fore again 20 years later. Responding to insistent demands on the part of the mainstream religious establishment, the Pakistani parliament passed in 1974 a constitutional amendment which declared the Aḥmadīs non-Muslims.

From the strictly constitutional point of view, this should have prevented the Aḥmadīs only from serving as president or prime minister of Pakistan. In practice, however, it had many serious repercussions. Aḥmadīs were dismissed from public service, were prevented from going on pilgrimage to Mecca, and were subject to various sorts of harassment. In 1984, within the framework of the general trend of Islamization, the anti-Aḥmadī measures of the Pakistani government went a step further—and a presidential ordinance transformed much of the religious observance of the Aḥmadīs into a criminal offense, punishable by three years of imprisonment.[1]

Ghulām Aḥmad Qādiyānī, the founder of the Aḥmadī movement, started his activities in 1880 as a rather obscure writer on religious subjects in a Panjābī town. During the first years of his activity, he also involved himself in numerous debates with Hindu revivalists, Christian missionaries and some Muslim scholars whose doctrines he wanted to refute. Later he stirred an intense controversy within the Muslim community by assuming a number of religious titles which, if acknowledged, would have ranked him above any recognized spiritual leader of the Muslim community. These titles included the *mujaddid*, a reviver of Islam on the eve of the fourteenth century of the Islamic era; a *muḥaddath*, this is to say, a person spoken to by God or by the angels, the *mahdī* and the *masīḥ*, or the Messiah. Finally, he also claimed to be a prophet of a certain kind. This last claim, which can be interpreted as contradicting the Muslim belief in the finality of Muḥammad's prophethood, understandably caused the most acrimonious exchanges between the Aḥmadiyya and the Muslim mainstream, and still stands at the center of the Aḥmadī controversy. Aḥmadī prophetology is therefore the main issue which made the Aḥmadiyya famous. This paper will focus, however, on Ghulām Aḥmad's Christology and on his claim to messianic status.

II

Ghulām Aḥmad's beliefs are steeped in classical Islamic thought and their significance cannot be properly appreciated without sufficient

---

[1] The history and religious thought of the Aḥmadī movement are the subject of my *Prophecy Continuous: Aspects of Aḥmadī Religious Thought and Its Medieval Background*. University of California Press, Berkeley and Los Angeles 1989.

reference to some elements of the messianic idea in Islam. In the classical Muslim tradition, the messiah is expected to appear just before the Day of Judgment. There is some discussion concerning his identity. According to a rare tradition, he will be "none else than Jesus" (*lā mahdī illā ʿĪsā*);[2] but most traditions maintain that he will be a descendant of the Prophet, by way of his daughter Fāṭima. Several traditions mention an additional characteristic of the messiah: his name and genealogy will be identical with that of the Prophet Muḥammad.[3]

The traditions identifying the messiah with Jesus are rare. It has been argued recently that it was highly uncomfortable for the Muslims to have an eschatological hero who was also "the god of another faith."[4] These traditions therefore lost much of their currency with the passage of time, and other messianic figures, clearly related to the Prophet Muḥammad and his household, came to the fore. However, even if Jesus gradually ceased to be considered the messiah, he was to play a crucial role in the events expected to precede the Day of Judgment. He will descend from heaven, and will kill the one-eyed false messiah (*al-dajjāl*) at the gate of the city of Lydda. He will also commit, at that time, a few violent actions designed to symbolize the destruction of Christianity: as the Muslim tradition has it, "he will crush the cross and slaughter the swine." In some versions of the tradition, these actions will be followed by the creation of religious uniformity and the establishment of an absolute and ideal peace on earth.[5]

---

[2] Ibn Māja, *Sunan, kitāb al-fitan 24*, Cairo 1972, vol. 2, p. 1341.

[3] ". . . The Prophet . . . said: The world will not come to an end until the Arabs are ruled by a man from my household whose name will correspond to mine." (*qāla rasūl Allāh . . . lā tadhhabu al-dunyā ḥattā yamlika al-ʿaraba rajulun min ahli baytī yuwāṭiʾu ʾsmuhu ʾsmī*). (Ibn al-ʿArabī al-Mālikī, *ʿĀriḍat al-aḥwadhī bi-sharḥ Ṣaḥīḥ al-Tirmidhī*, Damascus (?) n.d., vol. 9, p. 74); ". . . The Prophet said: If only one day remained of this world, . . . God would prolong that day . . . until he sends a man related to me—(or: a man) from my household whose name will correspond to mine and whose father's name will correspond to that of my father. . . . He will fill the earth with equity and justice, even as it had been replete with wrong and iniquity (*law lam yabqa min al-dunyā illā yawmun . . . la-ṭawwala Allāh dhālika al-yawm . . . ḥattā yabʿatha fīhi rajulan minnī,—aw—min ahl baytī—yuwāṭiʾu ʾsmuhu ʾsmī wa ʾsmu abīhi ʾsma abī yamlaʾu al-arḍ qisṭan wa ʿadlan kamā muliʾat ẓulman wa jawran*) (Abū Dāwūd, *Sunan*, Cairo 1983, vol. 2, p. 460).

[4] See D. Cook, *Studies in Muslim Apocalyptic*. M.A. thesis, submitted to the Department of Arabic Language and Literature, The Hebrew University of Jerusalem, 1996 (pp. 260–261 of the expanded version).

[5] ". . . The messenger of God . . . said: Jesus the son of Mary will be in my

The idea of the second coming of Jesus is related to the Muslim view of crucifixion. Echoes of docetic trends in Christian thought can clearly be discerned in these traditions. The Qur'ān says that the Jews claimed to have killed Jesus, but their claim is false: "they did not kill him, nor crucify him; it only seemed to them,"[6] or, according to another understanding of the verse, they crucified a man who was made to resemble Jesus. One interpretation maintains that all the disciples were made to resemble Jesus, one of them went out of the house where they were staying and the Jews killed him, wrongly thinking that he was Jesus. An alternative version maintains that one of the disciples volunteered to be killed instead of Jesus in order to gain Paradise. According to a third one, a traitor who betrayed Jesus for thirty dirhams[7] was crucified while Jesus himself was raised to heaven.[8] A variation of this idea is included in the Gospel of Barnabas, which is probably the work of a Christian mystic who embraced Islam in the medieval period.[9] According to this source, a disciple of Jesus sold him for thirty coins; as a punishment

community as a just judge and a righteous *imām*. He will crush the cross, slaughter the swine, abolish the *jizya* (variant: war), and abandon alms-giving. . . . Hatred and animosity will be eliminated. The venom of every scorpion will be removed. . . . The earth will be filled with peace as a vessel is filled with water. The declaration of faith will be one; nobody except Allah will be worshipped. The war will come to an end." (*qāla rasūl Allāh . . . : fa-yakūnu ʿĪsā b. Maryam . . . fī ummatī ḥakaman ʿadlan wa imāman muqsiṭan yaduqqu al-ṣalīb wa yadhbaḥu al-khinzīr wa yaḍaʿu al-jizya* (variant: *al-ḥarb*) *wa yatruku al-ṣadaqa . . . wa turfaʿu al-shaḥnāʾu wa al-tabāghuḍ wa tunzaʿu ḥumatu kulli dhī ḥumatin . . . wa tumlaʾu al-arḍ min al-silm kamā yumlaʾu al-ināʾu min al-māʾ wa takūnu al-kalimatu wāḥida fa lā yuʿbadu illā Allāh wa taḍaʿu al-ḥarbu awzārahā*) (Ibn Māja, *Sunan*, vol. 2, p. 1362). See also Abū Dāwūd, *Sunan*, vol. 2, p. 471.

[6] Qur'ān 4:157–158.

[7] In some versions he remains unidentified; in others he is identified as Yūdas Zakariyyā Yūṭā which sounds fairly similar to Judas Iscariot.

[8] Ṭabarī, *Jāmiʿ al-bayān ʿan taʾwīl āy al-Qurʾān*, Cairo 1954, vol. 6, pp. 12ff.

[9] See David Sox, *The Gospel of Barnabas*, London 1984, pp. 29ff., and P.S. van Konigsveld, "The Islamic image of Paul and the origin of the Gospel of Barnabas", in *Jerusalem Studies in Arabic and Islam 20 (1996)*, pp. 200–228, for a discussion of the origins and the history of this gospel. In recent decades there was a flurry of Muslim interest in the Gospel of Barnabas because of its apparent compatibility with Qur'ānic christology. See ʿAbd al-Ḥamīd Sirḥān, *al-ʿAqāʾid al-islāmiyya wa injīl Barnābā* ("Islamic beliefs and the Gospel of Barnabas"), Kuwayt n.d.; Muḥammad ʿAlī Quṭb, *Injīl Barnābā al-mubashshir bi-nubuwwat al-nabī Muḥammad* ("The Gospel of Barnabas, which predicts the prophecy of the Prophet Muḥammad"), Cairo n.d.; M.H. Durrani, *Forgotten Gospel of St. Barnabas*, Karachi 1982. For a Christian response to the Muslim interest in this Gospel, see *Injīl Barnābā: tafkiha fī maʿriḍ al-dīn* ("The Gospel of Barnabas: Jest in the realm of religion"), Cairo 1924. The last book consists of a number of articles disputing the originality of the Gospel of Barnabas.

for this, the physical form of the traitor was transformed into that of Jesus and he was killed in his place.[10]

According to a second Qur'ānic verse, "God said: O Jesus, I cause you to die and raise you to Myself, and purify you of those who disbelieved, and place those who follow you above those who disbelieved, until the Day of Resurrection."[11] The primary meaning of this is that Jesus was made to die before his ascension; it is in keeping with the standard meaning of the verb *tawaffā* used in the verse. However, this understanding is by no means unanimously agreed upon. The commentators differ on the question whether the death of Jesus occurred after the crucifixion attempt or not; whether it occurred, but was followed by a resurrection; or, whether it will take place only after his second coming at the end of days. Some commentators maintain that the verb *tawaffā* means that God did not make Jesus die at all, but rather took him in his sleep,—or just before the crucifixion was to take place—and raised him to heaven alive. Those who are inclined to the latter interpretation find support for it in a tradition according to which the Prophet himself told the Jews whom he encountered in the city of Medina that "Jesus did not die and will return to you before the Day of Judgment".[12] The idea that Jesus has been alive in heaven since his mission on earth came to a close is consistent with the role he is expected to perform at the End of Days. According to the classical Muslim tradition which we have seen above, he will then descend to earth, lead the eschatological struggle against the false messiah, and, by his death, will pave the way for the establishment of the kingdom of justice on earth.

III

Let us now move from the classical tradition to modern India and consider Ghulām Aḥmad's view of these matters. Ghulām Aḥmad's messianic claim was wide-ranging. Only a few weeks before his death (in March 1908) he said that God called him *mahdī*, Jesus and Krishna.

---

[10] *Injīl Barnābā*, translated and edited by Sayf Allah Aḥmad Fāḍil, Kuwayt 1983, p. 178. The medieval original of this work is not available to me. For the Aḥmadī interest in the Gospel of Barnabas, see Sox, *op. cit.*, pp. 22–25.

[11] Qur'ān 3:55.

[12] Ṭabarī, *Jāmiʿ al-bayān*, Cairo 1954, vol. 3, p. 289—on Qur'ān 3:55.

The reason for these appellations was that these were the three personalities who were expected by the three great communities of the time: the *mahdī* was expected by the Muslims, the second coming of Jesus was expected by the Christians, and the coming of Krishna's *avatār* was expected by the Hindūs. In this way Ghulām Aḥmad portrayed himself as the object of messianic expectations entertained by the Muslims, the Hindūs and the Christians. He also thought of himself as the person who would set right the errors which had crept into these three religions.[13] But most of his messianic thoughts developed as a result of his recurrent polemical encounters with the Christian missionaries. The personality of Jesus and the expectation of his second coming were at the center of these controversies. Ghulām Aḥmad became convinced that his ability to claim a messianic role for himself hinged upon his success in undermining the Christian view of Jesus, and, also, in introducing substantial changes into some prevalent Muslim views of him. Ghulām Aḥmad was convinced that the Muslim belief in the expected eschatological appearance of Jesus was disastrous for the spiritual well-being of the Muslims. He went so far as to claim that if thousands of Indian Muslims embraced Christianity during the period of British rule, this was because they pinned extravagant hopes on the second coming of Jesus; this belief made them close to Christianity and paved the way for their apostasy.[14] He argued that unless Muslims eradicated this idea from their midst and trample it underfoot, Islam would not recover its primacy. The life of Islam depended on the death of Jesus[15] which could be proven by Qur'ānic verses and prophetic traditions.[16]

The idea that Jesus performed a crucial role in the spiritual history of mankind, that he has been alive ever since and that he will return again in glory—left precious little room for any other messianic claim in the context of the Christian—Muslim polemics of late nineteenth-century India. If these ideas had been expressed only by Christians, Muslims could have dismissed them as plain infidelity, unworthy of any credence. The matter was, however, more com-

[13] Ghulām Aḥmad, *Malfūẓāt, in Rūḥānī Khazā'in*, second series, vol. 10, pp. 145, 222.

[14] Ghulām Aḥmad, *Tadhkirat al-shahādatayn* (in his *Rūḥānī Khazā'in*, vol. 20, p. 25); *idem, Malfūẓāt*, in *Rūḥānī Khazā'in*, second series, vol. 10, p. 57.

[15] Ghulām Aḥmad, *al-Hudā wa al-tabṣira li-man yarā* (in *Rūḥānī Khazā'in*, vol. 18, p. 320); *idem, Malfūẓāt*, in *Rūḥānī Khazā'in*, vol. 10, p. 257.

[16] Ghulām Aḥmad, *al-Tablīgh*, in *Rūḥānī Khazā'in*, vol. 5, pp. 377–378, 431.

plex, because the Christians could boost their arguments by relying on Muslim traditions that appeared to be consistent with some of their views. The existence of Muslim traditions which maintained that Jesus was alive in heaven and would appear on earth again placed the Muslim polemicist in an embarrassing and awkward position. This was especially true in view of the fact that the classical Muslim tradition had almost no comparable claims for the Prophet Muḥammad, and maintained, without much hesitation or doubt, that Muḥammad was a mere mortal who had died a natural death and was buried in the city of Medina. Ghulām Aḥmad lamented: "Is it death to our Prophet [Muḥammad] and life to Jesus? This is, indeed, an unfair division."(*a-li-rasūlinā al-mawt wa al-ḥayāt li-ʿĪsā? tilka idhan qismatun ḍīzā*).[17]

The comparison between the living Jesus and the deceased Muḥammad has been used in Christian polemics against Islam since the medieval period. We can find an excellent example of this usage in two verses from an anti-Islamic polemical poem, written around 956 A.D., and said to have been sent by the Byzantine emperor Nicephoros to the ʿAbbāsī caliph al-Muṭīʿ in Baghdād. The comparison is very explicit:

> Jesus—his throne is high above the heavens,
> and he who befriends him will achieve his goal on the Day of Strife.
> And your Lord [Muḥammad] is buried in the ground, destroyed by dust,
> crumbled, surrounded by decayed bones.
>
> *(fa-ʿĪsā ʿalā fawqa ʾs-samāwāti ʿarshuhu*
> *fa-fāza ʾl-ladhī wālāhu yawma ʾt-takhāṣumi.*
> *wa ṣāḥibukum fī ʾt-turbi awdā bihi ʾth-tharā*
> *fa-ṣāra rufātan bayna tilka ʾr-ramāʾimi).*[18]

The Christian missionaries in modern India were heirs to the same tradition, and still used this comparison, so odious from the Muslim point of view, in order to establish the superiority of Jesus over the Prophet Muḥammad. The issue of Jesus became therefore a cardinal theme in the writings of Ghulām Aḥmad. He repeatedly propagated

---

[17] Ghulām Aḥmad, *Āʾina-yi kamālāt-i Islām*, Qādiyān 1893, p. 379. This is a paraphrase on Qurʾān 53:21–22.

[18] Gustav von Grünebaum, "Eine poetische Polemik zwischen Byzanz und Bagdad im X. Jahrhundert", in *Analecta Orientalia 14 (1937)*, p. 50.

the idea that Jesus did not die on the cross but only swooned there. An impressive array of quasi-physiological arguments was marshalled in order to support this notion: a crucified person does not die as a result of the crucifixion itself but because he spends a long time on the cross and dies of hunger, thirst and exhaustion; Jesus was on the cross only for a short time and his bones were not broken. Furthermore, when he was stabbed by a soldier, there was a flow of blood and water: the blood would have been coagulated and would not have flown if Jesus had been dead when taken down from the cross.[19]

Ghulām Aḥmad also argued, in more general terms, that the idea of vicarious suffering, so central to the Christian dogma, is incompatible with divine justice, which would never countenance the punishment of one person for the sins of others. This is especially true when the punished one, in this case Jesus, is far superior to the sinners. On the basis of Ghulām Aḥmad's peculiar interpretation of the phrase *kī qilelat Elohim taluy*, "... for a hanged man is the curse of God"—in Deuteronomy 21:23—death on the cross is ignominious, and Allah would never allow one of His prophets to be killed in such a degrading manner. Jesus was therefore taken down from the cross, cured of his wounds with a special ointment known as "the ointment of Jesus" (*marham-i ʿĪsā*), went to India to look for the lost tribes of Israel, and died at the ripe old age of 120 years in the city of Srinagar in Kashmir. The Aḥmadī press of 1902 carried banner headlines, announcing the discovery of the grave of Jesus in that city.

Having proven to his own satisfaction that the crucifixion attempt was a failure and that Jesus died a natural death, Ghulām Aḥmad was now ready to address the issue of his second coming. Since Jesus is dead, he cannot be expected to appear on earth again. For this reason, traditions which predict his second coming must not be taken literally, but rather as a subtle simile. The person whose coming is predicted in these Muslim traditions is not Jesus himself, but a person similar to him (*mathīl-i ʿĪsā*). This person is Ghulām Aḥmad himself, whom God transformed into Jesus and sent to silence the Christians,[20] His decision to do so being announced in a special rev-

---

[19] Ghulām Aḥmad, *Jesus in India. Jesus' Escape from Death on the Cross and Journey to India.* London 1978, pp. 27–33. Cf. John 19:31–37.

[20] Ghulām Aḥmad, *Tablīgh*, in *Rūḥānī Khazā'in*, vol. 5, p. 367.

elation.[21] This transformation was intended as an irrefutable argument against the Christians[22] and as a punishment inflicted on them for the iniquities which they had perpetrated against the Muslim community. Ghulām Aḥmad became united with the "substance" (*ḥaqīqa*) of Jesus. The two became like one thing, bearing the same name.[23] The transformation of a Muslim (who has already come) into Jesus obviates the necessity of Jesus ever coming again, and serves also as a demonstration of Islamic superiority.

The affinity between Jesus and Ghulām Aḥmad is a cardinal part of Aḥmadī thinking and is also an essential part of his messianic claim. Ghulām Aḥmad claims to be the messiah, first of all, because God made him one and announced His decision in a revelation. But this is not the only basis for the claim. Ghulām Aḥmad was also convinced that he would effect a major change in the religious situation of the world by the refutation of Christianity, and by the restoration of the superiority of Islam. According to his understanding, he accomplished this task by proving that there was no crucifixion, that there can be no vicarious atonement, and that Jesus was dead and would never come again. By virtue of this assertion, he came to consider himself a person who deprived Christianity of the all-important crucifixion of its founder. In this he was following the classical Muslim tradition, though his conclusions about the denial of crucifixion were much more central to his thought than they had been to classical Islam. Then he went one step further: he claimed affinity with Jesus, and transformed him into a Muslim. By virtue of his purported success in this transformation, he attained for Islam another resounding victory: he deprived Christianity of Jesus and appropriated him for Islam.

The confutation of Christianity is the mainstay of Ghulām Aḥmad's messianic claim. Related to it is his transformation of the *mahdī* into a totally peaceful figure and the transformation of Islam into a totally peaceful faith. We have seen that in the classical Islamic tradition Jesus, who is sometimes identified with the *mahdī*, was expected to perform certain violent actions, designed to symbolize the destruction of Christianity. In nineteenth-century India, this theme was

[21] "I transform you into Jesus the son of Mary" (*innī jāʿiluka ʿĪsā b. Maryam*). (Ghulām Aḥmad, *Āʾina-yi kamālāt-i islām*, Qādiyān 1983, p. 426.)

[22] See Ghulām Aḥmad, *al-Tablīgh*, in *Rūḥānī Khazāʾin*, vol. 5, p. 373: *innā jaʿalnāka al-Masīḥ b. Maryam li-utimma ḥujjatī ʿalā qawmin mutanaṣṣirīn.*

[23] Ghulām Aḥmad, *Tablīgh*, in *Rūḥānī Khazāʾin*, vol. 5, pp. 436–437.

developed and widely propagated. Eschatological literature came into being and predicted the appearance of a *mahdī* who would carry the sword and the flag of the Prophet, conquer Spain and Constantinople, crush a huge Christian army, and establish the supremacy of Islam.[24] Such descriptions of the expected messiah, as well as the idea of *jihād* in general, were used by the Christian missionaries in order to denigrate Islam and portray it as an aggressive and militant creed. Ghulām Aḥmad was convinced that the Muslims who cling to the traditional content of this idea, and especially those who propagate the traditions about the so-called "bloody *mahdī*" expected to come and annihilate the infidels, supply the enemies of Islam with an effective weapon. He had no doubt that Allah had entrusted him with the obligation to restore the messianic idea in Islam to its original form in order to defend Islam against the attacks of its rivals. In his desire to attain this goal, Ghulām Aḥmad explained that the crushing of the cross must not be taken literally, but should be seen as a symbol for the confutation of Christianity by the force of argument. He rejected the idea that at the End of Days the *mahdī* would force all people to embrace Islam; he accepted, instead, that version of the tradition according to which he would "abolish war." Since Ghulām Aḥmad himself saw *jihād* as a war of words rather than swords, the "peaceful" version of the *mahdī* tradition could also boost his claim of affinity with Jesus. Jesus is normally not thought of as a person who considered the option of leading a *jihād* against the Romans in Palestine and for some reason rejected it; yet Ghulām Aḥmad views him precisely in this light. The rejection of *jihād* by Jesus, despite the fact that his community was subject to foreign rule at the time of his appearance, is used by Ghulām Aḥmad as a justification of his own acceptance of British supremacy in India, and of his abolition of military *jihād*; it is also intended to be an additional proof that Ghulām Aḥmad is, indeed, similar to Jesus and performs the messianic task. The final conclusion of this argumentation is that even if *jihād* had been justified in the past, it had now lapsed with the appearance of the *mahdī* Ghulām Aḥmad who is a peaceful figure and terminates all wars. Thus, the development of

[24] An extensive treatment of this subject can be found in Ṣiddīq Ḥasan Khān, *Ḥujaj al-karāma fī āthār al-qiyāma*, Bhopal 1291 A.H. The author died in 1890. He was a prominent member of the *ahl-i ḥadīth* ("People of the *ḥadīth*"), an Indian Muslim group whose members stood in sharp opposition to the Aḥmadiyya. See *Encyclopaedia of Islam*, new edition, s.v.

humanity reached its peak with the appearance of the Muslim *mahdī* after whose time military *jihād* would be abolished forever.

It may now be useful to consider some more general characteristics of the Aḥmadiyya and to see to what extent it is similar to, or different from, comparable Muslim groups. We should probably start by looking at the historical context. The fact that Ghulām Aḥmad made his messianic claim to a Muslim community which lived under non-Muslim rule and was exposed to intense missionary activity was a crucial factor in the development of his thought. His primary claim to spiritual eminence was made to the Muslims, from whom he eventually came to demand an unequivocal recognition of his explicit claim to prophethood. In all likelihood, if such a claim had been made under Muslim rule, it would have brought upon him the swiftest of retribution. British rule in India created the circumstances in which Ghulām Aḥmad was able to advance his prophetic claim with impunity. On the other hand, the Christian presence in the country created for him the opportunity to stand up to the Christian preachers and to defend Islam against their aggressive missionary endeavors. In contradistinction to other Muslim messiahs, he deemed it essential not only to establish his credibility among the Muslims, but also to undermine the faith and the preaching of his Christian adversaries. It would be very unlikely to find a Muslim messiah living under Muslim rule who would devote such a central part of his thought to the refutation of a Christian dogma, or to the refutation of beliefs which Islam had adopted, under Christian influence, in the formative period of its history.

One of the most striking differences between the Aḥmadiyya and most other Muslim messianic movements is the way in which Ghulām Aḥmad described his identity. The *mahdī* expected by classical Islam is supposed to bear the name and the genealogy of the Prophet Muḥammad. This prediction tends to materialize in the hagiographies of the various *mahdīs*. This was the case with Ibn Tūmart, the North African *mahdī* of the twelfth century,[25] with a Muslim *mahdī* in fifteenth century India,[26] and with the famous Sudanese *mahdī* of the late nineteenth century.[27] The case of Ghulām Aḥmad is essentially

[25] Goldziher, Ignaz, *Le livre de Mohammed Ibn Toumert*, Alger 1903, pp. 2, 15, 25, 53.

[26] Qamaruddin, *The Mahdawī Movement in India*, New Delhi 1985, pp. 30, 56.

[27] Saʿd Muḥammad Ḥasan, *al-Mahdiyya fī al-islām mundhu aqdam al-ʿuṣūr ḥattā*

different. While statements intended to create affinity between himself and the Prophet Muḥammad, saying that he is only a manifestation of Muḥammad[28] and describing him as Muḥammad's servant[29] can easily be found in Ghulām Aḥmad's works, the main thrust of the material points to his identification with Jesus. This is a substantial departure from the mainstream Muslim messianic tradition. Furthermore, while most messianic movements in Islam struggled for the restoration of pristine purity to Muslim religion and society, or for the political dominance of the Muslims, the Aḥmadī movement acquiesced in the political subservience of the Indian Muslims to the British, while striving with all its strength for the affirmation of the doctrinal superiority of Islam vis-à-vis other religions. Ghulām Aḥmad is probably the only Muslim messiah who devoted so much attention to the refutation of another faith. He also seems to be the only such messiah who was convinced that his purported success in this endeavour bestowed an aura of incontrovertible validity on his messianic claim.

al-yawm, pp. 200–201; Ismāʿīl b. ʿAbd al-Qādir, *The Life of the Sudanese Mahdī*, transl. Haim Shaked, Transaction Books, New Brunswick 1978, p. 56. The classical traditions which serve as a background of the Sudanese *mahdī*'s messianic claim are listed on pp. 51–53.

[28] See Friedmann, *Prophecy Continuous*, p. 134.

[29] In his *Tablīgh* (*Rūḥānī Khazā'in*, vol. 5, p. 388) Ghulām Aḥmad seems to explain his name as meaning "the servant of Aḥmad the Chosen" (*Ghulām Aḥmad al-Muṣṭafā*). Aḥmad is one of Muḥammad's names. Cf. my *Prophecy Continuous*, pp. 140–141.

MESSIANISM IN THE POLITICAL CULTURE OF THE WEIMAR REPUBLIC

Klaus Schreiner

Changes in language highlight transformations in a society's political thought; at the same time, language functions as a force which sets in motion and advances social and political changes. Therefore, on the one hand, the use of messianic concepts in both the political and cultural public spheres of the Weimar Republic refers to changes in political attitudes, which were characterized by an increasing degree of alienation from the values and institutions of the republican state. On the other hand, the use of the same messianic concepts in politics and culture served as an engine which effectively accelerated that very process by which parliamentary democracy would be replaced by an authoritarian *Führerstaat.*

In his novel, *Der Mann ohne Eigenschaften* [*The Man Without Qualities*], Robert Musil (1880–1942) describes concisely and vividly the ways in which anti-democratic attitudes articulated themselves in messianically charged language. In this unfinished work, General Stumm von Bordwehr plays the role of the vigilant critic who skeptically observes the increasing "popularity of the semantic complex 'redemption'".[1] Everywhere—in politics, in the churches and café houses, in art journals and books—there was talk of "redeeming," "the Redeemer," and "redemption." This novel semantic field expressed the "need for redemption" of an uncertain nation which believed that it was living in "a truly messianic age" and was therefore in need of redemption by a savior.[2] The "so-called people of intellect"

---

[1] Robert Musil, *Der Mann ohne Eigenschaften*, ed. Adolf Frisé (Hamburg, 1952), 519. Musil's novel describes a single year in the waning Danubian monarchy and its ailing society: the turning-point encompasses the time period 1913 to 1914. Yet, through the genre of the historical novel, Musil describes experiences of his own time. Musil wrote the first two volumes of his novel from 1930 to 1932. The citations in this article are from this time period. I am indebted to Werner Freitag, Manfred Hettling, Matthias Lentz, and Hans-Ulrich Wehler for critical readings of this manuscript and references to literature and sources. This manuscript was translated into English by Monique Rinere, Princeton.

[2] Musil 518–20.

became convinced "that everything would come to a standstill if some Messiah did not come soon. This was, as the case might be, a Messiah of medicine, who would redeem the healing arts from the academic research being undertaken while people fell ill and died without getting aid, or, say, a literary Messiah capable of writing a drama which would sweep millions of people into the theaters and would therefore be of the most unique intellectual and spiritual sublimity; and apart from this conviction that, in fact, every single human endeavor could be restored to its proper condition through the agency of a special Messiah, there was of course also the simple and in every respect wholesome desire for a Messiah with a strong hand to deal with the whole situation."[3]

In this novel, Musil broaches the question of what made people susceptible to the seductive powers of the anti-democratic formulas for redemption and salvation in the late stages of the Weimar Republic: the lack of orientation in values providing a secure sense of identity which could have given their lives goal and direction; the search for designs for living which liberated them from inner strife and social isolation;[4] yearnings for a strong man equipped with the authority and the consciousness of a messianic leader's mission who could bring about a change for the better in politics, the economy, and the society as a whole. A messiah for "the whole situation"—both for the wholeness of each individual's soul as well as for the unity of the state, the existence of which was threatened with destruction by the pluralism of party politics and party interests—was to restore order to German life, which had been stricken with afflictions of a critical nature.

The concept of waiting for a political savior was rooted in an atmosphere in which broad sectors of the population harbored doubts concerning the ability of parliamentary institutions to act with full authority. In an essay entitled "Vorbilder und Führer" ["Paragons and Leaders"], written in the period after the First World War during which there was neither emperor nor leader, the philosopher and sociologist Max Scheler (1874–1928) diagnosed the situation as follows. "[There was] an unprecedented yearning for leadership astir

---

[3] Musil 519f.

[4] See Manfred Hettling and Stefan-Ludwig Hoffman, "Der bürgerliche Wertehimmel. Zum Problem individueller Lebensführung im 19. Jahrhundert." In: *Geschichte und Gesellschaft* 23, 1997, 333–60.

everywhere. . . . That is shown perhaps most clearly in the countless new 'societies,' 'circles,' 'orders,' 'sects,' and 'schools,' which have suddenly sprung up in our country for all manner of vital interests, each with its own particular form of 'savior,' 'prophets,' and 'world reformers' at its center, each making all manner of lofty claims to improve the world and demands to convert."[5] "The immense religious yearning of the age," wrote the Protestant theologian Paul Wernle in 1921, "follows prophets who, unfettered by intellectual reflection and in need of no proof, are prompted by the voice of God in the very depths of their hearts to prophesy the meaning of the age and God's future ways for humanity."[6] In 1922, in Fallingbostel, a holiday resort in the Lüneburger Heide, village dignitaries erected a memorial to those who had fallen in the First World War and united the memory of the fallen heroes with hopes for the "return of the good old days." To them, the longed-for return of the past was synonymous with the arrival of a leader and savior who could liberate them from "disgrace and shame." Experiences of crisis generated hope.

In order to inform future generations of the suffering of the epoch and the yearnings of a people who felt humiliated and subjugated by the dictates of foreign powers, the patriots of Fallingbostel wrote: "Vast scarcity in all areas. . . . The republican form of government has been given to us while the promised blessings of the revolution are not forthcoming. . . . The political situation looks bleak. Jews and sissies rule in Berlin! When will Germany's savior come? . . . When will the time come when a strong man like Bismarck shall forge the empire anew and raise Germany to its old glory in defiance of all its enemies?"[7] The citizens of Fallingbostel believed that only a strong leader figure was capable of erecting the magnificent and glorious empire of which they dreamed.

Is it appropriate to describe as messianic the diverse forms of this widespread longing for a savior whose powerful leadership would

[5] Max Scheler, "Vorbilder und Führer." In: Scheler, *Zur Ethik und Erkenntnislehre* (Schriften aus dem Nachlaß 1) (Berlin, 1933), 151. "It is self-evident that the problem of leadership and followers should weigh heavily upon a people which has been robbed of its historical forms of leadership in every facet of life to some degree." (151) "The greatest question of the political present is whether to restructure the party system or take the path to dictatorship and restoration." (220)

[6] Paul Wernle, *Einführung in das theologische Studium*, 3rd ed. (Tübingen, 1921), 8.

[7] The City Archives of Fallingbostel, Findbuchliste No. 1.314 and No. 5.28.

overcome the inability to act of the democratic party? In other words, is it justified to unite the many manifestations of this longing under the concept of messianism?

I. *Problems with the Concept of "Messianism"*

Messianism as the sum total and system of ideas and expectations directed towards the future has its historical and religious roots in Judaism. Jewish Messianism is, in its origins and by its nature, a "theory of catastrophe" which emphasizes above all "the revolutionary, cataclysmic element in the transition from every historical present to the Messianic future."[8] Seen from the perspective of Judaism,

---

[8] Gershom Scholem, "Zum Verständnis der messianischen Idee im Judentum," *Apokalyptik*, eds. Klaus Koch and Johann Michael Schmidt (Darmstadt, 1982), 335. These sorts of political implications induced nineteenth-century politicians and authors to transfer the concepts of a messiah and messianism from the field of Judeo-Christian theology and religion to the field of politics and political theory. M. Höené Wronski (1776–1853), a Polish mathematician and philosopher who lived in Paris, wrote several works beginning in 1831 in which he outlined a program of reform of knowledge and society using the theme of the concept of messianism. The realization of such a plan promised an "avenir messianique de l'humanité." The titles of these works are: *Prodrome du Messianisme, Prospectus du Messianisme, Prolégomês du Messianism, Metapolitique messianique*, and *Bulletins messianique*. According to these works, if a nation were to transform itself into an "association messianique," the "epoch of man or of reason" would commence for all humanity. Such a transformation could only be effected by means of the "unification of philosophy and religion," from which a "new intellectual world order" would emerge. Quoted in Jürgen Gebhardt, "Messianische Politik und ideologische Massenbewegung, *Von kommenden Zeiten, Geschichtsprophetien im 19. und 20. Jahrhundert*, eds. Joachim H. Knoll and Julius H. Schoeps (Stuttgart, 1984), 44f. A book by J.L. Talmon entitled *Politischer Messianismus* concerns itself "with the expectation of a universal renewal which inspired people and movements in the first half of the nineteenth century." (J.L. Talmon, *Politischer Messianismus. Die romantische Phase* (Cologne, 1963), 1). The first two parts of the book bear the titles "Sozialistischer Messianismus" and "Messianischer Nationalismus." The book also addresses the subjects of "revolutionary messianism" (289) and "messianic totalitarian democracy" (2). This sort of conceptual expansion of messianism, which was also applied to designs for utopian societies in its extended form, resulted in the eventual characterization of social theorists and social critics of Jewish heritage such as Walter Benjamin, Ernst Bloch, Theodor Adorno, and Herbert Marcuse as representatives of "Jewish Messianism." See Michael Löwy, "Jewish Messianism and Libertarian Utopia in Central Europe (1900–1933)", *New German Critique* 20 (1980), 105–15; Anson Rabinbach, "Between Enlightenment and Apocalypse: Benjamin, Bloch and Modern German Jewish Messianism," *New German Critique* 34 (1985), 78–124. In order to justify the use of the messianism concept in this way, Adam Weisberg refers to "striking points of correspondence between aspects of traditional [Jewish] messianism and socialism." (Weisberg, "Gustav

redemption does not only refer to the need for redemption of the human soul, but to the unredeemed state of the world as a whole. "In all of its forms and manifestations, Judaism has always maintained a concept of redemption as an event which takes place publicly, on the stage of history, and within the community. It is an occurrence which takes place in the visible world and which cannot be conceived apart from such a visible appearance."[9] The idea that redemption must be thought of as an event which brings about societal and political liberation and takes places in the visible world belongs, even to the present day, to the tradition of Jewish Messianism.[10]

According to Max Weber, it was the "power of prophecy" which caused Israel to become "a people of 'expectation'."[11] Yahweh, who was allied with Israel, "was and remained a God of *redemption* and *promise.* But the important point was that both redemption and promise concerned *current political*, not inner matters. God offered redemption from the enslavement by the Egyptians, *not* from a fragmented, meaningless world. He offered the promise of a coveted ruling control over Canaan and a happy existence there, *not* the promise of transcendental goods."[12] Therefore, times of political distress and danger

---

Landauers mystischer Messianismus," *Aschkenas* 5, 2 (1995), 434.) He emphasizes the idea that "Jewish messianism underwent a process of secularization and gained entry into the essence of socialism."

[9] Scholem 327.

[10] In the 1920s, Zionism made use of the "language of Jewish Messianism" to express its visions, goals, and hopes (Michael Berkowitz, *Western Jewry and the Zionist Project 1914–33* (Cambridge, 1997), 121). The endeavor to erect a national homeland for the Jewish people in Palestine was described as a "messianic task" (90), as "salvation" (79), as "redemption" (78), as the fulfillment of a four-thousand year-old promise (88). Arthur Hertzberg, "a prominent liberal rabbi and scholar from New Jersey," said in November 1995: "In the aftermath of the Holocaust—the supreme moment of Jewish powerlessness—there was a feeling that some great messianic event would occur to restore this wounded people." However, he added critically that, under the conditions of the modern world, messianic ideas liberate anti-democratic ideas when they are taken as models of social self-description and principles of political action. Hertzberg emphasized that, "When you get into messianic thinking, you are at the opposite pole from democratic thinking. If you conceive of Israel as a secular democracy with a role for Judaism, then the government's decisions are to be accepted, but if you conceive of it as the first stage of the messianic age and drama, then a government that stands in the way is illegitimate." (Quoted in David Remnick, "The Jewish Conversation: New Yorkers Discuss Yitzhak Rabin's Assassination and the Lethal Power of Words," *The New Yorker* Nov. 20 1995: 40.)

[11] Max Weber, *Gesammelte Aufsätze zur Religionssoziologie*, vol. 3, ed. Marianne Weber (Tübingen, 1921), 249.

[12] Weber 136.

were also always times of raised hopes for an "eschatological hero,"[13] a "liberating Redeemer,"[14] an "Israelite Savior King of the House of David."[15]

The fact that messianic thought was of virulent relevance in the politics and culture of the Weimar Republic cannot be traced back to a relationship of causal dependence between temporally distant historical phenomena; rather, it was conditioned by similarity and structural correspondences. Fundamental to the Judeo-Christian concept of Messianism is the idea of waiting for a Savior and Redeemer who is endowed with extraordinary abilities, and able and willing to bring peace and justice to people who no longer have the wherewithal to save themselves. The hope associated with Messianism presupposes that the present is experienced as a time of crisis in which conventional mechanisms of negotiation and regulation are no longer sufficient for gaining control over the prevailing problems. Moreover, Messianism requires a people which feels in need of salvation and redemption. Messianism also involves a belief in the *kairos*, the "right hour," at which time the bearer of salvation appears in order to endow the age with a new quality through a miraculous, epochal act of salvation. Finally, and above all, a Messiah legitimizes himself by claiming a vocation and mission, something which must be believed and acknowledged by those to whom he directs his message. The eschatological hero does not need to be chosen by the many for he is acting on behalf of a higher, transcendental authority. Endowed with extraordinary gifts of grace, he claims to be capable of mastering the existential crises of the individual and the social and political crises of the community.

After the First World War, economic problems and a sense of political powerlessness were widespread. The sense of being overwhelmed by a life-threatening crisis led broad sectors of the population to desire to understand and change their cheerless lives in the light of interpretations offered by messianic concepts. The political and economic conditions seemed practically to demand a perception of themselves as a "people of hope" in need of salvation. The experience of a military catastrophe and the undesired transformation of the political system from a monarchy into a democracy evoked yearn-

[13] Weber 248.
[14] Weber 345.
[15] Weber 346.

ings for the One, a figure of a strong-armed messianic savior who would remedy the havoc wreaked by economic need and political disgrace. Promise and fulfillment, two ideas fundamental to the Judeo-Christian concepts of history which were charged with worldly expectations, nourished irrational longings for a heroic, charismatic savior and weakened political rationality.

Messianism remained a constant source of temptation to replace collective political responsibility with passive hopes for a redeeming savior. The manifestations of political messianism found in contemporary sources are the subject of the following investigation. It does not concern social utopias which promise a society without sovereigns and subjects. This investigation will identify, describe, and explain ideas, yearnings, and expectations, which, in the light of variously articulated assertions and perceptions, can be characterized as manifestations of messianism specific to the time and circumstances of the nineteenth and the early twentieth century.[16]

II. *Restorative and Revolutionary Messianism in the Nineteenth Century*

In one of his many sermons delivered in the 1880s, the Leipzig superintendent Oscar Pank asks, "In what sort of an age are we living?" He continues: "On the one hand, Rome beckons with the illusionary images of its external glory and sacredly ordained unity. . . . On the other, new messiahs present themselves before the masses and paint images of a golden future before their very eyes, a new kingdom of worldly happiness, a distorted image of the Kingdom of God established by Jesus Christ. Alas, both God and the Lord Jesus Christ are banished from this kingdom,—and how many, how many people are there who believe in these prophets!"[17] Contemporaries who wanted to learn something about the origin and meaning of the concept of messianism could read the following in Meyer's great

[16] The following investigation does not concern itself, therefore, with the question of whether Marx "secularized the concept of a messianic age in the representation of the classless society" (Walter Benjamin) or whether the belief in a society liberated from capitalistic exploitation can be interpreted as a "pseudo morphosis of Judeo-Christian Messianism" (Karl Löwith). The appropriateness or inappropriateness of a sociological conceptual explanation is not the subject here. This investigation seeks, rather, to present and examine cultural and political practices which were influenced by messianic themes, concepts, representations, and expectations.

[17] Quoted in Lucian Hölscher, *Weltgericht oder Revolution. Protestantische und sozialistische Zukunftsvorstellungen im deutschen Kaiserreich* (Stuttgart, 1989), 100.

Conversationslexikon für die gebildeten Stände [*Conversational Lexicon for the Educated Classes*]: The Messiah "was the name of the great Redeemer, Savior, and Restorer whom the Jews awaited to achieve the political and moral elevation of the people. They understood the rule of David and the world position attained through him as a model of its own destiny as a future world ruler." Israel's "messianic ideas," its "national wishes and hopes" could only "be formed among the people after the world position assumed under David and Solomon had been lost; when the kingdom was divided, beset by foreign enemies, and threatened with utter collapse; and when, along with the collapse of his political institutions, the retention of the religious and moral life developed through him in his characteristic way no longer seemed possible." They could not be saved from the threat of ruin by "a foreign and coincidental form of state," but by the "appearance of a virtuous ruler" who was "perceived" as a "messenger from God" endowed "with higher powers" or "as a product of the religious spirit which lived in the people themselves."[18]

The concept of a messiah evoked just such images and reminders when it was used by writers and journalists of the nineteenth century in order to characterize as messianic the extraordinary quality of political heroes and bearers of salvation. In an essay written in 1840 about Ludwig Börne, Heinrich Heine wrote: "Germany awaits a liberator, an earthly messiah! . . .—a king of the earth, a savior with scepter and sword." His ironically intended homage, "Oh dear, longingly awaited messiah!" referred to Frederick Barbarossa slumbering in Kyffhäusser, a figure whom the conservative bourgeoisie saw as the model and guarantee of a monarchical nation state. Heine's conviction that only a republic could save the Germans kept him from being led by the messianic hopes of an age which placed faith in myths. With the self-confidence of a republican ever conscious of liberty, Heine assures the reader, "No! Emperor Redbeard is not the one who will liberate Germany as the people are wont to believe. The German people are a people who are dreaming, addicted to slumber, capable only of envisioning its messiah in the figure of a sleeping old man!"[19]

---

[18] J. Meyer, ed. *Das große Conversations-Lexicon für die gebildeten Stände*, vol. 21 (Hildburghausen, 1852), 358f.

[19] Heinrich Heine, "Ludwig Börne. Eine Denkschrift," *Heinrich Heine*, vol. 11 "Ludwig Börne. Eine Denkschrift und kleinere politische Schriften," Helmut Koopmann, ed. *Historisch-kritische Gesamtausgabe der Werke* (Hamburg, 1978), 110.

While Frederick Barbarossa embodied conservative messianism, representatives of the democratic and revolutionary left, such as Wilhelm Weitling, Robert Blum, and Ferdinand Lassalle, personified utopian-socialist messianism. Messianic ideas derived from Judaism allowed for both a restorative as well as a utopian interpretation and realization.[20] Wilhelm Weitling, "Germany's first proletarian voice,"[21] was inspired by Proudhon's socialist ideas and desired to make all men brothers. Shortly before the *Völkerfrühling* of 1848, he promised a messianic savior. Dreaming of a time when a community of property and a blessed land of mutual brotherly love would exist, Weitling wrote: "A new messiah will come to realize the teachings of the first [Jesus Christ]. He will raze the ramshackle buildings of the old societal order, lead the sources of tears into the sea of forgetfulness, and guide earth into paradise."[22] He characterized the "leader," this "dictator of democratic provenance"[23] who would guide the way to an age of social harmony and political freedom as a "second messiah."[24]

After his assassination in Vienna on 9 November 1848, Robert Blum (1807–1848), a leader and symbol of the political left in the *Frankfurter Paulskirche*, was characterized and extolled as "savior," "prophet," and "political redeemer."[25] Present in the minds of his followers and admirers was Ferdinand Lassalle, the labor movement leader who would die in 1864. Lassalle was the "worker's savior"

---

[20] Scholem 329, 331. This work points out that Judaism's Messianic idea allows for both a restorative and a utopian interpretation and realization. It is equally capable of motivating "the return and restoration of a past condition which is perceived as ideal" as it is of presenting the "vision of an ideal" as "[the Jews] would like to see it realized" in the near future.

[21] Ernst Bloch, *Das Prinzip Hoffnung*, vol. 2 (Frankfurt a.M., 1959), 671.

[22] Quoted in Bloch 673.

[23] Dieter Groh, "Caesarismus," *Geschichtliche Grundbegriffe. Historisches Lexicon zur politisch-sozialen Sprache in Deutschland*, eds. Otto Brunner, Werner Conze, Reinhart Koselleck, vol. 1 (Stuttgart, 1972), 730.

[24] Quoted in Groh 730, fn 27. See also Paul Honigsheim, "Soziologie der Mystik," *Versuche zu einer Soziologie des Wissens*, ed. Max Scheler (Munich, 1924), 343 on the idea of the messiah in socialism. He writes that, in socialism, one had "first of all the consciousness of being called to the fulfillment of a mission of world salvation. Furthermore, one had the certainty of belonging to a collective messiah. For one perceived the proletariat as such with respect to its attitudes. Weitling and some of his contemporaries, no fewer but different socialist republicans from Munich and Budapest, were named as examples. It is such attitudes which, for a time, had great power to build solidarity."

[25] Ludwig Pfau, "Ein Todtenkranz auf das Grab Robert Blum's," eulogy, Heilbronn o.J., 21 Nov. 1848, *Robert Blum, Deutschlands politischer Erlöser. Ein Denkmal seiner Ehren zur Begeisterung Aller für die Sache der Freiheit* (Leipzig, 1848), 6–7.

and "messiah of the new age."[26] The messianic message conveyed by the leading spokesmen of the socialist and liberal movements read, "Notre Messie c'est le peuple."[27] The messianism of the people took the place of the messianic mission of a great world-historical individual. In that a people could liberate, reconcile, and bring about peace, it could achieve messianic feats.

Members of the conservative and nationalistic bourgeoisie hoped for the rebirth of Armin the Cherusker, Frederick Barbarossa, Frederick Schiller, or Bismarck. Memories of a heroic past nourished yearnings and wishes which the coming savior and returning heroes were to fulfill. In the period before the revolution of March 1848 (*Vormärz*), a call went out to Hermann the Cherusker: "Hermann [Armin], awaken, come and save thy people."[28] In ceremonies organized by civic festival committees in 1858 to celebrate Schiller's one-hundredth birthday, he was called the "freedom singer," the "messiah."[29] In the 1870s, when Emperor William the First, "Whitebeard [Barbablanca]," founded the second Reich, it was said that "Old Redbeard has awakened."[30] After Bismarck's death, he was remembered as a "redeemer," "hero," and "savior". The boundless reverence paid Bismarck articulated a longing for a strong man who could forcefully and decisively direct the fate of the German empire.[31]

---

[26] Heiner Grote, *Sozialdemokratie und Religion. Eine Documentation für die Jahre 1863 bis 1875* (Tübingen, 1968), 13.

[27] Talmon 244.

[28] Peter Veddeler, "Nationale Feiern am Hermannsdenkmal in früherer Zeit," *Ein Jahrhundert Hermannsdenkmal 1875–1975*, ed. Günther Engelbert (Detmold, 1975), 140, fn. 69.

[29] Rainer Noltenius, *Dichterfeiern in Deutschland. Rezeptionsgeschichte als Sozialgeschichte am Beispiel der Schiller- und Freiligrath-Feiern* (Munich, 1984), 113. Noltenius, "Schiller als Führer und Heiland. Das Schillerfest 1859 als nationaler Traum von der Geburt des zweiten deutschen Kaiserreichs," *Öffentliche Festkultur. Politische Feste in Deutschland von der Aufklärung bis zum Ersten Weltkrieg*, eds. Dieter Düding *et al.* (Hamburg, 1988), 250.

[30] Klaus Schreiner, "Friedrich Barbarossa—Herr der Welt, Zeuge der Wahrheit, die Verkörperung nationaler Macht und Herrlichkeit," *Die Zeit der Staufer. Geschichte—Kunst—Kultur (Katalog der Ausstellung Stuttgart 1977)* vol. 5 (Stuttgart, 1979), 545–51 ("Barbarossa-Euphorie nach der zweiten Reichsgründung"). Arno Borst, "Barbarossas Erwachen—Zur Geschichte der deutschen Identität," *Identität*, eds. Odo Marquard and Karl-Heinz Stierle, Poetik und Hermeneutik 8 (Munich, 1979), 17–60.

[31] See also Lothar Machtan, "Bismarck-Kult und deutscher Nationalmythos 1890 bis 1940," Machtan, *Bismarck und der deutsche National-Mythos* (Bremen, 1994), 14–68; Hans-Walter Hedinger, "Der Bismarckkult. Ein Umriß," *Der Religionswandel in unserer Zeit im Spiegel der Religionswissenschaften*, ed. Gunther Stephensen (Darmstadt, 1976), 201–214; Wulf Wülfing, Karin Bruns, and Rudolf Parr, *Historische Mythologie der*

The idea of waiting for a political savior expressed a sense of being powerlessly at the mercy of existential and sociopolitical crises. Authors, scholars, and political journalists borrowed from nineteenth-century messianic language and concepts to awaken hopes for a savior who could rescue them. They did not endeavor to meet the political and social demands of late imperial Germany with rational and pragmatic concepts. With the aid of messianic ideas and concepts, they sought rather to move people to place their trust in a polity guided not by the votes of many but by the will of one—a monarch, a leader, or a dictator.

III. *The Lost War and the Longing for the One in Academe and Literature*

It was in particular the loss of the war and the collapse of the empire which awakened the impatient expectation of a great individual capable of restoring honor and self-respect to the defeated nation. A charismatic bearer of hope who possessed the stature and symbolic power of an Arminius, a Redbeard, or a Bismarck was to raise up the defeated and humiliated German people once more. It was a commonly held belief that only a leader with extraordinary abilities would be able to eliminate the chaos created by the failure of an inept parliamentary democracy incapable of acting, to bestow power and glory upon the state, and restore prosperity and honor to its citizens.

The lecture halls in Germany's universities did not provide the proper soil for the sowing and cultivation of democratic ideas and principles. Among Germany's professors, *Vernunftrepublikaner* ["rational republicans"] formed a minority. To the majority, "Weimar [was] not a reality which furnished norms."[32] Resentment and disapproving attitudes towards the Weimar state predominated. Conservative, nationalistic, and *völkisch*-minded university professors harshly criticized the republican form of government and sought to convince their listeners that Germany's future depends on the establishment

Deutschen 1798–1918 (Munich, 1991); Rolf Parr, *"Zwei Seelen wohnen, ach! in meiner Brust!". Strukturen und Funktionen der Mythisierung Bismarcks* (Munich, 1992).

[32] Hans Rothfels, "Die Geschichtswissenschaft in den dreißiger Jahren," *Deutsches Geistesleben und Nationalsozialismus*, ed. Andreas Flitner (Tübingen, 1965), 97.

of an authoritarian state and way of life. Max Weber's lecture on "Wissenschaft als Beruf" ["Scholarship as a Vocation"] shows how widely opinions diverged when the significance of scholarship in politics and life were the subject of debate.

1. *"Lectern Prophets"*

Max Weber criticized the lectern prophecy of his academic colleagues and pleaded for a "heroism of objectivity." On 7 November 1917, Weber gave a lecture in Munich entitled "Wissenschaft als Beruf" ["Scholarship as a Vocation"] before the *Freistudentischen Bund in Bayern* ["Independent Students' Association of Bavaria"], a gathering of liberal students who were not members of a student society. In his address, he expressed his concerns about scholarship as a vocation. He then issued the following sobering announcement to the many attendees who awaited saviors and prophets to rescue them, give their lives meaning, and make sense of their situation: The "prophet for whom so many of our younger generation yearn simply does not exist."[33] Weber thereby dampened the young men's expectancies and enthusiastic readiness to embrace a cause fuelled by the belief that they were living in an age of undreamt-of possibilities for political and social renewal. Weber impressed upon his listeners, who stood at a crossroads between "revolutionary rebellion and a nationalistic cast of mind" that "only a prophet or savior" could answer the question of what "we should then do," "which of the warring gods" we should serve.[34] "If the [prophet or savior] does not exist or if his proclamations are no longer believed, then you will most certainly not compel him to appear on earth by having thousands of professors as hirelings of the state or privileged petty prophets attempt to usurp his role in their lecture halls."[35]

Quoting from the so-called Song of the Edomite Watchman, from The Book of the Prophet Isaiah (21,11–12), Weber sought to put the "lectern prophets" who practiced in the university lecture halls as well as all those "who awaited new prophets and saviors" in their place.[36] The Old Testament text quoted by Weber reads in its entirety:

---

[33] Max Weber, *Wissenschaft als Beruf 1917/19. Politik als Beruf 1919* (Tübingen, 1992), 105.

[34] Weber 105.

[35] Weber 105.

[36] Weber 110f.

Dumah: an oracle.
He calleth to me out of Seir:
"Watchman, what is left of the night?
Watchman what is left of the night?"
The watchman says:
"The morning has come,
And also the night.
If ye will enquire, enquire,
Come back again!"

These verses reflect the direness of the situation in Dumah. Dumah, an oasis in Arabia, was a place, like many others, in which the people grasped at any possibility of casting off the foreign rule of Babylonia. Night is an "image of a situation of distress and bondage, in this case undoubtedly foreign rule."[37] The question, "Watchman, what is left of the night?" was of burning relevance in this region as the Babylonian ruling government began to show signs of weakening.

The seer hears the voice come to him from Seir, the mountain range east of *araba*, the channel which runs from the Dead Sea to the Gulf of Aqaba. The repetition of the same question underscores the hope "that the great revolution would not be long in coming."[38] From the perspective of the seer, the revolution is already in progress. "The balance of power which has existed up to this point has been placed in question. Essential and radical changes are emerging on the stage of world history. However, nothing can yet be said about the particulars of the outcome. Therefore, he [Isaiah] entreats the inquirers to come again should they wish to know more."[39] The seer does not want to nourish false hopes. He knows, "the time is not yet ripe for a more precise assessment. Perhaps the situation will become clearer soon." The seer urges restraint. For, in accordance with the message of Isaiah's text to all ages, there are "situations in which the community of believers must temper their expectations until the situation has become clearer, even when it seems that something new is in the offing."[40]

Weber makes the critical possibilities of an Old Testament prophecy relevant and topical. He reminds his listeners that even today the

---

[37] Hans Wildberger, "Jesaja," vol. 2, *Teilband Jesaja 13–27* (Neukirchen-Vluyn, 1978), 795, vol. X/2 of *Biblischer Kommentar Altes Testament.*
[38] Wildberger 795.
[39] Wildberger 795.
[40] Wildberger 796.

people of Israel still await the promised Messiah. He also reminds them that "nothing is gained by yearning and waiting alone." To act differently means having to work. It means possessing "plain intellectual integrity," passionate longing, "to meet the 'demands of the day.'" It does not mean waiting passively for a prophet, savior, or messiah.[41] Weber did not give this lecture in a Munich University auditorium but in a bookstore lecture room in Schwabing, a district of Munich.

"After the countless revolutionary speeches by literary activists, Weber's lecture was like a redemption," reports Karl Löwith in retrospect, who was studying at the time in Munich.[42] Weber "shredded all veils of wishful thinking to pieces."[43] However, his words did not reach a majority of academic youth. The most aroused by war and revolution, sought "not the ordinary, but the extraordinary, not the sober teacher, but a hero or prophet, not scientific rationalism incapable of offering meaning, but a fundamental morality or the religious *unio mystica*, which clearly proved itself only all too often to be pseudo-religious."[44] The few voices of political rationality which made themselves heard were able to achieve little in the face of the prevalent belief in myths. The myth of a leader and the vision of an empire held the prospect of restoring to the state its sacred ordination, of replacing economic competition with policies of communal interest, and of making the German people once again the rulers at the center of Europe. These concepts found much broader resonance than the colorless, sober image of a constitutional state struggling for stability.

Weber's plea for intellectual integrity and sober pragmatism did not remain uncontested. In 1920 the cultural philosopher Erich von Kahler published a book in which he presented the case precisely for that "which Weber has declared as belonging to the ages of prophets and impossible for today."[45] Science, which serves life and the living and therefore assists in "determining the direction and

[41] Weber 111.

[42] Karl Löwith, *Mein Leben in Deutschland vor und nach 1933. Ein Bericht* (Stuttgart, 1986), 16f., according to which Löwith was present at Weber's lecture.

[43] Löwith 16.

[44] Wolfgang J. Mommsen and Wolfgang Schluchter, Introduction, Max Weber, "Wissenschaft als Beruf, 1917/1919" (Tübingen, 1992), 34.

[45] Ernst Troeltsch, "Die Revolution in der Wissenschaft," *Aufsätze zur Geistesgeschichte und Religionssoziologie*, ed. Hans Baron, 1st ed. (Tübingen, 1925; Aalen, 1962), 669.

conduct of our lives;"[46] the "whole person," who is at the same time "a knowing, desiring and acting human being" and recognizes no differences between "one's professorial and political dispositions";[47] leadership, which is able to overcome the "destructive divisions between the parties" and is in a position "to bring together to the fullest extent everything which has been torn asunder in the nature and character of the German." According to Kahler, only leadership could establish coherence for the living; the competition between opposing party doctrines caused only division and strife. He added that he was unable to perceive the "salvation of the German future" in parliamentarianism which he referred to as "this pitiful comedy."

Erich von Kahler did not expect this leader, someone of German essence and nature, to be a *völkisch* messiah sent by God. "A leadership capable of demonstrating to this concrete, particular German people the only right path in this concrete, particular, present hour must first be developed. It needs to be cultivated and prepared."[48] Kahler was not able to give an answer to the question of how this should come to pass. Behind Kahler's vague interpretation lies the outline of a charismatic individual who, by virtue of his education and upbringing, his moral authority and statesmanlike strength of mind, shall stand above the parties and perceive himself as responsible for the salvation of the entire people. According to Kahler, political pluralism, which required discussion, compromise and balance, contradicted the essence of German wholeness.[49] Kahler had high hopes for the renewal and salvation of both the individual and the society. The ideal for which he hoped was a life which knew no separation between emotional and rational powers and no division of society into rivaling factions and parties.

Erich von Kahler was among those conservative revolutionaries who, like Arthur Moeller van den Bruck (1876–1925), Hans Freyer (1887–1969), and Edgar Julius Jung (1894–1934), strived towards a "revolution from the right." Jung counted himself among those who prepared the way for the German revolution as tools of God, "who carry the coming Reich and the will to achieve it steadfastly in their

---

[46] Erich von Kahler, *Der Beruf der Wissenschaft* (Berlin 1920), 99.

[47] Kahler 40.

[48] Kahler 38f.

[49] For a discussion of the ideal of "Ganzheit" ("wholeness") in Weimar culture, see Peter Gay, "The Hunger for Wholeness," *Weimar Culture. The Outsider as Insider* (New York, 1970), 70–101.

hearts." With the pathos of a prophet, he proclaimed, "The time has come, when dissolution is complete, when the reality of the liberal world view has revealed itself to be illusory, when the mastery of life through abstraction and the rule of rationality have proven to be impossible. We see the world once again as it is not only because we ourselves are of this world, but also because we perceive the metaphysical and feel its presence in us as a cosmic law. Therefore, our hour has come: the hour of the German revolution." Jung's conservative revolution demanded the restoration of historical values and the establishment of a new order in which "the organic growth of leadership" takes "the place of mechanical selection." He described the will to the "coming new order" as follows: "We currently find ourselves in the midst of a German revolution . . . which will oppose the intellectual driving forces, formulas, and goals born of the French Revolution. It shall be the great conservative counterrevolution which shall prevent the dissolution of western humanity and establish a new order, a new ethos, and a new western unity under German leadership."[50]

2. *Messianic Ideas in the Liberal Arts and Social Sciences*

Historians of the Middle Ages who taught at German universities turned their glance back in time, to the spiritually closed world of the Middle Ages, to a world ordered by class which was led by the powerful will of a ruler. They were of the conviction that the political and economic burdens which resulted from the lost war could only be overcome and disposed of by means of the creative strength of the individual, not by means of parliamentary voting mechanisms. In the name of the scholarly study of history, it was said that the Germans had once again become a "people of yearning," "just as they had been after the days of the Hohenstaufen." Designs for the future which were created in the spirit of a past perceived as glorious nourished longings for a "new empire," "rule by the few virtuous," the "One," and the "great individual."[51]

Johannes Haller was a historian of Baltic descent who taught at the Universities of Gießen and Tübingen and had completed signifi-

---

[50] Edgar Julius Jung, speech, 1932. See Jung, "Deutschland und die Konservative Revolution," *Deutsche über Deutschland* (Munich, 1932), 380–383.

[51] See Schreiner, "Barbarossa" 521–79; and Borst 17–60.

cant and ground-breaking work in the field of medieval historical research. When he first published his book entitled *Die Epochen der deutschen Geschichte* [*The Epochs of German History*] in 1922, he wrote that he wished to describe the historically cultivated "countenance of the German nation," contribute to "national self-knowledge," and, in particular, "restore meaning" to German history. Haller's search for historical meaning ended by extolling the "magnificent age of glory" when Bismarck founded the Prussian Empire, an age "of fulfillment and happiness." The memory of Bismarck, whom the "nation recognized as its savior," was "to become the seed for the future which shall bear rich fruits when its time has come." Haller called upon his listeners and readers to hope—for the "right man at the right time" who would understand how to cure every affliction of the age "with the miraculous powers of a genius." Haller had the following prophetic promise imprinted on the title page of the first edition of this work: "The day shall come." The source of the quotation is not given. It comes from Homer's *Iliad*.[52]

Karl Alexander von Müller, a historian in Munich, finished a speech he gave in 1924 on Bismarck with the following declaration: "We are victims of the impotence of mediocrity and are crying in our time of need, as a deer cries for water for someone who shall lead us. The fact that his [Bismarck's] spirit has not yet died allows us to hope that he will one day rise again anew among our people, and that the hour will come in which the lightning of a genius shall flash through the dark clouds of our confusion and burn out the mountains of our shame."[53] Von Müller cloaked his hope for a new political genius in pseudo-religious language. The image of the deer crying for water had been used as a metaphor for the soul thirsting for God in the Psalms of the Old Testament. The storm metaphor conjured up a fateful process of purification which would restore clear political order based on leadership and authority. Thunder and

---

[52] See Schreiner, "Führertum, Rasse, Reich. Wissenschaft von der Geschichte nach der nationalsozialistischen Machtergreifung," *Wissenschaft im Dritten Reich*, ed. Peter Lundgreen (Frankfurt a.M., 1985), 230f.

[53] Quoted in Christoph Weisz, *Geschichtsauffassung und politisches Denken Münchener Historiker der Weimarer Zeit. Konrad Beyerle, Max Buchner, Michael Doeberl, Erich Marcks, Karl Alexander von Müller, Hermann Oncken* (Berlin, 1970), 255f. In his memoirs, written after the end of the Second World War, Karl Alexander von Müller characterized the "cult of the great political leader" as "the misunderstood experience of Bismarck" which had continued to have an effect on him as well as on his colleague Erich Marcks (Weisz 256).

lightning are among the mediums by which the God of the Old Testament proclaimed His will.

Karl Alexander von Müller was not speaking for himself alone. He had countless colleagues who shared his opinions and hopes. Their lofty language obscured them. Their backward looking prophecy, based as it was on concepts of fateful forces and higher destination operating in German history, contributed to the alienation of the bourgeoisie from the community. Erich Brandenburg, a historian who taught in Leipzig, began publishing a popular historical series in 1925 called "Die Deutschen Führer" ("The German Leaders"). The series was sustained by the belief that "a healthy people" in "times of danger also brings forth men whom it needs in order to overcome its spiritual, political, and economic afflictions." Brandenburg strived to reinforce in his readers the hope "that they will come,"[54] the men in possession of a leader's nature, the true heroes of the people, in order to bring about a turn for the better.

Ernst Kantorowicz published a biography of Emperor Frederick the Second in 1927. He wanted to call to mind the justification for heroic men of action. In an "age without an emperor," when "an interest in great German ruler figures begins to stir, [not only] in learned circles,"[55] Heroic biographies inspired their readers and found great resonance. "Our age," wrote Stefan Zweig in 1929, "wants and loves heroic biographies, for, because of its own lack of politically creative leaders, it is seeking a better example in past ages."[56]

From the biographical material of the life and works of Frederick the Second, Kantorowicz created the ideal of a "secret emperor" who would one day come to liberate Germany from its humiliation by means of a "secret society" of devotees. Kantorowicz's book is both brilliantly written and based on thorough and precise knowledge of the source materials. Yet, whether one deems it a "fascist classic" (Stewen Rowan), a contribution "to the hero cult" (Stefan Breuer), "history as political poetry" (Peter Gay), or "a breath of fresh

[54] Erich Brandenburg, "Deutsche Führer," foreword, *Der junge Luther*, by Heinrich Boehmer, vol. 1 of *Die Deutschen Führer* (Gotha, 1925), 9f.

[55] Ernst Kantorowicz, foreword, *Kaiser Friedrich der Zweite*, by Kantorowicz, 2nd ed. (Berlin, 1928). See also Schreiner, "Führertum" 213f.; *Eckhart Grünewald, Ernst Kantorowicz und Stefan George. Beiträge zur Biographie des Historikers bis zum Jahre 1938 und zu seinem Jugendwerk "Kaiser Friedrich der Zweite"* (Wiesbaden, 1982).

[56] Stefan Zweig and Joseph Fouché, *Bildnis eines politischen Menschen* (Frankfurt a.M., 1977), 12.

air in the muffiness of medieval history" (Felix Gilbert), the political message is unambiguous. It did not support the parliamentary democracy, but increased the longing for a heroic man of action who, supported by an elite of faithful, would effect a change for the better.

Historians were not alone; Germanists, sociologists, and jurists also nourished hopes for a man with a strong leader's character who, like the Messiah sent by God, would bring about epochal changes in both the state and society. In 1919, Gustav Roethe, a professor of literature in Berlin and temporarily vice-chancellor of the university, declared that, "out of the absolutely hopeless misery which has overcome us, only one single person will finally [save] our politically immature people once again." "Who can say" whether this rescuing genius will be a "king, military commander, statesman, poet, or an economist? We do not yet see him, nor does he appear to be far away. But he will come as the great individual, the true birth of German yearning and singularity."

Dreams of German heroism did not give rise to agreement with or understanding of a democratic way of life. To fight the evils of the age, that is, the "democratic disposition" and the "deplorable drive towards egalitarianism," the Berlin academic evoked images of the "hero," "this sacred German concept," which, he asserted, characterized and grasped the true German essence in crystal clarity.[57] Hans Naumann, a scholar of early German literature in Bonn, expressed his concerns about the situation in a work published in 1932 called *Deutsche Nation in Gefahr* [*The German Nation in Peril*]. He added current political content to the traditional model of expectation in order to interpret the vague presentiment of an imminent

[57] For further information on Gustav Roethe, see Schreiner, "Barbarossa" 553. For Roethe's political views, see Kurt Sontheimer, "Die Haltung der deutschen Universitäten zur Weimarer Republik," *Universitätstage 1966* (Berlin, 1966), 30, (Veröffentlichung der Freien Universität Berlin. Nationalsozialismus und die Deutsche Universität). Gustav Roethe, "whom neither the lost war nor the revolution had been able to move to a change in his militant reactionary disposition," bespoke in his lectures "the same spirit to which dozens of other university lecturers gave voice: the spirit of blind nationalism, the spirit of the German mission, the spirit of unpolitical deification of a strong authoritative state." See Theodor Eschenburg, "Aus dem Universitätsleben vor 1933," *Deutsches Geistesleben und Nationalsozialismus*, Andreas Flitner (Tübingen, 1965), 38: "The Germanist Gustav Roethe was an outspoken enemy of the Weimar state. He was one of the most respected representatives of his field and was adored by the students." Eschenburg writes as an eye-witness and from personal experience.

Wende in the age and its destiny in the interest of an authoritarian leadership. He included the belief in a hidden savior as expressed in the German saga of the emperor among the "enduring dreams" of the "eternal Teutonic nation." Waiting for a messianic savior was an "eschatology inherent" to the German *Volkstum* which spanned the ages "from the ancient myth and national sagas to the political relevance of the present."[58] Naumann did not perceive the order of the day to be the acceptance of active collective responsibility for a threatened democratic government; it was rather to prepare the way for a man gifted with charisma who would bring redemption and establish order. Naumann prophesied, "One is asleep somewhere, the hero and savior of our country, enchanted and concealed, who must be awakened. One is seated somewhere, gathering an army of chosen warriors for a future day.... According to all verdicts, a great battle will take place."[59]

In his work, "Gesellschaftslehre" ("Sociology"), the third edition of which was published in 1930, Othmar Spann, a professor of political economy at the University of Vienna, asserted as well that the "masses" had no existence without a leader. For "the leader is the only one who can give form to the opinion of the masses, i.e., who tells the voters both what they should instruct the leader to do as well as for whom they should vote." The leader, a blessed seer into the eternal order of things, through whom the divine reveals itself in history, must design the state in such a way that it becomes the "totality of life." Only when the people demonstrate their unconditional "will to revere and obey" could the leader become the "age's savior from evil powers."[60]

Liberal jurists perceived *Führerlosigkeit* ["leaderlessness"] as something intrinsic to a democracy, a system in which power is checked and controlled by means of the validation and application of laws decided by the majority. Anti-democrats like Julius Binder, a professor of the philosophy of law in Göttingen and the author of a work published in 1929 called "Führerauslese in der Demokratie" ("Selecting a Leader in a Democracy"), put their trust in the "spirit of the nation" which, in the history of a people, "proceeds more justly than an election committee and the decisions by the majority

---

[58] Schreiner, "Barbarossa" 553.
[59] Schreiner, "Barbarossa" 553.
[60] Schreiner, "Führertum" 172.

of those entitled to vote in a democracy." According to Binder, the idea of leadership by a leader who can be neither "made" nor "chosen" was in accordance with the spirit of the German nation. The "leader creates himself in that he understands the history of his people, knows himself to be the leader, and wills it."[61]

3. *Voices from the Field of Theology*

In his capacity as vice-chancellor of Greifswald university, the Protestant Old Testament scholar Otto Procksch gave a lecture on 18 January 1924 in which he said, "The name Versailles, a place over which an imperial crown once held sway, makes one's blood run cold today. For, from Versailles, we brought home merely a fool's cap; we are without an army, without defense, and without honor. Indeed, France itself broke the Treaty of Versailles a year ago, but we comply, comply, comply." Procksch recommended the following formula for salvation: "When the German way and the Christian faith join forces, then we shall be saved. For we shall work with our hands and await the day that the German hero comes; whether he comes as prophet or as king."[62]

Paul Althaus, who published a collection of essays in 1933, shortly after Hitlers "Machtergreifung", entitled *Die deutsche Stunde der Kirche* ["*The German Hour of the Church*"], perceived in the "fulfillments," in the resurrections and rebirths of the Third Reich ["kingdom"], an indication of the coming of the Kingdom of God.[63] According to his convictions, "every instance of historical liberation and recovery" was "a sign of the coming Kingdom [of God], an indication of it."[64] Every "earthly expectation and experience of a salvational figure" evidenced the Kingdom [of God] and would find in Him their fulfillment. Already, asserted Althaus, "we are experiencing the miracle of 'rebirth,' of healing, recovery, and new life, of the breaking

---

[61] Quoted in Kurt Sontheimer, *Antidemokratisches Denken in der Weimarer Republik, Die politischen Ideen des deutschen Nationalismus zwischen 1918 und 1933* (Munich, 1968), 219. For more on "Führerlosigkeit," which Hans Kelsen perceives as a "positive characteristic of a democracy," see Sontheimer 221. For further reading on Binder's concept of a constitution and a state, see Klaus von See, *Deutsche Germanen-Ideologie. Vom Humanismus bis zur Gegenwart* (Frankfurt a.M., 1970), 71f.

[62] Otto Procksch, "König und Prophet in Israel," lecture, Greifswald, Germany, 18 Jan. 1924, vol. 10 of *Greifswalder Universitätsreden* (Greifswald, 1924), 22f.

[63] Paul Althaus, "Drittes Reich und Reich Gottes," *Die deutsche Stunde der Kirche* (Göttingen, 1933), 26.

[64] Althaus 30.

of the chains—as we are experiencing this, should we not think of it as a sign of the coming of the day when we shall become 'like the visionaries' in the face of the one great rebirth!"[65] He justified his interpretation of the present, in which he was able to perceive a reflection of the "great rebirth," as the "application of knowledge gained from the Old Testament to the current situation."[66]

Althaus' essays included critical remarks as well. "In the last few years, political messianism, as professed by its preachers and many of its believers, has become a substitute for a belief in Jesus Christ, [that is] a belief in earthly salvation which the Christian faith must view as a mortal enemy, as it did the cult of the Roman Emperor." It was, however, not sufficient "that our theologians merely express the necessary objections to this political messianism, this secularized eschatology." Rather, he summoned Christian theologians to combat the "false messianic inflation of political expectation and experience . . . with the disclosure of the genuine and true relationship between political 'salvation' and salvation in Christ, between national 'resurrection' and resurrection through Jesus Christ."[67]

According to Althaus, drawing a correlation between the two was an attempt to conceive of "the history of our people as the history of God."[68] Christian eschatology, "which is not false, otherworldly, but realistic," did not need to be ashamed of its "relationship to the experience of the present." For, "the Old Testament, which intertwines concrete political hopes and eschatological expectations, grants precisely the right to such a relationship!"[69] In the Messianic traditions of the Old Testament, Althaus believed he had found an argument for establishing an inextricable connection between the concepts of political and divine salvation. Israel's hopes for the Kingdom of God had been "earthly, national, and concretely historical." Therefore, the Old Testament was especially helpful in preaching the "proclamation to our age," which the "political sermon" needed.[70] The people of his day were "a thoroughly political species," which was precisely why the question of salvation had taken on a political

[65] Althaus 30.
[66] Althaus 26.
[67] Althaus 29.
[68] Althaus, "Volks-Geschichte und Heils-Geschichte," *Die deutsche Stunde der Kirche* (Göttingen, 1933), 22.
[69] Althaus, "Drittes Reich" 30.
[70] Althaus, "Drittes Reich" 24; "Volks-Geschichte" 17.

dimension. If, in his age, the people were so deeply moved by the "prevailing question" of how to "overcome political difficulties," then, "in the face of such a question, the Gospel must be preached precisely in terms of its 'political' meaning, the Kingdom of God, and God's sovereign authority."[71] Under the conditions of 1933, resorting in such a way to the Messianism of the Old Testament amounted to endowing the National Socialist seizure of power, which was interpreted as a resurrection and rebirth, with a dimension of *Heilsgeschichte.*

4. *Messianic Thought in the Literature of the Weimar Republic*

After the defeat of 1918, historians, in the name of their science, characterized the Germans as a people of hope, determined by destiny to await a new political savior. Religious literature written by seers who sought to disseminate their visions of the future prophesied "a new empire" and "a crowned ruler" under whom the Reich would be returned to its old power and splendor.[72] Popular novels gave expression to hopes for a savior "Führer" or a "strong man from above" who would embody the "collective will of the people." Symptomatic of this is a novel by Adolf Reinecke of 1923 entitled *Der Erlöser-Kaiser. Erzählung aus Deutschlands Zukunft und von seiner Wiedergeburt* [*The Savior-Emperor. A Tale from Germany's Future and of its Rebirth*]. Reinecke had been the editor of the journal *Heimdall* since 1896, a paper characterized by racist and pan-German thought. He belonged to the National Socialist opposition which held the Hohenzollern regime responsible for the materialistic, liberal *Zeitgeist* and the "Judaization" and subsequent "'weakening' of the German national body." Reinicke prophesied an "emperor who was truly bound to the *Volk*" or an "imperial Führer," a Prince Frederick, who would wear a blonde beard like a pure Aryan, not a red one like Frederick Barbarossa, nor a white one like Emperor William the First. With a strong army, he would first conquer the Poles, then the English and the French. He would transform Germany into a world power in the face of which all other nations of Europe would be rendered politically insignificant. "Not only Poland, the Baltic, Bukovina, Bessarabia, Bohemia, Moravia, Slovakia, German-Austria, the Southern Tirol, Trieste, Switzerland, the Netherlands and Denmark,

---

[71] Althaus, "Drittes Reich" 27.

[72] Jost Hermand, *Der alte Traum vom neuen Reich. Völkische Utopien und Nationalsozialismus* (Frankfurt a.M., 1988), 104.

but Burgundy, Lothringen, and Flanders as well will become part of this new Reich." Frederick, "Emperor Blondebeard," worshiped and loved by all, would be crowned in Aachen's cathedral, a church "of Aryan salvation." The envoys of Germanic tribes would swear eternal devotion to him as the chosen and sent "savior" of the Nordic race.[73]

Longings for *Führerschaft* and a Reich can be found in rather more intellectually challenging literature as well. The origin of hopes for a better future expressed in these texts cannot be found, however, in the morass of racists myths. The growth of both the mythic as well as the poetic longing for a Reich and a Führer thrived in the well-cultivated ground of the prejudices against democracy. In 1921, Stefan George gave expression to a widespread attitude when he prophesied a time which would bring forth the "only one who will help us," "the man." George believed this man of action capable of breaking the chains, of affixing "the true symbol upon the National (*völkische*) banner," of sowing the seeds of the "New Reich" for "his faithful flock."[74] Characteristic of George and his circle was the "constant summoning of the great man and his salvational action"[75] and implicit trust "in the charismatic Führer." To George, far-reaching political reform only seemed possible by means of the strong will and acts of a hero and Führer. In his opinion, redemption could not come "'from below,' from the activities of political and societal forces, . . . but only 'from above' through the incarnation of redemption in a 'bearer of salvation,' through the 'union of cosmic forces' in a genius who would bring the new salvation for the new afflictions."[76]

Neither George nor his disciples and devotees were able to say what this "one" would look like or how he would act and work. Friedrich Gundolf, a Germanist of Jewish extraction who taught in Heidelberg, wrote in his book of 1924, *Cäsar, Geschichte seines Ruhms* [*Caesar: The History of His Fame*], that "you will not know what the future Lord or Savior will look like until He reigns." In an age in which "the need for a strong man is becoming urgent, when the people, weary of carpers and bletherers, make do with sergeants,

[73] Hermand 119f.

[74] See Schreiner, "Führertum" 213.

[75] Stefan Breuer, *Ästhetischer Fundamentalismus. Stefan George und der deutsche Antimodernismus* (Darmstadt, 1995), 235.

[76] Breuer 223.

rather than leaders," Gundolf wished "to remind those who were rash to judge and act of the great man to whom the greatest world powers have owed their name and their ideas throughout the ages: Caesar."[77] Gundolf argues "not against the political messianism of his age. He seeks rather to ennoble it with humanist ideas" by reminding his contemporaries of the "image of true greatness."[78] In Gundolf's view, Caesar, both lord and savior, had united intellect, power, energy, and morality.

Gundolf and George's formative influence can not be underestimated. As Karl Löwith reports in his autobiographical work, *Leben in Deutschland vor und nach 1933. Ein Bericht*, [*Life in Germany before and after 1933: A Report*], it "decisively shaped many young people of my generation." "The fates of those in George's circle reflect a common fate of the German as well as the Jewish intelligentsia. Its members formed an elite of German intellectual life. . . . They laid paths for National Socialism, paths upon which they themselves never trod."[79] Influenced by George's elitism and a belief in a Reich, many subsequently placed themselves in the service of the Third Reich. Among them was Claus Schenk Graf von Stauffenberg who later underwent a transformation from a nationalistic patriot who had sworn allegiance and devotion to the Führer as a member of the armed forces to a resistance fighter. He sought "to save the Reich" and "prevent senseless human sacrifice" by resolving to attempt the assassination of Hitler.[80]

IV. *Messianism in Political and Social Contexts*

1. *Messianism in the Youth Movement*

Characteristic of the German youth movement after the First World War was, in the first place, the flight "into an apocalyptic state of mind,"[81] and second, the longing for a hero who would give their

---

[77] Friedrich Gundolf, *Caesar. Geschichte seines Ruhms* (Berlin, 1924), 7.

[78] Ulrich Raulff, "Eine Figur des Imaginären. Friedrich Gundolf und Caesars magischer Name," *Frankfurter Allgemeine Zeitung* No. 159 (11 July 1992), "Bilder und Zeiten" section, 2.

[79] Löwith, *Mein Leben in Deutschland* 25.

[80] Harald Steffahn, *Claus Schenk Graf von Stauffenberg* (Hamburg, 1994), 81.

[81] Peter Suhrkamp, "Die Sezession des Familiensohnes. Eine nachträgliche Betrachtung der Jugendbewegung," *Die Neue Rundschau* 43, vol. 1 (1932), 111.

lives meaning and lead them into a better future with a strong hand. A "philosophy of destruction which would achieve the final annihilation of the bourgeois world"[82] summarizes their intellectualism.

After the First World War, representatives of the youth movement said and wrote, "In our misery, we long for a Führer. He will show us the way and the acts which will make our people honorable once again. This longing comes from the depths of our hearts."[83] "The true Führer surely has no selfish motivations, just one, regal motivation, that he must be the Führer because he is it by nature. . . . The Führer is not guided by the masses, but by his mission; he does not flatter the masses; he proceeds harshly, uprightly, and ruthlessly, in times of good and evil. The Führer is radical; he is wholly that which he is, and he does wholly that which he must. The Führer is responsible, that is, he does God's will, which he embodies, for every great human being is, to an extent, an embodiment of divine thought and recognizable as such."[84] It would be a mistake to speak of the "sovereignty of the people" here. "Only the one individual who towers above the masses is sovereign, the ruler, the Führer." "Leadership is brilliance, an act of God's grace."[85] Therefore, the urgent plea went out: "God, grant us the Führer and help us to achieve true fealty."[86]

According to their spoken and written words, young people who aspired to "manliness and heroism" were bound in fealty to the Führer. Fealty was "elective"; but "not in the sense of a ballot paper, but in the sense of hero-worship."[87] Therefore, "girls and women shall also show fealty to a man, a Führer, especially in public life, for the man is the creator of the state. He is its protector. The women shall also therefore follow the Führer and look up to him because they shall bear and raise sons, and because the imprint of a masculine personality, of masculine greatness is of service to them."[88]

---

[82] Suhrkamp, "Söhne ohne Väter und Lehrer. Die Situation der bürgerlichen Jugend," *Die Neue Rundschau* 43, vol. 1 (1932), 688.

[83] Käthe Becker, née Sturmfels, "'Führerschaft.' Eine Rede vor der Vereinigung 'Deutsche Jugend,'" *Deutschlands Erneuerung. Monatsschrift für das deutsche Volk*, vol. 4 (1920), 563.

[84] Becker 565f.

[85] Becker 564f.

[86] Becker 573.

[87] Becker 570.

[88] Becker 572. See also Harry Pross, "Führer und Gefolgschaft," *Jugend, Eros, Politik. Die Geschichte der deutschen Jugendverbände* (Bern, Munich, Vienna, 1964), 286–96.

The mission of male and female adherents was not to control the Führer, but to examine themselves constantly to determine whether their own nature and desires were in accord with those of the Führer.

In an article entitled "Führerschaft," which appeared in *Der Türmer* in 1923, young people who awaited the Führer were told, "As soon as the time is ripe, the Führer shall emerge as the bearer of divine powers of mercy and fate. He shall be [completely] free of any conviction with regard to his own intrinsic value. Whether he appears in the form of one person or as a collective power is immaterial." However, nothing precise could be said with respect to what "kind of person or from what class" this man capable of establishing the "new Reich" would be—"whether [he would be] a businessman, politician, or laborer, a scholar, writer, or a man without rank or name." Whoever though "snatches the spark from eternity to ignite this ideal of a new humanity shall be welcome and blessed."[89]

Members of the "Christliche Studentenvereinigung" ["Christian Students Union"] prayed and sang, for example, the following from a 1927 song book:

> To You we raise our hands
> in our greatest, most dire need.
> Lord God, the Führer do send
> He who shall our troubles mend
> Through his powerful command.
>
> Awaken for us the hero,
> Who, strong before all our woe,
> Shall move His Germany mightily,
> Shall lead Your Germany faithfully
> Into the morning dawn.[90]

By establishing an unmediated connection between the Führer and his followers, the youth movement sought to overcome the atmosphere of mechanization, objectification, and depersonalization which, in the eyes of those in these circles, determined the thoughts and actions of the bourgeois world. Spokesmen considered "the immediacy of the relationship between the people and a charismatic *Führertum*" particular to German values and achievements. "For," according to their convictions, "if there ever was a *Volk* not only in

---

[89] Paul Steinmüller, "Führerschaft," *Der Türmer*, 26 (1923), 4, 5, 6.
[90] Althaus 22.

whom a sense of the irrational and the emotional was united, but who also harbored the resulting yearning for immediate human solidarity and charismatic *Führertum*, it is the German. Everything opposed to it, such as the big city, bureaucracy, and a monetary economy, is of Romanic and Jewish origin imported in the Age of Absolutism and Enlightenment."[91]

Critical and insightful contemporaries were able to detect in young Germans of the early thirties an "odd combination of revolutionary rebellion against authority and tradition and blind discipline toward the 'Führer'."[92] In a 1932 essay called "Die Situation der bürgerlichen Jugend" ["The Situation of the Bourgeois Youth"], Peter Suhrkamp diagnosed the situation as follows: The "turn away from the liberal parties" goes hand in hand with an "enthusiasm for drills" and a "preparedness for anyone at all who will command them."[93] "Without heroes they feel nothing." According to Suhrkamp's conclusion, which was marked by a distinct sense of resignation, the young people who were "happier" than others had already found their heroes: "Lenin, Hitler or whatever their names might be."[94]

2. *The Common Man's Redeemers*

Countless "saviors of the twenties"[95] who achieved a position of "great significance especially in the years of inflation from 1919 to 1923 and then again during the Depression of 1929 to 1933"[96] were associated with the bourgeois and proletarian Youth Movement. These barefoot prophets of crisis and itinerant saints promising personal

---

[91] Paul Honigsheim, "Jugendbewegung und Erkenntnis," *Versuche zu einer Soziologie des Wissens*, ed. Max Scheler (Munich, Leipzig, 1924), 397f.

[92] Ernst von Aster, "Metaphysik des Nationalismus," *Die Neue Rundschau* 43, vol. 1 (1932), 52.

[93] Suhrkamp, "Söhne" 696. See also Hagen Schulze, "Die Versuchung des Absoluten. Zur deutschen politischen Kultur im 19. und 20. Jahrhundert," in his *Wir sind, was wir geworden sind. Vom Nutzen der Geschichte für die deutsche Gegenwart*, (Munich, Zurich, 1987), 123. Concerning the Youth Movement between the two World Wars, he writes: "The Youth Movement distinguishes itself with all its might from the values of bourgeois liberalism—restraint, societal forms, the belief in rationality. The standards of bourgeois civilization decay in the face of relentless rejection. The parents are conservative, national-liberal, or independent; the sons and daughters are becoming National Socialists, syndicalists, nihilists, or set out on a path towards a nirvana of interiority inspired by the Youth Movement."

[94] Suhrkamp, "Sezession" (above, note 81), 95f.

[95] See Ulrich Linse, *Barfüßige Propheten. Erlöser der zwanziger Jahre* (Berlin, 1983).

[96] Linse 34.

conversions, "who fancied themselves in the role of savior", were reacting to the existential fears and expectations of redemption held by a generation which had become skeptical, distraught, and uncertain. In an age in which "apocalyptic excitation and millennial expectation caught on even among the masses,"[97] these prophets preached the coming of a moral renewal which would bring about a new humanity, a new society, and a new political system. Their workplace was the street where they held meetings and organized protest marches.

In 1922, a Berlin correspondent for the *Kölnische Zeitung* [*Cologne Newspaper*] described how these "prophets of the street" appeared and worked as follows: "For the past one or two years, the advertising boards in Berlin have been covered with announcements of disciples of the future and prophets who are advertising their lectures (often at considerable admission prices). Catchwords and quotations from the Bible always play a role in the advertisements. The old constellation of ideas surrounding the apocalypse has gained new life, as it did in earlier times of crisis. From the mouths of eloquent speakers, it impresses itself anew in the minds of those who are frightened. The main characteristics are a heavy beard, neither collar nor tie, and imperturbable self-confidence." The correspondent noted the following with respect to the public's reaction and motives: "Even at this moment, the public is running into the lecture halls of these phantasts because it is looking for some sort of help, some consolation in its state of complete inner helplessness. A mood of boundless disappointment set in very shortly after the war, when the fruitlessness of all efforts had become clear. If the ever-increasing material privation and hopeless battle against rising prices continue as they have in the past few months, the minds of the public will become completely confused. . . . Everyone, especially those who are weaker by nature and cannot survive without help, is running toward the new-age, long-haired saviors and their bold fantasies. The existence of such prophets is a dangerous symptom of the mental state prevalent in Germany today. It must not be underestimated; it will be spread into circles it has not yet even touched. The age has gone awry!, as Hamlet says."[98]

---

[97] Linse 28.

[98] Linse 33f. See also Linse 33: "If we now recognize that the call for a Führer was a typical anti-democratic sign during the Weimar period, then it is necessary to

Experiences of crisis and existential fears had prepared the ground in which the messages of these "inflation saints" could take root. In fact, "contemporaries who were at the mercy of their fears did not necessarily seek their salvation in rational political and economic considerations and actions. Like their forefathers, many rather resorted to the social myth of messianic leaders. These were no swindlers; they truly believed that their coming would renew all things. Their considerable self-confidence also gave their adherents support and a sense of security and, at the same time, increased their willingness to suffer and sacrifice."[99]

One of the most prominent "saviors" was Louis Haeusser, who came out of the Pietist tradition of Württemberg. He considered himself a "helper to all ordinary people, the down-trodden, the weak, the oppressed." His followers, filled with religious zeal and social rebellion, called themselves "fools in Christ." Hauesser became a symbolic figure of hope "for those degraded proletarian and petty-bourgeois groups which united the anarchic rejection of the state with a cry for the strong Führer, and yearned for earthly salvation by means of a sword-yielding messianic savior instead of pragmatic politics."[100]

3. *Messianic Ideas in the National Socialist Movement*

On 19 July 1924, Joseph Goebbels wrote in his diary, "Great men make great ages—but not great ages great men." For, he added by way of explanation, "the age can only become great through the man. Alexander, Caesar, Barbarossa, Napoleon, Frederick, Bismarck. How wretched their age were one to imagine them absent from it. There is always an organic relationship between the age and man. If the great man is lacking, then the age is not yet ready."[101] As early as July fourth of the same year, Goebbels entrusted to his diary, "Germany longs for the One, the man, as the summer earth for the rain. The only things that can save us now are a last summoning of energy, inspiration, and restless devotion. Those are all indeed

---

recognize as well that the messianic expectations not only were incarnated in Hitler, but also inspired a multitude of itinerant preachers and prophets besides him."

[99] Linse 34.

[100] Linse 64.

[101] Elke Fröhlich, ed., *Die Tagebücher von Joseph Goebbels. Sämtliche Fragmente, Teil 1: 1924–1941*, vol. 1 (Munich, 1987), 44f.

miraculous things. But can a miracle still save us? Show the German *Volk* a miracle! A miracle!! A man!!! Bismarck, arise!"[102]

In his diary entry of 14 October 1925 Goebbels noted: "I am finishing reading Hitler's book [*Mein Kampf*]. With riveting suspense! Who is this man? Half-plebeian, half-God! Actually Christ or only John? Longing for calm and peace!"[103] In order to express what moved him, Goebbels employed the language of Christianity. "The only problem that Goebbels had was the question: Is Hitler the prophet, who prophesies the savior, or is he himself the savior, Christ with a whip?"[104] Goebbels did not find it difficult to answer this question. Hitler would only be able to still his enormous "hunger for light and salvation"[105] as "the warring and conquering Christ,"[106] not as a mere predecessor. Was Adolf Hitler indeed the Führer who, as Goebbels explained in his 1926 essay "Die Führerfrage" ["The Führer Question"], would find "the words of redemption for a whole generation in this age of deep shame and inner strife" and would therefore become the "pioneer and organizer of the yearnings, as yet vague, of German youths."[107] In order to characterize Hitler as the "fulfillment of a secret longing,"[108] Goebbels used "attributes which are associated with Christ in the Christian tradition."[109] Collaborators in Hitler's redemptive work were his "fanatic adherents." These "small, willful minorities, led and blessed by the will of a single individual" stand, as Goebbels asserted with zealous fervor, "at the turning point in history. They are spokes in the wheel of evolution which is rolling away from the abyss. They shall sweep through the land as the apostles of the new idea and shall achieve the miracle of redemptive liberation."[110]

Apocalyptic ideas came into play when Goebbels championed the view that the "Third Reich," the redemptive Reich of the future, would not come and assume its form peaceably; a battle would have to be fought against its enemies and adversaries. According to

---

102 Fröhlich 34.
103 Fröhlich 134f.
104 Claus-Ekkehard Bärsch, *Erlösung und Vernichtung. Dr. phil. Joseph Goebbels. Zur Psyche und Ideologie eines jungen Nationalsozialisten 1923–1927* (Munich, 1987), 94.
105 Bärsch 130.
106 Bärsch 310.
107 Bärsch 86.
108 Bärsch 87.
109 Bärsch 114.
110 Bärsch 87.

Goebbels, the National Socialists were tools of the divine will and, as such, were summoned to wage a final enormous battle "for the establishment of a future defined by redemption."[111] The outcome of the present "world struggle" between good and evil depends not on Germany being redeemed by the world, but on the National Socialists "redeeming the world through Germany."[112] The world's great enemy was international Judaism, whose capital threatened to subjugate and exploit all of Europe. On 26 June 1926, Goebbels wrote in his diary that "the Jew is indeed the Antichrist of world history."[113] If the attempt "to overcome the red plague of the Jews" was successful, "then our actions shall be immortal."[114]

In his speech of 27 April 1923, Hitler explained, "What our *Volk* needs are leaders, not of the parliamentary sort, but leaders who decisively accomplish that which they recognize as right before God, the world, and their conscience and, if necessary, against the majority. If we succeed in bringing forth such leaders from the masses of our *Volk*, then a nation will crystallize once again around them." The German *Volk* "does not yearn for majority decisions, but for leaders. The German Reich was not the work of a majority decision, but of a single man, Bismarck."[115] On 4 May 1923, Hitler prophesied the following before his listeners and party members: "The dictatorship of both the national will and the national determination are the things which can save Germany. The question then arises: Does the suitable personage exist? It is not our task to find this person. He is either bestowed on us by heaven or not at all. It is our task to create the sword this person will need when he comes. It is our task to bestow upon the dictator a *Volk* that is ready for him!"[116]

---

[111] Bärsch 309.
[112] Bärsch 124.
[113] Bärsch 127.
[114] Bärsch 135. Hitler considered himself a tool of the Almighty in the "battle for our self-preservation" as well, which made it absolutely necessary for the preservation of humanity to repel and combat the danger allegedly posed by the Jewish people. In his book, *Mein Kampf*, he affirmed his belief that "I act in the sense of the Almighty Creator. By warding off the Jews I am fighting for the Lord's work." (Hitler, *Mein Kampf*, vol. 1, "Eine Abrechnung" (Munich, 1938) 69, 70). When Hitler wrote this sentence, he invoked the power of anti-Semitic rhetoric. At this point, he had not yet begun to talk about the destruction and extermination of Judaism with the aid of state instruments of power.
[115] Quoted in Rainer Zitelmann, *Hitler. Selbstverständnis eines Revolutionärs* (Berg, 1987), 397.
[116] Zitelmann 401.

Hitler changed his political self-perception during his imprisonment in Landsberg after the abortive Munich Putsch of November 1923. He no longer conceived of himself as the man who paved the way for the savior. He freed himself of the idea that he was a man "of the nature of John" and now considered himself the coming Führer of Germany, resolved to establish a "true Germanic democracy" and to fight for the realization of Christian values. The "battle which the National Socialist movement wages," asserted Hitler in February 1927, was "now a true crusade . . . for the Christianity of the Lord."[117] In a meeting of the Munich NSDAP in December 1926, he said, "The teachings of Christ have been fundamental in the battle against the Jew as the enemy of humanity. I will complete the work which Christ began but could not finish. National Socialism is nothing other than practical compliance with the teachings of Christ."[118]

V. *The Year 1933 as Fulfillment of a Prophecy*

1. *Hitler's Claim*

If one follows the interpretations offered by nationalistic patriots and Protestant ministers and theologians, the German people had perceived itself as a people awaiting its "rebirth," "redemption," and "resurrection" since its defeat in 1918. According to their religiously charged rhetoric, the Germans conceived of themselves as a people chosen by God, as the "bearers of revelation" and as "agents of the salvational event,"[119] not as subjects responsible for their own politics and history. The self-perception of the people, defined as it was by religious ideas and metaphors, yielded a "people which experienced itself as passive, suffering, in need of redemption, and pleading for fulfillment. Hitler was therefore able to make use of these semantic

[117] Quoted in a letter of 4 Feb. 1927 to a Catholic beneficiary by the name of Magnus Gött who became a fervent member of the National Socialist Party after the abortive Munich (Beer Hall) Putsch of 1923. See also Paul Hoser, "Hitler und die katholische Kirche. Zwei Briefe aus dem Jahr 1927," *Vierteljahrshefte für Zeitgeschichte*, No. 3, 1994: 487.

[118] Hoser 487, fn. 114.

[119] Citation from the Protestant theologian, Friedrich Gogarten. Quoted in Michael Ley, *Genozid und Heilserwartung. Zum national-sozialistischen Mord am europäischen Judentum*, (Berlin, 1995), 165.

handicaps and perceive himself as the active leader commissioned by providence to save the people."[120]

In the consciousness of those who followed Hitler loyally, faithfully, and unconditionally, the National Socialist revolution assumed the character of a messianic event which would ostensibly fulfill the fervent longings of millions of people. Hitler himself saw himself as a savior chosen and sent by God's providence who was able and willing to overcome the existing crisis. He located the sources of the crisis in the liberalistic dissolution of moral values, in the domination of the world by the capital of international Jewry, and, last but not least, in the threats posed by the East, that is, the Bolsheviks' claim to be the leading power in Europe and the world.

Hitler endeavored to fashion his public appearances in such a way that onlookers and listeners would have the impression that they were standing before a statesman who was called and blessed by higher powers, who pursued a politics which was in the best interest of the German people. Critical contemporaries saw through Hitler's use of messianic allusions in his productions and viewed them as an attempt to exploit religious sentiments and expectations in order to achieve the goals of the National Socialist movement. Victor Klemperer, a brilliant scholar of Jewish descent who taught Romance languages and literatures at Leipzig university, remarked in his diary on 11 November 1933: "Yesterday from one to two o'clock, the 'ceremonial hour.' 'At one o'clock Adolf Hitler comes to the laborers.' The savior comes to the poor."[121] On 29 July 1934, Klemperer noted, "The philology of the National Socialists: In a speech before Berlin's city hall, Göring said: 'All of us, from the simple SA man to the prime minister, are of Adolf Hitler and exist through Adolf Hitler. He is Germany.' The language of the Gospels."[122]

Das deutsche Gebet [*The German Prayer*], a collection of texts which appeared in 1936 and was to be used in the National Socialists' morning ceremonies, stylized Hitler as a hero who could overcome all mortal powers. In order to lend the Führer's actions the character of a national act of redemption, it read, for example:

---

[120] Reinhart Koselleck, "Volk. Nation," *Geschichtliche Grundbegriffe. Historisches Lexikon zur politisch-sozialien Sprache in Deutschland*, Otto Brunner, Werner Conze, Reinhart Koselleck, eds., vol. 7 (Stuttgart, 1992), 410.

[121] Victor Klemperer, *Ich will Zeugnis ablegen bis zum letzten. Tagebücher 1933–1941*, ed. Walter Nowojski (Berlin, 1995), 67.

[122] Klemperer 127.

You walk among the people as its savior,
for you are possessed by faith . . .
No need for trembling or fear:
"When you believe it, I will have conquered death,"
you say to us, "even when my body decays."[123]

The ritualistic celebration and apotheosis of the Führer gave the celebrating community the feeling of being delivered through him, the new "messiah," to a new life. Like Christ, Hitler was seen and revered as the "revelation" and incarnation of a "command of a higher law" which "soars above us and in us."[124] In the political liturgy of the Nuremberg *Reichspartei* convention, Hitler was "illumined as the death-defying hero, as the redeemer. In performing the ceremonies, his followers were participating in the redemptive acts of the Führer."[125]

Indeed, from a psychological point of view, a "Messiah complex" is implied with respect to Hitler.[126] Historians also lend support to the following theses: Hitler saw himself as the "new messiah" who

---

[123] Klaus Vondung, *Magie und Manipulation. Ideologischer Kult und politische Religion des Nationalsozialismus* (Göttingen, 1971), 182. In one of his diaries, Thomas Mann states that the English press published a poem by a Hitler youth in 1935 which goes: "The merry Hitler youth are we, Christian virtue we do not need. For our Führer, Adolf Hitler, is our savior, our mediator. No parson, no evil one, can prevent us from feeling that we are Hitler's children. Away with incense and holy water basins!" (Thomas Mann, *Tagebücher 1935–1936*, ed. Peter de Mendelssohn (Frankfurt a.M., 1978), 198.)

[124] Vondung 183.

[125] Hans-Ulrich Thamer, "Faszination und Manipulation. Die Nürnberger Reichsparteitage der NSDAP," *Das Fest. Eine Kulturgeschichte von der Antike bis zur Gegenwart*, ed. Uwe Schultz (Munich, 1988), 366.

[126] In a study completed in 1943 called *The Mind of Hitler*, the American psychoanalyst Walter C. Langer (brother of the Harvard historian, William Langer) supported the view that there were signs of a "Messiah complex" which determined Hitler's religious and political world views to a significant degree "long before he had started on his meteoric career and become an open competitor of Christ for the affections of the German people." After his seizure of power, Hitler took great pains to be perceived and revered by the German people "not as a man, but a Messiah of Germany." (Walter C. Langer, *The Mind of Hitler* (London, 1973), 160, 55. See also page 217, where he writes, "He [Hitler] saw himself as the veritable Messiah of his people.") The American historian, James M. Rhodes, interpreted "The Hitler Movement" as a "modern millenarian Revolution." In light of such preconceptions, Rhodes writes that Hitler's programmatic work, *Mein Kampf*, proves itself to be "the best key to the mind of a millenarian 'messiah.'" According to Rhodes, Hitler had already made the conscious decision "that he was a messiah" as early as 1925. (James M. Rhodes, *Hitler Movement. A Modern Millenarian Revolution* (Stanford, 1980) 22, 68.) For other writers who define "Hitler's role as that of a religious messiah," see Sabine Behrenbeck, *Der Kult um die toten Helden. Nationalsozialistische Mythen, Riten und Symbole 1923 bis 1945* (Vierow b.Greifswald, 1996), 26.

would liberate humanity from the Antichrist;[127] he assumed the "role of savior" as the opponent of evil;[128] and he stylized himself both as a "figure of redemption according to the Christian model" and as "the savior-hero of the German people."[129] However, the following findings are remarkable and must be stressed: Hitler himself never characterized himself as a savior, redeemer or messiah.

---

[127] Michael Ley, "Apokalyptische Bewegungen in der Moderne," *Der Nationalsozialismus als politische Religion*, eds. Michael Ley and Julius H. Schoeps (Bodenheim b. Mainz, 1997), 25. In his book, *Genozid und Heilserwartung. Zum nationalsozialistischen Mord am europäischen Judentum* (Vienna, 1993), Michael Ley supports the thesis that Hitler, as the "new savior," as the "holy slaughterer," "carried out the killing of the Jewish people necessitated by the *Heilsgeschichte*." In this respect, the "annihilation of Judaism" took on the "aura of a sacred act" (188). According to Ley, the Holocaust was "explicable in terms of the sociology of religion" (239). It had its foundations in Christian apocalypticism which made the killing of the Antichrist a necessary prerequisite for the commencement of the thousand-year Reich. In this regard, the Holocaust is "an aspect of the Christian and post-Christian western world which is gladly pushed aside" (239). Ley's speculations do not, however, involve in-depth analyses of discourse, which entail weighing with expertise the relevance of views of history and philosophy to actions, careful consideration of the selective and fictional character of religious cultural traditions, and rendering an account of the constructive character of long-term continuities. Ley's thesis is not new. As early as 1961, Norman Cohn attempted to explain Hitler's resolve "to carry out the murder of approximately five million Jewish men, women, and children in the middle of waging an uncertain war at great expense with respect to labor, materials, and transportation" by using various disconnected cultural relics of apocalyptic provenance which he traced back to the eleventh century. (Cohn, *Das Ringen um das Tausendjährige Reich. Revolutionärer Messianismus im Mittelalter und sein Fortleben in den modernen totalitären Bewegung* (Bern, 1961), 272.) In order to criticize historians who believe they can explain historical events of their immediate present by establishing causal chains of events which span epochs, Marc Bloch spoke of historians' "Stammesgötzen" ["tribal idols"]. *Der Beruf des Historikers*, ed. Lucien Febvre (München 1985), 27f. Shulamith Volkov, a historian who teaches in Tel Aviv, argued recently "against the overemphasis of continuity in the history of German anti-Semitism" when attempting to make the "politics of murder by Nazi leadership" comprehensible by means of an analysis of anti-Semitic trends and undercurrents. She writes: "In order to explain National Socialist anti-Semitism, one should investigate more short-term developments. It would be counter-productive to view the entire history of the German-Jewish relationship only from the perspective of its final, horrific end." (Volkov, "Nationalismus, Antisemitismus und die deutsche Geschichtsschreibung," *Nation und Gesellschaft in Deutschland. Historische Essays*, eds., Manfred Hettling and Paul Nolte (Munich, 1996), 210, 217). Methodological premises such as this make it possible to approach historical reality. The reckless thinking of historians like Ley produces images of history like those in an already-antiquated type of intellectual history. It does not yield historical knowledge which illuminates history on the strength of its argument. Cohn and Ley still owe their readers evidence of a coherent tradition, whose adoption and transformation through Hitler into a concrete and precisely identifiable goal of action and caused the Holocaust. In order to lend his thesis plausibility (and following on Eric Voegelin's work), Ley sees in National Socialism a political religion. Whether one can and should grant a polit-

According to Hitler's own assertions, he perceived himself as a tool of "providence" or pretended "to act in the spirit of the Almighty Creator."[130] In Hitler's view of the world and history, providence and destiny were interchangeable concepts. He traced his calling to be the Führer of the German nation back to both destiny and providence. The "Almighty God" had to share His omnipotence with the "will of the gods"; he placed the "wisdom of providence" in competition with the power of destiny.[131] It is evident that he sought and desired distance from self-characterizations rooted in the Judeo-Christian tradition. In contrast to the concepts of the Messiah, Redeemer, and Savior proper to the Judeo-Christian traditions, the vagueness of Hitler's concept of providence protected him from the misunderstanding that he borrowed from the language of the Christian church or the Jewish synagogue.

Hitler legitimized his sense of a mission only by falling back on the concept of providence. In a speech given on 7 September 1932 in the *Zirkus Krone* in Munich, he asserted, "[I] know that I have been determined by providence to carry out my mission."[132] After the seizure of power, he believed that he was following, "with instinctive assurance," the path "providence bade me to go."[133] In Vienna,

ical movement which sought to legitimize itself with the aid of pseudo-religious semantics the status of a religion is a question of heuristic principles. Ley answers this question without reservation in the affirmative; I must, on principle, answer in the negative. National Socialism, in my opinion, was not a political religion, but rather a political movement which, on the basis of its claims to being a totality, politicized and misused religion as a useful ideology for its goals of amassing and maintaining power.

[128] Behrenbeck 117.

[129] Behrenbeck 463.

[130] Werner Hamerski, "'Gott' und 'Vorsehung' im Lied und Gedicht des Nationalsozialismus," *Publizistik*, vol. 5 (1960), 282.

[131] Hamerski 282f. For the interchangeability of "providence" and "destiny," see Hitler's speeches of 28 April 1939 and 30 May 1942. In April 1939, he said: "I can only express my deepest feelings in the form of humble gratitude to providence which summoned me and allowed me to succeed in rising up from the position of an once-unknown soldier of the war to that of the Führer of my beloved people." (Max Domarus, *Hitler. Reden und Proklamationen 1932–1945*, vol. 2, 1. Halbband, 1939–1940 (Munich, 1965), 1148.) In May 1942, he asserted: "It is for good reason that destiny has had me make this long journey from an unknown soldier of the World War to Führer of the German nation, to Führer of the German military." (Domarus, vol. 2, 2. Halbband, 1941–1945 (Munich, 1965), 1887.)

[132] Domarus, vol. 1, 1. Halbband, 1932–34 (Munich, 1965), 135.

[133] Domarus, vol. 1, 2. Halbband, 1935–38 (Munich, 1965), 606.

on 9 April 1938, he explained, "I believe that it was also God's will to send a boy from here to the Reich, to have him grow up, to raise him to the position of Führer of the nation, in order that he would be able to lead his homeland back to the Reich. There is no higher determination, and we are nothing more than its tools."[134] Hitler had a personal communication sent to Mussolini on 25 February 1943 which read, "I view it as a blessing of providence that I was chosen to lead my *Volk* in a war such as this."[135] He considered the fact that he had survived the assassination attempt of 20 July 1944 unscathed to be a "confirmation" of the "mission" granted him by the "hand of providence" to champion uncompromisingly the interests of his *Volk*.[136]

Hitler's "Lord God" and "Almighty" was not the God of western Christian history; he was the German national god who "let iron be grown" in order to make the Germans the ruling people in the center of Europe. The cultural formative power of religious symbols, sentiments, and values were employed to achieve political goals with the aid of ideological constructs labeled as providence. Hitler's recourse to the concept of providence was not the expression of a genuinely religious consciousness. In consciously endowing politics with sacred qualities or religion with political, Hitler sanctified his aspirations to and preservation of power. To subjugate all areas of life to the diktat of politics originated in the desire for totality and amounted to an attempt to reverse once again the processes of societal differentiation which had given modern society its unmistakable character. Hitler was characterized as a redeemer and savior only in public speeches given by party supporters and in poems and texts, which were used during public ceremonies. These appellations are among those used in the National Socialist movement's public language of worship and celebration, not among those used by Adolf Hitler himself. The messiah was a concept which held Judeo-Christian connotations; as such, it was neither used in Hitler's self-characterizations, nor among the linguistic resources of his admirers and party supporters.

---

[134] Domarus, vol. 1, 2, 849.
[135] Domarus, vol. 2, 2, 1994.
[136] Quoted in Steffahn, Claus Schenk Graf von Stauffenberg, 10.

2. *The Führer as Messianic Savior in the Religious Worldview of Patriotic-Germans and Nationalist Christians*

Messianism had an especially formative influence on the image of history and the present held by the "Glaubensbewegung deutsche Christen" ["German Christian religious movement"] which professed a "sort of belief in Christ" "in accordance with the German spirit of Luther and heroic piety."[137] Characteristic of this sort of devoutness was the conviction that Jesus had been an "Aryan Galilean" and not a "Jew by race." Spokesmen of this theology and piety felt obliged to battle resolutely against the Paulist-Judaic theology which had "made the heroic doctrine of the Redeemer into a belief system for weaklings and the Aryan hero into an oriental milksop."[138]

The "Deutsche Christen" considered themselves the "SA of Jesus Christ" and deemed it their particular religious duty to provide the National Socialist political program with recognition and legitimacy within Protestantism. To ministers who professed a belief system oriented around German ethnicity, "Hitler was the 'man sent by God to establish for Germany a community of the *Volk* from all walks of life and all classes, on a path consecrated by sacrifice.'"[139] In 1932, Julius Kuptsch, a minister from Riesenburg in East Prussia, published several editions of his work entitled *Christentum im Nationalsozialismus* [*Christianity in National Socialism*]. In it, he asserted, "National Socialism is utterly convinced that it is the tool and executor of the divine will in Germany."[140] Its "principles, aspirations, and actions" constitute the "practical application of the teachings of Christianity."[141] According to Kuptsch, this applied to the Jewish question as well. National Socialism realized "the teachings of Christianity when it seeks through words and deeds to put Jewry in its place, to remove it from all public offices and positions, and to call it to account for its atrocities;

---

[137] From "Richtlinien" ["Guidelines"] of the "German Christian Religious Movement" published in 1932. Quoted in Günter Brakelmann, "Hoffnungen und Illusionen evangelischer Prediger zu Beginn des 'Dritten Reiches': Gottesdienstliche Feiern aus politischen Anlässen," *Die Reihen fast geschlossen. Beiträge zur Geschichte des Alltags unterm Nationalsozialismus*, eds. Detlev Peukert and Jürgen Reulecke (Wuppertal, 1981), 129.

[138] Artur Diner, *197 Thesen zur Vollendung der Reformation. Die Wiederherstellung der reinen Heilandslehre* (Leipzig, 1926), 12. See also pages 31f.; 37.

[139] Quoted in Karl-Wilhelm Dahm, *Pfarrer und Politik. Soziale Positionen und politische Mentalität des deutschen evangelischen Pfarrerstandes zwischen 1918 und 1933* (Cologne, 1965), 203.

[140] Julius Kuptsch, *Christentum im Nationalsozialismus*, 2d ed. (Munich, 1932), 36.

[141] Kuptsch 19.

Jewry promotes animosity towards Christianity and mockery of Christian morality; it assaults the morality of the German *Volk* with its sexual literary filth and its journalism and arts (Piscator's stage and others)." In that National Socialism made it forbidden and impossible for Jews "to work in their anti-Christian and un-German way," he recognized himself "as God's soldier who engages in the decisive battle for the entire world against every anti-Christian and go less aspiration of the Jews and their Marxist henchmen on German soil."[142] In *Im dritten Reich zur dritten Kirche* [*Concerning the Third Church in the Third Reich*], which appeared after Hitler's seizure of power, Kuptsch asserted with prophetic pathos, "Millions of professed German Christian people of all confessions" have "correctly recognized" Adolf Hitler "as the savior, sent by God Himself, of both the German *Volk* and the Christian church."[143]

In the Thüringen church movement of "Deutsche Christen," Hitler was characterized as the "Führer of God's mercy," "who is sent to our *Volk* and our world to break the power of darkness."[144] The chorus "Now thank ye all our God" was made topical with respect to the "world transformation" achieved by Hitler in an updated refrain. It now read: "Now thank ye all our God, Who led our people, out of night and affliction to light, as we have recently seen! When did the yoke break? When was the clear peal at last heard? When God sent the man who triumphed for His *Volk*."[145] Hitler assumed characteristics similar to Christ; "Through him and in him we can see the savior in the history of the Germans." "Adolf Hitler is the word of a savior who shall become and has become flesh and blood in the German *Volk*."[146] Political mysticism displaced political rationality.

In a sermon given on 3 February 1933 in Berlin's *Marienkirche*, Minister Joachim Hossenfelder, the foremost theological leader of the "Deutsche Christen," interpreted the thirtieth of January, the day on which Hindenburg named Adolf Hitler the Chancellor of the German Reich, as the "great," "fortunate hour" granted the German *Volk* by

---

[142] Kuptsch 27f.

[143] Kuptsch, *Im dritten Reich zur dritten Kirche* (Leipzig, 1933), 10.

[144] Hans-Joachim Sonne, *Die politische Theologie der Deutschen Christen. Einheit und Vielfalt deutsch-christlichen Denkens, dargestellt anhand des Bundes für deutsche Kirchen, der Thüringer Kirchenbewegung "Deutsche Christen" und der Christlich-deutschen Bewegung* (Göttingen, 1982), 91f.

[145] Sonne 93.

[146] Sonne 93f.

God. He spoke of the "day of fulfillment" on which the German people's long-harbored political and ideological longings had become reality. Hossenfelder formulated his historical-theological explanation as follows: ["God acts] through Christ. Christ makes history through men whom He calls. To our German *Volk* in need He has always granted men who appeared before the *Volk* like a miraculous sending and who themselves knew something of God's mystery which was within them and was done through them."[147]

To the "*Volk* in need" in 1914, God had sent Hindenburg as its savior. In the present state of despair, He had sent "the best man imaginable, a man of a unified whole, cast of purity, piety, vigor, and strength of character, our Adolf Hitler." With unbroken faith in the divine sending of the new chancellor, Hossenfelder asserted, "In our time of need—in which not only mere existence is at stake, but much more, the soul of the German *Volk*—God created a man, one among millions of the World War, and gave him the greatest mission of our history: to wrench the German *Volk* out of the depths of its despair and restore to it its faith in life."[148]

The "Day of Potsdam" (21 March 1933), the day on which Paul von Hindenburg, the old President of the Reich, and Adolf Hitler, the new Chancellor of the Reich, shook each other's hands over the grave of Frederick the Great in the garrison church in Potsdam, was perceived by Protestant ministers and laypeople as "divine intervention in the world after an age of decline."[149] The organizers of the spectacular ritual thought of it as the symbolically represented alliance between the "Teutonic and Prussian worlds." Historians loyal to the party interpreted it as the "unification of the German nationalist movement with the old-Prussian elements." Protestant preachers saw in the event a religious and national awakening[150] desired by God, from which a new Reich of the future, the "Holy Germany" would arise.[151] In their sermons, Protestant pastors extolled Hitler's seizure of power as the turning-point in history through the hand of God.

---

[147] Quoted in Brakelmann, "Hoffnungen und Illusionen", 130f. Also Klemperer, 67.
[148] *Ibid.*
[149] Werner Freitag, "Nationale Mythen und kirchliches Heil: Der 'Tag von Potsdam'," *Westfälische Forschungen* 41 (1991), 410. Freitag provides a vivid depiction of this event (379–430).
[150] Schreiner, "Führertum" (above, note 52), 236, fn. 19; Freitag 411.
[151] Freitag 414.

In an Easter message of 1933, the head of the Berlin church proclaimed that God had spoken to the German people "through a great turning point [*Wende*]."[152] The press wrote of the "reawakening of the nation," the "great day of resurrection," the "old spirit of Frederick" who had arisen "against the spirit of Weimar," and of "the sending of Hitler" who "had come at the right hour."

It was not only in the cities that ministers and devout laypeople offered voluntary religious-political interpretations of the National Socialist dictatorship. In the provinces and the country there were many who did the same—in droves. In secular ceremonies to celebrate the opening of the Reichstag by Adolf Hitler on March 21, local dignitaries gave addresses which call to mind the religious pathos in the sermons of the German Christian ministers. In Lünne in Westphalia, Mayor Schlegtendal began "in a voice which resounded afar" his "striking address, which was often interrupted by spontaneous applause," with the following sentence: "On the twenty-first of March, the first day of spring, we greet the reawakened German Reich, the beginning of a new epoch of German history." He went on to say that it was Adolf Hitler, "the heroic man who, from small beginnings, created the powerful movement of National Socialism," who "has saved us with God's help. Let us welcome him with shouts of jubilation. May God protect his life and his work!" According to this speaker, Adolf Hitler had saved them from international Marxists and Muscovites, and from those of foreign races, who would no longer rule over them. They would henceforth only be ruled by "a German of German blood and with a German heart" and "according to German principles." There would be "no class war, but the cooperation of all," "not in the service of the individual, but in the service of the state." The speaker's summons to welcome the new Führer of the German nation with shouts of jubilation calls to mind the shouts of "hosanna" with which Jesus was met when he entered Jerusalem. Eschatology plays a role in his language when he quoting verses of Max of Schenkendorf ascribed to Adolf Hitler the task of once more struggling "in earnest spiritual battle" to conquer "the final enemy." In language colored by eschatological references, the last enemy was described as "anarchy, Bolshevism, the spirit of lies and internationalism, of inciting the people, and of factiousness."[153]

---

[152] Freitag 403.

[153] *Lünner Zeitung*, No. 69 (22 Mar. 1933). See also Freitag 416.

3. *The Führer as Seen from the Point of View of the History of Salvation [Heilsgeschichte] in Theological, Historical and Germanistic Studies*

Scholars of theology, history, and German studies lent support to the ideas which were presented to people in churches and public places concerning the messianic role of the Führer. The Protestant theologian Paul Althaus saw in the National Socialist Revolution the guiding hand of God. In the formation of the new state, the God of our fathers, who was identical to the "God of German history,"[154] had demonstrated His power to create history. For Althaus, it was therefore not difficult to welcome "the German *Wende* of 1933 as a gift and miracle from God."[155]

Similar attempts were made in the Catholic church to forge bridges between the church and National Socialism. To strengthen these bridges, however, Catholic authors did not rely on metaphors of *Heilsgeschichte* to make the Führer acceptable and worthy of reverence as a savior sent by God. Catholic theologians and writers sought and found access to National Socialism with the aid of the concept of *analogia entis* characteristic of Catholic thought. They also called attention to ideational and spiritual similarities between the two which gave the appearance that it was both advisable and imperative that the Catholic Church and the National Socialist state mutually view each other as partners of elective affinity with the same goals and interests. The "Reich" as an order of governmental and political life desired by God, the bearer of which could not be a republic, was a reflection of God's Reich ["Kingdom"], "a reflection of the supernatural," "a political analogy" to the "eternal kingdom." "The one Führer" corresponded to the "one God."[156] In March 1933, Ildefons Herwegen, an abbot from the Benedictine Abbey Maria Laach, maintained that he had identified values and ideals which established these similarities between the Church and the Third Reich. They were "gradation and structure," "authority," "leadership," "a spirit

[154] Althaus, "Volks-Geschichte" 20.

[155] Althaus, "Das Ja der Kirche zur deutschen Wende," *Die deutsche Stunde der Kirche* (Göttingen, 1933), 5.

[156] Klaus Breuning, *Die Vision des Reiches. Deutscher Katholizismus zwischen Demokratie und Diktatur (1929–1934)* (Munich, 1969), 193f. See also Breuning, "'Consecratio mundi' im 20. Jahrhundert. Vom Staat zurück zum Reich?," *Probleme der Entsakralisierung*, ed. Hartmut Bartsch (Frankfurt a.M., 1970), 136.

of community," "preservation of the totality," and "the totality of all relations in life."[157]

The Catholic Church historian Joseph Lortz (1887–1975), who became a member of the NSDAP in 1933, wrote an essay in that year entitled "Katholischer Zugang zum Nationalsozialismus" ["Catholic Access to National Socialism"]. In it he referred to the fundamental affinities between National Socialism and Catholicism, "to affinities which run astonishingly deep" and joyfully brought to awareness "how, quite unsuspectingly, from being earlier putative opponents, the best of our old Catholic strength is summoned to work along with the others on laying the new foundations of the 'Reich'."[158] Lortz named the following similarities which enabled German Catholicism to resolve "the problem of giving consent to National Socialism within oneself": "National Socialism is in its essence opposed to Bolshevism, Liberalism, and Relativism (a)."[159] "National Socialism is the avowed opponent of atheist movements and public immorality, both of which predominate as the continuing consequence of liberalistic self-indulgence and loss of self-control and make life un-Christian." National Socialism "acknowledges as fundamental the God-given structure of human society and rejects the leveling of society, which truly destroys life, as a fatal fundamental error (b)."[160] From the "Catholic affirmation of the natural order of creation," it follows that "every national, or rather, every ethnic individuality [is] desired by God" which is committed "to remaining true to this way of being desired by God and to perfecting it (c)."[161] And, he continues, "In his encyclic *Quadragesimo anno*, Pope Pius XI called for the construction of society according to station as a remedy for the seemingly irreparable damage done to society. After many approving and many useless speeches, he who shall realize this command has appeared in the National Socialist Party (d)."[162] For the Catholic belief in revelation, it was "of great value" that the significance of the profession to a *Weltanschauung* "is instilled to an unexpected degree

[157] Breuning, "Consecratio mundi" 141.

[158] Joseph Lortz, "Katholischer Zugang zum Nationalsozialismus," *Reich und Kirche. Eine Schriftenreihe*, 2d ed. (Münster, 1934), 9. The first edition of this series appeared in 1933 and included the essay by Lortz.

[159] Lortz 9.

[160] Lortz 10f.

[161] Lortz 12f.

[162] Lortz 13.

in the broadest social strata once again as a valuable pattern of behaviour"—a fact which should occasion the church "to welcome [National Socialism] gratefully as an ally of the first order (e)."[163] "National Socialism's rejection of intellectualism" and its demand for a spiritual life oriented towards the return to a unified image of man wondrously concurs with the principles of classical Catholic thought, for the purity of which it has been struggling with all its might for decades (f)." Through "its Christian teaching, 'Service before self'" as well as "through the general emphasis on the priority of the community over that of the individual," National Socialism overcomes the one-sidedness of subjectivism, "of the particularistic Germanic character," and brings forth a *Volkstum* which shall act as "native soil for the growth of the church."[164]

In an article for the journal *Germania* entitled "Unser Kampf um das Reich" ["Our Battle for the Reich"], Lortz appealed to the conscience of German Catholics. "Our *Volk*, our Reich, stands under its Führer in a decisive battle. The longing of a thousand years of German history shall finally be consummated in that this *Volk* shall become a unified whole. . . . 'May Your Reich come to us!' For us, this plea holds particular resonance and a certain obligation; for the coming of God's Kingdom shall fulfill and consecrate our Third Reich."[165] Like the concepts of the messianic savior and bringer of salvation evoked by Protestant theologians and preachers, the mysticism of the Reich which was cultivated by Catholic authors proved itself in political practice to be a reactionary and anti-democratic ideology.

Historians who interpreted the National Socialist revolution as the fulfillment of hopes and promises supported their theses using interpretive models of the concept of history from the Old Testament. In 1933, Johannes Haller, a historian who taught at the University of Tübingen, wrote in the foreword of the new edition of *Epochen der deutschen Geschichte*, "That which belief and hope once were has become a reality. The day has come." He celebrated the commencement of a new age through the metaphor for an epoch which had been used from the time of the Humanists to Hegel. "The night which engulfed us has yielded to a new dawn. The sun has arisen over Germany, more quickly than the most audacious hope had

[163] Lortz 13f.; 20.
[164] Lortz 14f.
[165] Breuning, "Vision des Reiches" 195.

dared to imagine. And its first rays promise that new bright day which will allow us to forget what we have suffered."[166] The function of prophet, which Haller assumed in 1933 as a historian, had nothing whatsoever to do with science. An inherently historical purpose had lived on in faith alone. The process of achieving it had been divided into ages of promise and ages of fulfillment. Haller expressed a secularized form of the messianism of the Old Testament, taken from the *Heilsgeschichte* and applied to world and national history.

Hans Naumann, a scholar of early German literature in Bonn, did the same. In his "Rede zum Geburtstag des Führers" ["Speech for the Führer's Birthday"] on 20 April 1937, he referred to the "individual heroes of our old sagas," the "dozen great figures of our history," and "Odin of myth," to describe the One, who was incarnated in the hero, Führer, and general, and was the moving and salvational force in the history of the German people. Because Naumann held the view that the "myth of remote antiquity" had come true especially clearly in the "most recent age," he allowed for no doubt as to whom fate had chosen as the savior promised by myths, sagas, and history. It was "our Führer of the new beginning, our master of the reconstruction."[167]

VI. *Objections, Opposition, and Critical Voices*

Hitler's rise to power constituted a German eventuality, not an inevitable German fate. The reality of Hitler's seizure of power was caused by many and diverse factors: political, economic, cultural, and historical. The pathological longing for a leader who would save the German people was unquestionably among the anti-western, anti-rational, and anti-democratic traditions and tendencies which made the collapse of the Weimar Republic possible, imaginable, and feasible. Those who voiced criticism and warnings against the devastating consequences of the myths of both Reich and Führer found little or no resonance. Their existence and attempts to be heard deserve, however, to be mentioned and remembered.

The sociologist Franz Oppenheimer pointed out that the idea that the world and history are created by heroes was "the last obstacle

[166] Schreiner, "Führertum" 231.
[167] Schreiner, "Barbarossa" 558.

to the political emancipation of humanity." The commonly held belief, according to which "powerful members of the master race made history" and, therefore, "strong characters" "will make history" again, would drive society "to commit atrocities in an unprecedented revolution."[168] Historians of the Middle Ages who supported the Weimar state and constitution issued warnings against the romantic glorification of and belief in the Reich, Führer, and fealty. They also cautioned against the attitude of mind which gave credence to the idea that the key to being saved from the state of crisis would be found in an authoritarian state ideal.[169] Carl Jakob Burckhardt endeavored to explain to his contemporaries that the flight into myth could be reconciled neither with the rationality of the modern world, nor with the rational principles of a liberally constituted state. "The secret emperor—the Hohenstaufen in Kyffhäuser—the unknown man with the sign on his forehead, in the middle of tumultuous throngs of the people! How long have such bearers of hope, these archaic images of souls, from texts ranging from children's fairy tales to opera librettos, been presented to this people as the fulfillment of their peculiar longing, a people who act rationally and objectively when they are in their factories and offices."[170] Burckhardt cautioned against rashly placing trust in the future of a heroic past, against romantic "hero-worship,"[171] against irrational myths and "unhealthy hopes for the future,"[172] as well as against the "feminine character" of the masses who constantly seek "the strong man, the father who will be in command."[173]

In an article for the *Neue Rundschau*, the philosopher Ernst von Aster wrote in 1932: "To the National Socialist agitation, Germany is the enslaved martyr among the people to whom ascent is promised if only it does not lose faith in itself; the turns of phrase, the words themselves call conspicuously to mind the messianic promises with

---

[168] Franz Oppenheimer, *Großgrundeigentum und soziale Frage. Versuch einer neuen Grundlegung der Gesellschaftswissenschaft*, Jan. 1922: 221f.

[169] Schreiner, "Barbarossa" 555.

[170] Carl Jacob Burckhardt, *Briefe 1919–1969. Gesammelte Werke*, vol. 6 (Bern, 1971), 81. (Quoted from a letter to Hugo von Hofmannsthal of 3 Jan. 1925.)

[171] Burckhardt 146. "It is not a good sign that the Germans now long for heroes and hero-worship. Should the heroes for whom they now long come, they will not improve the course of the world, quite the opposite." (From a letter to Hugo von Hofmannsthal of 9 Dec. 1927.)

[172] Burckhardt 142.

[173] Burckhardt 39.

which the Judaism of exile repaired its injured pride in orgies of fantasy."[174] The author was aware, too, of the hidden dangers which the "religion of today's nationalism" posed for the freedom of spiritual life.[175] "The desire to see and unshackle a 'religious' movement in today's modern nationalism," argued von Aster, "is tantamount to taking a step backwards, not just back through the nineteenth century, but back through the Renaissance into the Middle Ages. Yet back into the Middle Ages without Christianity, without the guiding concept of *civitas Dei*, which shall be replaced by a ceaseless battle of the peoples for power and *Lebensraum*—by the idea of a *civitas terrena* which, in the most extreme sense of the idea, leads to utter self-mutilation and self-destruction."[176]

The Protestant theologian, Richard Karwehl, a student of Karl Barth, published an essay in 1931 entitled "Politisches Messiastum" ["Political Messianism"], subtitled "Zur Auseinandersetzung zwischen Kirche und Nationalsozialismus" ["The Confrontation Between the Church and National Socialism"].[177] Karwehl wrote, "In National Socialism we have before us a secularized eschatology."[178] "The Messianism of Judaism" is being "replaced and surpassed by Germanic messianism" in the ideology of National Socialism.[179] The National Socialist movement, Karwehl continued, had borrowed "its essential concepts from the church and quietly transformed them. Original sin is now sin against blood. The Aryan prototype has come to be that which is created in the image of God. Banishment from paradise means the leveling of the race through 'violation of blood.' The party program is immutable and infallible just as the dogma of the church is. The Reich [Kingdom] of God is being replaced by the 'Third Reich.'"[180] Karwehl remarks critically that, "The prophecy of the church is so fully effaced that even Protestant preachers confuse the legitimate eschatology of the church's teachings with the secularized eschatology of the racial nationalist movement and enthu-

---

[174] Von Aster 44.
[175] Von Aster 43.
[176] Von Aster 47.
[177] Richard Karwehl, "Politisches Messiastum. Zur Auseinandersetzung zwischen Kirche und Nationalsozialismus," *Zwischen den Zeiten. Eine Zweimonatsschrift* 9 (1931), 519–43.
[178] Karwehl 539.
[179] Karwehl 540.
[180] Karwehl 540.

siastically fall in with the National Socialist front."[181] Karwehl reclaimed the politically unadulterated authenticity of Christian eschatology. He hoped to prevent his colleagues from improperly using Christian doctrine as a means of interpreting and legitimizing National Socialism.

Final Remarks

In the name of religion, history, and science, heroic images of the past and present, which were evoked and cultivated during the Weimar Republic, deprived the Republic of its legitimacy when it was struggling for its very existence. They reinforced the "latent willingness for charismatic leadership."[182] They articulated hopes for a leader who would make Germany strong once again, who would follow his own "genius," and whose decisions would not be limited and bound by a constitution and a parliament. They contributed to the definition of the political, economic, and social crises which came to a head after 1929, that is, the instability of the government, the world economic crisis, and the six million unemployed, as a situation which could only be controlled by the unrestrained employment and the extraordinary strength of a charismatic personality, not by parliamentary governing bodies. Societal ills, the danger of inflation, and the fear of one's very existence being threatened and endangered by communism created an atmosphere of catastrophe and apocalypticism, which allowed "the longing for a strong man and the heroic figure of salvation" to predominate.[183] Hitler found credence for his claim to be able to overcome the crisis. He presented himself as the savior sent and called by "providence." He did not develop a rationally thought-out program for overcoming the crisis, but rather promised that he would establish a completely new order. The religious metaphors in Hitler's speeches and the embellishment of his public appearances with mythic symbols and cult rituals contributed to his ability to move his listeners, spectators, and participants to emotional devotion to his person and his political goals.

---

[181] Karwehl 542.

[182] M. Rainer Lepsius, "Das Modell der charismatischen Herrschaft und seine Anwendbarkeit auf den 'Führerstaat' Adolf Hitlers," Lepsius, *Demokratie in Deutschland. Soziologisch-historische Konstellationsanalysen* (Göttingen, 1993), 100.

[183] Klaus Hildebrand, *Das vergangene Reich. Deutsche Außenpolitik von Bismarck bis Hitler 1871–1945* (Stuttgart, 1995), 515.

Stirred-up emotions, which quickly developed into thoughtless allegiance, displaced political rationality. Aesthetically mediated fascination, which abruptly turned into blind enthusiasm, prevented rational, analytical skepticism from prevailing.

The enthusiastic turn towards heroic figures and messianic leaders in the nineteenth and early twentieth century was not a characteristic particular to Germans. The worship of national heroes is a common European phenomenon; it is not a *Sonderweg* of German history. Nations desirous of unity cultivated images of heroic historical figures.[184] The belief in a leader chosen by fate or divine providence is found amongst all peoples over whom autocratic sovereigns and politicians assumed power in the nineteenth century. The leader "was not so much conceived of as a 'great man' in the sense of the Enlightenment or of German Idealism, but as a 'strong man' and was hoped for in times of crisis."[185] In a lecture given in Paris at the Sorbonne in 1882, Ernest Renan, a historian of religion, described the significance of hero-worship for the coherence of a nation: "A heroic past, great men, glory (I mean true glory)—that is the

[184] In May, 1840, Thomas Carlyle gave a series of lectures on heroes, hero-worship, and heroicism in history in order to furnish proof that hero-worship is the strongest and most tried and true way of stabilizing political and social orders. His London audience, "aristocratic in class and reason," was, as he later reports, "to a great degree astonished and delighted" by his lectures. They laughed and applauded without becoming aware of the fact that Carlyle's ideas contained "dangerous explosive material." (Ernst Cassirer, *Vom Mythos des Staates* (Zürich, 1949), 246.) When Carlyle's book, entitled *On Heroes, Heroe-Worship, and the Heroic in History*, was published in 1841 and translated shortly thereafter into German, it was read voraciously by the so-called German *Bildungsbürger*. The German translation, *Helden, Heldenverehrung und das Heroische in der Geschichte*, was republished no less than three times between 1846 and 1898. According to a political encyclopedia published in 1861, Carlyle's book corresponded to that "fundamental trend of our own age... which all too easily instills powerful minds with a belief in their own messianic destiny" and strengthens their conviction "that they are destined like Caesars for the throne." (Groh 740f.) After 1945, when searching for historical causes for Hitler's seizure of power, people made "Carlyle more or less responsible for the entire ideology of National Socialism." Carlyle's "ideas of political leadership" had, accordingly, effectively facilitated and promoted Hitler's seizure of power. Carlyle, therefore, counted among those men "who had accomplished the most for the future 'march of Fascism.'" In 1933, H.F. Griesson published a lecture on "Carlyle and Hitler," in which he used the example of Hitler's seizure of power in order to illuminate the conditions under which "the emergence of a hero, as Carlyle conceived of him, are caused or at least made possible." (Cassirer 247f.) As a young man, Hitler is said to have read Carlyle's book with great enthusiasm.

[185] Groh, 731.

social capital upon which a nation is established."[186] Experiences of crisis and longings for a good, secure life led to the formation of savior figures who were to lift up bowed nations and make personal happiness attainable. It was left up to the Germans to choose for the fulfillment of their hopes a hero and savior who led them to catastrophe.

[186] Ernest Renan, "Das Plebiszit der Vergeßlichen. Über Nationen und den Dämon des Nationalismus—Ein Vortrag aus dem Jahre 1882," *Frankfurter Allgemeine Zeitung* 73 (27 Mar. 1993) "Bilder und Zeiten" section 2.

LINES, CIRCLES, POINTS: MESSIANIC EPISTEMOLOGY IN COHEN, ROSENZWEIG AND BENJAMIN

Robert Gibbs

The impact of Messianism on epistemology appears most forcefully in the works of a set of German-Jewish thinkers. In their works we see the claim advanced that truth lies in the messianic future, and thus knowledge will be consummated in a future beyond our present. While what messianism promises for Cohen, Rosenzweig and Benjamin varies, all agree the truth is not known in the present, but can only be known in that future. The result is that the future orients all of our claims to know in the present and our claims to know about the past. In place of a view that holds that what is true is known in a present moment or that the originary past provides the truth, messianic epistemology holds out a hope for a future which can govern all knowledge. The significant result for each thinker, is that the task of knowing requires time, indeed requires history—because the future is temporally disconnected from the present. Temporalizing the truth leads to various ways of relating the past to the present. What the three ways share, however, is the sense that the need for historiography arises in the future, and in the epistemological implications of messianism. Only the future can make history true.

In some distinction to many of the interpretations of messianisms offered in this volume and in other historical writings, this paper will find that our ability and our responsibility to know history is distinctly messianic—and thus the possibility for historiography is in fact religious or theological, albeit in a somewhat unusual sense of that term. The study of history, thus, is part of an intellectual adherence to messianism. The three thinkers form a sequence that should not be seen as a progression. Instead, each offers a distinct model for interpreting history messianically. Of course, each thinker also has a much more complex interpretation of messianism. I have merely extracted the models from them, to indicate a set of possibilities that characterize the climax of Jewish thought in the period from the First to the Second World War.

I proceed by way of long quotations from the authors, each quotation parceled into smaller chunks for ease in reading. The chunks are numbered, and I have cited first the original German text and then the standard English translation for reference, but all translations are my own. My paper is a somewhat prosaic walking through a set of texts. I hope that the commentaries serve primarily to give insight into the models that are created within the texts of the thinkers. Just what sort of epistemology governs this commenting I leave for a discussion in another place.

Cohen's Line in Religion of Reason

The origin of this sequence is Hermann Cohen's *Religion of Reason out of the Sources of Judaism*, a work written but not completed during World War I.[1] The work proposes a rational construction of religion, but draws heavily on Jewish sources to provide its materials. Its ongoing problem is how to delineate the contribution that religion makes in distinction to those made by ethics. Both disciplines are rational, both address human action and interaction. The climax of the set of unique contributions made by religion is messianism—a vision of a world at peace in a cosmopolitan confederation of nations. Our interest, of course, is the epistemological significance of this vision.

> 1.1. 291–2/249–50 The messianic future is the first conscious expression of the opposition by ethical values to empirical sensibility. One can here simply signify it as the *ideal* in opposition to actuality.

For Cohen, Messianism is not merely a futural event. It is the future which stands against the present and the past. The very transcend-

[1] All citations are to first the German texts, and then to the standard translation, although all translations are my own. All of the quotes by Hermann Cohen are from *Religion der Vernunft aus den Quellen des Judentums*. Reprint of 2nd ed., 1928 (Fourier Verlag, Wiesbaden), 1988. English trans. by Simon Kaplan, *Religion of Reason Out Of the Sources Of Judaism* (Frederick Ungar Publishing Co., New York), 1971.

A helpful treatment of Cohen on history is found in Amos Funkenstein's *Perceptions of Jewish History* (University of California Press, Berkeley), 1993, pp. 270ff. In general, the whole volume provides the most extensive account of the issues discussed in this essay, albeit from quite a different viewpoint.

ence of ethics beyond our own memories and own present reality requires a temporality that is not just more of the same. The possibility, moreover, that the future can be used to judge both the present and the past makes a certain kind of cognition possible. The ethical vision is not simply a negation of the present. This is not the place to assess the viability of Cohen's pure idealism, an epistemology that is not as utterly out of favour as one might think. What we wish to see is how messianism enters into its general force-field. For messianism has a key role in Cohen's religion: the self-consciousness of the demand for ethics as other than empirical.

> 1.2. The ideality of the messiah, its meaning as idea, is shown in the overcoming of the personal messiah and in the solution of this visible image in the pure thought of time, in the concept of the *temporal age*. Time becomes future and only future. Past and present sink into this time of the future. This return into time is the purest idealization. Every existing thing disappears before the standpoint of this idea. Human existence sublates itself in this being of the future. Thus the thought of *history* arises for human life and for the life of the peoples.

But in this second chunk of text, we see just what this messianic future is: an age, indeed an age that is futural only, and as such becomes the transcendence of what ought to be against what now is only becoming. If the future is primary, as Cohen claims, then time itself becomes idealized, or becomes the schema of idealization. The transformation from a personal messiah to a messianic age is not described as an historical phenomenon, but as the production of a concept of time that privileges the ideal over the actual. A new age that is not now actual matters for humanity: it is the truth of existence. The past and present ages become significant only in the future age. The idea of history gains its salience because temporal change is the realization of the ideal. If we have a history, we can find the meaning in the future of the changes of our past and present.

> 1.3. The *Greeks* never had this thought of history, which has the future for its content. Their history is directed to their origins. Their history narrates their past of their nation. Other nations appear as an historical problem only for their travel narratives. A history of humanity is an impossible thought in this horizon. Humanity lived in no past and has not become alive in any present; only in the future can its form be brought to light. This form is an idea and no shadow image of a beyond.

And so Cohen uses Messianism to turn history around. The Greeks, and all the romantics, sought their origins. History looked back, often toward a Golden Age. Truth was in the past, and that ancient truth was under assault from change. Because humanity itself had never yet existed and did not exist in their time, the Greeks had no messianic vision of humanity. History could be told only about the past, not about the future. The knowledge proper to messianism is that proposition that what is to be known will only appear in the future. Again, for Cohen, this futural form is known through an idea, not by projecting an image from the present or past. The purity of rational ethics and rational religion produce a form which history can only foretell. History now must point the way towards a messianic future.

> 1.4. Even God's being becomes an other under the sway of this idea. The creator of heaven and earth does not suffice for this being of the future. He must create "a new heaven and a new earth." The being of previous history is also insufficient for nature; *development* is required for the course of things. And development presupposes a goal to which it strives. So the progress in the history of the human race is required.

The futurity of the idea of the messianic age now makes God change from merely a creator in the past to a new creator in a future. History cannot be an account merely of what has happened but becomes an account of the development of what has happened. Development, however, requires a goal. Cohen claims that the line we draw through the past events into the present is determined from a future point: the messianic age. Messianism, as the keen awareness of an ideal of humanity at peace, stands over against both the past and present, allowing us to discern in history a development leading to the future. The primacy of the future ideal determines the sort of history we can do: a linear developmental progress of the human race. History normed by the past, by origins, is marked by a decline and bears the sense that only what is the same is true. History normed by an ethical ideal in the future becomes a discovery of progressive development.

> 2.1. 306–7/262–3 Thus monotheism is in itself the immediate origin both for Messianism and for the concept of *World-history* as the history of humanity. Without the unique God, the idea of humanity could not arise. And without the idea of humanity history remains

> only a problem of knowledge of the past of peoples on the basis of one's own people.

In contrast to the historian who seeks the origins of monotheism, Cohen argues that monotheism is the origin of history, or rather of a specific sort of history: World history. World history requires a concept of humanity, indeed an historical concept of humanity. The world can appear as a world only through the universality of the concept of the human, a universality that is neither empirical nor static. Rather, humanity is an historical concept because its truth is in the future, in an ideal beyond what has happened so far. Cohen's claim is that only the unique God, standing against everything that exists in the world, provides the distance from our divisive and warring situation. Of course there is history that is not world-history, and it lacks a vision of humanity. Such history is turned only to the past, and to the past of one's own people. Such history lacks the ethical edge because it only bolsters one's particular people in its originary situation.

> 2.2. National history is thus generally not yet history. It cannot even have a methodical foundation, because it cannot construct a point of departure for a scientific orientation. Humanity must first become the object of *human love*, and thus also become the orientation for the problem of history.

Cohen, then, can take the bolder position and deny such historiography the status of history. What it lacks is precisely the philosophical conceptual resources to make itself "scientific", or we might say rigorous. While Cohen is not arguing that historians have to be theologians, he is claiming that the claim to be a methodical and rigorous historian will require an awareness of a norming goal for historical research. The goal is not a rosy picture of paradise, but rather an ethical vision of humanity, enlivened by a love of what is human, a love of humanity. Such a love does not simply embrace what is, but judges what is by what it should become. History becomes rigorous when the historian is oriented toward the historical materials by a goal of humanity. Cohen is arguing that such critical historical practice is only possible in relation to the goal, itself correlative with the unique God of monotheism.

> 2.3. *Deuteronomy* allows it to be known so clearly how the national history of Israel is an idealization from the historical point of its historical

> task, to be called to it for its future. Thus history, as literature of *historical writing*, here has such a naturalness and truthfulness. The idealization, if it is guided from a true idea, is altogether also subjectively the best instruction for truthfulness.

The paradigm of such history is Biblical historiography, particularly the Deuteronomical works, especially apparent in the canonization of Deuteronomy within the Torah. The repetition of the stories of the exodus and revelation, as well as the wandering, served as an innovation in the writing of historical literature. Cohen interprets the repetition, requiring a doubled reading of the two versions, as a self-conscious idealizing of the events narrated in the earlier books. The idealization does not portray the Jewish community in epochal terms nor as epitomes of virtue and righteousness. To the contrary, to call the community towards a messianic virtue, or at least towards a righteousness still lacking, the idealization is expressed as critique. National history is transformed into a story whose goal is not in the past but in the future. Typical of Cohen's idealism is the coordinate claim that not only is history now possible through idealization, but that such idealization is directed toward truthfulness. The historian gains truth not by a mere positivism, nor by a nationalistic recovery of origins, but by disciplining the events of the past for the sake of the future, a future that brings an ideal never seen before.

> 3.1. 311–2/267 The misery of Jewish history does not begin with the exile, because the loss of the nation state is already determined through messianism. But in the exile the *tragedy of the Jewish people* is grounded in all of its historical depth. How can a people persist and fulfill its messianic task if it is stripped of the universal human shelter, the state, in which the people develops? And nonetheless the situation of the Jewish people is such a form, and so also must be the meaning of Jewish history, if messianism constitutes this meaning.

Thus, the idealization of Jewish history, the source of all rigorous history—history that is world-history, governed by a messianic ideal—is a history of suffering. Idealization is not a spiritualization, despite a certain presumption that it would be Holy History (Heilsgeschichte) in which progress is marked by an ever rosier vision of humanity, improving in every era. Idealization requires an ongoing critique of what has happened. The progressive line seems to be attenuated by the consciousness that the ideal future will require the renunciation of force and power—which demands the very absence of national victories in the past and present. Despite, or perhaps because of, Cohen's philosophical justification of the state in relation to an ultimate international confederation, Cohen regards Jewish historiography as intrinsically a renunciation of the national state. Thus, he argues that the nation state must be historically removed from Judaism in order for the ideal of messianism to become operative. Exile is only a consequence of the messianic ideal and not its historical inception. Cohen's position is that the opposition messianism leveled at national history that seeks a past condition of perfection had to be translated into the suspension of the state for the Jews. The question of the meaning of history is raised precisely when a people insists that history has a meaning while renouncing the recognizable shelter in the storms of history, the state. If historiography is an expression of a messianic epistemology, then genuine history will be history that looks at peoples and institutions that are directed toward an ideal of humanity at the expense of having the national security that a state offers.

> 3.2. Whoever recognizes the genuine world-historical messianism of humanity as the task of the Jewish people, must catch sight in Jewish history the signpost for this goal. . . . Jewish history however, is understood as history, that is insofar as it displays ethical ideas, is an ongoing chain of human, of national misery. The servants of God were always despised and pierced, cut off from the land of life. And despite the astonishment at the continuation of this oddity amongst the people, thus remaining and thus always true, which is properly expressed in the original text: "And in its age, *who thought on it*?" [Isaiah 53.8]. The messianic people suffers as representative for human suffering. This perspective is no exaggeration of Israel's mission, if the messianic realization of monotheism is the historical task of the Jewish religion.

Hence, Cohen can claim that Jewish history will be the history that displays the way that historiography is messianic. But, in a somber expression of his piety, Cohen affirms that such history is not only messianic, idealizing, ethically normed, but is so as a line or chain of misery. He opts for a national historical interpretation of the suffering servant of Isaiah, even citing that text in the midst of this discussion. Precisely by lacking the state, by lacking material and imperial success in succeeding generations, Israel suffers as witness to the ideal that governs history, and thus historiography. When at any moment the present suffering is unobserved, the historical representation strikes astonishment in the world. Why should the Jews remain without the props of historical success? The mission of introducing the messianic ideal into the consciousness of the world is produced by surviving amidst suffering, but not only surviving one crisis, but rather an ongoing exposure throughout centuries of oppression. The line is a chain of misery, that the world may be astonished into recognizing that the Jews do not survive for the sake of national history, but for a history that judges the world, for the sake of all humanity. How can history become such an ideal history for the future, except by this chain of misery—for otherwise the power and success of the people or religion that bears the task would impugn its motives. While Cohen has a generally progressive vision of world history, the confrontation with Jewish history leads him to a mode of idealizing that is recognizably critical. A chain of misery is hardly what one normally associates with neo-Kantian ideal construction of historical meaning. The sacrifice in the present and the past that allows the future to bear the meaning of history, leads to a sacrifice within history that disrupts the very notion of progress that governs the view of the past and the present.

Rosenzweig's Circles in The Star of Redemption

We can notice in this somewhat difficult line of progress/line of misery that the task of narrating a history, born of a concern for the future, is normed by an ethical perspective, even as it is born of a messianic vision. But when we move to the second thinker, Franz Rosenzweig, we discover that the impact of messianism is not restricted to an historical narrative. Instead, the impact of the future on the present requires an act of hurrying the messiah. To accelerate messianism produces a different relation to historical time, focusing not on the chronological sequence, but on a calendrical socialisation of the hurry toward the future. While it is tempting to see Cohen's student, Rosenzweig, setting out to correct his teacher, I am afraid that such a view will not work. Indeed, the other tendency is stronger, at least in Rosenzweig's own reading of Cohen's final work: Rosenzweig interprets it as very much existentialist and as breaking away from Cohen's own system to belong together with Rosenzweig's own *Star*.[2]

[2] See "Einleitung in die Akademieausgabe der Jüdischen Schriften Hermann Cohens" in *Zweistromland* (Martinus Nijhoff, The Hague), 1984, pp. 177–224.

We will begin with a passage that forces the issue, where Cohen appears either as a typical believer in progress, or as a true messianic thinker who only dons progress as a disguise. The question, however, that governs this first text is how the future is the time of eternity and what sort of interruption such a future will bring into our experience of time.[3]

> 4.1. 252–3/226–7 For before everything this anticipation belongs to the future: that the end must be expected in each moment. It becomes the time of eternity thereby for the first time. . . . That each moment can be the last, makes it eternal. And even that each moment can be the last, makes it into the origin of the future as a series, each member can be anticipated through the first.

The nature of the messianic future, or as Rosenzweig terms it here, the time of eternity, is that it must be expected in each moment: it is not in the distant future. Unlike a future that could be extrapolated from a trend that leads from the past into the present, the eternal future will break into any such series. Any moment can be the ultimate moment of history, the real beginning of a future that we cannot predict. The discontinuity between what Cohen had called the ideal and the real is more marked. Not as a mark of insufficiency in the real—but only as a waiting for that stroke that breaks in upon our world. Messianism, in this sense, does not seem to direct us to draw a continuous function from past to present toward an ideal future.

> 4.2. This thought of the future now, that the kingdom "is amongst you" that it comes "today" this eternalizing of the moment is obliterated in the Islamic, as in the modern concept of temporal ages. . . . That every age is equally immediate to God, is also exactly the genuine thought of the pure historian, whose history has been extinguished into a mere tool for the knowledge of the past. Continuity, growth, and necessity appear most of the time to be at least as alive in the thought of progress as in the thought of the kingdom of God. But progress betrays its inner self through the concept of infinitude. If it

---

[3] All quotations from Rosenzweig are from *Der Stern der Erlösung* (Martinus Nijhoff, The Hague) translated as *The Star of Redemption* by William W. Hallo (Beacon Press, Boston), 1971.

A valuable study on these issues is Paul Mendes-Flohr's "Frans Rosenzweig and the Crisis of Historicism," in *The Philosophy of Franz Rosenzweig*, edited by Paul Mendes-Flohr (University Press of New England, Hanover and London), 1988, pp. 138–61.

> also will speak of "eternal" progress—in truth it is always means only "infinite" progress, a progress that always strides further on, where it has the guaranteed certainty that for each moment, more is to come into the sequence, and thus its becoming existent can be as certain as a past can be of its already existing.

And from this possibility born in the reality of the moment, making any moment the crisis point where the past is ruptured by something truly novel, Rosenzweig can level a critique of all attempts to homogenize historical time. I will ignore his basic contempt for Islam, but look instead at the interpretation of the "pure historian." Such an historian looks only to the past, and looks to the past merely to know. Like Cohen, Rosenzweig is trying to discern the aspect of historiography that imbues the practices of writing history with the depth of meaning that can justify the historian's own practices. Rosenzweig trained as an historian with Meinecke and knows that more is at stake than a merely contemplative relation to the past.

The difference between a progress that claims to lead toward a messianic future and a messianic future that comes and grows centers on the false claim that progress itself is eternal. Rosenzweig makes fun of it, pointing out that were progress itself eternal, it would be unending, infinite, without any possible closure. The homogenization of eras produces the notion that no era is capable of becoming the eternal time—the gap between real and ideal is structured so that the ideal is simply impossible. The real is denigrated, or perhaps elevated. Denigrated because it cannot become the ideal; elevated as defining the range of the possible. The world's exclusion of messianic time is achieved through continuity: any future moment is not eternal, not last, but must necessarily be followed by successors. There is always more to come, and so the certainty of a bad infinite of time is guaranteed. Rosenzweig thus connects the notion of a mere knowing of the past with a view of the future that excludes eternity. Only a future that can be last, that can conclude, is messianic.

> 4.3. Thus this genuine thought of progress resists nothing so much as the possibility that that "ideal goal" could and even must be reached, already in the next, yes or even in this very moment. It is the precise shibboleth, that the person who believes in the kingdom, who only in order to speak the language of the time uses the word *progress* and in truth means the kingdom, can be distinguished from the genuine worshipper of progress: whether he takes arms against the prospect and the duty to anticipate the "goal" in the next moment. Without

> this anticipation and the internal drive toward it, without the "will to bring the Messiah before his time" and the temptation to "force the kingdom of God" the future is no future, rather only one in an infinitely protracted duration, of a past projected forward. Because without such anticipation the moment is not eternal, rather it is one ever-enduring trudging on along the long highway of time.

Thus the vision of historiography bound to continuity and certainty takes a stance against the possibility that the ideal will be reached either tomorrow, or indeed even today. In a subtle comment, Rosenzweig indicates that one might only use the rhetoric of progress, but still anticipate the messiah in the next moment. I would suggest that for Rosenzweig, Cohen is just this one who only uses the word progress, but for us the point is to distinguish the one who is willing to anticipate, to be tempted to hurry the advent of the Messiah, and the historian who is certain that history must continue in a steady progressive motion. Such a view obliterates the eternal, but only knows an unceasing trudging through history. Such a trudger studies the past in order to make the future into a past, where no novelty is possible. Even if the line is at a positive slope and not merely always just the same, the constant slope means that the future is never capable of bringing the eternal. But how will history consider the past and temporality if it is to allow for a real future, an interruption of time by the eternal?

Rosenzweig's answer focuses on the way that the eternal is inserted into time by the calendar. In a hybrid of sociological and theological analysis, Rosenzweig argues that the repetitive cycles of the calendar allow for eternity to provide the social structure of our experience of time. The past becomes not a simple set of events, leading into the future, but a period, stretched-out in time, that repeats and recommences. Each week is the same week. Redemption arises precisely because the temporal creation of a community that can live together in its time is the first taste of eternity, or the messianic future. The week itself is given special interpretation by Rosenzweig:

> 5.1. 324–5/291–3 The week is set between the day and the year. By the orbit of the moon, it was based on heaven, but long ago it was disconnected from that, even where the phases of the moon still determine the measuring of time, and thus it became an authentic and purely human time. And purely human, is the change from work to rest day, that makes the week into a nunc stans for people posited as labor and contemplation. Unlike the day based in the changes of

> waking and sleeping, or the year in the change of sowing and harvesting, the week is without a basis in the created world, and for this reason in Scripture it is explained only as an analogy of the work of Creation itself. Thus the week with its day of rest is the proper sign of human freedom. Scripture thus explains it by its purpose and not its basis.

The social invention of the week arises in a willful disconnection from astronomy: the week is purely human because of the interruption of work with a day of rest. While the day follows the sun and its setting, and the year follows the sun through its seasons, the week is interpreted even in Scripture in terms of its purpose (rest) and not from its astronomical ground. Were people to live without the week, they would not know the rest that shapes the week, and indeed governs the workdays as well as the weekend. The goal of labor is rest (and not vice versa). Freedom is needed to set up the pause in working, freedom from working, but also freedom to ignore the nature that asks for work in its season.

> 5.2. The week is the true "hour" of all the times of the common human life, posited for people alone, set free from the orbit of the earth and thus completely a law for the earth setting the changing times of its service. It is to rule the service of the earth, the work of "culture" rhythmically, and to describe in miniature in the ever repeated presence, the eternal, in which the beginning and end come together, in the today of the imperishable. As a law of the culture of the earth made by people to set people free, the eternal is merely portrayed in the week, merely as earthly eternity. . . .

When Rosenzweig calls the week "the true 'hour'" he is interpreting the week as the key to temporal cycles. The hour is the unit that stretches out in time, having a beginning, middle and end, but then recommences. For Rosenzweig the hour institutes eternity in temporality: because eternity means that the moment can be the last, and thus will not be succeeded in a uniform sequence. The punctuation of the hour inserts the discontinuity of the future redemption, of the messianic age, into time. Cycles are neither linear nor simply the continuity of time. Rather, they represent the interruption and break-up of continuity. The week, with its Sabbath, rules our working life, our culture. The break of rest is "a miniature" of the break that the messianic era will bring.

> 5.3. In the everyday-every weekly—every yearly repetition of the circle of cultic prayer, faith makes the moment into an "hour", time becomes

> ready to accept eternity, and eternity, in that it finds acceptance in time, itself becomes—like time. But how then does the power to force eternity to accept the invitation reside in prayer?. . . Because time which is prepared for the visit of eternity is not the individual's time, not mine, yours or his secret time: is everyone's time. Day, week, year belong to everyone in common, are grounded in the world's orbit of the earth which patiently bears them all and in the law of labor on earth which is common to all. The clock's striking of the hour is for each ear. The times, which the cult prepares, are no one's own time without all the others.

The calendar of prayer not only gives shape to the work week, but it also allows eternity to enter time. The week becomes the central unit from which the year and the day are re-constructed. But if calendars insert eternity into time, how can that power belong to prayer itself? Rosenzweig notes that cultic time becomes common time through the fixed cycles, through the week and year. This commonality is the sign of eternity or of the messianic future. The Kingdom comes when the world shares in rest. The social nature of the calendar itself is the sign that cycles bring about redemption. The rest on the Sabbath, as foretaste of the messianic era, is not limited to the householders, but extends to the women, to the servants, to guests, and indeed to animals. The cycles interrupt time for everyone, and so hasten the messianic age.

And indeed, Rosenzweig is pointing toward not merely a social phenomenon, but a phenomenon that will allow us to see historiography differently. The cultic sequences of the year are the time by which we live, but also the time of memory. Historiography is not merely what is written on monuments and scrolls. History lives for a people in its calendar, lives not as past to be mindful of, but as a future and as the structure of the community.

> 6.1. 351–2/317 The eight-day holiday times of the Feast of Liberation from Egypt [Passover] and the Feast of Tabernacles [Sukkot] surround the two day of the Festival of Weeks [Shavuot]. Through these three, the procession of eternal history proceeds beyond the somewhat naturalistic eternal base of the year with its Sabbaths. Because they are only apparently feasts of commemoration [Erinnerung]. In truth in them the historical is utterly densely present, and what is said to each participant at the first one is valid for all of them: he must celebrate the feast as if he himself has been liberated out of Egypt. Beginning, middle and end of this national history, the founding, the climax and

> the eternity of the people—the old will be born anew with each new generation. No, with each new year's course and with each new year.

Rosenzweig's interpretation of Jewish time moves beyond the week with a consideration of the festivals that were pilgrimage festivals in Biblical times. Our concern is just how eternal history is instituted into the social time of the community. This history is not merely a sequence in the past (Exodus from Egypt, receiving the Ten Commandments at Mt. Sinai, and settling in the Land of Israel), but also is a theological sequence that leads the people from its founding to an eternal life (the messianic age). Thus the interpretation of these festivals concerns not only the community's relation to past history, but also its own theological experience. Rosenzweig's central claim is that to bear the full significance of eternalizing time, these events must not be merely left in a distant past. Because the meaning addresses the end of time, the future of redemption, what is celebrated is not merely the past working of God in Jewish history. The specific claim is that the Jew lives in the past event and does not merely represent a past event. The exodus is experienced: the celebrant was there! The cycling of the feasts is a cycling within one's life, not merely remembered, but actually lived both as history and as theological experience of creation-revelation-redemption. Moreover, the renewal of the people is not merely a question of generations, but instead is framed by the course of the year. Each new year brings the eternal historical sequence into the life of the community, in the guise of the history celebrated in the feasts. This importation of eternity into time structures history into a cycle that repeats. The promise of a messianic future does not make a line from past through present to future, but breaks lines. Interruptions, however, can become periodic cycles of time, and in each cycle there is a sequence of historical events. History in circles allows for the discontinuity of messianism to break into time, bestowing meaning and promise, without reducing the future to the past.

Benjamin's Points

The third member of my set of Jewish thinkers is Walter Benjamin, a critic, perhaps the model of what today is called cultural criticism. Benjamin represents a complex relation of theology and historiography. His last works were written in flight from the Nazi's, a threat that Cohen and Rosenzweig were spared by their respective deaths in 1918 and 1929. Benjamin did not write the sort of Jewish writings that either of the other did, but messianism figured in many important ways in his writings (not the least important influence is his friendship with Gershom Scholem, the pioneer in studies of Jewish Mysticism). But Benjamin refused Rosenzweig's circles as much as he rejected Cohen's idealistic linear progress. Before identifying the points that constitute Benjamin's epistemology, the vigorous refusal of Rosenzweig is worth a look.

> 7.1. Thesis XV (I, 701–2/*Ill.*, 261–2)[4] The consciousness of bursting the continuum of history is characteristic of the revolutionary classes in the moment of their action. The great revolution introduced a new calendar. The day, with which a calendar begins, functions as an historical time-lapse camera. And it is basically the same day, that always returns in the form of holidays, the days of remembrance [Eingedenkens].

Rosenzweig had recognized that revolution was a mode of hurrying the kingdom, of risking the violence against the old, as the very temptation of messianism now. Messianism is not merely knowing something, but also involves the possibility of a radical action in order to make the future happen now. Benjamin focuses on the bursting of the continuum—a theme familiar to us. But his point is that political action is keenly aware that consciousness must also be altered. The preferred choice is to initiate a new calendar. The calendar is built on repetitions in which the same returns each year. Moreover, the sequence in time that we had seen in Rosenzweig now has a perfect technological simile: an historical time-lapse camera. Benjamin does not simply contest Rosenzweig on the nature of historiography in the calendar. Rosenzweig had claimed that the holidays were only apparently commemorative. Benjamin, instead, considers them days of remembrance: in which there is just the

---

[4] Quotations by Benjamin are from two main texts: "Theses on the Philosophy of History" published in the *Gesammelte Schriften* in Vol. I, 2 (Suhrkamp, Frankfurt), 1974, and in English in *Illuminations*, trans. by Harry Zohn (Schocken, New York), 1969. Secondly, from Konvolut N of the Arcades Project, which was published in the *Gesammelte Schriften*, V, 2, and in English in *Benjamin: Philosophy, Aesthetics, History*, ed. by Gary Smith (University of Chicago Press, Chicago), 1989, translated by Leigh Hafrey and Richard Sieburth.

A valuable essay on Benjamin's Theses is Rebecca Comay's "Benjamin's Endgame". In *Walter Benjamin's Philosophy: Destruction and Experience*, eds. by Andrew Benjamin and Peter Osborne (Routledge, London), 1994, pp. 251–91.

re-insertion into the past, in distinction with mere re-presentation of the past into the present. In this text we see an invocation of the calendar with holidays, remembering historical events.

> 7.2. The calendar, therefore, does not count time like clocks. They are the monuments of an historical consciousness, and for a hundred years in Europe not even the slightest trace of them appears. This consciousness lingered in its own right when an incident happened during the July revolution.

The calendar with its cycles is a social monument, not quite a statue but a structuring of time: indeed, Benjamin recognizes that they are the monuments of a consciousness of history. The awareness of our history structures the time we live in. But, unlike Rosenzweig, Benjamin regards these cycles as obsolete. Modern Europe has ceased to recognize its own calendrical history. Perhaps Benjamin has in mind only the utter triumph of historicism and its sense of linearity and datability. But, written in Paris in flight from the Nazis, it is rather more likely that the kind of calendrical community, the community that shares time and in so doing hurries redemption is simply impossible. Rosenzweig's *Star*, was part of a program for revitalizing a dispirited Jewish community; Benjamin's life leads beyond any hope for such programs. Moreover, Benjamin's Marxist social critique alerts him to the more wide-spread dissolution of such community: the tyranny of consumerist capitalism, where the festivals are stripped of their historiographical meaning and of their redemptive sociological functions. Benjamin does linger over an event from the July revolution of 1830, which we will not explore. The calendar and its cycles neither binds a community together, nor is it the hope for our future. In its place is a less programmatic historiography, one that disrupts the continuity of time without building time upon a sequence of events.

> 9.1. N3,1 (V, 1, 577–78/50) What distinguishes the images from the "essences" of phenomenology is their historical index. (Heidegger seeks in vain to rescue history for phenomenology abstractly through "historicity".) These images are to be thoroughly delineated from the "historical sciences" categories, from the so-called habitus, the style, etc. The historical index of the images says not only that they belong to a determinate time, it says above all, that they first become legible in a determinate time. And indeed this "to be legible" is reached in a determinate critical point in the motion into its interior.

In the collection of notes on the theory of knowledge and the theory of progress for his unfinished *Arcades Project*, Benjamin explores non-linear models of historiography. And in a text that is widely cited, Benjamin identifies the relation of the past event to the present as a dialectic at a standstill. My interest with this fragment is the sort of connection between a past event and a present historian's account of the event. In other fragments, Benjamin addresses the way that the past event has to be blown out of its context, but here the specific relation between two points is examined.[5] Benjamin contrasts the images that constitute his historiography from both phenomenological essences and the positivist categories (like style). The historical index, marking a specificity in history, distinguishes his images from the other historian's concepts. But the indexicality is not a mark only of when something happened, but more importantly, of when it becomes interpretable in a historian's present. The two points are not simply fixed: the meaning of the historical event only becomes intelligible on reaching another shore. The points are, as it were, reserved for each other.

> 9.2. Every present is determined through these images, those that are synchronic with it: every now is the now of a determinate knowability. In it the truth is loaded with time to the point of exploding. (This explosion, is nothing other than the death of the intention, which coincides therefore with the birth of genuine historical time, the time of truth.) It is not that what is past throws its light on what is present or that what is present throws its light on what is past, rather the image is that in which the past and the present meet in a lightning flash in a constellation. In other words: image is the dialectic at a standstill.

The now of reading, of writing histories, is itself fully determined with a range of possible images, each coming from different points in the past and saturating the historian's present. What happens is not the calm prospect from a condescending present on the sorry past, nor is the truth unearthed in the past, a truth that has been true all along. The past and present meet in a lightning flash: each brings its own charge, its own energy, each contributes its own share to the image that now appears. Benjamin's interest in arresting the dialectic has much to do with stripping Marxism of its necessarily

[5] (N 10,3) (V, 1, p. 594/66).

progressive motion. The flash interrupts the present, inserting a new image of the past. It is the breaking in that resembles the messianic "today". In that interruption we have not an ideal that reveals the linear connection from the past through the present toward the ideal future, nor Rosenzweig's cycles that recommence through the interruption. But we have a lightning flash, an image of one historical point in juxtaposition with a now: revealing a new image through the rupture, the break.

> 9.1. Thesis A (I, 704/*Ill.*, 263) Historicism satisfies itself with establishing a causal nexus from different historical moments. And for just that reason no fact is really an historical cause. It became historical posthumously, through events that might be separated from it by thousands of years. The historian who moves away from this, stops letting the sequence of events run through his fingers like a rosary. He seizes the constellation, in which his own epoch is set with an utterly determinate earlier one. In this way he grounds a concept of the present as the "Now-time" ["Jetztzeit"], into which the slivers of the messianic are interspersed.

While there are many of Benjamin's texts that focus on the importance of messianism for the task of knowing history,[6] I will conclude with another thesis from the Theses on the Philosophy of History. Just as I could do justice neither to Cohen's nor to Rosenzweig's theories of historiography, I will plead serious incompleteness with Benjamin. But the stakes have risen through the paper. While Cohen would deny history to those who ignore the ideal found in Messianism, Rosenzweig saw cyclical memory as hurrying the messianic age. Benjamin can find no adequate disruption in either the circles or lines. He criticises historicism, which denies history by reducing each moment to a link in a causal chain. The historian merely documents the dead, safe from any future, indeed, insulated from his own future by the records of those who lie simply dead and gone. The con-

[6] Consider Thesis B (I, 704/*Ill.*, 264) For the soothsayers, who inquired of time what it hid in its lap, time certainly was experienced neither as homogenous nor as empty. Whoever keeps this before him, comes perhaps to a concept of how past time was experienced in remembrance [eingedenken]: namely, just so. It is known that the Jews were prohibited from investigating the future. The Torah and the prayer instruct them, in opposition, in memory. This disenchanted the future for them, to which all who consult the soothsayers for information are ruined. For the Jews, however, the future was nonetheless not turned to homogenous nor empty time. Because in it every second was the narrow gate through which the Messiah could enter.

stellation that the non-historicist historian seizes is charged with past and present, but precisely in order to interrupt the present with an awaited future. What I have called the points are a determinate past crashed up against the historian's present, producing the supercharged moment. While Rosenzweig sought a present that could entertain the eternal, through cyclical recommencement; Benjamin seeks to constellate the present with the past, as two points unbound, and in that moment to produce the now-time: a moment with slivers of the messianic future interspersed. The constellation of points from past and present is the place where the future can interrupt and act. But historiography brings that specific past into confrontation with a specific present with recourse to the splinters. Messianism is not plotted on a line that leads from past to future, nor is it inserted into a circular cycle, but it is dispersed in a set of points where the past and the present flash. The import of messianism for historiography, then, becomes the blasting of the past out of its context to supercharge the present, allowing the present itself to break-apart in expectation of the future.

The sequence of this paper, from line to circle to points, is not itself a line. The complexity of even Cohen's linearity, with a recurrence of Jewish suffering making good the messianic epistemology, should caution us against the linearity that the sequence portends. The influence from Cohen to Rosenzweig and then to Benjamin again might presume the judgement in Benjamin's favor. In the sequence of historical contexts, from the trauma of suffering in World War I to the utter dissolution of German-Jewry under the Nazi's, we see the hopes for anything resembling progress crumble into catastrophe. The steadiness of Cohen's tale of Jewish suffering gives way to a riskiness and vulnerability about time itself that disrupts Benjamin's life and thought at every moment. But surely the issue can be re-joined precisely by configuration or constellation: that the question is properly raised by the set (line, circle, points) because of their interaction. Messianic epistemology might be precisely the juxtaposition of these three geometries, where each disrupts both itself and the others.

What is more clear at the end of this essay is how the critique of historicism reflects the more profound discovery of the messianic dimension of historiography. These thinkers' recovery of messianism norms the historical enterprise in a way that is not simply pious. They raise the stakes for any discussion of messianism because they make the practice of studying messianism itself an issue. The historian's interest in the past is now guided and impelled by an urgent concern for the messianic future. That concern, however, has need of historiography not simply as a way of knowing, but rather as itself a social practice, a practice that challenges the present in its struggle for the future.

THE LUBAVITCH MESSIANIC RESURGENCE: THE HISTORICAL AND MYSTICAL BACKGROUND 1939–1996*

להפוך את הצרה לצהר

RACHEL ELIOR

I

The acute messianic ideology of Habad-Lubavitch was formulated during the Holocaust in reaction to the unbearable harsh realities of the death camps and the devastation of such a great portion of the Jewish people.[1] The tragic situation, which inevitably created a deep sense of crisis and hopelessness in the Jewish community, raised challenging questions as to the nature of God's omnipotence, and generated an intense attitude of skepticism about divine providence.[2]

Rabbi Yosef Yitzhak Schneerson (1880–1950), the sixth leader of the *Habad* dynasty,[3] is credited with effecting the acute Messianic

* I am grateful to my friends and colleagues Dr. Ada Rapoport-Albert and Dr. Mark Verman, who helped me in clarifying some debatable issues regarding the Habadic messianic phenomena. I wish to express gratitude to Prof. Ivan Markus and to Daniel Shtubel who brought to my attention important sources. My students who assisted in the different stages of assembling the sources for this study, Dr. Rivka Goldberg and Joel Kortick, deserve special gratitude. I also wish to thank my former student Dr. Kimmy Kaplan for his perceptive remarks. This study couldn't have been accomplished without the wide-ranging help and encouragement of my friend and husband Michael Elior and I wish to express my deep gratitude to him.

[1] See Gershon Greenberg, "Mahane Israel-Lubavitch 1940–1945: Actively Responding to Khurban" in: Alan A. Berger, (ed.) *Bearing Witness to the Holocaust 1939–1989*, Lewiston, New York 1991, pp. 141–163; Gershon Greenberg, "Redemption after Holocaust According to Mahane Israel-Lubavitch 1940–1945", *Modern Judaism* 12 (1992), pp. 61–84; Aviezer Ravitzky, *Haketz ha-Meguleh uMedinat haYehudim*, Tel Aviv 1993 (Hebrew), pp. 263–276, [= *idem, Messianism, Zionism and the Jewish Religious Radicalism*, Chicago University Press 1996, chapter 5]; Cf. Eliezer Schweid, *Bein Hurban LiYeshua* (= From Ruin to Salvation), Tel Aviv 1994 (Hebrew), pp. 39–64; 243–244. Earlier messianic speculations in Habad as reaction to Zionism were discussed by Ravitzky, *ibid.*, pp. 264, 377, n. 48.

[2] See Schweid, *ibid.*, pp. 10–14.

[3] For biographical details from the Lubavitch perspective, see Shalom Dov Ber Levin, *Toledot Habad be-Artzot ha-Brit 1900–1950*, Brooklyn 1988 (= History of Habad in the U.S.A.); For an autobiographical perspective see: Yosef Yitzhak Schneerson,

outlook which transformed the movement.[4] In the midst of the Second World War he took upon himself the heavy burden and the courageous responsibility to reverse and to restructure the deep sense of impotence, despair and helplessness that overwhelmed the Jewish community during the course of the Holocaust. In the attempt to decipher, interpret and re-define the meaning of reality in these most desperate of *irrational circumstances* he offered eschatological certainty and messianic purpose—what appeared to be the only *rational response* from a theological point of view. He further offered an apocalyptic reconstruction of the catastrophe—claiming that the horrors of the Nazi German occupation were the culmination of a cosmic scheme of pre-messianic tribulations which must necessarily precipitate and impel imminent divine redemption.[5]

After personally witnessing two decades of persecution and repression of Jewish religious life under Stalin in Soviet Russia, events occurring well before the Nazi invasion, Rabbi Yosef Yitzhak offered a mystical-apocalyptic reconstruction of reality. He viewed the calamities of the Holocaust as the final stage in the collapse of the old world order, thereby clearing the way for the inevitable redemption in the near future. He forcefully challenged the religious despair that emerged within the persecuted Jewish community by confronting a meaningless arbitrary reality imbued with existential horrors in the early 1940's. He reinterpreted historical reality by replacing existential helplessness with eschatological certainty, and by pursuing the messianic course, which entailed human hope and divine purpose.

Lubavitcher Rabbi's Memories (translated by Nissan Mindel), Otzar ha-Hassidim, Brooklyn 1971; for a critical point of view cf. Ada Rapoport-Albert, "Hagiography with Footnotes: Edifying Tales and the Writing of History in Hasidism", in: Ada Rapoport-Albert (ed.) *Studies in Jewish Historiography in Memory of Arnaldo Momigliano*, Supplement 27 of *History and Theory* (1988), pp. 119–159.

[4] Schweid, *ibid.*; Ravitzky, *ibid.*

[5] On the history and phenomenology of Jewish messianism, see Gershom Scholem, *The Messianic Idea in Judaism and Other Essays*, New York 1971; Hebrew version in Gershom Scholem, *Devarim Bego* (ed. Avraham Shapira), 1975, pp. 153–222, note esp. pp. 163–164; cf. Greenberg, Redemption; Schweid, pp. 14, 230. Various religious circles interpreted the Second World War as premessianic tribulations in the early forties as attested by Michael Zilberberg, *Yoman Warsha 1939–1945*, London 1969, Tel Aviv (1979?) p. 26, and cf. Schweid (n. 1 above), pp. 22–29 and Mendel Piekarz, *Ideological Trends of Hasidism in Poland During the Interwar Period and the Holocaust*, Jerusalem 1990, (Hebrew), pp. 21, 171, 262–264, 318, 335–338. However, no other religious circle reacted with an active ideological scheme and an engendered messianic movement which addressed a wide public and related to *Klal Israel* as a result of that perception—as did Lubavitch.

He contended paradoxically in 1941: "Every Jew should remember that it is not the people of Israel who are dying, God forbid, it is the world giving birth to twins—a new Jewish people and a new land of Israel are being born. . . . The birth pangs have started but will not last long."[6]

In this manner, existential death and a hopeless present were transfigured into a spiritual birth and into a future of hope while the meaningless torment and helpless impotence were transformed into predetermined messianic birth pangs—all culminating in the mystical birth of a new future for the Jewish people and the Jewish land. Rabbi Yosef Yitzhak was able to draw, in an elusive manner, upon a well known Talmudic dialectic conception of redemption which suggests that the Messiah was born on the day that the first Temple was destroyed.[7] This conception inherently links a crisis of historical catastrophe and a profound sense of impotence with the hope for redemption and messianic omnipotence. Likewise, this belief inseparably connects hopeless and catastrophic birth pangs with messianic revelation and the hopeful inception of a new era. Another notable Talmudic tradition suggests that the messianic era would be preceded by tremendous cosmic horrors and great world wars which would be known as the wars of *Gog and Magog*.[8] This metahistorical scheme which dialectically connected death and birth, was applied by various orthodox circles to the horrors of World War II, horrors which came to be conceived as pre-messianic tribulations.[9] According to the metaphor of birth pangs (*Hevlei-leida*), these pre-messianic tribulations were represented as cosmic birth pangs (*Hevlei Mashiah*) which

---

[6] *Hakeri'ah ve-Hakedusha*, Jerusalem 1942, p. 20. On this periodical and its various recensions and translations see notes 10 and 21 below. The full Hebrew version of the above quotation reads as follows:

חדש סיון תש"א,
"שום פורענויות חדשות, ר"ל, אינן צריכות לאבן את לבות ישראל! שום
השתערות של נחשולי אנטישמיות ונזרות רעות, חו"ש, אינה צריכה להטיל את האדם
מישראל לתוך יאוש! יתחילו נא היהודים מעתה לקבל איש את פני רעהו בברכה
המשמחת "לאלתר לנאולה" וכמה שלא תצר חלילה, השעה האחרונה, זכר יזכר כל
יהודי, אם איש ואם אשה, שלא עם ישראל נוסס, חלילה, אלא שזה התבל כורעת ללדת
תאומים: הולכים ונולדים עם ישראל חדש וארץ ישראל חדשה! . . . הגואל את ציון
וירושלים, אל עליון, הולך ונואל את ארצו ומקבץ ומביא את בני עמו. תקפו צירי
היולדה אבל הארך לא יאריכו".

[7] *Jerusalem Talmud*, Berakhot 2:4; *Eicha Raba* (ed. Shlomo Buber, Vilna 1899) 1, pp. 89–90; cf. Devarim Bego, p. 165.

[8] Pesahim 118; Sanhedrin 97 b.

[9] Schweid, p. 14.

would inevitably hasten the birth of the Messiah and precipitate the revelation of redemption.[10]

II

Habad Hasidism was a *mystical* movement established in the late decades of the eighteenth century which possessed *no messianic* character at its inception.[11] The Habad movement always strongly maintained a mystical acosmistic belief that God alone is the true essence of reality, that through Him all things are but a manifestation of the divine being, and that every human experience is imbued with the all-encompassing divine presence. The infinite divine entity which permeates all existence is grasped as the vital force of life and the source of its being, whereas the physical world is interpreted as the illusionary cloak for the expanding divine vital force. The paradoxical nature of the divine presence is perceived as a mystical "unity of opposites" or as an eternal dialectic process being simultaneously revealed and concealed, creating and annihilating, being and non being, a process which transcends all constraints of rational perspective concerning time or place.[12] The desperate circumstances of the Holocaust were a severe spiritual challenge for those who attributed absolute being to the Divine Presence and absolute nothingness to

[10] *Hakeri'ah Vehakedusha* (hereafter HK), vol. 1, no. 1 (2 October 1940) on this periodical cf. Greenberg, Redemption, p. 76, n. 2; Greenberg, Mahane, pp. 142–148. Levin, *Toldot Habad be-Artzot ha-Brit* (n. 3 above), pp. 344–346.

[11] On the mystical nature of Habad and its virtual indifference to messianic leadership and national salvation see: Rivka Schatz, "Anti-Spiritualism baHasidut, Iyunim be-Torat Shneur Zalman mi-Ladi", *Molad*, no. 171 (1962), pp. 513–528; Issiah Tishby and Joseph Dan, "Hasidut", *Ha-Encyclopedia ha-Ivrit*, vol. 17 (1965), pp. 769–822; Rachel Elior, *Torat ha-Elohut ba-Dor ha-Sheni shel Hasidut Habad*, Jerusalem 1982; Rachel Elior, "Habad, the Contemplative Ascent to God", in: Arthur Green (ed.) *Jewish Spirituality from the Sixteen Century Revival to the Present*, pp. 157–205, in: *World Spirituality*, vol. 14, New York 1987; Naftali Loewenthal, *Communicating the infinite; The Emergence of the Habad School*, Chicago 1990: Rachel Elior, *Torat Ahdut ha-Hafakhim: ha-Theosophia ha-Mistit shel Habad*, Jerusalem 1992 (Hebrew); for English version see, Rachel Elior, *The Paradoxical Ascent to God: The Kabbalistic Theosophy of Habad Hasidism*, Albany 1993; Roman A. Foxbrunner, *Habad: The Hasidism of R. Shneur Zalman of Lyady*, Tuscaloosa 1992; Joseph Dan, "Hasidism", *Ha-Encyclopedia ha-Ivrit*, Appendix volume III, Jerusalem 1995, cols. 412–419.

[12] In addition to the sources mentioned above in n. 11 see further comprehensive discussions on Habad mysticism: Louis Jacobs, *Tract on Ecstasy*, London 1963; *Louis Jacobs, Seeker of Unity-the Life and Works of Aaron of Starosselje*, London 1966; Miles Krassen, "Agents of the Divine Display: New Studies in Early Hasidism", *Religious Studies Review*, vol. 20, no. 4 (October 1994), pp. 293–301.

its worldly manifestations—all the more so since this catastrophe threatened the very existence of the entire Jewish nation.[13]

The *mystical acosmistic perception* of Habad—which negated the autonomous existence of reality and accentuated God's immanence by emphasizing the eternal ongoing dynamic divine presence in the world[14]—was radically *transformed* by Rabbi Yosef Yitzhak. He advocated an extreme *apocalyptic perception* of history, orientated towards a transcendental messianic turning point which would inevitably occur in the very near future.[15]

The creation of this messianic mythology that reshaped history and promised immediate redemption was the result of a transformation in the very heart of Habad mystical theosophy. Messianic theodicy, or the apocalyptic justification and rationalization of God's apparent helplessness and *impotence* in light of the Holocaust—replaced mystical acosmistic theosophy of the *omnipotence* of God that had prevailed continuously in Habad since the end of the eighteenth century.[16] Only a belief in the concealed messianic significance of the events could refute the cruelty of their revealed meaning and resolve the tragic plight of a seemingly impotent divine providence in the light of desperate human experience.

III

Rabbi Yosef Yitzhak Schneerson escaped from Warsaw, Poland, in 1940, arriving in New York as a refugee from the devastation of Nazi Europe. He had personally witnessed the persecution of the Jews throughout his adult life, first in the Soviet Union, including the ongoing crisis of the war as well as the hopeless fate of the Jews living in Lithuania, Latvia, and in Poland during the first half of the twentieth century, a crisis which reached its horrible culmination in the Holocaust in the Second World War.[17] Rabbi Schneerson was

---

[13] Schweid, *ibid.*, pp. 39–40.

[14] Elior, The Paradoxical Ascent to God, pp. 49–102.

[15] See *Arba'a Kol Kore meAdmor Shlita Milubavitch,* Jerusalem 1942–3; cf. HK, Brooklyn 1941 nos. 9–11 (Yiddish and English) partial Hebrew version in: *Covets Maamarim translated from the periodical Hakeri'ah vehaKedusha, by Mahane Israel Jerusalem,* Jerusalem 1943.

[16] On Habad acosmic theosophy see Elior, Torat ha-Elohut, pp. 25–60; *eadem,* The Paradoxical Ascent to God, pp. 49–79; Loewenthal, Communicating the Infinite, pp. 50, 137, 147.

[17] On Rabbi Schneerson's rescue from bombarded Warshaw at the end of 1939

motivated both by the trauma of the disappearance of European Jewry and by his perception of the great spiritual poverty of American Jewry. Upon his arrival to New York, he therefore resolved to utilize the realistic existential tragedy as a hoist, elevating man beyond the horrors of exile towards redemption. As the leading messianic theologian of his age, he called upon the American Jewish community to urgently reassess the situation, to accept responsibility for the fate of Jewish lives in Europe, and to realize the urgency of penitence—*Teshuwah*—and to realize the inevitable immediacy of redemption.[18] Rabbi Schneerson engendered a wave of messianic resurgence with the publication of four urgent appeals *kol kore* (קול קורא) in both the Yiddish and English language Jewish newspapers. He used repeatedly the declaration "*lealtar lege'ulah*" לאלתר לגאולה meaning "redemption is immediate", "it awaits just beyond your door".[19] He assured his readers and listeners, with both great enthusiasm and with great desperation, through the most radical messianic texts to spring from the Jewish world in the twentieth century, that the apocalyptic scheme was reaching its end, the messianic process would soon be accomplished, and that redemption could be achieved immediately.[20]

> Immediate redemption! Is our call, and this is because it is the call of our time. This is not merely a consolation for those who despair. Even more, it is our good news about actual "salvation which is to come soon" (Isaiah 56:1). We must prepare ourselves in heart and soul to welcome the righteous redeemer. We call upon *all* Jews to join the "*Mahane Israel*" which, with the help of the Blessed Name, is being organized, for this purpose. "Immediate redemption!" Be ready for redemption soon! It is approaching rapidly although you do not see

---

and his departure from Europe see, Yehudah Koren, *Yediot Aharonot* (15.4.1996); on his arrival to America in 19 March 1940, see Levin, *Toldot Habad be-Artzot ha-Brit*, pp. 166–172. On his life in Russia see, Shalom Dov Ber Levin, *Toldot Habad beRussia haSovietit baShanim 1917–1950*, Brooklyn 1989 (= History of Chabad in the U.S.S.R–1917–1950); David E. Fishman, "Preserving Tradition in the Land of Revolution: The Religious Leadership of Soviet Jewry 1917–1930", in: Jack Wertheimer (ed.), *The Uses of Tradition, Jewish Continuity in the Modern Era*, New York and Jerusalem, 1992, pp. 85–118. On other aspects of the writing and activities R. Yosef Yitzhak see Rachel Elior, "Vikuah Minsk", *Jerusalem Studies in Jewish Thought* 1:4 (1982), pp. 179–235; Rapoport-Albert, "Hagiography" (n. 3 above).

[18] Levin, *Toldot Habad be-Artzot ha-Brit*, pp. 304–344.

[19] *Arba'a Kol Kore meAdmor Shlita mi-Lubavitch*, Jerusalem 1942–3; cf. HK, 1941, nos. 9–11.

[20] See Yosef Yitzhak Schneerson, *Sihot Kodesh*—1941 (eds. Hozzat Otzar Hasidim) Brooklyn 1964; *idem, Sefer Hamamarim*—1940 (eds. Hozzat Otzar Hasidim) Brooklyn 1955; HK, 1941–1945.

> it. It is near at hand! The righteous Messiah is already around the corner, and the time for self-preparation is already very short.[21]

Rabbi Yosef Yitzhak employed the mystical authority invested in his person as a Hasidic mystical leader—*Zaddik*[22]—to state that the divine decree had already been issued and only true repentance was required to end the pre-messianic tribulations and to bring the Messiah.

In his words, repentance preconditioned the last stage of redemption and, in order to realize the apocalyptic process and the messianic prediction, only all-encompassing repentance was needed.[23] In order to strengthen and to facilitate this apocalyptic arousal, Rabbi Yosef Yitzhak established a Messianic Society that was called "Mahane Israel" (hereafter MI) or "Camp of Israel" and he founded a periodical—"*HaKeri'ah VeHakedusha*"—that voiced his views.[24] Together they formed the apocalyptic messianic response to the Holocaust as it occurred. MI took upon itself the task to disseminate Judaism within the Jewish secular community, as well as to propagate and

---

[21] "Kol Kore Fun'm Lubavitsher Rabbin" HK, vol. 1, no. 9, 26 May 1941, pp. 15–16. An English translation appeared in HK, vol. 1, no. 11, 24 July 1941, pp. 2–3. A Yiddish version was published in the New York Yiddish newspaper *Morgen Journal* on 26 May 1941. On the different publications of this Kol Kore see Greenberg, Mahane Israel, p. 160, n. 20.

[22] On the mystical authority of the Zaddik see Gershom Scholem, "ha-Zaddik", in: *Pirkei Yesod be-Havanat ha-Kabbalah u-Semaleiha*, Jerusalem 1976, pp. 213–258; Samuel Dresner, *The Zaddik*, New York 1960; Arthur Green, "The Zaddik as Axis Mundi", *Journal of the American Academy of Religion* XLV (1977), pp. 327–347; Ada Rapoport-Albert, "God and the Zaddik as Two Focal Points of Hasidic Worship", *History of Religion* 18, no. 4 (1979), pp. 296–325; Rachel Elior, "Between *Yesh* and *Ayin*: The Doctrine of the Zaddik in the works of Jacob Isaac, The Seer of Lublin", in: Ada Rapoport-Albert and Steve Zipperstein (eds.) *Jewish History: Essays in Honor of Chimen Abramsky*, London 1988, pp. 393–455; Joseph Dan, "Hasidism: The Third Century", *World Union of Jewish Studies, Newsletter* no. 29 (1989), pp. 39–42; Rachel Elior, "Between 'Divestment of Corporeality' and 'Love of Corporeality'—The Polarity Between Spiritual Perception and Social Reality In Hasidism", in: Israel Bartal, Ezra Mendelson, Chava Turniansky (eds.), *Studies in Jewish Culture in Honor of Chone Shmeruk*, Jerusalem 1993, pp. 228–241 (Hebrew); Rachel Elior, "The Paradigms of *Yesh* and *Ayin* in Hasidic Thought", in: Ada Rapoport-Albert, (ed.) *Hasidism Reappraised*, London 1996, pp. 168–179.

[23] On the role of repentance-*Teshuvah* see, Schweid, pp. 53–58; Greenberg, Redemption, pp. 62–67; Greenberg, Mahane Israel, pp. 141–157.

[24] On the various activities of *Mahane Israel* see, Greenberg, Mahane Israel, pp. 148–151. On HK see notes 10 and 21 above. On the esoteric and exoteric nature of this publication, see Greenberg, Mahane Israel, pp. 141–163; Levin, *Toldot Habad be-Artzot ha-Brit*, pp. 304–344; Naftali Loewenthal, "The Neutralization of Messianism and the Apocalypse", in: Rachel Elior and Joseph Dan (eds.) *Kolot Rabim, Memorial volume to Rivka Schatz-Uffenheimer: Jerusalem Studies in Jewish Thought* 13 (1996), pp. 2*–14* (English section).

to strengthen devoted religious life within the observant community, specifically to generate the essential repentance which would in turn generate the redemption. HK communicated its messianic message from 1940 to 1945, throughout the war years, and generated acute messianic arousal and apocalyptic hope. The periodical presented two fields of battle—in Europe the struggle centered on rescuing the Jewish body while in America the struggle focused upon rescuing the Jewish soul.[25] MI and HK aggressively disseminated the messianic world view, demanding both material support in order to rescue the persons of the victims in Europe, and spiritual repentance, in order to rescue the souls of the victims of heresy and secularization in America. Through these actions the Habad movement claimed mutual responsibility for the sins of exile and the hopes for redemption.[26]

The dissemination of the apocalyptic spiritual message and the messianic activities in the 1940's were interpreted in a fourfold manner: 1. As expressions of *Exile* of both body and soul co-relating the punishment of the "Old World" in Europe with the sins of the secular "New World" Jews in the United States 2. As interpreting the inception of *Pre-Messianic Tribulations* which signified the collapse of the prevailing order and the birth of a new one. 3. Describing the birth of the new era as *The Imminent Redemption* 4. Relentlessly propagating the demand for an all-encompassing *Repentance-Teshuvah*—perceived as the *reversal*—that which will turn the descent of Israel

---

[25] HK cf. Schwied; Greenberg, Redemption.

[26] The discourse and talk that Rabbi Yosef Yitzhak Schneerson gave on Purim 1941, indicate that he saw the Jewish suffering in Europe partly as a result of the sins of Jews around the world, particularly in America. It seems that he believed that because one part of the Jewish people were sinning, particularly those in America who had an extremely poor level of religious observance, the Jews of Europe had to suffer: "Jews in America . . . you must know that the sorrows which those Jews across the ocean are suffering are not by chance. This is a decree from heaven, and the decree is *a punishment for something of which you are guilty*, something for which *you are in part to blame* . . . Jews in America . . . you are being called by God's call to repentance. The moment is much more serious than you can imagine". Yosef Yitzhak Schneerson, *Likkutei Dibburim*, Brooklyn, 1972, vols. C–D, p. 386 (English version vol. 3, pp. 62–63). By telling the American Jewish community that they are to blame, he also called on them to repent and in this way to save their fellow Jews in Europe. I am grateful to my student Joel Kortick for his help in clarifying this point. It is interesting to note the history of the causal link between the sins of the Jews and their sufferings in the rabbinical historiosophy that justified the destruction of the Temple in this self-blame. Apparently, the sages preferred self-blame over the possibility of an irrational world which has no correlation between good deeds and evil destiny.

from the verge of death and forsaken exile towards divine providence and assured survival. The passage from the old world into the new world, the passage from the torments of exile into the promised redemption—could only take place through collective self-determination which will lead to repentance.

The mystical-apocalyptic reconstruction of reality as proffered by Rabbi Yosef Yitzhak transformed the *coercive existential death* of the Jewish people and their experience of meaningless torment in a helpless situation within the chaotic reality of the present into a *predetermined divine scheme for redemption* which, though entailing premessianic tribulations, will definitely lead to the aspired mystical birth of a new future.

By 1945 it had become obvious that the predicted messianic events had not occurred and that the period of pre-messianic tribulations had indeed brought immense torment and calamity but, alas, no redemption. The HK ceased to appear, an indirect admission of failure for the prophecy of immediate messianic revelation, and Rabbi Yosef Yitzhak did not use the slogans לאלתר לגאולה anymore. Further, the political establishment of the State of Israel in 1948 was passed over and ignored with complete silence thereby divesting the new state of any messianic significance. Rabbi Schneerson's prophecy may have failed from the point of view of predictive accuracy but had overwhelmingly succeeded from the point of view of building lasting social institutions from the cohesive experience of apocalyptic anticipation.[27] The messianic prophecy relating to the physical salvation of the Jewish people failed, but Rabbi Yosef Yitzhak did not give up his vision regarding the salvation of the souls and the apocalyptic anticipation. He was determined to create through his own efforts a new Jewish people, a nation which would be worthy of future messianic revelation. Further, he wished to establish new Jewish

[27] See Leon Festinger, Henry W. Riecken and Stanley Schachter, *When Prophecy Fails*, University of Minnesota 1956: References here are to the Harper Torchbooks edition, New York 1964. The authors delineate perceptively the common response of believers to contradictory evidence occurring in millennial or messianic movements: "Suppose an individual believes something with his whole heart; suppose further that he has a commitment to this belief, that he has taken irrevocable actions because of it; finally, suppose that he is presented with evidence, unequivocal and undeniable evidence, that his belief is wrong: what will happen? The individual will frequently emerge, not only unshaken, but even more convinced of the truth of his beliefs than ever before. Indeed, he may even show a new fervor about convincing and converting other people to his view". (*ibid.*, p. 2)

communities, replacing all those which had been destroyed, in order to found a Jewish people befitting the messianic age.

After the Holocaust, Habad adopted a twofold role, one professing a testament and the other, carrying a mission.[28] Habad followers were called upon to attest and to bear witness through extreme personal devotion and self-sacrifice to the world that passed away in the Holocaust, reconstructing that which had all but vanished. They pledged a mission to build anew, through an all-encompassing educational process, to include *Kelal Israel*, that is, the new religious Jewish community forming over the world. Unlike other Hasidic communities that were trying to rejuvenate their own remnants out of a result of urgent existential motivation and hopes for survival, Habad people were reaching out into the entire Jewish community. They were motivated by their all-encompassing messianic expectation (which had no particular date at that stage) and acted according to the objectives of still concealed agenda for imminent redemption.

Rabbi Yosef Yitzhak and his son-in-law Rabbi Menachem Mendel Schneerson who, in the eyes of their followers, were endowed with a divine charisma of mystical piety and an incomparable spiritual authority, dispatched emissaries to nearly every Jewish community on the globe, transcending all social, ethnical, cultural and geographical borders, taking upon themselves a responsibility for the entire Jewish community.[29] Their goal was to reach out, in an unprecedented manner, to attempt to establish a connection between the non-religious and the religious communities, in order to attract a wider following for more observant ways of life. They were battling religious invalidation, heresy, assimilation, desperate predictions concerning the future of the survivors, material constraints, the weakening of socio-religious bonds and the general sense of estrangement and rejection of the observant life style that emerged in the wake of the Holocaust. They utilized every means of active promotion, aggressively promulgating Judaism by drawing upon a charismatic Hasidic leadership and a mystical heritage, providing educational

[28] Schweid, p. 64.

[29] See, Menachem Mendel Schneerson, *Sefer HaShlichut*, Kfar Habad 1989; Mordechai Laufer (ed.) *Sipurah shel Shlichut*, Kfar Habad 1990; Levin, *Toldot Habad be-Artzot ha-Brit*, pp. 209ff., 369–373. On the missionary nature of the emissaries cf. Menachem Friedman, in Martin E. Marty and R. Scott Appleby, *Accounting for Fundamentalisms—The Dynamic Character of Movements*, Chicago 1994, pp. 328–356.

needs and assisting in comprehensive family welfare and social care.[30]

The emissaries, who were eagerly seeking the presence of supporting co-believers in order to recover from the disconfirmation of the messianic expectation of the war time, concealed the outspoken messianic vocation of the 1940's, and replaced it with the concept of קירוב *-keruv-* (drawing together), reaching out to all members of the Jewish community everywhere, through an educational network, social welfare services, and an intricate religious campaign. Their efforts integrated explicit spiritual and social rehabilitation and implicit messianic hopes that were preconditioned by repentance. Once again Rabbi Yosef Yitzhak transformed a profound sense of powerlessness and despair into a powerful socio-spiritual action, and yet behind the open educational actions and social reaching out there was a still hidden messianic design.

It should be noted that through the transformation of messianic hope into practical activity, the Habad leadership came to realize that in order to maintain the belief in the coming redemption they would have no other choice but "to return to history," in the very Zionist sense of the phrase.[31] They came to adopt a full devotion to every earthly concern and all mundane human activity—in order to influence and to hasten the divine redemption. In many aspects they created a religious parallel to the secular *Zionist* ideology for which they professed a bitter resentment dating from before the Holocaust. Zionism was perceived by broad religious circles as a secular heresy—an ideology that demanded unlawful human arousal into specific action and deed that must necessarily precede any divine intervention into history—human action which would overlook the traditional prohibitions regarding hastening the end of exile and aim to bring about the yearned for redemption. Habad was willing to adopt different degrees of pragmatic realism and rational politics, combined with a practical orientation towards political organization, educational systems, economical resources and a communication network—in order to engender religious arousal, and repentance, and to precipitate redemption.

Rabbi Menachem Mendel Schneerson (1902–1994), assumed the Habad leadership in 1951,[32] one year after the death of his father-in-law,

---

[30] See, Levin, *Toldot Habad be-Artzot ha-Brit.*

[31] Cf. Schweid, p. 234; Ravitzky, p. 271.

[32] Rabbi Yosef Yitzhak suffered during the last few years of his life from a stroke,

Rabbi Yosef Yitzhak. Rabbi Menachem Mendel represented the seventh generation of successive Habad leadership and maintained that his generation, the seventh generation, inevitably had to be the generation of redemption.[33] He further contended that this generation was the last in exile and the first for redemption, since there could be no preconditions or reservations: the time had arrived. He assured his followers that the Messiah would come in his generation and consequently he never conceived of the possibility of an eighth Habad leader. He maintained that Habad would accomplish what others would or dared not attempt: he dispatched thousands of emissaries to disseminate Judaism and Hasidism, often at great personal danger, in many places around the world to hasten the expected redemption.

This combination of comprehensive educational activities striving to reach every member of the Jewish community and the possession of a definite messianic inclination, nourished by a charismatic leader who encouraged the use of all modern resources in order to achieve mystical and messianic goals—succeeded in raising a wide following of Jewish proselytes—*hozrim be-teshuvah.* The Habad movement has thousands and thousands of members who joined as the "newly reborn", a group which was attracted by the religious awakening, drawn to the messianic orientation of the 1980's and the 90's and determined to carry these spiritual impulse and social conviction ever further.[34]

---

from multiple sclerosis, and apparently from a form of aphasia and was not able to express himself. The passage from the sixth to the seventh Rebbe was not immediate and not without complications since R. Yosef Yitzhak had no sons and there were several candidates to choose between, among them the two brothers-in-law who were married to his two daughters—Shmaria Gur Arie and Menachem Mendel Schneerson. Yet another relative, Schneur Zalman Schneerson, was also mentioned. There is no critical biography of Rabbi Menachem Mendel. However there are many biased biographies and hagiographies. See, e.g., Shaul Shimon Deutsch, *Larger than Life—The Life and Times of the Lubavitcher Rebbe—Rabbi Menachem Mendel Schneerson* vol. 1, New York 1995. On Hasidic historiography and hagiography, see Ada Rapoport-Albert, "Hagiography, (n. 3 above); Israel Bartal, "Shimon ha-Kofer"—A Chapter in Orthodox Historiography" in: *Studies in Jewish Culture in Honor of Chone Shmeruk*, (n. 22 above) pp. 243–268 (Hebrew): Hayim Solovetchik, "Rupture and Reconstruction: the Transformation of Contemporary Orthodoxy", *Tradition* 28:4 (1994), pp. 23–75.

[33] See *Kol Mevasser* (n. 35 below). On the messianic significance of being the "Seventh Rebbe" who leads the seventh generation of Habad, see Loewenthal, *Neutralization*, p. 11. The origin of this retrospective tradition is debatable and further study is needed.

[34] On the role of the "Jewish reborn" *Hozrim betshuvah* in the Habad Messianic campaign see William Shaffir, "Jewish Messianism Lubavitch-Style: An Interim

With the establishment and expansion of Habad centers all over the world, starting from the fifties on through the seventies, Rabbi Menachem Mendel Schneerson, commonly known as "The Lubavitcher Rebbe", was able to regenerate the acute unqualified messianic expectation, all through the 1980's. He asserted repeatedly that this was the "last generation", the generation of redemption and consequently demanded that all his followers broadcast the imminent appearance of the Messiah.[35] He required his emissaries from around the world to prepare the Jewish people for this expected redemption as he emphasized again and again that all was entirely dependent upon the Habad activities ("כי בנו הדבר תלוי"). He further maintained that there was a direct connection between the promulgation of Torah and of Hasidism and between the hastening of the coming of the Messiah, repeatedly saying in public "גאולה בקרוב ממש" "redemption is veritably very close". The messianic prediction was proclaimed with vigor and accepted by many convinced followers who then acted accordingly: they committed themselves by constant propagation in the messianic prediction, by uprooting their lives and going to new places where they built new Lubavitch communities, attracting new adherents and disciples every day; by preparing spiritually and

---

Report, *The Jewish Journal of Sociology*, vol. XXXV:2 (December 1993), pp. 115–128; and see note 45 below.

[35] See, M. Zelikson [Slonim], ed. *Kol Mevaser Mevaser ve-Omer: Kovetz Hiddushei Torah: Ha-Melekh ha-Mashiah ve-haGeullah ha-Shelemah*, 1983; Ravitzky, pp. 265–270. Naftali Loewenthal has pointed out that two different concepts of redemption were simultaneously expressed in R. Yosef Yitzhak's writings and public discourse: the theme of *Geulah Kelalit*, the general redemption which will take place after the apocalypse of the war, and that of *Geulah peratit*, achieved through intensive contemplation in prayer and through strengthening normative Judaism. He further asserts that in the teachings of R. Menachem Mendel one aspect of redemption is a preparation for the other. See Loewenthal, *Neutralization*, (n. 24 above) pp. 1–14. The messianic tension in Habad had different expressions. There were various messianic publications by different Lubavitch writers who expressed private initiatives which reflected a certain public atmosphere. In 1965 Avraham Pariz published an announcement that claimed:

"קול מבשר... בשמחה רבה יכולים אנו לבשר לכם כי הנה מלך המשיח... כבר נמצא עתה כאן אתנו, הנה הוא הרבי מלובביטש... הוא אינו צריך את בחירתנו מפני שבחר בו השם"

In 1970 A.Z. Slonim planned to publicize the messianic identity of R. Menachem Mendel but was contested by some Habad leaders. In 1983 M. Zelikson-[Slonim], published *Kol Mevaser Mevaser ve-Omer: Kovetz Hiddushei Torah: Ha-Melekh ha-Mashiah ve-haGeulah ha-Shelemah.* On the nature of this publication the editor attested in the introduction:

"פריצת דרך בקביעה ברורה בהתאם לפסק דין הרמב"ם על אופן התגלותו של המלך המשיח ובעיקר מי הוא מלך המשיח"

materially for the coming of the Messiah and by disseminating the idea of imminent redemption in every possible way.[36]

It is interesting to note the gradual intensification of the messianic message and the expansion of its public scope: In the decade of the fifties, R. Menachem Mendel continued the messianic language of R. Yosef Yitzhak in a more subdued tone. In the sixties, the Lubavitcher Rebbe said: "The coming of our righteous Messiah is veritably close" ("ביאת משיח צדקינו בקרוב ממש"), in the seventies he declared "Here, here, the Messiah is coming" ("הנה הנה משיח בא!"), in the eighties he announced: Messiah Now!! ("משיח עכשיו!") and "Get ready for the Coming of the Messiah" ("היכונו לביאת המשיח");[37] in the early nineties he promised the imminent coming of the Messiah by the end of the Jewish year 5751 (1991) ("הטוב של הגאולה האמיתית והשלמה על ידי משיח צדקנו עוד בסוף שנת תנש״א מלכותך")[38] and he stated in an unprecedented way that he had done everything that he could do to bring the Messiah and that now it was up to his followers to do their best:

> What more can I do to motivate the entire Jewish people to clamor and cry out and thus actually bring about the coming of Mashiach? All that has been done until now has been to no avail. For we are still in exile. . . . All that I can possibly do is to give the matter over to you. Now, do everything you can to bring Mashiach here and now, immediately. . . . I have done whatever I can: From now on, you must do whatever you can.[39]

---

[36] A further study is needed in order to assess the full impact of the phenomena of the *shelichim* and the significance of their overt and covert social and spiritual activity. Inner Habad sources which document this activity should be consulted.

[37] See sources for the different stages in Zelikson, Kol Mevaser, pp. 14–17.

[38] Admor mi-Lubavitch, *Iggeret ha-Kodesh for the new Jewish year* תשנ"ב 1991–1992. In this year R. Menachem Mendel said further "ודאי ודאית ללא כל ספק וספק ספיקא שכבר הגיע זמן הגאולה"... זוהי השנה שהמלך המשיח נגלה בו... שעומדים כבר על סף התחלת ימות המשיח, על סף התחלת הגאולה, ותיכף ומיד המשכתה ושלמותה" שיחת השבוע (19.7.1991, 238) = "There is no doubt that the time of redemption has arrived. This is the year of the revelation of the king messiah . . . we are standing on the verge of the beginning of redemption and very soon upon its continuation and completion". . . (weekly discourse 238, 19.7.1991).

[39] *Sicha* (Discourse), April 11, April 18, 1991 (= the 26th of Nissan 1991) Martin H. Katchen, "Who Wants Moshiach Now? Pre-Millennarism and Post-Millennialism in Judaism". *Australian Journal of Jewish Studies* 5:1 (1991), cf. Shaffir, p. 119; Katchen is quoting a Fax from Crown Heights, 11:15 PM, April 18, 1991; Shaffir quotes this as *sicha* (discourse) from April 11 according to *Sound the Great Shofar: Essays on the Imminence of the Redemption*, Brooklyn 1992, p. 7. Two external political events contributed to the escalation of the messianic expectation and eschatological prediction at the end of the eighties and the early nineties: In late 1989 the Soviet

Habad followers responded by an overwhelming commitment to live constantly with a renewed and invigorated messianic consciousness, to study messianic teachings, to publish endless treatises, pamphlets and books on redemption, to write and to publicize in every manner on the immediate redemption, and to prepare both night and day for the coming of the Messiah.

When taken together—the inherited messianic vocation that the Seventh Rebbe received from his predecessor, the mystical consciousness originating from the charismatic leadership, the commitment to the dissemination of messianic expectations, the resultant overwhelming messianic awakening coupled with pragmatic realism, all borne by the thousands of emissaries and new followers—it is no wonder that the messianic resurgence rose to such new heights.

In the course of the eighties and nineties, Habad followers, including the multitudes who had responded to the wide religious arousal and the vital outreach activism, enthusiastically carried out a messianic campaign unprecedented in its amplitude. The outcome of this process was the replacement of the *general* expectation of imminent redemption in the near *future*—by an expectation of a *personal* Messiah embodied in the figure of the Rebbe who would reveal himself in the *present*. In the eyes of many of the Habad followers, the messianic tension was sharply concentrated on the Rebbe, and the fact that R. Menachem Mendel Schneerson forcefully proclaimed the imminence of the redemption and encouraged the cry "We want Moshiach now!" strongly implied that he himself might be the redeemer. He was often depicted in words and praises that transcended human nature and was described in concepts that Jewish tradition reserved for God and God alone. Unprecedented mystical descriptions from the eighties and the nineties relating to the divine nature of R. Menachem Mendel attest to the extremity of this development:

"עצמות אינסוף התלבשה בבשר ודם; היותו של הרבי עצמות אינסוף
שנתלבש בנופו של הרבי"

Union reversed its policy of prohibiting Jewish emigration and began to allow Russian Jews once again to leave. The unexpected collapse of the Soviet Union was perceived as a sign that the redemption was near. The defeat of Iraq in the Persian Gulf war in 1991 as well as the unexpected fact that in spite of severe Iraqi missile attacks on Israel there was no widespread injury, raised hopes and expectations for messianic imminence and were further perceived as an apocalyptic victory. For the use of dramatic events as a turning point, see Shaffir, 118–119.

("The essence of the Divine Infinite was invested in a physical garb: The Rabbi himself is the essence of the Divine Infinite that was enclothed in the body of the Rabbi").[40] The ambivalent role of R. Menachem Mendel himself within the messianic movement as both instigator and as restrainer as well as the level of his participation in the personalization campaign as the embodiment of the Messiah remains uncertain and will probably never be unequivocally answered.

According to all indications, R. Menachem Mendel, while most certainly fulfilling the role as a messianic activist, refused in the 1970's and the early 1980's to grant permission to publish messianic texts that proclaimed him as Messiah and nominated him as *Melech HaMashiach.* However, while he did not necessarily see himself as Messiah, he said nothing and did nothing in the early 1990's to dissuade his followers from their belief in his messianic stature and certainly did not attempt to curtail the messianic campaigns proclaiming him to be the Messiah. There can be no doubt that he ascribed great religious significance to the messianic awakening that swept his followers, although he refrained from any open, explicit proclamation of his own Messianic vocation. The majority of the texts proclaiming him as Messiah were published and disseminated only at the time of his final illness and incapacitation when the apparent refutation of the messianic prediction increased the enthusiasm and activity of his followers.

In the last decade before R. Menachem Mendel's death, the movement divided into the *messianic majority* who pronounced R. Menachem Mendel himself as the Messiah, and into a self-proclaimed *sane minority* that strove to keep a measure of respectability and reason, urging a restriction of messianic hopes. The messianic group, known as *meshichistim,* was engaged in the enthusiastic activity of obtaining new followers,[41] and spared no effort in bringing the Messiah into

[40] M. Zelikson, ed. Kol Mevaser, pp. 32, 48–49; cf. *Iggeret LeYadid,* note 42, below, p. 17. See also Shalom Dov Wolpo, "Nahamu Nahamu Ammi—Nehamah be Kiflayim", *Kfar Habad* 106 (5743), 6–7.

[41] On the significance of recruiting ever greater numbers of believers when a growing cognitive dissonance is occurring cf. When Prophecy Fails (n. 27 above) p. 28: "If more and more people can be persuaded that the system of belief is correct, then clearly it must, after all be correct"; see also *ibid.,* p. 229 "The presence of supporting co-believers would seem to be an indispensable requirement for recovery from such extreme disconfirmation".

the public arena, disregarding the mounting criticism and condemnation. In opposition, the non-messianic group, known as the *shfuiem*, "the sane ones", unsuccessfully attempted to restrain these activities to internal Habad circles and to avoid exposure to the public eye.[42]

The division in Habad created opposing sides, those who held to unrestrained popular "exotericism" (i.e., the public proclamation of the Rebbe as Messiah following his stroke in March 1992) and those who held to "rational" discreet "esotericism" (i.e., the insistence that the Habad mission was only to declare that this was the messianic time, denying any need for a public proclamation of the Messiah). The division was more tactical in nature, not really substantive since both factions believed in different ways that R. Schneerson definitely was or certainly might be the Messiah.

The messianic "exotericists" were acting with great enthusiasm, irrational persuasion and unbounded energy under the inspiration of imminent redemption ("We Want Moschiah Now!"), expressing complete disregard for the undeniable refuting evidence pertaining to the temporal present and near future. They spread their urgent messianic message in the journals "Kfar Habad", "Beis Moshiach", "Sihat HaShavouah", and in the weekly pages of "Parashat Hashavouah" and by various means in public campaigns. This group was headed by the spiritual leader, R. Yoel Kahan,[43] assisted by R. Shmuel Butman, the director of the Lubavitch youth organization and chairman of the international Moshiach campaign (who was planning to publicly anoint the Rebbe as Moshiach). Yosef Yizhak HaCohen Gutnik financed the international messianic campaign and was involved in effecting political consequences in Israel.[44] The Messianists enjoyed

---

[42] For an internal critical view of the extreme messianic course see Yehoshua Mondshine, *Iggeret LeYadid* (= "A Letter to a Friend") Jerusalem 1993 (a circular letter aimed to Habad people, typed on a typewriter) Scholem Collection 6710.1, Israel National Library. The writer is a Lubavitch Hasid who resented the messianists and described with detail the developments from an anti-messianistic point of view. For an external report informed by inner circles see Nadav Ish Shalom and Yuri Yanover, *Rokdim U-Bochim, The Truth on the Habad Movement*, New York 1994 (Hebrew).

[43] See Mondshine, *Iggeret*; cf. *Rokdim u-Bochim*, pp. 70–73.

[44] The messianic arousal had a profound effect on the political position that Habad advances in Israel and is still advancing. Habad holds to an extreme right-wing policy and supports both politically and financially right-wing conservative policies and political parties. See Yosef Yizhak HaCohen Gutnik, *Shlemut ha-Haaretz, The Rabbi of Lubabitch: Al haSakanah bi-Mesirat Shithei Eretz Israel* (On the Danger of Giving Away Areas of the Land of Israel), Brooklyn 1996.

the support of popular circles, of enthusiastic women groups, and of the proselytes known as *hozrim betshuvah*.[45] The "sane" circles, those who were interested in the future of Habad as an accepted religious movement and as an international educational order, were headed by R. Abraham Shemtov and R. Yehudah Krinsky, a senior secretary of the Rebbe. They were supported by the educational establishment and by some members of Agudat Hasidei Habad. The "esoteric" circles, while acknowledging the importance of the messianic idea, were not usually willing to consider the practical consequences of imminent redemption and resented the fusion of the intimate mystical world of Habad messianic vision and the pragmatic reality of unrestrained public religious activity. Their opinion was transmitted primarily through the publication and the distribution of private correspondence since they claimed to be suppressed and persecuted by the dominant messianic majority. The non-messianic circles were guarded in their approach, believing that the messianic propaganda would lead to contempt, defamation, and to a devaluation of all public Habad activities. They further maintained that an overemphasis on messianism would generate an estrangement from God in broad Jewish circles and will cause many to drift away from the Hasidic world.[46]

---

[45] The central role of *Hozrim beTshuvah* and women groups in the messianic arousal was noticed by students of sociology and anthropology who studied the current Habad phenomena; their work is in preparation. The uncompromising enthusiastic position, which transcends the accepted religious common denominator, was propagated to a great extent by the *Hozrim BeTshuvah*. Adam Tchubin discussed this aspect of his work on Habad community with me and suggested that the newcomers find the messianic enthusiasm a promising avenue for their religious activity since it "compensates" for their own relatively low status as newcomers to the ranks of Habad, devoid of the spiritual authority shared by elders or the prestige of those of distinguished Habad descent, cf. eye-witness description: "The split in the movement is between mainstream messianists and radical messianists. The mainstream messianists tend to be older and remember the previous Rebbe. Most were born into Lubavitch families, believe that the Rebbe is the best candidate for Moshiach in this generation and say that the way to bring him is through greater Torah study and *mitzvot*. . . . The radicals tend to be younger, Israel-based and *ba'alei teshuvah* . . . They believe that the Rebbe is the Moshiach and the way to bring him is to crown him and to force the hand of God. They see the Rebbe more in their mind's eye than in person. They are the ones who have sponsored full-page ads in American Jewish newspapers and street signs in Israel, 'Welcome King Moshiach' with the Rebbe's picture", Yosef Abramowitz, "What Happens if the Rebbe Dies?", *Moment* (April 1993), p. 72. I wish to thank Daniel Shtubel for drawing my attention to the article of Y. Abramowitz. The central role of Lubavitch women in the Messianic circles still awaits a comprehensive sociological study.

[46] Cf. Mondshine, *Iggeret leYadid*, note 42 above. Indirect aggressive response to

IV

In March, 1992, Rabbi Schneerson suffered a major apoplectic stroke.[47] The *Meshichistim* increased their messianic fervor following the physical refutation and apparent disproof of their belief. They emphatically invested the stroke with redemptive significance following the Biblical tradition of the suffering servant of God in Isaiah 53 which culminates with the verse: "He will be taken from the land of the living, and will be wounded for the sins of his people" (*ibid.*, 53:8) an astonishing exegetical tactic, in view of Christianity's usage of this text. The messianic circles transcended all the major physical consequences of this condition by turning them into a mystical omen, arguing that through his suffering the Rebbe was atoning for the sins of the entire nation and thus was preparing them for redemption. They further contended paradoxically that the Rabbi would not die at all and would imminently be revealed as the King Messiah.[48] They concluded that they must take the initiative and to give the messianic wagon the last needed push, through relentless written and oral actions, and to effect the open and declared revelation of the Rabbi as Messiah.[49] The messianists, driven by the deep conviction of the immediate messianic revelation of the Lubavitcher Rebbe—sought wide public acknowledgment of his messianic identity. The public campaign culminated in the anointment of the indisposed, paralyzed and speechless 90 year-old Rabbi Menachem Mendel as

---

the author of the Iggeret was published in *Beis Moshiach* 60 (November 3, 1995), p. 28.

[47] On the grave medical situation and its grim consequences regarding the divisions in Habad see: *Rokdim u-Bochim* (n. 42 above).

[48] The anointment and the public campaign that took place in 1992–4 received wide public attention and were described in Israeli and Jewish newspapers from an *outsider's point of view* in various critical tones. See Allan Nadler, "Last Exit to Brooklyn". *The New Republic*, May 4 (1992), p. 32 and see below.

[49] Expression of the later stages of the messianic resurgence written from an *insider's point of view* can be found in Habad periodical publications such as *Kfar Habad; Sihat haShavoua, Beit Moshiach* and in volumes such as Levi Yitzhak Ginzburg, (ed.) "Messiah *Now*" (Kfar Habad 1993–4, III volumes) Levi Yitzhak Ginzburg, (ed.) "*Long Live the King Messiah*" (Kfar Habad 1994); Pinhas Maman (ed.) "*The Torah of the Messiah*", New York 1993: Menachem Brod, *Yemot HaMashiach*, Kfar Habad 1992; Mordechai Moshe Laufer, (ed.) *Yemai Melech*, Kfar Habad 1991; Yosef Yitzhak Havelin, *Sha'arei Geulah*, Kfar Habad 1992; Yosef Avraham Heller, *Kuntres Hilketa Lemashiha*, Brooklyn 1992, and many other anonymous messianic titles such as *Mevaser Tov; Kol Mevaser, Torat HaGeulah, Maaiaanei Hayeshuah* and many others in Hebrew, English and Yiddish, all of which are collected in Gershom Scholem Collection in the Israeli National library in Jerusalem.

Messiah followed by a campaign to "Prepare for the Coming of the Messiah Menachem Mendel". His advanced age and great illness made the urgency of the public campaign a pathetic spectacle that transcended all constraints of Jewish tradition.

This paradoxical decision that ignored immediate reality and challenged all physical and medical probability was further complicated by the public subscription of many thousands of followers to a petition expressing their enthusiastic support for Rabbi Menachem Mendel in his new position.[50] The Messianic circles simultaneously maneuvered on both rational-traditional and irrational-apocalyptic levels. They were moved to seek Halachic support for their messianic claim and to issue a rabbinical verdict proclaiming Rabbi Menachem Mendel's messianic character, arguing a Halachic-legal basis for their messianic claims through the tradition found in "*Hilchot Melachim*", the messianic guidelines laid down by Maimonides.[51] At the same time they demanded "להגביר הלב על המוח" that is, the abandonment of rational considerations that cast doubts on the current fulfillment of the messianic agenda and the disregard of all events which might seem to refute the messianic belief.[52] R. Yoel Kahan, the head of the messianic faction, claimed that anyone who cast doubt on the messianic identity of R. Menachem Mendel had cast doubt on the very existence of God. At the same time his followers published a long list of books that strove to grant Halachic, mystic, and religious validity to the public campaign. They presented the mystical background through the "*Holy Epistle of the Besh't*"[53] which

---

[50] In the course of 1994, full-page advertisements pledging subscription to the Messianic role of R. Menachem Mendel were published in Israeli and American newspapers. One example from *Yediot Aharonot* 23.3.94 reads as follows:

"נזור ושלח אל מטה הגאולה האמיתית והשלמה. . . אנו מקבלים עלינו את מלכות
הרבי מלך המשיח שיחי'ה לעולם ועד, ובשעה גורלית זו פונים אנו בבקשה נפשית
לבוא ולהציל את עם ישראל וארץ ישראל ולהביא את הגאולה האמיתית והשלמה.
[מקום לחתימת שם וכתובת] יחי אדוננו מורנו ורבנו מלך המשיח לעולם ועד"

[51] See Shalom Dov Wolpo, *Yehi HaMelech HaMashiach*; Kiriat Gat 1992. On the paradoxical use of the Maimonidian passage in Habad Messianic arguments see, David Berger, "Messianism, Passing Phenomenon or Turning Point in the History of Judaism?", *Jewish Action* (Fall 1995), pp. 35–44, 88. The argument is written from an academic-religious-orthodox point of view. On the social impact of the messianic campaigns from the Habad point of view, see Shaffir (n. 34 above), pp. 114–117.

[52] See *Yemai Melech*; introduction.

[53] See Israel Ba'al Shem Tov, Iggeret ha-Kodesh, In: *Shivhei ha-Besht*, Yehoshua Mondshine (ed.) Jerusalem 1982; English translation and discussion. Louis Jacobs, *Jewish Mystical Testimonies*, New York 1967, pp. 150–151; Ben Zion Dinur, *Be-Mifne*

advocated widespread dissemination of Kabbalistic and Hasidic ideas as a vital precondition for the coming of the Messiah. The early issues of the anonymous newsletter "*Beit Mashiah 770*" (*mi-yomano shel ehad ha-tmimim*) that bears the interesting subtitle "private—with no responsibility whatsoever" is the pathetic culmination of the messianic expectations.[54] The newsletter regularly described the daily experiences of the Hasidim who lived around 770 Eastern Parkway, the Lubavitch center in Crown Heights, New York, waiting for messianic announcements on their electronic Moshiah beepers.

Through all these unprecedented written and oral campaigns hailing the Rebbe as Messiah, by utilizing every agency from Messiah bumper stickers, leaflets and booklets, public pronouncements, massive signs and posters on homes and highway billboards, full-page advertisements in the Jewish and general press, to the most advanced means available from satellites and international media through Internet communication and computer graphics, Lubavitch sponsored and demonstrated an ingenious and aggressive use of the mass media[55]—from an outsider's point of view—in order to announce the imminence of redemption. From an insider's point of view, they strove to generate immediate miracles, to bring about the deed which would transform the speechless impotent, elderly and stricken human Messiah into the omnipotent eternal divine entity, there, in their immediate presence, in their own day and time.

The messianic circles were living an ongoing tragic paradox, ignoring the sad physical and mental condition of their sick, paralyzed, coroneted messiah and adopting a completely irrational viewpoint, demonstrating the overwhelming power of messianic expectation and its total immunization to the shortcomings of physical reality. The Messianists expressed a total indifference towards any events refuting the messianic belief as well as a complete disregard of any expression of criticism pertaining to negative assessment, rational or biological

---

ha-Dorot, vol. 1, Jerusalem 1954; Isaiah Tishby, "Messianic Idea and Messianic Trends in the growth of Hasidism" (Hebrew) *Zion* 32 (1967), pp. 1–45; Moshe Rosman, *Founder of Hasidism, A Quest for The Historical Ba'al Shem Tov, Berkeley*, 1996; Allan Nadler, Last Exit . . ., p. 34; Rachel Elior, *Rabbi Israel Ba'al Shem Tov—Mystical Image and Magical Background* (forthcoming).

[54] *Beis Moshiach* 770 a computer printed circular (not to be confused with the above mentioned *Beis Moshiach* which is a weekly magazine).

[55] The influence of the massive use of the media for religious purposes by the American Christian fundamentalist organizations might have played a role in the decision to use this media for the public campaigns of Habad.

facts, religious concerns or disparaging reaction to their messianic campaign—from within the Habad Lubavitch circles or from without, that is, from the broader Jewish community.[56]

It should be remembered that the Habad movement always believed in the paradoxical nature of the divine presence, perceiving the divinity as a mystical unity of opposites, as being simultaneously revealed and concealed, present and absent, as a dual process of creating and annihilating, as being and non-being, as transcending all constraints of a rational perspective of time, place, and conventional perception of reality.[57] Thus, by applying the dialectical *divine* paradox to the hidden-revealed *human* Messiah, Habad could envisage a messianic movement which incarnated the mystical paradox within human dimensions. The analogy to the *Sabbatean* precedence of paradoxical faith in an apostate messiah and in the dialectical interpretation of reality as revelation through concealment—can hardly escape the eye. However, while both messianic movements do share a paradoxical belief in an inner messianic reality transcending physical con-

---

[56] Rabbi Eliezer Shach, the head of the ultra-Orthodox "Lithuanian" yeshiva faction (stemming from the historical "opponents" of Hasidism) headed the attacks on the rising Lubavitch messianism in Israel and Rabbi Moshe Teitelbaum, the anti-Zionist Hasidic Satmer Rebbe, headed the attacks in the United States from his seat in Wiliamsburg-Brooklyn. The attacks in Israel were published in "Yated Neman" the daily newspaper of the "Lithuanian" faction, where Rabbi Eliezer Schach denounced Rabbi Schneerson as a false messiah. For quotations of growing criticism from opposing religious circles that compared Lubavitch messianism with Sabbatianism, see Ravitzky, p. 370, n. 105; Mondshine, *Iggeret*, p. 22 and see below.

An example of comprehensive academic-religious criticism on the Messianic claims of Habad can be found in Allan Nadler's article mentioned above. See also Allan Nadler, "King of Kings County", *The New Republic* (July 11, 1994), cf. note 40 above. A grave concern from religious point of view is expressed in David Berger's article mentioned in note 51 above. Lawrence Schiffman, professor of Hebrew and Judaic Studies at New York University, wrote in an open letter to his friends in the Habad-Lubavitch movement in the *Long Island Jewish World* (January 29, 1993): "What you risk in your messianic pretensions is not your own Jewish observance, but the continued role of Chabad-Lubavitch as a major catalyst of Jewish observance in the wider Jewish community. If you turn yourself from an outreach movement into a false messiah movement, many of those who have gained so much spiritually and religiously from your work will find themselves unwilling to follow your future". Habad was criticized from all directions—Orthodox, Hasidic, Mitnagdic, academic and secular circles as well as from inside and outside factions who all expressed their concern, resentment and reservation in different tones. Cf. *When Prophecy Fails*, pp. 19–22 for the response of the members of messianic movements to sharp criticism.

[57] Elior, *The Paradoxical Ascent to God*, pp. 97–100.

straints, spiritual disproof and rational consideration and do cultivate a dialectic perception of the parity between the inner truth and the disappointment of external reality—they do not share practical conclusions. *Sabbatean messianism* transgressed all borders and restraints of the traditional Jewish world with a debatable religious awareness, through provocative spiritual expectations and by emphasizing paradoxical traditional practices while Habad remains solidly within the Jewish tradition in spite of its paradoxical mysticism and acute messianic perspective.

In conclusion I would like to argue that inherent in the Habad movement are three principal elements that nurtured its messianism:

1. A tradition of *paradoxical spirituality* perhaps the key to the acute mystical messianism—that which can transcend reality and ignore physical constraints and rational qualifications.[58]

2. *Mystical leadership* drawing on a dynastic heritage invested with unlimited mystical authority that transcends constraints of reality, influencing both the Hasidic community and the heavenly spheres.[59]

3. *Social creativity*: from its very inception Habad demonstrated interest and capacity in the establishment of new social institutions and outreach systems which would attract and initiate newcomers through education. In the second half of the twentieth century, the social creativity that was directed to the entire Jewish community transcending all local borders and traditional differences and ultimately hoping to generate repentance and redemption, thus bridging the gap between history and metahistory.[60]

The merging of these three elements, richly supported by written mystical discourse and oral deliberation combined with the desperate historical circumstances of the first half of the century, generated a messianic movement founded upon catastrophe.[61] By the second half of the century, after the positive historical experience of the nearly unlimited material security and spiritual freedom of Jewish life in America, the catastrophic messianism faded, leaving behind a messianism of affluence which could utilize the innovation and freedom of modern material society for its own spiritual ends but which

---

[58] *Ibid.*, pp. 49–100.

[59] Cf. n. 22 above.

[60] Cf. Levin, *Toldot Habad be-Artzot ha-Brit*; Ravitzky, n. 1 above.

[61] See Schweid, cf. Scholem, n. 5 above.

would require ever-expanding new goals and achievements in order to sustain messianic tension.[62]

Habad has been living with the cognitive dissonance of a constantly changing focus for the last fifty years. Its *initial* stage was marked by the paradox of the impotence of the omnipotent God during the Holocaust which was temporarily resolved by a pre-deterministic messianic interpretation of history. Its *second* stage was the moment of disillusionment that followed the disproof and failure of the immediate messianic prophecy in the wake of the second world war. The unequivocal refutation of any messianic hopes in 1945 was not only a paradoxical moment of despair, but also a moment of great creativity since in the wake of the failed messianic prophecy came an unprecedented religious arousal marked by great outreaching activity and spiritual commitment. Habad turned that moment of despair and disconfirmation into a moment of great social creativity by turning to the broad public and adopting the missionary role. The movement took upon itself the task of disseminating overt Judaism and covert messianism all over the world through appointed emissaries in order to prepare a generation that would merit a future messianic revelation. The immense educational activity carried by the Habad emissaries all over the world formed the *third stage* and brought about a resurgent wave of religious devotion and repentance that nurtured acute messianic expectations. In the *fourth stage*, that which occurred in the 80's and the early 90's under the direct inspiration of Rabbi Menachem Mendel, the messianic expectations were inflamed and concentrated around his own figure. The paradox of an old and sick, bedridden and speechless Messiah marked the *fifth stage* in which the messianic movement recruited all its resources to transcend the constraints of time and place in order to compel heaven to transform the mortal epitome of messianic expectation into an eternal divine Messiah. The *sixth stage* was the cognitive dissonance experienced with the final illness and death of the promised Messiah, the event which expressed the paradox of the tragic impotence and temporal helplessness of the expected omnipotent redeemer and eternal saviour. It is premature to fully assess the spiritual and social consequences of the messianic prophecy that failed.[63] However it

---

[62] See Ravitzky, pp. 266–267.

[63] Several months after the death of the Rebbe, leaflets and books were published in Hebrew and English which purported to explain the grounds for contin-

seems that this striking disconfirmation did not halt the movement, but rather gave it new life. Once again, as in other messianic and millennial movements, we note the appearance of increased enthusiasm and conviction after a sad and seemingly hopeless refutation. Habad is experiencing now the *seventh stage*—in the wake of the new stage of "when prophecy fails" it has splintered into many smaller interrelated groups, often at odds one with another. They continue to speak of the Rebbe in the present tense although he passed away some years ago, on June 13, 1994. Some of the more extreme messianic circles deny the fact of his death, arguing that there was no passing away and claiming that "The Rebbe lives and exists *hai vekayam* among us now exactly as he did before, literally, literally, *mammash mammash*".[64] They continue to expect his immediate reappearance as the messiah and keep publishing daily announcements in the newspapers concerning his immediate revelation. The members of the Lubavitch community are living with his *past* audio-visual and written messianic heritage, while continuing the vast educational commitment and social activity of the *present* and are seeking to relocate the messianic revelation in the *future*. Unlike some other followers of messianic movements that gave up their beliefs and witnessed their movement disintegrate in dissension, controversy and discord until it virtually disappeared, Habad followers seem to withstand the unequivocal refutation of the messianic agenda. They hold to the messianic nature of the Rebbe and to the equivocal nature of his death and consequently entertain hopes for his resurrection, but it seem to have no immediate relevance to daily life as these beliefs are not specific anymore nor are they concerned with the real world, where observant ways of life and the daily educational work are taking precedence.

The messianic resurgence occurring in Habad during the course of the twentieth century still awaits a comprehensive theological analysis which could draw on the full textual evidence and historical

---

ued faith. Notable among them are *Ve-Hu Yig'alenu*, Brooklyn 1994; *And He Will Redeem Us*, Brooklyn 1994; Shalom Dov Wolpo, *Hanissayon ha-Aharon*, Kiryat Gat 1994. On the immediate reaction to his death in Lubabitch centers in Crown Heights and in Israel, including total denial and expressing hopes for immediate resurrection, see Nadler, *Kings*, pp. 16–18.

[64] See Levi Yitzhak Ginsburg, "Hirhurim Likrat Yom Malkenu Meshihenu, Yom ha-Segulla Gimmel Tammuz", *Beis Moshiach* 41 (June 9, 1995); 13; Levi Yitzhak Ginzburg, *Le-Havi Liemot ha-Mashiah*, Kfar Habad 1995; Michael Friedman (ed.) *Melech Ha-Mashiah*, Safed 1996. Cf. Berger, p. 39.

documentation and include a comprehensive sociological evaluation reflecting the complexity of the religious and social phenomena that sprang from this spiritual inspiration and paradoxical mysticism. The historical-chronological descriptive outline offered above, and the preliminary theological observations that sought to point out the complexity of the different aspects involved in the Habad messianic phenomena, should be perceived only as the very beginning of a long discussion.

PATTERNS OF THE END: TEXTUAL WEAVING FROM QUMRAN TO WACO

James D. Tabor

> For surely Yahweh does nothing without revealing his secret to his servants the Prophets
>
> Amos 3:7

I have been invited in this paper to focus in particular on the apocalyptic messianic views of the Branch Davidian community and that of their leader David Koresh, who tragically came to international attention in the Spring of 1993. Since my training and work is that of an historian of the Mediterranean religions of late antiquity, I am stepping far out of my chronological period. Most of my research has been on late second Temple Jewish apocalyptic systems of thought, particularly those of the Qumran community and the followers of John the Baptist and Jesus. Nonetheless, since I was directly involved in assisting the FBI negotiators during the Waco crisis, and I have subsequently studied the apocalyptic teachings of David Koresh in the light of the systems I know from late antiquity, I trust that these reflections and analysis will prove fruitful for our collective deliberations on Messianism.[1] Throughout the paper I call attention to some of the major thematic parallels between the apocalyptic belief system of the Branch Davidians and that of the Qumran community, as reflected in the Dead Sea Scrolls. Both groups located their history and experiences in the prophetic texts of the Hebrew Bible; understood their community as the elect and chosen saints living at the "appointed time of the end;" and were led by a "Teacher" who claimed a definitive and ultimate role as God's final revelatory messenger. My aim is to isolate some of the main elements in a common process of interpreting texts that I describe as the "dynamics

[1] See my account of the whole episode in the work I co-authored with Eugene Gallagher, *Why Waco: Cults and the Battle for Religious Freedom in America* (Berkeley: University of California Press, 1995).

of biblical apocalypticism."[2] That the two communities, and their respective Teachers, dealt with and appropriated some of the same texts in strikingly similar ways, yet are separated by two millennia, is a testimony to the enduring power of such textual dynamics in the life of apocalyptic movements of this genre.

By any scholarly reckoning Daniel 11:20–28, which purports to be a prophetic vision of the events that will usher in the "end of the age," concerns the early military campaigns of the Syrian ruler Antiochus IV Epiphanes (175–164 B.C.E.) into Palestine and Egypt. Here, in thinly veiled language, the author covers Antiochus' deposing of the pro-Egyptian high-priest Onias III in favor of his Hellenizing brother Jason, his partially successful march against Egypt, and his subsequent plunder of the Jewish Temple in Jerusalem (see 1 Macc. 1:10–19; 2 Macc. 4:7–17). That the "contemptible person" of Daniel's vision, whom he also knows as the "king of the North" (11:21,40), is none other than the "sinful root" whom the author of 1 Maccabees identifies as Antiochus IV, is beyond dispute (1 Macc. 1:10). The problem is, the events that the author of Daniel subsequently describes, and obviously expects to take place at the "time of the end," culminating in a cosmic judgment and resurrection of the dead, simply never happened—neither in the career of Antiochus, nor that of any other potential candidate for "king of the North" down to our time (11:40–12:4).

The prophetic scenario set forth in this vision of Daniel 11–12 is surely the most detailed found in the Hebrew Bible, echoing the specifics of Antiochus' political, military, and cultural activities in the region. One might think, for this very reason, that the text would have fallen into disfavor or at least disuse, in view of its blatant "failure" in the capricious light of historical events. But such has not been the case. Although it may be true that a more general sketch of "end-time" events (e.g., the proverbial wars, famines, earthquakes, pestilence, and persecution) appears to escape the possibility of historical falsification, and thus offers itself to every generation anew, it is also true that such stylized apocalyptic scenarios lack the gripping imaginative potential of a text like Daniel 11–12.[3] The detailed

[2] I use the term apocalypticism in a restricted way here to refer to the view that the end of time is imminent, with the signs of the End unfolding according to an interpretive scenario revealed in the prophetic texts of Scripture.

[3] An example of such a generalized text is Isaiah 24. Such texts are highly elas-

visionary materials one finds in Daniel, particularly in chapters 7, 8, 9, and 11–12, sets it apart from most other apocalyptic/prophetic texts in the Hebrew Bible precisely because of its highly specific references to geographical setting, chronology, actors, and events. Here one reads of mysterious composite "beasts" with multiple heads and horns, representing successive kingdoms and rulers. One finds tightly linked chronological patterns such as the Seventy "Weeks" of years (490) and the successive periods of 1260, 1290, 1335 and 2300 (or 1150) days. Details of battles set in precise geographical contexts are carefully described. All of these elements are related to what the text repeatedly calls "the appointed time of the end." When understood on its own terms, according to its own internal claims, as an inspired, and thus an inviolate, revelation of end-time events, Daniel becomes a text that simply can not be wrong. Like some type of prophetic "template," devout interpreters have applied it countless times over the past two millennia to some anticipated unfolding of historical events, always looking for an "Antiochus-like" candidate who will fulfill things to the letter.

The apostle Paul, writing in the mid-50s C.E., but echoing the precise language of the prophecies of Daniel, had recommended celibacy to his communities, warning them that "the appointed time had grown very short" (1 Cor. 7:29). The followers of the apostle Paul in the late 60s C.E., judging from 2 Thessalonians 2:1–11 (and likely Paul himself a decade earlier), anticipated a repeat of Caligula's aborted attempt to set his own statue in the Temple at Jerusalem, perhaps by the emperor Nero, thus fulfilling Daniel 11:31–36:

> Forces from him shall appear and profane the temple and fortress, and shall take away the continual burnt offering. And *they shall set up the abomination that makes desolate* . . . And the king shall do according to his will; he shall exalt himself and magnify himself above every god, and shall speak astonishing things against the God of gods. He shall prosper till the indignation is accomplished; for what is determined shall be done.

The early followers of Jesus interpreted the first Jewish-Roman Revolt in the light of the same texts. Indeed "*the* sign" of the End was to

---

tic, lacking specific references to actors, events, time, or place. The "four horsemen" of John's Apocalypse appear to reflect the same stylized scenario. The Synoptic "Apocalypse" of Mark 13 is most instructive in this regard in that it actually *combines* the general (vv. 3–13) with the highly specific, drawn from Daniel (vv. 14–23).

be the dreaded "desolating sacrilege" set up by the "king of the North" in the holy place of the Herodian Temple:

> But when you see *the desolating sacrilege set up where it ought not to be* [Matthew's gloss: "spoken of by Daniel the prophet," 24:15], then let those who are in Judea flee to the mountains . . . for in those days there will be such tribulation as has not been from the beginning of the creation which God created until now, and never will be" (Mark 13:14,19).[4]

This imminent apocalyptic expectation of Mark, which was repeated in a relatively intact form by Matthew (chapter 24) a decade or so later (80s C.E.), is recast by Luke into a decidedly non-apocalyptic form. Rather than the expected "desolating sacrilege" leading to the final events of the End, Luke interprets the Roman destruction of Jerusalem and its Temple in 70 C.E., as well as the further dispersion of the Jewish people from Palestine, as the signs of a new dispensation that he views most positively, namely—the "times of the Gentiles" in which the Gospel of "repentance and forgiveness of sins" would be proclaimed to all nations (Luke 21:20–24; 24:47). Following the disaster of the second Jewish Revolt (132–135 C.E.), and Hadrian's rebuilding of Jerusalem as Aelia Capitolina, the hopes and expectations that had been fueled for more than two centuries by these prophecies in Daniel largely waned.[5] After all, with neither Jewish Temple nor Judean State, the land of Palestine could hardly serve as an arena for the literal fulfillment of texts such as Daniel 11:29–39. In this regard the words of the post-Exilic prophet Habakkuk offered a perennial comfort to both Jews and Christians:

> For still the vision awaits its time; it hastens to the End—it will not lie. If it seem slow, wait for it; it will surely come, it will not delay. Behold, he whose soul is not upright in him shall fail, but the righteous shall live by his faith (2:3–4).[6]

---

[4] This text is a *pesher* on Daniel 11:31–12:1. The flight to the "mountains," was understood to be the trans-Jordan area of the Decapolis, designated in Dan 11:41 as an area of safety ("main portion of the Ammonites") that would escape the invasion of the evil "King of the North."

[5] See the primary sources cited in F.E. Peters, *Jerusalem* (Princeton: Princeton University Press, 1985), pp. 107–130. The book of Daniel was denied a place among the Hebrew Prophets and relegated to the *third* section of the canon, that of the Writings (*Ketuvim*), while the book of Revelation came near to being excluded from the New Testament corpus entirely.

[6] This text was cited by the Qumran community as a way of dealing with the

The apocalyptic systems that we can subsequently trace, particularly among Christians, found it necessary to develop more allegorical and symbolic ways of reading texts such as Daniel and Revelation.[7]

It was only in this century, with the establishment of the State of Israel in 1948, and more particularly, the Israeli capture of the Old City of Jerusalem in 1967, that prophetic hopes that had been dormant since second Temple times were revived.[8] This was certainly the case in the latter months of 1990 when Iraqi leader Saddam Hussein invaded the tiny Gulf state of Kuwait, resulting in the massive military response by the United States, Europe, Egypt, Saudi Arabia, and their allies.[9]

David Koresh was one such interpreter who had his attention fixed on these events in the Middle East. He was the 30 year old "prophet" of the tiny Branch Davidian sect, which had broken with the Seventh Day Adventist Church back in the 1940s and lived

---

apparent failure or delay of their own prophetic schemes to develop (*1QpHab* 7:1–8). It is used by the writer of Hebrews much to the same end (10:37–39).

[7] See the various movements surveyed by Norman Cohn, *The Pursuit of the Millennium*, Revised and expanded edition (New York: Oxford University Press, 1970), and the texts compiled by Bernard McGinn, *Visions of the End* (New York: Columbia University Press, 1981). Jews had a greater tendency to continue to read the prophetic texts of the Hebrew Bible rather literally, but for another time, perhaps in the distant future. Thus when the emperor Julian (361–363 C.E.) offered a possibility for a return to Zion and a rebuilding of the Temple, concrete plans were made, funds were raised, and old prophetic passions were certainly reawakened, see Peters, *Jerusalem*, pp. 145–147. However, the Jewish apocalyptic texts from the Medieval period, collected by Raphael Patai, tend to move in the direction of the allegorical and the increasingly fantastic, see his *The Messiah Texts: Jewish Legends for Three Thousand Years* (Detroit: Wayne State University, 1979). It is worth noting that the seventeenth century Jewish Messiah Shabbatai Zevi, and his prophet Nathan, did take quite literally the notion that the Davidic Messiah must facilitate the return of the "lost tribes" of Israel (based on Isa. 11). They sent delegates to the east to contact these legendary apocalyptic players and rumors of their imminent arrival in Palestine helped fuel the messianic hysteria that swept the Ottoman empire and the Jewish communities of central Europe (see Gershom Scholem, *Sabbatai Ṣevi* (Princeton: Princeton University Press, 1931).

[8] Paul Boyer, *When Time Shall Be No More: Prophecy Belief in Modern American Culture* (Cambridge: Harvard University Press, 1992), has done a masterful job of tracing the rising interest in prophecy among evangelical Christians after 1948 and 1967.

[9] See the popular news article by Jeffery Sheler, "A Revelation in the Middle East," *U.S. News and World Report*, November 19, 1990, pp. 67–68. Not only were leading evangelical Christians speculating as to the "prophetic significance" of the Gulf War but Rabbi Menachem Schneerson, leader of the Orthodox sect known as Lubavitchers, declared it the definitive beginning of a series of events that would lead to messianic times. On the underrated influence of "prophecy belief" in American culture in general see Paul Boyer, *When Time Shall Be No More.*

communally outside Waco, Texas, in a settlement they called Mt. Carmel. The group anticipated the imminent and literal fulfillment of biblical prophecies, and the establishment of the Kingdom of God on earth, beginning in Jerusalem. Koresh had often told his followers that Daniel 11 was the most important prophecy in the Bible.[10] He understood it to be the "master key" to the entire biblical prophetic corpus. For Koresh, as well as many other evangelical interpreters of biblical prophecy at the time, the close match between the latter part of Daniel 11 and events in the Gulf was all too obvious:

[There] shall arise a contemptible person to whom royal majesty has not been given (v. 21a)[11] *Interpretation*: The ruthless Iraqi leader Saddam Hussein whose cruelty had become proverbial in the Western media.

He shall come in without warning and obtain the kingdom by flatteries . . . he shall act deceitfully; and he shall become strong with a small people (vv. 21b–23) Interpretation: Saddam Hussein obtained power by a coup that put his tiny Bath party in control and installed him as absolute ruler in Iraq. He declared his reign a rebirth of the glory of the ancient empire of Babylon, with himself as a new Nebuchadnezzar, ancient destroyer of Jerusalem and the Kingdom of Judah.

Without warning he shall come into the richest parts [or among the richest men] of the province . . . scattering among them plunder, spoil, and goods (v. 24) Interpretation: The invasion of oil-rich Kuwait by Iraq with the resulting plunder and destruction.

And he shall stir up his power and his courage against the king of the south with a great army (v. 25) Interpretation: Iraq threatens both Saudi Arabia and Egypt to the south, massing forces on the desert border for an invasion.

And the king of the south shall wage war with an exceedingly great and mighty army (v. 25) Interpretation: The massive response of the United States and its allies, led by Egypt and Saudi Arabia.

His army shall be swept away, and many shall fall down slain (v. 26) Interpretation: Utter defeat of the Iraqi army by the Allies with massive casualties inflicted.

And as for the two kings, their minds shall be bent on mischief; they shall speak lies at the same table, but to no avail; for the end is yet to be at the time appointed (v. 27) Interpretation: Sudden halt to the Allied invasion of Iraq,

---

[10] The views of David Koresh largely survive on audio tapes made prior to his death in April, 1993. I have documented his overall spiritual and prophetic outlook in *Why Waco?*, pp. 23–79.

[11] Biblical quotations are from the Revised Standard Version, although when I deal closely with Koresh's exegesis of the biblical text I use the King James Version, which was the only translation he endorsed.

General Schwartzkopf ordered to pull back all forces; a fragile peace agreement is signed.[12]

And he shall return to his land with great substance, but his heart shall be set against the holy covenant (v. 28). Interpretation: Saddam, who had vowed "to turn Tel Aviv into a crematorium," and even fired Scud missiles into Israel, formally withdraws but blames global "Zionist" forces for his defeat, vowing revenge.

The key phrase in this entire section of Daniel 11 is found in verse 27: *for the end is yet to be at the time appointed.* The phrase "at the time appointed" occurs again in verses 29 and 35, while verses 35 and verse 40 speak of a series of events designated as the "time of the end."[13] Koresh was convinced that the Gulf War marked the "beginning of the end," but that Saddam had been providentially spared in order that he (or a similar successor) might fulfill the next phase of this prophetic scenario described in verses 29–45—the actual invasion and near defeat of Israel by this wicked "king of the North," the leader of modern "Babylon."

On Sunday morning, February 28, 1993, two years *to the very day* after the defeat of Saddam Hussein, as if prompted by some cosmic cue, the Federal Bureau of Alcohol Tobacco and Firearms carried out their ill-fated raid on Mt. Carmel, the communal center of the Branch Davidians a few miles outside Waco, Texas. Thus began a 51 day siege that ended in the incineration of the 74 inhabitants that had remained inside throughout this period. David Koresh spoke about being "in the fifth Seal" the very day of the BATF raid. He was referring to his particular understanding of a sequence of events to unfold before the End, drawn primarily from the Seven-Sealed scroll of Revelation 6, but connected to a host of related texts throughout

[12] Menachem Schneerson, the Lubavitcher Rebbe, was quick to point out that Gen. Schwartzkopf was strangely ordered to halt abruptly the Allied advance on Thursday, February 28, 1991, the very evening of Purim, as synagogues around the world were celebrating the defeat of Haman, ancient foe of the Jewish people. The Kabbalists were also quick to point out that the Gematria (mystical numerical value) of Saddam Hussein's name in Hebrew equaled 240, the same number as that of Amalek, the ruthless enemy of Israel from the time of Moses. Indeed, the synagogue readings for Purim focus on Exodus 17:8–16 where Yahweh declares that the forces of Amalek, though battling against God's people from generation to generation, will be utterly blotted out in the end.

[13] This notion of a "set time," ordained by Yahweh for his intervention and final judgment is common in Israel's post-exilic literature (Psa. 75:2; 102:13; Isa. 60:22b; Hab. 2:3–4; *1 Enoch* 10:12; Testaments of the Twelve Patriarchs 17; Jubilees 22:8–21; Testament of Moses 7–8).

the Bible. What is operating here is a series of interpretive dynamics, well known to scholars of Jewish and Christian apocalypticism, that have played themselves out countless times in the past 2500 years. An understanding of these dynamics would have provided what appears to have been the best hope for a peaceful resolution of the Waco situation. Biblical apocalypticism involves the interplay of three basic elements: 1) The Sacred *Text* which is fixed and inviolate; 2) The inspired *Interpreter* who is involved in both transmitting and effecting the meaning of the *Text*; and 3) the fluid *Context* in which the interpreter/group finds itself. The *Text* functions as a kind of "map" of things to come, setting forth an "apocalyptic scenario" of end-time events. Koresh's "Text" was of course, the entire Bible, but particularly the books of Daniel, Revelation, the Psalms, Isaiah chapters 40–61, and the Minor Prophets, which he had woven into a prophetic complex that had deeply impressed his followers and convinced them that he was a prophet himself.

Although the *Text* itself is fixed and unchanging, mirroring in advance an almost fatalistic reflection of what "must happen," there are two variables in this scheme of things, allowing for a high degree of flexibility. First, the *Interpreter* is doing just that—*interpreting*—both the *Text* and the outside *Context*. And second, outside events are always changing and changeable. This was the key to effective negotiations during the entire 51 day standoff at Mt. Carmel. The government largely controlled the *Context*, or outside situation. Given this dynamic, this means that the FBI actually held within its control the ability to influence Koresh in his interpretations, and thus in his actions. Unfortunately, *everything* they did for 51 days, following the standard negotiation strategies and tactical quasi-military maneuvers developed in response to what they called "Hostage Rescue Barricade" situations, simply confirmed Koresh in his initial perception of the situation on February 28th—that they were "in the fifth Seal," and that the entire situation might well have a tragic ending. In other words, the FBI played the perfect part of "Babylon" throughout, validating in every detail the interpretations of Scripture of both Koresh and his followers.[14]

[14] Koresh, like many devout prophetic interpreters since the early Christian period, used the term "Babylon" to symbolically refer to the political, social, and religious system of the dominant culture.

The fifth Seal of the book of Revelation was chilling in its potential implications for the situation at Waco:

> And when He broke the fifth seal, I saw underneath the altar the souls of *those who had been slain* because of the word of God, and because of the testimony which they had maintained; and they cried out with a loud voice, saying, "How long, O Lord, holy and true, wilt Thou refrain from judging and avenging our blood on those who dwell on the earth?" And there was given to each of them a white robe; and they were told that they should rest for a little while longer, until the number of their fellow servants and their brethren *who were to be killed* even as they had been, should be completed also (Rev. 6:9–11).

This fifth Seal takes place shortly prior to the cosmic judgment of God, the Great Day of the Lord's Wrath, which is to be revealed by a massive earthquake and various heavenly signs, introduced by the sixth Seal (Rev. 6:12–17). In other words, it is the last major event leading up to the end of human history. The text speaks of a group of the faithful being slain, followed by a *waiting period*, prior to the slaughter of the rest of the group. Koresh connected this with Psalm 2, which tells of a final confrontation between the "kings of the earth" and an anointed one or "messiah." Based on this possible interpretation of events, the killing had begun on February 28th. From the Branch Davidian point of view, the six members of their family who had been killed had died for no other reason than they were studying the Bible with David Koresh, and thus branded as part of a "cult." In other words, they gave their lives "for the word of God, and for the testimony which they held" which is precisely what the book of Revelation says. Accordingly, the group is now told *to wait* for a "little season" until the rest would also be slain. The martyrdom of those remaining inside Mt. Carmel would lead to the sixth Seal, which would bring on the judgment of God to the world. As long as Koresh and his followers believed the fulfillment of this fifth Seal was upon them, based on this particular prophetic scenario, they would view their impending deaths as inevitable.

It is obvious that David Koresh himself was confused by the events which had transpired. It is true that his prophetic scenario did call for a final fulfillment of this fifth Seal. However, Koresh had taught for years that this was all supposed to happen at a later time and in another place. The setting was supposed to be in Jerusalem, in the Land of Israel, not in Waco, Texas. Also, the group was expecting the final confrontation to come in 1995 or even beyond, not in 1993, based on their calculations of the end-time drawn from the book of Daniel. Koresh had told his followers that he, as this final Koresh/Christ figure, would be inevitably required at some point in the future to die in a battle. The latter verses of Psalm 89, which Koresh mentioned on the day of the initial BATF raid, predict just such a fate for such a Davidic figure. However, beginning in 1990, and particularly following the Gulf War in 1991, Koresh began to speculate that at least a portion of this final scenario might be fulfilled in Texas rather than Israel. Although Saddam Hussein had not fulfilled the latter part of Daniel 11, it certainly appeared that he had inaugurated the process. This shift in focus from Israel to Texas was increasingly discussed, according to surviving Davidians, as Koresh became more and more convinced that those living at Mt. Carmel might well be challenged by the Federal authorities for their behavior. It was this uncertainty which offered the best hope for a peaceful resolution of the situation. At one point on the afternoon of February 28, the very day of the initial raid, Koresh spoke live on Dallas radio station KRLD with the station manager. He asked Koresh how he felt about the BATF agents that were killed and wounded that morning. Koresh answered with emphatic passion, "My friend, it was *unnecessary*." He goes on to say that the whole thing was regrettable, that innocent lives had been lost, and that he would have peacefully submitted to any governmental investigation of the weapons he had purchased.[15] In the KRLD conversation Koresh describes his cordial relationship with local McLennan Country Sheriff Jack Harwell and other law enforcement officers, including undercover BATF agent Robert Rodriguez who had tried to infiltrate the group earlier that year. The 911 tapes, made on the same day, within minutes of the BATF raid, also reveal a panicked group inside Mt. Carmel who desperately wanted the authorities to back off. On March 7th the group recorded a one hour video of Koresh with his wives and children. In this video Koresh addresses the federal authorities in a most

[15] Indeed, it is the case that nearly a year earlier, in July, 1992, when BATF agents had questioned Waco gun dealer Henry McMahon in their initial investigation of the Branch Davidians, Koresh had actually invited them to come out to Mt. Carmel and talk. He later faxed copies of his arms purchase receipts to McMahan to assist him in responding to the BATF inquiry. See the interview with Henry McMahon, in "Waco: Behind the Cover-up," *Soldier of Fortune*, November, 1993, pp. 36–41, 71–72.

accommodating manner, stating his desire to peacefully resolve the situation, while still sharply blaming them for initiating the entire encounter. At the end of the tape he says "Hopefully God will grant us more time."

All of this indicates that Koresh did not see the February 28th confrontation as some inevitable fulfillment of the final prophetic scenario which he had proclaimed to his followers in such detail. Some things did not match, other things were open-ended and yet to be determined, and surely the *major* fulfillment of his prophetic scenario was to take place in Jerusalem during the time when the "king of the North" made his next move. Still, Koresh had been wounded on February 28th, six members of his group had been killed, and he was now confronted by official agents of the United States government, whom Adventists had historically identified as destined to lead the forces of spiritual "Babylon" at the time of the End. It is clear from conversations with surviving Branch Davidians who were inside Mt. Carmel that they feared the overwhelmingly superior government forces might come in forcefully and slaughter them all at any moment. Given these ambiguities, Koresh was convinced that the attack on February 28th was at least related to the final sequence of events foretold in biblical prophecy, but he was uncertain of what he was to do. So, although the apocalyptic *Text* was fixed, like a script written in advance, the *Interpretation* and the precise *Context* were variable. Koresh was "waiting" for two reasons: because he understood that to be required by the "fifth Seal," but also because he was seeking his "word from God" which would clarify for him the ambiguities and uncertainties of the situation.

The one thing that was consistently reported in the media regarding Koresh's teaching was his claim to be able to "open the Seven Seals" of the book of Revelation. Most biblical scholars would date the final redaction of this mysterious final book of the New Testament around 90 C.E., associating it with the terror filled reign of the Roman emperor Domitian. In Revelation 4 and 5, John the visionary, is taken to heaven where he sees God sitting on a throne, holding a scroll in his right hand, sealed with seven wax seals. At first, no one in heaven or on earth is worthy and able to open this mysteriously sealed book. Then a great proclamation is made: a Lamb with seven eyes, who has been slain, is declared worthy to open the seals. In chapter 6 this Lamb proceeds to open the book, removing one seal at a time. As each seal is sequentially opened, an episode ensues, described in veiled, symbolic language: successive riders on horses that are white, red, black, and pale, followed by a scenes of famine, martyrdom, heavenly signs, and an earthquake—and finally the Seventh Seal itself. However, the Seventh Seal turns out to include another sequence of seven events—the Seven Trumpets (chapters 8–11), which in turn lead to a final series of seven, the Seven Plagues, poured out from vials upon the earth (chapter 16). The entire book is an unfolding sequence of dramatic events which usher in the Kingdom of God and the reign of Christ on earth, as described in the latter chapters of the book. In other words the Seven Seals actually comprise and initiate the unfolding of the entire book, step by step. Consequently, to be able to "open the Seven Seals" is to explain and set forth the entire book of Revelation.

Yet Koresh understood much more by this phrase. And here my model of apocalyptic dynamics, built upon *Text, Interpreter*, and *Context*, must be modified and expanded somewhat. Koresh often said he had been sent both to "explain and *to do* the prophetic Scriptures." In other words, opening these seals involved explaining their mysterious meaning, but also actually bringing them into historical reality. So to "open a seal" was ultimately *to usher in* its actual accomplishment on earth. This has to do with Koresh's self-understanding and identity. As he saw things, he was not merely one interpreter among many, but *THE* final Interpreter of *all* the mysteries and revelations of God. He began to identify himself with a certain "Prophetic Voice" that runs through specific texts of the Hebrew Prophets and is also found in the Psalms. I think there is good evidence that other "messianic" types in Jewish and Christian history have identified with these same texts, and sought to appropriate this Voice—including the Teacher of Righteousness at Qumran and likely Jesus himself.

Koresh claimed to be that Lamb who takes and opens the sealed book as portrayed in Revelation chapter 5. But this claim was not a denial that Jesus Christ was also a "Lamb" of God. The Lamb is described as the "Lion of the Tribe of Judah, the Root of David" (Rev. 5:5). Christians have traditionally understood this as a clear and exclusive reference to Jesus Christ. Koresh argued otherwise. He pointed out that the entire book of Revelation, though revealed by Jesus Christ, and written by John in the first century, was only to be understood and accomplished shortly before the end of history. The opening verses of the book say it was given to "reveal to his servants things which must *shortly* come to pass" and that "the time is at hand." As Koresh explained it, this could only refer to a time far into the future from that of Jesus of Nazareth, when the events described in the book would be "at hand." In other words, Revelation would remain a closed and sealed book *until* the appearance at some future point of a "Lamb," who would open, and ultimately usher in, the entire sequence of prophetic fulfillment. Koresh held that the entire book was written from the standpoint of a later time, so that it functions as a kind of proleptic message for the last generation.

So, Koresh did understand himself as a "Christ" figure, but not in the sense that he thought he *was* Jesus of Nazareth, the "Christ" whom he believed that God had sent in the first century. As he often told his followers: the English word Christ, taken from the Greek word *Christos* comes from the Hebrew word "messiah," It means one who is anointed or chosen. It is a title, not a name, and is commonly used in the Old Testament or Hebrew Bible for all the kings and priests of Israel. Koresh believed that just as God sent Jesus of Nazareth as a "Christ," to his generation, to accomplish a certain mission, there would also appear, prior to the end of time, a final manifestation of a Christ figure. He pointed out that according to the book of Hebrews such a Christ figure had also appeared two thousand years before Jesus, in the person of the enigmatic priest Melchizedek, in the time of Abraham (Heb. 7:1–4). Accordingly, the Branch Davidians understood the term "Christ," not as a single historical figure, but as the manifestation of the "Word of God" (John 1:1), through a human agent, who thus *became* the anointed Son of God. Koresh claimed to have that same "Spirit of Christ," that is called in the book of Revelation, the "Spirit of prophecy" that came upon Jesus of Nazareth at his baptism (Rev. 19:10). In some of his tapes, as he attempts to explain this metaphor of the Lamb, whom he believed in a certain sense also referred to Jesus Christ, he put it like this, "The Lamb [Jesus] *has* a Christ, the Lamb sends a bird with a message." So he could affirm Jesus as the Lamb, but he believed that now another manifestation had appeared.

Koresh relied chiefly on the Psalms to show that such a manifestation of "Christ" could not be limited to Jesus of Nazareth. In Psalm 110:4 a descendent of David, king of ancient Israel, is addressed as "a priest forever after the order of Melchizedek," which for Koresh provided the link between the "Christ" of Abraham's day, Melchizedek, and subsequent manifestations. This understanding of Melchizedek he found supported in the New Testament by the writer of the book of Hebrews, who presents him as:

> He is without father or mother or genealogy, and has neither beginning of days nor end of life, but resembling the Son of God he continues a priest for ever. See how great he is! (Heb. 7:3–4a).

The Dead Sea scroll community shared this exalted view of Melchizedek, and expected him to appear as an anointed redeemer figure in the end-time. It appears, based on a fragmented but precious text from Cave 4, that they also identified this heavenly Melchizedek figure with the anointed "Messenger of the Spirit" predicted in Isaiah 61:1–4—the one who brings "Good Tidings" (see *11Q*13, Col. 2). There is every reason to conclude, based on this citation, that they are identifying the role of their Teacher of Righteousness with that of the exalted Melchizedek figure. Such a view is hardly surprising in view of the astonishing language of heavenly exaltation found in several other related fragments from Qumran. Indeed, these texts appear to reflect the claims of the Teacher himself to have ascended to heaven and taken his seat among the Holy Ones above (*4Q*491, frag. 11; *4Q*471b).[16] Of course the early Christians cited Isaiah 61 as well, applying it to Jesus, and indeed, Luke alters Mark's Gospel here and centers his opening scene for Jesus' ministry in Nazareth on the fulfillment of this very text (Luke 4:14–30). The Isaiah 61 text clearly lies behind the pericope in the Synoptic Q source where John the Baptist sends word *from prison*, asking Jesus whether he is the "one to come or should we look for another" (Luke 7:18–23). One of the tasks of this figure was to "set free the captives," so John's query is certainly apropos. As it turns out, the precise wording of Jesus' reply to John in this text from the Q source is one of our closest New Testament parallels to a Dead Sea text, namely *4Q*521, that specifies the role and task of the Messiah.[17] This point

[16] Michael Wise has convincingly argued that these texts, that apparently belong to a collection of songs related to our Thanksgiving Scroll (*1QH*), celebrate the career of the Teacher in autobiographical style ("Seated at the Right Hand of God," paper delivered in the Qumran Section, Society of Biblical Literature Annual Meeting, New Orleans, November 24, 1996). This view is now supported in the official publication of the text in the Milik Festschrift, by Esther Eshel, "*4Q*471b: A Self-Glorification Hymn," *Revue de Qumran* 17 (1996): 175–203.

[17] See my study with Michael Wise, "*4Q*521 'On Resurrection' and the Synoptic

was extremely important in Koresh's theology because it showed that a "Christ" had appeared 2000 years before Jesus Christ, and so, he concluded, it surely would not be so surprising that one would appear 2000 years after. According to Revelation 10:7, which was an absolutely crucial verse for the Davidians, it was "in the days of the voice of the seventh angel (or messenger), when he shall begin to sound, the mystery of God should be finished, as he declared to his servants the prophets." Koresh claimed to be that final seventh messenger, and thus it would be to him that the full mystery of the prophets would be revealed. It is significant that the Habakkuk Commentary from Qumran speaks of the Teacher of Righteousness in a similar way:

> [This passage {Habakkuk 1:5} refers to] the traitors with the Man of the [2]Lie, because they did not [listen to the words of] the Teacher of Righteousness from the mouth of [3]God. It also refers to the trai[tors to the] New [Covenant], because they did not [4]believe in God's covenant [and desecrated] his holy name; and finally, it refers [to the trai]tors in the latter [6]days. They are the cru[el Israel]ites who will not believe [7]when they hear everything that [is to come upon] the latter generation that will be spoken by [8]the *Priest in whose [heart] God has put [the ability] to explain all* [9]*the words of his servants the prophets*, through [whom] God has foretold [10]everything that is to come upon his people and [. . .] (*1QpHab* 2:1–10 emphasis added).[18]

Koresh argued that the reference in Revelation to the "days of the seventh messenger," was an unequivocal reference to the last times, *not* to the time of Jesus. Just prior to this pivotal verse another angel declares that "there should be delay no longer" (Rev. 10:6b), so obviously, Koresh emphasized that these matters apply to the last days of human history. What is so striking is that he might just as well have quoted the Qumran commentary on Habakkuk and applied the language to himself—the result would have been the same.

This expectation of a succession of "Christ figures" is not unique in the history of Christianity. Some early Jewish-Christian groups, such as the Ebionites, apparently held views that were somewhat

---

Gospel Tradition: A Preliminary Study," in *Qumran Questions*, edited by James Charlesworth (Sheffield: Sheffield Academic Press, 1995), pp. 151–163.

[18] Quotations from the Dead Sea Scrolls are taken from the translation by Michael Wise, Martin Abegg, and Edward Cook, *The Dead Sea Scrolls: A New Translation* (San Francisco: HarperCollins, 1996).

similar.[19] They believed that the "Christ Spirit" had appeared in numerous forms through the ages, in figures like Enoch, Noah, Abraham, Isaac, Jacob, and Moses. As they expressed it, "the Christ [True Prophet] from the beginning of the world is hastening through the ages." (*Pseudo-Clementine Recognitions* 2.22). Of course they held that Jesus of Nazareth, at his baptism, received this "Christ Spirit" in a fullness that made him unique. He was the "beloved son," whom God had chosen as Messiah. Psalm 2:7 was very important to such groups. There God declares to his anointed (Christ) "You are my Son; this day have I begotten you. Of course the Ebionites did not believe any further "Christs" would appear after Jesus. For such groups he was the final and ultimate manifestation of the phenomenon—the fullness of the Spirit had "rested upon him." Accordingly, Koresh's assertion, that the two appearances of Christ (the First and Second Coming) involve two separate human individuals—first Jesus and then himself—is somewhat unique.

Psalm 45 is the key to the First Seal, according to Koresh's interpretation. Here the King is anointed, that is made "Christ," and rides his horse triumphantly (verses 1–7). This is parallel to Revelation 6:1–2 and 19:7–19—so this figure is none other than the Lamb. After conquering his enemies, the marriage feast takes place. This Lamb marries virgin "daughters" and has many children who are destined to rule with him over the earth (Psa. 45:10–17). Jesus of Nazareth, though anointed as Christ, never fulfilled this role 2000 years ago. Accordingly, Koresh believed that Psalm 45, along with several other key Messianic texts, could not apply to this appearance of Jesus Christ of the first century. Jesus never married and had children, as this text requires. Koresh maintained that Psalm 40 also speaks of the same figure: "Then said I, Lo, I come; in the scroll of the book it is written of me, I delight to do thy will, O my God, yea thy law is within my heart" (verses 6–7). The text goes on to speak of this one as having "iniquities more than the hairs of mine head" (verse 12). This so-called "sinful messiah" is none the less the one written of in the scroll—that Koresh connected, obviously, to the Seven Sealed Scroll of Revelation 6. Koresh further argued that the same figure is mentioned in Isaiah 45:1 and called

[19] On their history and theology see H.J. Schoeps, *Jewish Christianity* (Philadelphia: Fortress Press, 1969), pp. 68–73 as well as the texts collected by A.F.J. Klijn, *Jewish-Christian Gospel Tradition* (Leiden: E.J. Brill, 1992).

by name: "Thus says the LORD, to his anointed (Christ), to Cyrus (*Koresh* in Hebrew), whose right hand I have held, to subdue nations before him. . . ." This Cyrus, or Koresh, is called Christ. His mission is to destroy Babylon. Historians have understood this text to refer to the ancient Persian King Cyrus, who literally destroyed ancient Babylon. But there is a deeper spiritual and prophetic meaning according to Koresh. The book of Revelation appears to designate the religious-political system of the Roman Empire as "mystery Babylon the Great" (compare 1 Peter 4:13). Koresh quoted Revelation 18:2: "Babylon is fallen, is fallen," to support his view that "Babylon" must fall twice. Accordingly, the last Babylon is defeated by the last Christ/Koresh.

Koresh found his role described in great detail in Isaiah 40–66. Some of these texts in Isaiah appear to be addressed to an individual, the very figure Koresh claimed to be. It was as if such Scriptures had been written just for him. For example, "Assemble yourselves and hear, which among them has declared these things, Yahweh has *loved him*: he will do his pleasure on Babylon, and his arm shall be on the Chaldeans" (Isa. 48:14). This text was of particular importance to Koresh as a succinct statement of his mission: that God loved him, and as the arm of Yahweh he would bring down Babylon. The text goes on, with God speaking in the first person about this figure:

> I, even I, have spoken, yes I have *called him*, I have *brought him*, and he shall make *his way* prosperous. Come near to me, and hear this: I have not spoken in secret from the beginning; from the time that it was, there am I: and now the Lord Yahweh and his Spirit has *sent me* (Isa. 48:15–16, emphasis added).

This verse was instrumental in Koresh's understanding of the notion of Christ, as explained above. Here Yahweh sends one with his Spirit, that same Christ Spirit, that was with him from the beginning. It is as if that Spirit, speaking through Isaiah, takes up the first person, but then switches to the third person—in other words the prophetic "I" who is with Yahweh in the beginning, embodies the "him" who is sent. The text goes on to say: "Go forth from Babylon, flee from the Chaldeans . . ." (v. 20), which the Davidians understood as yet another reference to their upcoming flight to Israel.

There are dozens of references to a mysterious "servant" of Yahweh in Isaiah 40–55. Most of these appear to refer to the nation of Israel, who is called, metaphorically, God's Servant (e.g., Isa. 42:21). However, the four sections of Isaiah that biblical scholars call the "Servant Songs," are distinguished in both style and content and have often been understood, by both Jews and Christians, to refer to single individual (Isa. 42:1–4; 49:1–6; 50:4–11; 52:13–53:12). This individual is, in fact, contrasted with the Servant nation, that is said to be deaf and blind (Isa. 42:19). The New Testament applies each of these "Songs" to Jesus. In the Dead Sea Scrolls, particularly in the Thanksgiving Hymns (*1QHodayot*), these texts and ideas were applied to the Teacher of Righteousness as well. The author declares, "These things I know through your understanding, for *you have opened my ears to wonderful mysteries*..." (*1QH* 9:21). And further, "For You, O my God, have concealed me from the children of men, and Your law You have hidden in [me] until the time you reveal Your salvation to me" (*1QH* 13:11). In one section he clearly appears to have the role of the figure addressed in Isaiah 50:4 in mind: "[And] You, my God, have appointed me as a holy counsel to the weary. You [have taught me] Your covenant, and my tongue is as one of Your disciples" (*1QH* 15:10). It is clear in the Scrolls that the community's expectation focused on the arrival of *the* "Prophet like Moses." He was not understood to be merely one among many, but the final revelator, who would inaugurate and orchestrate the events of the End. In our main copy of the *Community Rule*, the group is clearly expecting the arrival of such a one, flanked by his two anointed assistants:

> They shall govern themselves using the original precepts by which the men of the *Yachad* began to be instructed, doing so *until there come the Prophet* and the Messiahs of Aaron and Israel (*1QS* 9:10, emphasis added).

This idea of the two messiahs, one Priestly and the other Davidic, appears to be drawn from Zechariah 4:14, but appears to have been modified somewhat with the arrival of the Teacher of Righteousness.[20] The anticipation of the arrival of the Prophet, as reflected in the *Damascus Document*, the early copies of which I take to be written *before* such a Teacher had arrived (in contrast to Text A, Col. 1, that looks back on his career, as does the fragment of Text B), ap-

[20] All the references in *CD* Text B are singular, one not two messiah. The same idea of two messiahs, flanking Jesus as the center Figure (the Lampstand) is found in the book of Revelation (11:4).

pears to base its hopes for this "coming one" on the texts of Scripture. Numbers 21:18 and 24:17 are both understood to predict the arrival of an Interpreter (*Doresh*) of the Torah, who will "teach righteousness in the last days" (*CD* Text A, Cols. 6:2–11; 7:17–19), and Deuteronomy 18:18 is directly cited in *4Q*175. It seems clear to me that in *CD* Text B, the *Community Rule*, and the *Habakkuk Pesher*, he has not only appeared but has been killed, fueling the certainty of the community that there were indeed living in the last generation (final 40 year period, see *CD* Text B, Col. 20:1; *4Q*171). Indeed, the *Habakkuk Pesher* appears to focus primarily on the crisis of faith sparked by the failure of the End to arrive. The text promises a reward to those who hold steady in their faith in the Teacher of Righteousness, which means in context, not abandoning the authenticity of his mission in both predicting and bringing about the End (*1QpHab* 6–7).

David Koresh, as one might expect, tried to demonstrate that these sections of Isaiah addressed a final Christ figure, namely "Cyrus," conqueror of Babylon, who was to appear before the end of history. This teaching was of enormous influence upon his students, who became convinced that these texts did not and could not apply to Jesus. Given their unfaltering faith in the inspiration of the Bible, they became convinced that David Koresh was indeed the one he claimed to be, a final Christ or "Servant" of Yahweh. Koresh argued, for example, that the servant mentioned in Isaiah 49:1–4 is actually introduced in the previous chapter as the one who will lead God's people out of Babylon and eventually even destroy the Babylonians (48:14–20). The text also says this one will "raise up the tribes of Jacob, and restore the preserved of Israel" (Isa. 49:6). Certainly Jesus never did this, and Koresh connected such a task with Revelation 7, where the "messenger from the east," the very one he claimed to be, gathers his 144,000 from the twelve tribes of Israel.

Koresh found every detail of the origin and mission of this figure meticulously described in Scripture. For example, this one is to come from the north and the east (Isa. 41:1–2, 25; 46:11). The one who comes from the "north" is the one who comes from God's throne, which is said to be in the north part of the heavens (Psa. 48:2; Isa. 14:13; Job 26:7). When John has his vision in Revelation 4 he is told to "come up hither," to heaven, which would be, in the cosmic configuration that Koresh imagined, to ascend to the north. Koresh believed that he too had been before the throne of God in the north, and had now returned with the sealed book in his hand. Koresh claimed that the reference to the "east" referred to his own revelation in Israel in 1985—a far country to the east of the United States. Since the United States, in his view, was the very "seat of modern Babylon," this figure comes from Israel to the United States to deliver his message. Koresh connected these references in Isaiah to Revelation 7:2: "And I saw another angel ascending *from the east*, having the seal of the living God. . . ." This one from the east was to come to "Babylon," and call out the faithful ones, first spiritually and later literally. Koresh expected that his followers, who would eventually number 144,000, would someday move to Israel and actually participate in the final events of the end described in Daniel 11:40–45 as set forth above. All of these events, described in such detail in the prophets, the Davidians understood in the most literal way and constantly discussed in great detail. They often referred to Isaiah 2 and Micah 4, and the actual kingdom or government which God was to set up in Jerusalem, in the Land of Israel, following the events of Daniel 11.

Koresh found reference to this second "Christ" figure, whom Isaiah calls a "ravenous bird from the east" (46:11), in other biblical texts that have not traditionally been understood in an apocalyptic context. For example, Ecclesiastes 12 contains a number of poetic images such as the sun being darkened, the "keepers of the house" trembling, the "strong men" being bent, and the "grinders" being few (12:2–3). These appear to be fairly transparent references to the obvious characteristics of old age: dimming eyes, trembling hands, stooped legs, and loss of teeth. However, in verse 4 there is a reference to one "rising up at the voice of the bird," whom Koresh equated to the "bird from the east" in Isaiah. On this basis Koresh saw the entire chapter as an apocalyptic poem about the end of the age. The "evil days" of verse 1 he took to be the tribulations of the end of history, rather than old age. The heavenly signs, with sun darkened and stars falling, mentioned in verse 2, he paralleled to the Sixth Seal of the book of Revelation, and also to the "Synoptic Apocalypse" in which Jesus predicted this precise sequence of events (Rev. 6:13; Matt. 24:29). The "keepers of the house trembling" would then refer to the kings and rulers who will tremble with fear when the great Day of Judgment is manifested as described in Revelation 6:15–17:

> And the kings of the earth, and the great men, and the rich men, and the chief captains, and the mighty men . . . hid themselves in the dens and in the rocks of the mountains and said to the mountains and rocks, Fall on us, and hide us from the face of him that sits on the throne and from the wrath of the Lamb.

The text in Ecclesiastes goes on to say that "they will be afraid of that which is high," which Koresh saw as an apt description of this very passage in Revelation.

Koresh further expanded this concept, pulling in what he felt were parallel images throughout the Bible. For example, this "bird" or messenger from the east, mentioned in Isaiah 46:12, is also called the "arm of Yahweh" in related passages such as Isaiah 52:10–12 and Isaiah 40:10–11. In other words, he is the instrument who gathers this final remnant people from Babylon and takes them to the Land of Israel (Isa. 52:10–12). To establish that this metaphor of the "arm of Yahweh" refers to a specific individual, Koresh would incorporate other texts, particularly from the Psalms. Psalm 80:17 says: "Let your hand be upon the *man of your right hand*, upon the son of man whom you made strong for yourself." Psalm 89:13, 27 directly speaks of this Davidic ruler or Messiah: "You have a mighty arm, strong is your hand, and high is your right hand . . . also I will *make him* my first born, higher than the kings of the earth." Accordingly, the Davidians believed, that this "man of the right hand" is none other than the son of David, the Messiah, or Koresh, conqueror of Babylon.

According to Koresh, this figure is also called the Branch, or sprout of David. Isaiah 11 gives a sketch of his career (vv. 1–2). This "Branch" figure is also mentioned in Isaiah 4:2, Jeremiah 23:5, and Zechariah 3:8. In each of these contexts Koresh would attempt to show that the accomplishments of the figure were not those of Jesus, but would be those of the final Christ. To connect this "Branch" figure with the "arm of Yahweh" mentioned in other texts, Koresh used Psalm 80:15, which speaks of the "Branch that you have made strong for yourself," and in the following verses speaks of this one as the "man of your right hand." The name Branch Davidian, of course, is connected to these ideas; namely, that one from the line of king David would reign literally in Jerusalem. It was unnecessary for David Koresh to claim literal, biological, lineage from king David, which is the historical meaning of this language about the Branch figure. In Isaiah 11:1 the "Branch" comes from the line of

Jesse, the father of King David of Israel. This is why the New Testament writers go to such pains to demonstrate that Jesus of Nazareth is of this lineage (Matt. 1; Luke 3). Koresh argued, for example, that the servant of Isaiah 49:1–4, is actually introduced in the previous chapter. He is the one who leads God's people out of Babylon, and actually destroys the Babylonians (48:14–20). The text also says he will "raise up the tribes of Jacob, and restore the preserved of Israel" (49:6). This Koresh connected with Revelation 7, where the "messenger from the east" gathers his 144,000 from each of the tribes of Israel and preserves them from the forthcoming wrath of God's judgment. He maintained that Jesus never did any of these things, yet they would be accomplished by this final messenger.

In my judgment there is much we can learn from the career and self-understanding of David Koresh in our studies of Messianism. Beyond the more general characteristics of this particular apocalyptic community, that I find to be fairly commonplace in the history of such movements, Koresh's appropriation of a specific set of texts from the Hebrew Scriptures, that in his judgment addressed him directly and personally, is most worthy of analysis. He becomes for us a contemporary example, if not in personality and style, in exegetical strategy, of how such claimants to the messianic texts of the Hebrew Scriptures, appropriate and live within their parameters. The notion of a living Prophet, who is at the same time "more than a Prophet," but indeed, *the* Prophet like Moses, adds significantly to our understanding of the dynamics of such apocalyptic systems.

INDEX OF SOURCES

INDEX OF SUBJECTS

STUDIES IN THE HISTORY OF RELIGIONS
NUMEN BOOK SERIES

4 *The Sacral Kingship/La Regalità Sacra.* Contributions to the Central Theme of the VIIIth International Congress for the History of Religions, Rome 1955. 1959. ISBN 90 04 01609 0
8 K.W. Bolle. *The Persistence of Religion.* An Essay on Tantrism and Sri Aurobindo's Philosophy. Repr. 1971. ISBN 90 04 03307 6
11 E.O. James. *The Tree of Life.* An Archaeological Study. 1966. ISBN 90 04 01612 0
12 U. Bianchi (ed.). *The Origins of Gnosticism.* Colloquium Messina 13-18 April 1966. Texts and Discussions. Reprint of the first (1967) ed. 1970. ISBN 90 04 01613 9
14 J. Neusner (ed.). *Religions in Antiquity.* Essays in Memory of Erwin Ramsdell Goodenough. Reprint of the first (1968) ed. 1970. ISBN 90 04 01615 5
16 E.O. James. *Creation and Cosmology.* A Historical and Comparative Inquiry. 1969. ISBN 90 04 01617 1
17 *Liber Amicorum.* Studies in honour of Professor Dr. C.J. Bleeker. Published on the occasion of his retirement from the Chair of the History of Religions and the Phenomenology of Religion at the University of Amsterdam. 1969. ISBN 90 04 03092 1
18 R.J.Z. Werblowsky & C.J. Bleeker (eds.). *Types of Redemption.* Contributions to the Theme of the Study-Conference held at Jerusalem, 14th to 19th July 1968. 1970. ISBN 90 04 01619 8
19 U. Bianchi, C.J. Bleeker & A. Bausani (eds.). *Problems and Methods of the History of Religions.* Proceedings of the Study Conference organized by the Italian Society for the History of Religions on the Occasion of the Tenth Anniversary of the Death of Raffaele Pettazzoni, Rome 6th to 8th December 1969. Papers and discussions. 1972. ISBN 90 04 02640 1
20 K. Kerényi. *Zeus und Hera.* Urbild des Vaters, des Gatten und der Frau. 1972. ISBN 90 04 03428 5
21 *Ex Orbe Religionum.* Studia G. Widengren. Pars prior. 1972. ISBN 90 04 03498 6
22 *Ex Orbe Religionum.* Studia G. Widengren. Pars altera. 1972. ISBN 90 04 03499 4
23 J.A. Ramsaran. *English and Hindi Religious Poetry.* An Analogical Study. 1973. ISBN 90 04 03648 2
25 L. Sabourin. *Priesthood.* A Comparative Study. 1973. ISBN 90 04 03656 3

26 C.J. Bleeker. *Hathor and Thoth.* Two Key Figures of the Ancient Egyptian Religion. 1973. ISBN 90 04 03734 9
27 J.W. Boyd. *Satan and Māra.* Christian and Buddhist Symbols of Evil. 1975. ISBN 90 04 04173 7
28 R.A. Johnson. *The Origins of Demythologizing.* Philosophy and Historiography in the Theology of R. Bultmann. 1974. ISBN 90 04 03903 1
29 E. Berggren. *The Psychology of Confession.* 1975. ISBN 90 04 04212 1
30 C.J. Bleeker. *The Rainbow.* A Collection of Studies in the Science of Religion. 1975. ISBN 90 04 04222 9
31 C.J. Bleeker, G. Widengren & E.J. Sharpe (eds.). *Proceedings of the 12th International Congress, Stockholm 1970.* 1975. ISBN 90 04 04318 7
32 A.-Th. Khoury (ed.), M. Wiegels. *Weg in die Zukunft.* Festschrift für Prof. Dr. Anton Antweiler zu seinem 75. Geburtstag. 1975. ISBN 90 04 05069 8
33 B.L. Smith (ed.). *Hinduism.* New Essays in the History of Religions. Repr. 1982. ISBN 90 04 06788 4
34 V.L. Oliver, *Caodai Spiritism.* A Study of Religion in Vietnamese Society. With a preface by P. Rondot. 1976. ISBN 90 04 04547 3
35 G.R. Thursby. *Hindu-Muslim Relations in British India.* A Study of Controversy, Conflict and Communal Movements in Northern India, 1923-1928. 1975. ISBN 90 04 04380 2
36 A. Schimmel. *Pain and Grace.* A Study of Two Mystical Writers of Eighteenth-century Muslim India. 1976. ISBN 90 04 04771 9
37 J.T. Ergardt. *Faith and Knowledge in Early Buddhism.* An Analysis of the Contextual Structures of an Arahant-formula in the Majjhima-Nikāya. 1977. ISBN 90 04 04841 3
38 U. Bianchi. *Selected Essays on Gnosticism, Dualism, and Mysteriosophy.* 1978. ISBN 90 04 05432 4
39 F.E. Reynolds & Th. M. Ludwig (eds.). *Transitions and Transformations in the History of Religions.* Essays in Honor of Joseph M. Kitagawa. 1980. ISBN 90 04 06112 6
40 J.G. Griffiths. *The Origins of Osiris and his Cult.* 1980. ISBN 90 04 06096 0
41 B. Layton (ed.). *The Rediscovery of Gnosticism.* Proceedings of the International Conference on Gnosticism at Yale, New Haven, Conn., March 28-31, 1978. Two vols.
1. *The School of Valentinus.* 1980. ISBN 90 04 06177 0
2. *Sethian Gnosticism.* 1981. ISBN 90 04 06178 9
42 H. Lazarus-Yafeh. *Some Religious Aspects of Islam.* A Collection of Articles. 1980. ISBN 90 04 06329 3
43 M. Heerma van Voss, D.J. Hoens, G. Mussies, D. van der Plas & H. te Velde (eds.). *Studies in Egyptian Religion, dedicated to Professor Jan Zandee.* 1982. ISBN 90 04 06728 0
44 P.J. Awn. *Satan's Tragedy and Redemption.* Iblīs in Sufi Psychology. With a foreword by A. Schimmel. 1983. ISBN 90 04 06906 2

45 R. Kloppenborg (ed.). *Selected Studies on Ritual in the Indian Religions.* Essays to D.J. Hoens. 1983. ISBN 90 04 07129 6
46 D.J. Davies. *Meaning and Salvation in Religious Studies.* 1984. ISBN 90 04 07053 2
47 J.H. Grayson. *Early Buddhism and Christianity in Korea.* A Study in the Implantation of Religion. 1985. ISBN 90 04 07482 1
48 J.M.S. Baljon. *Religion and Thought of Shāh Walī Allāh Dihlawī, 1703-1762.* 1986. ISBN 90 04 07684 0
50 S. Shaked, D. Shulman & G.G. Stroumsa (eds.). *Gilgul.* Essays on Transformation, Revolution and Permanence in the History of Religions, dedicated to R.J. Zwi Werblowsky. 1987. ISBN 90 04 08509 2
51 D. van der Plas (ed.). *Effigies Dei.* Essays on the History of Religions. 1987. ISBN 90 04 08655 2
52 J.G. Griffiths. *The Divine Verdict.* A Study of Divine Judgement in the Ancient Religions. 1991. ISBN 90 04 09231 5
53 K. Rudolph. *Geschichte und Probleme der Religionswissenschaft.* 1992. ISBN 90 04 09503 9
54 A.N. Balslev & J.N. Mohanty (eds.). *Religion and Time.* 1993. ISBN 90 04 09583 7
55 E. Jacobson. *The Deer Goddess of Ancient Siberia.* A Study in the Ecology of Belief. 1993. ISBN 90 04 09628 0
56 B. Saler. *Conceptualizing Religion.* Immanent Anthropologists, Transcendent Natives, and Unbounded Categories. 1993. ISBN 90 04 09585 3
57 C. Knox. *Changing Christian Paradigms.* And their Implications for Modern Thought. 1993. ISBN 90 04 09670 1
58 J. Cohen. *The Origins and Evolution of the Moses Nativity Story.* 1993. ISBN 90 04 09652 3
59 S. Benko. *The Virgin Goddess.* Studies in the Pagan and Christian Roots of Mariology. 1993. ISBN 90 04 09747 3
60 Z.P. Thundy. *Buddha and Christ.* Nativity Stories and Indian Traditions. 1993. ISBN 90 04 09741 4
61 S. Hjelde. *Die Religionswissenschaft und das Christentum.* Eine historische Untersuchung über das Verhältnis von Religionswissenschaft und Theologie. 1994. ISBN 90 04 09922 0
62 Th.A. Idinopulos & E.A. Yonan (eds.). *Religion and Reductionism.* Essays on Eliade, Segal, and the Challenge of the Social Sciences for the Study of Religion. 1994. ISBN 90 04 09870 4
63 S. Khalil Samir & J.S. Nielsen (eds.). *Christian Arabic Apologetics during the Abbasid Period (750-1258).* 1994. ISBN 90 04 09568 3
64 S.N. Balagangadhara. *'The Heathen in His Blindness...'* Asia, the West and the Dynamic of Religion. 1994. ISBN 90 04 09943 3
65 H.G. Kippenberg & G.G. Stroumsa (eds.). *Secrecy and Concealment.* Studies in the History of Mediterranean and Near Eastern Religions. 1995. ISBN 90 04 10235 3

66 R. Kloppenborg & W. J. Hanegraaff (eds.). *Female Stereotypes in Religious Traditions.* 1995. ISBN 90 04 10290 6
67 J. Platvoet & K. van der Toorn (eds.). *Pluralism and Identity.* Studies on Ritual Behaviour. 1995. ISBN 90 04 10373 2
68 G. Jonker. *The Topography of Remembrance.* The Dead, Tradition and Collective Memory in Mesopotamia. 1995. ISBN 90 04 10162 4
69 S. Biderman. *Scripture and Knowledge.* An Essay on Religious Epistemology. 1995. ISBN 90 04 10154 3
70 G. G. Stroumsa. *Hidden Wisdom.* Esoteric Traditions and the Roots of Christian Mysticism. 1996. ISBN 90 04 10504 2
71 J. G. Katz. *Dreams, Sufism and Sainthood.* The Visionary Career of Muhammad al-Zawâwî. 1996. ISBN 90 04 10599 9
72 W. J. Hanegraaff. *New Age Religion and Western Culture.* Esotericism in the Mirror of Secular Thought. 1996. ISBN 90 04 10695 2
73 T. A. Idinopulos & E. A. Yonan (eds.). *The Sacred and its Scholars.* Comparative Methodologies for the Study of Primary Religious Data. 1996. ISBN 90 04 10623 5
74 K. Evans. *Epic Narratives in the Hoysaḷa Temples.* The Rāmāyaṇa, Mahābhārata and Bhāgavata Purāṇa in Haḷebīd, Belūr and Amṛtapura. 1997. ISBN 90 04 10575 1
75 P. Schäfer & H. G. Kippenberg (eds.). *Envisioning Magic.* A Princeton Seminar and Symposium. 1997. ISBN 90 04 10777 0
77 P. Schäfer & M. R. Cohen (eds.). *Toward the Millennium.* Messianic Expectations from the Bible to Waco. 1998. ISBN 90 04 11037 2
78 A. I. Baumgarten, with J. Assmann & G. G. Stroumsa (eds.). *Self, Soul and Body in Religious Experience.* 1998. ISBN 90 04 10943 9

ISSN 0169-8834